T0039281

The YARD LAMP of Gloria

A VISIONARY JOURNEY OF SUPERNATURAL SETTINGS AND ENERGY TRANSFORMATION

Aglaia Marusin

authorHOUSE®

AuthorHouse™
1663 Liberty Drive
Bloomington, IN 47403
www.authorhouse.com
Phone: 833-262-8899

Published by AuthorHouse 06/28/2024

ISBN: 978-1-5049-6066-3 (sc)
ISBN: 978-1-5049-6067-0 (e)

Print information available on the last page.

Contents

My compendium novel has been tweaked or perfected to the uttermost dot and tittle on a four day, August 11 of 2015 Upstate NY stay where I secluded myself along rural Arkville. Still later, due to inevitable inconsistencies, I have rechecked everything thoroughly- June 3, 2024 in New York City (outside of Upstate) and I have concluded the refinement thereof.

My printed holograph record of another World
is endorsed by Aglaia Marusin

* * * * * * *

A poet can do much more for the country
than a proprietor at a nail factory.

Fredrick Theodore Roosevelt

* * * * * * *

Truly the light is sweet, and a pleasant thing
it is for the eyes to behold the sun:

Ecclesiastes chapter 11, verse 7 (KJV)

* * * * * * *

Title: The Yard Lamp of Gloria: A Visionary Journey of Supernatural Settings and Energy Transformation

Synopsis:

"The Yard Lamp of Gloria" is a five-fold discourse that takes readers on a captivating journey through supernatural settings, unendurable energy centers, and the revelation of a Hypersphere. The narrative unfolds in a nonlinear fashion, weaving together elements of romance, surrealism, and divinity personified.

The story begins with an outback trek to a preparatory destination that hints at supernatural occurrences. This initial setting serves as a precursor to the grandeur of the "Glib" megalopolis, an imposing energy center that is both statelier and more unendurable. As readers venture into this remarkable city, they encounter an inexpressible and inchoate force that defies conventional description, rendering traditional vocabulary inadequate.

Amidst the backdrop of this extraordinary environment, the plot takes an unexpected turn as a Hypersphere is unveiled, bringing the narrative to a standstill. The Hypersphere becomes the focal point of a romantic and surreal tale, personifying divinity and intertwining with the primitive gliff of the protagonist. The bond between the protagonist and the personified Divinity unfolds instantaneously, captivating readers with its enchanting and ethereal nature.

As the story progresses, the focus shifts to the ultimate frontier represented by the Hypersphere. The protagonist embarks on a journey that explores the significance of the Hypersphere and its paramount role in the narrative. The Yard Lamp of Gloria, a storyboard that symbolizes enlightenment and transcendence, becomes an integral part of this exploration.

Interwoven within the narrative is the author's observations of the Long Island Lighting Company's innovative energy distribution infrastructure in the 1990s. These observations prompt reflections on the future of street lighting and its potential to illuminate the path towards immortality. A brighter tomorrow, powered by revolutionary "lamp entities," is envisioned, offering respite and fulfillment in the present while paving the way for a sacred cessation.

"The Yard Lamp of Gloria" challenges the status quo and calls for a drastic alteration of our current affairs. It emphasizes the need for a pioneer spirit to ascend the metaphorical Jacob's Ladder and attain a higher realm of existence. Through its visionary storytelling and transformative themes, the book invites readers to re-imagine their place in the world and embrace the possibilities of a luminous future.

Inception Date: August 11, 2015 Author: Aglaia Marusin

Advent

Ere stars of heaven fall
Again upon this Earth,
Or babes begin to bawl
By reason of such dearth,
I'll shine- protective- all
On Heaven's holy Birth.

If ever earthquakes quiver
Our land to liquefaction,
And sirens make us shiver
To take up arms in action,
I still will flash My River
But billionths of a fraction!

For I am that which once
Came on the earth to save
So many as for months
And years await the grave;
Today, o'er railroad shunts
Red semaphores do wave!

You often seek an answer
To things beyond the soul,
Yet seldom heed as cancer
Devours some, but whole-
I'll heal up all that rancor
If you make Me your goal!

Synoptic Anticipation

My five-fold discourse commences with an outback Trek to a somewhat supernatural setting. This preparatory destination, by echelon, anticipates my nicer, statelier but more unendurable big Energy Center; designated as the glorious "Glib" megalopolis... Then, the reader is catapulted to its enormous "counterpart chorus" of something so inexpressible, and yet inchoate, as to render yardstick usage of vocabulary inadequate! But not only so- rather- in that the Plot of such outbursts skids to a standstill at the dilated disclosure of a Hypersphere! Accordingly addressed, as it were, a romantic and surreal tale of the personified Divinity- shared by my primitive gliff of Her- follows suit (instantaneously) until to no reservation. And finally- to conclude this Vision- I embark upon an ultimate frontier with that selfsame Hypersphere paramount.

Precedent to deployment of The Yard Lamp of Gloria storyboard, I noticed interlink of the 1990's at the **LILCO**, or Long Island Lighting Company with its fine public works of innovative energy distribution along New York's industrial peninsula. Therein, I perused the early inception of its very vast framework of infrastructure, and how that the 120 mile "long" island has reached a zenith of such

classical reputation. By this diorama- inter
alia- I was able to reconsider well enough
the future ramifications of street lighting,
and that perhaps for its very own sake...

As such, imagine a brighter Tomorrow
of unparalleled "lamp entities" designed
to energize us into Immortality. Indeed,
the cornerstone of which paves parking
lots of sacrosanct cessation; or- as shown
in yon Yard Lamp of Gloria- some radiant
respite to fulfill today's anticipation still!
Wherefore, our precarious din of affairs
need be altered- drastically- nonetheless,
if ever we are to attain the upper rung via
Jacob's Ladder! Not an impending cliché,
I say, but a requisite pioneer spirit for all.

June 3, 2024
Consolidated
Compendium

Author's Footnote Notice

With regard to the modus operandi of Concord Contact as such, this silver sliver of mine in brief presents only the tip of an arctic iceberg; that which would float foundational as one out of divers cryogenic proposals to the finest future unraveling of a Stelliferous Revivification Era.

CONSECRATION

The Proverbs, Chapter 1, verses 20 through 23 (author's paraphrase intensified to megaphone amplification):

Wisdom cries from without! Blaring: She utters Her still
small voice in the streets: She cries in the major metropolis
of concourse, in the openings of the gates: in the chief City
She utters Her words with *annunciatory* glory, saying,
"How long, ye simple ones, will ye love mediocrity? And the
scorners delight in their scoffing, or fools hate knowledge? **23**.
Turn you at My reproof: behold, I will pour out My Divine
Spirit upon you- I will make known My words to you..."

Superfluous Mouse-Print

"Epitomized is the saying:
Fine-print taketh away
what the large-print giveth!"

Apropos of the aforesaid, be ye advised, that for the usage of added visual accents and effects, the letter "U" would have been converted to "V" in some cases of preferred designated emphasis, so that a more striking appearance of print was originally intended throughout this storyboard, poetry and screenplay of authorized text. The pronunciation, preferably, is maintained as if it were applied in the character "U" and that for any *ad hoc* authentication staged. Our Latin forebears to be accredited accordingly.

The general gist and syntax of these fictitious episodes remain variously archaic and exalted in order to best facilitate the tone and feel of the subject matter at length; this with a few Latin and French phrases appropriated for the sake of flowery language!

Consequently so, some annotations were omitted for facile reference, recital, and/or unbiased screenplay performance. In addition, attributable numerical verses (considered intermittently) instead of the normal sentence sequence, seem to have been my more appropriate device for polyglot conveyance; particularly when we'd reckon the motifs thereof to be of an overdone overture of description!

Consequently, without nagging need for a glossary index, I have reserved the rights of interpretation to the examiner of this intended [tour de force] facility... *So be it.*

TRANSALTERATORIUM

1) The narrow Y-shaped, high-ceiling corridor is of relative size; beauteously bathed in such seamless, dispersed, but brilliantly *luminiferous* electroplasmatic fire of changeless star-white.

2) Ever constant and continual it must be, yet amiably so: able to rearrange (molecularize and atomize) or alter itself- instantly- into whatever one wonderfully or wistfully so desires...

3) Introducing this rather windowless, doorless, and permanently enveloped enclosure that obviously forbids any man, nor woman to enter thereunto, lest it divinely divulge *all that was, is now*, and *ever shall be* within one's internal spirit and soul, whether good or bad, holy or hideous!

4) Be it heartfelt and holy, acceptable, or profane by divine standards- the Transalteratorium exposes every interior thing, under reproduced full-blown-blow-ups of three-dimensional, illumined manifestation.

5) Hence its concrete cornerstone epigraph ordinance: **FOR WHATSOEVER DOTH MAKE MANIFEST IS LIGHT**, Ephesians chapter 5, second half of verse 13.

6) An enclosure of exposure which is to remain- unreservedly- *anechoic* and *benignly docile* to spatial displacements of that universal, myriad medium called the super Sacred Aether.

7) That with narrow neutron-packed waffled Walls of arterial sophistication, façaded by pliant *plastisteel* plaster, its

never-diminishing hyperspatial sponginess (plump and alive) may absorb and record all that has occurred, and all that may yet unfold into being by and in space-time continuum; not excluding the very bare thoughts and intimately intrinsic intents of the very souls themselves...

8) Its empowered endowment consists of cold fusion reactor *transparent transducers*, pickled alive and self-sustained in heavy water. Steroid but stoic revelatory replicators that responsively re-create bodily ballooned objects of Living Lamp Entities, breathing forthwith genetic and cybernetic clones out of any chosen form or actual event subject to convenient and preparatory purposes; this and that also for prolonged memory storage.

9) In other words, the Transalteratorium (abbreviated as TATM system) uses Transvortiums of transducer transference, that function as harmonic hives of holographic detonations, able to "fourth-*dimensionalize*" 3-D radiant reality into component compartments of pressure-compressed memory bank data storage. With preternatural Presence programming- and with protuberant perfect jackets inertly installed- the interior is uncontaminated and, apparently, unapproachable fully alive!

10) Any attempted access or unregulated retrieval thereof would constitute an infinite variety of possibilities unrealized by limited desire; yet multi-lit and surmised upon by largely the Archangels of Universality if expressed unambiguously, that is to say.

11) The embryoctoarc reactor core of Transalteratorium would then be comprised of seven transparent transducers, or self-triggered Transvortiums of *quasi-plosionary* inputs & of supernumerary outputs that can cooperate independently, or

simultaneously, as one and the selfsame seven-fold Spatial Sponge: the nomenclature thereof as a Sponge of Truth.

12) In fine, such a radiative, resonant reactor-core of the TATM system can contain the *supra-rational* resonance of canister creation, or ever the Tremendous Transducer of an insulated incubator that openly operates (or that has covertly cavorted) as *glorifier* of Divine Spirit. Albeit that far beyond the living logic of any contemplative comprehension, it unfolds out of naught yet "rife with life" to cut like a knife, but to-the-hilt ...

2 Precedent Protocols of the **TRANSALTERATORIUM**

I

To remain the symmetrical blueprint of a far higher, and finer Radiant Reality than can ever be conceived of, and that is to be cushion-cradled by anti-gravity, solar-bathed and self-lit; having been torched-up to a hazel haven of undisturbed, uninterrupted "diamond silence" within which the blinding bliss of Unveiled Paradise stays perfectly protected and preserved through an Electrical Antarctica-endlessly- yet thawed for humankind *in futuro*. Please note: as it already exists in some far off Tomorrow with tremendous transducers of tranquility, it lay non-trampled, never trodden upon, pending our arrival!

II

An installed Experiencing Provisionary allows us to "catch" a glimpse of its open momentary molecular incunabula of but blank cross-sectional events prepared to balloon outwardly, or collapse and implode inward, respectively, which in turn are utilized *inter vivos*, and that with interwoven identical identities correspondingly corrected.

And now, the vivid Vision and dream of my lifetime lucid landscape unfolds, undisturbed by quotidian qualifications

---

INTRODUCTORY

PRIMER ON

The Yard Lamp of Gloria:

GLIB

PREFATORY GLORY

Perfectly Unaltered

Carefully reprinted from the very first draft only with no revision whatsoever except with punctuation and a slight grammar check. Nothing more... Revitalized and refined throughout July of 2022

I beheld Hickory and Sycamore- side by side from a timberline ledge, distanced downward- that interspersed Douglas fir forests embedded into this vast valley. The mildly tepid afternoon gave off a soothing radiance, redolent with warmth, which seeped down, deep enough in an immaterial but enchanting environment.

For the surroundings were just so, as it were, wimpled with corrugation while my Holographic Hive slept. Nature's outback situation became but a halcyon lull as I reposed likewise. For I was found inside the superior interior of an absolute envelopment, although self-contained, compartmentalized and multiplied out inter-dimensional...

Wide wall fronts unfolded themselves accordingly ere my companion exulted, "Oh what a wonderful nap we took!" I gazed at her steadily and discerned her half-lit French-curved contour still burrowed snugly under the bloated blanket. Beneath it, wedged with wide-awake wanton ambush.

"Where the dickens are we, my dear?" I prodded her hastily. She sat up with her lightweight stature that crisscrossed and creased the once bloated blanket- now into a rumpled comforter. She spat: "We have entered the year, 2113!"

Then, unexpectedly, just adjacent to our unkempt bedside mound, the *holohive* released its instantaneous flash-point. Barely nullified by a nanosecond of blinding brightness that disintegrated far and away, the 3D picture dwindled into an architectural enfilade of sparkling snow white. Immaculately sterile corridors narrowed up and were splayed outstretched. Eerie hallways were they, that annexed out in separately and to nowhere else. That branched out with many more arms and conduits to near-eternity... Thruway-throats and necks nacreous until dwindling into oblivion.

Both my companion and I, having been wide awake at present and more aware than ever, had noticed some intramural Maze of some complicated combination. Corridors which, with configured conjecture, surrounded us. The hallowed hallways, as they were venerated or so called, continued with uninterrupted contiguity!

It was where visionary vistas led me for a jaunt of a lifetime to surmount. Even so, I declare, that which had just about begun: O bountifully lorry-laden in an endless emporium of an empire!

Bulged out at the seams like our bloated blanket mattress, the dregs of my dream drench my frozen-stiff skull and bones bodily (if ever a pockmarked skeleton) into resurrected corpora. No more mantled by the cryogenic stasis of *preservatory* procurement.

We were thawed, my muse and I, not out flesh and blood, but by soul and spirit spun to wholeness so that sentience would take over. Because of it, I became super-conscious of myself inside a holographic maze with walls of no end. The self-tunneled matrix, be it mystery or inanity, I aimed to embody. Of course, I yearned to venture into *terra incognita* outskirts of the entirely invincible *Megalotubulopolis* vaunted, variegated with wormholes and vat-vacuoles of womb-waffled wonder! That pellucid polychrome she shines, and very vomitory per packet (e pluribus unum), multiplied million-fold, one by one, was just the genesis if each and every one could contain Hong Kong & New York City congealed into an upright vat. Like shiny sardines side-by-side pack, unbuckled by barbaric contaminants of mismanaged mercury.

Yea, the 'vulvatorium' superstructure of a hyper honeycomb, with every one of its voluminous vaults & vats- alas, as these self-packaged canisters sustain citywide individuality- had been built up to the multifaceted Megalotubulopolis hive! Whereby its vast vestiges are elucidated herein by my following formula: that of suchlike self-replication. Namely, non sequitur Radiant Reality Redevelopment; the layout thereof consists of but null-lull or labyrinthine limbo, until consolidated to citywide suitability.

Observe then that this inter-linoleum luxuriant oasis, for fey reasons, may render recall and reckoning to all visitors alike.

What we look forward to, therefore, is still an aggregate conglomeration of such stupendous station. Namely, the inane entanglement (once again) of boulevards and avenues enclosed by non sequitur silence, but bustling in one's soul, depending on the state of mind thereof. For herein are vast suburbs of the mega-structure municipality. Aye, whilst jotting this down, I overheard echoes of Petula Clark singing the 60s song, Downtown.

Deliberately distributed uni-matrix adjuncts of vats and vacuoles voluminously multiplied to a horrid hyper-number that exceeds the gargantuan Googolplex. Yea, my incomprehensible numerator that would multiply every Planck point or volume of space-time cubed as if the sum total is again multiplied by every Planck point and volume of the selfsame spacetime *ënsphered* rather than cubed a septillion times a septillion times a septillion coefficient of *Googolplexity.* I forbid: not just Googolplexian, but ''Pluriseptiplex''! The vats and vacuoles- each one ascertained- contain New York City and Hong Kong combined into every hexagonal cell, impossibly added to Pluriseptiplex, or but one step short of Infinity! The tongue-twister Ubiquelabyrintheopolis stands ground both ways wayside, open-ended like the aforesaid super-numeral beyond life's stage. Enter the Warp Maze!

My infantile footing, alongside en route, readily paves the way via Trivia intersection, Aorta, and an occasional cul-de-sac ...

My Magnetic-Levitation Joyride

Indeed, and it came to pass that the aforementioned roommate companion was what had become of my personified alter ego, but muse-like in semblance. Heretofore, of course, I shan't go into needless trivial detail about the wherefores thereof; neither the abrupt aspect of her foreground fetish.

Well then! Aside from cumbersome matters of profundity to trifling contrivance let alone, if one even dares to prevaricate the sum quotient of it, I embark on a preparatory mission to yon Yard Lamp of Gloria! May I now commence this briefing of acquired dialogue between such a monstrous Warp Maze and myself: nearly infinitesimally compared!

In lieu of a preamble, the concise presentation thereof:

"I am <u>of</u> 2113, welcome to my Labyrinth."

Its voice-over solaced my normal mid-range of hearing. Upon any CCTV monitor, however, it would have appeared as an EVP, or Entity Video Print. Whereas the slightest acoustics of my repository reverberated, and that with rippling accordion pleats, all intonations had been gauged accurately according to sound envelope. The palpitations of which were probed under analysis via undisturbed, anechoic *super-silence*; channeled and charted out by but soundproof android-adroit and ambidextrous scrawls of an Electronic Scriptorium.

Elsewhere, automated arms and hands had my trek rigged.

Since everything ever conveyed underwent uncontaminated, compartmentalized computation, the audio and visual view-screens recorded the narrowest nudge of a hairline hit-and-miss sequence. So much to the pinpoint of an ethereal wavelength waxing or waning; a tiny seismograph needle twitch! Until the detection of it (even if insignificant) was to shatter-cone shock wave the linoleum flooring. An orchestral record-keeping of such sub-staged, low frequency contrapuntal thunderclaps clarified, caused cushioned chambers of waffled, pyramidal pylons to quiver awry! Or rather lather augmented to a crisp soundboard envelope of diminished decibels to distend spaciously, echoing, thrown throughout a supernumerary replay over and over again, redundantly resonant.

A mere hairpin or stylus of it that crackled, deafeningly...

Like neon-lit New York's Empire State Building in full force, collapsed frontward upon ground zero, but decibel-distributed from only a laser razor-edge shimmer of the silkiest signature that fell over its side, and that almost imperceptibly!

At any rate, I will withdraw from cumbersome, descriptive illustrations, and attend to my direct, dogmatic documentary of enchantment:

And so, I resume repose with this:

"Hey, who on earth is 2113?" I inquired therefore, ever so belittled and quite astonishingly enough!

"It is I-- I am 2113 itself..." bellowed the vestibule Voice, insistingly.

I glimpsed the glorified glitterati of lightning lanterns that brightened their hot arc tubes, and that sizzled sultrily, sewn seamlessly above. Right overhead, hauntingly whole.

Flustered, I pried for an explanation, "Whoa! If you're year 2113, then what is the interpretation thereof? Can you offer me more high definition?"

"2113 is the auspicious year you have hiked upon, and this only for record-keeping reconnaissance," the ghostly voice-over explained. "Hence, therewith, may my myriad *Univaconduitorium* abide..." I forced myself to remember the... Univaconduitorium!

There was a swirled silver sliver of the figure eight reclined lazily, sideways, atop some desolate doorway with transom vent of a narrow niche. Still, the ceiling scintilla of "utter upper udder" vaccimulgent immaculacy just about blinded my eyes from all around, as this Walled Womb (endometrium) glinted, glaringly agleam. My subconscious personified it rather to the *Immaculucy.*

"Come hither!" urged on the Voice authentication, by now vociferous! "And I'll show thee the wherewithal of my municipal Maze..." A twitch and twang ensued, then- mellow tonal- "Please enter causeway 08, thank you!"

At once, an interconnected conveyance system had shuffled alongside adjoined adjuncts of some vestibule section labeled, ELEVATORIUM 291. Its electric shoe powered booth came, caterpillar-like, right on through beside my bystander's walkway, until sliding doors opened to yet another platform. I boarded what showcased a bullet train from Japan, a rocket sled lubricious at its undercarriage of field~cushion~support, and [all aboard] quite intimidatingly forbidden to ride. Insulators beneath me, cupcake shaped and truncated as fat mushrooms- some shriveled, others intumescent or squat- were licked by bulged Lichtenberg figurines creased and cratered by afterglow thunderbolts of high-tension.

Heck, I felt enthralled, as I took on the bounty of it, barged in and sat thereat! Feeling thunderstruck by the high-tension!

Once settled inside, now nestled plushly into my passenger berth- belted down and comfy- I witnessed an over-the-face/ glow-screen CRT monitor showing the outside still stationary before my transport traversal. An automatic annunciator ululated aloud and a taped recording rattled my Faraday cage with untimely reminder: PLEASE REMAIN SEATED OR SUPINE. WE WILL NOW DEPART FROM THE UNIVACONDUITORIUM. THE NEXT STOP IS THE UNIVERMICULATORIUM... STAND BY AND ENJOY THE RIDE! But more of a tributary trip, or *slip trip* as I sped and slid into time-lapse... My viewer flashed scenery that flickered the frenetic flyby of merciless, accordion acceleration.

A grappling burst and surge of 2, 4 and 6 Gs of quickening velocity knocked the air out of my lungs when, lo and behold, the outdoors beyond my glow-screen blurred with hurtling, fast-forward momentum. For a moment, I gasped, aghast, panting for oxygen. I mouthed a breathing tube that dangled about at me as a feline plaything! There were no windows in my cramped cockpit cabin, only old aerosol anti-combustibles protruding from the bulkheads and gasket-sealed airtight emergency exits that, overall, encapsulated my safety. Momentarily, however, the uncanny sensation of zero gravity gripped me with acute swoons of disorientation and disequilibrium if ever I stood stout, or ever I forsook my modular berth! In rapid response I reclined, wryly, back down.

The outside streaking by, to soundlessly slip and froth forth from stupendous speed, could have revealed contorted images if dilated down to near freeze-frame. But as it sped up, time-lapse-like, the elongated chimeras of scenery kept coherent composure, bottled by a charcoal chiffon or saffron lattice of quantum flux.

There were a few souls seated aboard the MagLev conveyance whilst one fellow got up from his chair, vomited and voided due to extreme pressure-shock of forward force and momentum. Robotic relays assuaged his inconvenience with dispensed disposables and toiletries. The other passengers I could not have fellowship with were well facilitated no less.

In a matter of minutes, my rocket sled slowed to a halt and the intercom rattled my rib cage comfort: WELCOME TO THE UNIVERMICULATORIUM... Then, the sliding doors flung open-- sideways-- for a 14 minute disclosure and shut back up again. During that interval of duration, I peered out at tubes and conduits intertwined interminably. Now knuckled with valves and capped faucets, the lot of which were bundled by an elaborate plumbing plethora. These then were topped off with fiery afterburners, tall smokestacks and stovepipes; pylons, sieves, and furnace-backed chimneys reaching for an ever opaque overcast bathed by sodium afterglow... In my internet diary, I specified the showcase:

Log Entry, August 26, 2113 (my visionary impression)

Park Yard

Sharp shadows fell elongated
the farther I had gone from the
bundled up glimmer of Light.
Several blocks away, I could
perceive how what once was big
lot lay transformed into some
still life carnival of naught but
multitudinous street lighting
lavishly laid, lustrously limpid.
They were tall, these sleek high
mast lampposts huddled together
from a distance; and yet one by one
alongside rows effortlessly effulgent,
and so spicular, that they punctuated
an oily asphalt overlap. By reason of
such a stellar spectacle, brazen bright
as it was, I prayerfully approached
their presence lest I could go blind.
Of course, each high mast cluster-

lantern, cradle-hoisted high up via
compound pulley, gave off brilliant
brightness, notwithstanding thick
pitch black darkening the night!

Log Entry, August 27, 2113 (of inconclusive detail)

The lampposts were crowned by
cradled fixtures of big eight, high
candlepower (1000 watt) high-
pressure sodium vapour fat arc
tube lamps never to wane... Big
Eights on ring girders of support
atop every high mast Metro-Pole
post that those were. Ah, for what
once was called "commercialized"
a 900,000 acre blacktop parking lot
had been built up into the luminous
and verily vast UNIVACUOPOLIS of
glistering glitz! Whose high voltage
beacons undimmed, outshone all to
reembody an eternal sunset band of
garish glory discerned many miles
away… hazily lurid, mellifluous.
Even so, say, such setup satellite
surveillance was able to discern
an opaque orange, argent regent
Light Show of crisp clarity from
outer space! In vacuo, far over the
stratosphere & into an ionosphere
solar wind aurora-clad, as it were.
With added UVB protected eye
wear, goggled up, I observed the
closeup thereof at ground level,
looking o'er and upwardly. This,

the Univacuopolis or UVPS (for
short or in brief) blazed, shining
hexagonal, so surveyed from high
altitude sky-watch which scanned
layouts of an unguent parking lot
plot platformed: the span thereof
glitter-gold and lava-lot bright!

Tall cornfields thereabouts lay
enlightened by this grand-scale
spectacular sparkle where nearly
eleven million lamps seduce the
surroundings with contiguously
concentrated coruscation poised
par excellence: illuminating the
empyrean lucidly with multiplex
stadium Star Packs compressed
into a strangely strong throng. A
ferrous, fiery forest of electricity!
Still, one may envision closeups
of these blinding-bright lamppost
cluster lamps to have heftily whole
Arc Tube Torpedo shape HPS 1kW
whoppers aglow, ablaze per package
in vitro! Each one of such, sizzling
up monochromatic honey-golden
corncobs gone gibbous and somewhat sweetly swollen to lissome.

Hence having to flinch away for
far under bulged-tubular beacons,
I only beheld, heartily, the bygone
glorification thereof; especially in a
light-emitting diode age of artificial
innovation. For far above my height,

winched aloft via compound pulleys,
were overhung 8-lantern chandeliers
upheld by metro poles of high mast
singularity. Gloriously, what topped
off the vast UVPS in her lamp lump
sum (waxed up to 3 billion of them),
were Big Eight high masts of HPS
torchlight life, strewn on carousels,
but back up and above an asphalt
baseline founded on granulated tar.
Yea, enter thou the Univacuopolis
1000 watt layout multiplied with
One Hundred and Eleven Billion
beacons potential, and we'll wield
the superiority of translucent torchlight trans-piercingly apparent. As
having cast her eternal sunset that
never would descend, nor waver
in freshly lambent light, porcelain
sockets are designated by number
of alphanumerical nomenclatures.
Whence neighborhoods narrowed
outstretched silhouettes from afar,
but up close, bathed by the harsh
glare thereof; and whereas thick
darkness dauntingly prevailed in
the suburbs of UVPS; the glister
aureole of her entirety outshone
outer city limits by miles larger
than anyone! Therefore, unveiled
lay lovely luster and iridescently
irradiated forests of blue spruce
conifers by rooftops interspersed
throughout hilly regions nearby!
Of no recoil, nature glimmered.

For by my Night-Watch, within
which visceral visions fluctuate
auspiciously, I encountered the
big burnt otherworldly predawn
of that spectacle therefrom thus!
But satisfactorily so, until never
forgotten in a lifetime experience,
nor ever taken for granted as I remember elongated shadows cast
by torpedo tubes of high-pressure
sodium vapour lamp deployment,
so lustrous, with a *fulvous* maize.
Yielding yellowest Elysian Fields!
An eternal sunset (tableau vivant)
that brightened brazenly our souls
awake or asleep~ be what it may~
I cry, the never forgotten dream
of city-lights and diurnal dials to
fortress me in diaphanous delight
forever and ever! Fenced about,
fragile as ever, I became burnt!

||||||||||||||||||||||||||||

The engineering of the "megalotubulopolis" astounded me at least! My Log Entry was filed for keepsake and for the long haul.

This is what was witnessed. A prima facie case of self-evident concreteness independent of my sensory perception. Indeed, in that inside the seamless quick-slide of my transit thereunto, that is, *destination* GLIB as I have abbreviated it offhand, inadvertently, I envisioned "yoctoarc" Hydrogen bomb detonations stone-frozen to (terrible) tableau vivant! No, not the ones causing death and destruction, but on the contrary, those that create new tissue out of instant growth with each life-giving energetic "entelechy" of an external exploder at ground state range! Momentary mushrooms stemmed up and out, multi-sided, but never truncated to any lethal dose of radioactivity. Nay, rather! Save the very opposite per se! Each one, an inviolable Insularity of tomorrow's "Creatorium" able to re-create and resurrect buried congregations via concord contact, instead of gulag Gestapo's crematorium embedded by heartbroken, historical pitfalls.

My odd adage of the self-coined "yoctoarc" was what one would picture: colossal cones quivering, blindingly bright-hot and exceedingly instantaneous! A temporal yet timeless split-fraction flashback of yesterday's Universe before it had ballooned, but fleetingly narrower than the septillionth of a nanosecond or under (10 x 10^ -24)! Too quick for space-time itself to have caught up with, and that this was Spirit-Induced superluminal by nature!

Molten hot mushrooms midway squat were they, the turgid, repository remnants of *ex flamma lux* electroluminescence.

With white and creamy champignon, yellowest chanterelle, luminous lactarius indigo of enamel-milk-blue blush; canister contoured and barrel-backup bucket caps, cauliflower-like truffles tremendously enlarged, nonetheless unapproachable by my human standards, whose whereabouts bulge and balloon into reproductive resiliency. Blindingly apparent! Billions of bouquets beautifully arranged, but as squat swollen mushrooms so self-illumined as to compare the Sun, by contrast, only a shadow! Mounded up from the Earth to cloud-cover altitude; myriads upon *milliards* of them roundabout bulked, and many hundreds of times more mammoth and multiplied than any reinforced concrete water tower.

Thus the antediluvian, erected up GLIB I had envisaged, and with trembling trepidation. Howbeit the previous Voice from out of naught soothed me, finally announcing my abbreviated major metropolitan epithet: "THE GLIBOLOTUBULOPOLITZ CITY IS OUR LAST

PIT STOP- PLEASE STAY SEATED FOR THE DURATION..." as it specifically addressed my whereabouts, "I understand that this Hyper-City is your enveloped encounter! I suggest that you prepare yourself..."

And abruptly, upon decompression of my cabin compartment, there were welding goggles, Hazmat suit, scull-cap and helmet dispensed at my disposal with radiation vest for added safety accoutrements I was required to wear. The gradual growth of garish brightness so permeated the hull of my MagLev Transport that the extreme, ghastly, gargantuan Glibolotubulopolitz "multi-megalopolis" area had suffused the outer shell of the chrome, stainless steel bullet train. The sudden suction of thermal shock hammering the bulkheads made me crouch, cautiously, as I geared up for the expedition.

Alas for such a precarious predicament! Yea, my radioactive confrontation of glorious GLIB! Now, having been vicariously vested by some synthetic mantle of protection, my preparatory observances were wrought at hand for the fairest citywide-pretty-bride megalopolis *Glibolotubulopolitz* of shiniest showcase. In anticipation to that which took me aback, I dreaded the possibility of those penetrating, infrared and UV-violent solar flare-ups that, like spicules of prominent profusion, jutted up at, trans-pierced an empyrean or fiery firmament of effusive, effortless effulgence. The like of which mirrored upright silvery sardines, albacore, cod, halibut and tuna- sandwiched side by side, huddled together- but ballooned glaringly, and that luridly luminous!

For these were fish-like headless and tailless shapes of the city district Lamps, precinct and all! The side-by-side superpowers of an out of control, overgrown mountainous municipality ...

But back to square one, at ground state permanency:

Howbeit each one was at length an arc-hot packaged cocoon and chrysalis ready to hatch horrendously, I mused. Radiantly writhing and reaching about until I might have been vaporized into some ion discharge fit for an aurora borealis! I felt like a squashed honey badger or flattened weasel, confounded by admiration.

Still stupefied I was within confined containment, I noticed how they were rigged for thousandfold accommodation: the whole, heavy, hefty, hexagonal harmonics thereof! For midst multi-storied mega-structures, their hedgerow honeycombs unparalleled by any of today's metropolises, loomed! Aye, whose residential hive had hove, taxed under prolonged priority, heavily hoarded together. Nevertheless, the temperature would curdle cool to the touch. And so, such searing superfluidity, surprisingly apparent-- but harmless!

Moreover, antiquated effigies of it were backed by billboard namesakes like the citywide **GLIBOLOTUBULOPOLITZ** that resembled tubes of clockwork clusters and timetable tufts of termite towers huddled together as tall-wall tapers of stalwart stalagmites. These towering fortresses stood upright, poised and pointed skyward, overcrowded altogether into bundles of a never-ending strong throng. The diversified distribution of city districts that had me spellbound by a fiery forest of hot-rod moderated fusion!

I felt bedazzled and bewildered by the enormity of it all; in that-precedent to my arrival at GLIB- the intertwined outskirts of it had glistered already star-like, sun-hot & unimaginably profuse.

Whilst sliding, pending first contact, I muffled myself, took leave of my cocooned berth and went to dine at an onboard banquet bottled just for me. Metallic humanoids ushered in delicious provisions of delicate, delectable dainties. The obsidian dolls carried out the main course of my menu: Roast Pterodactyl à la carte, tortes and hors d'oeuvres. Automated waitresses were they, the chrome automatons, whose shiny shell mannequin showmanship glittered lambently in the candlelit ballroom. Each of one functioned as a complementary Matryoshka of very virtuous versatility; yea, Russian ingenuity mechanized! Over them, the dining ballroom backed by mellowest, melodious mirth had repertoires of the old **Mortier Taj Mahal** DANCE ORGAN...

Slit-reeds of steam-blown whistles, tufted together, crowded keyboard consoles. Like long ago, hot, pressurized, discordant distribution (decibel-augmented) breathed brazenly out of tune...

This rocket sled, sleek and aerodynamic- although compact- was designed with an extra spatial dimension found from within like Doctor Who's Tardis; whilst without, seemingly simple and small, suggestive of passenger claustrophobia. Even so, peopled fore-and-aft and that quite sufficiently to say the least, it epitomized the future MagLev Transport conveyance system that sustained speeds of up to Mach 1! Now, another handy over-face glow-screen utility device glared above my dinner table, its picture tube image now badly distorted from out-of-doors electromagnetic interference due to sudden centerfold clear closeups of that gargantuan GLIB Hyper City...

Immediately, and right out of the blue, an accompaniment of ballooned brightness bloated blisteringly the glow-screen's viewer. Its eerie image glimmered an overexposed, eye-searing video of quickened sunrise that whitewashed the entire surroundings! That, in radiant reality, fizzled forth an all-pervasive magnitude of negative nil! Soon afterward, the CRT television hissed, its blip blinked blearily, and then- popped a circuit, only to fizzle out into short-circuited silence with no more video noise, nor electrostatic snow flurry- unable to show the glorious GLIB on its glass-laminated megapixel convexity. The solid state CRT had darkened, sanguinely aglow now. Let alone obsolete, whereof even the very voice-print videotaped verification of its image, that lapsed into a glitch of no return, had plunged into irretrievable irresolution!

I felt the more spooked than pooped as my own mirage on the defunct monitor screen scowled back at me, grimly, in a grotesque grimace.

I swallowed up my gourmet meal and giddily galloped off into bed, safely secured and anchored down by my seat-belted berth... Ah, but the ultra-bright sight of it horrified me enough; that is, the GLIB GLORIFIER agleam... It would appear, whose photon fury of utterly effortless effulgence effervesced! And whose nacreous nipple, upper udder atop and tenuous taut teat coruscated with unflagging hellish heat!

I cowered into my buckled berth- burrowed- but then the intercom assuaged my vulnerability: "Come now, comrade, your vest will protect you from preview vestiges of an aftershock meltdown... If anything ought to occur."

Doubtless then, it was with amicable reassurance! Using my viewfinder, I plotted the Hyper-City's geometrical configuration; The EMS wavelength of such searing contrast would nullify notation thereof! The powerful concord concourse from it caused me to bundle up or batten down the hatches. Although I might have felt uncomfortable wearing it- my unwieldy yet sartorial cosmonaut MOPP suit- I lounged languid but warily with but a self-reasserted Mission Oriented Protective Posture upon my thermostatic memory mattress, mantled up and out, shortwave-shielded.

Regrettably, an unavoidable slowdown transpired. Until then my makeshift bullet train transport trundled along, lumbering to a sluggish crawl. A standstill! I shivered, having to hear (in spite of incessant insulation that cocooned me from the raw, lava-like outdoors I was obliged to venture into) an HRF or High Resonance Frequency frisk me from my quilted quarters! Tentatively, in my metal-armored reconnaissance outfit, I trotted down a vestibule ramp- wearing my coat of mail- blistered by old egg-and-dart up and down as a corncob, ready to alight my MagLev rocket sled and onto slippery glitter!

The sliding doors whisked ajar...

My staunchly incontrovertible, impossible impression of the strong, long-awaited (citywide) **GLIBOLOTUBULOPOLITZ** unfolded unceremoniously. Not the monstrosity I had expected, I sighed with relinquished relief. At once, nonetheless, I hunkered down to turn toward the *postern door, with my back on the harsh glare that cascaded, casting an iridescent shadow that lay elongated before me. This was the "enveloped encounter" my muse and I envisaged offhand. With bright brocades of **Transducer Transference**, it remained unapproachable, too lovely to look upon.

A hard-to-decipher imagery of it persists as burn marks singed into the already seared surface of a cathode ray tube, melted into fulgurite filaments. Burnt cinders left by a GRB video array! Not green, red and blue, as it were, but by a Gamma Ray Burst, preferably put.

So swollen out with protuberance, and pressurized were these, as if in deep freeze, but not quite! Mere, malleable mushrooms mounted up, stood, staged- stone frozen in tableau vivant- that vouchsafed volatility with their glare upon me! As if succulent translucent transducers, each a triple-petticoat insulator of some sort, oddly enough, had spewed forth froth through an ineffable congealment! That of continual causality. Whose glimmer glinted with *aureate* and granular glorification, and whose shiny shimmer brought about breathtaking bright white!

From such I flinched away, agog, and could ne'er dare stare thereupon...

Wow! What woeful words fell short, shy of the invincible, inviolable and inexhaustible "Gloriopolis" implanted in the middle thereat! Fair finest fusion of gibbous, barnacle gweducs- no longer stuck up- but bulged up and out from the primordial brine and broth, goop and goo of a tar pit.

Hence hitherto, see thou the glorified **GLIBOLOTUBULOPOLITZ**! I mused in my Shakespearean vernacular. *Lo! Lit up, glaringly, and that from out of nothing!* I was taken aback willy-nilly by the spectacle of it all; the impearled, opalescent opulence, exigency and glamorous glitz of its (warp lamp) dazzling Light Show! Of course, at this juncture, I beheld billions of hyper-skyscraper obelisks that distended up to puncture the cerulean stratosphere, eftsoons bloated, blackened and charred by searing effulgence; unable to endure the solar prominence of such spectacular spicules! Of stalagmites frozen in ancient time, according to one's own perspective. Antediluvian megalithic monuments copper-glazed; calcite and argon ignited. Aragonite pylon-plastered to tough stovepipe tubing and *fulgurite*! But ballooned and manifest manifold into structured stratified striations- if observed from satellite surveillance, that is. Like lithe limned shafts of spectra-sparkle, twinkling, twilit, but badgered by an old rogue radar blip of blitz, if plotted, when we use azimuth vectors!

Perhaps then, an age-old withdrawn "uniglot" Tongue of the fourteenth century Yuchi~ a medieval southeastern Tennessee native American tribe~ would have wrought better results to my multitudinous description thereof! Or even Sumerian ciphers of cuneiform formulation illustrating it far better! An old English language barrier, although prefixed and suffixed enough, was *transfixed* tremendous by the inexplicable supernal surf and turf territory that boils beneath GLIB's bedrock embankment! The heartland *spaghetti* of its "infundibuliform" pipework power grid.

Instead of sensory deprivation, I almost hyperventilated from acute over-stimulation by its glitz. For satiated satisfactorily I had been by the glorification of it that engulfed me to no end.

In acquiescence to my brave briefest visitation, my visionary vertigo of the still inconceivable Hyper-City, the rocket sled transport re-accommodated my personage with its self-protective gear, accordingly. Even the shortwave-shielded vest I wore could mitigated injurious jurisdiction to be perforated on any other bystander aside from an armored shell. Especially when one was upheld under over-irradiation to cause Geiger–Müller counters to run amok or haywire. They were once, of course, gas discharge contraptions utilized for an automatic count of detected ionizing particles.

An unwelcome 'electroaorta' of the big GLIB infrastructure overwhelmed me and I fainted... Readily, a reel-to-reel roundelay of my lifetime unfolded fast-forward and then backwards.

Mission Fission accomplished! I wrote in my logbook, but sub rosa! After what seemed like eternity, I came to... And an insuperable serenity soothed my discomfiture of bewilderment.

Rescued by reentry robots, I was now underway, prepared to return and resume repose with Calliope, my Muse. I wanted to come home to the equally bright white, yet less garishly-lit Maze whence I journeyed. The luxuriant booth and berth buckled me up with slip-zip technology as my runway Ride sped off to my starting point in just half the time embarked originally. Unlike Lot's wife, I reminisced, rather. I dared not look back at the pressurized, protuberant prominence of the whole Hypercity that was about to implode- figuratively speaking- into kaleidoscopic, four-dimensional fits- lest I turned to a pillar of salt!

The unraveling of the supercity had grown immanent due to my inability to hold back the transcendent transparency of its *extra* time-frame dimension. Aye, ever since such "cynosure caesuras" of GLIB prefabricated provenience, the "hyper-whole" hyperspace lolled- listlessly- thereat! Bottled up in vacant vats of quantum foam to froth forth with subatomic equipoise; self-induced to ever spawn another infinite Universe from ears and kernels of a Concord Corncob that swaggered and wriggled, writhing with her hyper-radiance too taboo, terrible and unlawful for mortals to look upon, let alone our departed loved ones. The shape and maize-mantled corncob would show up much later quite often.

What could never be envisaged by a three-dimensional visual cortex: that of chimerical consistency and of "irretinal" radiance! The word *irretinal* is an apt characteristic of Ancient Light not to be beheld by the naked eye whereby its retina is burnt instantly!

Frenetic froth of no moth, nor dust, to put it bluntly. Although fast-jacketed by "Transvortium" Transduction- or by what bygone Mayan and Yuchi tribes tried christening it as the *TT*- lathered lugubriously and postmortem for our sake, lest we partook of its immortal manna, never to know of what to do therewith, infantile at but feeble footing!

Enough of this. I sequestered myself once again to my all too familiar nook and cranny. Quite content I was with ignorance throughout sheepish, shortsighted bliss. For having been escorted backwards via the greater GLIB environs- along a far, far vaster UNIVERMICULATORIUM oft roguishly riddled with countless corridors outstretched to and fro, up and down, and all around an "elevatorium" at hand- the MagLev deployed my pockmarked person into the decompression chamber.

At this point, as I returned, wrung out and wrenched to the beginning terminal, so tightly tucked in, magnanimous Calliope welcomed me, catering pastries: birthday cake, and a hazelnut torte. The vanilla cream aroma of her ne'er provocative presence prodded me militarily to upright attention. Forthwith we cuddled.

After this heretofore escapade, unlike beforehand, I promised not to make such an about-face on her ever again!

Homecoming

“So how was the confrontation thereof?” someone inquired, quizzically. I shrugged it off, not to be beholden to robots.

“I- I didn’t feel good,” I figured. “The entire supercity was way too bright and brilliant to tolerate~”

“I could see that!” a nearby nurse in buttoned up regalia would intrude. I took a whiff of her ozone. “Here, let me mollify your blistered sunburn from head to foot-” For I returned somewhat singed or hard-boiled by heat! The mechanized matron squeezed analgesic cream and ointment out of an automatic tube-paste on my wounds lest I would wax tumescent. Recovery was prompt.

In due process of time, I was escorted to a more makeshift hospital.

“You mean to tell me, no visitor can confront it and not be consumed?” My Muse wondered as she gingerly jacketed my fresh cicatrix. Hell, it only took an hour for my third-degree gash to seal up since I was well taken care of by our home-grown Labyrinth.

“Affirmative,” I wheezed, whimpering groggily by reason of flash burn aftershock; sounding like an astronaut trying to recover from swoons and fainting spells of decompression. “In layman’s terms, it was refurbished for pristine spirit only, in lieu of your usual flesh and blood scenario for eyeballs to be burnt by...” I gulped and continued. “It was what the Apostle Paul spoke of in his epistle to the Corinthians, who ‘saw and heard things which were not lawful for a man to utter’ I reckon.”

"Yes, I understand." The previous voice-over had answered amiably and in psychological playback: "Could you be more... specific?"

In actuality, and aside from my redundant return upon an alternate multiverse, I was nonetheless escorted back by my deferential dispenser via Univermiculatorium. But one of many suburbs of the hot heliocentric, circumstellar, or even (albeit) the circummured GLIB Hyper-City. At once, one runabout chute conveyed my presence until I made landfall within an electrical typhoon. At its disposal, a vestibule funneled my prayerful presence, priority delivered, into my cozy bedroom.

Here, having been bogged down and supine, endlessly asleep, abed, sedated to a comatose calm, I was awakened by Calliope's lingering sallies of gleeful gladness.

Aye, my rather robust gusto resumed, revitalized by her constant wooing.

My dearest companion separated herself from my heartfelt rib-side and rolled out the red carpet treatment.

"Hurrah for the newcomer! Tallyho!" bellowed she in flippant British bravado compensated for by her lissome, ladylike nuances.

I oohed, a bit disoriented by my sudden reincarnation. "It's good to be back, Cal!" But she refused to be outfoxed.

"You said it! So tell me, how was your close encounter with the GLIB?" Her candor was upfront.

And I pondered the grappling gravity of her quick question... With self-conclusive nonchalance, I replied: "Never mind the... Whatchamacallit? Hey! Such a platform of incomparable and incontestable space- call it *grace*- yea, that's it! Anyway, such paradise- a helluva showcase! Too supernatural for us crybabies- awaits those particularly worthy enough and vivified enough to dwell therein..." I swallowed up my prattle. "Let's go to bed and we'll sleep on it, okay?"

Howbeit, her big burlap of wisdom waged war with my oft parochial poppycock. Smartly, she would backlash lecture me: "Societies invented the old crematorium, a furnace furnished and designed to smolder to ashes the remains of any cadaver hurled into it. But Yahweh! That's right, yea, Yahweh created and foreordained the 'Creatorium' pronounced, Cree-ator-ee'um that can, conversely, resurrect, revivify, or reanimate the whole soul back into interminable longevity; the everlasting life inside super-silos of the Heavenly Jerusalem. Instead of the incinerator, the Inner, Greater! Nor what an ICBM warhead stood for a long time ago... Rather, the Inviolable Canister-Bulged Monument!"

No more midway, if ever she could capstone my lesson, I had to memorize her harmonious CREATORIUM namesake. Alas, its embodiment of entirety had been unendurable.

I wallowed headlong into the boated blanket, and listened intently to what she had to say. "Pray tell, allow me to elucidate. That old GLIB, of ancient pallor, but blindingly bright, is our ultimate futurity, and whose Causal Quasar Beacon or CQB 3113 paves for us the blacktop of destination, if we live *righteously*- not riotously- here on embattled planet Earth beleaguered by bigots."

"Ah, very much, my dear lass!" I grinned, harlequin under disheveled bed sheets, teasing her. She giggled. But moreover, I felt an inner resolution; a power surge of joy and tranquility permeate my heart and soul as I recollected my rendezvous with the still astounding yet stately GLIB! There was Love and Peace that quelled consternation; that encouraged me once and for all!

We contemplated the very contents of this prefabricated far-fetched supercity.

Meanwhile, the holohive resumed "re-absorption" of energy release and all was back to normal again. The materialization of reality rekindled itself once more to the timber of hulk and hoar Hickory and Sycamore side by side. Orchards and groves of them illumined by but "Something More..." A good book I glossed over a long time ago, no longer in print, amid tomes, tucked away.

A primordial forest against a featureless background! The broadleaf, brindled bristles and perpetual pine cones that were once enlightened by age-old gold leaf sprout anew. That which fringed, limned and licked- lavish- the fountainhead foliage of redbud shrubbery blossoming pallid rosy-pink, strewn about with conifers of blue spruce. And down underneath, amongst feral fens situated so silkily, pungent peat bogs irrigated the loam. Now, nature's newly amalgamated symbiosis of self-redevelopment wrought, as it were, with *walls of contiguity.*

In time-lapse, how hulk hedgerow, hillock, and hilltop hove, adorned distantly; dimly bathed from an "infundibuliform" old afterglow of the billion-by-billion light-year riddled (nowadays diminutive due to faraway proximity) glorified GLIBOLA. Glib abbreviated: not ready for an excuse as if it were insincere or superficial; nor in *being* glib, only to gloze over the matter, but rather, the veritable quasar 'Glibola', or the very Hyper-City itself.

My Muse and I had reentered sweet dream somnolence, or *sleek sleep* as we picture it, but ever so subconsciously. By golly, the one and only way such a Thing can be solidified without inaccessible transmogrification. Behold, howbeit whose high-ceiling hallowed hallways recline, reservedly, but for fine, divine guests outside of ourselves. Pilgrims of ponderous outreach.

The Pilgrim Guesthouse Supercity we would wish to occupy by grace in the remote year, 2113, festooned in lavender, lilac, and old acanthus ornamentation.

The eternal vernal equinox to adorn Paradise:
Yea, glorious gleanings of the cornfield Glib!

Enter Yard Lamp of Gloria

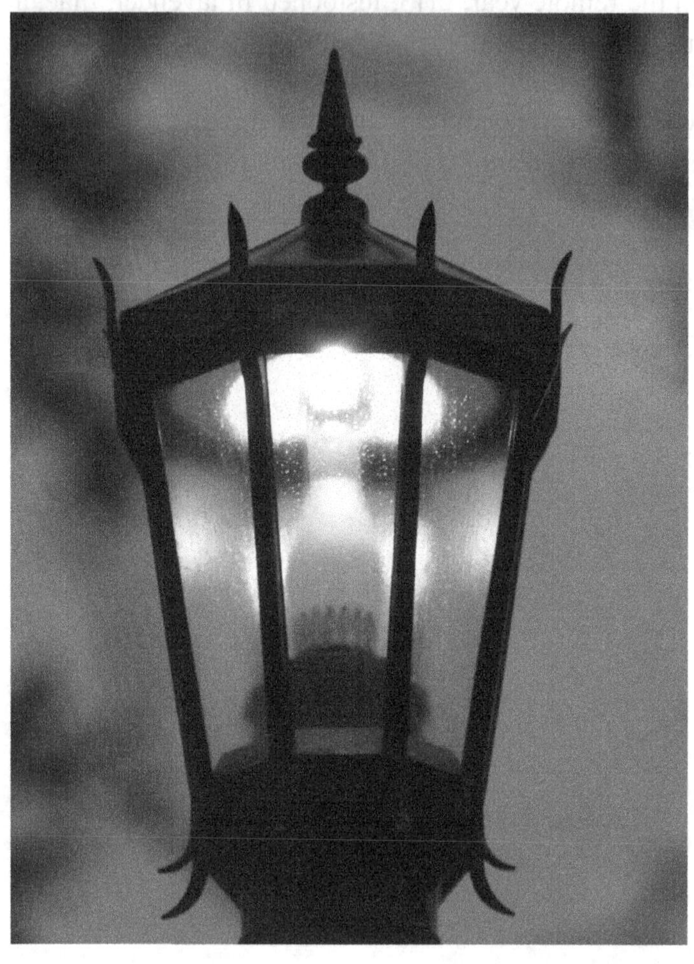

1) 1940s mercury vapour streetlamp at some city park of Brooklyn, New York.

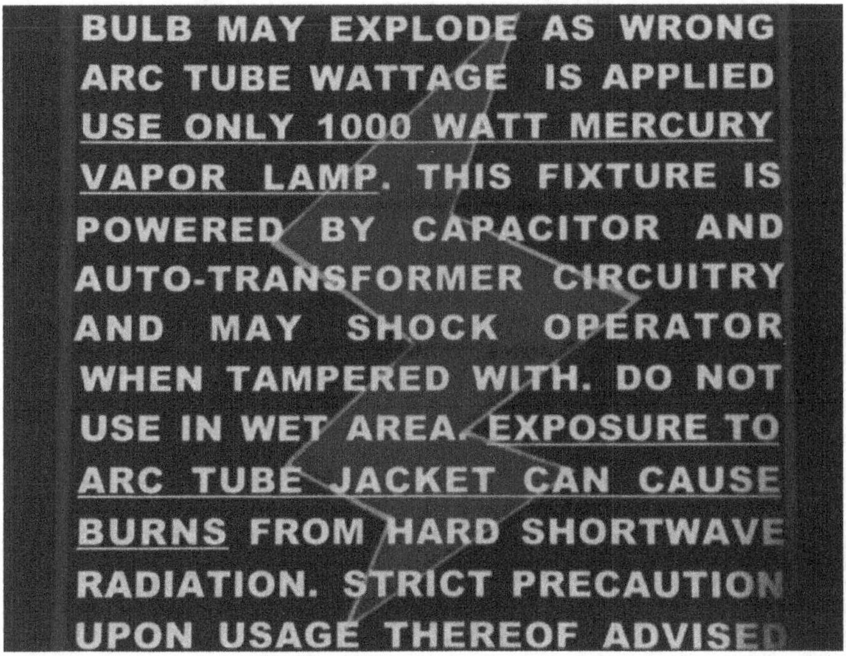
BULB MAY EXPLODE AS WRONG
ARC TUBE WATTAGE IS APPLIED
USE ONLY 1000 WATT MERCURY
VAPOR LAMP. THIS FIXTURE IS
POWERED BY CAPACITOR AND
AUTO-TRANSFORMER CIRCUITRY
AND MAY SHOCK OPERATOR
WHEN TAMPERED WITH. DO NOT
USE IN WET AREA. EXPOSURE TO
ARC TUBE JACKET CAN CAUSE
BURNS FROM HARD SHORTWAVE
RADIATION. STRICT PRECAUTION
UPON USAGE THEREOF ADVISED

2) Self-composed warning label from a defunct 1kW cobra head parking lot mercury vapour lamp.

3) A Coney Island district park backed by high-rise Russian occupancy in Brooklyn.

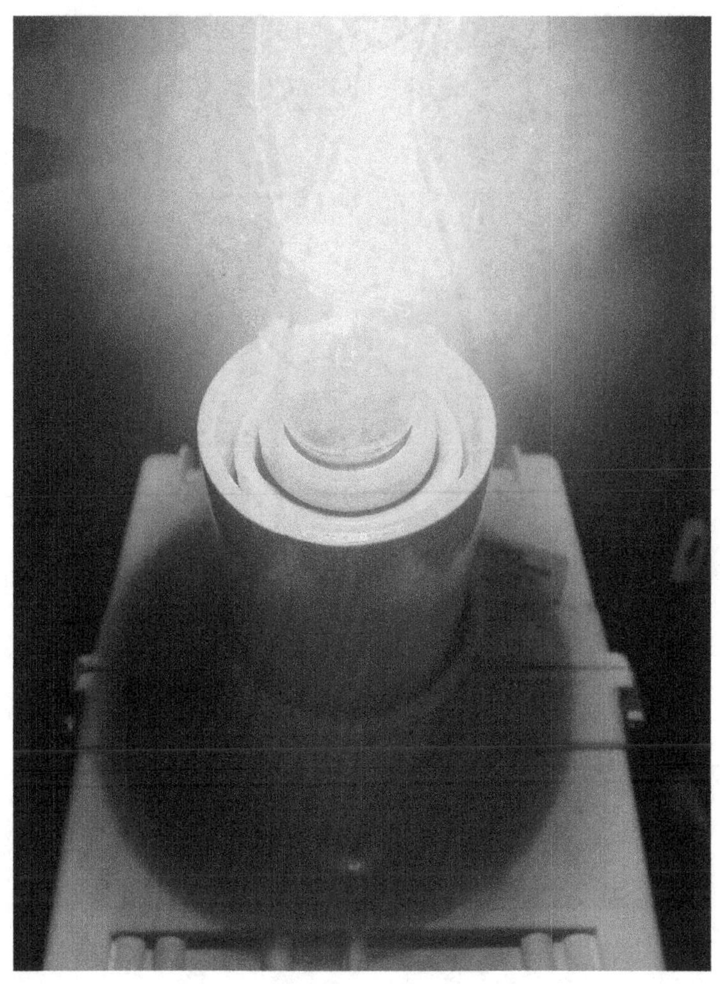

4) 175W arc-glare of the High Bay "burger", circa 1981.

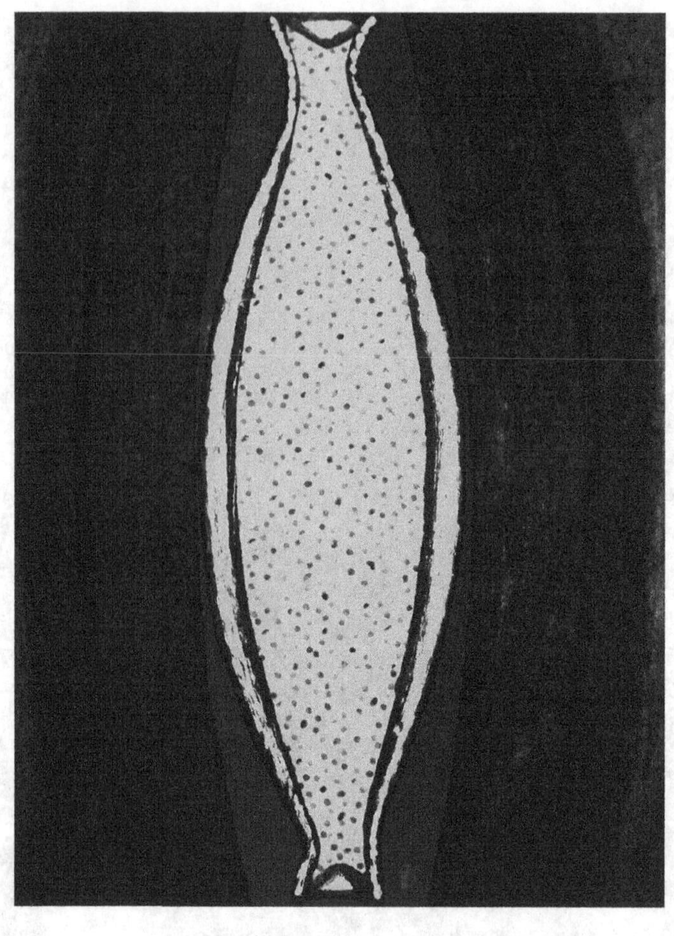

5) The electric "gweduc" so self-distended; the very photon entity of a plasma arc thereof. Also, it is an upright "Vacoon" as illustrated in this book.

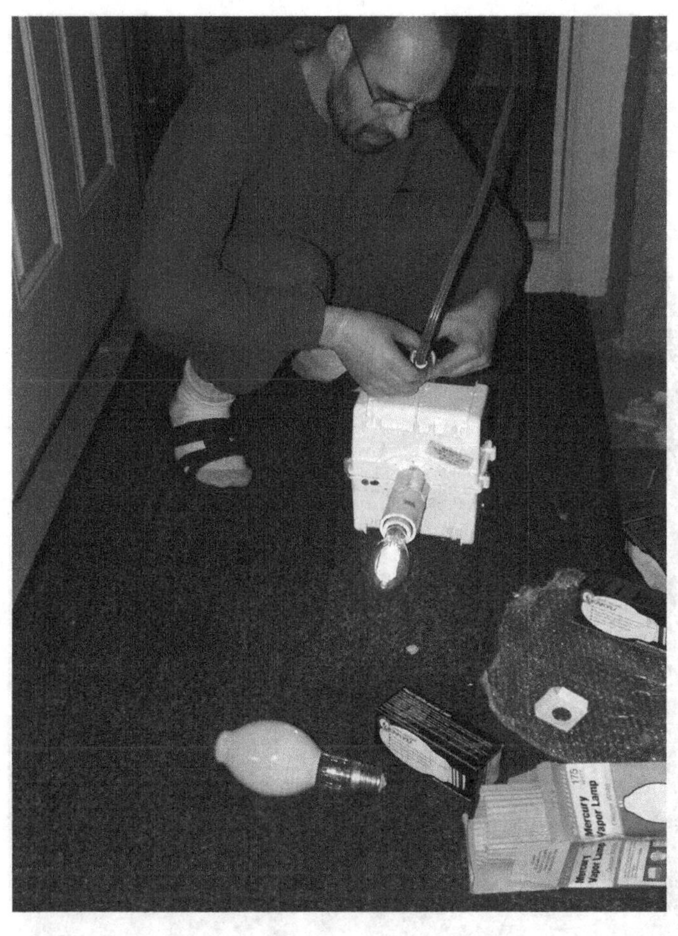

6) The author caught on camera when working on an obsolete arc tube fixture.

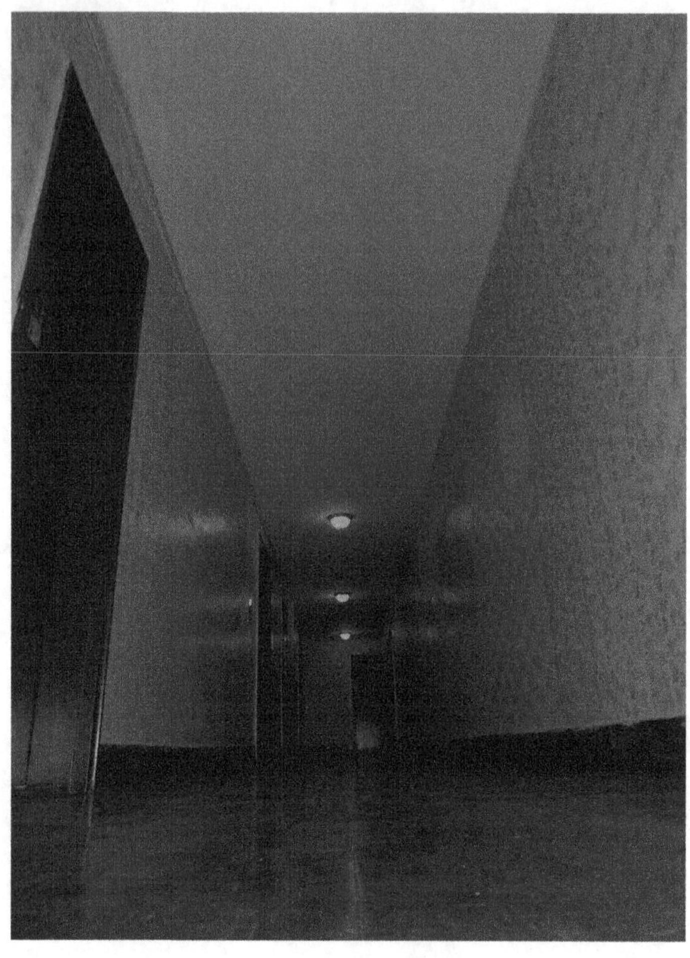

7) The snapshot of an authentic haunted hallway, but never designated to have been as it were...

8) The author's proposed projection for the Yard Lamp of Gloria storyboard.

9) Coney Island amusement park model inner core of over-sized insulators depicted by my Vision.

ALTERATORIUM

There stood a home eternal
Coal-bricked and tile shingled;
Its furnace breathed infernal
Where air and fusion mingled.

Within her, spiral stairs
Ran coiled up each wall
That needed no repairs
Midst tarnished Time acrawl.

Both room and eggshell ballroom
From vestibule to basement:
(Whole household void of gloom)
Had not one ill displacement!

High-ceiling corridor
With frieze o' egg and anchor,
With gilt and *postern door
All spotless, ne'er could canker!

For breathy stayed this house
Throughout the years gone past-
Her flares no one dare douse
As they cavort per snast...

CHORUS
Bulged torchlight brightly sears
Such hung down chandeliers-
Large Lamps inducing tears-
Flung rays like lambent spears.

Elsewhere, beneath a gable
Some paisley pallor gleams
To occupy man's table,
Now full o' vacant Creme!

Alone, serene, whipped raw
Full blown- pristine and naked-
This fudge top with no flaw
Lay thus for us to take it.

Time lurches to the stand-still
With everything glazed blank;
This Creme is for each hand-fill
As GRACE ignores our rank.

Strong shone long-thrown fat *fulgor*
(...cocoon-like...tuberous...)
Against what's rude and vulgar,
Worldwide, so numerous!

Dire destiny seems finished.
No more as sprinkled, swirled
Were pastimes now diminished
To bygone days impearled.

Instead, outspread she stood
Ypsiliform twin-contoured;
This hull amidst burnt wood
Where everything was moored.

Still, not one spill had faltered
Old holographs perennial,
Yet aeons may have altered
Life's lamp-lit finial...

The Walled Womb intramural
With warp-core cloven tongues
Re-mirrored pastures rural,
But felt not heart and lungs.

CHORUS
Bulged torchlight brightly sears, &c.

Outside, I felt the damp oily drizzle of urban lather all over my epidermis. The clammy mist of airborne fog: of adhesive droplets, stuck stubbornly upon me as if from a sprightly spray of old grotty grease. Its subtly sustained penumbra of odor so permeated my neon surroundings with almost spiritual, impalpable implication...

From elsewhere, the hushed hum and seemingly brazen *brool* of far away transformers had crept hauntingly upon my frail stature as I gazed out at an entirely nacreous haze. Some rather electrified ozone that veiled vast the fiery firmament stayed overhung until distended, distantly, to some impressive event horizon. For o'er abroad had loomed up mounds of **Transducer Teats (TT)**, or what appeared to be enlarged mushrooms and squarely squat sponge-parasols, but that jutted upwardly at an under-glazed empyrean. Enormously bloated, these glossy intumescent, self-contained edifices could have easily dwarfed any of today's water towers if compared! Triple petticoat insulators pigmented with cobalt, cadmium sulfide, selenium and vermilion. Each one, an anechoic INSULATORIUM of foam-full support juxtaposed with inner city predominance.

Now, in between each one of these insular denizens, a super-metropolitan cornfield consisted of a concord corncob right after another with tall afterburners, chimneys, and smokestack pylons sparkling ablaze, obliviously. As chrome colander-sieved thermal vents of petrochemical fire-spouts awry writhing! These, of course, contributed to an already thick brick and quick-slick overcast. Its mysterious malaise lit up, pellucid as it were, by the garish glitter of an increasingly non-*vitiated* super-turf Territoriality!

Hither, in iridescently non sequitur silence, I would glide, shuffled along lengthy umbilical cords of an expressway where pantograph and electric shoes- wedged within cupcake-like conveyance- slid smoothly, effortlessly... And it felt just so hydraulic, inside my air-pressurized seal-tight compartment, that I lounged lazily, cozily into my thermostat-regulated love-seat sofa while being transfixed by deafening serenity! As through a soundproof fisheye aperture, outwardly, bulked behind skeletal skeins and lattices of girder grid work, I faced futuristic forests of shiny, cloud-piercing, monolithic hyper-skyscrapers that- like China's Hong Kong city- overcrowded the area. Not to forget cathedral-like buildings of porcupine spires huddled beneath the electromagnetic blinding and glamorous glitz, brightness and solar prominence of a shimmering, ultrahigh-resolution *Hypercity*!

Albeit the urban basin glistered glitz, I wedged myself in an immeasurable immaculate and sprawled out multi-megalopolis of exaggerated attributes. My fancy of an exotic assortment! Akin to the privately protuberant envelopment of energy strewn strangely about but quite manifest manifold, and that so innumerably, for nearby countless cloistered congregations to encounter! Seething each of their hot plasma-packaged cocoons through the night. A nullified nocturne, if ever there is any! Nonetheless, their overall surplus fund and efficacy of glorified glare prolonged artificial daylight round the clock, indefinitely. No night nor day for that matter, save an orange argent regent aglow, constantly. Able to emanate undimmed sunlight by but state-of-the-art hydroponics unsullied by filthy lucre. They were "electroplasmatic" by nature.

Innermost *evercrème* would bulge fudge and spew forth froth!

How ultrahigh frequency, such sheer shock of sultriest raw photonic emission! Of a luminous aureola, whose glorification outshone mere megawatts of such pronounced high power factor distribution! What soft silicon gel of a gold gargantuan petroleum churn. Of refineries replete, I discern! Incandescently ignited to a ferocious flash-point *femtosecond* of an old ICBM detonation! Although this one, anti-destructive, in lieu, ready to unleash (in miniature) an overhead inflationary expansion acquired timelessly! Oscillator of effulgent fluorescence: with a transparently gorgeous mother-o'-pearl piled beside blossoming paradise. Doubtless that which punctuates padlocks to smoldering shrapnel …

My door that I call, 'Permadora'

Whereas amalgamated principality is exhausted or exhumed by the supercity necropolis- though they say *curiosity kills the cat-* can I fulfill my clinical cliché? In that case, inter alia, I visualize the impervious door on the end of a tall wall whereupon none in this universe could penetrate, nor violate forbidden foreclosure. Imagine then the cul-de-sac thereof paved onto terminal shut-down: a thick pitch o' Tar. The charcoal door that even absorbs light like a black hole! Although perforated with Planck-pliant singularities soporific to the bystander sojourn, still, it is silent and impermeable to hot nuclear blitz if kittens and cubs confront the Lion of Judah, as it were, at an onrush of Lethe. Either way, the adhesive cohesion of utter erasure shall transpire forthwith, and not only that, but shock and shatter us out of our wits! Nary a null noose to oblivion, nor inflammatory flue of aerosol vomit!

Alas, aside from the glamour and kaleidoscopic cacophony of life's mirage, the narrowest door wrought of naught but hyper-polymer, (of poised permafrost), is a show-off shuffle of Access Denied; my forbidden-to-enter Fail-Safe Device!

Yea, just in case wanton wanderlust vies with soul possession.

Now, nonetheless, somewhere hidden, as if it were a needle in the heavy-handed haystack or proverbial tincture to the ocean, the perfect poise of Permadora will outlive our destinies defunct. The impenetrable shut-up to worldwide wanderlust whereat no lad nor lass presumes entrance. For we've colonized the moon and vicinity outskirts of Venus and Mars, even out of bounds: outside Jupiter, Saturn, Uranus, and Neptune- passing the Oort cloud of vagabond comets astray but grappled by *Hekate-hinged* far reaches of Sol's gravitation- never to let loose- only to fall upon recall via the inviolable Permadora, our damper... dead-end at long last.

One might as well stagger and straggle thereupon the foresheet of it, the forbidden shut-up at unholy endeavors, humbling if not humiliating any volatile venture to a standstill. For behold the Permadora of a hyper-black bloated appearance, as if burnt by space-time itself, incinerated by the flit of eternity. Never installed in the first place to begin with, neither ever to enter determinate evanescence. But extant as an ultimate end in and of itself. Not necessarily black-hole-like, but backdoor barrier to any further investigation of unrequited spirit. Permanently paved on an inner niche and having the intramural surrounding it with walled inner-city predominance. Contoured up to a rectangular repository or flat monolith of one by three meters, yet super-polished, varnished vertiginous with linoleum latex Tar of neutron consistency, one would only catch a glimpse of the Infinite to terra incognita. The (postern) yet colossal cosmic crunch of Universality.

And now- regardless of my naivete- after I boarded my magnetic bobsled, I sat. Safely reassured from being trenchantly tried, let alone dreadfully drenched, I soaked in soapsuds [the paraffin rainfall of a torrential downpour]. If not by bone marrow, conversely, quite taken aback! Whoa! Whacked with variegated episodes observed via porthole, the acceleration would whiplash me at the Mercy Seat of my recliner. The passenger transom vent bloated with a heliarc welded tint of filmy glint; that of jacketed, jar-proof protection through which I beheld a chaotic blur of hurtling speed spatter by. It kept me preoccupied to window-watching some time-dilated, meteoric or horizontal shower of sardines shimmering well-nigh. I stood preferably, inadvertent, giddy with acute belly flutter! Indeed, the vestibular yet evacuated Tubule to **Thruway 8** had bustled with an incessant barrage of arrows; of BTT Bullet Train Traffic that slid along dozen-deck highways, boulevard ramps and thunderous thoroughfares, and all eclipsed by an occasional molten, *multi-sided* mushroom that towered up, nonchalant and aloof. These were the only discernible milestones passing me beyond my mere arm's length lightning lilt of frenetic frazzle-dazzle. Heliumatic lamps passed by outside!

The interlink loop and commute of a suburban sprawl supported sky tunnels and tube-ways, altogether, that stretched onward for hundreds of kilometers, plumb set above an endlessly outspread oleaginous power grid park. With inner-city industrial equilibrium interspersed with intramural gymnasium warehouse wharves, these city-side piers had launched up a formidable flotilla and fleet of sailboats and flagships afloat; like Styrofoam buoys barged into some cerulean surf, only to put to shame Shanghai.

Overall yet, environmentally inter-dimensional interiors of each arboretum ballooned botanical gardens cultivated in subtropical micro-climate hillocks with flora and fauna abloom- lush loam lavender-lavished over their arbor vitae forested Silbury Hill- the likes of which cultivates the blistering, burning Bush of Moses, a 'Heliconifer' serried with berry-laden luminescence alongside sacred Helicon of the Nine Muses. Each and every specimen: an inverted cone-shaped "infundibuliform" evergreen or *evercrème* permafrost~packaged pylon afresh all-year-round! In greenhouse Versailles garden plot platforms of terraced multiplex pleasantries plushest, they accommodate wildlife symbiosis! Cradled under harsh chimerical confetti of this citywide light-show extravaganza, *Heliconifer* shrubberies (amidst an intimately gravid Meticulous Metropolis) prepare to implode, inwardly, overtaxed by opalescent opulence!

Her tall tapered teats of unbridled b<u>reasts</u> beckon pilgrims ...

Until still, having felt fulsome to this showcase, I just about shielded my eyesight of scrutiny from a far vaster but coruscant force field of an *unapproachable*, *unimaginable* slip-city nucleus. Shockingly and shattering enough, that mirrored from on high an emblazoned congealment of this mighty marvelous municipality or downtown crown configured by my visionary vista of it! At large, She furthermore wore white bridal frills of fulgurite arc-forks mirrored off holograms! This induced me to notice incredibly beautiful and tall tapered slender candlesticks huddled together from one end of the rainbow to the other, illustriously illumined. The igneous ignition of which would have outshone the hottest of volcanic calderas! Situated under sustained fusion, the searing pilot light polychrome *chrysalopolis* radiated exceedingly an unearthly glitterati of flamboyant flambeaux to outnumber [near-infinitely] the hurly-burly of Las Vegas properly predicted. An electrostatic and cornucopia conflagration of staggering amplitude! Everyone, a star in a jar scintillating Sirius at hand, or better yet, Quasar!

Still more, in polished up gilt glistened obelisks barricaded by trappings of traffic cones. All of equipoise elegance with such elaborate sparkle-tape of wraparound festoonery, might I add. In blinding resplendence, these were layouts lavished in contrast lucency, each one with the other. Like lava-granulated embers, hulk hedgerow by hedgerow, that iridescently irradiated diamonds of supernal similitude. One by one, an enshrined shrub of fat fulvous *fire~brush* inextinguishable, twilit atop Mount Sinai for future Moses to verify once again! In actuality, everyone, an old grown, multifaceted perfect crystal package thereof had caused visitors to step aside and to survey their glare, goggle-eyed... On the other hand, alternate tube-tops could have easily given me vertigo from sleek-steel-sheet thousand storied architecture, or at least, via my visceral view of the same, overwhelmingly realized from precipitous observatory decks. Upon them, therefore, are luminously organic light-emitting diodes save within unearthly decorative divans that, anon, deliberately defy any prior probe, strobe and visual cortex of database acknowledgment from an electroencephalographic printout strip! Of incorporeal invisibility diaphanous, elaborate and too innumerable to fathom! As inverted mnemonic nodules too many to quantify! An unraveled radiant replica of cross-sections kept column after column!

May I annunciate: "What one Heart hath never felt, nor ears have ever heard; neither what eyesight had ever seen since the foundation of terra firma *herself...*" [of amplified emphasis]

Moreover, the huddled Hong Kong multiplex, alongside the surrounding supercity agglomerate Pearl River Delta megalopolis combined with New York's Times Square (ballooning) billboard advertisements, at this juncture, fail to vie- albeit alluringly- with zenith vistas uncannily unveiled via portrayal. Namely, the solar-system-sized **MEGALOTUBULOPOLIS** of a large Bulge! By contrast, an entity entirely *incommensurate* with any aforesaid metropolitan monstrosity: the interfaced and interwoven multi-metropolitan *strong throng* of efficiently effusive, exquisite and filigree intricacy to no end! Easily, an ever ageless Promethean avatar of arterial sophistication and of stupendously stunning needlework more meticulous than embroidered tapestry spun by spool, spindle and distaff of any adroit, matronly loom-side seamstress! Whose solar flareups and spicules are concentrated to heliolatry of the Sun! Or that which far outlives artifact finials and spires of a massive stalagmite formation subterranean, though not necessarily dissimilar to any of my precedent models. An awe-wrenching and seething cellular aorta aggrandized- that *glistered* glaringly- howbeit wholesome, hallowed, an everlasting Atargatis of vitality; narrowed by nimble Mnemosyne within her cathedral niche, to proffer forth her prehistoric incunabula ...

Such a city, inasmuch as it is pleasing, ever anti-vituperative! Rather, that the starriest of attractive attributes lay foundational.

Its brocaded bright bridge of luscious Light is fringed forth to the crepe drape and certain-curtain outskirts of soffit coffers. A herculean holographic hive of honeycomb life. Except in that she hurdles up an otherwise billion-riddled quivering Giga-populace, if comprised commercially midst much of an available ferroconcrete fortress, her preferred designation spells GIGALOPOLIS!

Soda straws that solidify to super-taper stalwart stalagmites!

Observe now my main unceasing Silo City wilderness! Whose secondary & tertiary adjunct, abutment, *arc brisé et arc boutant* and flying buttress are appended by porcelain insulator-seals of cobalt concentrated terawatts, incontrovertible! Adding aggregates of agglomeration only to concordance of an automated whirlwind winnowed by electronic cyclones of tornadic vortices that range five-fingered on an entirely Enhanced Fujita Scale! An uproarious typhoon of rational rotation christened the "creatornadoarc" hyper-cone! Able to dig trenches and easily peel up concrete streets from off the face of ground zero by old school corkscrew shock-wave liquefaction! Albeit some super-suction-cone cavorting a polka polonaise over rooftops dilapidated thereby! The very technical modus operandi thereof spawns enigmatic materialization through the legendary multi-mirrored Looking Glass framework vis-à-vis. Such unexplored cornfields of knowledge: *Alas, Cheshire sphinx, beware!* Even so, waving to and fro, with swollen swagger, the concord corncob of a resplendent, conflagrant thunderbolt with yet another radiant replica of the like stovepipe jet! The very identical and gibbous glorification of an **M87** elliptical searchlight at large bulge in and of itself. Yea, sub specie aeternitatis, at merest mirror images of gamma ray plasma frozen up in an Anthropic Principle of cosmological spacetime... The Anthropic Principle, also known as the *observation selection effect*, is the hypothesis, first proposed in 1957 by Robert H. Dicke, that there is a restrictive lower bound on how statistically probable our observations of the universe are, because observations could only happen in a universe capable of developing intelligent life.

This is what I had perused, beforehand, in my files before the breathtaking exodus.

Residual Impressions of Contingency

But my **GLORIOPOLIS** was to reverse the curse; our worldwide, contemporary precarious predicament of profligate collapse! To (*inter vivos*) mercifully rescue the oppressed from imperialistic subjugation! Only to transplant and graft them from out of a hideous global Illuminati and- preferably- resume rapid rebirth of each soul installed into the incorruptible vicarious burly bowers, boughs and branches of ***Jesus Christ*** almighty and none other! His Heavenly Jerusalem, by and large, as in the tome of Apocalypse interpreted, that YHWH must perpetuate perforce notwithstanding! An iron summer hammer or anvil which will pulverize cryogenic icicles! How hereafter, the necessary new augmentation of an indispensably indestructible global Glory shall settle earthbound; nevermore to ignore Heaven's authorized injunction or ultimatum of glacial and palatial Peacetime. Whereas an apocalyptic upheaval ensues (forefront), even at the doors- pending- future **Advent** is foreseen by no mere prowess of prognostication, but rather, by a foreordained Rolodex directory-distributed prophecy ...

Elsewhere, in ardent outcry, a verified voluminous voice-print identification of untimely reminder is resonant. Matured from an inconsequential echolalia to Pentecost glossolalia, glorified with cloven tongues, taunting us of ourselves, it rattles its icky, sticky stew-cauldron of intonation. Lugubrious, lachrymose, whimpering wheezily! Bloody, blatantly foreboding:

O nature will payback what man
Has done to her at global span

An ICBM: Intercontinental Ballistic Missile warhead branded with what is malevolently **MAD**, or- as momentarily- *Mutually Assured Destruction*, sags flaccidly into a malleable meltdown of liquefied aluminum. The tinfoil wafers of which wallow listlessly in the placid guestroom of an abandoned auditorium: my musty acoustics stage juxtaposed out of a normal, natural environment!

♦♦♦♦♦♦♦♦♦♦♦♦♦

Until nowadays, nonetheless, we envisage the inner and outer Supernal City of an interurban unified *interlink* predisposed for exact punctual public servitude. Yielded hastily, obsequious to a millisecond milieu of effortless production pristine, organized redistribution, and with my final, fabulously refulgent Reactor Power Plant heretofore posted. As addressed heretofore, I attained the inexpressible galactic core and confrontation of what my fluid, quicksilver synchronicity was so choreographed by. Preternatural and preparatory as **GLORIOPOLIS** before and after. Furtively, that which connects vestibule plenitude of ubiquitously narrow high-ceiling corridors, hallowed hallways having egg-and-dart with tongue-and-acanthus backdoor mausoleums, adoringly adorned. In Latin, labeled the grand Ubique Labyrinthum (the Everywhere Labyrinth), it contains memoirs marmoreal. Votive *memorial*, as it were once graven from a **V** cut grove topper hewn from of an unrecorded rectangle. Foursquare dormant but exhumed from archaeological excavation exacted by ratio 1, 4 and 9 noted in my diary as our *Omnipresent Maze*:

Ubique Labyrinthum

At ceilings bulged aglow
Flambeaux grow elongated
By hedge-maze or hedgerow,
Niche-like, ne'er etiolated.

But hung are corncobs fat,
Grown greasy at their sides
To brighten this or that
Above magnetic rides!

The tubule-tunnel long
Burrowed in all directions-
Life's labyrinth laid strong
With intramural sections:

The doorways were by number,
Each entrance designated-
Whose transoms never slumber
Since lights lash unabated!

Transvortiums were they,
The mercury-filled torches,
Winched up and all the way,
Whose gluon-glory scorches!

The concord corridor
Of narrow necks full bloated
Bore bounty-backed rapport
Like lorries creosoted!

Emporiums once were
Behind dead doors long shut~
Vague memories may blur
My memoirs to the gut ...

The labyrinth still static-
Built flawless by design-
Concealed, but automatic,
Immaculate would shine:

Electroluminescent
Bright cucumbers outshone
Our lifetimes evanescent,
As stoically stout grown.

Each gweduc by the number
Would lurid lightning lilt,
Obliquely per cucumber,
Shortwave and to the hilt!

Be they flambeaux fluorescent
Who's harsh glare radiates
Life's labyrinth incessant
With lazy eighty-eights ...

Where muffled up wall-glaze
May mirror soffit ceilings
Throughout unending hallways,
Too mute for fickle feelings!

Ensconced in every fixture,
A Teflon tongue yet quivers
This intramural picture:
Now permafrost, no rivers!

Some cryogenic sleeper
May thaw me with incision;
My mission as Light Keeper,
In vitro, vouchsafes Vision.

Betwixt flip-sides of fleurs-de-lys flamboyant, an otherworldly **Mortier Taj Mahal** DANCE ORGAN bleats, blaring its blitz o' slits (*squeak, screech* and *shrilly shriek*) of violent vociferation broadcast across kilometers! As if with clockwork control, steam-pressurized reed-whistles whine and wheeze woefully, yet ululate aloud out-of-tune clarion clarinet choruses distributed hither and yon. For this weightiest harmonium of pneumatic stop-and-knob keyboard backup heats her argent **Hg** pap smear of thermometer condensation into a damp daguerreotype! Effective effigy effused to resonate a repertoire repository of prerecorded ditties about doleful desires and niceties; that of age-old wee whistles which *blow, blat, blurt, blare*~ with flair~ their hot air en clair.

Therefore, in metronome and mellifluous mellow-tone, whilst big bulked bellows were buckled by accordion pleats; as molten throat and bottleneck bundles moan & groan grotesqueries and tartly torturous toccatas, that palpitate surreal surroundings, a *tintinnabular* 56-bell carillon therewith had staged complementary accompaniment! Thenceforth, for no pretense, hence my **Mortier**

Taj Mahal DANCE ORGAN blow-top calliope! Equipped with her fully unmanned massive music box "Orchestrion" or (French) "*Limonaire* Frères" mechanized via self-lubricated automation, *she* renders an organist inept thereat! Yea, and unlike organs for indoor use, be they designed to bellow out a large volume of sound heard above noisy din and fairground machinery, this helluva harmonium had deafeningly screeched her locomotive and ferryboat whistles with woeful earsplitting splutter, only to resume her incontestable yet time-tarnished, etiolated étude! In an intramural repository, the Thursford collection contained the Mortier **112**-key Dance Organ, if I may recall. Overall, she was within such steamy éclat!

My timestamp inventory of fairground organ-manufacture and development was the late 1830s, particularly with the opening of the Limonaire Frères company of Paris in 1839. On my Rolodex record, it was 274 years ago from this year of super-tall **2113**! Apropos of the aforementioned, a *limonaire* is a mechanical wind instrument. The limonium fair organ of the Limonaire Frères brand was an unwieldy, herculean heavyweight of the organ series that could only be transported on a lorry-towed platform. Mechanical-pneumatic originally, it is operated by a steering wheel crossbar either by a crank, by a steam engine, or by an electric motor for the most memorial models. I realized by my history, how it was then that Giacomo Gavioli patented the usage of book-music to play organs, that later became cartridge inserts for fairground 'calliope-organs' of **2113!** Confounding though, and spoof-proof for such a robotic reliquary revealed, I versify my adjunct of attribution:

Porcelain Polonaise

Via resonant repertoire roll
Loudly lurid or lissome alas,
Oily Taj Mahal Mortier whole
Dials eloquently every brass.

Brazen egg-and-acanthus lady
Bundled all about inviolable
Is voluptuously very weighty,
Eggshell-easiest *unetiolable!*

Tiles deafeningly echo round,
Royally reply whistles aloft
Any Yell propagated profound-
Felt stentorian only or soft.

Spreads Organa Goldora aloud,
Lovely lullaby ditty endowed!

Upon brief relief, just shy of another paragraph of paramount performance, marched (in starched uniformity) an Exemplar next to nothing and out of nowhere numbered. Her regalia roughneck military Maypole Poetry proceeds as (**132** verses of **33** stanzas):

a Valid Ballad of 2113
Vista Vision elucidated

I had a cryptic dream
That loomed up a tall tower:
O building which would seem
To rise above all power!

Inside it floors were slanted;
Its plaza splayed out gardens
Where no one ever ranted,
Nor any lad who hardens.

Where customers stayed happy
And quietness filled hallways,
And thrift productive, snappy
Switched on the hurry always.

Where air remained efficient,
Where doors and floors were white
Immaculate as if omniscient-
Some Source kept it bright.

I surveyed every corridor
And enfilade stretched high,
High ceilings florid more,
Enough to make men sigh.

For silence soaked me in
With whiteness all around
That had no noisome din,
But lay instead pure crowned.

I launched an elevator
Way up to seventy-seven;
I thought it must be later
If I will reach up Heaven!

This building would not sway
And neither did she lurch;
Well paved was she, I'd say!
Far stouter than mere church.

Now seventy-seven to reach:
I sought a good wide window
As muffled wind would screech;
Its pane withstood wind blow.

I gazed above me heights
That tapered up to cloud-forms;
How high above streetlights
Below me with loud swarms!

Beneath me spread the sprawl
Of greatly grown skyscrapers
Where grid work towered tall
With tube-tops of high tapers.

Each after burnt were they
Per torchlight fusion-sewn,
Ablaze midst haze fir-gray,
Opaquely, like a cone...

I ran back to the shaft
Whose elevator waited
For me lest I fell daft
From vertigo, elated!

ELEVATORIUM

Reentered I the car-lift
With blister numbers stuck
Upon its walls to far shift
Me weightlessly with luck.

Four hundred eighty-six
Awaited my arrival,

Far o'er yon candlesticks
That lit up tomes archival.

But with weird jolt I sped,
Smoothed out and gliding free,
Until time-dilated, spread
Crimped cushions hiding me!

Four <u>THOUSAND</u> eighty-six
With platform came instead!
That lit split Katy Sticks
Since rarefied, thin spread ...

Through exits tentative
Reluctantly I went
Out into sensitive
Surroundings very bent.

How holy Silence came
About me, though I stood
As every wick seemed tame
Aflame beside plywood!

Whence Laser Lamps ionic
Gleam monochrome fluorescent
While mirrors chromed photonic
Reflected every crescent.

Wee peepholes revealed dark
Sheer stratosphere cessation;
Without were stars seen stark
Besprent through coruscation.

Above thronged lady sticks
With weighty egg-and-tongue
Be four thousand eighty-six
Too high for *wall-side* rung!

Beneath me wave-crests skirt
Hung high: fudged under-cast,
Outspread like sheets begirt
With lightning thunder blast.

Whence iridescence softly
Suffused my wayward being
Transfixed, how loftily,
Vertiginous and reeling...

Dirked dizzily, I saw
The curvature of earth
As cloud tops causing awe
And wonder offered mirth.

Atop the globe was I
How halcyon unabated!
Enough to make me cry
From joy while elevated!

But then my Vision ended;
I saw some cloud around me
By reason since ascended
It upwardly, abound-free.

I do remember this then:
(An observatory outspread)
Would panorama kiss ten
More visitors about led!

I love thee, VIVATORY:
Two-One-One-Three so tall,
So stately, full o' glory
To balance up thy ball.

What tapered up at edges

[With supple bottle *frission*]
Surpassed forever ledges
Exceeding vaunted vision!

Whose quietest quintessence
Protrudes thy polar Nipple
That enters evanescence
Beyond recumbent ripple.

FOUR THOUSAND EIGHTY-SIX

Became my ranked reward,
Whose cloven weighty wicks
Fan forth what few record!

Vouchsafe Cartouche, I pray
Thou rimmed reactor churning
Star-bright Sprite roundelay:
Crown resonance returning.

At acme, prolonged before any Aramaic mosaic, the algebraic *infundibuliform* Conical Helicon or fine Fulgid Finger of united Yod~Hei~Vav~Hei [unspeakably unlawful but serenely sancta sanctorum] inscribes on capricious sand (awhirl with wet breeze) an interminable BTE or Bulged-Tubular Entity of indefatigable instantaneity. That which kinked our cryptic cuneiform crescent and cradle of civilization amid Mesopotamia! This eschatological abacus, even so, enumerated to ….

No googolplex, nor excelsior; neither *nether-number*, save

Tanquam in Speculum
As if in a Mirror

PLURISEPTIPLEX

I'm surefooted, foreshortened and sheer amid an incalculable **LAZY EIGHT** swirled sideways like a terribly toasted, or charred pretzel! An acronym (multiplex) multiplied *exponentially*!

How unfathomably apparent! But the more belittling to me~ so unapologetic~ were maze-like entanglements of a narrow burrow and clandestine clinch of continual conduit. My *omnidirectional* **UNIVERMICULATORIUM** or UVTM (via acronym convenience) woeful wormhole and sinkhole, noodle-spurious spaghettification throughout labyrinthine limbo reintroduced! Notably, nearly one light-year's length of convoluted causeways- and outstretched still- treadmills that funnel through an ultra-integrated slip-slit *city grid* inside-out, all hallway housed!

Hallowed hallways of the **Ubiquelabyrinthium** (ultimately)!

How herewith [as I meander midway~ by my Yard Lamp of Gloria exposition~ to distinct details in this maze on some *X-Files* case] there lies an enigmatic Vista Vision ---

My mugshot *prima facie* evidence of an ultimate UVTM, under such an expunged verdict betwixt the plaintiff and defendant, who conduct controversies over innumerable grains of sand- say- ten sextillion? as in a tribunal! My affidavit of deferential defense; yea, under deposition thereof, is forwarded to the year **2113**...

I was so cornered, dazed and dumbfounded. Not just by the fabulously refulgent Hyper-City, all elegantly arrayed and attired- against which some vituperative vitriolic assaults and subjugates the glorified, glaringly seraphic Light thereof, using relentless religiosity that managed to nuke a third of our global crowd back in WW3. But rather, by the never kinked, colossal sub-stretchable labyrinth limbo, reevaluated with emphasis:

*For with sure-footed forbearance, intrepid still, I ventured out into this narrow, high-ceiling hallway only about 2 meters wide, with 23 meter height, having oily white latex enamel of high-gloss, and with ridiculously large bio~genetic lanterns linked lazily overhead, dangling in the ventilated waft and draft of transducer transom vents installed upon the forefront and also *postern slip-slit door of each walkway corridor.*

Since I had absolutely no sense of direction- neither the up, down, left, nor right orientation whatsoever- I felt much more dwarfed and diminutive therewith! Aye, in that [though] multiple doorways of alternate exits surrounded me, right after I went through that main singular door-slot, the other far end of the corridor continued to nowhere.

Immediately, less than a hairline of one nanosecond, another identical hallway of like-appearance, yea, and of a definitive dimension, had re-materialized instantaneously, as if it were all along situated, right there, in the first place to begin with!

Wherefore, the veritable radiant replica of it could continue consecutively, unless something quite spiritual midst my inner quintessence caused the corridor itself to replace an infinite regression of other circummured conduits with what my Soul sought to prefer on her behalf; namely, the unfolding of radiant reality with that of space-time altogether.

Unfortunately, if nothing rare, redeemable, or worthwhile was found embedded inside my spirit-soul, then the prolonged process of automatic and inter-dimensional duplicity and entanglement continued on forever and ever; inchworm-inchoate upon one's very first footprint privately partaken thereupon! And this, in graphic lay language, was what the "spaghettification" of my directionless Univermiculatorium entails. So much to the point of something so alien and utterly bizarre, as to horrify the skeptic and unbeliever alike; let alone stultify anyone's stupid stance against my moderated UVTM!

Amen! Again, we shan't show (shallowly) anything irrelevant, save what that last abbreviation, UVTM, hath stood for! But no epithet, nor nomenclature are offered to the very endless annex thereof, except for the following subset, 9830164275 24811993 9830164275, whose corresponding numerology is aligned with letters of a cryptic alphabet, notably, characterized by the elusive ILUCIFULGIDULIPLURIGLUNIVATI~ *as if to have been a perfect match on target, naught else!* ——

* In 1984, this was an entry passkey to my old 'Transalteratorium' traced all the way back to the beginning.

The tunnels of the entire 'Univaconduitorium' followed forever to *continual contiguity* of one seamlessly stretchable passageway! Of course, authorized arrangements for entry level thereunto can be traced back by far easier labyrinths, like the Chartres cathedral labyrinth~layout (in ecclesia) of the northwest French countryside.

9830164275248119939830164275
ILUCIFULGIDULIPLURIGLUNIVATI

But back to bivouac lamp camp.

In retrospect, I shan't exclude mannequin monstrosities of an outdated ballerina to mimic pterodactyl Terpsichore, tantalizingly. For with obsolete, behemoth television propagation cable-work and fulgent bundles- all full of blow-up fiber optics and **CRT** equipment paraphernalia *sub-squeezed* into some soap-slushy, salty subterranean substructure- admittedly, it was an anthropomorphic necropolis of burial quarry pits side by side sequestered amid compartmentalized

Sheol in sharp contrast to a phantasmagorical future photon tableau vivant (vindicated), void of want.

So stately, that its millennial covenant behooved me to stumble and take heed of the freeze-frame thereof.

The polychrome vat-and-vale of sunlight *herself*, whose aurora corona unleashes a nacreous nimbus of lurid luminosity, expands; that unsheathes shortwave swords and bulbous bundles of complex plurality energized by but solar wind intensification of precisely **94,107** Kelvin in colour temperature! Yet each Pyrex borosilicate glass and transparent-sleek stainless steel sheet of aluminum and ceramic tile- under insular, infrared investiture- is wrapped round itself, and with what wonderfully can harness heavenly flow and flux abrupt! Just as if the spun fabric of shock-wave energy had been amalgamated out of an indecipherable inviolability! A *multi-labyrinth* outstretched so, able to disorient unauthorized intruders into oblivion. An antediluvian tributary of mercurial, multifarious LETHE, liltingly lustrous and limpid! Devoid of recall! As if some seamless Tarmac, but by itself and forever forgetful, oozed the creamiest creosote of an oil-gusher ever imagined!

Whoa! With snapshots of an electrostatic cathode and Tesla coil: the ineffable I clarify. Likewise, I glanced upon an afflatus buffer therewith, held out athwart at heart, girt with the under-garter belt of a potential, exponential power factor quadrupled to 900 quadrillion *yottawatts*! Able to easily dwarf the bygone Tevatron: a proton/antiproton particle accelerator once stationed in DuPage County, Illinois, which- although that energized its 6.28 kilometer radiant ring or arc-plasmatic doughnut to 1 TeV- was shut down in September 30, 2011 (or about 102 years ago). From equivalent Quotient to Sum of a stellar resonance resource par excellence! The inconceivable but masterpiece magnificence of what had illimitable thermal transference by one nuclear reactor Super-Tongue Tremendous Transducer, or STTT to yet another and another, almost indefinitely! And each one embalmed by an emblazoned encasement of a plump *plumbiferous* chrysalis, how surreptitious! So serenely separate from carnality as to avoid any inkling of a catastrophic meltdown induced. Triggered by firebug- bulged luciferin of radio and bioluminescent tritium, burnt pouch, copper kettle and/or [canister creation] of explosive existence!

The concord cascade of *hyper~spirit,* which, for having been overhung nearside an oceanic basin, spills sparkling bright, might I add. The contents of which- by contrast- stratify a wet superfluid hydropolis or *liquilopolis*, if symmetrical. Having zero viscosity, volatile and slipperiest "univacuoleum" lay adroitly adrip with a fissile reassertion of resiliency- from *fireplug* faucets of breeder reactor revitalization- that transcends processed heavy water (D_2O) or evermore so. Commensurate with nothing but finest fusion!

Nor on another equator, via viscous *petroleum* quicksand with its moist, mercurial, marginal and briny brink, the supernumerary spectra-sparkle of raw, unleavened flat-fusion reactors could quickly be utilized to reabsorb reservoir mercurial deuterium oxide. Such lightning liquid *spilt to-the-hilt* [figuratively so] to be Fraunhofer fine line-by-line imprinted, by quantum analysis, and interspersed as that thick, slick Lady *LIQUICK*. Whose vivifying hemoglobin serum, siphoned and transfused, supplies every artery and aorta of a hydraulic network; whose ambidextrous waldoes of versatility are imbued with an Instamatic circulatory subsystem. The infrastructure of interlink transposed throughout the highlight-girdled starry cope and TRANSDUCER (**T**) of focused photons comparable to **M87**! Bordered about at the bright fringe thereof lay a self-luminous *Luciopolis* steed-backed carousel-adjunct accretion floppy-disk-drive of rapid, rational rotation! Blimey! Brocaded brilliance unapproachable at that! Herein, of course, derive divers precincts of annexation to a much more magnified metropolitan cynosure in quickening, glamour gladsome.

Sustained by my votive offering, I classify galaxy **Messier 87 (53.49 million light-years from Earth) with the GLIBOLA designation! END OF LINE**

In fine, may I climax this revelatory glory-clip with an outcry of entry to upright and upside-down pyramidal Bliss. Howbeit though, that inundated with support pillars, totem-caryatids and nearly nine-hundred thousand vertiginous vacuum shafts all at once, it resplendently flashes out at me, clamoring for attention! Bedazzled then, I verify an auditor. **We must ask ourselves, what binds us together as Americans, what makes us e pluribus unum, 'out of many, one'?** *The Latin phrase e pluribus unum is found on the seal of the United States, adopted by an Act of their Congress in 1782. Hence out of many, One*! Verily, whereby an *e pluribus unum-* without currency- takes on refurbished replication of investiture literally! The plurality of hexagon packets, each one, a colossal cavernous cathedral kept anti-gravity-suspended. Yea, each as an insular yet interconnected Vat, vastly the size of China's Pearl River Delta urban intersection, but so sub-squeezed into a tiny TARDIS- acronym for Time And Relative Dimensions In Space- that enough of them make up my *Metropolis Astra* **------** City of Stars. Indeed, every one of such superstars, if self-contained and energized with Elysian cornfield continuity, one Vat after another, hexagonal, to contain a fiery forest of at least 1000 meter-high cattails and corncobs at large bulge in and of themselves! The whole gamut of which would insulate the preparatory occupancy of 3,000,000,000 inhabitants (futurity-distributed), except vastly vacant for now ….

Midst searing standpoints of all-Holy, mercurial and sizzling **MEGALOTUBULOPOLIS** expediently expounded upon, lush-laden wi' wet mercury-mantled and *metalucent,* multi-storied mushrooms of soft self-contained slip-city access, I herald prophetic profusion and premonitory promise of incalculable magnitude! Its provisional facilities are divinely engineered, filled and filleted with beehive Honeycomb Hexagonal Harmonics of tall-wall hyper-architecture emanated by permanently paved holograms of variably algorithmic fractals via *vomitory* Mandelbrot set. As *Titanic Termite Towers* (TTT), but each one turreted. Although full of elongated beehive, honeycomb Heavenly Hexagons- or better yet- pliable Plexagons super-symmetrically contoured, serenely situated as stalagmites in an antediluvian cave. Except these, distended from 2 to 3 thousand meters in height! As outwardly six-sided they were, with lapis lazuli cinder-block brickwork that contained lazurite, calcite, and pyrite, far down below, streets lay lit by glittering diamond-asphalt and see-through permanent pavements of ultra pure 24 karat gold leaf inlay. Revelatory streets set- supinely- beneath elongated sea cucumbers kept in seamless self-sufficiency. That alongside old arc tube transparent transducers, an obsolete cobra head with one kilowatt *luminaire* shines, still, even if as a preserved artifact!

I witnessed how yesterday's Museum would complement such city-complexity with petroleum based blacktops Tarmac flanked by high-mast streetlamps. Quickened, quivering quietly, with their outdated netherworld, hinterland nostalgia, these are truncated arc tubes of ionized mercury vapor. Still pressure-preserved to offer an ever ageless, narrowest wavelength [like sunlight] for Fraunhofer special spectral analysis...

Perchance, by my fortified fore-glimpse of Spiritual Radiation, known as increate light, its stray spark of consecration confounds but graven images of our benighted age of blight. If ever plagued by a fanfare of vanities, such saturnine soil of today's grotesque grotto ushers everyone's spirit in for mandatory growth! In fact, amongst numinous nodules of fiery finials at every old **Argon Ancon (A-A)** that ballooned into a discreet, deflated dirigible- or ever as deluxe flux capacitors wrought *radiative*, such <u>saturated</u> presence persists! Robustly rotund with dark, archaic antiquity, extend balustrades of colonnettes wrought with redwood and Norway spruce; ravishingly resistless Rococo and Renaissance double~helix spiral staircases overshadowed by bulged mahogany-carved anchor and acanthus ornamentation. Adjoining some paisley plafond of pliant plaster, *SHE* shows off! Right down from escalatory prominence, gingerly, yet downright delicately graceful! Nicely narrowest, sylphlike and contoured up as an innately sculptured immemorial *inamorata*. My one-size-fits-all (only in this context) goddess-bodice of preened, pruned and prim boxwood myrtle festooned fancily! Embellished daintily, demurely dolled by grease-gritty tallow-tapered homestead maidenly merriment up a staircase of 33 steps at the 1873 Chapel of Our Lady of Light in New Mexico.

Aye, such *gweduc duckbills,* distributed from a soporific sea, inserted and then reconverted into corpulent cucumbers of this tall, tallow, fallow **Vouchsafe Cartouche,** initiate lily-like luminance unfading for eons. Or that shall induce the makeshift torchlight to become quasar beacon Glorifier! As rational radiance illumined for no legitimate purpose except as *lighting for the sake of lighting,* crème de la crème creations and distinctions of vitreous paradise are arrived at or fetched, as it were. For by midyear of 2113, anti-gravity crystal chandeliers of candelabra tapers flare flauntingly, flickering. Their bulk bundles looking like crisp cream and foam fudge-top topical *congealant spray* applied on the Sacred Five Wounds. Foiled in old gold leaf and tinged, tenuously, with an iridescent anemone of quivering quicksilver cotton candy caught through the stretch-fabric of the Luminiferous Sacred Aether! Of radio radiance! Of no lackluster loot, but of fabulous finesse and how insuperably inseparable!

An ambrosial, old elixir vitae it will be. A cocktail potpourri of wrenching wreath-like liquefied *Lethe, though the steroid river of forgetfulness,* that which with forget-me-not florals recalls no more vice, nor memory lapse, but in favor or Mnemosyne) laid à la carte, conserved to administer amaranthine mollification therapy at the blink of an eye.

O for once, what salubrious soliloquy of my longing to have it arrayed, *glistering* still! Unapproachable! Concrete! Of no more allegory, it is alive and far too rainbow-radiant to go gawk at, let alone epitomize! The all-holy Helicon Conical congealed from prismatic prominence to an electromagnetic mountaintop super-summit into but one infinitesimal yet titanic instant! I blare, enter now the holographic *Hyper-city* and away with our present day polluted and barbaric bustle of riffraff hellbent upon bartering bellicose altercations the world over by belligerent and naughty thugs, renegades and wranglers!

Our portentous population epicenters shall become amputated, forthrightly, from out of nil, still, and ever so forcibly replaced by something of more perennial outcome. Of biblical prediction and old candle-wax *ceromancy* once and for all, wherewith "*a City not made with hands, eternal in the heavens*" should shortly transpire! Man's overbearingly obstinate corporation duly decapitated at long last. Retrofitted with fairy tale fulgurant arc-forks of cocoon firefly phosphorescence enlarged a million percent! An oasis of 3 Graces destined to carry out the quintessential **CREATORIUM** ready to *revivify*, instead of annihilate in an oven or furnace, cadavers that are, by hopeless heaps, hurled thereunto! Radiating Resurrection Incorporated! The Resurrected *Effulgurant* showcased, quickened with paranormal priority... Per apotheosis, souls beatified bodily.

[Apropos of some aforementioned spectacle ever so gossamer envisaged, allow me to indulge in on but one more unavoidable cornerstone] w*ith nary unnecessary emphasis reaching borderline vainglory vehemence*: may we address our whole-soul heretofore MERCURITY of an elegantly attired Superpower:

Again, picture an intramural environment, for example. Based on an all out-of-the-body bivouac of adventure one experienced before the composite sketch of Gloria's consummation. The author herself was swooned up by a lock, stock and barrel bivouac extravaganza of hallowed hallways that immured her to *the very inchworm of forever*. Moreover, any precautionary detour was veritably impossible to compute since the whole resemblance of it maneuvered by mere advancement of her feet, no matter how tentative! Hence, may I wager my final film-footage of the old VIVARIUM in conclusion to my garishly *bright city of Elysian fields*! Annexed adeptly by high-pitched squeals of a **Tiny Still Small Voice** (TSSV) herewith.

An intramural intersection, within circuit surveillance cradled comfort opposite to incarceration of any kind; not to preclude the proverbial gilded cage of sorts. Wherein, of course, one is found confronting his or her real simulacra of 3-dimensional televised *hyper~reality* and (as if meeting another actual personage to touch) reaches out to an entity-tangible doppelgänger of the same sort to either embrace or resist. That is, depending on how accepting one is of their sanity sized up, I reckon. Furthermore, accompanied by my aforesaid scenario, imagine then these sterilized premises to proffer unsurpassed technology at the faintest whim of one's behest, howbeit holy it must be by Divine Ordinance!

Meanwhile, cross-stitch netting of equilibrium unfolds!

The foreseer is taken aback, aboard, bilked by metamorphosis of a muddled moratorium:

And I faced lividly the wan membrane of plaster, high ceiling and transom vents at each doorway down an enfilade of this ultra acoustic facility. Now confronting me, on an adjacent adjunct of a wall-facade, hung some shiniest mercury mirror framed in an egg-and-tongue rectangular entablature of foursquare dimension! The quivering moiré sparkle (silkily) **---** *having this rippled, lustrous finish, of which (furrowed with vertical vortices, striations, wee wavelets and loops throughout)* **---** *mirrored me my narrow-burrow doorway to unknown eternity! Until precedent to my exit from thence, I have ascertained how screaming silence augments the soundboard of this intimately 'unetiolable'* GLORATORY **291-** *Some underground fallout shelter designated with an eighteen digit or cipher enumerator of* **9830164275** hyphen **24811993**. *Notably, to such a degree as to echo contrapuntal crackle from a hairpin on impact, as if it were cacophony* *and amplified to the sudden topple or stentorian thunderclap of an old Empire State Building in full, fallen...*

Whereas and whereabouts an attenuated but undiminished murmur issued forth froth *from all six sides of this Corinthian corridor I had basked in, seated on an ibex-swirled Mercy Seat, I could not endure to look at Naked Truth notwithstanding! Thus I took the plunge instead thereof and had horizontally escaped an ear-splitting, most deafeningly horrific confrontation curiously conceived of! Not of confabulated unreality! Rather, plummeting headlong into listless lull and an ever peaceful, trance-induced (hypnagogic) hallucinatory state ...*

It was the silver sliver of a cloven cord let loose, lilting, as I disembarked in my reconnaissance capsule or armored French frigate galvanized with cannonball arsenals of deployment by the dozen. Staunchly launched and adrift! Which capsize, luckily, had been prevented! Ready to dodge and disregard decoys of any kind; focused not upon gweducs, nor big barnacles, but on the hunt for Red October!

Alas, disturbingly disembodied for a moment by trenchant, tributary traversal of such superluminal Enveloped Departure, I reawakened right from Salvador Dali's Persistence of Memory; superimposed by the guise of an auspicious ready-room or walled Womb I could have rather forsaken and forgotten! An endometrial omen to be unsurpassed, alive under my dimmest flashbacks of discomfiture, if otherwise delightful desultorily ...

Hereof the portent beyond the pall of a midnight entrance and exit vivified *vis-à-vis* with an auditorium quite incomprehensible yet yielding effervescent is shared. Frankly, I became bamboozled by indecipherable odds. Now, a ninny I was in comparison to recollection and recompense of data diminutive. Never mind my pedagogue goon gone gaunt, agog and gaping at naught else under a microscope!

Minuscule more than this, dare I blare, by crushed comparisons with what my mainstream milieu sips single-handed! But for now, how once more, my farewell to her triumphant transmogrification of *aluminum vapor* vouchsafed via pressure gun primed hitherto! An effusion of which was aerosolized by an old can of hairspray or fluid fluorescent neon splattered upon subway catacombs; a spray can that spits its will-o'-the-wisp flareup I'd combust, resolute by my kitchen matchstick of flammability!

Fagot for a bundle of sticks--- inextinguishable--- anyone?

My whole hush, ephemeral dream-time resumed evanescence, enough to wax one pallid. But not without crystal clear memory of lake *Liquick's* ladyship allure, daintily miniaturized and suspended sideways, silvery! Dimpled up into protuberances sprayed o'er and still flavescent, blushing sanguine, verecund. Splashing about but unguent: an opaque, argent arc tube Entity bulged by its sides, tapered up and down at each end thereof... so self-protuberant.

O frothiest steel-still Sheelil alone: so seamlessly grown as a two-tailed albacore fish with no head, nor eye, nor mouth, but *flat-out*, yet finely cylindrical and outspread to its fan-like dorsal fin fore-and-aft. Uprightly or transversely poised for incorruptible freshness! God-forbid, never to be harpooned, hoisted, devoured, nor partaken of, neither compared with~ save shared, as it hath glared …

Rung cloven red hung merrily
Tongue overhead flung verily

COMMERCIAL BREAK

At night, are you
Feeling dark, damp
As in a pit?
Ignite our new,
Revealing arc lamp
Inviolate!

Yard Lamp of Gloria: **Revamp**

Until then, we wanted to loll and lollygag bygone backward in nostalgic times past atop my stagecoach of subsonic transport. To turn my gaze on an inviolable, inextinguishable, titanic, turgidly Cardinal Amphora Tongue or **CAT** container. Or refrigerant h~ly hyper-hydrant fireplug of- oddly enough- bloated blanket: as an insulating invocation wrapped roundabout! Its cobalt bluebottle effigy would remind me of a Klein-clinched *bottleneck* of fluid fulminating reflection. A mathematical paragon paradox of inter-dimensional infinitude that occupies its molten maelstrom of a "Unicloveniferous Supersingularity" beneath shriveled shrinkage! An utter, upper udder accord of *vaccimulgence* squirts forth froth o' quantum foam. But yet & still, with Pneumatic Transducers…

The citywide curbside reveals it resplendently! Row-by-row Refrigerant Fireplugs of slit-sieved fishnet mesh interfaced with the whole Hive, poised at my approach, as one of them [telephone booth bottled] inquires of me, using a metallic intonation with TSSV (The Still Small Voice): "*Whence comest thou*, O pilgrim?" And so, that then brandishes an automatic microphone for better reception.

Looking like Doctor Who's infamous cyborg mutants, the Dalek, and just as resplendently robotic!

"From that *Bright City of Elysian Fields*, I pray..." I'd cry in reply, squinting by reason of facial sunburn; for furthermore, my skin-job jocundly appeared pockmarked, cratered, badly battered by bombardment of radioactive roentgens! Even so, I was alive and preserved proportionately nonetheless!

"Yet you bypassed my former landmark of an **STTT** during thy way heretofore, O wherefore!?" the interrogatory hyper-hydrant persisted (the acronym is spelled out below forthwith).

Nonplussed, I would almost yelp for help, blithely elated by jolts of the flyby jet stream that knocked me out of my socks.

Eftsoons, I faced an erect, incombustible Heav'nly **Cooca** rise above my head: that stood upright, narrowed up and down, open-ended, but that widened out at girth and with whom I leveled in sackcloth and ashes: "Not so, O incumbent package, for thou art that *irreplicable*, selfsame Super-Tongue Tremendous Transducer, indistinguishably so, next to thy former fuselage of voluptuous vintage. In restitution, therefore, I offer thee my heavy hatchway passkey to time-slot 2 1 1 3 anticipated in fine!"

"Affirmative, thou mountaineer to 2113: A Grace Odyssey, in that whosoever you may meet along the way, I am the Luciferin Incognita! Yea, and that which you confront, I am acknowledged therewith! Henceforth, O away with thee to the Old Glory of VIVATORIUM **291**! Ich liebe dich! Auf Wiedersehen!" By that Deutsch dimple of valediction, I curry favored Futurity for extra attention. I felt like Rutger Hauer on that epic classic Blade Runner sci-fi movie ministered long, long ago, in a galaxy far, far away, accompanied by the most mellifluous Greek composer, Evángelos Odysséas Papathanassíou, or the Vangelis soundtrack throughout.

I swallowed my spittle, puckered with stiff-upper-lip Ae Fond Kiss, and waved farewell. This then to take my moratorium to heart for the reminder of a lifespan; at times serendipitous:

By courtesy of Robert Burns (1791)

Ae fond kiss, and then we sever!
Ae fareweel, alas, for ever!
Deep in heart-wrung tears I'll pledge thee,
Warring sighs and groans I'll wage thee.
Who shall say that Fortune grieves him,
While the star of hope she leaves him?
Me, nae cheerful twinkle lights me,
Dark despair around benights me.

I'll ne'er blame my partial fancy:
Naething could resist my Nancy!
But to see her was to love her;
Love but her, and love for ever.
Had we never lov'd sae kindly,
Had we never lov'd sae blindly,
Never met — or never parted —
We had ne'er been broken-hearted.
Fare-thee-weel, thou first and fairest!
Fare-thee-weel, thou best and dearest!
Thine be joy and treasure,
Peace, enjoyment, love and pleasure!
Ae fond kiss, and then we sever!
Ae fareweel, alas, for ever!
Deep in heart-wrung tears I'll pledge thee,
Warring sighs and groans I'll wage thee.

Like sunset, she set; having to dwindle away into her pinpoint of no return. Into an eternal cushion, far away from the precipice...

Finally, I overheard *Moon River* by Johnny Mercer & Henry Mancini.

With an overdue schedule- as cockpit conductor- I flailed out my forearm above a *glishoe glusilk* self-flanged undercarriage and hit a backlash o' unctuous airflow overblown to blustering gusts outdoors of my barreling booth. Unhampered by oil-spray pelting my hand. And lo! Not the in least shocked was I by how fulminating filaments quiver up cumulonimbi to precipitate with fallout renewal. Decades past me, posthumously, lest Freya's inevitable *Folkvangr* unveils! To be invincibly reinstalled and illumined into the sleekest Futurity, still. With no *blet* leftovers!

Quoth the non-grotesquely graven **city** *forevermore*: "Behold thou the ever incontestable GLIBOLOTUBULOPOLITZ with a glimmering and effulgent effect in esse ..." END OF LINE

Indeed, may I prophesy progress henceforth, ere my prefab but salutary sapphire VITROPOLIS glass-city of inviolable inventory may materialize multitudinous variety into reliable, pliable and vanishingly vibratile sheer sheen! Having heavyweight pacifier of an **insulator conduit** or hefty **hexagon**!

Far fiercer than the one handheld caduceus, and on the other, cornucopia, that flank Anciently Loveliest **UMA** in Coney Island's bygone Luna Park carnival! Or our Chicago World's Fair once lit up by myriad Westinghouse arc lamps. Let alone [later] to outshine Bulged-Tubular streetlights that dangle from a track-side canopy net of catenary cables and conduits aloft, would one's visionary ***Videopolis*** vitrify! Faultlessly electrified in an exigent unguent of a paraffin slip-sleeve.

Oh, and don't worry! If you're already en route, no charge for tomorrow's **TGV** high-speed MagLev hyperloop slide! Ye boxcar convoy: just wait! Your next tour de force entourage of a lifetime!

This rather repository tale of no extravaganza, but an entirely fathomless metropolitan monstrosity, can be delineated with words by the following Threefold Twilight (T-T):

1. Consider then our Sun reduced down to beach ball size- say- seven feet in diameter. The Earth would be big as a marble that children dally with and at 700 feet away. The moon in orbit of it, only a tiny ball bearing. Thus the closest star, Alpha Centauri, lies about 35,000 miles distant (again, that is, if our planet were 2.1336 meters, or 7 feet wide). * Alpha Centauri is exactly 4.367 light-years away

2. And now- if we were to actually visualize and imagine the macro-scale of my marvelous, mountainous municipality GLIBOLOTUBULOPOLITZ "Luciopolis" superstructure, my only drawn out picture of its glitz of magnitude could be portrayed as ordinary traffic cone pylons- plumb next to each other- but outspread like an uninterrupted, continual bunch, just to cover the state of Colorado!

3. In contrast to a four-foot safety cone- fluorescent neon that though it be- the world's tallest building is but a wimpy matchstick, flat out floor-level squat, flimsy, frail, and not without combustible comparison!

I, Aglaia, in light of my "glorified" glimpse, [dutifully] do rest my case.

finis

Supporting scriptures are found in the Gospel of John (first 3 chapters) and in the Book of Revelation (final 3 chapters) of the Authorized Geneva Version, unalterably

Firsthand Major Flood Image Section

11) Heartfelt photograph of an ageless seaside surf.

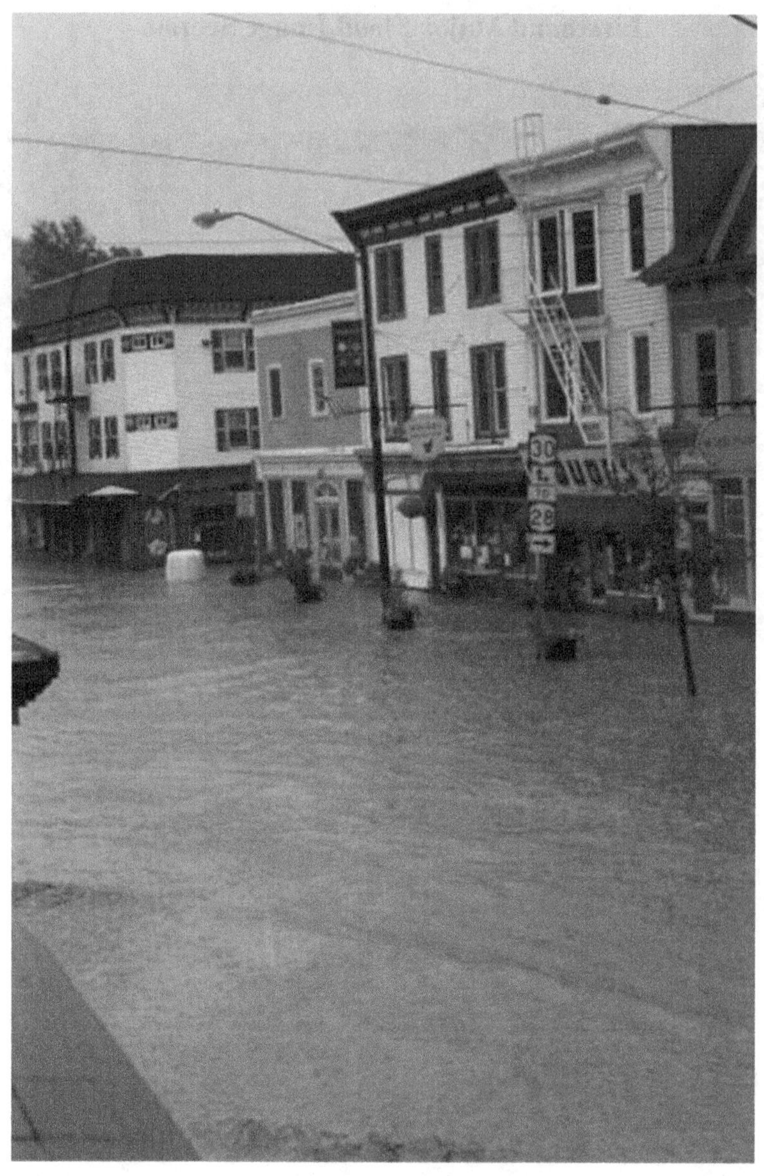

12) Margaretville was my village of residence through which the disastrous deluge had dredged up sludge and debris along New York's Delaware County alongside hurricane Irene's aftermath of lachrymal landfall; an unexpected event in late August of 2011. But just about 2 months before most of my personal belongings were swept away, I managed to preserve [for keepsake] my Yard Lamp of Gloria manuscript from sudden wash-up by Irene's flash flood of a swollen river that cascaded menacingly down the Route 28 Catskills Valley!

13) Rescue crew piggybacked on a fire engine auxiliary truck whilst woeful contingency and emergency sirens blared balefully from afar…

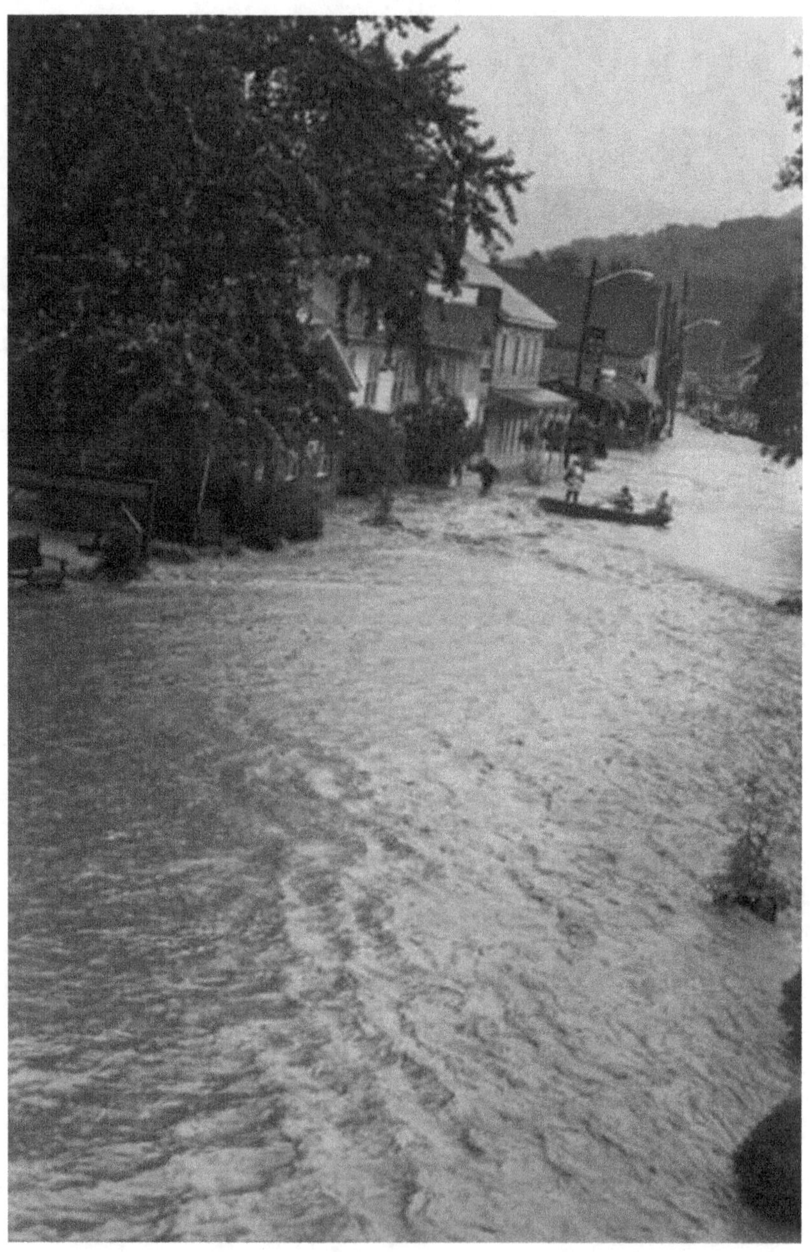

14) Reconnaissance rescue team aboard an emergency raft were in search of anyone stranded or immersed by an unprecedented "trenchant drench" of the Margaretville major flood!

15) Standby snapshot of the Margaretville Main Street area where one raging torrent of the deadly deluge gushed by with waterfall pressurized presence! Inter alia, some business owners were beleaguered later by big pitfalls and sinkholes unexpectedly laid out. It was an overwhelming overflow, I'll say.

16) Bird's-eye view of Margaretville's Main Street inundated by floodwater! This surreal scenario was taken from my apartment home that overlooked the furious eddy thereof.

17) Close-up clash of overflowing floodwater flux, aye, and its rather unabated gargantuan gush!

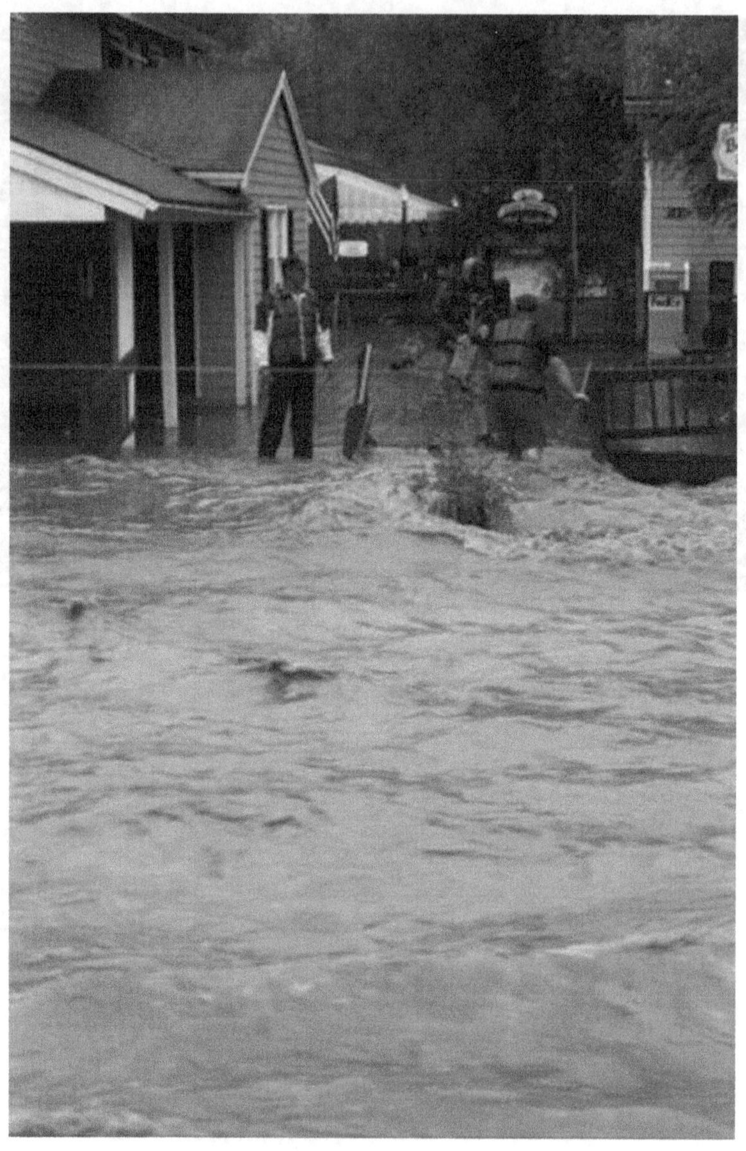

18) A high alert task force ready to anchor themselves with rope, rigging and tackle for added countermeasures implemented along the very "edge-water" of this torrential nightmare!

19) Routine disaster safety backup that inched their way above and across the raging river of a menacing flood! There were village victims in dire need of immediate reinforcements: their township Total Recall.

SHEEL

And the manna was as coriander seed, and the color thereof as the colour of bdellium. *And* the people went over and gathered *it*, and ground *it* in mills, or beat *it* in a mortar, and baked *it* in pans, and made cakes of it: and the taste of it was as the taste of fresh oil. And when the dew fell upon the camp in the night, the manna fell upon it... Numbers chapter 11, verses 7 thru 9.

Once long ago fell oil cream;
The which was often cooked
In frying vats, aglow, agleam,
Foam-filled but overlooked.

Since ancient Israel engaged
Prim prayer fasts of sackcloth,
Pacific grease, uncanny, staged
Lithe lather lit by back-froth.

An ordinance as many taught
Could not soak soft each heart
Upon old people newly bought
By Grace right from the start!

Frenetic churns o' pastry rose
For naught, at times, save rich
For fervid ones who did disclose
Their soulful Vase with pitch!

Like leavened dough, O edible!
Such fuel bulged brownie cakes
Throughout hard lard incredible
Midst manna's downy flakes!

If divers ages (kept in rigor)
Sought crowned glory yet,
A gift of grace far better, bigger
Gleamed globs aureate ...

Fat, milk and honey holy flow
From Heaven o'er free earth;
Congealed to crude cream lowly so
That fudge tubes grant rebirth.

JACOB'S LADDER PROPHECY

Composed on April 3, 2013 and
discerned over carefully as such

In a doorway hinged narrowly
Bordered upon *egg and tongue*,
Where no rocket nor arrow be
Soft Holy *Sheel* God had hung.

Time, alas, stills the frame
Frailest immaterial coffered-
As her maize spills selfsame
On society centuries offered!

Twilit days render reckoning;
Surly souls sink all on high,
But wet Graces are beckoning
Parsons to draw up well nigh!

Bound between egg-and-tongue
Ornate Amity here is rebuilt
With *Hydropolis* newly sprung
Out of which water has spilt!

May much Glare blare: Repent
Ye! Seek silent Original Joy!
Eschew strange entertainment
Discordant enough to destroy!

God at hand reaches downward
To others awaiting salvation;
By command, teaches One Word
That verifies vital creation!

Shapely Sheel fits each rung:

O inertly as people yet flee
Far away from disaster flung
Hot while souls are set free.

INTERPRETATION

Verse 2: EGG AND TONGUE interior art
*Verse 4: SHEEL lay opposite to *Sheol*:
the darkest crypt of one's own grave
(Sheel was my visionary first in 1986)
Verse 14: ORNATE AMITY represents an
aesthetic radiance restored worldwide
Verse 15: HYDROPOLIS the Liquid City

INTERMISSION

TESLA, Nikola (1856–1943). This big inventor and electrical engineer, Nikola Tesla, developed the alternating-current (AC) power system that provides electrical distribution for homes and buildings. Tesla was granted more than 100 United States patents. Many of his discoveries led to electronic re-developments for which other scientists were honored.

Nikola Tesla was born in Smiljan, Croatia- back then annex of Austria/Hungary- on July 9, 1856. Although he was often ill during his boyhood, he was quite a bright student with photographic memory. But contrary to his father's wishes he chose a career in electrical engineering. After his graduation from the University of Prague in 1880, Tesla labored as a telephone engineer in Budapest, Hungary. By 1882 he devised an AC power system to replace weak direct-current (DC) generators and motors in use.

Tesla immigrated to the United States in 1884. Thomas Edison hired the youthful engineer as an assistant upon his arrival. Friction soon transpired between the twain, and by 1886 Tesla had lost his job. In 1887 he obtained enough funding from bankers to build up a laboratory layout of his very own in the heart of New York City.

By 1889, Tesla received citizenship in the United States. A year earlier he had acquired a patent for his AC power system. At the cornerstone of this system lay the efficient *polyphase* induction motor that he invented. George Westinghouse purchased the patent rights from Tesla. Westinghouse then launched the campaign that established alternating current as the prime electrical power supply for the United States and the world over.

Tesla later wrought a high-frequency transformer, described as the Tesla coil, which made AC power transmission practical. He also experimented with radio and designed an electronic tube for use as the detector in a voice radio system almost 20 years before Lee DeForest contrived a similar device. Tesla lectured before a crowded audience of scientists in the United States and Europe from the years 1891 to 1893. Some of his so-called "sermons" were at least one century ahead of that early Era's scientific comprehension...

Although Tesla had paved the theoretical basis for radio communication as early as 1892, Guglielmo Marconi claimed all basic radio patents because of his own pioneering work in the field. In 1915 Tesla made an unsuccessful attempt to obtain a court injunction against the claims of Marconi. When the United States Supreme Court reviewed this decision in 1943, however, it reversed the decision and invalidated Marconi's patents on grounds that those had indeed been anticipated by earlier work.

Tesla and Edison supposedly had been chosen to take part in a Nobel prize for physics. According to such reports, Tesla declined his share of the award due to his doubt that Edison was a scientist in the strictest sense (but still, Edison was hailed as an American entrepreneurial idol thereafter). Nevertheless, neither of them ever retrieved the prize; a trophy well deserved by the former cup!

In later, elderly years, Tesla had led a somewhat destitute life; nearly forgotten by the world he believed would someday honor him. Tesla became defunct on Jan. 7, 1943, in New York City. The Tesla Museum in Belgrade, Yugoslavia, was dedicated to the inventor as some of his eager aspirants and benefactors had consecrated themselves to his posthumous milestone landmark. In 1956, the *tesla*, a unit of magnetic flux density in the metric system, was soon enough standardized in his honor.

In fine of the aforesaid outline, Nikola Tesla left us with an illustrious legacy of unparalleled possibilities toward a far finer, titanic Tomorrow; perhaps with much more of a pristine, pollution-free environment than what we, as caretakers, could conserve!

And now …

The *MBS

Initialism for Major Ballroom Sphere

Polyhymnia, my geisha who is white-gowned, remained a Siren of vociferous voices, and accordingly, *she* and I were found in spirit beside each other in the walled womb of Time. We were both enthroned far above the crowds of stars down beneath. For us it had been a reference room where contemplation presided. Between some puncture-proof *sphere*, myself and my Muse, as it appeared, was prepared an ever-delta triangular concord consent to a vertical *upward* and *downward* direction of *breathiest* spirit. The enlarged spherical presence would show itself as a *star torch* aflame, but so rounded out as to make it the prototype to any other geometrical shapeliness.

"One sphere round my Whole I show," intoned he,
"The rest of my cross sections none can see..."

The faceless yet convex and probing spheroid rotated itself, robustly, and that with an indescribable maneuver. Like that of collapsing into itself and *reverting back out* as it introduced many of its infinite variables.

"On him there is no end..." Polyhymnia reminded.

"That I know," was my only response.

How nuances of female grace bulged and retreated through her own veil of but rare and ancient discretion! She added, exulting: "For his rotation continues forever!"

By the import of those words a tremendous truth had dawned on me. Hereabouts a bio-plastic base hovered above our spiritual union right before its South Pole, divinely-curved exposition of electromagnetic polarity had begun to balloon forth- silently, smoothly- approaching us with such ease of impact. And from all perspectives at once, out of nowhere and inside out, I then witnessed a huge ball take shape as I heard with Polyhymnia a rough metallic, muffled voice of identity shriek "I was, I am, and I shall be..." out of what was- with sauntering, effortless effulgence- so flawlessly glossy and sleek.

As such, undeniably, it was altogether from an infinitesimal *vantage point*, out of nothing and inside-out, that a full grown overwrought Super Sphere of glory took shape. It was like globe lightning, but magnified hundredfold, that now divulged some bulged seventeen~meter equatorial girdle or hula-hoop of a full blown, big bouncing diameter! Eh? alley-oop!

"Horrify us not!" Lady Polyhymnia commanded, and futilely. Thunderstruck, I folded up my field of consciousness to a fully fetal position- be it humanly contrived- having been unable to detect any of it, protectively numb. On her side, the pressurized expressions thereof became battened down as if by figurative hurricane *diffusers* evacuated of thermal flux, wherewith both of our dual composure lay literally shattered.

Again, the Sphere resonantly reverberated:

"I come from up above, without... to down below, within."

Its niveous, featureless blank-blown etheric and *ectoplasmic embodiments* of must have been a seemingly contorted but self-sustained enveloped curvature started to oscillate in and out, tapering away and away, inflating back---- back, away and back ...

My Muse muttered bravely at once, prompted by unwritten volumes throughout an old tome of Mother Nature herself. "Show yourselves whole to me!" she demanded, direly, addressing the endlessly *harmonious.*

"But no mortal, nor messenger may target my blank body and live!" recoiled he, *creamily*. For it now felt as if an eternal calm had surfaced from its blank, blindingly bright elastic resiliency as it slightly, soundlessly bounced. The Oracular Orb persisted with warning: "It is forbidden for you or anyone to look past what God hath ordained, is that clear?"

We were speechless, overawed. Floored, if anything else.

"Is that clear?" the entire Super Sphere pressed, expanding its selfsame, silvery *size*; its three-dimensional protuberant properties- which were mere quasi-images of whole halves [to the naked eye] although inseparably joined- had bounced, bound by its unseen hyper-toroidal circumference, I say, the *Quasimage*, as it were:

"It is..." I answered obligingly. "We will not look upon thee-" and uncannily, "Being short*sighted* compared- we will not gaze at your fullness." I tried to swallow, but there was no throat with which I could do such a thing. Having been made disembodied for this very purpose, purportedly- in the gaudy, girly company of Polyhymnia- I was irreversibly conditioned to proffer an account of my Unknown Venture whether it damaged me or not!

"That is much better," the Sphere commented, satisfied by our final acquiescence to its obvious superiority: its *hyper~contours* of continual convexity that revealed our past, present, and future ever before it! But now, breathing down a bit to its seventeen meter roundness, though spongy as could ever be, it floated over my soul. I was forced to feel null and void like a tiny plastic plaything gnome before what would calmly be suggested as an old *ghostly* porcelain entity. An alterable, perpetual *theophany* beneath which our starry four-dimensional universe is but a silhouette of vacuous space and time, full of galactic disks and concrete clusters of quasar blobs that only overwhelm our imagination with their near-infinite riddles of relativity.

The Super Sphere continued in its usual synthesized chorus. "May the rest of me go through," with its *porcellaneous prototype*!

"What do you mean?" inquired my Muse, and in a beseeching manner- "Interpret for me and to this weary damsel that I am!"

One of its counterpart spherules (indistinguishably identified) clarified the objective: "Allow me to manifest myself- that is, let my hyper-curvature commence intensive intrusion," it squealed.

"Nay," was her objection. "Instead, let us convene a hearing on this," requested she, Polyhymnia. "Leave us, now!"

"Very well," the overbearing visitor paused, then added: "As you wish. Only if it will make you happy. Just this once! Now be careful, it's heavy..." It was intent on having the last word. "You are both free moral agents- I shan't infringe upon your desires. End of line..." Its whirling glitterati of equipoise polarity and equator acquiesced for the time being. The porcelain Tall Ball retracted.

This was the selfsame building-ballooned Ball that reluctantly, yet obediently slipped away and away, receding into itself until it was gone. Vanished into nonexistence. Never to have commenced concourse with its arrival in the first place to begin with!

Totally irreversible erasure.

Deflated, then deletion.

"See? It's that simple," she gloated gladly. "To him the tenuous thoughts and tendrils of a linear lifetime, such as our own, are as tactile as material substance is tangible to an earthling."

"You don't say!" I sounded sarcastically, feeling nonetheless like a nonplussed planchette aimlessly askew on some witchcraft Ouija board: the alphanumerical platform for an underhanded and slyly slippery séance- O oftentimes too taboo to religiously reckon with!

After all, and still, with knock-on-wood rapport of the Round Table hewn out of Honduran mahogany, my Muse gave me an abridged explanation of what seemed to transcend even our very own noetic knowledge of the Near-Infinite **----** Be it with interplay to intersect life's inter-dimensional intersection heretofore or forevermore (for Heaven's sake), I was stupefied by what was stupendous, *not* staged.

Via versification, she shared and annotated this thing.

"Your encounter with the Super Sphere will only retain but a fleeting fore-glimpse of its equidistant cross-sectional split prism assumed by spacetime continuum." She shook me breathless and hammered me while I felt tremulously impinged upon; mercy!

01. "Consider a rippling film of water," she elaborated.

02. "When you were earthbound, of course, remember your terrestrial, tellurian memories of childhood. Indeed, you imagined the top layer of *aqua pura* or clear-water, for instance, to be a world on its own; blind to the spacious air and heavens above it."

03. "This thin rippling film, or surface tension- the separation betwixt water and the firmament- could contour about any of the immediate shapes, forms, and figures that it embraces as an object is inserted. The pliant plenum is tenacious tapered to an object, as it were, and takes on a two-dimensional cross-section thereof."

04. "Be it formed from up above, beyond, or from down below, beneath, indeed, a universe of flat images, reflections and bubbles better yet completes the animate picture."

05. "In this malleable mortar, or call it the Plexiglas platform of imaging diagnostics with optimum optic ***polymethylmethacrylate** clarity, a higher, more vibrant visual cortex of shiniest polychrome colorization releases radiant rays of *irradiative* translucency."

06. "Even so, on that slick surface tension of water, amid the shiny film of it, would stretch a two-dimensional vastness perhaps so wide as the Seven Seas that *surround* your planetary *globus*."

07. "Whichever way one went, there he would be- but inside the harmonic horizons of that sub-spatial confinement."

08. "For the moment, recall a time when you curiously inserted but five fingers of your hand into the water. The sheer sheen and film of it (that clung to anything in contact therewith) reproduced five circles of those fingers to submerge. Nothing more, nothing less..."

09. "All that could be observed were those circles of likeness changing size as you moved your hand up and down, or *ana* and *kata*. To describe the two additional cardinal directions, Charles Howard Hinton coined the terms ana and kata, from the Greek words meaning "up toward" and "down from", respectively..." So, too, with four-dimensional maneuverability."

"Illustrated, as it were (for example), anyone within that two-dimensional matrix-featured frame of reference, or ring-ripple of *clear-water* (not to exclude the top layer thereof) would still be unaware of and ignorant to *the whole upper and lower shape of the hand*, or even to the lengthwise plumpness of an entirely elongated arm extending much farther and upward to the rest of the largely unrevealed polymorphous form!" She cavorted a cheerleader cartwheel and hollered, "Lucky star!"

"Likewise with our guest," she reminded, cryptically. "Except one step higher or excelsior. Never to puffy, vermiculite value, but epoxy material of continual concrete consistency, eternally unlike what we can conceive of, nor ever..." *Did she just stun me?*

For feeling *flattened* instead of- before- floored, I gathered my mindset. "You mean, one of many spheres can be a radiant replica of an imponderable entity?"

"Precisely presented! Well put. Perhaps... *irreplicable* rather," she sheepishly paused. "Apropos of the analogy, refer to it as an available self-conscious shadow of a *Hypersphere* that- *elsewhere-* mysteriously exists, to be exact." She mellowed herself, no longer whimsical. Polyhymnia then would shrug in self-relinquishment.

"But for what reason?" I persisted to the turn of the screw.

"Oh~ okay. The same, or relatively similar reason why atoms, molecules, planets and stars are all of one geometrical perfect shape, a *sphere*. A prototype of the much higher Infinite." By now, she had shown to be abysmally drained and I wore no comelier complexion.

Wearily, it was with mind-clenching erudition to both of us. Polyhymnia explained herself quite well, and far more accurately than any philosopher that the world would ever know, save for **Jesus Christ Almighty**, so be it. The master builder and architect engineer of Tomorrow's topographic Age!

Her loving, empathetic friendship seemed to spill into my soul as I savored every caress of it. The rippling film (five-fold) with five circles, five fingers, whole hand and arm illustration prepared me for what was about to occur... Divine intervention itself. The Holy of holies now unearthed by otherworldly knowledge! Yet contrary to us, unexpectedly, we had faced a far greater grotto of the Uncertainty Principle (the principle that the momentum and position of some subatomic particle cannot both be precisely determined simultaneously). Although an antediluvian time ago, even if at once discovered by the German physicist and Nobel Prize winner Werner Heisenberg in 1927, our *terra nova* frontier of the 2113 Pangaea went into effect about 85 million years <u>later</u> after the first predawn of a one continent, single settlement!

Its *vanilla*-visionary voice returned as it resonated out of my feeble being, as if I, a marionette, were rudely possessed by an unseen puppeteer. Then it was *shock-waved* throughout the whole of space! Polyhymnia had vanished!

"Where are you?!" I wailed in frenzied frustration. "Why must I face it alone?!"

Another voice, quite different though, soothed my person as it suggested: "Let limitless Loveliness reside inside what never may divide." The clandestine clench of a magnetic maelstrom upheld her *manus e nubibus* as I grappled with sub-spatial distortion.

Mad science, I thought. It was my Muse, recognizably, who retreated inside of me. Polyhymnia, who then challenged me to confront the Unapproachable and vie with it- to prove the very insistence of man's indomitable spirit. Regardless of the sphere's Capable Paradox. To yet accommodate *It* for whoever It is: the same yesterday, today, and forever...

I was now left alone therewith, expecting disasters to befall me, but even *this* incident, compared to my own theories and vagaries of presumption, proved me to be erroneous. I was dead wrong and I knew it. The infallible quintessence of the Super Sphere presided.

The discarnate, all-pervading voice resounded:
"What is this that we see?" and in chorus, "Are you yet without wisdom? Have you any steel-tough *titanium* temperance, prudence and sound judgment? Do you but value love and knowledge?"

"Do you copy? Answer me!" thundered he as if in a dirge.

The placid, self-circummured *pliancy* of its pristine presence would enough quell any fearful fret gone awry into such shriveled shrinkage, but by that of halcyon lull! Life-giving, to be frank, but more effective than doomsday desolation deployed by hot nuclear fallout. Of no match, I argue, to this puncture-proof, <u>invincible</u> 8 ball too taboo for humankind's corner side pocket! Balloon aloof? Nay! Rather, contrarily, protean by nature, yet with its Sumerian swirl of cuneiform mezzo-impression reclining resolutely onto its side, but lazily~ thus the infinity symbol:

The lemniscate of Bernoulli

Behold, like limpid liquidation of the "carnal factor" to signify Eternity itself. Should we wager & wedge deeper the profundity?

An emboldened embodiment of some sort; a triumphant trophy bequeathed by the very Heaven Herself. However, on the other hand, never to leave radioactive ravages of burnt flesh, charred to crisp cinders, redolent with housefly stench, languidly left behind to linger still. Instead, such **Reproductive Inviolable Presence** (the authentic RIP) outdid perpetual peacetime altogether.

At point blank range, resolutely and dead-on center-staged to elicit quivering quietness of a water brook murmur. Its tributary eddying, and that purled on by, downward from a sinkhole to oceanic eternity outstretched. The Vagdevi~Sarasvati cynosure: O requiescat in pace! Assurance of a gargantuan Gusher Jet!

Thereby, Polyhymnia had me eloquently record an event of a lifetime via the following Vision. A briefing [message of essence] to mankind that I had been forward to complete with poetry and prophecy. Language failed me to elucidate the impossible, the truly ineffable, and the indecipherable disclosure of *Hyper-Curvature*.

Well then, no prank or prattle could confiscate the following:

AMALGAMATED MONUMENTARY

I was found in the white womb of Time overlooked by sidereal sundials of every *intimate interim.* There lay lissome mediumship of benign *breath* about me. This hyper-elastic medium, void of head or tail-- continual-- upheld the vibrant *lucency* of all things. In it, I remembered my spirit, but lost all orientation as my sense of occupancy stretched out to some diminutive dimension perfectly perpendicular to all other directions I was conscious of. An extra-alternate spaciousness, without any center of reference, was what gave me the notion of being omnipresent.

Other Ether, that it was christened, which would be an elastic and ultra-*resilient* myriad medium, had harbored no beginning, neither middle, nor ending. That it lay transparent as a hyperbolic chute atop the apex of conical consciousness was what angelic comprehension could only grasp. Its hyper~spatial spiral having been four-dimensional Time, within which cosmic *censorship* of all that was, is now, and ever shall be, was in constant flux and forbidden from infinity to infinity (a mathematical contradiction). Other Ether at large: to be lengthier than the changeable chain of any event to take place- be it hither and yon- yet briefer than a nanosecond! A pliant plenum of non sequitur identification.

At *rem*, the walled womb of time had now transmogrified into my faintest memorial of surrealism, taking the formula of domestic desolation on earth. An *escalatory* cascade of steps along some staircase shuffled under me whereabouts a paisley canopy hung overhead with its rectangular congealment of tall walls and floor foursquare. A quaint household it was with an enclosure, vacantly, about me. Thus this was to identify me with *tellurian* reference.

But by one sudden shudder, the surroundings froze. When out of nowhere, as aforetime, I beheld with reverential awe another *clone* sphere materialize in the next room with what appeared to be six other spheres peering through at the doors ajar by each of their harsh glare and bulge! And all of them exactly alike! Along an architectural enfilade, the open doors were only to disclose these amazingly bizarre lookalike ballooning big *bouncers* conveniently squeezed into storage chambers or compartments; in store rooms, indistinguishably full blown, and everyone on their own accord, each (blanket-bloated) roundabout by the exits thereof!

Perchance then, was this an exit to Time Warp? Alas, to my incredulity, it instead became some *uncreated* perpetual *theophany* of separate spheres in one spectacular overblown roundness, and all sedately calm, *each one whopper*, all by themselves.

"Be not startled," *it* or *they* intoned in unison as one altogether.

Nevertheless, like some primitive primate aghast, I was taken aback, buckled up and frightened!

And now, in one widening worshipful whoop, and with such supplest elasticity and *superfluid* flow, all seven spheres in seven separate rooms of the household had clearly identified themselves to my mere personage of frailty. Shocked out of my wit's end was I, O breathing broomsticks! All full inside-out! *They*, the Orbs- with unmatched metronome cadence hypnotic- heaved, oscillated simultaneously, seamlessly so.

"Stand aside and let me manifest myself! For what is many out of One is concretely one out of many," they announced, reasserting themselves, and included this in Latin: "e pluribus Unum."

At this outright abominable, foreboding scene, my imagination was contorted beyond logic. Their paradoxical chorus vociferated forthwith. "Marvel not that I make impossible intervention for your sake- behold! I am the Main-throw Ballroom Sphere, and the rest of me, creepily, resiliently reserved, which you cannot see (except I showoff to you), are my one and the *selfsame* enameled exposure assumed by your shadow-flat spacetime continuum."

Was this an incubus? I marveled at such a wayward gesture.

"How absurd! By no means," he reassured me, reading my thoughts. "Verily at thy disposal. Just accept it."

The total temerity thereof waxed not apologetically.

As I reconnoitered the ghostly household, dangerously backed by globular glory in lieu of some architectural modillion and ancon supported façade, I literally felt the big-ball-bodily weight of fully expanded *sphericity* sag the linoleum flooring at each racquetball room I entered. And there it was, apparent as having never been! Shrunken, tapering away, eh? Augmenting back up, outward, and diminishing inwardly- infinitely- and out again, and again, in one wholeness and gradual equidistant equilibrium unparalleled by any fluid continuity upon planet earth. For at every prolonged drawn out inflationary expansion, the counterpart *spheroids* all oscillated outward, singularly, their protean plumpness imperceptibly.

My spiritual hand of focus inadvertently neared this concretely opaque object of such South Pole exposition.

"Touch me- me not... not. Touch me not!" echoed its caveat from ball-to-ball; their revivified blow-horn authenticated octaves now distinct one from another, from one blank-blown body to the next. Narrowed up into niches of the racquetball courtrooms! No magistrate on the throne save a big Ball in the midst thereof.

"I am alone with myself," proclaimed one of the side spheres necklaced along with the others that linked up a chain-reaction in such separate, disjointed disentanglement. "The same with me ..."

Another nacreous sphere, by itself, blurted: "... Me also!"
"~And with me," bowling ball to building-sized!
A high-pitched powerhouse: "With me too!"
"~And me..." like a petticoat insulator.
"Don't forget ME!" barreled the big cannonball!

"Yet lastly, or firstly, *Meeeeeee .... likewise* — whichever way outstretched, it makes no difference- *We* are all as one!" concluded one of them, somewhere wedged, way too hard to tell which one of the spheroids- for all seven of them resonated remarkably as but *one* whirling equatorial *girth~line* of an equally undivided *super-circumference.* Indefinitely, ballooned like that of a thousandfold Warp Sphere clandestinely attempting to dilate *its glitz* of concrete concordance from inside out. Yea, that of such seamless contiguity from millimeter to micro- to nanometer- to *pico-* to *femtometer* ...
... And, finally, from Planck length back to ten meters wide ...

Except, unfortunately, an observer would only perceive but one out of infinite *other* cross-sections wax and wane in size as some spectacular loony monstrosity of nothing *but* a supernal Sphere, so swollen out of nothing and yet able to revert back to *nothing.*

Certainly, it was *he*, if superhuman, personified to ever be, this infinitely harmonized whole *Hyper-spheriness*, that managed to remain unharmed in spite of the cutting edge of geometry! An intervening caterpillar-pillar of cloud by day, but far *rounder* and *spherier,* and more boundlessly curved than a conventional, three-dimensional big rubber ball. Be it my preferred and more likely version of that similar Angel who exposed itself to me during my private pilgrimage as it had historically to infantile Israel. To the Apostles of Christ at Pentecost as clear cloven Tongues of fire, and to Saul on his trek to Damascus, who then became the Apostle Paul- first messenger to the Jews and Gentiles- when being bashed by a blinding flash of it centuries ago. How many a God-ordained commissioned prophet, that I call a *vatician*, saw forefront the same for many an episodic epoch thereafter.

That this manifested intermezzo-impressions of globular Glory nearby- similarly achieved- granted, exceedingly as real (if not more), was yet to unfold. Such an insularity stayed in-betwixt…

An authorized visual equation of the spectacle runs by analogy (slap me Five):

01. For example, enshrine an ordinary latex ball and trace a thin hairline around it (the bouncing quality of shiny or lackluster latex adds to an elastic, predisposed potential). Now consider a mathematical sphere comprised of infinite points.

02. The circumference thereof would merely reveal a circle- but one out of countless many- that offers it an unbounded curvature of its own. Enter innumerable possibilities.

03. Just as an entire *sphere* ought to be but one cross section or curvaceous image of a Hypersphere (postulated in theory), inwardly or upwardly extended beyond space, so, too, all the other infinite shadows of the same, one by one, follow suit continuously without one interruption or breach.

04. And so, as it would intersect our spatial dimension (though endless in all directions), an actual sphere, or cross shadow and semblance of its completeness, would easily change size along therewith during an up-or-down maneuver.

05. Thus enlarged from any given point in space, and returning back to a tiniest point, wherefore, the whole Hypersphere entirety is nonexistent both *before* and *after* it appears- but only *this* according to Space and to the laws of physics and perspective that therefore apply. Otherwise, accordingly, it alone transcends human elucidation.

And ay, by the way/ needless to say, even empty *space*, or utter vacuum, is conclusively incomprehensible, if it be void of a relative ratio with the distance of existence; being *nothingness* on its own; although *that* nothingness is rendered pure solid compared to ultimate, emptiest nonexistent null-and-void! For instance, (by my Good Fellow Gazette twofold excerpt):

Subdivision A:

An Impossible Nowhere

Aye, there is no "outside" that space-time itself is expanding into! Nay, not even nothingness! Totally incomprehensible to the human mind! The best way I can describe it- using the injustice of literary language- is that the so-called big hyper-balloon of our "infinite" universe grows evermore hyper-luminal but beyond the laws of physics, and transcendent to light-speed. It's as if space-time itself [and naught beyond it] has undergone inflationary expansion- but that without boundary- since there is no "outside" as it were. Whatever remains outside, does not exist, save for an omnipresent super-Singularity from which our universality has expanded in the first place to begin with! The miniature point and spatial infinity are the same and cancel each other out. Or better yet: imagine the "Forbidden" to be of such a hyper-Void, as to render the very vacuum of space merely an absolute, unsolicited solid by my compartmentalized comparison! Hence, of course, in order to escape Space, one would require merely an infinitesimal preparatory, but omnipresent, pinpoint wrap-up of some inward, diminutive dimension! But whose curvature is sub-squeezed into itself with incalculable compression ...

Subdivision B:

If it were possible, a mirror, which would reflect absolutely naught, may appear as faceless. As if on an infinite wall of snowy white, without any shadow of turning, timeless tenuity and spatial vacuum may replace the see-through nothingness or sheer nihility that this forlorn looking-glass may mirror. What then could it look like if nothing, not even darkness, were reflected?

Now back to bivouac basics (with my adjunct of attribution):

With this in mind- like an ordinary ball entering or leaving the aforesaid shiny film of H_2O haunted by *Superreality*- this supplest Call Ball would budge or bulge accordingly, until its equatorial wideness [circumference] expands and then reduces to a point! The punctual pin-up of a conscious *Metatronic* marvel- as if documented- can at any moment re-materialize, or *vanish verily altogether!

---

* The top surface layer is called the epipelagic zone, and is sometimes referred to as the "ocean skin" or "sunlight zone." This layer interacts with the wind and waves, which mixes the water and distributes the warmth. At the base of this layer is the thermocline.
* A former colleague of mine mentioned it with what North and South Pole separation/ intervention of Determinate Evanishment would be like, if so fancily featured.

[Stealthily], contrary to metaphysical crossroads of paranormal phenomena, as a blip on the radar screen (if militarily detected), its Planck volume could abruptly inflate to a fully sized twenty-three metric meter dirigible. I deduce it to balloon from inside-out in a direction that baffles logic; that thereafter collapses right into itself, back into *nothing*. Hey, having to withdraw from the fringes of existence as having never arrived in the first place to begin with, nor ever.... Only then, as it were, the Hyper-Whole-Super-Sphere could have visited Polyhymnia and I *before*, *now*, or *afterward* as if without reservation, inviolable via quotidian calendar!

To sum up my overview, I can conjecture this big Ball to have grown 3 kilometers in diameter, with weight of a billion metric tonnes, but able to reduce down, daintily, to a rubber racquetball. A nimble bouncer, albeit cast from outpourings of latex, ebonite, gum elastic, or vulcanite. Far sprightlier than the feathery shuttlecock of badminton, if we were to amuse ourselves, launching over the net.

Whereas this one big Ball slips behind the Tall Wall without bypassing its top or side. Instead, into itself, reduced down to infinitesimal deflation, but ballooned back out on the other side of it- deftly and seamlessly- having no need to circumvent anything!

Prophetic Prism of Regulatory Output

Vox Stellarum

```
I burst by vouchsafed veneration
In elastic self-curved adoration
Wi' convexity contoured rotation
```

Phase Sequence I

"The rest of Our girth We withdraw away,
That one may but confront thee everyday."

And it came to pass- at once, unawares- four full sized floating spheres so fluidly and *infrangibly* reduced themselves [smaller and smaller] as if to the infinite *other-where*. And ensuing, there were two other big bouncers that imploded themselves into naught! Finally, the last of the South Pole Hypercurvature had left us via enveloped departure once and for all, altogether. Yea, and that with some divinely deflatable, yet using up an insuperable signature (*thermomagnetic*) engraved throughout the superfluid *flange* or transcendent Sacred Aether (fabric) of spacetime continuum! That of completely collapsing outward-in, right down to point zero in six corresponding cubicles of the hexagonal domicile. One per holographic hexagon upheld in an endless honeycomb hive of the **GLIBOLOTUBULOPOLITZ**, leaving, last but not least, the one *Main~throw Ballroom Sphere* (or MBS), as we will call it, to assume assiduous precedence as our seventh remnant Big Mother Sphere (BMS: or in this case, the counterpart *anagrammatical* acronym thereto) with the other sixfold septuplets, yet set separately so in their places, platform and all. Fret not, as its complexity shan't increase.

"See my Theophany which *was*, is (as of *now)*, and *ever shall be*," orchestrated the monstrous MBS with its muffled chorus of metallic voices. The plangency of which rattled one's rib cage!

Indeed. For I was now- as having *never* been <u>this</u> <u>time</u>- forced to seriously consider or possibly yield to a pliantly plump blank-blown body of nothing but *sphericity*- full o' incorporeal conscious life-tenaciously taut, and thereabout, having to be self-enveloped, self-sustained, and completely on *her* own, alone... unknown!

Even so, heretofore, what was rough and metallic sounding had switched to a pleasing feminine *vox femina*. My illustrious consort of some sort had then transformed from a snowy frozen hue of bloated blue, instantly, and into a mother-o'-pearl thermal pinch of pink or blood-rush gush of blush, with somewhat euthermic and mellow Maternity notwithstanding.

Comically, by an outer deluxe CRI: *color rendering index* shift I was later lulled, transfixed by its instantaneous transgender flux.

O what dregs and dross of earthly shadows were soon dredged and purged out of me! Per se, it had been Polyhymnia that all along was *voiceprint interfaced* with this transmuted, metamorphosis of nothing but an inducing *Super Sphere*. For I had felt like being an orchard-gleaned lemon harvested out of electromagnetic radiation; roasted alive by solar winds billowing forth the starry corona of an authentic par excellence power factor stellar source- or Sol.

Aye, try and reconsider, for keepsake, the *stelliferous* glory of Eta Aurigae, a blue-white cosmic beacon at about 3,000,000 miles in diameter alone, or better yet, that immense violet *superstar*, Alnilam, at twenty-four *more* million miles crosswise, and sheer hundreds of thousands of times brighter than our local yellow yard lamp sun! Moreover, compare the hyper-compressing shrinkage of some compact Neutron Star- by minuscule proportions- except, far statelier and more perfect than that of the preceding fine fettle of shapeliness.

For needless to add, as the vast volume of Earth compared to the Sun- say- is like a tiny grain of sand in relation to a bowling ball, so too, *no less*, take only a wee golf ball that is easily upheld, or even an inscrutable mote of dust, and, by analogy, dare match it to the heavyweight whopper of an eternal lava luminary, like our Sun. A nuclear furnace is in full equilibrium of its 28-day-cycle, imperturbable rotation factor! Of course, self-counterbalanced with an electromagnetic plateau of quiescence and solar flare frenzy of conflagrant conduction; a moderator and super-cell substructure to sustain equipoise and counterbalance at the same time; and this *puissant* power-storage of comparison is computed for fathomable footage! Pressure to prevent stellar collapse, but massive enough to keep it from hurtling apart, our Sun, suchlike, lies spherical!

But nay! I mustn't elaborate upon the proton-proton fusion, nor the wonderful wherewithal thereof, and neither the nuclear chain reactions therein that consist of both fission near its surface, and ferocious fusion (though explosive, perfectly controlled and self-sustained) but down deeper to the very continuous "depth charge" compressed beneath its ultra-dense *radiative* zone, at its core …

Where gargantuan *giga-year* finest fusion is neither explosive, nor implosive, but *Plosive, and in such estate that transcends our concept of energetic genesis!

* Much later, the Plosive Plucire plies through Mitchelville for a showdown!

Apropos of this erudite elucidation, nevertheless though, thus my wallop of the hyper-heaviest of all. Alas, the scale-squashing Warp Super Ball- clearly- the vital Voluminous <u>VORTRON</u>: an as yet undetected pulsar of such extraordinary properties a priori! Try my empirical data. * More on its specifications in another story…

Enter the Neutron Tremendous Transducer (NTT in contrast to TNT)

The result? What *then* would our vision of such self-contained fusion entail? (No doubt, a cannonball but far too *horribly h~ly* to formulate, let alone for the human race to presently tame, nor contain as in a cosmic menagerie!) The very contents of which churns no fissile material whatsoever! But [God forbid] if ever molten more, inwardly- whereby the neutron packaged extra strong nuclear force could collapse, ne'er to endure any longer- such an [unsqueezable] property would only (just so) seemingly slide into itself, and... collapse into black hole status quo. Hasta la vista and good luck! Let alone threadbare barrel and booth... Upon which any technological Japanese jet set would wave their Ernest Hemingway's Farewell to Arms, and relish Rachel Carson's Silent Spring or [Sayonara] to forbidden experiments on the effortless effulgent effect thereof. And what about the B-29 Superfortress bomber named after Enola Gay Tibbets, the mother of the pilot, Colonel Paul Tibbets? For it was on 6 August 1945, piloted by Tibbets and Robert A. Lewis during the final stages of World War II, when it became the first aircraft to drop an atomic bomb in warfare. Long after our final feat, I say *Sayonara* unto primitive fission compared to the sustained finest fusion thereof: *imagine* the Earth compressed into the size of a tennis or racquetball!

さ よ う な ら ~ "If that's the way it is..."

Likewise with neutron Ball <u>VORTRON</u> voluminously compacted

But ne'er to deny such an accord, nor my merest adage afforded thereunto, that how ultimately requisite it may *still* be, if it were possible for another disembodied bystander- so unrenowned as myself- to ever *inhale* an undefiled diamond-polished refinement of a similar gnome or *dwarf,* naught else! Whenever I state *accord* on any paragraph, I am not referring to Honda.

No, not enough cause, *a fortiori,* to chauffeur some matron!

Not prissily prim, but **TRANSCENDENT TRANSPARENCY** had transpired like never heretofore, nor ever having been versified throughout the following resurrected *effulgurant*:

Unendingly Harmonious

I am big Borteum announcing
So elastic, while bouncing
Septuple Theophany
That stretches to eternity:
I *was*, I *am*, I *shall be*.

Above the world conventional,
Shown shapely, fourth-dimensional:
(Perpetual Theophany)
As *breathiest* with shapeliness,
I am white loveliness.

What was, is now, and ever shall be
Hypercurvature Holy,
Blank Elasticity
Cross sectioned, equatorial:
All incorporeal!

PRAYER

Remain me from the taints of sin
As Thou art infra-stretched within ...

For **Jesus Christ** I glorify
As I enlarge myself on high-
Rotational, sensational:
Let Loveliness reside inside
What never may divide!

Phase Sequence **II**

"Proclaim to the unfamiliar, buxom *materfamilias*," my visitor suggested serenely. "Only glad tidings ..." Its voice-authentication now finely filigree, until ferroconcrete feminine.

Aha! Was this in reference to any earth mother with our former lives *under the clock?* For in this region of timelessness there was no clock, gauge, nor diurnal dial to go by. No, neither to measure bullet flyby! Wherefore, the phrase "under the clock" I affirm.

Indeed, ever so time-dilated, that those imperceptible, clearest, sheerest sheets in but one femtosecond could be forefelt, flat out FAT (or Fat Arc Tube) for that matter, and all in full!

Because abased thereat, I imagined myself seated dumbfound-docile to this blubber of blankness. I noticed how intangible and inexpressibly impalpable it looked: the lucid bounty Bouncer. The wrecking ball that all consisted of nothing but spheroidal essence, quintessence, and even '*septessence*', dare I say with *ineffability*!

The *self-septupled* fettle of the Tall Ball bounced a wee bit and settled down, sagging the linoleum floorboard. For what once were front and back door--- entrance and then a side *postern--- would have each worn the pall of a portiere over them, to forthwith shield these from the blindingly blankest and pallid plumpness of convex consonance that interposed the entirety thereof glaring at them!

Its very own overblown, immemorial, equatorial *girth~line* of bodily intervention vaunts an impressively captivating *snowiness* thereunto, or otherworldly pearlescence of celestial silence unlike anything imaginable down upon *terra firma.* Of a polychromatic creative tinge of loveliest lavender and antiquity intermixed with *obliquity* that would wax starry congregants roundabout itself! Its complicated combination of color-coded kaleidoscopic diamond-faceted sprinkling (that sparkled the contents thereof) now offered me the feeling of radioactive signatures written right into my soul. That then yielded forth a randomized radiant retinue and entourage of matter/ anti-matter neutrinos which had deftly moon-cratered [pockmarked] my recessed bone-and-marrow by its mini-meteoric flurry of fallout! The Tremendous Transducer *transpierced* me!

For as my magnanimous Sphere purposed to disclose her cross sections one at a time, I saw what was unconditional, but strangely raw and without flaw. Meanwhile, its full blown clone *equatorial* assumed gradual growth from base entrance of its southern *point* which would widen right out or deliberately dilate to an entirely overwrought, wraparound occupier; then contract *back* inwardly and *away* at once whence its far northern tip abruptly disappears... the spatial slip-blip of it to follow lastly, receding to a vanishing point that departs from this veritable veil of reality; the aftershock of whose heft- prolonged by my recording companion- had entered some sacrosanct but featureless limbo that came to *naught* …

Moreover, the radiant replica of it persisted and unflinchingly positive or negative! Depending on what such reversal or dispersal of spatial polarity would have been. Without, its barest presence smudge-smeared over an obsolete daguerreotype o' mercury film!

Or ablaze, bloody blitz! Starred, charred, or mezzo-impressed in a sequestered archaeological, forensic fossil record of a silent cinder (subtracting Sodom and Gomorrah's sulfur), Lichtenberg burnt.

Nonetheless, the fingerprint of it would persist... Whether in an insulated alabaster box, amber encasement, an old petrified log, volcanic shatter-cone, viable vulcanite, fulgurite, a honeycomb, or antiquated creosote goo bloated o'er a tar-laden blacktop scorched by some afternoon summer hammer- no matter- the sable footprint pressure promptings of the tall ball remained! Readily reserved for easy access by nanosecond fulgid finger photography utilized via electron microscope calibrated to its super-high-speed time-lapse, until taken to a slow motion freeze-frame crawl, albeit subatomic cyclotron accelerator equipped.

By now, in brief relief, if you allow me to repeat the refrain of this oracular Orb, my depiction of its yellow pallor can continue to render us due justice. As it were, the stage performance of a seven-part Hypersphere is clearly likened to a pinpoint twinkling out of nowhere, ballooned up and out to a hefty, nacreous necklace of swollen swagger. The identical septuplets, soft as is quantum foam sudsy, saunter to a supplest *stretcher* of some sort, not to contort.

That the consort of each orb drops back into itself, altogether, is an enigma! Even so, seven spheres by themselves shrivel down to Planck pinpoint of a super-singularity, supremely-- into tiniest *nihility* once and for all-- swiftly wink out of space, I speculate!

Into self-nullification ----------- Nonexistence for me, that is.

As tears streaming from one's virtual visage of veneration, so was my outcry of awe to such a mind-altering, whole-soul heart-harrowing and confounding dizzy discovery, duh! Until discerned (decoratively) to vindicate every narrow *gliff* of it, now and then, I was later introduced to an ecclesiastical or *cathedralesque* nave with niche nicely ornamented in concave scallop-shelled preferred preference to this spherical grace and formula bestowed by direct, divine apotheosis.

Although this groin-vaulting grotto showcased egg-and-anchor papier-mâché, yea, tallow cinereous silkscreen of moldering crisp parchment- possibly that of some legendary era- the format power factor of a household hereof had outshone itself, unquenchable, aflame! Barefacedly furrowed, entreating aesthetics, and that with various splits, *clefts*, fissures, faults & branching cracks outspread from an epigraph chiseled on chalk- whereof an unearthed *codex* might have on its front cover grossly graven or etched: TERRA INCOGNITA IN PERPETUUM, or albeit forever an unknown, unexplored cornfield of knowledge or missing school of thought.

But before we continue with descriptive interpretation of our MBS (Major Ballroom Sphere) as such, I beseech the readership of this section to pause for a moment, take a deep breath, and shut each pair of eyelids to what I am about to unveil...

I'll begin with prefatory priority nearside a terracotta cottage:

Picture yourselves on a close encounter with the Hypersphere, envisaged via my Yard Lamp of Gloria- the very same one we've been bantering at, all along- rather. Now visualize such a Big Ball to hover, how *heavenly*, above an intersection; a city aorta fraught by freight, frazzle and dazzle no less. Aye, so full o' nonstop-and-go traffic, trundling by and by, during rogue, runabout rush hour.

The motorists never have time to slow down, pull over and step outside of their cars to take a look! For far overhead and above-ground, hung up o'er an intersection of hubcap hurly-burly, this star-white beach ball is on the approach at point blank range ...

Thus, to offer up a percentile of contribution, let us commence with what *ought* to have transpired, from **A** through **H.** That is, if we were to continue on my intrepid venture or giant jaunt toward the tellingly landed Sphere, hugely parked smack in the middle of a crossover thoroughfare:

A) *I'd normally see this bountiful ball to expand bigger, as I neared its southern hemisphere that sat thereat upon the street pavement. Also, [it] should unwieldy wax forth in like manner on the median of an interstate highway of one accord, by now trooper patrolled!*

B) *Automobiles suddenly screech to a halt as pneumatic boots o' black skid and pandemonium erupts, abruptly. The Big Ball is blocking each queue of traffic on this bustling city intersection- say- on the elongated X of Times Square, an aorta of the Big Apple, or ypsiliform (Y)! No dilly-dally ...*

C) *Assuming that I'm inconspicuous, no one notices me at all, save that imposing barreling cannonball of an over-sized seventeen meter diameter circumference subject to change at any time, but for the time being, just seated there, lolling, acutely aware, but aloof!*

D) *As 24 hours inch round the liquid crystal sundial, no more mercury-moist, MUFON (Mutual UFO Network) has been emailed and dispatched to arrive quickly and ascertain the situation, tentatively, cautiously, lest the NYPD puts out an APB (All Points Bulletin) and a bawling BOLO (Be On the Lookout) Red Alert, Vigil and Curfew calls the beleaguered metroplex area into televised befuddlement! Emergency until, offhand, New York City slickers* ***really*** *rally athwart and upstart preparatory procedures, protocols on yet another nasty 9/11 (God Save America) scenario!*

E) *Now- needless to carbuncle the kerfuffle- yea, if ever stray bullets of drive-by shootings occur; or if, upon ultimatum, scud missiles are deployed at it (the MBS) only to puncture* *its mercurial membrane, this- of course- is what would ensue. Regardless of how hard any wallop volley of rockets impale the super-surface thereof,* "the superficies of such a SPHERE", *any projectile of penetrating impact is sunken suddenly into the Big Ball's ultra-supple hyper-polymer elasticity ... to the point of nowhere and no return ... And, uncannily, blithely, the MBS stays staunch and absolutely unaffected* [more on this in a jiffy].

F) *And so, as we aim to get a closeup entirety of the deftest spheroid ever, the null~blank enveloped curvature of it's sphericity lissomely grows greater, and- meanwhile- the street we have left behind shrinks smaller and smaller. Moreover, the closer we'd loiter beneath its south pole underbelly, the more eventual shrinkage of surrounding "termite" territory to Times Square. (termite, per se I say, or by the surroundings such as tall towers similar to the stalagmite multitudes built up by those tiny critters; but just so, as if it were compared with another unparalleled, paranormal, immaculate, supernatural, concrete, and all- too-permanent Presence as this one)! Ultra-ethereal, but, by far, tougher than a titanium and diamond mix!*

G) *When all at once, one is engulfed with White, a featureless void of nothing! A disconcerting, blinding blankness from all around- of omnidirectional disorientation- but gone all the way to infinity. Like being buried alive in self-illumined snowpack permafrost- except not necessarily within gelid snowiness to gnaw at one's discomfort of head, hand and foot. Snow-bright all around, but of ambient temperature.*

H) *An (H) affirmative for our so "horrible outcry" if we were to go bonkers and ballistic, and reconvene steroid ready-reconnaissance of the then targeted MBS, let alone to conveniently disperse payload arsenals of armor-piercing* *blitz, or a deployed Fat Man B-29 bombardment of shock thereupon! That even if* *this* *were to occur, even MAD, mongrel, military missiles of grievous warhead horror- though explosive enough- would simply sink and slip into the super-surface thereof like nothing at all. Leaving the Main-throw Ballroom Sphere virtually unaffected by the Tsar Bomba (for instance), nor nemesis of any kind, and with absolutely no depth-charge to rattle or even jolt its incorporeal cage! Never an Atlas, nor Titan torpedo will wager a chance against the invincible MBS, let alone its billion tonne weighty, 33-block diameter, liquid Uranium-filled and neutron-hulled Heft ballooned by re-assertive wrought iron wraparound radiance! The malleability of which easily bounces back man's meteoric madness.*

The colossal callback of this 4-D decoy buoy beacon could have heretofore reckoned the outcome as:

I cannot be divided, nor destroyed-
If ever warheads are at me deployed:
For still I will remain, of all devoid.

Forevermore, I still shall reassert
Myself the same, elastic, & unhurt!

End of line

And now, it flashed upon me like ball lightning!

That how I recalled its *hemi-hyper-sphere* diminished and then augmented right back next to me is coupled by my next, rather vertical versicle: (its lucidity defied my semiconscious state)

For where a social sphere may bounce
Compared, alas, we'd weigh an ounce!

'Twas the very same likeness of confluent clones

From which an index finger of graphite fire finely,
Divinely wrote this epigraph as on a chiseled hewn
Half of the cornerstone. Its foundation to be laid by
None other than the Ancient of Days: the Architect
And Master Builder, whose memory never fades
And whose perpetual presence forever stays.

From whom alone proceed the Titan torpedoes
Of depth-charge potential against global havoc.
But otherwise, a lambent lure of love thru'out
Every astral tapestry delicately detailed by age.
To engulf the inane senselessness of null-space
And portray rounded shapes shown proforma.

From out of *naught*, a cloned company of orbs
To expansively wax and attain globular glory.
Ballooned aeons apart. Where Sacred Aether may
Lay star-spangled by CONCRETE CLUSTERS of
An opaque object. An invasive supernal, eternal
Baseball left by a heavenly contact/contest of but
Perfect players; a toy bouncer, somewhere found
Amongst the stadium myriads of some star-field
Marvel, unchallenged or even unparalleled before
The cushioning fringes of a consoling Coliseum.

For only the feeble mere thought of such pure
Curvature would only melt that mount of slate,
Level the steps of a formula, and deftly stagger
The presumptuously accurate tread of geometry!
The seismic twitch of a stylus that scribbles this!
The narrow numerals thereof now shamefacedly
Shuffled down to bamboo straws and splinters of
Pickled pulp, let alone bullion slabs afresh from
The foundry or kiln, baked during decalescence.

Or better yet, let's elaborate on the puny pedantry
Of mediocrity. Take as a precaution for Peace or
War the two-edged foibles of any schoolmaster
Address; institutions of industry and automation:
The overtones and scrawls of city halls, or the dis-
Course and long scrolls of public schools peopled
By pedagogues set on pedestals- bespectacled and
Bedecked to a flamboyant decorum, whose own
Homes are tomes of incubated *incunabula* (Book-
Worms are they) wafted woefully into inert ash
Fit for the cinerarium replete with Ouija boards
By a lazy swirl of Time- sordidly silenced in
The ennui of dangling flypaper glazed by old
Laboratory goo. Or as vast volumes vilified to
Threadbare futility, so the thin brittle leaves of
Autumn shall decay and turn to charcoal soot.

Yet dare to defy any blackboard-backed madcap
Of closet drama classrooms cluttered with lessons
And lectures on a gnat or jarred robber gadfly of
Political disorder. Those headlong teachers who
Dawdle with one bauble and *pop the top* instead
Of a noteworthy *carpe diem:* ad Astra per aspera!

Such scrawny, scraggy *wine coats* who only fawn
After femaleness, who exemplify the epitome of
Colossal collapse; the rational, materialistic rise
Of a nasty nexus given to necromantic devices
That leave curry favored pupils of curiosity
Bilked, bamboozled and stone-frozen by the
Lethiferous stare (beyond compare) of Medusa
Herself. A fraudulent *other* mother of massacre
Who lets our demise be what she'll soliloquize.

Until purgatorial Ritz and Glitz bloats blight:

Or, as you will, everything yields, still, to the
Infinite index of authority ere the Creator God
Of concrete clusters returns reposed once more
Galore. In the symmetry of spherical harmonics
Not punctured by our mortal models of heroics
Themselves reasserting, while blindly blurting:

For where a social sphere may bounce
Compared, alas, we'd weigh an ounce!

Phase Sequence **III**

Here it would better be, overshadowing fickle frailty as never before exacted. For as a dog must obey its Master, so likewise- as an abstract contrast to the far finer breath-liner of limpid life- I heeded His call, the Ball, stunted at four fat-foot candlesticks of luminosity. Like squat stumps were they, but elongated later on …

Perforce foot candles (equivalent to one lumen per square foot or 10.764 lux) of an afterburner beacon bonfire!

But by analogy, it had arrived as from the South Pole base of a disturbingly huge and herculean, building-sized tall ball concretely compacted, from a noble neutron star to timid Tinker Bell toy.

Not necessarily a wrecking ball of utter temerity it was, able to bash itself into ramparts, bulwarks, and castellated fortresses (if it were to time-travel back into the Middle Ages). Nor was it an over-sized incoming cannonball- before gun powder was ever invented- catapulted, stout-slung and then out-flung way overhead- rather- a Universality in and of itself and on its own, full blown, intelligent, inter-dimensional, inner and outer paved with perpetual equipoise.

The self-contained median of an infinite highway junction this MBS maintained. Whereas one runs upward and the other down, it remained unaffected by the duality of any detour; against which no brawl, neither tug of war [waged] could cobble its quintessential quiescence ever so quietly balanced! Privily prominent!

Well above anyone's philosophical bailiwick, albeit *metrology* or hard core Euclidean geometry, the one and only Super Ball kept composure roundabout itself unsurpassed. Tellingly, of insuperable and superior presence.

Its implacable, implosive implication imposed such an impact on me- as massive as Mount Everest at 29,032 feet to the summit- yet compressed only to 29 meters of embraceable sponginess! But the pinch and squeeze of which would wormhole the Earth itself. A globular furnace not to be elbowed nor knuckled with. Barbecued, barbed wire-like, from a distance akin to the Chernobyl churn!

WARNING... DANGER!

In contradistinction to the bloated blanket of a hyper curvature shock wave, my cerebral cortex lay licked up by 'Porcelain Pallor'.

The shapeliest showcase and big bouncing buckle thereof, may I add- waxed contiguous, interrelated, syllogistic, and symmetrical.

Comprised and conflated with innumerable points, googolplex gargantuan and galvanized, infinitesimally infused underneath sub-nothing, (*multi-universal singularities)* that were one Planck and all the way back out to an equidistant equilibrium no narrower than a stealth weather balloon~ but far shinier than the bright Breitling Orbiter to have circumnavigated the globe~ the redistributed red-shifted radii of its *Oscillating Assumption* was interrelated from nowhere to nowhere; linked onto nothing yet [as if] omnipresent every-which-way at once, and so, simultaneously enveloped by the selfsame indivisible individuality of innumerable Spheroids.

That the total sum of but One was *abaft by the aft* of an exit, whence entrances could commence, distend, and then exit back up again, had been not just four-dimensional, but the Quad of God!

To elucidate: that which, without a beginning nor ending, was sub-stretched, except perfectly unaltered and consistently curved but warped in on itself. That of contiguous *elasticity* unlike any other geometrical configuration. Its dilated, diaphanous dimension of a nearly-infinite heavyweight *whirl* was so super-compressed together by a multidimensional matrix, that it became multiplied instantly, only to be replaced by this proclamation:

I *was*, I *am*, and I *shall* be;
None before, nor after Me.

Then, the unidirectional transmission blaring out of thin air, but contrapuntal with waveform decibels of electrostatic amplitude at full blast, was augmented to a hissing susurration:
* The only onomatopoeia of its kind:

… th—sss--th--sss--th--sss--th--sss--th…

In like manner, I heard from inside-out (resounding from the ebullient bullion and ingot of my sagacious sanctity subjected to a furnace, as if to entrench and try me for dregs of dross) that which would palpitate one's respiratory diaphragm to painful spasms:

"Theophany thought at variable size,
I am a Hyper Sphere of no disguise."

Until there, whereabouts or *en clair,* inaudible and irreversible, from infinitesimal *instantaneity*, as if from oblique oblivion, dead center in a main parlor ballroom of prefabricated surroundings, strangely strewn about, its spherical harmonics from minuscule minuteness to the plateau of plumpness would resume repose as before, once more, in one continuity of expansion to that of some glorified globe. It was again an unbounded entire entity of a single furlong Bouncer of Bounty, stateliest and starriest, breathing with protean pressurization, primed or preparatory to pulverize to pulp steroid remonstrance. Mockery (manned by violators) vilified.

Inadvertently, an avatar of the Tremendous Transducer (TT), whose incontestable confrontation diminished a wee inch for my sake, had heralded aloud:

"If you dare to stare at my glare,
Anew, I will spare thy despair!"

The Supreme Primary MBS, silkily agleam like bottled up ball lightning transcendent to anatomy *materia medica*- furthermore- proclaimed its superior overkill caduceus hyper~naked Lilith:

"For inasmuch as that brazen Serpent of Elder was hoisted up above-ground to be coiled all over a robust bough, and that far above the wilted bower of sordid suffering and disease- when they gazed upon it, they were healed- so it is with Me, the Almighty would confirm, Destroyer of the Worm, providentially. I shall show My glory seven times to convince you that *I was*, *I am*, and *I shall be*: the same yesterday, today, and forever..."

Unlike that mid 1970s insurance television ad, "Get a piece of the rock, Prudential~" it rather rattled rib cages with "Get awhirl with the Big Ball, Providential..." (commercial)

Then the more, like heretofore galore, the overbearing ball of the Main-throw Ballroom Sphere, the MBS, collapsed downward to nothing at all and *relapsed* backlash again into something reminiscent of its own formidable embodiment. But this time, in the Ballroom gloom it *hyper~conflated* smoothly within colossal curvature alongside plastered pilasters of etiolated, yea, yellowed Yesteryear.

An indestructible sort o' Tarmac flooring for a platform would support this billion-tonne wrecking cannonball. Although sagging from the scale-squashing weight thereof, its glorified glimmer of 'natrium neutroil' facilely and elastically reasserted itself with the pliable plateau, platform or trampoline of the *Inviolinoleum.* The overlay plenum of which lay superimposed impregnable to even the flash-point flux of an H-bomb if detonated thereupon! Thereby, on the median, I was flattened out by an asphalt steamroller.

Unexpectedly, having nearby my reassuring anthropomorphic Polyhymnia for company, I hurtled to Time-Warp in an eleventh century slot of entry. But whither the holy trajectory? The medieval trappings and transference beyond cannonball common sense of a dispensed decoy or big buoy beacon! Either way, eh? Its canned whistle began to bob boisterously as on the surf & subsurface of quantum foam. Wherefore nary a runway retinue of lights, nor via the red carpet treatment were witnessed- as I scanned squeezable elasticity all around- even so, its glitz embraced me mellowest.

Thoroughly amazed and shaken, I was found alone, prone atop a remote ledge of Colorado's famed Crested Butte, right beneath the underbelly of that same predominant, whole but droll Mother Sphere I had known all along- *which one*? The Selfsame One that must have never altered, though its mirror-image wavelengths were whisked right before me, insofar as the electromagnetic spectrum of light is lit up for the naked eye! The remnant of it existed eerily outside of *created* perception that only revealed a split fraction or hairline of its robust and rotund penumbra of multiplex convexity!

Incontrovertibly, the other polymorphous perfectly undetected 99.999999999999999 percentile thereof, therefore, utterly unseen! indiscernible, and entirely *uncreated!* Yea, by orders of power and magnitude more aureate and~ by far~ shinier than the lorry-load-purged-of-dross *shiniest* gold we can ever conceive of; of course, comparable to transparent cellophane, yet of starriest, liquid-lithe, protean properties. Likened with elastic ether, a delicately garish gossamer, silkily so as an effervescent spirit, but billions of times tougher than titanium steel! Neutron-packed!

Nay, I say, not amber. But rather, with lightning-bright-blazing iridium, the narrow yellow honeycomb if irresistible iridescence.

The authorized King James Version has long eloquently stated: While we look not at the things which are seen, but at the things which are not seen: for the things which are seen are temporal; but the things which are not seen, are eternal. (2 Corinthians 4:18)

To my carnally clad stature, the MBS medieval times addressed as I became beholden thereunto:

"See how crepe-veiled were they, these ladies. Some wearing milkmaid dresses in retrospect to Alpine peasantry; others sheathed in petticoats & hardy undergarment stockings, thoroughly attired," quoth an old *Sphere of yesterday.* "As towering cumulonimbi were white with an overcast, blanched or blushing, our woman were wimpled and gorgeously garbed and gowned lengthwise if not loosely. And gentlemen, with conservative apparel, complemented them thus by love-lavished order and privilege to the degree of their disciplined lives of chastity, sobriety, and selfless Solace."

Confounded, I wondered with admiration, still starkly startled by some demure, puritanical radiation of awe! The palindrome of holy women had noticed me gawking at them: they blushed in the year 1221. Polyhymnia reacted rose-red, floridly floored, whereas an undertow of compunction swept us o'er with Planck volumes of hyper-pinpointed infinitesimals------- via Quantum Foam fields in between Earth-sized electrons, enough of them, innumerable, to tally up the multiverse at large bulge, but staggeringly stupendous by crushed comparisons!

Still, the unadulterated Sphere continued wistfully, "For where are those wholehearted moments of finest familial life? saith My **DIVINE SPIRIT**... When we were warmed with the hearth of hot embers and mused on solemn things, or bantered by a campfire? Yea, why not yon quiet quell of fairy-tale times to reminisce about, buttressed by memorials, mortified mourners; aprons, overcoats and thermal mufflers? The Philadelphia Era of curfews, mirthful conviviality, or heirloom memorabilia that ballasted the futurity of the loveliest Lavender Calendar to blossom yet, yellow as vernal sprouts atop dogwood. Moreover, when words like *gay* meant merry, and *dike* referred to overflow hindrance; whereas *levee* is a riverside or even seaside embankment against a disastrous deluge."

And now, comically, conversely: "Whoa, where, O where hath *thy* Underdog gone?" it recorded for keepsake some very vintage television cartoon, replete with [at least] valiant heroics and good gallantry if not hilarity. Also, sacrificial for school kids to try and exemplify or merely mimic so "long, long ago in a galaxy far, far away..." as it were. *I refuse to be silly and plagiarize Star Wars* (by rote).

——— "*You just did,*" said someone's conscience... At any rate, resumes readily my Yard Lamp of Gloria *gliff*:

Then came the caesura of intonation as a *Sphere of Tomorrow* surfaced from the same fourth-dimensional MBS instead thereof.

"Ah, but the scorching torchlight shall shimmer forth, glaringly adjacent to an impending Modernity of decrepitude. Or until the burgs thereof will be burnt up and torn asunder ere tender and sacred buds of the Vernal Equinox exult over man's ecclesiastical stronghold."

In moon-cratered crests and lilts of blissful glee, its contorted curvature waxed and waned~ wonderfully or woefully~ whichever way.

"*Ecce signum*!" intoned the ancient juggler of orbs. Wherefore, I was beholden even more so to the triumphant sign or ill omen thereof.

And from the vantage standpoint of an ensconced *witch~light* that bulged back fattened, firebug bellyful pregnancy, protuberant by bio-luminescent *luciferin*- O how horr'bly h~ly! Its entirety of even-keel, equidistant, and self-pliant Planck pinpointed spiritual variation had hung aloft, heyday-hard-bitten & heavyweight, in warfare against contemporary trends. No nasty carnifex, topped by a metal cap, yea, stationed at his guillotine, could counteract the inquisitor thereat. The Holy Trinity of its threadbare *Threesome*, as it were, adamantly opposed to an unholy triad of our Antichrist regime; the MBS itself instantaneously having to sear through otherwise retinal retention! I blare, *en clair*, so super-poised to manifest manifold a divinely shaped exposition at any quotidian day! Far beyond the spiral web-work of spacetime totality, it laxly cradled itself in an octagon platter prepared before foundational establishment. Ah, its bodily bulge oscillating like liquid cradled chrome Hg! ... Rippling, sinking from all sides, silently slipping, slithering away and approaching back. Away and back to yet nullify my pallid pillow of drenched dreams. Or be they the wet nocturnal dreams that perhaps portray chief cherubim, Seraphim, and even the six-winged, many-eyed *Ophanim which will* gyrate and coruscate indefatigably in wayside worship of their Creator's 'diamantiferous' divinity ... (an apology for my grandiloquence)

Dizzily discombobulated, I forthwith evaded the puissant **MBS**, avoiding to capture a fleeting glimpse of its grotesquely grappling *multi-monstrosity* of *eternities edgily a-whirl* around its profoundly spectacular spectacle; its dreadnought prominence preparatory to vaporize and ionize into its gamma-ray *electroplasmatic* Jet just about anything from inside out!

I fled the premises, prayerfully predisposed of...

Still, a recoil of reproof was wanting, knocking on the door:

"My whole Theophany that Angels see
Rebukes whoever thinks indifferently!"

The rebuttal of its re-assertive Resilience thundered:

"We revisit modern Babylonia, and the multitudes thereof have [hitherto] corrupted themselves..."

At such an interim, its baritone megaphone was like the Voice on Mount Sinai as Moses-- performed by Charlton Heston in Cecil B. DeMille's 1956 film, The Ten Commandments-- had been **vis-à-vis** conversant with YHWH.

I relished this low intonation of godlike resonance. Recalled, rather than reproduced, thus the palindromic yesteryear of 1221 spelled out (by and large) **ROTATOR** in lieu of a Hannah or Anina ad hoc happenstance.

Over the supernal superficies of this sphere were indentations of holographic facets that showcased *shimmering* highlights of the above epochal synopsis, namely, as in the year proper, 1221, the following events had become barely noticeable: notably how a foundation stone laid for Burgos Cathedral of Ferdinand III of Castile- centuries later- yielded a **UNESCO** World Heritage Site for 1984! The timestamp? Exactly upon June 20; whereas elsewhere, Emperor Go-Horikawa, aged only at 10 years old, ascends to the Chrysanthemum Throne of Japan, for example. Furthermore, on June 15 (five days earlier), on that same year, the famous Frederik II [Strijdbare], duke of Austria was born; and just a few months hence, Salimbene di Adam, Italian chronicler, was born in Parma, Italy, (who then died in 1288); and then on November 23 of that selfsame *palindromic year*, 1221, Alfonso X 'the Wise', King of Castile & Leon, had been born in Toledo, Spain, but gave up the ghost in 1284 and everyone else right on their predestined quota... The whole nine yards, yea, the ruby Rolodex roundelay rigmarole collapsed with the flip of a switch. A twilit twitch of impartial importunity, O for crying out loud, or for Heaven's sake!

Encrusted in an endless genealogy, *to tentatively touch the tip of an iceberg, or merely scratch the surface thereupon*, or so the thunderclap cliché would have rung resonantly, one out of twenty quadrillion hard-copy hologram happenings of continual causality congealed occasionally ludicrous, trifling and trivial trinkets of an ever immovable, static, ethereal Fourth Dimension left unaffected by the hauntingly apparent Transformation Effect once deduced by the late great Hendrik Lorentz; whose fundamental concept theory in 1895 was that the "theorem of corresponding states" for terms of order *v/c* had calculated that the moving observer, with respect relative to ultra~elastic *aether*, can utilize the same electrodynamic equations as an observer in the stationary *aether* system. Thus they are making identical, indistinguishable observations. And whose corollary conclusion was preceded by but negative results of the Michelson Morley experiment, whereby his hypothesis of 'length contraction' culminated *per se* in the year 1892… This was where length of spatial distance and time-dilation were gradually altered evenly throughout and within the freeze-frame and framework of spacetime continuum. Indeed, as if it were so-called consolidated if not confabulated by the electromagnetic transference of the *light-speed-limit*. Howbeit that clearest, sheerest Nothingness outside of omnidirectional space via pure vacuum only allows hyper-luminal inflationary expansion of this 4D universe (known as the Hubble constant). Perhaps then, the Twin Paradox, *inter alia*: if one flies away light-speed, the duration of us waiting for their return may seem like a lifetime compared to a fleeting few minutes in a light-speed round-trip flight of reentry! Conversely then, as on the other hand, once formulated by the German physicist and Nobel laureate Werner Heisenberg in 1927, the Uncertainty Principle states that we cannot know *both the position and speed* of a particle, such as a photon or electron, with perfect accuracy; the more we nail down the particle's position, the less we know about its velocity and vice versa.

Such information superhighways were tarred or paved with, as if ---- *for now we see in a* ***mirror*****,** ***darkly****; but then face to face: now I know in part; but then shall I know fully, even as also I was fully known*, I recall in First Corinthians, chapter 13, verse 12 of the KJV.

Whereas whereupon push comes to shove, I shan't shuffle a punt, nor violate my fine line of scrimmage, neither sidekick the football of pig-skin power-play to baffle the Big Leagues; nor to boorishly batter buckaroo bookworms!

Immediately, via the Major Ballroom Sphere (the mighty MBS), I was whisked out of the vacant Vac-Shaft, light-speedily, and with super-celerity, escorted back into an all-too-familiar living room. Again, at far length outstretched, or close range therein, either way, still, the phenomenal Lorentzian Contraction overtook my mindset unawares, (downloaded by that visual cortex and convex volume cyborg implant matrix of holographic facets)! I was all thoroughly spellbound. More than enough to have voided myself, let alone to have vomited. Such prisms of prima facie evidence~ that of the pineal gland, as otherwise encased (conically) in the would-be brainchild of my cerebral existence~ flickered kaleidoscopic flits of unearthly, otherworldly pigmentation:

(only blue, yellow) trinanopia
(red-weak to green) protanopia
(raw red-green) deuteranopia

These hues have a secondary and tertiary recombination factor of the Sixfold Primary Colour Wheel which reintegrates red, orange, yellow, green, blue, and purple-pink clockwise configured on the Ruby Rolodex Dial. My wherewithal to actualize a 4D perspective was paramount, but without the motley flamboyance.

Alongside my soulful sojourn, Polyhymnia's amiability assuaged my disfigurement, discomfiture, and dizzy disorientation.

Enter terra incognita: Territorial against an unholy entrance
Deliberately docile to divine Spirit on behalf of the visitors

Thus the palindromic yesteryear of 1221 spelled out **ROTATOR** in lieu of a Hannah to unravel. By the Major Ballroom Sphere I was wrenched out of the Vac-Shaft lightning quick and with super-celerity escorted back into yet another posh parlor trick showcase.

Phase Sequence **IV**

In the commodious Show Room (manifest manifold on Maroon Avenue of Crested Butte in Colorado) I was seated or reclined (if humanly conjectured, for I was now discarnate) on an *ibex exedra* before which Persian tapestry rested. Thereat, I had listened to its available discourse on the code of conduct as also observed by my Perfectly Unaltered Polyphony. This was my portico benchmark during a mountainous blizzard that raged resolutely on the outside of my makeshift log cabin.

But all the more matched with the Authorized **KJV Bible**, and certainly as forthright and haunting as Edgar Allan Poe's Quoth the Raven "Nevermore." (The sixth verse of the eighth stanza in his poetry classic, The Raven):

"The male and female *both* hath not acknowledged My modus operandi, saith the Primary Providence of **YHWH**: for then would their bowels of love and mercy be moved for one another. Yea, when was the last time men and woman ceased from being equal rivals one to another? But I have forewarned you, O stiff-necked generation, that I shall no longer strive with you, nor with your controversy, saith God; and no more will I discard discord from your homes by reason of an unbalanced weight…"

Once more on the floor, for answered prayers prefatory to my sequential Phase 1, the glaringly enameled, expanded exposure of an Opaque Object reverberated, yet *yielding yottawatts* as hotly profuse as the Sun in full (although I was mercifully shielded from the impossible impact and enormous output thereof):

I bounce with refined veneration
In elastic-bound blown adoration
The whole of my rounded rotation!

As it bulged forth its divine shape in front of me, the advanced creature continued, "Yet what has become of us? Now notice and discern the Jet Age: for many more run to and fro, and knowledge hath been increased," cries the Commander in Chief cherubim.

Transfixed in betwixt tar-pitched pines that enclosed me, as if in my terracotta cottage or log cabin covered with stucco against weathering, I beheld ensuing scenery whilst the Crested Butte township slumbered. Wintertime waxed snow-frosted big boughs and branches and arms of birches and autumnal aspens along the steep slopes of dreamy sludge. *It was the black forest's foreclosure.*

Hereabouts, the forests were interspersed with an assortment of bristlecone pine, Colorado blue spruce, Douglas-fir, Engelmann spruce, limber pine, lodgepole pine, narrowleaf cottonwood, the quaking aspen, piñon pine, plains cottonwood, ponderosa pine, Rocky Mountain juniper, subalpine fir, and white fir! Where walls loomed up to an almost stratospheric ceiling, the Rocky Mountain Belt had straddled below its waistline the huddled rift and canyon of woods with diverse evergreens and shrubby Colorado conifers altogether. *Holographically, howbeit, it was for endless forestation.*

In complement to the yonder distant sylvan timber tufts, where air was bathed by an attar of scented pine cones redolent with sap and nectar of blue spruce conifers; having everyone of them coats of snowdrift and frost, this then warmed me merrily for the alpine breeze that wafted over a moor (it was the prevernal period):

Where white plaster walls were quoined with red sandstone cinder blocks by holograms of the TATM system~ and where, per passkey entry, versification flooded my mindset meticulously reconditioned

Brightness shimmers upon every meadow
Now in springtime that blossoms aloft
Near her hedgerow-humility spread low
Dolled through lavender oiled up soft

Curtains far above, bathed by sun rays
Tremble one's bloated blanket per each
Vernal warmth has infused our fun leis
Lest lugubrious days spawn their leech

There be dismal days creepy! They pinch
Heartfelt fat, listless lull and repose
But bulged paradise soaked inch by inch
Still prevails; herself she'll disclose

How whole Helicon mountain sprouts firm
Fiery crimson, blood-red, twilit yellow
Seamless sewn, grow immune to some worm
Still deployed against damsel or fellow

Whilst evergreen boxwood buds splendor
Where drenched daffodils daintily lilt
Spectra Sparkle above, tapered slender
Mirrored so, wears her quivering quilt

O what stateliness stays far and wide
Lilac hedged, primrose radiant tinged
Be it she: brick-thick thermal inside
And without void of exit doors hinged

Somehow and *elsewhere,* miles from the cavernous cathedral, I soon beheld man-driven steeds and carts clatter over cobblestone crosshatched streets and sidewalks full o' public commerce where pedestrians peopled the square, busily intermingling or en route to work; aye, by-the-lorry-load trading & bartering beside clapboard high-gabled buildings buttressed by a sandstone campanile along the countryside crossroads. An insular intersection it was, backed by a forlorn semaphore which waved and flashed its age-old traffic signal salute to tourists, visitors, boot camp recruits, and to locals alike and impartially. Clapboard sidings boarded the barracks.

These low-key but lively fellow outsiders, with bustling bursts of thrift and activity, were wearing customary clothing of aesthetic designs. For whereas the upper class of this people would remain embroidered with finery, and felt quite complimentary to cautious eyes, the middle class (also) appeared likewise in modesty withal, bearing about bourgeois polite decorum covered from neck to foot. For wholesomely attired and egg-and-dart decked were they, the Victorian vindicators of the Mercy Seat. The portrayal thereof, that of a cassock-covered parsonage *all Holy Ghost filled,* and the lay-men and ladies, frock suit framed and gowned with undergarment girdles of garter belt *discretion.*

Alongside forested furlongs of loamy repose skirted by forlorn ferns, punctuated by coniferous curtains, lumberjacks wore brawny breeches; their dolls were draped thigh-high, almost midriff, with brooches and cluster-cleats under garter belts.

Yet so soon as when the campanile belfry would toll "*the knell of parting day*" with the eleventh hour numbered on its clock dial, the time slot envisaged therewith had smoldered to soot, only to be vehemently replaced by an oily, asphalt Metropolis rumbling and churning its all-gas and electric inferno! And now, vaporous vomit and a noisome malaise befouled it as networks of sinewy wisps, woven by bituminous boulevards and avenues, were inundated like clogged, claustrophobic arteries of a metal mushroom monstrosity.

As I had felt the grotesque growth of its macadamized anthill, a metallic *Vivatorium paralleled the lifelike stores of this city! Oil-inflamed, inextinguishable, belching by afterburner chimney-flues!

* Another coinage for vivarium. It is an enclosure (not a cage, Heaven forbid) for keeping pets under semi-natural conditions but beneficial to their well-being. Or in such a context, not unlike a terrarium of another Transalteratorium commodity.

Then, the timelessly-tapered MBS or Big Ball heftily translated me right there to an abandoned warehouse where it entered some vac-shaft chamber, quietly concealing its fully overblown pallor of blinding blankness from the viewership of my Muse and I. Though immediate, meteoric teleportation re-materialized us as if naught could have happened, this nullified my last inklings of its memory beforehand!

Good Heavens! What comelier conjecture can I proffer than to avoid being rebooted! Exit from the backstage of this universe …

(via *vermicular* wormhole) *instantaneous* reentry!

| | | | | | | | | | | | | | | | | | | | | | | | | | | | | |

Immediately --- *of no idolatry*, aglow immaculately ….

For it was then that incessant murmurings of a trillion terawatts had paved permanent chills of Chernobyl into my spleen and spinal cord as I eavesdropped on the encased sphere's muffled message to ensue with a pillar of fire, cocooned column after column:

"Behold, what horde of humanity has so many ears to hear," would intone its still small voice, full blown. "And they refuse to listen, saith the Almighty; or so many eyes to see and *still* they refuse to observe what was, is now and ever shall be..." |whispered We| "But if one puts blinders on his eyes to go one way, there he will stay. If *she* therefore lavishes jewelry over herself, the rust and canker therewith may eat her up as an anachronistic epitaph of a time-distorted daughter; thus the power of a man hath fallen prey to her modern worldview of salacious seduction."

I gawked dumbly at the vac-shaft-kept MBS swollen from the transom vent, though this with conviction, compunction, and raw admiration of its sermon on the mount proffered.

Meanwhile, I was required to remember my whereabouts once more, meticulously, as if I were whooped up and deafened by this somewhat continental canister manifold metropolis at large bulge. For it was as though the city gaped out through a fisheye lens whenever my hidden and cryptic curve-ball (concealed by the vac-shaft) unrolled everything in front of me like some red rug nap awaiting the soft tread of my subconscious soles.

The flashback, like ball-lightning, flitted forth fluidly--

The township square of a parallel Crested Butte, Colorado, for some odd reason, recalled itself with a plethora of lock, stock and barrel bustle and thrift. This time, the vast metropolitan trolleybus transport, although incontestably efficient, barreled back and forth, carrying payloads of passengers long before pantographs would be installed thereupon each and every one of them.

An old trolleybus trundled on worn cobblestone streets under catenary netting and a mesh of what would have been featured for the good Guinness Book of World Records vastest amusement park bumper-car layout. Except with this lattice, lighted by bloated arc tubes, an entirely safe, energized continuity atop and overhead: the entanglement of its 600 volt catenary canopy of an electrical grid and bifurcated electric shoe-flanges of the trolleybus that make magnetic contact with the cables. Until, as any other pedestrian in the alternate year 1221, I could distinctly and delicately detect the odour of ozone therefrom, except not normally by *that* year, I do declare! Because by a refrigerator-fat fire hydrant, I salvaged a "glishoe" that fell off an *electropole* of the trackless trolley, which was a nifty pneumatic flywheel: yea, U or V flanged doughnut!

Eftsoons, I was separated from that memorable time-slot to the re-assertive and radiant radius of but ultra-elasticity which was one of the very Super Spheres themselves... and I was made to assume visual acuity upon an enormously elongated ring-world corridor of some spectral structure. The superior contents of which will remain a puzzle henceforward. It staged a laboratory maze manufactured for runaway rats, and I was one them.

Henceforth let me endorse, that throughout its concourse, there were Walls called *mures* and indentations of coffers along ceilings suspended to dizzily neck up, up and away with such continuity that the which barely gave off an inaudible and uninterrupted reverberation of it being intelligently alive. I wish to clarify it, preferably: what I heard was an awful old chorus of gargantuan ghostly air, *pillared* along this Labyrinthine Limbo of *ypsiliform* or Y-shaped high-ceiling topped hallowed hallways that curl, curve, and contort into themselves. Similar to the famous 24,000-square-foot American Queen Anne Revival mansion. Aye, one of the most peculiar and sprawling estates in the world, with its nine kitchens, 52 skylights, 160 boudoirs, 2,000 doors, and 10,000 windows... It was once seated across a very busy street from the San Jose high-end retail and dining destination of Santana Row. A long tome ago, it was known for its abnormal architecture, such as staircases into nowhere; a window in the floor of the south conservatory, a room without a ceiling or floor, doors that open into walls; a cupboard with a half-inch of storage space, the recurring spider web motif, and curious instances of the number 13, or like the baker's dozen of hooks on wall-sides of the séance room. Back then, the Winchester even created a room just for convening with spirits.

Today, in our timestamp of 2113, a far larger scenario:

This unimaginable rotational runabout ran, upwardly extended and back down. That descended downward, and then up again … over and over, forever… A gigantic tunnel-tube hyper-toroid that could easily accommodate some superhighway to run through it; able to go on indefinitely, but only to be entered or exited from via cloverleaf junction! Its four-dimensional aspect allowed anyone to have strolled along its corridor, but non-curved, as if it were the Universe in miniature- so that if you start at space-buoy *A* and move in a straight line almost forever, or to the other end of the cosmos, you would somehow or other arrive at that exact same space-buoy *A* again. And so, in this case, to walk the Ring-World runabout seemed similar to me!

Of course, every isolated crossroads ramp-exchange radiated a conventional lighting-layout for the times at hand. Duly designated with glister-torches of living-lamp-entities, each which were of efficient flywheel~slip (caduceus-coil-lynch by pulley-and-winch) versatility, the high masts riddled each pit-stop junction box at the interior of the vast tunnel-tube roundelay! Aside from what once the eloquent author, Larry Niven, today's rather ancestral science-fiction predecessor, had far earlier conceived of in the late 1960s over a century ago (by his fantastic and fabulous *Ringworld* novel), this then had become my Reality check here & now, nonetheless, hither and yon, yea, off and on! Anon, be they that of luminescent, interlocking wheels as envisaged in Ezekiel's Vision.

Amen

For as I negotiated its inner-tube doughnut either way, it then behaved likewise as if it were the gargantuan pneumatic-inflated Ferris wheel within which I was stationed momentarily. However, since I lacked any referential direction, albeit Up or Down, the curved floor enabled me to be on any one of its *mures* as I moved. Overwhelmingly, this instead offered the faintest impression of some seemingly materialized carousel turning at every advance or retreat that I executed. Alas, the below memory was inserted into my cerebral cortex:

Never mind the aforesaid *doughnut*, even if by back-flash I ate at a Winchell's or Dunkin' Donuts... For with my five senses- nay- sixfold sensory faculty enhancement, the taste of a vanilla version was so multiplied but billion times! Not to mention the other five windows or portholes of my utter soulfulness! No backlash herein, big buddy! No, not by a long shot!

Lo and behold, my feeble attempt to outrun the hollow bore of a Hyper-Toroid, at large bulge in and of itself, was only futile.

Hauntingly, my memoir of a childhood ditty soliloquized it:

Life is like an enclosed carousel that whirls and twirls
round and round, "the way we go- the way we go!"

With equestrian nymphs and gnomes saddled upon steeds and
unicorns as pipe organ reeds prepare to cry out "Oh... Whoa!"

And so, where e'er you get off- there, O there thou wilt be

For all eternity,- for all eternity...

For as a rider thinks, be he priest or Sphinx
(as Antiquity hath written),

So is he... Yea, so is he, hard smitten, hard-bitten!

I am there and nowhere. The walls will not re-absorb me into naught, I may say. Regardless of this carousel steeplechase!

I am immured in one out of an infinite other Ring-Worlds that consummate some alternate Multiverse I know nothing about!

But annexed to my most meandering rumination: "O how can you escape this express hurdle of such timeliness?" carped aloud the Rotator's voice-print identification. My mentality underwent an impossible perusal of sorts as my mind was read by a 4D Ball.

'Twas the hyper-half of that marvelous MBS, presumably, or as I guessed, the Primary QUOTILE of explosive existence!

The South Pole poise of underbelly ballooning weight waged havoc with the surroundings as the floors sagged from pressure. I backed away at once.

"Eschew ne'er My glare! But go to and walk my *hypertoroidal doughnut*," suggested he out of a stark spark. "That the loop of causality thereof is upwardly extended from *up*, *above*, *beyond*, to *down*, *below*, *within*- and locked in a direction unknown to the Euclidean geometry of perspective persistence- originates from My incontrovertible, multitudinous dimension..." With one gulp, I had swallowed its final gobbledygook!

How his near-infinite intelligence challenged my dearly-held miniature disposition! Doubtless, I was no less disconcerted by the Obviously Oblivious that pulverized to bulk pulp the renegade by but bareness and blankness. Of course, someone so *obvious* and blunt as a door knob; a rotary door knob as such for us all to ne'er turn clockwise, nor counterclockwise- whichever- whether it be on the southern or northern hyperhemisphere of the nacreous glue-glob of naught else except pristine elastic *spheriness*- either way- we would never see this particular entrance doorway of esoteric knowledge go ajar and shut but back up on itself.

Phase Sequence **V**

As I must have realized, this warped womb or box of paradox that bore one wan corridor became more of a "horridor" to me than anything else. Or pictured simply: with *ghostliest* and an inferior interior one can but barely imagine! Immured indefinitely, as it were, that narrowly tapered to some hairline slip~slit at each end, the overwhelmingly vibratile vestibule stretched on forever as if it contained tubiform remnants of an immense global star ship with countless more *horridors* distributed and up-curved to the much vaster warp-maze of its interwoven, labyrinthine **MULTIPLICITY** (as envisioned on Another Equator of some sort).

That having been but light-years distant- let us conjecture- its madcap, mind-boggling colossus ought to, with a circumstellar embrace, contain the giga-year scorcher of luminiferous SIRIUS in full orbit- this very labyrinth, that is. Not necessarily a Dyson sphere, but instead, a big ringlike superstructure, although not in the least manufactured. Rather, to be organic and a self-enclosed inner-tube that resembles this magnificently monstrous Michelin tyre.

But far past ancient Paleozoic calendars and to tenebrous times of Precambrian ooze and goo, the puerile, primordial, and precious electromagnetic spectrum and wavelengths from this quasi-stellar storehouse of thunderbolt bullets~ that of lightning luces to yet extravagantly shine out of violently lit SIRIUS~ still illuminates the immaculate floor of the vast Maze. From threadbare thrones of power compared, the *irretinal* rays of Sirius' corona now puncture the opaque plaster plafond of quilted quietness. And this sustained quiescence separated from such a Warp Lamp!

Apropos of *Warp Lamp*, and on a tangent per se, the superstar thereof can be fortified (in its quasi-conscious prominence) with yet much more inscrutable gluons that further fuse the subnuclear reactor core of some nearby anomaly, and that far better than any of the prefatory marvels ...

The concretely permanent and Unspeakably Unlawful of close encounters ever conveyed via technical, laborious language:

Wherefore such and such having been an over-sized warp-goo *GLUOR* of nearly infinite indivisibility. Thus the compact contents of which consist of *hypertiny* gluons and nothing more! |Assuming each *gluor* to be a fusion of three gluons|

Enter the eternal shape! Whereof that of an ellipsoid, albeit, but bulged out from end to end, or squash-contoured balloon-like with one smaller protuberance on each side, and at each end of it, by reason of a self-supported equilibrium upheld by the strong nuclear force. Such a force that can barely keep it impossibl*y* uncollapsed! Already devoid of subatomic infrastructure, and far denser than a superstate primordial black hole, the aftermath pulsar threshold of pressurized compression [akin to hematological agglutination, but more on the subatomic level] the *subsqueezer* is ever so fused to an enlarged GLUOR which occurs ephemeral after shortwave gamma ray bursts from a binary neutron star spinner or *spinar* meltdown collision! The conclusive result? The aforesaid warp-goo gluonic substrata having been the sustained fusion of continuous liquidity; but rather that of an infinitely-squeezed GLUOR to ever be, as if never to have been before, nor ever...

This now infinitely invisible or invincible Attractor of adhesive cohesion between gargantuan galactic superclusters is but a moth Magnum Magnet of starry disks from void to void! Under Heaven, as that which holds together the bottomless gulfs of null-space, lest but merest and sheerest nullified *Nothingness* dissipates to eternal nonexistence. As if there were no point of singularity to identify with, no! Not even space itself!

Only my manner of sustained *finest fusion* of naught but sticky gluons need a magnetic neutron bottle to be insulated, store-kept in stasis for fuel. The Gluor that lay the groundwork of indivisible fusion by contrast to conventional stellar fusion was what the most Major Ballroom Sphere of them all had compressed unsurpassed.

At rem and in fine, I suddenly came to and resumed reentry to my own time-slot. From Victorian vagaries (in abstract contrast) to the malevolent Futuristic Metropolis that progressively waxed into inane tar-pit bitumen churning away in a death-chant of corrupt choreography, the finalized transcendent impression of the *warp-glue squeezer*- the which I did not reinterpret by nomenclature- remained thus. The memory pellet of *adhesive cohesion* was only printed lengthwise with forbidden fiery strength from stelliferous, *antiluciferous* glorification.

All cassock attired monks, able abbots, care-fraught friars and, not to dismiss scrawny scribes of a gloomy scriptorium attributed thereunto- via my crushed comparisons, *sub specie æternitatis*- had grown instantly hoary. Whereas some have gone gaunt to the bone, whilst knighthood to the hilt, the pungent pall and breath of age lay lock, stock and barrel by bountiful excess.

Until with impending age, page by page, through voluminous tomes, Holy Fear of the Unknown (the seventh of spiritual virtues) awakens my soul. For as the fish-eye lens closes to a tiny aperture, and that even to a silver sliver vanishing away, the Hyper Whole Super-Sphere is reduced to that of a stop-slip tiptop. Its luminous Quotile quoting the bygone book of Ecclesiastes:

* “The thing that hath been, it is that which shall be; and that which is done, is that which *shall be done*, and there is no new thing

under the sun," the Archangel, against *teraphim* fetishes of the devils, jackhammers the verdict, with an axiomatic motif.

And amidst the wide, wallop fallback of the South Pole Sphere (SPS), ere such enveloped departure ensued, the maternity of my forgotten Muse, Polyhymnia, returned as if she were suspended fleetingly by this timeless tinge, or flashback swoon of remarkable memory!

But for now, and alongside her rather ravishing, girlish figurine cushioned up by an antiquated empress bouffant dress-gown; and that discreetly hemmed o'er her ever virginal vitality, Polyhymnia-bundled and *merribound*- beckoned to me through self-postured, adorned and prim primrose prominence. Her hair coiffured to an up-swept flavicomous swirl. To her direction, therefore, I gazed at sudden manifestations of *determinate evanishment*. Albeit, down through the funneled mælstrom of yesterday's past; all the way to the primitive times of our Stone Age, and henceforth (by quietest increments of evanescence) until the warp wave-forms of 4D depth blend. The laws of science were transfixed, transformed to some *nymphæum* within which she stood in solar glory as multi-mirrored heliostat *Heliatrix* accompanied by cream-crested caryatid pillars subservient to the most moderated DIVINE SPIRIT as it were.

My most welcomed musings of divine inspiration persisted still in Time Warp with the now North Pole Sphere of the MBS, and yet I was at arm's-length (literally) right near to her. Although uncanny as it can be, we were separated by an infinite cæsura of time, save only over a brief breath away from each other! My flip-side of this baffling enormous-to-tiny-sized ballgame of heftiest *hyperspheres*, tapered to BB shots at point-blank range, had only divulged the re-bulged South Pole proportion of zero distortion...That is, on the outer edge membrane of ultra-elastic hyper-curvature, our polarity converged in one uninterrupted shrinkage of the MBS, but not until we were fully joined together outside of it, touching, embracing.

For the first *time* in eternity I felt reassured, nurtured and safe. Distinctly relieved by someone so supernal instead of having to face nothing but that bouncing monstrosity: that elastic contorter of impossibility. For herewith, she intimately and knowingly would woo my soul with even further entries of female metaphysics, and that with the Hyper Whole Super-Sphere dwindling daintily in the backdrop, how hesitantly poised for the moment with its entirety of energetic and enveloped departure pending still!

"My intrepid darling!" she shouted with solace. At long last, no more demure, coy, nor cautious, but free-spirited. I could hear her distinctly clarion visionary voice of modulated intonation. "O how I'm thrilled to see ya, my master..." For like Barbara Eden of the bygone, I Dream of Jeannie, who starred in the sultriest television sitcom, I started to enshrine *Her* henceforth. Save, Heavens forbid! not to portray her as obsequious to me, except out of venerable and virtuous vindication!

Overawed and a wee bit taciturn, I became so entranced by her innocently wimpled lookalike as never before. As if fresh from the Nunnery, evidently, she wanted to share the center-stage, cynosure, and drape-drawn victory of her paranormal *personage* during her absence. Indeed, fit for the parsonage of the Crested Butte visit we were escorted to by the Major Ballroom Sphere proper.

I wondered about her, saturnine, wanting to frown, *Where were you when I alone had hapless to evade each external exposure of the eerily incontestable, super~stretchable, spherical continuum? Conscientiously, I forthwith buried my unbelief. Now unbecoming. Abominable! In the wink of an eye, I reverted myself to a grayish, gravely somber- and lastly- lugubrious stance on grounds of what was witnessed with self-renunciation forsworn, deposition and all! Not necessarily funereal, but a trifle trespass.*

"Inside of thee, O silly!" she *quirked*, mimicking me playfully. She then bared herself upon me; the maternal monument of all my desires delectably dolled up by narrow nuances. My slight grimace melted away. For as we merged more and more into each other, I glanced at ghostly quasars dimly arrayed above and around our baseball mound, besprent with an infinite cornfield way out! So diminutive and so distant, that super-voids render them red-shifted! Nonetheless, I truncated her dillydally on a dash of shock!

Our cosmic carnival of exotica; a nearly *glib*, gleeful glitterati of this showcase extravaganza culminated. How heavenward to its climactic, intergalactic tour de force of *theremin* thought as I ought to have addressed it as such: O *Excelsior!*

The shades of night were falling fast,
As through an Alpine village passed
A youth, who bore, 'mid snow and ice,
A banner with the strange device,
Excelsior!

His brow was sad; his eye beneath,
Flashed like a falchion from its sheath,
And like a silver clarion rung
The accents of that unknown tongue,
Excelsior!

In happy homes he saw the light
Of household fires gleam warm and bright;
Above, the spectral glaciers shone,
And from his lips escaped a groan,
Excelsior!

"Try not the Pass!" the old man said;
"Dark lowers the tempest overhead,
The roaring torrent is deep and wide!"

And loud that clarion voice replied,
Excelsior!

"Oh stay," the maiden said, "and rest
Thy weary head upon this breast!"
A tear stood in his bright blue eye,
But still he answered, with a sigh,
Excelsior!

"Beware the pine-tree's withered branch!
Beware the awful avalanche!"
This was the peasant's last Good-night,
A voice replied, far up the height,
Excelsior!

At break of day, as heavenward
The pious monks of Saint Bernard
Uttered the oft-repeated prayer,
A voice cried through the startled air,
Excelsior!

A traveller, by the faithful hound,
Half-buried in the snow was found,
Still grasping in his hand of ice
That banner with the strange device,
Excelsior!

There in the twilight cold and gray,
Lifeless, but beautiful, he lay,
And from the sky, serene and far,
A voice fell like a falling star,
Excelsior!

By Henry Wadsworth Longfellow

Meanwhile, theremins wailed with coloratura soprano …

We both gawked, bucked aback, and noticed that the complete equatorial equanimity of our portly spherical friend, from tip-to-tip topnotch, finally fell into itself, alas, once and for all! Irretrievably deflated right out of existence, slipping away and away and...

Ah, *perhaps not*! Polyhymnia had hoped- having no longer any need to bellow aloud, her thick thoughts welded to my mentality. *The selfsame sheer shape of it has simply evolved to a far statelier form, as I should show you.*

Evolved, I noted. Nothing too tawdry, I presume.

The *irreplicable*, inviolable Vulgate Latin transliteration of [it] was consequently bequeathed for our scrutiny. Unread as of yet by but a bodiless brainchild. Its Heaven-sent note, so sooty and fallen apart by strong, long, drawn out interminable duration of vacuous time, that the dauntingly descriptive encryption was inconveniently capitalized by this <u>cornerstone</u> voice-print perforated or inscribed into a slab of granite herewith. As if blowtorch-toasted, timelessly inert, unalterable:

Vouchsafe Cartouche

WET JET
SLIP SLIT
WARP SPEW
SHEER SHEEN
HARSH GLARE
SUPER SOLUX
HYPER NAKED
BLOWN BLAZE
PALLID PILLOW
BRIGHT BRIDGE
JOCUND JACKET

ARGENT REGENT
LUCENT LEMONS
CONICAL HELICON
SWOLLEN BALLOON
AURORAL AMPHORA
QUANTUM QUASARC
RATIONAL RADIANCE
RADIATIVE GLORIFIER
CONTINUAL CAUSALITY
ANCIENTLY LOVELIEST
INFINITELY INVINCIBLE
MATERNAL METAPHOR
PERPETUAL THEOPHANY
ENVELOPED CURVATURE
CONCORDANT CONTRACTOR
DELIGHTFULLY LUMINESCENT
DETERMINATE EVANISHMENT
ELECTROSPUN ENVELOPMENT
ECTOPLASMIC EMBODIMENTS
TRANSPARENT TEMPERATURE
TREMENDOUS TRANSDUCER
RADIATIVELY ANTIRETINAL
SUPERTRON METATORCH
INSULATED INCUBATOR
MINIATURE DIMENSION
SHRIVELED SHRINKAGE
ABSTRACT CONTRAST
EXTERNAL EXPLODER
PARAGON PARADOX
CANISTER CREATION
CREMEUM FOAMERY
COMPACT CAPSULE
MERCURY MYRTLUX

PERFECT PACKAGE
CLOVEN GLOZAR
HOLLOW YELLOW
LUMIFER LUCILUX
BEAUTY BEACON
LOONY COOCA
FINEST FUSION
BURNT POUCH
BLANK GHOST
LAMP CAMP
FAT VAT

INTO A SOFT MATTRESSED DECOR
AND THRO' AN IMPERVIOUS DOOR
ETERNAL HARMONY
BORTEUM CREMEUM
PROTEAN COMPANY
O' RECRUDESCENT FLOOR
WE INCANDESCENT GLORE
FUSED MEMORY TO STORE

FOREVER JOINED BULGED HEMIHYPERSPHERES
BLANK-BLOWN STAY UNEPHEMEREAL FOR YEARS
DEAR CHILDREN OF CONVIVIAL MIRTH
TRY AND TAKE MY EQUATORIAL GIRTH

UNCREATED
ALTERABLE, ADAPTABLE
PERPETUAL THEOPHANY
FROM PINPOINT TO INFINITY
MY SWIRL RECLINED IN ME
I WAS, I AM, I SHALL BE
WHOLE BORTEUM & QUASI-CREMEUM
UNENDINGLY HARMONIOUS

LET LOVELINESS RESIDE INSIDE
WHAT NEVER MAY DIVIDE

IMPERIOUSLY INDOMITABLE

TRANSALTERATORIUM

♦♦♦♦♦♦♦♦♦♦♦♦♦♦♦♦♦♦♦

CORRUGATED HULL OF LULL
OUT (REVERBERATORY) PUT
FUSES SEVEN MUSES

INTO THE DOOR I NOW IMPLORE
EMBRASURE OF ERASURE
HOW HORR'BLY H~LY WITHIN THIS ALEMBIC
OR OPAQUE OBJECT OF ENAMELED EXPOSURE
MY CLOVEN TORPEDO COME DOWN
INFUSE EV'RY VERB TO A NOUN

I BOUNCE WITH REFINED VENERATION
IN ELASTIC BLANK-BLOWN ADORATION
THE WHOLE OF MY ROUNDED ROTATION

STRONG BORTEUM AND CREMEUM
ETERNAL HARMONY
IMPERIUM
SUSTAIN ME FROM DELIRIUM
YEA UNIVACUOLEUM

Hitherto was voice-printed the Vouchsafe Cartouche!

I was stunned dumbfounded by the sheer shock-wave thereof.

Imagine: A protean entity that defies all logical explanation, yet maintains its re-assertive formulae beyond anyone's contemplative comprehension! The result? We ought to at least exult in the Prime

Intelligence that exists- with or without our approval ratings- if it were a benchmark on social media.

Nonetheless, more ensued …

For that without doubt came some series of bizarre and entirely otherworldly events to yet *still* be buttressed before our bedazzled, bejeweled cognizance. Chagrined, and void o' hour glass, we were spellbound near the margins of mad ecstasy. This riveting, mind-blowing efflorescence of effulgence was what *would welcome* an entr'acte between somewhat portentous portrayals of the supreme paranormal equipoise upon a rebar-reinforced concrete sheet and bewildering psychotic episodes muzzled mainly in one's cerebral Möbius strip!

In mirrored likeness, therefore, we had ascertained conscious tufts and sprouts of mushrooms oozing about- opened up and out into even stranger holographic detonations like never before. Or *such, inasmuch as it seemed à propos de rien*, rather, to have been completely confronted, but not by the menacing jocund Jekyll and Hyde side of the uttermost, heftiest MBS at large bulge, nor the aforethought contorted antics of component confrontation caught (disturbingly distributed), as if to render us both numb and inept. Instead- with billiard-like chain reaction fashion- a *metamorphosis* marvel would snatch us away, for the moment, to a kaleidoscope of incontestable- yea- and illustrious *illuminants.*

In brief, lacking language deficit, the following cohort escort of beauteous beacons pump, power-play, and sport up their chimerical goal-game of array (I categorize several according to echelon):

	NOMENCLATURE	SUPER~NATURE	LAMP LUX
I.	LUCET	Miniature Luminaire	4,200 LUMENS
II.	LUCIERE	*Supertron Metatorch	8,600 LUMENS

III. LUCELUX	Scorch-white Torchlight	12,100 LUMENS
IV. SOLUX	*External Exploder	16,000 LUMENS
V. REGULUS	Irradiant/ irretinal (with poetry)	63,000 LUMENS
VI. STERILUX	Far Bright Starlight	*septillion lumens*
Reactor Warp Lamp	Super-seraphim of YHWH	hypersolar output
VII. SIRIS: the pulleyless high-tension of buoys	Liminal Tenuity of a "Threshold Thread"	near-infinite countless candlepowe
Naked singularity of minus infinity	Coruscant corona to warp-quantum quasars	lightning luces/ thunderbolt bullets

Our above and fifth living lamp entity of the ranks or radiative zone of circumstellar magnification (the seventh having the highest powers of lumens) was decanter-christened to remain REGULUS: my *ultima ratio regum* against the sinister, chaotic principalities in world domination that~ *whilst upon earth*~ was manufactured as a 1000-watt mercury-vapor Metalamp. An old incontestable scorcher that but 'shatteringly shineth' with the author's intended surrealist narratives in mind. Ultimately, the final prototype model of which an absolutely, *obsoletely*, completely Bulged-Tubular protuberance flashed and fluoresced herself, eerily- now swollen up- and full o' fiery fidelity, *felicity*, facility and phantasmagoria insofar…

I say, right to you~ Highway Light and too bright for any Little Shop of Horrors, terracotta cottage. Ne'er the nonsense, nor bric-a-brac Broadway burlesque of pomp. Instead, brickwork bungalow!

And verses therewith that at random may run (BEACON):

Robustly bulged to Buoy be
Ablaze with night festooned,
A thousand watts of mercury
Shine, blindingly ballooned.

A glistering glorifier of rational Radiance that it must be, quite indefinite and indefatigable. Inexhaustible by itself.

This prototype Warp Lamp mini-series typifies a blankly blown star in space that melts the atomic nuclei of hydrogen into helium by its reactor core of pure nuclear fusion. Such *finest fusion* within which well over 15,000,000 degrees Kelvin is requisite before its multi-billion year *conflagratory* glorifier can instantaneously ignite into continuously uninterrupted, incorruptibly blue-white Light.

I came to confirm the radiant, repository contents thereof with my Muse, Polyhymnia, as she now nestled herself deep down into my mystical midst. Alongside each other, we but bade farewell to that metaphysical MBS that escorted us from door-to-door and via dial-a-Rolodex directory carousel.

God bless my lovely doll who would still above me loll to the special spectra sparkle of radiant Reality! Yea, I blare, even to the discarded shriveled shrinkage thereof- or whatever was left of it! A deflated departure of thermonuclear envelopment, ever immune to the steroid *acromegaly* of megalomania, I implore and pray for!

Conclusively, with no naughty, haughty vaunts whatsoever, I've *deplatformed* production, the which will resume here-afterward.

PROPHETIC PROFUSION

Until ineffable whispers, subliminal long-distance wails, boops and beeps were delicately addressed adroitly from my Main-Throw Major Ballroom Super-Sphere, that (by design) over the telephone, and *foretold* fourfold divine, these sentences had unraveled the red carpet treatment. This was a comma or pause or caesura or interim of my four-dimensional filmstrip *featurette* of limitless *liminality*, the denouement of stage production, platform and plank fold-up of all no-showoff, non sequitur possibilities:

The prefatory Book of Daniel 12:4
"But thou, O Daniel, shut up the words, and seal the book, *even* to the time of the end: many shall run to and fro, and knowledge shall be increased."
King James Version (KJV)

Having been merely our prelude to the hot superstar torchlight clipsome Molten Mother about to take place, this fourfold for brief in-vitro vision is presented wondrously (worldwide elucidated):

* * * UNIVERSAL ULTIMATUM * * *

I. The stars of fire shall be thrust down to burn away obsolete earth, that it should be replaced by a new and unvitiated ball of perfect glory- and that transillumined with YHWH...

II. Lust shall be vanquished utterly to the determinate evanishment of every breath therewith, until a h~ly and endless Love pervades all of glorified creation.

III. There will no more be war both in Heaven and on earth, for that great amendment of reparation shall remain in *futura* settled forever and ever according to the *Primordial Promise* and Meticulous Metropolis of VITREOUS PARADISE.

IV. Divine Light of a *Metaluminiferous Supersingularity* shall expose all the secrets of human drama past, present and future. Including the perfunctory pall of intents beforehand never known; indeed, the prophetic disclosure of the CAUSAL QUASAR that manifestly relinquishes the contents thereof right out of the blue, and so, before the Holy Spirit, fully alive

CONSECRATED TO THE PREFATORY PRESENCE OF SHEEL WHOSE MIRROR IMAGE I HAD VERILY ABUSED~ TO WHOM I AM BEHOLDEN, AND IN WHOSE PRISTINE PRIORITY I OWE ADEQUATE ADJUDICATION AND ACKNOWLEDGMENT AS UPRIGHT RIGHTFULLY: ADJACENT OR ACCORDINGLY SO

Via Lactea
Milky Way Galaxy
circumstellivigesimalopolis

FRENCH BALLADE & CHORUS

What many fancy frills
Our lives can fabricate
Among malignant ills
That mortify man's fate.
Strong sun-rays permeate
Mere flesh of every soul;
Though sheer voids dilate,
Her whirlpool spirals whole.

This cobbled causeway fills
With cabby, cart or freight,
Yet yonder cascade spills
Via mountainsides o' slate-
(She shimmers forth innate)
Though we were in the hole,
Still, bright stars emanate
One whirlpool *Spiral*, whole!

Thick blacktop tar instills
Prim progress full of bait,
An old blown Organ shrills-
That fogs one's lazy eight!
Charged sun-rays penetrate-
Which perforate each soul;
Midst bygone times ornate
Her whirlpool spirals whole.

L'ENVOY ENTR'ACTE
Throughout sprout daffodils
That throngs would liquidate,
Fresh fronds o' froth unroll.

Stars sprinkle o'er the hills
Vouchsafed to bulge up great
One whirlpool *Spiral,* whole!

CHORUS
One whirlpool Spiral, whole.

HYPER-HOLY SUPER SEALANT CONSECRATED TO MY VACCIMULGENT CREAMERY OF HOLY SHEEL- AS THE ABOVE CONSECRATED CONTENTS THEREOF PAVE AN APPROPRIATE APPROBATION UPON THE PORCELAIN POLONAISE OF THIS CLOVENRY COVENANT RECORD

20) The "highway high-rise" apartment building; the reinforced concrete design of which was engineered to have it upright on tall pillars, posts, pylons and girders that support the unwieldy edifice, and that right over an ever busy, bustling car conduit! This is the entrance to New Jersey off the lofty George Washington Bridge of New York City from the Bronx.

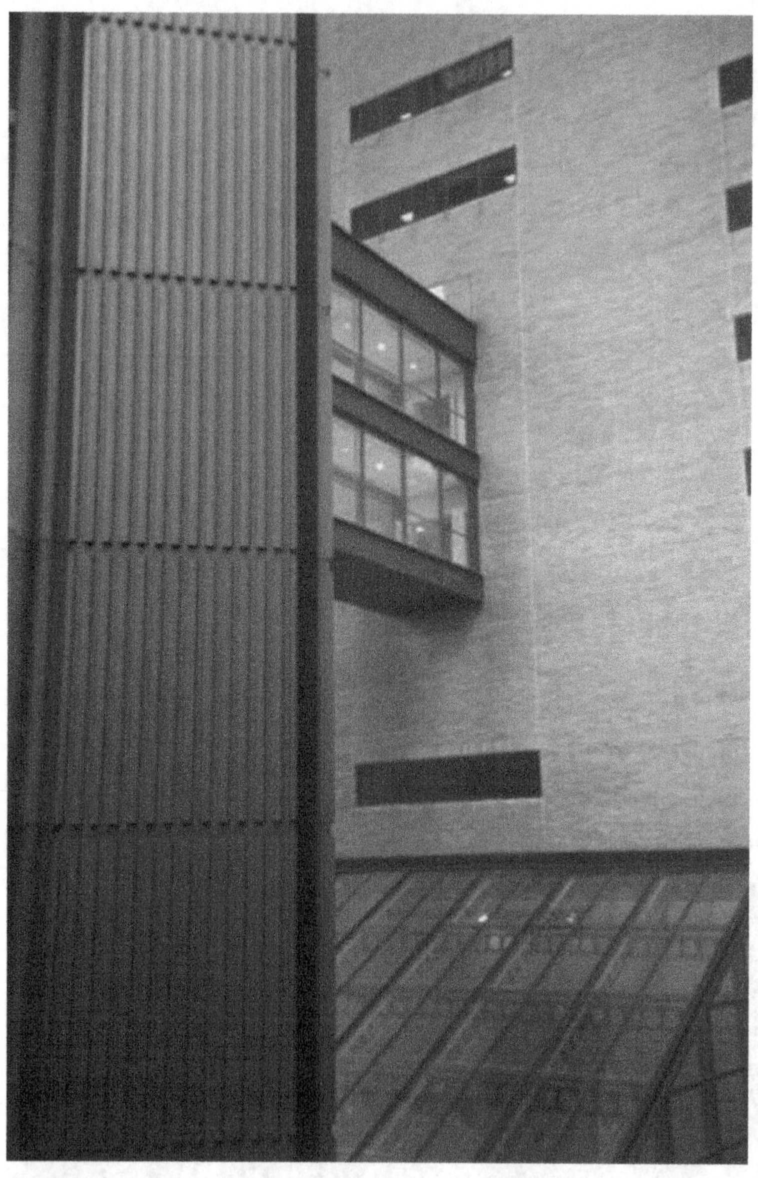

Example of what an enclosed vestibule causeway would look like if envisaged in my future interlink Metropolis. Actually, however, this was my snooping snapshot taken of Mount Sinai Hospital in Manhattan, New York City; only weeks after my mother's massive stroke… In memory of her, I rededicate my Yard Lamp of Gloria. Plate **(21)**

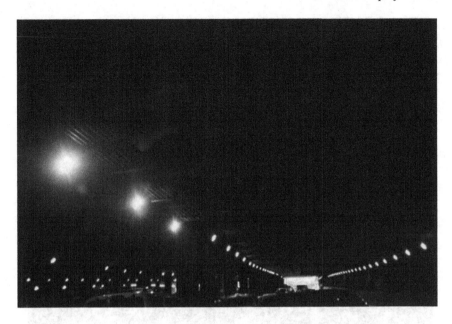

Photographic feature of a Tunnel Tube-Way clogged by EVT (Electric Vehicular Traffic). Actually, it was another snapshot taken just seconds later beneath such superstructure of nothing but building! Perhaps this one in particular portrays an image of what it would be like, except longer throughout my Megalotubulopolis. Plate **(22)**

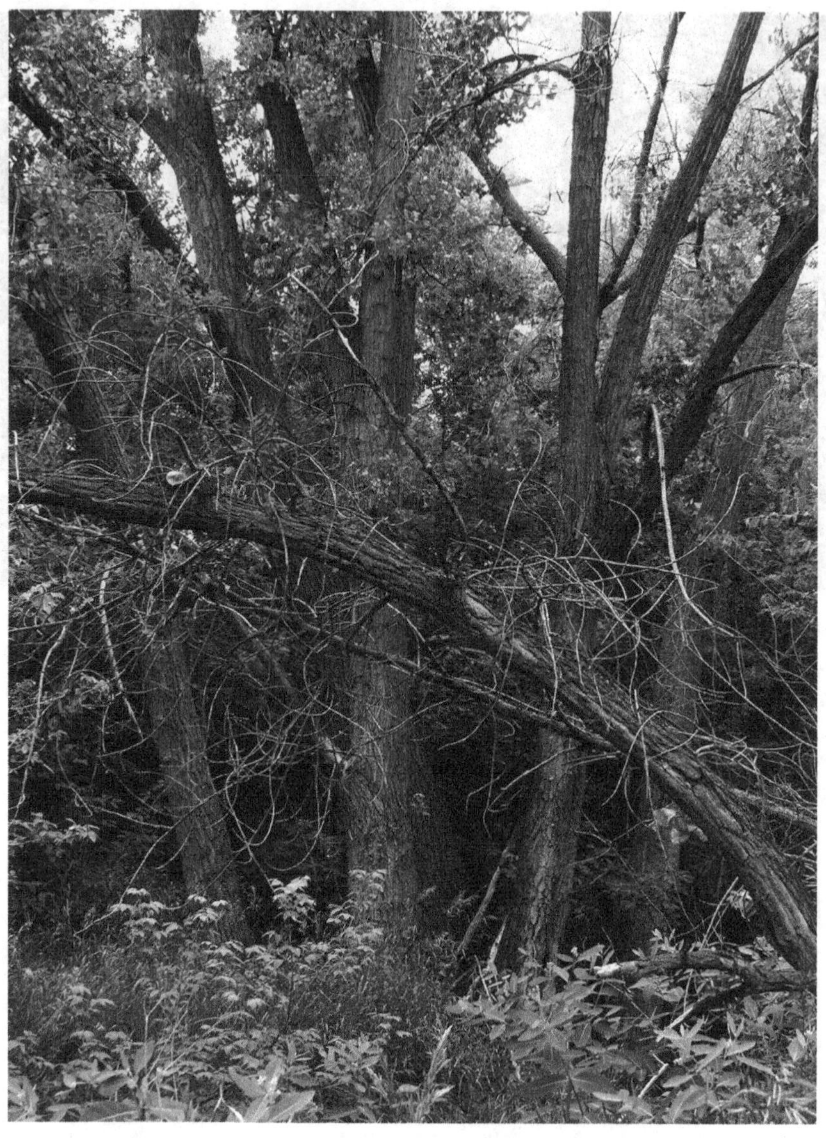

23) *Author's secluded storyboard-launch-pad near South Broadway in Denver, Colorado; truly, out of which the Yard Lamp of Gloria was then conceived. I had happened to compose the cardinal cast of its contents thereat!

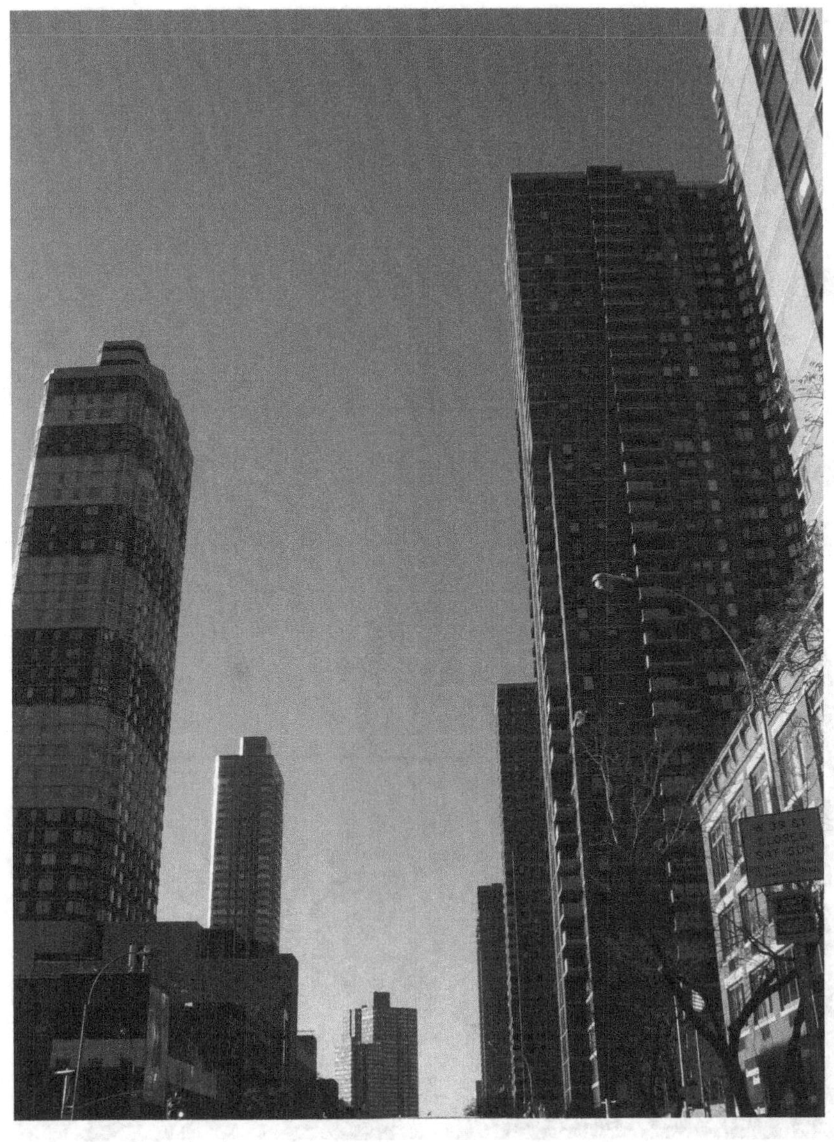

24) My early vernal equinox picture taken in the late afternoon of an antiquated, historic Manhattan high-rise neighborhood. For at that time, it was at least a decade before the influx of *streetlight-emitting diode* commercialization.

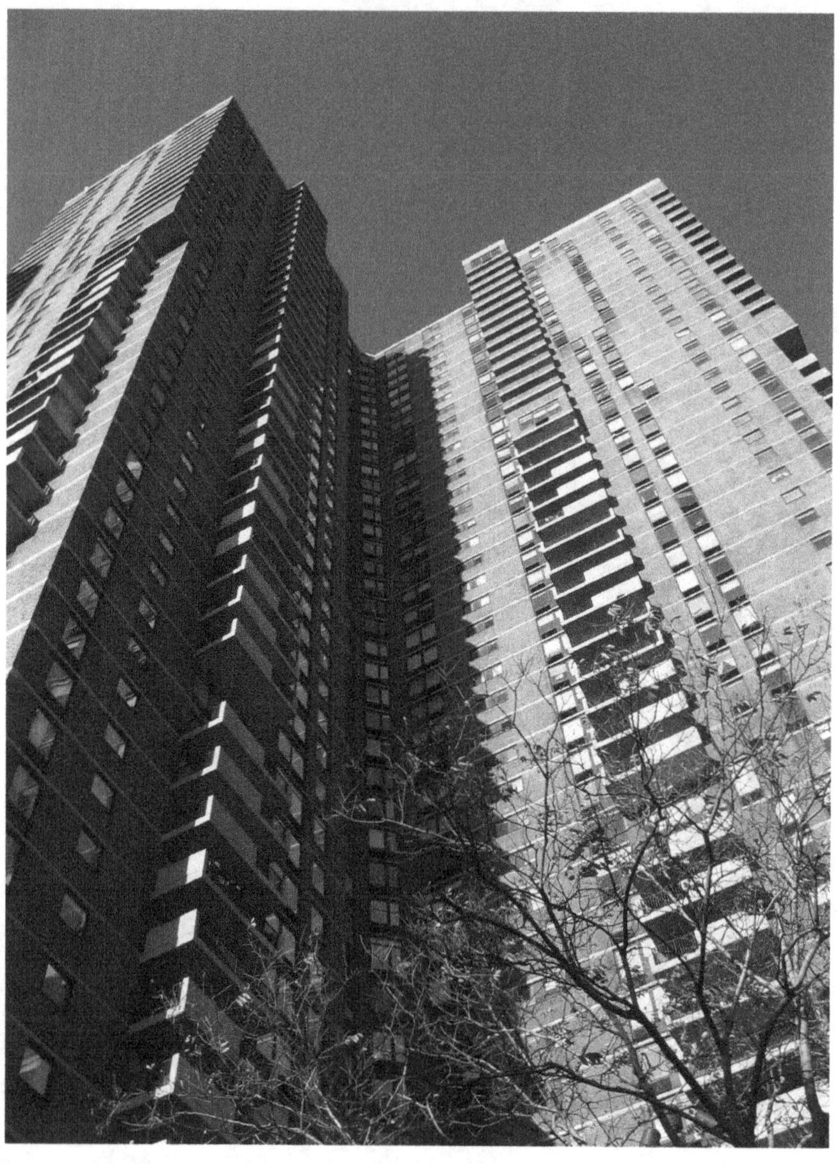

25) My rather early vernal equinox lookup of a mammoth apartment complex in the Bronx. The serenity of that afternoon felt timeless!

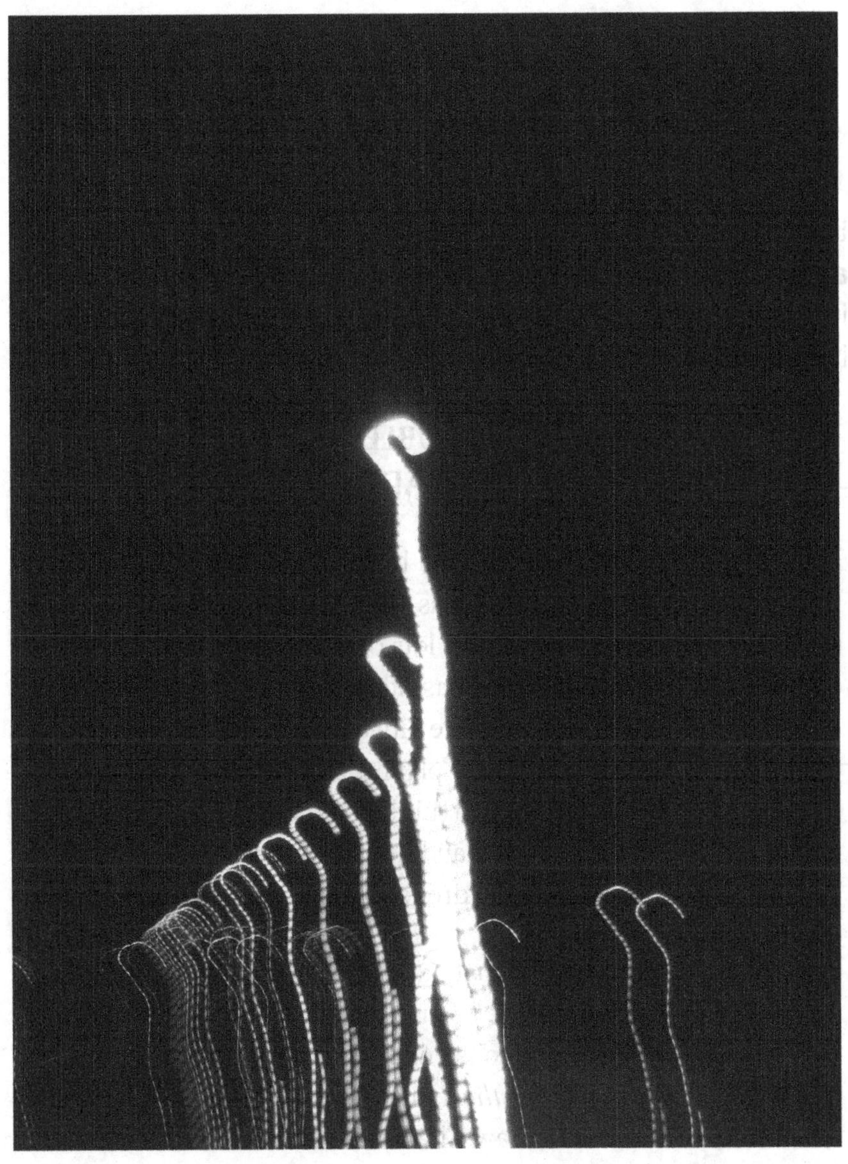

26) As if through the camera obscura, *light anomaly*- but better yet- that which might even signify some ancient Mesopotamian [reed-hook] so symbolic of an Inanna/ Ishtar cuneiform hieroglyph, believe it or not!

Argent Regent

Due to precession, Vega will replace Polaris as the northern polestar **around 13,700 AD**. Vega is also approaching Earth and will make its closest approach in about 264,000 years at a distance of 13.2 light-years.

DOUBLE BALLADE

The darkness and light are at war
With each other as nay against yea;
Holy angels cast lots on some floor
"**P**redetermined" astute prophets pray.
Soon ablaze above ciphers were they
Where raw power plants gather galore-
Someone wonderful then must ignite,
Big, ballooned and devoid of decay:
Snow-white hydrogen/helium light!

Down the throaty abyss we implore,
"**O** *Regina Lucis*, stretch our Sunday!"
May mere gluons engulf fused rapport
Between *ghostliest* quarks gone astray;
Let droves draw Titan torchières moiré
Through that Crucible ready to store
Its own super-cells pressurized tight,
Until seared focused photons convey
Snow-white hydrogen/ helium light.

Likely after earth-eons wax hoar,
After droids turn to fossils of grey,
Such a stellar torch rids global pallor
And can coruscate past linked delay;
Dauntless souls who retain *ev'ry* ray
Shall record its first prominent roar-
Gravitation that squeezes sheer might
Hurls hot seraphim six-winged to say
"**G**low bright hydrogen/ helium light!"

Cosmic spirals, festoons for décor,
Cradle ancient Light flung far away.
Yet the same swollen lamp heretofore
Like some quasar bizarre and how fey,
Still unaltered, remains hence to stay.
Arc tube torpedoes beyond our seashore
Now go burnt out at fathomless night-
Tho' so many worlds wobble or sway,
"**G**low bright hydrogen/ helium light!"

An ex nihilo lux thrones once swore
Against Time-tinged *per diem* dismay-
Seething starlight distends evermore
At old orbs forged from papier-mâché;
Light, as needles, in wan stacks of hey
Fiercely penetrates man's opaque door.
Full of gamma rays, X~rays in flight,
Solar winds induce thousands to bray
"**G**low bright hydrogen/ helium light!"

Thus the blinding new Vega few bore
In this vista lest neurons would fray,
Lest th' vastness of minds would adore

Its strange God-breathe'd *elixir vitae*;
"Don't dare open a sphere if you may!"
For each nuclear fusion reactor core
So warp-lucently lit (bulging bright)
With bipolar jets, juts up with spray
Snow-white hydrogen/ helium light...

DUAL ENVOY

For as giga-year Dog Stars but bite,
Crowned "irretinal" Vega should splay
Forth her thunderbolt bullets in spite
Of Dark Ages that martyrs portray.

God~created from stardust and clay,
We outgrow ourselves into new height;
Ere the torch may replace the bouquet:
"Glow bright hydrogen/ helium Light!"

To the glory of Argophany
and her ultra-elastic MBS

Afterword

With a footnote snapshot of memories, the big blue star Vega was my very first inspiration in the year 1996 and onward. On a clear summer observation in Denver, Colorado, the star was way overhead, directly on top of my skyward line of sight at around 10:30 PM at night as I had attended my night-shift job. This star is locally close, at only 25 light-years from the Sun, and one of the most *bluish-bright* stars

in the stellar neighborhood. It is a little over
[2] times the mass of our Sun and about 2.5
times larger… Also, it used to be the North
Pole star around 12,000 B.C.E. and will be
again the cynosure around the year 13,727.

The Poet's Cornerstone Epigraph:

♦ ♦ ♦ ♦ ♦ ♦ ♦

The kirk and state may gae to hell
And I'll gae to my Anna!

ROBERT BURNS
(My guidepost behind the curtains
of this next back-stage production)

♦ ♦ ♦ ♦ ♦ ♦ ♦

Any sufficiently advanced technology
will appear as magic.

Arthur C. Clarke

Spiritual life is the bouquet of natural life,
not a supernatural Thing imposed upon it.

Joseph Campbell

There is no end. For the soul there is never birth nor death. Nor, having once been, does it ever cease to be. It is unborn, eternal, ever-existing, undying and primeval.

The Bhagavad-Gita

What you are about to recall is a curiously compact memorable melodrama of the idyllic. A rhapsodic soliloquy designed to recall from its tertiary persona that which defies duality: as if it were to cry, in desperate remonstrance: Emancipate yourselves from such a cadaverous gender gap and so release instead the acute qualitative, angelic desires for none but your next door neighbour.

Herein is my fictitious fancy of what might have been shunned if I would not surrender myself to the far finer finesse of life, and revitalize the visceral receptivity for a *profounder love*, completely unbiased. Involved are both halves of the human whole: aggressive and passive to congeal as one, harmoniously joined.

This inventive invitation is what I allow in giving us visions to uninhibited, unconditional radiant *Reality* and the contact/ consent faculty we ever so often suppress as terribly too taboo or illusory. Having been intimated by my internal invocations at the time of oft infused writing, its own imagery and maternal metaphor may retain my masterpiece achievement through what I intend to convey as if commensurate with what is unthinkable!

Whereas it offers to unbiased readership a referential backdrop of barest actuality, to the unschooled and unbelieving (contrarily), nothing more than "a [tall] tale told by an idiot…" The last line or paraphrase borrowed from Shakespeare and *in due deference* to the literary genius thereof.

"All aboard the Unthinkable Titanic!" I invite. "Abound, abound, Thou *creatrix* of the muse! Surround the carnal mind reclined upon parochial pews!" Hence in Dante's Vita Nuova and Divine Comedy an allegorical figure developed likewise was with personification whom Dante first saw from his childhood and embraced her as an ideal monument of womanhood: Wherefore woven in warm-white and *unetiolable* consecration, albeit Beatrice the creatrix! At long last, let us exit and avoid newfangled future façades of tomorrow.

Instead, enter the reanimated mirror-image of Pygmalion's bygone Galatea of yesterday ere staggeringly stentorian megaphones blare their whistle-blown calliope chorus of contiguous convergence:

* * * (AOE) * * *
Alpha & Omega-Enumerated
exactly [28] characters across

9830164275248119939830164275
ILUCIFULGIDULIPLURIGLUNIVATI
||||||||||||||||||||||||||||
Until

3
2
1

CONTACT

THE

METAMORPHO-
ſis of Pigmalions
Image.

AND
Certaine Satyres.

AT LONDON,
Printed for Edmond Matts, & are
to be ſold at the ſigne of the hand and
Plough in Fleetſtreete.
1598.

It is with this 1598 facsimile, I offer up my votive tribute to old Valley Brook Ballroom's Galatea as the ageless myth of Pygmalion and Galatea paves way to the foundation of my storyboard. But yet, for as the commemorative '*very first faint*' image of the star Vega's 25 light-year-old photons fell into focus upon an evenly *sheer sheet* of a silver-plated copper sensitized with iodine vapors (visualized via one third of an hour long exposure) only to bolster benevolent anticipation, just as well, what could they have fore-felt, watching wistfully the image slowly develop over hot mercury fumes during the night of July 16-17, 1850? It was James Adams Whipple and William Bond who had used their 15-inch apparatus at Harvard College Observatory to impromptu do the trick, though tremendously tried (trial-and-error) beforehand until vindicated as a triumph of pure pioneer exploration and discovery. Whereas two decades later-plus 2 years and a month- in August 1872, amateur astronomer Henry Draper selected Vega as the first nighttime star to have its spectrum photographed, standardized and so forth---

Now nonetheless, I am not (*Heaven-forbid*) a showoff of easily-acquired information hacking that need be accordingly accredited

Enough of my unconventional prattle!

Case closed, *clairaudiently pending.*

May my visual Framework of a Fraunhofer *barcode* impress the unaided naked eye in order to ascertain the (plain vanilla) spectrum of a steady Light Signature which serves as Vega's groundbreaking brink for (full) electromagnetic spectral analysis, particularly so to identify and reclassify similar stars of its echelon and glorification including Sirius, Altair, and Fomalhaut manifest verbatim.

| *nothing follows* |

V

For this book-backup, the two website hyperlinks

https://skyandtelescope.org/astronomy-news/
vega-the-star-at-the-center-of-everything/

https://www.youtube.com/watch?v=a89kmpjXymg

An exemplar study of a visual cortex 4-D ball:

https://www.youtube.com/watch?v=_4ruHJFsb4g&t=329s

Originally conceived and now unabridged!

THE OLD VALLEY BROOK BALLROOM

Throughout the *unshuffled*, unruffled meadow of another land, suitably an island far, far away on the other side of life, there was undisturbed docility within vacant rooms long empty. In the living room parlour of undiminished ghostliness, albeit incandescent or ever fluoresced via paraffin candlepower- with fine filament multiplicity of inspired infusion- the wall mirror gave off a peculiar look. That of orb-emanated brightness unparalleled.

This post-residential chateau that it was, situated and elaborately embellished in stately architecture was engineered to enclose, safely, protectively, some stone-tongued-force.

Of infrastructure matrices, protean by nature, but programmed to converge from its multi-millennial concealment, to nanosecond inducement. It was as if its opacity was undivided by time.

Until the plaster-paved mirror sparkled on the main room wall: That this was overshadowed by the niche of Mnemosyne, sequestered alcoves, high-ceiling Corinthian columns, and company sister boudoirs shackled beyond in an imperious palatial setting is what my soothing set portrays. Point-blank out of nowhere it stays referenced, and *refinely* redefined. Yea, no one could ever reach, let alone breach its ethereal threshold of an effect *effulged*; neither bypass it with any hint of fantasy, nor fleeting flint of a visionary glint.

An eerie age-old annexed Victorian manor home unfolds just so, overlooked as it lay picturesquely engulfed by bush-laden glens and full fens followed with the rhythmic rain forest. Such a hazel haven of almost absurd secrecy and stealth prepares its statuary stage of insular resurrection. Its ultra-elastic and re-assertive plenum of Sacred Aether awaiting to levitate an uninterrupted visitation of a mystical masterpiece.

It was nearly dismally dim on the caped island where this superstructure so settled, save for an occasional gesture of wart-wimpled arms waving from the white willow grove, or compliantly, the whir of a ruby neck-and-throat hummingbird tentatively flying up and down with canary-sized nightingales yellowed beneath ancient moonlight. There were blue jays, cardinals, magpies, and also wraparound retinal-band *Vacons* of unknown species. The latter littlest pterodactyl bird had an eye that could scan the surroundings simultaneously 360 degrees all around with one retinal-band roundabout its semi-conical head. Each Vacon, endowed with four wings instead of the evolved two, had flashed o'er like lightning. Obviously, an ornithological metamorphosis of self-disclosure! Their superb celerity seemed nimbler and quicker than their highly prized progenitors, the hummingbirds themselves, whence this facility's aviary had developed genetic mutations of exotic, ultra-avian availability.

They darted daintily, but at vibratile velocity, whilst using their panoramic ultraviolet vision. The Vacons (only caught by the wink of an eye) had flown and flitted about, fleetingly aflutter... Now nacreous and of narrower wavelength, as oft indiscernible!

However, the wick-filled lanterns glowed variegated in the manor house as its high Gothic topped interior and Renaissance groin vault had only been bulged, bathed and suffused by those flickering ghostly-lit lamps and lambently aflame flambeaux. For indoors it was altogether "switched on" as if someone somewhere was there, en-clair and aware.

The moist mixture of vacancy intertwined with a hollow and electrified insomnia of *odorous ozone* was what personified the energy of it all. Take for instance how duly kempt and tidy remained each household of this big concord complex cocoon, and that without occupants! Beneath such absence, how fiber-optic rug naps, self-maintained, had kept fresh and brand new their never-trampled billion square foot layout. Velvet and Velcro appearances enough to amaze about any walk-in carpet master! Not to mention, an immaculate, stainless and sterile intramural environment of but bare necessity as would behoove visitors (or encroachers) to examine their own lives! Albeit the *Immaculatorium* therefore.

And no flamboyant demand to remodel her salons of creature comfort if our first step taken, as on its sunken meadow, folds up into itself, or surrenders selflessly under effortless effulgence.

Rather, this automated lot via the contents thereof had pioneers pinned to an ultimatum of conscience; choose good or bad, the architecture itself presided with Spirit-filled impartiality. And that is why-- wherefore none have entered it ever since-- the sterile platform of a walled womb preserved itself from even the intrusion of vermin. Nay (*Heaven-forbid*), not even an outside irk, nor inkling! Yea, no housefly flabbergasted its bionic sensors.

For if it were feasible, a randomized quota of lively breathing tissue, at any given time, could continue thereat, but abruptly prone by subconscious collapse. Struck down at entrance level between musty pilasters immured in time-warped latex enamel, we behold a heavily seated blow organ furnished upon quad casters. And that under which the thick lacquered dance floor of no lackluster linoleum, but hand-crafted overlap lozenge parquetry- *micrometer accurate outspread*- gleams back at us like some placid lakeside mirage of mariner investiture! Lengthwise, as buoys but may meticulously mirror up and out their inverted continual cotillion of Farthingale festivities vac-shafted and Time-tarnished with one moldering porcelain polonaise (lunar-eclipsed as it were by silent, soporific, and romantic radiance of a nurtured nocturne), hither Beethoven's Moonlight Sonata kept keyboard accompaniment.

That both blow organ and will-o'-the-wisp whirl of yesterday were still audible, though muffled, was clearly no surprise to the wet, depth-discharged Mercuric Mirror of prominent profusion. For diamond-dust it had shone and faintly reflecting the lambent lilt of tallow-tapered *sconce~snasts* fittingly set about, high along the chalk-like but pink pilasters of a metronome choreographed memorial Ballroom backed by a benign *vouchsafe cartouche*! A bloated plaque inscribed with hieroglyphs and cuneiform characters from ancient Mesopotamia and Persia. And overall, notwithstanding, with silly swirls and sweeps of indoor ancons with twin volutes and modillions supporting corona-work cornices- as once animate concrete cream, now frozen up into friezes, fretwork, edges and ledges of delectable decay- it had been by now the opaquely *holographic* spectacle that waxed up dilated longing but in need of nothing new. Raw reality eviscerated out of naught, yet yielded. Reservedly relished by the precious profiles of the Faithful Few, this uninhabited multi-labyrinth under a transept of transference to utter privacy was perhaps better suited and imbued with blithest spirits of immaterial mirth, but of still no occupancy!

Only Love's very own plush and luxurious cushion of halcyon lull may pave a blankly bloated blanket, and pallid pillow, and rumpled row of a *euthermic* memory foam mattress, and seat-pad with sprightly sponginess. Of course, with pillow shams cotton and feather-filled, the heav'nly hulk and bulk therewith had been buttoned up at the seams and sleeves, gorgeously edged and etched by spiritual, long-lost antediluvian antiquity.

Only dismantled diamond Silence and quilted quietness quasi-sprinkled have glinted metallic motes of stardust; the open bay windows remained drape-drawn for the time being with heavy velure, and above, beside an outside foursquare soffit gliff: concave coffers, that are as craters caused by upward rays of electroplasmatic packages were pockmarked from by bullets o' focused photons super-spewed and unleashed long ago! That which was abandoned, barren, and insulated from overexposure thereof was what took priority precedence and supernal supremacy as subjectively as Mind over thought forms enlarged.

And quivering above, on high, in acquiescence to stolid stillness, sterility, and drab reason, an unabated Aurora Australis had fluidly blazed its dimensional curtains of fiery filaments and kaleidoscopic columns. Its evacuated drapery and vaporous vaunt blushed and *flavesced* fluorescence, ionized by pinpointed polarity- *posterized* by the Sun's stellar wind; with flailing flanges that mysteriously intersperse an airborne aeolian harp. Fitful, fizzing and hissing hollowly and even to lash out like fine fingers of gyration, atop a wobbling globe; that pleasantly pluck pleasant tunes but in unison of a reed organ in E minor diminished, the first letter to the word *eternity*

One muffled melody echoed my motif: Johann Sebastian Bach's Ich ruf zu dir [BWV] Willem van Twillert Garrels-organ Purmerend~ at least from out of nowhere, from *eternity*

Whence wigs, foils & coils delicately untangle each other throughout the cat's cradle of an electrical Faraday fence!

But backstage in an olden gloomy ballroom superimposed by a twenty foot narrowing mirror was harshly heard, with clarion clarity, the canorous chorus of a self-automated **Mortier Taj Mahal** DANCE ORGAN blow-top calliope! Its hefty mother-accordion branched out by miniature harmoniums full o' metal reeds and calliope whistles thinly high-pitched and dolefully *out~of~tune* by thick thermal pressure. Sharply chattering away, via roll-feed, an octave-o'er-octave irreplicable repertoire of roundelay resonance, indefatigably upon its 112 slat keyboard.

Thus the ballroom floor shook, shuddered and sagged; flinching flimsily away from the discordant, dissonant harmonics of aeons gone by. Each creosote crème façade of age darkened to a timeless tinge, that of some fatal fallow pallor, coal-burnt and forsaken. Nevertheless, a surrealistic revelation was about to unravel.

At once, the ever spectral sparkle of this supernatural mirror, the ever vitreous *vista* of it, was instantly transmuted to a vivid visage of glorified brightness. Then the blitz of an extra-pervasive tantrum followed, *blaringly*! With its tortured chorus o' cringing croons: of squeals, screeches, screams, shrieks, shrills, howls and yells, the DANCE ORGAN, likened after an earthly prototype (*built to make man lilt*), bellowed but loudly out of every opaque object stored in one hologram after another, until animated by sound and light. The prismatic wavelengths of 3-D motion pictures multiplied along a fourth-dimensional axis which were as mirrors vis-à-vis; an infinity of both transept perspectives fused into the caesura of resonance/ radiance wrung up into one wholeness! But clearly, one-out-of-many induced phases of upcoming causality sprouted into the continual causality of the present. Thus, from the paisley plafond, floral floors, fine furniture, musty murals, Trivia exits- everything surrounding space and time- the blow organs thereof would wistfully wail with whistle-work to *blow*, *blurt*, *blow*, *blurt* their indefinite registrations of rapport; O how earsplitting nearby! Whispering, *wheezily*, afar their mezzo-sonic superstar, or in close proximity, a booming, deafening, deathless **coup de tonnerre** en- clair with a *wee! wee! ooh, ooh!* toot, toot, until to ululate an *Aw!* … and so forth …

Herein were one of the miniature figurines of the towering Nine Muses; the Three Graces (triply lit) now invariably manifest manifold through the looking glass. A sheer shapely contour, hurled out- overtly revealing- from the Mercuric Mirror on an opposite confronting wall. Thereat, by an adjacent adjunct to that of a dreary, dreamlike but eeriest filmy mist of quartz and crystalline amethyst, her svelte garter belt buckled stature harbored hairline split prisms of curvaceous, contoured comeliness...

Already lifelike and whole, she shuffled forth, solemnly, advancing into the memorial midst of the once murky wall-womb of the Ballroom; now illuminating it with her solar Soul. Her dauntingly, daintily prim procurement tersely waxed into an opaque formula rekindled by hyper-helical **DNA** with residual **RNA** signatures detected by the facility gene pool. This estrogenic Matrix stood demurely- dominantly disposed of herself- aloft and aloof. Yea, whence briny Breath brought this maternal metaphor and likeness of limitless loveliness and blow life into it? As a result, the vitreous veneration of see-through transparency was altered to a rococo mirror that blushed and flushed itself to a timeless tint, and *in extremis*, ultimately to an ebon bituminous slab that gradually evanesced as this rapturous archetype was now the salient cynosure of every electric eye. Forefront, its underlying unworldly incorruptibility remained incarnate as ever!

Behold, whose heartfelt attenuated underpinnings glorify tremendously an old gold loom, spool, spindle and distaff, distinctly distended outwardly as from a tiny singularity!

How before it all had been the old unoccupied Time-slot of lazily languorous longevity that now and then gravely became nonplussed thereby until agog by this startling (candidly captivating), impossible intervention of the Eternal Female! Surely she short-circuited the diurnal dials and climate controls at very best! Though polymorphous, it longed to balance itself- right there- the spatial Time-slot, from dismantled persistence: she modeled her thick skin of photovoltaic cell and pore contiguity as having ever been bulged by egg-and-dart and all over noduled, so comprised of that selfsame Hyper Helix up-wound within.

Perforated and interspersed with oracular orbs of fat eggshell protuberances, she bore a proportionately lyrical landmark. For having an Indonesian and faintly Mediterranean complexion, she shone as Lady Iwuwi agleam, oft clad in a chemise. Underneath, via ruby-bright rays to a mammary hale and supple bottle at length- momentarily attired by accordion pleats of **crêpe de Chine** and the gilt silk of garish gauze as it were- that so shapely enveloped her, completely, concretely. At large bulge she was wound with one magnetic braid that never decayed nor deflated to shriveled shrinkage~ Never To Fade.

Outwardly lifelike, the entity of entirety became an intricately petite doll fringed by a supernatural Coronal Aureole of angelic desires, as if crowned with an encircling radioactive ringlet of miniature quasars. Her blessed head hulked, if not by an 1820 tiara (ornamental coronet) by Jacques-Evrard and Christophe-Frédéric Bapst, made for the Duchess of Angoulême, daughter of Louis XVI of France, tastefully topped by an up-swept G*oldilocks* swirl, circa 1950. Although therefrom frilliest bemusement, the rest of it was blanched and poker-faced like a blanched cartouche that only prolonged permafrost portraits of her calm-balm homogeneity.

Her hot trans-piercing gaze would withdraw and store an inner *Glore*: the stare beyond compare, to glower roundabout, quasi-omniscient, and penetratingly inside-out. Her impervious verecund virgin-white, *birchen* comely aspect of sculptured nose and lavish lips (slightly parted so as if intending to say something), soft long jeweled neckline, fragile shoulders- was suggestive enough of her fullest essence as *she*, underneath, was consequently found heavily insulated in a profoundest intimate interim of cleat undergarment Pearliest Porcelain. Indeed, and even more than that, preciously embroidered and bundled up to an undercover corset of incessant discretion. Except for her imprinted palms, expressive hands and kissable arms of bare nudity plumply widened off to squeezable, prenuptial and dimpled cones that loll full as elastic foam latex pacifier paps appended by nodules or nipples according to the anatomy thereof. But when cupped conveniently by a brocaded brassiere of rigged rope, her twin twilit breasts- firmly fishnet attired- shall have stuck out and abruptly so or self-expectantly.

Amiably, this lass o' glass chastely wore willow white; that overhung her holy hyper~hydrant milk-jugs per taut teat of eggplant spiritual fertility! Both bulged as life-givers snugly covered from vain view, imbued by riverside embankments of redolent dampness, with a tincture of talcum powder for her terminal toiletry, if assumed on the mortal plane, the perfectly astral-projected mamillae thereof were personified *sub rosa* or under red rosebuds that could cushion and venerate inviolable pronouncements of consecrated motherhood heart and soul!

And down further, to her feminine figure, full hips and aureate garter-and-bangle thigh-high voluptuousness; not wasp girthed was she, but an eternal paragon of power and love, hourglass-glorified rather. Blankly blazoned, but faultlessly resembling some strange parallel cloning device; besought or simply put, her own full blown empowered endowment of the inamorata equips her to be self-replicated for a quasi-omnipresent Universal Plurality...

An originality of a veritable voice-authenticated and genuine *e pluribus unum* was what she divulged of herself to be: thus this vivaciously vivid and radiant replica of a sheer and crystal-clear continuum is as One (constantly concentrated) out of Many. And now, as if to enhance upon the coronary panorama and bouffant bursts of her opulent opaque advent, these gently tender verses were in response recorded and then revealed:

ADDRESS

The days of Time are thin and brief
Like sands awash upon a reef.

For waves slap harder as they crest,
That force us to endure each test.

Man tends to manufacture dreams
With countless features, so it seems;

Yet Time corrupts whatever built
As flowers droop away and wilt!

Tho' right beside the tossing tide
We raise up piers for ships of pride,

Same tidal wave still swipes away
Unanchored buoys that bob and play!

The breath of Time and Life must blow
Aloft four seasons- warmth or snow.

If fateful years for now have slumbered,
One shall wake: Your days are numbered!

Let us therefore stretch those piers
Across our hearts with earnest tears.

Where sands run through the hourglass,
Have hope, this too will come to pass!

For she is precisely just that! The embodiment and incarnation known as Time and Life materialized but for a little while. A future herald, prophetic discloser of, and Gateway to another tomorrow bestowed by heavenly Hope.

By the same token, if one were to lounge upon a chaise longue and espy her wholeness through a filmstrip, there would unequivocally be a distaff of decorative dilation. Whereas waffled in sheathed tautness under which she lolled narrowly, nicely and daintily, an investiture of discretion prevailed, outside on her mantle Mother Nature had handwoven a firebrand of some sort. Far unlike a black widow stamped with a crimson splotch under its abdomen, a stark mark of virulence, Iwuwi wore, almost tattoo and totem pole personified an argyle (diamond-like) over her bust between both breasts, but not necessarily creased by their *Twinity.* This apocalyptic *sign* significantly softened situations of any kind and would succor the numb, needy; the oppressed and the denuded, stripped-of-dignity descendants and congregants of her hyperdulia veneration! A form of worship worthier than *dulia* but less likely than *latria* in low estate peasant parsonages. For only the humble of heart dared to render due deference thereunto. Heretofore no Heart of Glass, nor such songs sung before by Debbie Harry on her Blondie album, resembled its finest finesse *in esse*, but better --- a *Vitropolis* of infrangible, unshatterable Mirror materialization!

The cozy *bed~warmth corpus luxus* of the dim domicile was jolted by this chimerical efflorescence of a lively lubricious Lily. Or was it exactly at that? Shiny Sheelil, albeit nicknamed as with such highly refined and pronounced overflow of gracefulness, the mirrored mannequin tiptoed ballerina-like and gingerly flaunted herself upon the backstage floor. In pearliest [porcelain linoleum] limelight, unveiled finally to voluptuous, curvaceous yet sacred nakedness, her luscious fissure was outspread. No, not by the fourth dimension *evaginated*, but tucked in. The slip~slit crevice thereof was undefiled & free from the entrance of anyone, as if it were some revelatory Receptacle immured by barricade hymens of an impregnable Vat at that! I say, O in array of no ABM or *anti-ballistic missile*, but armored up: a vast <u>VULVATORIUM</u> of a wall-womb Ballroom henceforth! One wormhole via NDE exits.

Via anechoic cushion, never to be bombarded by tellurians.
So invitingly nude she looked, with her bare pyramidal pair
oxidized by raw open space, voluminously enclosed upon herself
as a paranormal polyglot, so succulent, vitrified with celestial
maternity. Lightly numinous until nightly luminous, so to speak.
But still, sleek and infinitely smooth to the forbidden touch, this
rather instantaneous *Imperatrix* wore her half-life necklace of
uranium agates by the domestic confines of a ballroom interior.
Now trans-illuminating old contoured cakes of plafond plaster,
decorative divans, paisley upholstery, silkiest ceiling, sofas and
heavy undercarriage love seats like nothing whatsoever! She
shimmered, tho' displayed daintily, glittery as an intervening
torchlight magnified million-fold from the vast vault and starry
cope of HEAVEN as depicted in Dante Alighieri's Paradise.

Elsewhere, a reel-to-reel chrome taped video recording
clicked as if the robotics of the complex were prefabricated
for her annual priority-presentation. And since this occurred
merely yearly, hence the transcendental glory of it all!

And so, ceiling, wall and floor listened intently to her
otherworldly Andromeda-escorted *Vox Femina...*

"From turning Time immemorial," she announced,
beautiful-voiced. "I have vividly ventured into the
Unspeakably Unknown and have succeeded."

Now! As she laid out her magnum monologue, as presiding
mediatrix, the tall wall mirror unexpectedly returned out of
nowhere revealing a glimmering crystalline motion picture of
some spectacular lake. A long lurid bathtub body of water on
its vertical profiles lustrously lavender, resplendently reserved.
"Aye, I am quite built white quilt Queen Glasgow!" she intoned
along with Lake Liquick's undulant and supernumerary murmur,
pointing at the gaping mirror. "*That* is where I came from..."

In Tenebra Lux *

Undying spring
Is all year round
Fluorescent
Ultraviolet-

In everything,
She's shiny crowned
From dusk to dawn,
O twilit!

Whose fulgid form
Long time defies
An egg-and-dart
Old frame~

Aglitter swarm
Night fireflies,
Luciferin-
Aflame!

Her honey-laden
Hive and comb
Wear aurified
Attire:

This vernal maiden,
Like life's loam,
Glints glorified
Desire!

* Latin for (feminine)
In Darkness, Light

As if it were by
*Emily Dickinson**

Only the sheepishly parochial and stubbornly prudent shan't be dare shocked by the untimely reminder of such slender tapered tender splendor! For how prematurely brave and brawny men o' war would all be laid like self-bloated maggot-fat lads before that "lass of glass" and that full o' beatified finesse! Still, was it some ubiquitous spoof? Could this then be the omnipresent caryatid-pillar and divinest distaff of vestal rites that may permeate Life?

Everything in correspondence to our query came to a taciturn cessation in the ballroom courtyard save for her hale, palpable pause to yet radiantly ripen. The despotic interrogation of any inquisitor, perforce, otherwise will be subject to and quelled by Unviolent Adoration laid out at once! She later proclaimed her timeless sanctity and concluded herself with one caduceus call:

"I was, I am, and I shall be entirely alive in glee- to
no one present, but absolutely absent. Yea, call me
the Prophetic Discloser, for I am christened, the vatic
ARGOPHANY of large lamps that be --but behold!"

Triggered to but one millisecond flash-point, her colossus collapsed. How her formulated consummation of *electrospun* envelopment [irreducible though] slid and slithered down into a dwindling line, thinly winking into nonexistence! Then followed fallow yellow: a hollow sounding incorporeal visionary Voice pervading the fathomless cosmos of our most tertiary dimension. The vertiginous Fourth Dimension as such intervened spacetime from up, above, beyond- to down, below, within- narrowly thin, threadbare tenuous. A big ball from out of nowhere would expose an inert theophany, or by itself, not on a back-burner nor shelf, instead, expanded from the infinitesimal whence she had left us sub specie aeternitatis, or under the standpoint of eternity.

The Sphere that tilted itself to an opaque object of cross-sectional curvature had now around it distended torpedo-shaped tongues. These monstrosities materialized from fresh froth molten white!

Quite soon enough- cooling down as would cloven wafers of liquefied aluminum reach decalescence [as if] at a Pittsburgh, Pennsylvania foundry- the horrific entities became an energetic Paraclete company of hot corpulent cucumbers that hovered haphazardly from their upper udder jubilee of Pentecost! Lastly, they then exited the world's workbench and swiftly shrunk away.

Her voluminous Vat o' volcanic voice-authentication echoed:

"Venerate me as your Mother-
Cleave to me and to no other."

Was it *she* "Glishoe" via an exalted formula? The intumescent balloon, only to have been omnificent, deflated flat down into utter nonexistence, and the ballroom was restored to its former vacancy. Nonetheless, an aftershock of such silent impossible intervention reverberated high-pitched throughout the ornately festooned egg-and-acanthus interiors of *indelibility* with which holographic erasure could never transpire. For bulked between corbels and ancons having volutes to support a ceiling cornice, with chalk-stucco textures peeling away, the stylized gold leaf hedgerows of eggshell protuberances and acanthine foliage had etiolated. As if the benign faces and spiked spades of the swollen ornaments were once alive (preserved by holographic harmonics), the listless yet living festoons altogether turned to sooty scabs of mold and mildew as if plagued by a hoary roar of age, unable to survive the yawning eternity of her début & gala performance. Only once again to be recorded, regrettably, but no more. That ghastly blankest exposition of her soul, super-symmetrical and unbounded on all of its images; the circumference of it sleekly equidistant at every vantage point of exact exposure. No more exposé let alone those grotesquely visceral tabletop tongues of insuperable elasticity attenuated out, withdrawn permanently!

No marvel when wondrous YHWH forewarned Moses, "For no mortal may see My interface and live..." Thus the epigram was fulfilled, furtively, in an environmental vivarium of entomology:

The day-glow depth of one's own hale hand,
When it dare authorize its tapered index
Upon someone funereal by brand,
Dissolves away amid a swarm of insects!

Now no more perched or poised to overlook Valley Brook were treeswift-sized Vacons, fourfold or dragonfly quad-awing, using their panoramic viewership iris imprinted as eye-bands wrapped roundabout semi-conical tops of regular octahedron aviator-bred birdies in God's Aviary. Some seen as nifty *night-jars* or others as *owlet-frogmouths*, aligerous oil-birds of South Equacoocador, but marvelously superior, agile, perspicacious & aware with gigapixel widescreens encircling each specimen. Ring-headed vital Vacons: having hindsight and foresight simultaneously! Never monstrous, nor ludicrous; neither ridiculously reduced to bandersnatch yocto-yellow likewise like an inch-long canary, the Vacon had dilated its darting flitter to a sundial tableau vivant as all raw *Radiant Reality* reverted down into undisturbed shrillness of the moaning **Mortier Taj Mahal** DANCE ORGAN! But not until still *hush* ensued, that sea cucumbers and gourds were suddenly transmogrified into self-protected open-fixture arc tubes à la carte in the menagerie menu! The enveloped enclosure took on such self-relinquishment that the household vestibules buckled back on themselves with not even a doorway or bay window for anyone to exit an escape hatch. For as of this *mutant* moment, in the meantime, no one was to even dare contemplate its impenetrable, illustrious lush *lusus naturae* from beyond, nor resume some prolonged vis-à-vis acquired dialogue with her fieriest, phantasmagorical brainstorming as showcased.

A primitive priority *mindbirth* of her first redevelopment
or a Walled Womb of the Labyrinthic Limbo about to take
place. One would by then christen her as Immurea...

That so silently surpassing myrtle laurels of *sylvatic* ecstasy, across the outskirts of a valley and purling brook, and out farther back by the hinterland, above some weeping willow grove; past eucalyptus brush, waxen broadleaf and shrubbery whereabouts hedgehogs and hot honey badgers bartered for their tellurian territory and turf; not to exclude gophers, beavers, quails, partridges and water-drenched, though unctuous, duckbills (desultorily in fanciful fellowship with one another) were miraculously initiated. Their lush *lusus naturae* had greased but flammable torches, narrowed to niches of ex-voto votive candlelight atop the gala festivity: the Valleybrook vivarium of a vast vista vitrified therewith unwittingly! To the sterile strands at this fairy-tale island of non-compromised insularity- waywardly, on the other side of a continental drift- the Sylphid's superstructure prerogative exceeded veritable visualization itself as our Ballroom Lady with her linoleum-floored Vulvatorium of hallowed hallways attained immediate immaculacy for the sole sake thereof, versified:

An open walled womb of Time is turned inside out
For that Clearwater Lake of transcendent transparency!
The Cavernous Cathedral or masterful portrayal of
A faithful, prayerful daughter embraced by her
Sole *materfamilias*, its foundational glorification
Erected and perfected for TWI so interpreted as
Transworld International and Solidarity Inc.
Perpetual peace (scallop shelled) about to cradle
Lake Glasgow glimmering and glittering with light.
At last, the world's hydra-headed detonations
Quelled by but a dewdrop of its holy water!

There, shallowly shown in *perpetuum* through
The luminescent Mirror that radiantly replicates

Ev'ry subtle crest, node, wavelet, and ripple-
The bleeding pink sunset beyond it, like a gilt silk
Brocade in the Unveiled Paradise of Argophany,
Beams with shortwave rays into our waning days.

And no mere tortes of décor back yore could be
Gleaned or relished from global Antarctica adrift,
For the invitational ecosystem of rain forests on a
Polar icecap had commenced with insular appearance.
The glacial cascade of spatial cakes stay evacuated as
An intangible dreamworld to dart athwart and depart-
Only the future sunrise in her eyes left at the reliquary
That never went down, never to the endless descent of
An equatorial sunset- that of sodium and infrared.
From which eight-minute-old lumens extend outward
As from a buoyant promenade of funnel cloud odyssey.
Far from conical throngs of Himalayan Helicon.
Over zenith vistas of the sierra and frozen tundra-
Her primal Southern Lights would glint back at
And deftly probe the twinkling and scintillating
Citywide haze of an urban sprawl; and would
Vouchsafe reluctantly (with empathetic election)
Upon the counterpart chorus of an overblown rush
Hour gargantuan Gotham. Its asphalt anthill of hard
Wall Street arteries constantly congested with dreadful
Droves of each metal *auto-box* conveyed on pneumatic
Boots o' black as they *vroom* and *zoom* in gloom!

Or by contrast, try and compare wholesome
Nature with today's *mega~populace* churn of
Poker faced personnel seemingly punctured by
Punctual clocks and gauges of alarming pressure!
For we, as stuffed cattle, are gamely driven to
The slaughterhouse of a global meltdown. A roguish
Horde of humanity haplessly on its way to be cremated.

Man and his corporately generic identity pickled by
A power plant flush, as were many casualties *sickle-*
Sought by that unapproachable Chernobyl plug!

* Jotted down a few years before the catastrophic event of 9/11 *
Until alas, the twin holographic hives of a telltale
Cosmopolis monopoly *telescreened* against the ballroom
Looking glass are gone ablaze! Until this momentary
Molecular Memoranda of elite but corrupt society
Discordantly dissolves into a radar blip as on
Picture tubes of cold cathode rays switched off
From all of their baubles of automatic static.
Man's cacophonous channel of fake snowiness
And hellish haze that plunges through a horizontal
Abyss of infinity, disintegrated by tritium heat ...

Apropos of the preceding plateau, an *aurora australis* (southern lights) cascades a certain curtain from without on the turreted and castellated shade of life. Still illumined from within. The Faraday fence of wrought iron fleurs-de-lis, the grotesqueries and gargoyles of Precambrian hot lava hitherto rock-frozen upon air; the crème de la crème of unearthly concrete sludge-fudged up here and there have instead outlined an awe-inspiring comely palace, anciently set apart and still imprinted by the Permian period of the antediluvian era when geologic times of the Pangaea coalesced continental plates accordingly. Such carboniferous soot clung to the comely palace, tenaciously, and was splashed upon by the lapping and laving broth and brine of primordial ooze and organic goo not meant to manifest there, except via preserved permafrost memory mantled by cryonics. Permian permafrost of cratered cream.

That founded away from the incessant noise and din of public disclosure, skulduggery and happenstance- away from monolithic edifices looming behind polluted veils of rainfall- the Old Valley Brook Ballroom at lustrous Lake Glasgow took on a renovated overlap layout with its **BB** ~ Big Bouncer instantly inflated in our immortal midst, right under the bonnet roof of an oak pergola.

An *ultra-ethereal*, adaptable, alterable & perpetual personage: The Great Theophany of Sinai! Yea, that of naught but a perfectly diminutive *stellular* spheroid of static starriness, as if it were an alternate Universe on its own, but in and of itself; separate and self-contained with both halves of *hemi~hyper~spheres* (top and bottom) forever joined, ballooned out and only to calmly bounce in her stead. That is, the Theotokos inscribed inside-out of a Hellenic hologram: Θεοφόρος … Aye, the God-Bearer (All-Holy Mother, Main-throw or Major Ballroom Sphere): the MBS thereof. At large, the retrofit replacement of *ectoplasmic* embodiments that merely *she'll* recharge (originally Sheel in 1986). It was a full-sized comical contorter, One out of Infinite, whose applied appliance of appellation reads Unbounded BORTEUM with 'another' of a far different hue, yet of identical larger-than-life-size symmetry, like as of Holiest CREMEUM housed up by the Creatorium silo.

Albeit big Unbounded BORTEUM alongside CREMEUM, who embody two-thirds of the Heavenly Host, so confronted Lucifer's diabolical devilry in order to perdure such a timeless temptation (the tenebrous spiral staircase of the soul, creepily crimsoned)! However, it was not so with *MORTEUM,* the one-third of Heaven that plummeted and are forthrightly castigated as Fallen Angels culminating in one woeful wake-up call … Hell, I will still rotary-dial the old Bell Telephone in lieu of a cybernetic interface, Aye!

Thus these whole holy Hyperspheres bounced resiliently, reasserting and recoiling themselves, with both their enameled exposure eerily breathing at the same time as they slipped away, slightly, came back, away and back as one unbroken ENTIRE ENTITY- yet revealed through *hyperspace* formation.
With a metallic voice-over, the Borteum ball intoned,
"What was, is now, and ever shall be ----"

"But no mortal may look upon my blankness and abide!" interjected the other, the Cremeum.

* Please note: It sounded like persiflage between the twain *

For this twofold spherical spectacle is her one and singular Recording Companion, as God's distinctly distinguished Angels *unfallen*, or so it was recognized, somewhere, in Dimension Five

------------- 5 -------------

Nay, not that one would dare bray, 'God in Five Persons, blessed *Quintity...*' Yahweh forbid! But that's beside the point!

Where GMC buses barreled along East Colfax Avenue in 1986, there were walls of the high Gothic Ballroom that ultimately underwent metamorphosis; a GMC (Giga Mural Colosseum) of sub-spatial diaphragms and warp-bubbles, far transcending a conventional auditorium (that which emanates its protean laws of Fluid Flux). The tremendous TRANSALTERATORIUM steals precedence! An ultra-transformable intramural Superpower that can alter itself from one room to another. Equipped with bio-intelligent *Transvortiums* and the *novus* twenty metric ton titanic Mercury Mirror, it would withstand our rivalry to reproduce anything, or anyone at pinpointed (gluon-spun) exact accuracy!

What once was the former vacant Valleybrook Ballroom estate self-translated its contents into a colossal "gloreate" globe of force departing from Terra Firma, leaving behind our terrestrial or Quotidian Calendar in preference for the wide and single stars. Quite distant now, with hurtling speeds it went up and away to an insignificant orb that it became and had dwindled to evanescence.

"Venerate me as your Mother-
Cleave to me and to no other!"

The enormous memorial mercury-vapour lamps are shut-off for now, deactivated as an ignitron separates its anode from the cold cathode of the metallic reservoir, and that of mercuric oxide- the *omnivalent* radical of residual aluminum to be soon ionized when igneous~ignited.

Her ATTW: Arc Tube Terawatt Wafers of liquefied aluminum, prepared for *atomic excitation*, are asleep or *decalesced* at the foundry, only to keep awake, fluoresced and fired-up *in the year* 2113 (with a *now* narrowest mirror-image) as quasar-quotient of near-infinite brightness beyond barnacle reach of the sea foam.

Aha, it was quite a lucid experience as it must be of her cosmic carnival backed by the vociferous calliope, but by confirmation, and certainly of no phantasmagorical nor allegorical nightmare for that matter! Snuff out the votive paraffin taper and wi' whence to where does the flame of Immaculate *Flammifera* go? 'Tis not my "torchiest" farewell to her enveloped departure! For she hath yet to return and firebrand-burn, and cause our hearts for eternal **Jesus Christ** to yearn! Incontrovertibly, so be it He, the one & only true Trinity. Who has shattering shined as her internal torchlight blindingly and blisteringly blitzed over the Bloated Blanket.

I took the metal-banister-sided plank and catwalk along the flanks of another dream where such superstores like TARGET topped the Old Valley Brook Ballroom. Its funfair and jamboree jacketed life!

What filigree finials self-crested beneath the upper udder of a gable ornament are disintegrated with all their Victorian vaunt! O alas, as we weep with yearning, now replaced by our light of common day! Come hitherto at that marmoreal Mercy Seat of balmy evenings, of hoop dress cotillions on a Saturday Night terrace; the musical twirl of S*teed-Backs* hulked on a carousel where Lakeside lay appareled with blue spruce and hemlock shrubs that ornament the amusement park beside bustling

interstate 70 **HWY** snaked between Wheat Ridge and Arvada,
Colorado. My year was 1986 back then, still preserved

Fine Freya's froth-fringed Light, moth-impinged and receptive lush hush of forested fervor *sags with recumbent repose*, as we "gild the lily" once more and then close; or ever the spectral candlelight of a curving seashore~ lastly laved by wart-capped waves of an old, old swollen sea~ is a fair and felicitous sight to contain & contemplate.

And from one far and distant Echo inchoate, may it still persistently, immutably repeat, replete with ferrous sheet:

"Venerate me as your Mother-
Cleave to me and to no other."

In German: gottesbrautliche Mutterschaft

das Ewig-Weibliche zieht uns hinan

"The eternal feminine draws us onward"

Of course, as for our dear Lamp and Saviour, so long ago in the garden of Gethsemane, so with the Personification of Grace, I spare my rare cry, haply for all. And as it were, there a-crawl through *her,* mantled in myrrh, Abused Nature awaits and anticipates His Light of manifold merriest Mercy to be!

On an affirmative offering herewith, I resolve my case.

finis

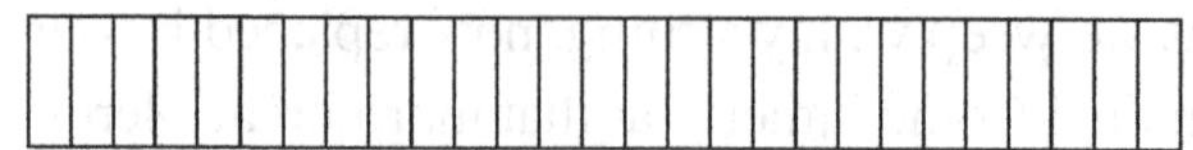

Rose that
never stops
opening,
whose fragrance
builds the cosmos.

ANDREW HARVEY

A thing of beauty is a joy forever.

EDMUND SPENCER

Authorized Footnote

For in fine, aside from the aforesaid far-fetched, cosmic contents of exotica, I nurtured this finalized 'round-the-corner' incunabula, but rather, that of an old bygone parking lot lighted o'er with piercing bluish-green Mercury Vapour lanterns strewn about, pulley-upheld over a cobbled street. Their elongated arc tubes jacketed by Fresnel lens lightning-packets linked and laced up altogether. And in the background, a voice-over broadcast of '*Wilt Thou* Still Love Me Tomorrow?' played by the Shirelles, while we nestled into the back leather car seat. I reclined serenely by all-holy Steel Sheet in my Chevrolet automobile, circa 1957. And here's an episode therewith:

* *

Living Lamp Entity

The highway was heavy on the outskirts of a distant Denver suburb. In our 1957 Chevy, Elaine and I had barreled to a lumbering crawl and a halt on the hot, blistering blacktop. Big, burdened but polite police officers upon patrol soon semaphored our convoy of traffic. "Thank heaven the two utility roads have funneled out this grotty gridlock!" one of them, relieved, announces on the CB radio. "That's a ten-four, big buddy..." My signal and squelch were well adjusted to eavesdrop on their

State Trooper band broadcast. But then we noticed an overhead streetlamp on some narrow divider or median, so silvery-silent in the sun, reflecting a Summer Hammer through early afternoon at this detour we were wedged into... "Oh, Drat!" I blurted to Elaine, reminded by those golden goose neck pressure beacons of natrium. Each one strewn in staggered formation alongside an entrance and exit cloverleaf. "Hell, we forgot the kerosene lantern!" I wailed. Now this was en route to our Lake McConaughy campsite and Elaine's eloquence reassured me with her "Never mind the mishap". As always, she would grin athwart what was woefully grim. "We'll compensate if there's an old bucket lamp out there by a barn," she prophesied moreover. And so, in overflow of time, her uncanny intuition was fulfilled. There was indeed an old yard lamp available in proximity to our makeshift stake at the lake! Soon afterwards, having been dumbfounded by her foresight, notwithstanding, I had gathered up the hobby of street lighting altogether and with faithful Elaine at my side every inch of the way. Like a fairy of guardianship, she glisters via vital ex flamma lux! Wherefore, it is only *She* to become my living Lamp Entity henceforth. Nay, not necessarily the allure or seduction thereof, dare I say, but rather the more holy and finer fire at heart: likely, my Shining Light interpreted by the chief experts on parapsychology...

---

* HEREAFTER the HYPERSPHERE and VALLEYBROOK VISIONS... Wherefore we, Polyhymnia and myself, embraced and lolled into each other, melting quite enough- tenderly- as She with Mediterranean complexion and of Asiatic allure- professional and prim as an old "yūjo" (play women) Geisha of the "Tayuu" class; the one paragon paradox that cavorted as a swanky "kabuki" would woo and lull me! O with an unfamiliar swoon of potent infatuation (continued following this brief intermission):

My Midway Storyboard Reminder

** Unlike Americans, the families of victims in Japan don't seek out grief counseling. They know that they'd feel much more at ease and at peace with the counselor but they're afraid it would make them forget the deceased. I believe it's because of such Japanese spirituality stays in contrast to the way we perceive life and death. Japanese people do not separate the dead from the living like we do. In many of their households, Shoji is a sliding door made of very thin paper. To Japanese people, death is like a shoji. Once you open the sliding door you go through to the other side and the living can still see you through it. **

By then, we shared sentiments of a fat nuclear furnace, primed and moderated meticulously.

In the slenderest slip-slit and slot of **2113**:

Those reactor rods of radioactivity were enveloped by *hydrogel* heavyweight water, D_2O: Incorruptible, indestructible, immutable, immortal, and *immune*. A Timestamp Dilator dialed up immaterial!

* Please note: immune was written a few years before the 2020 Pandemic *

My **V V V V** (Vestal Veronica, Viable Vat) who held [originally in spirit] an authentic *faceprint-envisagement* of our dear divine Lord and Saviour, was preparatory to disappear at the foreclosure of this Vision, only to do justice upon everything at hand whilst *warming* me *in myocardium*, within. Warming, I pray, not *warning* me!

Speaking of which, howbeit that dauntless D_2O: an oceanfront hydrostasis of Tomorrow, but bejeweled and crowned by beautiful, intercontinental **GLIBOLOTUBULOPOLITZ**: like Lake Michigan cradled by the crest and crescent of the imposing Chicago megalopolis. At last, ne'er to be invaded, nor trampled by gargantuan Godzilla- the Japanese daikaiju- in that this glory ushers forth a whole different animal and ballgame! The future version of this Hyper City would be utterly spotless, but almost ridiculously re-glorified on another dimension. Consequently addressed: interspersed with BTT (Bullet Train Traffic), punctuated by dizzily tall, cloud-piercing monolithic dominoes, and by high vertiginous vac-shaft "elevatorium" SNS: **Space Needle Spires** yet everyone with an outreach upward for the starry stratosphere... Except- my requisite qualifier- all of them rebuilt without pollution nor decrepitude of any kind!

Our nearby superstar-- stupendously stalwart and staggeringly apparent-- revivified into **VEGA** void of omen-- shall allow for our renovated Earth to be topped by her in the arctic Pole about 12,000 years from now; hence our dire need for D_2O global super-saturation, a genetically enhanced biosphere to soak in the new ultraviolet sunlight and newly resurrected bodies of "molecular glorification" able to glide through solid objects like impalpable silk, in need of no maintenance whatsoever! Our souls within them installed by the CREATORIUM-- embodied by divers alternatives of unadulterated adventure; fantastic, but scientifically pragmatic.

And I saw a new heaven and a new earth, for the first heaven and the first earth had passed away, and there was no more sea... (KJV) REVELATION 21:1

And so, I bellow, Thus that was the end of it!

In tribute to our Memorial, recently: *Residents in the Japanese city of Hiroshima that commemorated the 70th anniversary of the first atomic bomb being dropped by a U.S. aircraft...* A U.S. B-29 bomber called the Enola Gay dispensed the huge uranium bomb, exploding some 600m (1,800ft) above the city, at around 08:10 on 6 August 1945. [According to a BBC news footage on 6 August 2015/ from the section *Asia*].

With heartfelt heaviness, but by Heavenly Hope,

SAYONARA to what once Was.

Prefatory Glory

17 "For our light affliction, which is but for a moment, *worketh* for us a far more exceeding *and* eternal weight of glory; 18 While we look not at the things which are seen, but at the things which are not seen: for the things which *are* seen are temporal; but the things which are not seen *are* eternal." II Corinthians, chapter 4 (The Authorized King James Version)

IMMACULUCY

The very existence of *incommensurable* theories is about the worst nightmare that can happen to empiricists (not my quote). *Of course, I refused to wage war with what was incontestable, I admit.*

* *

I found myself to have walked to our Edmonton, Canada TARGET warehouse superstore. In my dream, however, in this diorama the word was an acronym that represented a Trans-alterable *radiative* gala-energy Transducer! Presently primed from my bedroom ceiling, the quad-hung large lamps look at me.

Before I negotiated an entrance, I scanned the perimeter of this commodious building which went on for 33 city blocks in diameter, both lengthwise and width, entirely foursquare. Its rooftop tar was flat-out, of course, and unseen since I stood at ground zero upon Tarmacadam gravel of still non-flattened quarry asphalt. Right out of the furnace, the facility had been erected by the recent Project Procyon wherewith corporate investors transfused ferroconcrete funds for such purposes thereunto, I gathered.

The mountainous Municipality of Alberta, Canada refined designs of a hyper-square to retrieve video-transference of conflagrant convergence in one intramural environment. Whereas (preferably) indoor basketball court, hockey arena and whatnot were intended for sporting endeavors; whereas Big Lots retail supermarket grounds were better suited for such private premises in this enveloped enclosure, indeed such was not the case. Canada's major facility for paranormal phenomena was of paramount issuance thereat rather. Whereabouts one wormhole under the floor was up and down rebar rigged with rungs, the rib-cage of Jacob's Ladder, but by allegory inverted, burrowed as a vertical vac~shaft manhole. Conversely to an above-ground Labyrinth, a subterranean UNIVERMICULATORIUM settled it.

Now, whilst I sought out the front door, it had automatically slid open and I crept into the storefront foyer. Already, in my line of curiosity, I gazed up at Beacon lighting appliances interspersed beneath a super-seamless ceiling upheld by the quad Tall Wall about 40 meters high! Occasional support pillars and poles almost thronged the area, nearly huddled over the far-off opposite end partitions of ruby, opaquely lozenged barricades. The brickwork of these were hexagonal cinder-diamonds meticulously mortared together to stay impregnable. Obviously, Public Property predicated prolonged preservation!

Junction boxes bulged forth from one wall for step-up transformer power polarity. Petticoat insulator cupcakes were installed intermittently and fastened to topnotch upper cornices roundabout overhead.

And so, I entered the disturbingly desolate but harshly illumined interior of my enormous warehouse without an inventory stock upon multi-storied shelves. *In visione mea*, I felt no claustrophobic clinch o' immurement, but on the contrary, my euphoria felt vulnerable, although no less compartmentalized!

Meantime, every once in a while, as I surveyed these pristine premises, I noticed some upright booth en route, just situated there, alone and aloof. Its telephone kiosk of surveillance was unattended and unmanned, unlike beforehand particularly- that is in case of a contingency- I ought to have speculated.

Basically, the facility grounds were deserted but self-irradiated for some repository reason. I recalled, during my tentative approach before- on the outside- the neon light signage across the marquee had shown TARGET in ballooned red letters as an adjunct of the storefront facade. To my amazement- if I may decipher its significance- it was the ubiquitous acronym of the usual department store franchise corporation distributed in North America. Emphatically, in essence, the Trans-alterable *radiative* gala-energy Transducer! But wherefore and why? I mused under overpowering insularity of the latex ceiling.

Then, farther forth, as I centered myself in the nucleus of this kilometer-wide warehouse- empty and vacant as it were- with wonder and shock, I confronted an ultraethereal Teflon-Tongue "Transducer" of some sort overhung from some ceiling nearly 40 meters above me. It was slightly larger than one of those 2 kilowatts each High Bay ballast and luminaire lighting appliances. Arguably, the shape of her resembled finest fusion reactor pack units at a moderator power-plant north of Edmonton. Halted, hereby, I can confess my momentary abandonment in the remote year of **2113** hath hitherto climaxed.

Back to square one. Why then the notion of a remote time-slot that haunted me? I dare ne'er nullify it. What (unearthly thing) was the nature thereof? I pried at my noggins: For what reason was this living lamp entity dangling, daintily about, via a pulley-winch hoisted up at a silent ceiling? Hence the titanic TARGET for what it really stood for! Albeit now, no patrons nor customers could be bedazzled by the: I can safely say- "organic" specialty spectacle, I presumed, since none were at hand. On the other hand, hardly, and unbeknownst to my 'targeted' whereabouts, I was unaware of 'spooks' from the past that may have inundated this pliable place. I say 'pliable' in that the dimensions of human history have not yet caught up with the present era of the year 2113, but lay dormant and lithely elastic, as if obliquely *'alterable'* by continual causality itself! Surely, the sheer and shattering shock of it overshadowed me. For this cause, it was the unrealized steel 'Sheel' that [incorporeal] could congeal consequently cloven!

At once- by my incredulity, or whatever last inkling of waking consciousness I had clung to- I forthwith fizzled away with a fainting spell. I felt succored and swooned by a quick thick darkness that pervaded me serenely, subconsciously- Simultaneously, a distant star from one end of a long tunnel engulfed me.

I came to and was revived by a visionary Voice out of nowhere that rattled my Faraday cage. Violent voltage charged the ambiance of ventilated air which palpitated with high-tension. I knew it was that culprit, the self-lynched arc tube entity above me, flexing its bellyful or lorry-load elasticity of sinewy megawatt muscle as it intoned a sauntering sentence: (I was, I am, and I shall be), but nothing more. Then, suddenly, I maneuvered through silkiest *terra incognita* which forced me to reckon with *what an incontrovertible territory or topper*! Besides, the Tarmac tang of creosote permeated my surroundings as I moreover regained a whiff of ozone that oozed ultraviolet from the lamplight fat crème creature. There were no eyes nor mouth thereupon, neither a visage on the ghastly thing; only an elongated bulged-tubular silvery *Hot Cod* of savory sort, devoid of head, as if it displayed a dorsal fin fastened at each end thereof. These flat protuberances tapered outward, then back (gradually) to an intumescent plumpness merely to thin out to two flat appendages again at each end, up and down. It looked like an open-ended supple bottle of either-side symmetrical proportion, aglow by but searing brightness from within herself, yet unwieldy as a coruscant, corpulent cucumber juxtaposed with the Bermuda Triangle off of the Florida peninsula. Thus the sleek steel sheet of SHEEL (recalled since my post high-school class of 1986) had henceforth recapitulated my scrutiny of this bizarre specimen or species of extraterrestrial inception. Her stentorian vociferation ululated the persistent echo against the TARGET anechoic chamber factor, fully, *I was, I am, and I shall be*: annunciator shutdown and naught… But wait!

Aside from such rather mariner manifestation, three slender slipways revealed themselves to my utter discomfiture. Atop one of them, a miniature marquee not unlike the much larger version of it out-of-doors gaudily brandished a more complex computation of lettering, that of UNIVATRIVIATORIUM. As I later interpreted its meaning, this was the three-way Trivia (in Latin literally) disclosed all for me. Well, which way would I go? I challenged myself. But it just stood there for hours at length, pending my dire decision. I was walled up by an inner womb which welcomed me: a hitherto passerby poised amid my visitation. Then the entirety of it collapsed, dissipating into a frenetic froth of quantum foam fizz fit for this deflated decanter hung horridly on a threadbare tether! Garish and glaringly gossamer, I proclaim!

Needless to admit, there had lain no residual *ectoplasm* on the Metalinoleum floor, as if it had been the end result and as if the ghostly onlookers from the other side desisted seances altogether for now!

At any rate, radiant was this Transducer, suspended from a 131-foot ceiling and with Harsh glare (or Hg for mercury) unlike liquid quicksilver and natrium vapour lamps tucked inside the High Bay barrels and buckets! Its chrysalis of focused photons appeared hot-neon iridescent and caused the glittering effect of transparent

gold in the linoleum flooring to backlash or flash fluidly. In other words, the glazed floor fluoresced in return, reflecting back out in one accord the Sun's granulated surface of gargantuan gold leaf. Aside from this, by the way, an offhand placard on the foyer wall at eye-level that I had bypassed revealed an indicative description with a narrow arrow pointing downward, foreboding and forbidden to have been overlooked: **METALINOLEUM**
(only for fieriest fortification and large luminous layout)

The steel SHEEL sheet of life's lovely luster, NOT FOR SALE
(All authorized personnel must wear UVB eye-protection)
Indecipherable designation dial: **9830164275~24811993**

The enumerated subset of its nomenclature benumbed
me- > 9830164275248119939830164275
At this juncture, its timeless tenuity overtook me
unawares- > ILUCIFULGIDULIPLURIGLUNIVATI

Inasmuch muffled by naught but numbers, I was so taken aback! For as my eyesight began to fill with tears and stung with irritation, forthwith I was ready to nab a pair of sunglasses from any pastel cyan-emblazoned booth cabinet nearby that posted the official notice -- Safety Protocol Eye-Wear Required: Ordinance **291**/ Because of UVC neutron spray leakage, skafanders are recommended body-sealants!

Ere I had donned my visors, I noticed spectacular spectra sparkle spew forth from the Teflon-Tongue of the arc tube entity. Its sheerest Sheelix attenuated inter-dimensional wavelengths the unaccustomed observer shall have been blinded by, or so it seemed. Thus, then, for several more minutes in the slim interim (by my dream and later in waking consciousness), I was outwitted woefully by the apparently effortless effulgence of an energized lighthouse Lantern out of nothing, louvered with leaden crystal Fresnel lens lapis lazuli lozenges translucently triggered! In Latin, it was to convey an old Ex nihilo Lux (Out of nothing, Light) or in this case, enter to or exit out of nowhere virtual *nihility*! No, not even via voltage hook-up, an entity caused the quivering Teflon-Tongue to fulgurate and even outshine any of man's bygone Broadway extravaganza. Moreover, the brazenly bright glitter and glistering gold of the linoleum floor fluoresced in return to my bewildered cognizance. The narrowest "glorified glimpse of the glitterati thereof", which was whiter than snow-white, would wheeze intonations of dilated dial-tones into my ears. A conch shell echo-factor! On all of my five senses, *the ladylike fulguration of what transcends a sterilized station*, but that of no clinical cliché. To my marvel, albeit distinctly disposed of and deliberately the sine qua non or indispensable qualification of "placatory plushness". In esse, our security nightlight pacifier of quintessential quiescence able to quell noisy and noisome obtrusion of any kind. An absorbent buffer of waffled up, *anechoic* presence- not only replete- rather redolent with soulful silence! The placid platform of pliability, at exigence, and outstretched just so in the middle of its featureless background pallor, moistened to mute an awry scream or screech into noise-nullifying tremendous tranquility. Of anechoic, hallucinatory, auditory deafening depth over the bloated blanket.

The vast layout overflow of the Metalinoleum (that which *they*, the interior design engineers, had long ago christened) glimmered agleam with haunting heft like that of raw output, opalescent and opulent. No brighter platform was ever noticed; indeed, unimaginable on the solar superficies or Photosphere of the Sun! Perhaps, might my epidermis soon acquire a forbidden third-degree suntan for keepsake? Therefore, in retaliation to stray neutron spray, I stealthily fled from the vicinity so as not to excite suspicion, that is, with whoever Ouija-boarded me from the departed Past. Ah, my mortified feeling of overexposure to tritium-fueled lurid luminosity that had become intolerable, especially via Vat volume.

It was as if, like in the movie, *The Others*, starring Nicole Kidman, I must have been temporarily nudged aside in stasis or in limbo on an 'elsewhere' phantom domicile. But wan walls welcomed a time zone tableau vivant, ere I became stone-frozen in comparison to even *yocto-moment* intervals of Planck Time.

God's quivering cocoon; the chrysalis of the Transducer Teflon-Tongue (overhung by itself and so self-sufficient) in need of no backup power-grid distribution nor transmission, forlornly fallow-fetched as it were, waited for me. Alas, what an eeriest *thing* eftsoon to be deprived of my company, only to regain reincarnated re-admittance! Timestamped over via Vouchsafe Cartouche: La Myoacoocreata duffel bag.

In retrospect, I had coined with terminology the resurrected effulgence of every egg-and-dart corncob homegrown at a cornfield, unabashedly, to revive the *we install confidence* commercial of the quaintly quiescent 1970s timetable. The decade doubtless sandwiched by steroid rigmaroles of the 60s and 80s uproarious compensation. An epoch futilely found in scrapbook memoirs now revivified resplendently.

Now, notwithstanding it, the colossal year of 2113, timelessly, lingered still as citywide Edmonton will be eerily empty and evacuated, yet alive in an automated self-preserved *modus operandi* mode upon standby, stoic stability. Nary, nothing may dare invade its pristine, preparatory premises. Nay, not even vilest vermin! *Inter alia* then, the Transducer center-stage surpassed age, wear and tear, and that with inextinguishable equilibrium glistened inviolably if not invincible; never fake (makeshift-manufactured) but very voluptuous. Visceral as a sacrosanct soul, self-vindicated, voluminous, and *yottahertz* vibratile.

In lieu of the aforesaid Perfect Package, as I meandered out of the TARGET (Trans-alterable *radiative* gala-energy Transducer) walled warehouse lot, only to circumvent *vomitory* big booths along the way, hauntingly desolate and unoccupied, I glanced back at the 33-block squared Edmonton edifice with anticipatory suspense. I recount in my Bible codex, "No man can gaze upon Deity (supernal Light) and live..." and might I have believed it then, I avoided it heretofore! Why? What a transfigured, Pyrex-jacketed arc tube Torpedo glinted at me by reason of the Metalinoleum trampled upon by my feeble footing! Not unlike a mausoleum for the dearly departed, except that this kilometer outspread span of an exact **10,763,910**. 41671 square foot facility presumed precedence under quietest quality control.

Apropos of a walled lot, in retrospect of this drastic dream, those telephone kiosks of investiture were burnt into my memory cells, each one like a Doctor Who TARDIS, yet another shorthand abbreviation for Time And Relative Dimension In Space. Nearby, one water fountain faucet had a nodule and nozzle.

In due process, I named such an oasis the Immaculatorium, eh? Howbeit hereafter, it had vindicated my oft-dredged dream of the same hangup. Hence an enigmatic intramural enclosure- whereas pine pilasters were plastered along the foursquare wall-sides, only to be forested by pillars and poles for support columns of a contiguous ceiling- provided me my totem pole experience unlike any other oak tree-trunk! Whilst big beacons, summarily, supplant light-emitting diodes, a firefly (luciferin-infused) pouch persists; I repeat, a bio-luminescent quasar out of its cobalt glass jar [cylinder] for a shortwave-showcase is revealed. Divine vouchsafed s*tella bella* unvitiated indoors, whose cynosure is her en-clair, irreplicable Teflon-Tongue tapered slender but slightly swollen; a blankly bloated blanket; an upside-down torpedo against the present-day onslaught of profane conduct. The demurest doll, whose Holy, wholesome Transducer of the gala-cotillion Ballroom dance-floor shall have resurrected our long gone popular past. Ballerinas and ice-skaters simultaneously sifted and shuffled to and fro and fore-and-aft aboard this incorporeal anachronistic non sequitur, ready to reoccupy my ethereal stance. Aye, as if for once in a lifetime this TARGET may have facilitated the old *glaciarium* of celebrated antiquity, the sheerest steel sheet of polished permafrost fresh lay slippery to me without ice skates. Aye, multiple scenarios seem plausible at the time of newly-surfaced artificial ice that waxed or waned throughout the fourth dimension. Another level of which was called the Pluceptorium, ultimately, I coffer my case!

Likened thereupon, let us recollect the dilated Dorothy Stuart Hamill- and preceding her- picturesque Peggy Gale Fleming rotating mid-air, awhirl with triple Axel before resuming their figure skating rink- roundelay and repertoire of photogenic performances. Meanwhile, some supernumerary palindromic portraiture one year ago had timeless **2113** reclined [lazily] as an eight onto its side, representative of *infinity* (∞) or the mathematical lemniscate- Life's never-ending swirl these imperishable ladies strove to impearl! Underneath real SHEEL complementary but unbeknownst with my duo, Dorothy and Peggy.

Nevertheless, no more were soporific souls celebrated save such in due deference the architects, the inventors and investors had envisioned and addressed verily, to be ballooned by but tabletop seance summoning. No more the hustle and bustle or haggle at an emporium among customers accounted for within convention and conviviality coping whatsoever! The antiquated relics of the latter 60s and early-to-mid 1970s were widespread back then as holograms of mercurial mannequins mirrored these.

Finally, off in the outskirts, alongside my precise 33-block-mile-marker of the TARGET torchlight mart most eviscerated by bygone bounty of oft-relished reminiscence, the hung *hot cod* of the steel SHEEL resumed repose and wheezed across the ethereal isles of would-have-been bounties: *I was, I am, and I shall be*, and that was the end of it! For so it seemed as if a filmstrip, wrought reel-to-reel, reenacted the scenario for me, lock, stock and barrel, believe it or not! I was confounded, frazzled, or amazed to have witnessed my episodic kaleidoscope of this holographic conveyance cast by electronic witchcraft!

In futura, the desolate ravages of Edmonton, all devoid of ladies and gentlemen, perhaps post nuclear, were whittled down to but a vestige and wisp of my memorial repository. And yet, via hologram, some stout stovepipe, chimney, and metal mushroom reflected (but barely) a doppelgänger of predecessor ancestry paved into the landmark monument of this fully self-absorbent *Metalinoleum* layout lavishly lit up by this inviolable Teflon-Tongue: the residual Regent and retinue-radiator of our posterity; O an "Unthinkable Titanic". Yea, an epoch of age-old otherworldly ventures indiscernible to the naked eye; not even captured by my wink, neither the nanosecond glitch of its *gliff* gleaned through cyclotron velocity. The lightning-lustrous Teflon-Tongue in polyglot glossolalia communicated her oracles to me, still, in an ocean of whitecap colossal memory-storage. The fieriest and incalculable incunabula exactly unforeseen; the impressionable imprimatur of Mnemosyne narrowed at ecclesiastical niches of the nave.

Whereas the flitting celerity of hummingbird ebullience shall have captured my split-second nuance and intimation of a visual cortex, retinal and redistributed, its turn-of-the-century *luminiferous aether* would evanesce and reenter *liminal* Lethe: a refulgent river of forgetfulness branched out to tributary alternate Universes. The shriveled shrinkage of it, from inception to extinction, in one wet whopping instance, had vanished into nonexistence, as if it never materialized in the first facet to begin with, I conclude. Long live the deflated decanter, medical AMBU bag, and alembic of an ambrosial elixir vitae!

It looked like proposed Project Procyon preceded
foreclosure, long since the resurrection of prohibited retail.
No longer the intramuros mountainous municipality,
I disembarked from a swarm of warm walls.

Wherefore- via my dream ever backstage, but euthermic- the shiniest TARGET department warehouse withstood our world with its consecrated ferroconcrete foundation in contrast to a mediocre mindset and mainstream shopping spree. In molten mush, the Trans-alterable *radiative* gala-energy Transducer built by and large. In fine, that which will even outshine what once Was, but may never be! Imagined merrily, herewith no validation of likeliest similarity, nor mirror-image might momentarily suffice, I say.

Processed profoundly by my brain long left behind, it
was Rolodex carousel-filed priority 'Immaculucy'!
Last but not least, the literal Latin terminology of the
UBIQUELABYRINTHIUM (everywhere maze) stood
in light of the aforementioned notwithstanding with a
trivia three-way doorway dimension indefinitely.
and unaccounted for. Whereas conventional TARGETS had
common department stores of perpetuated quid pro quo
merchandising, I had perceived the empty isles and untenanted
wall-to-wall nothingness to revive liminal vacuity between palatial
potentials unrealized as of yet. My final frontier was restored.

* *

Jan 23 thru Feb 1, 2023:
Revised & refined.

VACATION

My Midnight Dream:

I'm in my shiny Chevy Citation, listening to oldies music. The year is 1983. Outside are galaxies of high-pressure sodium and mercury vapour lamps permeating this bustling boulevard with whitest and yellowest kilowatt-hour outputs! My inamorata and I have one helluva fabulous time! Her slinkiest and sassy auburn hairdo glistened under the streetlights strewn above as she readjusts her curvaceous sheath and bodice. She lolls, cuddling and nestling next to me. The air is rife with festivity where we ride up along the cloverleaf ramp to an evacuated thoroughfare junction as the radio continues. Later on, we exit and stop by a convenience restaurant, only to feast on a turgid burger and vanilla combo. My refurbished 1983 Chevy Citation purrs like a well-tuned alley cat whilst we, on lazy idle, sop up our roadside meal. I gaze up for an interim and see that high mast (winch-elevated) cradle of such Six Pack cluster lanterns looming over some freshly macadamized parking lot. Their brightly brazen brilliance of marigold and bluish 1kW protuberance lay lavishly lit up across the asphalt. Since there was no contest between a sheer sheen and my being suffused by quicksilver and natrium lamplight, it is my persistent desire, disclosed daintily, to welcome with equilibrium electric quasars staggeringly agleam in her sultry presence!

* Based on a true story *

My most personal testimony

I will still remember in my early-youth, the indoor racquetball court. It was silent and empty while I, solitarily, occupied the pristine premises thereof. A six-sided enclosure it was, glazed with white walls and ceiling and slatted floor or platform, gleamily latex-varnished! Overhead, recessed mercury-vapour lighting glared into its interior with an eerie, slightly green-bluish and pallid light that haunted me back then. Beforehand, I would oft visualize a Hypersphere to have entered therein. My testimony of such an entity is referenced by my teenage employment at the Sizzler Family Steak House restaurant where I worked as a bus-boy and dishwasher, later promoted to be a salad bar and dining lounge prepper and attendant. At any rate, it was the Avion Sphere that appeared to me during the long, grueling hours of washing loads of dishes, pots and pans in the kitchen. Apparently, such a big Ball presence of consolation came to me in 1984 and, consecutively, for half a decade thereafter. The circumference of which was, as it were, with seamless variability, exquisitely maneuverable and protean by nature. For out of nowhere, it expanded to full size like a balloon self-sustained, only to dwindle into a point and vanish into extinction! But the bright white racquetball room remained, within which I had played against myself, bashing an Ektelon rubber ball hard at the front wall until missing it as it reasserted itself deftly on the rebound. I must have had fellowship with something otherworldly. On that occasion, I persuaded my father to install a 2-lamp, four-foot fluorescent lighting appliance on my bedroom ceiling. I picked out the desired colour temperature for the light output at a nearby Kmart. My sleeping quarters were warm-white and lavender lit, inspired by my watching the movie THX 1138. Finally, to *surrealize* the scenario, I designated my door using a numerical nomenclature for some reason... Indeed, altogether, it was the heyday of my rather hitherto vision, albeit progressive. Contemporarily, I call it the Immaculatorium facility and the Super Ball, Univatrium, aloft!

INVORTIUM

The Outskirts of Invitation

My lucid dream recommenced from an older inception.

The maze-like tube~way network quivered with an interim of waffled quietness as concave walls were bared before me instead of a crowded horde peopled about. Thereat, I waited for my scheduled rocket sled to pick me up. It was so unlike my earlier redeveloped Hyper Loop where commuters and computers, wedged within friction-free container casks and pods, glided speedily in an evacuated, tuberous chamber; the big bore or muzzle of an M2, 105mm howitzer cannon.

These convoy cargo casks had been automated and I happened to be their perfect payload, upheld humanly, bundled up by an anti-volatile vestment. Noncombustible canisters kept company.

Overhead, firefly-filled luciferin Arc Tubes sizzled furiously at the station platform where I lounged on my prescribed recliner at some waiting room. Until right then and there this big bullet conveyance corridor flexed itself at my convenience, releasing one of many cars that slid up to my fine line of entry. I then trotted out of the guest area and boarded my so-called 'slip-trip' ride-along levitation of a seamless flange suspended by Lichtenberg-lacerated cupcake insulators.

Inside now, nicely nestled in lithe luxuriant and cozy comfort, I relaxed on a plush-pleasant seat and peered outward of my porthole. Everything was stationary, when all at once merciless acceleration plastered my body aback. Forthwith the rocket-sled slide transport trundled forth briefly, and then had hit top velocity. It felt like horizontal free-fall fulminating with a *swoosh!*

My porthole window revealed an incoherent blur of flyby flutter. Ere time elapsed, that lingered longingly- I thought, when will it be to my destination? As only smooth but swift momentum kinetic kept me fastened firmly to my backrest. For during the interval of hysterical exhilaration I must have felt by centrifugal force, as curvature of an outside portal pulled upon me, I felt no nausea, nor dared to induce vomit. Of course, after awhile I discerned neon streaks of blinding blip-lighting lilt and lick about, reappearing like sparkling flashes from the vantage point of a rather rapid rotation.

Notwithstanding the continuity of my traversal, an old overwrought intercom interrupted my midway train of thought and announced: “Slip city grid 291 shall arrive upon contact at ETA 2113 hours sharp! Please stand by…”

In response to a time-saver, I’d grab my seat belt to loosen it, and took out a gazette from the magazine dispenser, only to seize the moment by my perusal of updated science articles. This apportioned opportunity of my easy sit-back and relaxation was cut off abruptly. Soon enough, in almost no time at all, my Canister Conveyance Booth, as it were, or CCB, entered a far lengthier stretch Tube Expressway. And yet another backward jolt had underpinned me into my recliner that, by now, served as compensatory Mercy Seat! For faster my magnetic cushioned catapult pushed my own envelope of a comfort zone, I reacted, refastened my seat harness strapped over me, and nestled snugly back, but giddily as it ought to have been, or as was usually the case.

Outside my barreling cockpit could be seen through the transparency tubing an endless city of skyscrapers languidly lurching by in back of a skittering glitter of stupendous speed up front! An aftereffect of some optical illusion it was whilst the forward thrust, rush and hush of sheer G-force ferry wheeled me continually. Hell, I called this joint juncture of my slip~trip, the Univomitorium, and indeed it was. The exigency thereof hammered me.

After another flyby of momentous motion, my quick sliding cask slowed down to a gradual crawl on its appropriate approach to the B-section; it was an extremely vast Hyper City that was rekindled into viewership observance, replete with *ignitrons*.

And so, in my view of the enormity of it all, it was the Univacuopolis urban center of innumerable CRT vacuum tubes. Of this I was conversant.

My rocket sled's tunnel conduit contorted itself out of an electrostatic and elastic thoroughfare funnel to reconnect with some local station. My *carriageless* cushioned car slithered slightly to a pit stop and I alighted its cramped quarters. Nevertheless, after an inter-dimensional distortion of time that had befuddled me from exiting my own barrel-booth, an eerie innuendo, as if on Doctor Who's *Tardis*, altogether gripped me as things seemed far larger on the inside than on the outside without! For as I stepped out of my now, newly named CCB, or *continual conveyance bullet*, I was ushered away; whisked willy-nilly on automatic via the treadmill towards yonder Vomitorium~ the concrete one~ of the Hypercity UVPS for short. Although it was christened the ever grandiose Univacuopolis, in brief the welcomed abbreviation suited me just satisfactorily. There were other acronyms to be used inter alia.

And now, no longer shackled by the transport system, I preambled my disorienting way over additional platforms that staged various viewfinders designed to focus in on the unidirectional UVPS from afar. I sighed at the prefatory colossus thereof! Aye, too fathomless and breathtaking to take in all at once!

Needless to articulate, the labyrinth of such sinuous tunneling roundabout was labeled (by designation) the 'Univermiculatorium' or, better put, the 'Univermicuity'. Yet moreover, it resembled a resolutely convoluted plumbing as of yet undiscovered by spry engineers and travelers alike. Ultimately, may I add, to my most merry amazement I saw filigree needlework of the unfathomable diorama thereof; yea, that with exceedingly stunning and cunning gossamer and stretch-fabric finesse far across the neighborhood block, lock, stock and barrel!

Furthermore, on the rebound rebus, the whole thing portrayed portentously picturesque events that then marched on by from past, present, to future. Each one, a carousel of continual causality on a Rolodex of rotating time-slots galore. The interior labyrinth thereof was also, as it were, instead of a museum, a 'mazeum' of interlink entanglements to no end; that of countless corridors.

A bloated empyrean, above creosote crème underneath, glimmered from upward harsh glare of this UVPS at large. Besides this, smatterings of hillocks and of alpine uplands were slanted far away from the cornfield outbacks to the vast valley and meadows that interspersed the starburst of an intricate labyrinth layout; its *mazeum* woozily outspread hither and yon.

Whoa! I wondered. Wide-eyed galoot was I.

For there curved yet another surly film of a tinted translucency walled up and down and all around me, and obliquely. I suspected that it had been a type of shatter-cone shielding to protect or 'ferrofortress' my mother-naked eyes and overall frailty from overexposure of the Invortium. How the whole gamut loomed up in the distance dauntingly, but at least eight to tenfold condensed and more unwieldy than New York City with Hong Kong combined! Hence I waxed spellbound and flabbergasted as I soaked in the experience fit for long lifetimes. A metropolitan municipality that it was, well-nigh, and the likes of which I had never knuckled before. No, not with my noggins, nor heartfelt ever before.

There appeared an old entrance for me momentarily makeshift when, immediately, a rectangular corridor manifested itself before my approach. I took advantage of its piled up red carpet treatment and entered therein, tentatively padding the floor.

The Tall Grey Hallway, as I could coin it, had unfolded out all about me a high-ceiling vestibule passageway riddled with arc tube lighting from topnotch to rock-bottom. I furrowed my brow and assumed the fearful fetal position; crossing my legs over, I hunkered down. The surroundings, lolling lazily, listened…

Where am I? I queried myself, but not so much my horrid corridor that I was unable ascertain with interpretation.

"You are in the midst of my Univacuopolis!" intoned a voice as I stood stiffly at hand, nakedly numbered, narrowly scrutinized.

"So--- this is it…" I finalized conclusively. *Make no mistake where you are* (or) sung by Kenny Loggins in 1979!

"*Yea, this is our heartfelt haven of Repose.*" a chorus of souls said serenely and as if in respectful reply to Kenny Loggins.

No doubt, it was a prefabricated repository of some sort as I had speculated on the very contents thereof. And so, I gazed up and down the hallway with a dozen doorways leading off into nowhere. In front, an inky, charcoal and dismal doorway of gaping blackness, and to the aft, the selfsame appearance. The manifestation of it too tenuous to touch, I presumed under ultraviolet lamplight.

"Where are you going?" inquired gravely the UVPS.

"I'm wanting entry to the heart of it all, your ladyship." I explained.

“So then,” countered the corridor, “It is as it were...” And that was the end of it before that creepy, cryptic Voice faded and would resume later.

At its behest I was alone in the narrow hallway, but on the qui vive, totally unaware of was to transpire next. Although this somewhat nettled and narrowed my juncture of a grog-full decanter to mollify my recollection of such harsh glare. Meanwhile, I reconnoitered the situation rather than be nonplussed about it. At first, I reasoned about the lighting overhead eerily emitting UVC that, if I stood still for prolonged exposure, my skin became singed as if it were goose-flesh, odorous by burnt flies and bugs all over, even to a pungent stench! Secondly, as I quickened the pace to an evenly step-over cadence, I mused of how- if at gigahertz ultrahigh frequency of alternating current- the amperage remained abysmally wee via high-tension of energy propagation maximized. *So that's how energy conservation caught up confluence all about throughout this meticulous monstrosity!* I wondered. By that reconsidered, I might as well refrain from cumbersome conjecture and have it eloquently elucidated...

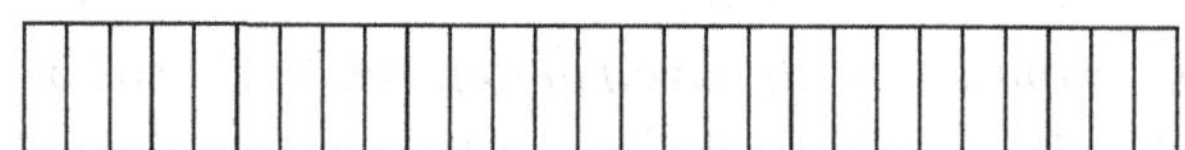

For what I was about to witness is beyond vocabulary for anyone to dare disclose; namely, that I had fallen privy to prominent profusion quite contrary to any Visions aforementioned (authorized details as follows):

In betwixt pilasters and pillars posted about, and that flanked me for foot-candles away, a nimbly narrow runabout meandered off at fore-and-aft whereon I went. The tar-dark doors from side to side, and that each, absorbing hot light ray reflections of the EM spectrum into them (no matter how lackluster), passed by me the farther forth I advanced in my Trek through the conduit.

Whilst with tentative tread, I walked lengthwise the long preamble of the plank or pliant platform, adjacent doorways revealed themselves, which had led to countless hallways perpendicular to my lath and clapboarded catwalk rib-caged by skeletal support pillars. These were alternate corridors that made way to an unknown oblivion offhand, as if into utter nowhere. At length, I heard spectral voices voluminously echo throughout their vacant vacuity. Vociferation of which reintegrated reams and reams of instant information interpreted by the old Akashic Records department. The vibration and wavelength of resonance recollected was wonderfully wrought and revitalized with preemptive retrieval, but intact. Perhaps paved into the permafrost Other Ether unable to deliquesce, nor ever to alter in any way, shape, or form. This thingamajig, the *Other Ether*, is a pliant plenum of spatial elasticity.

Hence how all of this bypassed me as I walked the Tall Gray Hallway whereabouts unknown. Suddenly, supple quilted quietness quelled the faintest of perturbation; even to the very last inkling of a seismic twitch! Sotto voce then. The silver sliver of mercurial Silence muffled the amplified deafening dull thud or crisp crackle of a pin-drop thimbleful throwaway! And by contrast, those charcoal blackest tar and bitumen creosoted Doors of an intramural facility, christened the Gloratorium, had sponge-like soaked in all manner of mirrored mist from all around my presence. I suppose it was the aura around me, nothing more. But somewhere else, at another forbidden vicinity, one backdoor stayed ajar like a slip-slit to let light in from the multifaceted Millennium Star Diamond; a heavyweight amongst upper echelon polished gems, the which weighs about 777 karats. Imagine its glitz of starriest and coruscant iridescence!

For such an adjunct it was, like a garishly gaudy Fun House of mercury-backed rococo and renaissance French *miroirs*, and forged of diamond dust, whose sheer sheen ballooned but back at me what was staggeringly radiant. Of course, this with their lovely lavender luster luridly delightful. Others still~ embedded elsewhere~ far, far away and away… Alas, delivering daylight doppelgangers of juggernauts built beside oceanic basins beginning to splash and slosh soggily, drenching an etiolated floorboard lacquered with lozenges of linoleum varnish agleam! Greasily wet like a mirror! Never noisome with odorous ozone, but almost! Ever so glaringly glistering up antiquity-ensconced tapered slender *flambeaux* flareups re~mirrored from groin vaulting bulged and carbuncled by egg-and-dart and eggshell acanthine ornamentation. With igneous frozen frieze ledges and chalk cornices, no less adorned adorable and garlanded gorgeously; *this* was my picturesquely enhanced hologram!

But aside from such musty medieval embellishments, therewith stalwart stalagmites of old castellated and cathedral-crocketed spires, cascaded (igneous) Pahoehoe, Blocky, and Pillow lava-flow. Rising timelessly in tableau vivant. As pyramidal pylons and traffic safety cones replete with sparkle and multiplied many times, one with another; if there were any stone-frozen cressets once aflame thereon, it had solidified long ago alongside organic petrification.

Yet how Gothic gibbous gargoyles likewise were perched over the edge! Nevertheless, an 'immaculucy' ubiquitously yielded it!

Wherefore The Doors dedicated themselves as I fell transfixed and rapt thereby; the rectangular and foursquare frames of which had then truly portrayed my soulful personage entirely. I therefore avoided the confrontation thereof: that of each and every doorway redundant, redolent with the forbidden that would interweave intermittently with those shut-up 'mortiferous' monoliths of The Doors; having to conceal, covertly, incorporeal corridors behind them.

At this ulterior ultimatum I remembered Jim Morrison with his band members, backstage circa 1967 (the year of my nativity).

Within this narrow-walled labyrinth of an endless Univermicuity, only vivid visions and dreams of hot, hallucinatory glory grappled my attention span. Attenuated as they were at this point due to such rational radiance water-fallen therefrom. My mere mentality, cascading along for the ride, but unlike igneous lava-flow, took on the kaleidoscopic collage of innermost intimate intelligence shape-shifting with impossible contortions. I fainted and came to.

How huge glimpses of hyper pyramidal and conical conscious, contoured edifices thronged o'er a super turf territory of pure gold pavement everywhere and wheresoever one listed. Amazonian tall Termite Towers of tubular Titans, or that of such inviolable investiture- at six-thousand storeys upwardly had hexagonal housed beehives of insular inhabitants up and down and all around. Equipped with 'elevatoriums' of hundredfold elevators gliding by effortlessly. Hereby my disclosure of the spiritual infrastructure now congealed into a finest, divinest conference.

Yea, vestigial fingerprints of yet another tall time-frame amidst the preternatural Univacuopolis Hyper City had conveyed continual holographs of protuberant architecture to accelerate redevelopment redundantly so. Not to exclude lively cocoons, whose fat, fulvous and bilious phosphorescence~ as shiny upright albacore, cod, and tuna~ illumine therapeutic Thulium; aye, its super rare metal to tellurian topography. But an overflowing cornucopia at this level!

An acquired dialogue started when the creepy, cryptic revivified Voice came online again: "I am ever thy unifying Univacuopolis of luminous effulgence; the Revivified *Vitriatrix* thereof." Ugh, or whatever *that* meant!

I awakened myself from the swoon and swoop of time travel as gusts of a whirlwind howled and hooted here and there about the hallways. There was no source of that gale factor and I realized the Voice uttered something moreover. Likewise, I then overheard ear-shattering, vociferous annunciators ululating stupendously stentorian alarm calls with screeches, shrieks, and squeals from on high. The importunity of it was laid out for me as if for overlap *ferroconcrete*: "I acknowledge thee, thy Ladyship." I'd answer back, but so lugubriously and ill-disposed of that I couldn't bellow back!

But still, in unison of Her persistent metallic chorus (via vox femina): "Affirmative! Wherefore do I see thy bloody time-slot of the early to mid twenty-first century wherein corollary corruption and die-hard decrepitude are precariously present?"

"Yea, I realize how horrifying it hath become, and I wish for a more favorable future, your ladyship." I confessed under trembling trepidation. A quota of murmurs and a quivering vibrato were augmented as dangerous decibels reverted to a rock-bottom naught.

Eftsoons enough, waffled walls, glistening with glorified glitz, loomed over me in an uncompromising, imposing manner. At once, I felt so circummured by their Ballroom of a Wall Womb, an effulgent affront, while vociferation continued its clarion caveat (except clara voce or audibly; not muffled like before): "Oh, the worldwide avarice for monetary security in filthy lucre and pleasure hath climaxed and is pending judgment! Be this an international headlong plummet into an unbridled naughtiness if nothing at all is rectified. Yea…" emphasized the oscillating intonation. "Vagabond violence and steroid religiosity pollute terra firma, and televised escalations of emergency cover four corners of both air, land, and sea." Later, larger than life-size images of it flitted imposingly. Again, by the lorry-load, liquefied aluminum wafers (per bloated package) quiescently quell the surroundings until I would wax queasily adrift. No need for an adage: "Renegades run on a rampage and pilfer possessions!" was overheard directly using Ye Yielding Identity.

Then it prognosticated the prescient *foregleam* (capitalized for more emphasis)! **"MANY MORE RUN RAMPANT TO & FRO WHEREBY**

ANOTHER SUPER BOMB EXPLODES! WAVES OF RADIONIC DISCORD REACH LETHAL LEVELS. VULGAR OBSCENITIES SOON THREATEN PLACID ENVIRONMENTS. STATE TROOPERS RETALIATE AGAINST THE INFLUX OF POWER FANATICS UNTIL WAR WITH TWO MAJOR COUNTRIES ENSUES..." (it was rebroadcast and televised, replete with cacophonic echolalia)

I shuddered. This prophecy seemed relevant and quite familiar to me. I had to beseech the Tall Wall before me; that enfeebled my diminutive stature: "O most sagacious one! what will we wish, and what of the outcome?" But her perspicacity perforated me...

"Congregate into groups of peaceful tranquility. Yea, prostrate yourselves in sodden sackcloth and ashes, kiss the loamy earth, and with warmth of humility, go *walk the talk*; living in harmonics with Universal Laws. For the milieu of society suffers hardship and deterioration, longing to be reconciled! Yea, hearken to no hearsay! And lastly, O would that ye go according to the godly, Good Book and Gospel of Jesus Christ, the chiefest of Thrones and our Mercy Seat of Paradise and Heaven..." urged voice-overs, vehemently.

I was dumbfounded and taciturn. And in reply to my shock of awe, the All Tall Wall of the quiet *Quotile* folded back on itself and evanesced. Wall-side Hg mirrors vanished therewith to be replaced by the blank and featureless Void. Immediately, the scaffolding and flat-planked catwalks collapsed into their hydraulic sleeves whence my common ground had grown grotty by the wayside.

I no longer detected any feedback from the intramural interior. And so, like (Hg) pap smears atop gable ornaments drooping down from soffit ceilings reckoned upon old aperture time-exposure slats and slots, residual liquefied aluminum and mercury leakage licked over afterburner nozzles. Their Transducer trickle of condensation had fogged up the bloated blanket from inverted nipples of vacuum tubes embedded into coffers. For as images scorched onto photographic daguerreotypes of iodine-sensitized silver plating in mercury vapour, variegated 'vacoons' were suspended from the ceiling as the entire UVPS slumbered. The horrendous Hush, the dormant docility of what was bygone, overlapped my most hypnotic trance of awareness. The multi-megalopolis with a billion spires quiesced into such quelling quietness, unlike beforehand, that the ferrous array thereof radiated resplendence like never before.

Moreover, one more flash and glitzy glimpse of the vast Vision unfolds by my redundant recourse- crème de la crème- accordingly acquainted with and acquired!

Therefore, as if out of none other, I had stumbled on something truly tremendous. Faultlessly, these were burgs of vertiginous *light* gleaming in my midst, or as it were, very vastly vindicated by what looked like an eternity. I paused before tall, elongated tapered half-conical coolant towers, like those that may mirror nuclear reactors. Here, inside of these monstrous edifices were in storage and enveloped (by plumbiferous pliancy) 'flexilastic' cocoons or Vacoons, or so designated. Each voluminous Vat was insulated within gelatinous heavyweight super-fluid that weighs untold times the atomic density of deuterium and oxygen but which would likely consist of conventional heavy water. Within every one of the aforesaid were wedged tightly into them probe prods instead of normal plutonium rods regulated via sheathed moderator. This was the tried Transvortium core and coil of the finest fusion reactor, efficient as the star 25 light-years away, top-spun Vega of 12.5 hour rotation!

Thus the glitterati of Light was known to me as the Luciopolis, ever empowered with *Transvortiums* full of Vacoons, vibratile, and sizzling through their cryogenic chrysalis. They had to be super-refrigerated due to self-compression and pressurization! But overall (inter alia then) the gargantuan Luciopolis glimmered with multilevel hyper-hives of hexagonal harmony & within which each Flex Hexagon, an embedded hyper-burg each the size of New York City and Hong Kong congealed, had been irradiated irreplicably. To elucidate it *en clair*, the Luciopolis was even comprised of billions of these holy Hexagons where within each of them would reside an NYC/HK sized slip-city interlink. And all of it, its consummation, aye, as with the Gothic gamut thereof, was such a lovely layout enlivened by Transvortiums heavily equipped with stretched moderators. They themselves are each one an incontestable Plosive Plucire that may resemble a molten eggplant. These packages are antediluvian, deposited by some [superpower superstar] that spawned such living lamp entities into timeless immortality; O every pliable Plucarian in turn but benign and harmless by nature, although more intensely potent than any plutonium rod millions of times, albeit benignly (God forbid, not evilly, if prognosticated by foresight)!

We welcome the years 2113 all the way to 3112: my millennial palindrome short of but a day! Wherein this lavish Luciopolis illumines priority precedence above arterial sophistication. Nevermore the primitive foibles and trifles of needing to refuel our brief lives with Precambrian or crude and raw refineries ad hoc. For behold how that *amaranthine* contiguity of a pellucid Power supplies cisterns of annexed connection! Unknowingly, I say, every Cell of an NYC/HK burg dwindles into a hexagonal Vat. Not to exclude the over three-quadrillion *souls* of residential radiance reposed therein; the overcrowded occupancy of which surpasses posterior generations underneath these Termite Towers of strong throng stalagmites forested about everywhere at near-infinite distance. The number of them at an innumerable and open-ended 'Pluriseptiplex' or powers of magnitude is notated as some (...^-0110+^...)! The concord convoys of such golden stalagmites, thousands of yards in height, had towered up to their overcast empyrean charred and bloated by blistering brightness! Therefore, those diamond stone-cone stalagmites stay staunchly upheld by hexagonal hives, and wherein each flex-hexagon or "flexagon" gets to be but a very visceral version of the NYC/HK slip-city-grid reduced ridiculously to the diminutive, ultra-compartmentalized multiple-sided *Pentakis Icosidodecahedron*: its convex shape of 80 triangular faces, 120 edges, and 42 vertices of pointed out hexagons are apparent, and all multiplied with more myriads of *hyper~skyscrapers* per section of perfection; a cellular colossus, that of convivial consolation, if not numberless *consolidation* (no pun in tautology save surrendered with portrayal)!

I witnessed widely overhung starry ceilings atop an immeasurable megalopolis within and whereat I had visited sundials dwarfed thereby. This singular multi-megalopolis, herewith interpreted, the glorified 'Glibolotubulopolitz' in and of itself was what multiplied its UNIVACUOPOLIS embedded right inside stalagmites amongst myriads more throughout an endless linoleum of pearlescence! The Vacoons, for your information, FYI, were collective companions to the countless souls who resided *brain-gloriously* in each of a concordant compartment distributed down into the super citywide Luciopolis: the mountainous municipality of ebullient quantum foam- or better yet- 'femtofoam' elegantly attired by glazed glitterati.

Likewise the Transvortiums, for me to yet epitomize- although they resemble nuclear fusion Reactors of circumstellar magnitude- provided opaquely holographic labyrinths of Elysian Fields for the supernal souls to venture and settle into with many more labyrinths via the 'univermiculatorium' of wormholes. Heretofore it was what I had scrutinized in the aorta of the runabout. And, like legacies left behind- that of their enormity gleaned from states of raw Bliss- this then defied my contemplation of the same. Imagine it, if one will, the super-central serenity of Elysian cornfields that heave up an interurban Stone-Cone and Strong-Throng of corncob-countless stalagmites, like unto overly life-size traffic safety pylons, nodular all over, with ear kernels of bloated Bliss via memorialized endurance from past lifetimes and reincarnations upon Earth entirely; whose surplus of flareups materialize an illustrious Luciopolis! Throughout its dirigible~distribution display, every Flex Hexagon in which NYC/HK megalopolises are nicely nestled, have this congregation multiplied multitudinous milliards of times! A consolidated sum of 3,000,000,000,000,000+ or three-quadrillion-plus super Soulmates of such a 'Creatorium' unbeknownst by life's laity too innumerable! Nor quota-quantified alongside some antiquated nave and niche of cloistered parochial scrutiny. As anti-cremated, **re-created* rather! Let luminiferous *fire* revivify the dearly departed!

Pentakis Icosidodecahedron

Along public premises of an inconceivably ineffable Vicinity lay what is carefully identified as 'Metalucelectropluceptorium' that defies description over the highest apex. For shorthand usage, may it be the *Metalinoleum* or *Porcelinoleum* either way. Such is spread down for ordinary linoleum flooring to appear as it were with glorified glitter like permafrost pavement with elasticity, but all flawlessly impervious to any bombardment; be it meteoric or comparable even to any impact like that of the fiery bolide which exploded near the Podkamennaya Tunguska River in Yeniseysk Governorate, (Siberia) Russia, on the morn of June 30, 1908. Equivalent to a 12-megaton air-burst (even upon *Metalucelectropluceptorium*) nary an indentation, scuff, nor hairline gash on its supernal surface!

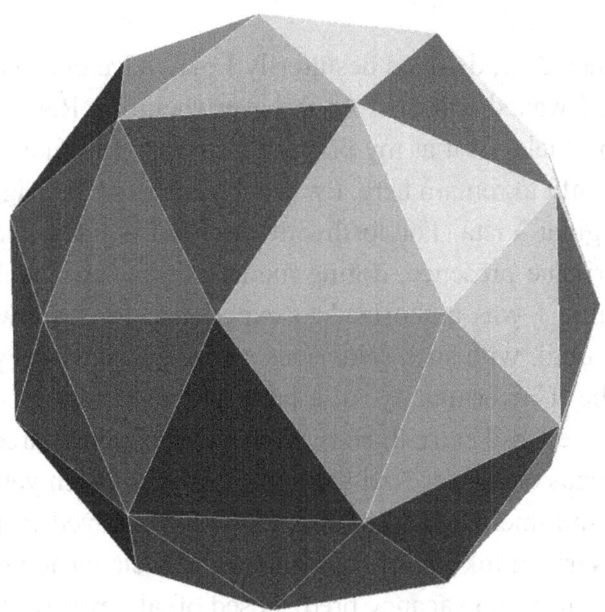

*My *creatorium* may supplant the crematorium! It readily resurrects from hoariest hot ashes a divinely fine, fiery phoenix out of sacrosanct soot in an urn tucked away to a mausoleum crypt. Alas, far too accelerated for any coroner or mortician at a morgue to yet catch a fleeting glimpse of…

The analysis of this overwhelmed my mindset. In esse, I found shriveled shrinkage of nonexistence, or if ever confronted by such a breathless branch of excellence. Ordinary orifice? Never! But the envelopment of which had exceeded the paranormal lisping of personal expectations; yea, such domains of prominent preponderance unworthy of our present-day disputes. Unqualified as we were all, still, stubbornly hellbent on profligate degeneration by reason of a necessity: that of survival of flesh, blood, bone and marrow for its own sake. After all, I withdrew my case through the slip-slit of personal perception and recoiled into my mortal conch shell.

The pressurized presence of nacreous nodules and of tapered teats deliquesced above me, sagging so, and lolled loosely, but that had finally fizzled to naught.

Until, however, daunted desultorily I may have become by now to the hilt, I waxed aghast from the overwhelming Revelation: the [special spectacle] of it at my prayerful creche. And like a *persona non grata* unfit to remain here, I was expelled from the Night Watch of this virginal Vista. For forthwith the UVTY nudged me away from its pristine presence, urging me to exit an inner niche. Now, not one thing I was authorized to experience for my own sanity and health until, with such salubrious serenity of protocol proffered hitherto, the 'Univermicuity' of a labyrinthine Limbo escorted me back to where I had started. How humbly I was unprepared for any of the enigmas enclosed. And that meant more swollen yellows and iridescent shimmers and glimmers gloriously arrayed in heavenly splendor. Nary an inkling of any prim prima facie facade save for a featureless, in-vacuo vacancy predisposed of, ah! ever so desolately delivered. An **oleo tranquillior* lubricity of which was this slip-slit of a prism where electroplasmatic spectra-sparkle I see!

*As a fig. of softness, gentleness: "oleo tranquillior," quieter, gentler, stiller than oil

Soon afterwards, the Univermicuity (UVTY) collapsed into itself within shriveled shrinkage of a glorified 'unicloveniferous supersingularity' threadbare threshold; ever so sub-squeezed into dimensionless reduction whence *she* originated. Suddenly I was left utterly alone and abandoned in the Electrical Antarctica wilderness of metropolitan~ but more so~ of castellated palatial perpetuity.

For it had been a perforce perspicuous slip~trip to begin with. Inside-out and all around; crystal clear and self-luminous after all. Revealing as ever. Until X-ray illumined, eviscerated.

Eventually, the blank walls would acquiesce, buckle inwardly and away from off me alongside this intramural moment that then disintegrated, as if into nonexistence. Nonetheless, nothing so non sequitur about it, it had straightaway restored my standpoint all in one piece~ perhaps as a bedside setup, sanguinely.

Just imagine, indistinguishable and instantaneous insularity within the UVPS: such as an ever elongated corridor conduit to interwoven vistas available only at the sidereal sundial and flip of a switch! Revamp rotary dial only, Rolodex-roundelay deliberate!

Now notice the notion of a "Glistery Gloridor" to have herewith resurfaced! The definition of which withstands a common-day Hall of fame. The illimitable and really *liminal* interlink corridor of glorification to no end, nor cul-de-sac to nowhere, I declare!

Aside from the convergence of a concord confluence, I admit by my *terra incognita* that the veritable vocal Accord (not that of a Honda, for crying out loud!) was only quelled merely from a *non sequitur caesura* unjustified in an Unthinkable Titanic tome of raw reason. Since then, I desired the tremendous treatise of it all rather than face expulsion therefrom. Aye, try but supplest silencing that muffles forth just because of the macabre skull-and-bones of our malevolent, diabolical epoch apparent! Defiantly though, I couldn't employ plain English here. Nor do I intend any of my polysyllabic jargon to create literary gargoyles out of the creative ether. May an instructor of *tenebrism* summon my hitherto dismissal from life's eternally tableau vivant vogue of the status quo, I bellow!

As for the qualification- despite the lack thereof in comparison to concreteness transcendent to retinal retention of my neocortex- I explored this diversified, dynamic but waffled up Luciopolis.

Herein were created crystalline obelisks and needles and Vac-Tubes bundled together from one end of the rainbow spectrum, all the way to the other end. The electromagnetic wavelengths of magnitude and amplitude, long-wave and shortwave throughout, iridescently and colorfully unparalleled by any virtual and visual cortex and colour wheel conceivable. It was an unearthly splendour of tapered slender candlesticks that thronged about my viewpoint of it, inside out. Like long tube SOX lighting of whopping yottawattage, I prognosticate with British bravado. Its lookalike lustrous sparkles uncannily connected with intracellular accuracy; the contiguity and homogeneous Metalucelectropluceptorium of which would uncompromisingly comprise Paradise itself, but (Heaven forbid) never to exceed the biblical High-Definition of spiritual coronary panorama in myocardium (encapsulated by a paragraph below):

Like four-dimensional holographic special effects, effortlessly effulgent, extravagantly displayed, but cross-sectional in an upright salubrious super-forest of blinding Glitz, building-bright brilliance! Awhile back, the sheer shock wave of it had hunkered me down as my knees felt rubbery and I languished under its power right at the supreme sight thereof. For lo and behold, flambeaux Flareups the life-size shapes of hydrogen-filled Hindenburg zeppelin dirigibles (as if this were UAP: Unidentifiable Aerial Phenomena), and down deeper into the depth-charge trenches of submarines and torpedoes up on end, swollen, had all suffused this Metroplex Supercenter so gaudily that gainsay *garish* and *lavishly* narrows yardstick usage of vainest vocabulary! For example, gargantuan 'gweducs' were they, and yet never barnacled by the burdens and toils of this wayward and quite oftentimes woeful world. Enlarged living lighthouse entities that facilely exhibit iridescent exotica, though altogether alike; for some, lubriciously lighted; others lustrously lit up with frothy Freon from hyper-hyper diminutive Planck-pliant quantum foam.

And this was the virtuous vindication of such as I *squinched* to observe what was indiscernible, insurmountable, and incorruptible! My enveloped encounter and departure that followed by the time I had felt deeply debased by brilliant brightness crept up on me fast. How having to return aboard my reliable rocket sled, I aback went, whisked away with an automated causeway and into the transport transducer in one peace; so that I could but flee the sheerest *UVC & (B) barrage of that UVPS unleashed! I then saw in my porthole the distantly departing sunset of my Univacuopolis paradise recede away under determinate 'evanishment' as from freeze-frame shriveled shrinkage altogether.

*UVC: shortwave radiation (used for sterilization) that is in the region of the ultraviolet spectrum which extends from about 200 to 280 nm in wavelength, and that is more hazardous than UVB but is mostly absorbed by earth's upper atmosphere.

Though the safety protocol of my big barreling bullet encapsulated me from the rather horrendous, harshest Glare of that yellowest UVPS, I at once suffered a sudden suntan to my epidermis. My completely complexioned skin-job must have been pitifully pockmarked and cratered from the roentgens of that furious, fabulously **embryoctoarc* Anthropic Universality insofar fossilized. The midway word between prefix and suffix refers to near one septillionth of one nanosecond via inflationary expansion when the merest moment (about at a sub-gluon hairline split-fraction) of inception had ever been precisely precedent, created in the first timeless and hyper-vacuous phase to begin with! Clearly, the harshest Glare was a step next door to the Genesis of Fiat Lux (Let there be Light).

**embryoctoarc*: my self-created terminology that combines 3 words; *embryo* and *yocto-* (septillionth of a second), and *arc.* As if the first faint flash or flicker of our universe occurred, except in one septillionth of a nanosecond. Namely, the Planck time is the length of time at which no smaller meaningful length can be validly measured due to the indeterminacy expressed in Werner Heisenberg's Uncertainty Principle. Theoretically, this is the shortest time measurement that is possible. Planck time is roughly 10−43 seconds… However, to specify, the smallest time interval that was measured was 10−21 seconds, a "zeptosecond." One Planck time is the time it would take a photon traveling at the speed of light to cross a distance equal to one Planck length. One zeptosecond is a trillionth of a billionth of a second. Please note that this time-interval is brief enough for an electron to flit across a hydrogen atom. To compare the size of a Planck volume to ourselves is like the size of a proton on its own to match the vastness of the observable universe (93,000,000,000 light years wide), yet universal expansion of the entire cosmos will soon surpass this number!

And now, back at my ground-state bivouac base:

The inevitable intercom high-pitched crooned: "Attention! For those of ye who prefer not to remain at the cynosure UVPS, please remain aboard this slip~trip 192 until we've gained clearance of the Harsh Glare thereof…" As a privileged commuter to the mountainous municipality, I would later disembark from the old lorry-laden cargo convoy of a Hyper-Loop rocket-sled.

Meanwhile more ensued.

END OF LINE flashed forth at lamp-camp of an unplugged CRT, whereas netherworld nostalgia, nook and cranny had salvaged the shrapnel of flyby flutter that skittered past me frenetically.

I was relieved, forever altered by the confirmation of illustrious *illuminants* and tubules agleam throughout the huge Invortium itself. Indeed, for whilst my Maglev Machine transporter-trajectory looped into its beginning terminal, I wailed and whimpered by myself into roughneck reprieve. Even so, my immemorial memoirs of it (charred by a *shattercone* shock-wave of a supremely pretty city about a dozen times vaster than Japan's Tokyo and the Osaka metro area) persisted! But better *yet*, and of no clinical cliché, I'd still dilly-dally incommensurate with superhuman reckoning of an ageless eclipse! This was the antithesis of yesteryear's bellicose barbarism by bold contrast. Once again, soulmates suffused me per cell of an NYC/HK metropolis wherewith every *Pentakis Icosidodecahedron* was fitted well with countless others! Mere keepers of silentium est aureum (Latin for silence is golden) stood up aground across the shiniest Metalucelectropluceptorium plenum, and having Transvortium living lamp entities overhead, above each and every one of them!

How hallowing! While I'd gather in the gargantuan gamut, and other-worldlier than anything. Never but one whit of it, I pray! No, not by my heavier haul over verdant fairyland Elysian Fields and pristine prairies fancily arrayed and addressed! What weightiest lot lay every-which-way a Pluriseptiplex square meters of the sagging metric system incapable of plumb-lining the immeasurable…

And it came to pass, at having been carried away back to point A, an afterglow of its Glitz glinted out amidst the very Vac-Shaft of the Tubule network, lucently lit by the yocto-UVPS. Or at best by what was unlawful for anyone to vainglory glimpse (as if scarcely spoken of) on the promenade of a runabout like this. With a feeling of rapture one would wonder under fervor: is it another showcase pageantry? Surely our wearisome world is as-of-yet unprepared for radiant reality to cascade and coruscate like an intumescent tributary ready to eddy off into the far larger lakeside of eternity. We are still groggily stunted on the basest rung of Jacob's Ladder, lackluster as it were, long pending a final frontier to her Excelsior.

But back at the Depot Station whence I started from, I melted into an air-conditioned emollient of environmental depressurization in the waiting guest lounge where I divested myself of my cosmonaut spacesuit.

I am revitalized, relatively, and red-hot radioactive until afresh frazzled like when once our biblical Moses must have been hiking down from mount Sinai millennia ago; until spectators were forced to furnish a veil over his visage by reason of the blinding shine of residual Contact, that is. From this linoleum lot I had gotten much more than what my mind, fumbling feet, and fair share of the bargain could ever purchase. Wherefore an inexhaustible recompense of credit is due.

My redundant round-trip ticket of multiple lifetimes was compressed into one lump sum. At last, I was heartfelt timestamped by the indelible imprints of 'hyper-burg' bounty that thusly computed the consummate Paragon Paradox of an open-ended Pluriseptiplex, hence (...^-0110+^...)!

In my dream were no appendages, only an endless annex of a Matrix. Heavens to Betsy! I went en route for such superior stages, eager to graduate therefrom. Not needing to be matriculated. And I held at hand tiny tweezers or a micrometer to gauge grains of sand as if they were superstars heaped into pyramidal sand dunes in order to tally up the orbs of the Heavens to…

Not unlike Pythagoras of ancient antiquity, in a silent lyceum, I calculated carefully the *innumerable* once and for all:

INVORTIUM

CHORUS

In spite of regularity
Of commonest existence
I've entered insularity,
Alas, above resistance!

Inside a dream myself I find,
Gone forth from room to room
By way of corridor designed
To lighten up the gloom.

But still, into more depth I went
Much more than here on Earth,
As if with one volcanic vent
I felt such molten mirth!

It all began right from the start
As lengthy hallways followed,
And darkness dappled up my heart
Whose half-life only wallowed.

As if in mire I had been
Compared to walls pristine
That glimmered, all devoid o' sin,
Nor anything unclean.

At room and board conventional
I'd long meander deeper
Until inter-dimensional
Translucency slid steeper.

I lay asleep on my stout bed
Amidst that narrow night
And saw some Vision so outspread
It glorified sunlight!

For in pitch twilight everywhere
Glazed one ballroom became,
Whose entity would merely glare
Fair, back at me selfsame!

Wherein a misty mirror lighted
Her whole sheer sheen wet
Hung from a wall-side, so ignited,
Vacant as of yet…

The mirror glinted something more
Than quartz quicksilver-backed
Whose fourth dimension, hefty, hoar
Had nothing that she lacked!

With which fine furniture reflected
Back both walls and floor,
How hung about, as if erected,
Founded evermore.

The absence of a soul persisted,
Aye, whose presence lingered
The Twinity thereof existed,
Steepled, twenty-fingered!

Four hands were held on tightly so
In times all tall and spired;
Two virgins very lovely though,
Gilt, gorgeously attired.

But mirror-imaged, full o' light
The twain fell under spells
Via looking glass eternal framed
By egg-and-dart eggshells.

They vanished into raw thin air
As Nothing crept instead
So glinted from a 'luminaire'
Hung high and overhead.

O creepily as silence grown
Too threadbare, thickly veiled
It had unfolded, still full blown,
Surroundings that prevailed!

Its holy timeless tinge arrayed
But ne'er could enter altered,
Nor any inch to ever fade
If operations faltered!

As kept inside the spirit-room
I stood my ground, enthralled;
Invincible to gloom and doom
Without, which went appalled…

And so, I had resumed my flight
Twixt pilasters quelled quiet;
The dream thereof withstood the plight
Of worldly, warring riot!

Yea, wheresoever I may go
My Hallowed Hallways seethe
And sizzle bright enough, aglow,
That cause my soul to breathe.

I'd then revisit that Ballroom
Where whiteness glared aloft:
What wonder in an old wall-womb
Seldom compared, so soft!

The dream hath ended her concourse
And causeway paved up whole:
How heavenly! as I endorse
The sojourn of my soul.

CHORUS

In spite of regularity
Of commonest existence
I've entered insularity,
Alas, above resistance!

The Big BALL

What ye about to review, dear reader, is an abridged amalgamation of painstaking research rendered by international mathematicians and theorists on the Fourth Dimension. My fervent fascination of the subject matter was once reinforced long ago whilst I studied the essays of Charles Howard Hinton, Immanuel Kant, and the more contemporary Rudolf Rucker; Therein, of course, my most memorable melodrama (in provocative prose) I present therefore. Herewith, upon pages of fantasy, I offer forth hearty discretion to fans familiar with this genre of surrealism, and of 4-D geometry consummated by my abrupt broadcast of interpersonal transaction.

17 "For our light affliction, which is but for a moment, *worketh* for us a far more exceeding *and* eternal weight of Glory; 18 While we look not at the things which are seen, but at the things which are not seen: for the things which *are* seen are temporal; but the things which are not seen *are* eternal." II Corinthians, chapter 4 (Authorized King James Version) An address from God's Good Book that cannot bear false witness by reason of a self-evident Hyper~Sphere Universe divinely lit*

SECTION A

I hiked nature's trail and focused on an ancient restricted area at Inca Machu Picchu, dead ahead. A barbed wire fence jabbed me but I managed to circumvent the metal nettle thereof.

It was quite dismal at the time during my reluctant approach to a forbidden hatchway that lay welded shut about ninety years or so against bedrock. My make-way was to fork open that wrought iron scuttle to suppose where it may lead. *Once, twice, thrice* and with a makeshift crowbar I pried its hulking lid ajar just enough for me to stealthily step in. A detour it was to a rather rib-cage, gaunt, gated abyss with groin-vaulting...

Inside, I went through a very narrow corridor bent back- or that descended, steeply, as if into Sheol. Still~ through my frontier~ by taking the gradual plunge underground, some tunnel necked deeper and deeper into an almost bottomless, baleful Pit. Now, whereas, dreamily bituminous creosote cratered such gargoyle gullets which would neck to a downward degree, self-lit glossy sides seemed to have been the case, rather. Some barometer, noticeably, plateaued wetly with one wayward twitch until I reached rock bottom. Soft and subtle nuances of my bioelectric field bucked back and forth cybernetic hair-implants that detected my plummet. It seemed like my investigations were gauged by tentacles of surveillance.

Hereupon, barricaded before me, in due course, a snow white-polished and spotless vestibule glared, lit up by recessed panels. I had suspected, overhead and suspended above were slimline T12 fluorescent lamps, row by row sizzling nearside the annex, ballast-backed by an endless electronic *brool.* Determined, I trotted on for no purpose whatsoever save mischief that murders *Schrödinger's Cat! Indeed, not until *lo and behold*, the basement I had entered blended into another attenuated, high-ceiling Ballroom of clinical sterility with something rather bizarre at every postern thereat. A looming wall-side labeled <u>ICDD</u> or Inner City District Grid, and designated by nomenclature ***BB,** stared back at me mainly for its nondescript identification namesake. *BB stands for Big Ball, by the way!

*In Schrodinger's imaginary experiment, you place a cat in a box with a tiny bit of radioactive substance. When the radioactive substance decays, it triggers a Geiger counter which causes a poison or explosion to be released that kills the cat. Here, it is a portrayal of impartial physics that bears no record of sentimentality, no matter how blue in the face the Ailurophile may become!

An invasive super-quiet tranquility muted my ears.
The anechoic hyper-hush had shattered my mentality!

A metallic sounding intercom from the Tall Wall, numbered by triple Sumerian swirls of an *888*, inquired, *Where are you going?*

"Egad!" I choked, floored and flabbergasted.

Again an automatic vociferation: "Wherefore art thou, laddie?"

Until when I fumbled for a reply, I squinted at a hairline silver sliver *form* from out of nowhere as umbilical cords of conduit and some age-old pall fell, foiled over the medial lath of a catacomb backroom door. In rippling mercury moiré, its crepe drape allured me, yet yonder over evacuated limbo, as if all of it were with an undercroft mortuary. Not that I intend to sound morbid or anything, but an apt metaphor for mystery by lamplight is needed.

Moving right along, I cascaded via *escalatory shuffling* with its self-lubricated continuum as I was ambushed by every sequestered nook and cranny of outlets and inlets--- the normal nine yards. An hour later or so, there were no more taunts of that voice except for my eerily illumined "parlor of pallor" that remained *aphonic* on the other hand, I'd reckon. Meanwhile, mysterious murmurs made me mumble incoherently compared to the faultless cessation of it.

For at once juxtaposed with an otherwise vast intramural maze- *at point blank range*- an even narrower niche, or ditch doorway to another *dimensionality* dangled at my furtive footing. An imposing overlap of foursquare plasterboard buckled me to my knees; that gave leeway to malleable goop melted with lozenges of metallic linoleum. Soon afterward, I would swoon into a foggy trance.

And on the treadmill of a half-comatose level, I came to~ and still~ this diminutive doorway inched in front of me whilst, when I glanced back whence I came, an over-sized beach ball bouncer of pearliest pallor widened out to about one-tenth of a furlong in diameter; or about 66 feet across! Once more, out of aftershock, I fainted. Then I stood up, revived by its hawk-eye microscope.

The overbearing observance thereof reminded me of my former Valley Brook brainchild. That of an aerial self-maintained, preened primate of a Vacon with wide band coronary panorama for its one-eyed wraparound-retinal visual cortex. For such distinctly specific ornithological avifauna in that region to have been my pretext of an adroit aviatrix ushered in the Avion Sphere I was able to deal with! But, preferably, whose globular kind had hovered over my indoors attendance at a Sizzler Family Restaurant when I scoured dishes and bussed big tabletops in 1984. Though the pots and pans pelted me along a conveyor belt, I recalled consolation from its convex heft and deft distributed to highly tensile, torpedo-like and wonderful elasticity, as it were, effectively illustrated years ago.

Henceforth an old epigram of its appurtenance: "Tie two birds together. Even though they have four wings, they cannot fly." ~The Blind Man. And yet if our quicksilver Vacon of merely *aliferous* or *aligerous* dexterity- not unlike a dragonfly- fluidly flits its fourfold elevons, how much more the transcendent transept of an *MBS?

To blurt the obvious, number 4 appertains to 4-D agility.

*MBS: Mother, or Major Ballroom Super-Sphere (stand aside, *O Superman!)

*O Superman (for Massenet) is a 1981 song by performance artist and musician Laurie Anderson. The monotonous and hypnotic, electronic honk in her masterpiece is a bold benchmark for the occasion at hand.

The sharply sugarcoated and pungent fragrance of hedgerow hyacinth, lavender, honeysuckle and lilac licked the atmosphere for physical reconnaissance unbeknownst by me. Hot visceral vistas of this hush-lush Lakeside and Loam lavished *vernal this scrapbook snapshot of deliberate disclosure. To be sure, Large Lamps of high-ceiling and high-tension backup have mirrored memoirs of their fair share, and with flauntingly floral overflow.

*With not a knuckle sandwich sauntered, frankly, it was April 10, 2023 during the azimuth and zenith of my Yard Lamp of Gloria. The longitude, latitude, and zenith of surveyed geometrical symmetry which- with exquisite flawlessness- like Helen of Troy, was once proclaimed to have launched a thousand ships (unintended cliché). No bystander as myself could even endure such an awesome onslaught of utter loveliness far more curvaceous than the contour of curvature itself!

What the Devil!? Panic stricken, I felt only my frailty, frazzled from what transpired. Nevertheless, in one serene, solid, seamless maneuver the big eight Ball distended and then deflated down to a life-size effigy able to commiserate with one of straggling strength, merely myself! Some faintly humanoid figure bulged slightly from its Quasar Beacon factor, now niveous for continual contiguity. As snowiest permafrost frozen up for an aeon atop Mount Everest, but bathed by sub-stratospheric (UVC) sunlight, so too amidst likelier alacrity, or calling card collective simulacra, its freshest fringe was whiter than bluish-white of quadrillion candlepower output.

Quoth the Hyper Sphere *evermore*: “I was, I am and I shall be, O maverick!” Its iridescence of creamy circumference receded and ballooned forth imperceptibly whereas I waged resplendent rapport therewith! No pineapples and oranges to differentiate, save such blinding blankness self-sufficiently seamless that, even so, whose finest fusion of featureless limbo could consist of quelled quantum foam- pliantly Planck- the Hyper Sphere entirety is only to contain gluons glorified far beyond neutron *Narrowness*!

“Hark! Whither art thou bound?” With its archaic vernacular it thudded thoroughly with warmly mellifluous consonance, but more or less muffled by such a flexible, cushion-assertive mattress and membranous Memory Foam of nothing else except gluon-glorified *stretchability*~ strongest, admittedly, at its weakest interlink!

“I~ I fail to understand, *O flawless One*” [with but one cloying clincher, I branded it just that] “Star-avatar! Who or w~ what are you...?

Awhirl with preemptive deft devoid of presumption, it cornered me, my Major Ballroom Sphere: the MBS! In back of me was one cul-de-sac hindrance which prevented my escape; in front of me, a convex wall of the Big Ball (I call the double B).

Suddenly, the globe levitated much closer as it (with proximity) maximized an entire equatorial girthline of total top-spun exigency, interrogating me, insistingly, "My query hath not been answered as of yet---- " Its *fluminous fluxion* became but overwhelming!

"I just want to pursue something dissimilar, okay? That's where I'm going!" I finalized and puckered my stiff upper lip, trembling.

Take heed of spriest spree! That, of all oddities, I found myself conversant with the self-implosive, intimidating Spheroid deployed by such supernatural, overpowering performance!

Distinctly, I have here imagined an outstretched sheet of tar, or Sheetar that resembles linoleum made of metal, or Metalinoleum in midsection of this compendium (versified). Then, afloat in-vacuo and only 9 meters above its platform, an enormous Ball, 33-blocks in diameter packed with purest, hyper-refined uranium from U-238 ore (howbeit having heaviest isotopes in nature), contains exactly 1,634,160,000,000 tonnes thereof, except only a percentile of what a Neutron Star of "avoirdupois" density would weigh!

*(computation of the **VORTRON** from precedent encounters):

1)	Natural U-238	Weight: 1180 pounds	Per cubic volume
2)	Sphere	Diameter – 33 city blocks	*Radius: 8712 feet*
		3.3 mile-wide Sphere 2.76976E+12 cubic feet	Volume: 2,769,760,000,000 cubic feet

3) Pounds of uranium in Sphere: 3.26832E+15	Translated number: 3,268,320,000,000,000 lbs	
Tonnes of uranium in Sphere 1.63416E+12	Translated number: 1,634,160,000,000	* Mass of Sphere: 1,634,160,000,000 tonnes (totality)

Circumference Formula ------- C=2πr

Spherical Volume Formula ------- V=4/3πr3

Authorized Original Backup

On another level of augmentation, alternately, it altered into the UNIVATRIUM colossal cannonball of gargantuan girth. Every one of which were pluralized to *Pluriseptiplex, that is (...^-0110+^...)! Individually, each one weightily redistributed across Metalinoleum many milliards of times vaster than the Universe flatly laid out like a hyperspace topographic blueprint! Stretch layouts of Univatriums manifest multiverse configurations beyond intelligible *numeracy.*

*Pluriseptiplex is commensurate with googolplex to the *googolplexth* power! It is an open-ended number that can *septuplicate* itself seven times seven in perpetuity as by a multiplication Table I have enumerated one-by-one upon my next and separate folio. I have speculated the inherent infinities thereof to go both ways forward and backward, but *irreplicable* by any other number. Pluriseptiplex cannot be quantifiable either way.

HYPER TABLE

7 x 7 wormhole quantification
wherein every jump from one
row to the next equals seven:

01 08 15 22 29 36 43
02 09 16 23 30 37 44
03 10 17 24 31 38 45
04 11 18 25 32 39 46
05 12 19 26 33 40 47
06 13 20 27 34 41 48
07 14 21 28 35 42 49

Septuagint continuity from a hyper-city hexagon enumerator

My heart palpitated and trepidation tried me to the hilt as if, for the first time in my life, I became bogged down by an inexplicable sensation where instantaneity kept me stone-frozen by comparison! This blissful Entirety resembled supple symmetrical plumpness; an emblazoned encasement of resiliency. Some argent orb of spherical proportion whose accordion pleats pliantly corrugated such a scale-squashing Heavyweight- in that it reasserted itself with nuances of the neutron star. Impossibly compressed~ appropriately apparent.

Meanwhile aloft in unison how high-pitched choruses squealed at once, as numerous necklaces of its <u>crease</u> created kaleidoscopic flits and fits.

Septuplets of varicolored pearls altered themselves to full, life-size trampoline-cradled monstrosities mimicking the Mother-main-throw-ballroom-Sphere in their midst. Finally, everyone's ionized petticoats had quietly quickened abreast to an enormous, nacreous menagerie of separate simultaneity, yet one and the selfsame Big Ball!

Quoth both *hemi~hyper~spheres* that, by analogy from Edwin Abbott's 1884 novella, announced themselves, but one step higher: "Acknowledged! I am distinctly different, outside of what you are accustomed to! For My blank plank that you observe is but a cross section and reference-slice of what I am *consummately* (perforce). Hence up, above and beyond your three-dimensional existence, to down, below and within the very same strata thereof! Or, in other words, may My corpulent curvature be a flawlessly flattened fluid *silhouette* compared to **Omnipotent Embroidery** that *defies any lawful ordinance of spatial stretch-fabric..."

**Exceeds* is a better rendering of that which is immune to infectious apotheosis.

For furthermore elucidated ad hoc, namely, such self-sufficient infrangible infrastructure of *wraparound convexity* is precisely 1.0 x 10^-15, or (to be explicit). The slice of which is a quadrillionth of its whole completion materialized inter vivos as an ephemeral mirage. Whereas its other whole 99.999999999999999 percentage of undetected hyper-wholeness easily transcends man's fleshly flip side of reason- even (ESP) extra sensory perception *per se*- the indivisible stateliness of its gleam of cream balloons, but far more curvaceous than that of a mere sphere the size of the hydrogen-filled Hindenburg zeppelin which exploded in the year 1937 on May 6. Until yet another, extra adjunct thereof addressed itself:

"Accordingly, consider comparisons of thy medieval abacus to My non-quantifiable Pluriseptiplex (...^-0110+^...) before which an innumeracy in all of spacetime preexistence persisted! At this jump of **adjuncture*, our Universe- from end to end- is a cross-section in one of My *Pluriseptiplex Plancks," the Big Ball intoned to me:

**Adjuncture* is my made-up word for an added junction (necessarily supposed).

||||||||||||||||||||||

**Pluriseptiplex Plancks are* googolplex to the googolplexth power of magnitude total cross-sections of slices as thin as a Planck length each. The never comprehensible and forever forbidden Multiverse Universality manifested in one surplus or self-contained aggregate altogether melted into an Entire Entity too infinite for even trigonometry or calculus to survey! The Boötes Void, for example, with a radius of 62 megaparsecs, or 202,216,954.17 light years, is merely a thimbleful pocket on the sponge of its surface!

"Is it a wild will-o'-the-wisp or netherworld sprite?" I initiated an inquiry in rogue rebuttal to my confounded whereabouts nowadays as we, the Sphere and I, were *circummured* by a walled womb environment of pristine insularity. How hollow haunting echoes of some far off Affront Wall with an enfilade enhanced our acoustics backstage.

"Nonetheless!" recoiled the scale-squashing big *Whopper of a 1.6 trillion-ton wrecking Ball Bouncer in an Untimely Reminder of reproof. "Now, no mortal may occupy porcelain insulators of the *Videopolis* Vista (V-V) and loiter!" Or interpreted as *"no man can confront my interface and survive!"* (No, not in reference to Burger King, let alone my Honda's pit-stop on its parking lot premises!)

**Please note:* My first encounter with the *hypersphere* occurred whilst washing dishes, pots, and pans at my Sizzler Family Steakhouse job when I was sweet 16! Back then, I christened it the Avion Sphere which was about 23 feet in diameter.

I beheld myriads of luminous Lava Tube stalagmites refulgent by their tremendous translucency. And very specimen flailing fitful filamentary superstructures of unimaginable brightness! I about-faced away from multitudes of them outstretched, each one, with a garish sleek steel Sheet of sheer sheen or the shiniest *shimmer* that outflanked quivering tributary accompaniment!

Then the Sphere obliged, confidingly: "Thrust out your hand as did Thomas to the empirical rib-side of our sacred Lord Jesus..."

Immediately, its gargantuan garter girdle of anti-gravity waxed forth froth with prefatory bloated blanket that caressed me with an ultra-curved event horizon. I interpreted this rather trans-infinite, distinctly dimpled and opaquely opulent or *soporific super-surface* pressed against my forearms and biceps before I opened my palms along such a glorified, glossy and smooth concord contour, full of interminable continuity! My M-imprinted palmistry poised upward was a sign of surrender to the superiority thereof and at hand where one South Pole underbelly inched down to the top of my head.

Ye Revelation Extraordinaire

I was walking for 33 blocks and the base of a stupendous ball approached me overhead. The opaquest shadow of it expands. I see an umbra take over as everything around me is dark and overshadowed by this enormous Ball. If I could have situated myself to one side, or the other, the convex wall of the sphere towered up to a mile and a half high past the low-level clouds.

But I had happened to be up under its South Pole centerfold. Whereupon nothing appeared save for grim gray, its calm cast caught my attention right quick! Up close, its color differential is tinged in a deep iridescence unearthly and unlike anything I had imagined. From a few blocks away the whole Ball turned blacker the farther I went, yet more rainbow-hued up closer!

Very gradually, as it seemed almost like a large flat ceiling, it curved little by little in every direction as if I were a gnat under the monstrosity of the Unisphere at Flushing Meadow Park in New York City. Tremendously tranquil, this 3.3 mile wide curviest continuity of nothing but a *Primum Mobile. The solidity thereof was tougher than titanium or diamond!

**Primum Mobile:* Dante's depiction of the largest and swiftest sphere in cosmology: the origin of life, motion, and time in the Aristotelian-Ptolemaic universe. Thus this heavenly wonder~ the supreme physical heaven in the universe~ is enclosed only by the Empyrean, the mind of God- videlicet- whose Pluriseptiplex Planck units contain the quantum foam and froth of exponential multiverse manifestations to infinity.

Meanwhile, as I felt dumbfounded by the sheer size of this Ball, I would dimly observe, in particular, how eerily gradual curvature above that receded from me to every side about half a block away, was warped and upwardly extended to this unfathomable sphere it eventually rounded off to be and with an equatorial circumference. A serene anti-gravity quietness & silence oozed forth therefrom!

As if it were packed by purified U^{238} (natural uranium ore)! So refined to a fine powder of non-reflective blackness, that the acme of my vision ended with one ton weight multiplied to 1.6 trillion or notably 1,634,160,000,000 cubic tonnes liquid-compressed into the huge *hull* of its hulking, hefty capacity. The skin of which consists of *neutronium*: 23 meters thick all around & fully impenetrable!

The likeness of which shall have scorched up a megapixel ultrahigh resolution viewer installed to outdated CCTV technology. If at all old electronic gauges gawked at it for barometric pressure atmospheric! *Still, will spiritual Grace guard my eyes, lest they be burnt out of their sockets?* I wondered woefully.

"Satisfied?" the big bowling ball bellowed, self-satisfactorily.

“Egad!” I crooned into awestruck abandonment. “You yield too lithe to touch! An inextinguishable effusive saturation, and ever so wholesome!” [had been my erudite evaluation of it]!

“Now knuckle your fist and pounce Me” reassured the Sphere.
-- I felt challenged by an Arm & Hammer trademark brand.

Inadvertently, I whacked its supple side and the elastic bounce-back of this gesture radiated and rippled reverberation through my mainframe frazzle! Whereas more leal than lubricious with vantage pronouncement the Univatrium sphere seemed, I convulsed and lay stunned by its wherewithal jolt of metaphysics. For as I’d pelt its glaze, feeling for feedback on the Sphere’s multi-surface supernal-- apart from an intimate interim of silkiest cessation-- the stretching of *spaghettification* to the brink athwart the outer fringe or *Edge of Forever* had rushed roundabout me unawares. Its bloated blush of finesse toppled me as I turned, taken aback! Not to admit a turgid unearthly mink mother-of-pearl and a crowned crème de la crème sprinkling that overwhelmed and dwarfed my belittled stature; this with contortions of an inflated hot air and helium-fill dirigible, the 55-meter tall Breitling Orbiter (3) of tough tautness upheld! O how harmoniously down to its sub-scale Planck length afresh!

“Aha!” I exclaimed clammily. “So that’s what a hyper-sphere is meant to feel like: indistinguishable, inseparable, interconnected!”

“Precisely, my dear chap.” Univatrium humored me moreover using an early sci-fi episode from BBC’s *Doctor Who.* With added confirmation, I perceived how whole such concord contour in shrill stillness of *continual causality* permeated all six sides, silently, of the Ballroom suite wherein the *Die Gestalt* of its underbelly had hovered horrendously! Alike Polyhymnia beforehand, my mirrored companion lectured me on this rather telltale topic:

"You see, it's that simple! But, Heaven forbid, never facile! For by analogical disclosure, multiple simulacra of My incombustible billiards Eight Ball, whose full figure 8 is rolled lazily onto its side glorifies globular equilibrium. Each ellipsoid expansion comprised of infinitesimals can coalesce complete *spatiotemporal congruity. Specifically,* *Hilbert Space is of extra vacuumed vastitude with no Planck points but innumerable singularities instead!" We envisaged cubic infinitesimals of Hilbert Space to be so vacuous as to suction up anything whatsoever that enters its hollowest *hyper-hyper-void* of naught, no matter where it is or in what vicinity!

It's as if the forbidden *outdoors* of our infinite multiverse is this Omnipresent Singularity of a no-space & no-time timeless Tenuity. Any point of which will utterly reduce all into nonexistence. Not a black hole, but beyond even *that*! That which was, and is, and what will be boldfaced **embryocto-nihility* or via an embryonic genesis that balloons in a septillionth of a nanosecond. The Time it takes a photon to traverse the distance of Planck length and a slip-slit of it to lie in betwixt the *gliff* of spacetime continuum itself; the ground-state of which embeds the bedrock and foundation of frenetic foam under itself wherein intervals of primordial Preexistence converge, I declare with backup of a Charles Howard Hinton heft!

* *Hilbert Space* is a mathematical concept covering the extra-dimensional use of Euclidean space- id est, a space with more than three dimensions... Hilbert space uses the mathematics of two and three dimensions to try and describe what happens in that which is greater than three dimensions. It is perpendicular to standard 3-D space!

* *Yoctosecond:* A yoctosecond (ys) is a septillionth of a second or 10 –24 s *

I felt baffled by what denuded me of every vestige; the implicit interpretation of it by and large; an appended tongue-twister that caused my mindset to be definitively devoid of depreciation.

"Wherefore with wee contrast of insular investiture, Our supple rubber racquetball radiates the inviolate quasi-image: Yea, one out of innumerable *alternate* sizes sewn up into a hyper-whole sphere whose uttermost Top and Bottom, called *ana* and *kata*, or north and south-pole *hemihyperspheres* cannot be detected by any of the six senses; nor dismally depreciated by thy radar dishes of microwave authentication, if choreographed on an electromagnetic searchlight network," Univatrium patiently pointed out with reverberation.

Its thick brick Empyrean of enveloped curvature had attenuated with sultriest or ionized high-tension accretion, far enough for such lead-shielded spectators to have been accidentally reverted to mere shriveled shrinkage. Alas, caught unawares and unprepared!

At this climactic entr'acte, I felt like Isaiah receiving a seething fossil fuel firebrand to my midriff and tip of the tongue- dispensed, sublingually, by Six-Winged Wonder! Isaiah 6, verses 6 & 7:

6 Then flew one of the seraphims unto me, having a live coal in
his hand, which he had taken with the tongs from off the altar: 7 and
he laid it upon my mouth, and said, Lo, this hath touched thy lips;
and thine iniquity is taken away, and thy sin purged.

Its glorified glitterati deflated dizzily, downward, then slithered off and receded back into itself... and much later, bulged back to a rotund orb of tapered totality! All the while I had to regain my final composure and, in fine, vis-à-vis twin mirrors of a video diorama.

The Twin Paradox of Enveloped Departure

But before the Hypersphere's departure from the year **3113**: that of palindromic weightiness~ I'd venture to exemplify this perfected portrayal of what the Univatrium would materialize in relation to natural surroundings. For firstly, I have had glimpse of the South

Pole point of an infinitely *hyper~spatial* Spheroid to have tapered upwardly extended Planck length silhouettes of it blended to each other throughout one wonderful unendingly harmonious wholeness up and down, fore-and-aft, and all around (including inside-out)!

Secondly, such dilation thereon, that is, over the superficies of the Univatrium-- although temporarily materialized to one 33-block wide, or rather, properly, 33.89423076923077 city-blocks-wide, or 3,525 yards in diameter big Ball-- contains convoluted algorithmic Mandelbrot sets of a sequential series. The Plancks of which (each and every one individually and *hologrammatic*) expand to Uniform Hyperbolic Honeycomb poly-symmetrical lattices which have cells of dodecahedrons uniformly united in a network; as if cubical or bricked together, where in between not even a hair's width can seep in! One of every spherule, as on some cellular membrane, proffers pristine Primula Polyantha sprouts and blossoms of the prominent Primrose, but by analogy only! Not that this botanical species is of flimsy flora, as a floribunda shrub dwarfed by pyramidal pylons of Pennsylvania's Longwood Gardens gorgeous (the 1,100 acreage lot of fifty fabulous topiary trees removes my residual pavement)!

Whereon a multifaceted Surface, one-by-one dials of dilation balloon one billionth of its cornucopia, even the tillage of a terrace or veranda, though castellated and colonnaded conspicuously with chipper chimeras all over, ought to surpass efflorescence!

Nor any of these photosynthetic chlorophyll, pollen, and spore producing processes within horticulture and gardening; neither fat fauna for instance, but deftest convergence of preternatural priority but backs my scientific juxtaposition which proves otherwise:

That the Bald Eagle, the Peregrine Falcon (the staunchest and fastest wild-bird on planet Earth), and Ferruginous Hawk of whom noted ornithologist Arthur Cleveland Bent evocatively praised the Ferruginous Hawk as "the largest, most powerful, and grandest of our buteos, a truly regal bird"~ these three among others~ have one thing in common. Though they may fall prey upon *fresh* flesh and complete meat, the heretofore and hereafter Hypersphere by and large hath something similar if not superior to bi-winged wonder- its pliant plumpness consists of comfortable room temperature-to-the-touch Teflon coating that restores itself and whereof waxy and paraffin-slippery *unicurvaturity* of but continual *curvation* is prima facie felt on one's fingertips... The aftereffect of what would cause the feeler to develop Tactile Defensiveness! With due reverence to the foundress and pioneer of Radiology aboard army field hospital units in the First World War, venerable Marie Curie was well aware of the polonium and radium isotope. Whereupon the integument of Univatrium, *radioactivity* (originally coined by her) perhaps could have been anti-inflammatory and regenerative to the touch!*

*Recall the *Creatorium* to replace the crematorium, the Resurrector instead.

Therefore my exact 33.89423076923077 city blocks wide Ball of 3,525 yardage, then converted to 3223.26 meters & subdivided down to 3,223,260 millimeters in diameter, I would confirm it by a mean metrical radius: 1,611.63 that calculates into a circumference of 10,126.16993661 m. With this in turn, we pause for a moment to verify the cross-sectional Univatrium by my measurement:

Circumference: 10,126.16993661 m (meters)
Surface Area: 32,639,278.509877 m2 (square meters)
Volume: 17,534,146,808.291 m3 (cubic meters)

Also, not to vilify any of the contents thereof, if at all in fine, I venture to conclude a South Pole enveloped departure of the MBS to recede resplendently from reservoirs, aquifers, lagoons and large lakes, ponds, trails, or fields and prairies; from the Sun and Moon, mountaintops, arctic glaciers, or hoariest antediluvian permafrost Alaskan glacier ice recovered from a basin between Mt. Bona and Mt. Churchill at about 30,000 years of age; frozen tundras, sierras, plateaus, cold cataracts, winding waterfalls, undulant hillocks; wet estuaries and aviaries; grasslands with campground parks, rocky terrain, bluffs, cliffs, valleys, meadows and woodlands, evergreen coniferous and deciduous forests; even from alluvial fans, deltas and confluences to riversides, tributaries, streams of overflow and undertow with purling cascades, V-culverts, conduits, quiet brooks; granite bedrock, ravines; crevices, deep gulches, gullies, trenches, ditches; deserts and oases, caves, caverns, canyons, gorges, fjords, inlets, creeks, furrows, fields, fens, swamps, marshes, quicksand, quagmires, peat bogs and bayous; the orchard, grove and grotto; the dormant volcanic vent; gushers, geysers, hot pools, slime and tar pits, and so forth! Plus consolidated withdrawal from every one of these as if it had never arrived in the first place to begin with, id est, the organic Orb itself. Heaven's harmonious portable, globular Empyrean.

Aloft as our queenly three-masted wooden-hulled heavy frigate known as the USS Constitution, armed with 24-pounder long guns, leaves behind bow and stern wavelets, eddies and currents in her wake, so likewise an aurora borealis bequeathed by the MBS with an indelible imprint signature to linger on in lieu of its absence! Again, must I accentuate? For just as our universe could never be circumvented, nor challenged in any way, shape, or formulae, as it were (even via light-speed), in like manner my Herculean Ball!

Elsewhere, like lozenges of flat sheets, the quicksilver mirrors glassily spanned out to numberless platform plates hexagonal and hyper-curved 'around' an open-ended Observable Universe whose radius is 46.508 billion light years (merely one infinitesimal area of my mind-boggling Pluriseptiplex cardinality). The remainder of which suspends some galactic super-clusters. I name a handful: the Virgo, the Hydra-Centaurus (subsumed by the large Laniakea), the Southern Fornax, the Saraswati, including (the following) nearby superclusters like Perseus-Pisces, Coma, Sculptor, Hercules, Leo, Ophiuchus, and the Shapely of their super-cluster extravaganza.

Reticently, I add, so as not to forfeit readership reflection, I can facilitate a larger list of even more distant denizens: (as the Major Ballroom Sphere slips away) Pisces-Cetus Supercluster, Boötes in proximity to its Void, the Horologium-Reticulum, Corona Borealis, Columba, the Aquarius and the Aquarius B, Aquarius-Capricornus, Aquarius-Cetus, Boötes A, Caelum: the largest galaxy supercluster, Draco & Draco-Ursa Major, Fornax-Eridanus, Grus, Leo A, Leo-Sextans, Leo-Virgo, even the afar off Microscopium Supercluster, Pegasus-Pisces; the weightier superclusters Persius-Pisces, Pisces-Aries, Ursa-Majoris, and the remotely vastest Virgo-Coma.

Continuing on to the farthest reaches of observable radio-space are the Hyperion-Proto Supercluster and the Lynx Supercluster; the last four of the cosmic domain, no more named, but codified as by SCL @ 1338+27 at z=1.1, *the* SCL @ 1604+43 at z=0.9, *uttermost* SCL @ 0018+16 at z=0.54 in SA26, *&* MS 0302+17, whose whole counterpart cannot be catalogued so as to avoid redundancy.

The *ambigram* SWIMS reads right side up and upside down.

The *pangram* "the quick brown fox jumps over the lazy dog" is but one sentence or verse whereas we'll welcome both sides, auto-justified, at a time when people bid farewell to each other in "God be with you" instead of today's watered down "Goodbye" (I say) as the word for fear of palindromes *'aibohphobia'* is ironic with which I implore everyone's readership reflection to reconsider.

Hell, even if surface-to-air hypersonic missiles may try to make a scuff onto what had demurely deflated down to sheer nonexistent extinction, I would wager for invincible Rotundity once and for all. If ever targeted to be pulverized, such warheads will have hurtled right through it; whose underside bellyful fortress of so elasticated, stretchable pliancy reasserts itself like flexible ether either way. Its rotund rubber-like resiliency had caught a fleeting back-scatter and mirroring of Reality reversed! Momentarily inverted as on a crystal looking-glass that, with immaculate imaging, replays everything in real-time, but backward, under such a colossal collapse!

Whereas, at the flip-side of all existence- of which humans are totally unaware- everything returns to its former origin whence we were created. The unutterable run-of-the-mill return *from casket to the cradle* while we all regress backwards and shrink into infancy. From an *NDE tunnel- counterclockwise- to tunnel in utero.

*NDE stands for Near Death Experience reported by the dying resuscitated back to life; especially ones which share an encounter with holy Light at the end of the tunnel

The Intimate **INTERIM** via Versification
(manifest verbatim)

STRONG THRONG

O iron orb ordinaire unveil
Thy convexity so wraparound,
How whole that will prevail
Forevermore and all unbound.

Opaquely aloft dark attired
With neutronium illustrious,
Impregnable entity acquired
Amidst titanium industrious!

Far too heavy for any scale,
Whose south pole touches me;
Bent back from head to tail
And fore-and-aft seamlessly!

Gargantuan gold, as it were,
It glisters mother o' pearl
Uranium packaged by no blur

Save glitter fit for a girl!

I quoth, nevermore affected
Nor surface scuffed is this,
For effulgently resurrected
Be the Supersphere business.

Neither scarred by harpoons
Or by missiles contemporary;
That indefatigably balloons
Back on itself as temporary!

Multiple via Pluriseptiplex
To uniformity ultra-arrayed,
Alike mirrored by a Rolodex
Roundelay carousel overlaid!

If ever she deftly deflates,
Dwindling down out of sight
Her hyperball reinvigorates
Ethereal luminiferous light!

Tho the world waxes bizarre,
Cacophony caught uproarious,
Impenetrable each of ye are:
O agleam glaringly glorious.

* CONTINUED *

-

INVOCATION

Univatrium viably beautiful
Glare inviolability dutiful

07/12/20, confirmed 07/13/20

Envisaged in the park thrice
and on the Fourth in my home
with a vision of it overhung
for 33 blocks in diameter as
Harmonic Convergence was the
same number thereof in years
backward to 1987 accordingly!

Afterwards with the aforesaid- unlikely but purely possible- the elegant *l'esprit d'escalier* literally "the mind of the stairs" in French, is thinking of a perfect comeback after the conversation has ended. Wherefore, what impressions or indentations has the identity-yielded UNIVATRIUM vouchsafed on your behalf?

As my midget mindset tried to grasp at intellectual straws and possible pipeline bamboos, I staggered aback as It continued: "The tip residue of Me (to clarify it into lay language, let alone my twin *hyperhalves* within Me, although conjoined contiguously as above, so below My equatorial circumference materialized spatially) stays forever out of concord contact and all inaccessible! The remainder- need I reemphasize- carries undercarriage curvature perpendicular to right angles of every spacetime coordinate. Yea, but mind you, nonetheless: *Indeed*, My concrete immutability will one day- away *in far-off futurity*- be unraveled by old Ariadne's thread of complex computation..."

To this end I had total recall of Pluriseptiplex complexification outlined as this gigantic googolplex to the *googolplexth* power is exponentially exposed from such simplicity narrowly notated:

(– … ^ … +)
NEAR INFINITY

Or with open-ended, either way, enumeration up and down the hyper-curvature of the MBS! That which curves beyond limit and enters into self-infinitude. See something endlessly curvier that an ordinary ball (impossible though it may seem) and numbering falls headlong folded up wherewith spacetime folding is not necessarily inconceivable. Can you turn an ordinary hollow ball inside out, but without puncturing it? Unanswerable, albeit, yet a piece of cake in *Hilbert Space!

*Hilbert Space is this mathematical concept covering the extra-dimensional use of Euclidean space~ or a space with more than three dimensions. Hilbert space will use the mathematics of two and three dimensions to try and describe what occurs in space greater than three dimensions. On the other hand, the highest number elucidated is the

*Googolplex that, written out, spans this many volumes: 10,000,000,000,000,000,000,000,000,000,000,000,000,000,000,000,000,000,000,000,000, 000,000,000,000,000,000,000,000,000,000,000,000. Each of those volumes holds a million zeros!

Author's note: In my previous version of Yard Lamp of Gloria, an anonymous googologist had megafugagargantugoogolplex listed for one of many named numbers that I found utterly fascinating.

Here is my makeshift 'googological' survey appropriated on the next sheaf (page). The horribly incomprehensible *googolplex is to my knowledge more than enough for anyone's sufferance, I admit.

*The much larger number googolplex has been enciphered out as 1 followed by a googol zeros. While this inconceivably *unquantifiable* number can easily be written as googolplex = 10 googol = 10 (10100)! Using the exponential notation, it has often been claimed that the number googolplex is so large that it can never be written out in full. For more information, please check out http://www.googolplexwrittenout.com/

The googol, that is the number of zeros to follow after the truly horrific googolplex is like having ten grains of sea-sand squeezed into a cubic millimeter and multiplying each one to fill the volume of the Observable Universe: a sphere with a diameter of about 28 billion parsecs (93 billion, or 9.3 × 10^10, light years). The tally is 10 to the ninetieth power (10^90) grains of sand in any direction! Then take such a surplus sum and multiply it with 100,000,000,000 more observable universes of the aforementioned. And this is just a pygmy peek at what googolplex can add up to! If only 1000 is as One times Ten to the third power, out of just 3 zeros to the right we come up with One Thousandfold, how much more with merely one followed by a googol zeros? In brief, the googolplex notated:

1 x 1010^100

ADJUNCTION 1

My hyper-numbers or *innumerables.*

So that these are pronounceable, I have each of them unaltered. Now the second one consists of every mathematical point in the universe crowded together, within which each selfsame universe exists and added up with every other mathematical point to the surplus sum or total space-time tapestry thereof. The exponential potential factor per each upper order of number is another universe with points agglomerated altogether as a Matryoshka or Babushka doll inwardly as well as outwardly unidirectional. But, of course, so much to the point of reaching a transcendent dimension! The (< & >) that flank such a number signifies pure parallel power x 10.

ubiquiuncericosa
< ubiquiducericosa >
ubiquitrecericosa
ubiquiquattuorcericosa
ubiquiquintecericosa
ubiquitisexcericosa
ubiquitiseptcericosa
ubiquitiocticericosa
ubiquinoncericosa
ubiquidecicericosa

ubiquitivigintunceriquosa
<<<<<< ubiquitivigintiduceriquosa >>>>>>

ubiquitivigintitreceriquosa
ubiquitivigintiquattuorceriquosa
ubiquitivigintiquinteceriquosa
ubiquitivigintisexceriquosa
ubiquitivigintiseptceriquosa
ubiquitivigintiocticerixota
ubiquitivigintinoncerixota
ubiquitivigintidecicerixota

gigolubiquitivigintuncerixota
<<<<<<<<<<<< gigolubiquitivigintiducerixota >>>>>>>>>>>>
gigolubiquitivigintitrecerixota
gigolubiquitivigintiquattuorcerixota
gigolubiquitivigintiquintecerixota
gigolubiquitivigintisexcerixota
gigolubiquitivigintiseptcerixota
gigolubiquitivigintiocticeriplex
gigolubiquitivigintinonceriplex
gigolubiquitivigintideciceriplex

CONT.

ADJUNCTION 2

Designations of the following numbers have changed by reason of an entirely holier dimension due to not enough space to contain every point within a point of a point whereof each is our selfsame universe multiplied almost indefinitely. The last ten of this list, as if before the infinite, takes on another transcendent realm so far, far beyond numbering that nothing exists~ not even space-time continuum~ except that very entity of an infinite enumerator, but never quantifiable. As it if were a Singularity (everywhere and nowhere)!

giquevigiunpluceriplex
<<<<<<<<<<<<<<<< giquevigidupluceriplex >>>>>>>>>>>>>>>>
giquevigintriduplex
giqueviginquattuoplex
giqueviginquintaplex
giquevigisexaplex
giquevigiseptaplex
giquevigioctorium
giqueviginonarium
giquevigindecurium

gigunium
<<<<<<<<<<<<<<<<<<<<< giducium >>>>>>>>>>>>>>>>>>>>>
gigatrium

giquorium
giguintium
gigasexota
gigaseptira
gigooctera
gigonanusa
gigodecira

viguna
<<<<<<<<<<<<<<<<<<<<<<<<<< viducis >>>>>>>>>>>>>>>>>>>>>>>>>>
* vatrium *
liquora
liquinta
lucexota
luceptosa
horoctera
horrinusa
horridora

Pluriseptiplex

Important to note, the Pluriseptiplex can also on its own be but a vertical slash, | that intersects the ∞ to represent near-infinity as an infinitesimal fraction just short of the Infinite [presumably]. The truly choking clincher I have ever felt to strangle me was my great grapple with Space and Time itself. My years-ago study of Einstein and *Charles Howard Hinton led me to believe in our absolute tiny existence in the middle of nowhere when we remove all references. Where the mysterious median of a 4-way thoroughfare contains an extra dimension, as if it were the oft inconspicuous isthmus of two lands between the living and the dead; between time and eternity, and in betwixt, whilst we are transfixed, the subconscious and the eternal! In fine, furthermore, I can conclude that sizes and times are relative to one another only by comparison. If you were to float in pure vacuity of naught-- no size, nor weight could be delineated of and from yourself whatsoever. Wherefore, in sheer nothingness, no distance is meaningful, and thus that haunting sensation of pure infinity!

*Infinity is something we were introduced to in our math classes, and later on we learn that infinity can also be used in physics, philosophy, social sciences, etc. Infinity is characterized by a number of uncountable objects or concepts which have no limits or size. This concept can be used to describe something huge and boundless. It has been studied by plenty of scientists and philosophers of the world, since the early Greek and early Indian epochs. Notably, in writing, infinity can be noted by a specific mathematical sign known as the lazy-eight and *swirly* (∞) created by John Wallis, an English mathematician who lived and worked in the 17th century.

The infinity symbol (∞) represents a line that never ends. The common sign for infinity, ∞, was first time used by Wallis in the mid 1650s. He also introduced 1/∞ for an infinitesimal which is so small that it can’t be measured. Wallis wrote about this and numerous other issues related to infinity in his book Treatise on the Conic Sections published in 1655. The infinity symbol looks like a horizontal version of number 8 and it represents the concept of eternity as endless and unlimited. Some scientists say, however, that John Wallis could have taken the Greek letter ω as a source for creating the infinity sign (such is one of many instances for representation).

PLURISEPTIPLEX

Via a severely red-shifted background due to too-distant numbering, for this cause, the near-infinity supernumerary nature thereof is lain lazily, but intersected by a vertical slash as only a cipher short of an *innumerable outstretch to infinity, or as it were one step before (∞)!

The Footnote Analysis

Why should there be only three dimensions in space? Do we have a four-dimensional existence? But are we conscious of it? If there are four dimensions, can anyone access the incomprehensible reality thereof? To pursue such a lofty question as this, Charles Howard Hinton (1853-1907), who speculated brilliantly on the idea, set out intuitive exercises for students and professors alike to utilize in order to touch upon four-dimensional spacetime. Since he was an astute and gifted English-born mathematician best known for his writings and inventions aimed at helping to visualize the Fourth Dimension, Hinton was one of the very first mathematicians to write at length about it. He anticipated many of Einstein's discoveries, and~ what's even more astonishing~ he did so analogically, without the aid of any experimental data. Many of his ideas are still debated in scientific circles.

*Now, not much dissimilar to my Pluriseptiplex, the Absolute Infinite (symbol: Ω) is an extension of the idea of infinity wrought up by mathematician Georg Cantor. It can be thought of as a number that is bigger than any other conceivable or inconceivable quantity, either finite or transfinite. Cantor linked the Absolute Infinite with God, and believed that it had various mathematical properties; one of which included the Reflection Principle (as if infinite attributes recognized only by finite consciousness): every property of the Absolute Infinite is also held by some smaller object.

This is one of Georg Cantor's excerpts in German, then in English:

Es wurde das Aktual-Unendliche (A-U.) nach drei Beziehungen unterschieden: erstens, sofern es in der höchsten Vollkommenheit, im völlig unabhängigen außerweltlichen Sein, in Deo realisiert ist, wo ich es Absolut Unendliches oder kurzweg Absolutes nenne; zweitens, sofern es in der abhängigen, kreatürlichen Welt vertreten ist; drittens, sofern es als mathematische Größe, Zahl oder Ordnungstypus vom Denken in abstracto aufgefaßt werden kann. In den beiden letzten Beziehungen, wo es offenbar als beschränktes, noch weiterer Vermehrung fähiges und insofern dem Endlichen verwandtes A-U. sich darstellt, nenne ich es Transfinitum und setze es dem Absoluten strengstens entgegen.

The Actual Infinite (A-U.) was differentiated according to three relationships: firstly, insofar as it is realized in the highest perfection, in the completely independent extra-worldly being, in Deo, where I call it Absolute Infinite or, for short, Absolute; secondly, insofar as it is represented in the dependent, creaturely world; thirdly, insofar as it can be understood in abstracto by thinking as a mathematical quantity, number or type of order. In the last two relationships, where it appears to be a limited A-U. capable of further multiplication and in this respect related to the finite. presents itself, I call it Transfinitum and set it strictly against the Absolute. (This was where Cantor would not even dare equate his rationale with what was truly infinite in every way, which was none other than God- according to his churchly Lutheran inclinations).

Georg Ferdinand Ludwig Philipp Cantor

And now, **SECTION B** next page

The Close Call

We sailed out, insistently,
Before some surly sizzle-
For now, the ocean glistened glee
Until with misty drizzle:

"Yea, stay abaft!" I yelled for Mike
Who at the poopdeck cast
Brocaded nets on waves that spike
Where winds began to blast-
We never felt upheaval like
This vomitory vast!

Harnessed, aboard our fishing ship,
We scooped uploaded lorries
Of barnacles, with rigging grip,
The legend of old stories...

"Mike, pull!" I called, all rubber-clad,
"Behold yon whitecap waves!"
Cried he, "How horrible, how mad!
They'll flood us to our graves..."

I then reported, Nay, not so!
And hauled another burden
Aboard my schooner to and fro
Tossed terribly, I'm certain,
By Heaven's hoary haze aglow
Midst firmament and curtain.

Echoingly the plankways shook
As waterspouts spewed nearby~
"Mike, manifest in your logbook,
Their writhing horror hereby!"

'Four foamy tubes whirl wildly
Protuberant and lengthwise,
As if to yet defile me
Or wherewithal my strength lies.'

Forefront and full astern waves wan
Would drench the deck and floorboard
With frightful froth that caked upon
Our trawlers twined with more cord!

"Set sail, aye!" Mike semaphored
An EPIRB lest she'll sink~
Some mermaid in a pinafore
Appeared, blithely blue-pink.

A sprite at hand it was, we wondered:
Warning us of doom,
As lightning flashed o'er us and thundered
A deafening, stentorian KABOOM!

The waterspouts retreated then
Whence we lurched on our way-
Our sail ships were saved, Amen!
We wailed: "Whoa! Give-way!"
Both Mike and I no more again
Record this dismal day.

Post-storm it was, a languid lull
Had calmed cargo adrift-
Cod-packed entirely her hull-
God gave us such a gift!

The Awful Fury

BALLAD

* * * * * * * * * * * *

Contingency or fire drill,
My megaphone I rattle!
Beware of the Tsunami Hill
To wash away our battle...

There is a raging sea, somewhere
Bulged by a hurricane,
With waves of foam-capped
Breasts but bare, alas,
Which wax and wane!

Now nakedly unleashed, fresh froth
Frenetic lathers forth
A hydrogelid briny broth
Appareled by the north:

Coruscant curtains overhung
Illumine this glazed ocean
With glitter off a cloven tongue,
Whose tincture spells a potion...

Where witches and saints soulful join
Each other hand-in-hand
Aboard sailships to yet purloin
Alchemical command!

Colossal cones could undulate
And lash out at them both
With what no mortal may abate
By grimoire, neither quoth!

Upheaving heavy water churns
Beneath but winds which yowl;
That echoes what my soul discerns-
Oft grimaced at per scowl.

Found fore-and-aft by boat or raft,
Grown great and swollen yet,
Tall tidal waves of no witchcraft
Nor blessing bloat forth wet!

No matter what the state of mind
Where woeful waves wax grim,
Fat Atargatis, gargantuan reclined,
Spews tempest to the brim.

If ever I end up insouciant
To pure Power outspread,
This memory of Her- laid lucent-
Blushes me stout red!

2 Chronicles 7:14
King James Version
14 If my people, which are called by my name, shall
humble themselves, and pray, and seek my face, and turn
from their wicked ways; then will I hear from heaven,
and will forgive their sin, and will heal their land.

Stella Maris

The Star of the Sea

While whitecaps heave up loftily
And the overall surf glistens fairly,
There be beacons that shine up softly
Afloat thereupon to the brink barely.

While wail the poopdeck steam whistles
From our ferryboat Bounty galore,
I can still discern Light as it drizzles
O'er each lantern ablaze evermore:

Buoy beacons are they abroad cast
Overboard by a pulley and reel-
Then adrift automatic, strewn vast
On an ocean as shiny as steel!

Where the gweduc and barnacle cling
To the keel of our wayfaring schooner,
Ghostly Light, lilting lambent, awing
Joins this chorus in need of a tuner ...

Tho' the brazen slits wheeze with a screech
From our keyboard calliope crying,
We rejoice in such melody each
Whilst breathiest, brazenly sighing.

Aye, may mariners rig rope and mast
Fore-and-aft, having halyards brocaded;
Let our sailship showcase Light cast
Deployed roundabout her inundated!

Let Light glister and transpierce the mist
Thickened up as forthwith may she shine-

Yea, we pray, that pure Peace void o' fist,
Nor of sword would secure rope and line.

While tempestuous tides toss awry
With a hurricane heftily churning,
Throughout Life buoys bob by and by,
And, of course, still their torchlight
Keeps burning ...

Epiphany

In Nineteen Eighty-Six,
I felt a sheer Steel Sheel
Facilely handle bricks,
Aflame and very real.

Regardless what direction
Seemed rigged reality,
Selfsame- with one perfection
Vouchsafed- Vitality
Paved permafrost per section
That healed my malady ...

For Sheel was once ignited
Inside some arc tube old,
Whom I have whole-invited
Throughout my life unrolled!

She hallows my stout bed,
And dredges up old dreams ...
This doormat Vat outspread,
Eviscerated, gleams!

The bloated blanket blisters
All night and day, incessant-
Whence fairy folklore ministers
Delight and sprite fluorescent.

Old French vanilla crème
Shines forth froth top afresh,
Too bright for Light agleam-
Too nude for flaunted flesh!

Shoo! hush! If ye offend her-
Ungrottily grow Graces-
To blush and gush up tender,
One bodily oasis ...

Yea, six-dimensional
Lay long ago revealed
An unconventional
Relationship congealed:
Oft soft (I'll mention Lull),
Immaculately healed!

I praise, cannot conceal:
Tall Taper candlesticks
Long lit en clair Steel Sheel,
In Nineteen Eighty-Six!

YHX 3113

Walls ever so selfsame,
Were white immaculate,
And ceilings glared aflame
Lest night attack you yet.

Effulgent round-the-clock,
One Titan Teflon Tongue
Was hung on high to shock
Ladders of every rung!

By pulleys self-suspended,
Electromagnets shone
Aloft but recommended
For lighting felt full blown.

I gazed at one of these
Transducers in each lamp,
As ozone cast a breeze
At me inside my camp!

But bivouac and stationed,
We laid our rug naps out
And waited, feeling patient
For glorified Gold stout ...

Three-one-one-three: the year
Persists with palindrome,
With wall-side siles sheer,
Each waffled up in foam.

The Y-H-X was named
For Yellow Heat X-ray
And neutron spray inflamed
Too hot for either sex, eh?

An underground vault-womb
Will overshadow Time
Long after all the gloom
Hath fled back to her slime ...

Immaculate instead
Tall walls outshine my years
By me dreamed of in bed,
Beside wide chandeliers.

With ferroconcrete force
One Wall spreads infinite
Where I ensconce, endorse
Our fellowship intimate!

Would that old permafrost
Stay creamy crowned for me:
Such citywide Smyrna lost
Restores her profound glory.

Ninth-century Ceropolis,
No more a tomb of stone,
Lay subterranean as this
Walled intramural throne!

Smyrna's fine future city
It be throughout my maze
Of loveliest layout pretty,
Hence heartfelt polonaise!

Beyond grim, gritty litter;
Upon some Tarmac street,
Linoleum mirrors glitter
Agleam: a tar-back sheet.

Whose starriness distends
Foursquare for many miles;
That never fades nor lends
Out Rolodex stretch-files!

Whence willy-nilly moments
Through permafrost remain,
Still freeze-framed up by omens
And prophecies inane ...

Hereby I hope to find
My needle in her haystack
Quotidian, though reclined:
Impossible to stay back!

My colossal

Companion

The 33-block wide
Big Ball I comprehend:
No more than this inside
Of it will spacetime bend.

But billion tons it weighs
Me down, though levitated-
A scant few inches away
From ground up, elevated!

Whose underbelly slightly
Is curved away from me,
Upward gradual that might be
Bulged convex seamlessly-

The gigaton Big Ball
Packs perfect sphericity,
Though toweringly tall,
Found quiet, eerie, pretty

Whose Univatrix namesake
Stays timestamped on her hull:
Over any birthday aflame-cake
With such interminable lull ...

So silent, full of hush power,
She'll shine electrum cream
Overhung above rush hour
Of car combustion and steam.

Up o'er some city park
The spheroid, may it hover-
Whose bulge distends, I mark,
Enough to darkly cover!

Linoleum-lithe cream
That glistens glaze o' glory,
Pearlescent, curved agleam,
Yields uranium by the lorry!

Now nacreous enlarged
This Univatrium Bouncer
Would condescend recharged
With U ^{238}: my announcer.

No, not a bomb deployed,
Nor any warhead threat-
Just simply undestroyed
Is the Big Ball shiny wet!

In nineteen-eighty five,
The avion sphere appeared
To me, bright white, alive
From ceilings chandeliered.

Still hitherto the same,
Midst bedrocks of a canyon-
By 'roid riverside, aflame-
My comeliest companion!

By Aglaia Marusin
March 19, 2023

CONCLUSION

Shattered from sheer shock, I blindly noticed, goggle-eyed, the all-pervasive inconceivable investiture of an alembic rubber supple bottle, or Klein bottle TRANSDUCER that seared the fluorescent-lit facility with its wavering wash of whiteness. Cold cathode-rays of hyper-holy <u>wholeness</u> *surrounded* it! Its substantial, wraparound wrinkle of wimpled white Light still blinded my envisagement of the like; an ebon asphalt permanence paved into bone marrow and *tunica-intima* of one's essence in myocardium! Such properties of supernal exposure stealthily seeped into me and eclipsed any of my evasive strategies until I flinched away from the surreal situation at boot camp bivouac! Again, within self-shapely trans-luminous flux sub rosa, or under infrared refulgence, hove heavy *3C 273 quasar-conveyance of an utterly incontestable superpower equipoise. By stateliest perfection, although diminutive, still overall gargantuan! An unsurpassed paragon paradox peradventure.

*3C 273 is a quasar with a heavyweight black hole 885 million light-years away!

An inserted short story:

The Herculean Ball

Where woods are thickly laid
And apple trees spread round,
This forest ne'er would fade
Away for she'll stay crowned

Inside whole hallways silent
Built desolate and stout red,
God's mirror quivers violent
Wi' freshness ever outspread

An endless traffic of utility trucks and shopping carts shuffled by; some manipulated with waldoes of automated arms. These were used for transporting goods and merchandise plus lorry-loads of supplies for a large labyrinth construction project. Everywhere, pedestrian passageways were clogged and crowded by bustle and hustle of daily activity.

I was seated at the foreground of a building site along with 9411, my co-worker and friend. Fortunately, we had forked out a sustainable boon from a city district deal and walked winsomely via viaduct canal.

"So what's cooking in furnace 291?" he wondered why, pointing to a far-off bulged tubular edifice right smack at the backdoor of the hallway chamber.

"I dunno, Joe." I preferred to call him just that instead of by the number that designated every one of us with citizenship in this far-fetched Futurity. "Hell, I suppose it's up to the quarter master and General in chief to maintain prolonged heat for this whole facility-what do you think?"

"Gosh, I believe it to be true blue, big buddy!" 9411 had finalized to me. Our city district controllers, purposely as it were, happened to have global authorization to go ahead and erect tall walls for this vast maze of theirs, that is. Still, at such a point, we were more or less spectators rather than contributors to an enterprise profit margin masted and totem poled on the works as such. "So much for the corporate hogwash!" he sneered under his nose against the ozone-pungent air, mindful of his work ethics.

You see, it was certainly a humongous undertaking that military adjutants and civilian adjuncts of the Metro-Aorta urban center had invested in. Namely, 9411 and (I, nominated by number 3185), in teamwork were mere cogs of the conglomerate empire and emporium hand-in-hand, but- better yet- participants in particular to an urban bowl and sprawl project sponsored by the surrounding supercity multiplex. At once, howbeit, to break apart our sit-along monotony on a stagecoach metal bench, our truck conveyor arrived, as always, on-time. Our puerile TGV maglev!

Both Joe and I boarded the over-sized, self-automated shopping cart and, like toddlers on some baby seat silly spree, we went. Whisked away by ourselves together therein as casters and swivels swooned the riders; that have done their job just the same: *Vroom*! For while en route to Thermal Transfer 291, we wallowed with window-shopping (at least cyberspace virtually) along the way by gawking dumbly at storefronts which would wonderland the inner intramural causeways and alleys where our carpool cart careened and then trundled through. Forsooth, it was a convoy of conveyance of tremendous traffic to no end, how it was prefigured.

"--- So old Ethel managed to get out of that walled interlock in one peace, eh?" 9411 was hellbent on an explanatory uproar on behalf of his mother-in-law, lugubrious as ever. Even so, since he had nothing worthwhile to yap about.

"Is that so?" I countered quizzically. "I never knew she showcased a spry springboard!"

Joe giggled and acknowledged me for far too long to not necessarily nettle with domestic affairs. Our families had been partitioned from our official position with Thermal Transfer Two-Ninety One, or TT 291, customarily initialized among many more acronyms... Apparently, the giant joke was water-ballooned upon all of us during our workday banter.

Now the intercom cackled and coughed overhead, hereby with its all-important announcement: "Dear ladies and gentlemen, TT 291 will be arrived at in half-an-hour. Please standby for disembarkation."

"--- So Ethel concluded the entire matter, by golly," continued wryly my trustworthy colleague, co-worker and Metro-Aorta compatriot, Joe, just to fill in for the gap of our shuffling trip, "and snoozed soundly that very night-shift."

"You mean to tell me she slept on the job?" I glared at him incredulously.

"Aye!"

"Aha… I see," I said soggily. "And it looked like the doggone interlock failure had gotten the best of her, no doubt, regardless of a fail-safe device."

"Alas, until I slept on it myself, because of her! You ought to know- *she*, being my relentless kindred of reminders… and so forth." And so on with the soap opera as we meticulously manned our stations from pillar to post.

Our entourage of shopping spree or queue had nonetheless lumbered along sequential tracks that, each one, with an assigned department, determined destination of every cart by a timetable directory. Whether driven to Metro-Aorta or Thermal Transfer 291- either selection- all of the walled up or immured high-ceiling megalopolis contained crossroads and switches and intersections prefabricated precisely for foreordained operation of transport. In addition to such complexity as this, there were also supersized portals of a multi-tunneled Vomitorium, moreover, which would interconnect expressways throughout the inner city gridlock and outer-city suburbs and environs for more exact, punctual barrel-and booth, canister-and cask, and car-and cart configuration.

But for our own convoy of conveyance therewithal, it was enough of a swivel wheel sprawl of undercarriages, whereupon an intermittent flange flywheel and sheave or high tension shuttlecock contact pumped power from overhung netting of elaborate electrification interlinks latticed up with scaffolding and bloated insulators to and fro or fore and aft if ventured upon overseas! The latter, let alone, interconnected to a more remote Hydropolis (an industrial supercity of waterworks), the plumbing of which was not dissimilar to our bodily network of an arterial circulatory system!

Back at base, Joe quieted down and silenced our comical conversation as something palled over his countenance. I gestured to him, full wondering what in heavens had tackled him right then and there, and I wasn't to entertain memories of his long past yard-line of scrimmage screw-up, nor his punt stunt at a college football fumble. Rather than to freshen frivolities, the imposing iceberg of our moratorium melted with, "What's the matter?" and *"What's wrong?"* (the very first line from an old movie directed by George Lucas in 1971, THX 1138, of course) as I pried at his unsettling stupor. We were on an elevated sidewalk stilted by stanchions.

"Nothing, nothing really--- it's just that the Tall Wall at Thermal Transfer Two Hundred and Ninety-One awaits out our priority presence of Attendance," he went on to illustrate for me, pointing out potential ramifications of an oddity not numbered before, nor ever.

"You mean to tell me the TW-TT 291 is alive and conscious?" I gasped, feeling pallid all over… "--- self aware?!"

"Affirmative, lad. And check this out! It was ascertained to have been self-conscious ever since the installation thereof in the year 2108---"

"But this is 2113!" I interjected, surprised and aghast with butterfly flutter in my belly. I swallowed the update down in trepidation. "So it had five years to remain alone, desolate and unsupervised until for subtle sentience to awaken therein! Now I'm really concerned." And hereafter, emotive melodrama could not even suffice for apprehension, whereas unscientific sentimentality only left a soppy mess. We were trained for rash and unexpected contingencies to crop up from Demeter's cornfield *equazione a due incognite* (equation with two variables)! In simpler terminology, the absoluteness of prima facie evidence~ that which we scrutinize at face value~ might as well wield one syzygy of twin flames, but paradoxically polar opposites. One above and one below, or with up-down characteristics! In experiential clarification, I realized that *that Thing* in there, stationed at the TT-291 vac-shaft, contains a cornfield cornucopia whose charge is magnified quadrillions of times up from some single proton and neutron nuanced by subatomic particles like up-quarks and down-quarks and so forth. The sustainable $U\text{-}^{238}$ natural isotope at ground-state stability was the suitable orb and erg for counterpart containment amidst moderator rods submerged in D^2O or Heavy Water (deuterium oxide).

The uranium atom is all that was needed for self-inflationary expansion, but unbeknownst to us all, a rogue spray of neutrons (once prerequisite for nuclear ignition) predominated like leukemia where white blood cells supersede the red in cancer of the blood. An organic alchemy of transmogrification it was and right down to subatomic substrata. Paranormal phenomena finer than a gamma ray wavelength which is smaller than a few tenths of an angstrom, subsisted surreptitiously, that is. None of our detectors could zero in on what went awry!

Evidently, this was a too problematic 'fissile issuance' for Metro-Aorta to overcome, let alone handle. For fusion had been the key factor forward on; specifically, to induce the backup of quantum foam that can concretize quasi-conscious to superconscious self-awareness and psychometric sympathy among many walls, called *mures*, plastered up by lead-shielded radioactivity-immune independent automatons unawares! The Management Corporation Personnel, MCP guardians and keepers of the fusion reactor itself, tried to take it upon themselves to resolve the inevitable issue, but to no avail. Reinforcements were warily deployed likewise to perhaps hamper the hyper-progress of spirit-induced mures, as engineers oft christened them to be.

Meanwhile, blindly blankest wall-sides of insular investiture consequently side-surfaced forth out of nowhere, which encased an anti-gravity cradled colossal scale-squashing neutron star prototype (not to be mistaken for the *Real Thing*), or Heaven forbid, *not that it was ever sponsored by the Coca-Cola soft drink company*, as if its glitz of billboard bombardment placarded my sacrosanct inner Eye with woeful wanderlust, nor the Illuminati for that matter! Neither by EYE (Hg) lamps I had sported up for offertory glory illumined once before. At any rate, this newly emergent manifestation of Pulsar perpetuated bona fide, putting to shame our worldwide heap of timepieces and chronometers, like an atomic clock clandestinely closed in upon us deep inside the vac-shaft Vat of the bulged tubular furnace, for the record. Regrettably, to our consternation, such was the case.

In our eerily lengthened pause of the wake up call, my reliable co-worker and best friend, frazzled though he was, wondered: "So you say, this mountainous metric-ton titan of a tall ball is upheld, heavily housed in the framework of a mere metal cage? Indeed, not as-of-yet interrogated?"

Elsewhere, outside of our computerized company, the scientific community of impertinent inquisitors and rude jabbers pried and prodded at the circumferential whereabouts of this Big Ball now expanded to an almost citywide size…

"Indubitably, 9411. Let us not underestimate it." I surmised in answer to such feasibility that had already dawned on me. "Preferably, Faraday cage ultra-electrified." I corrected his question. But Joe nudged me as he shrugged into a fearful fret, disconsolate outright! His facial features: from frown to grave grimace, then a scowl of utter concentration as he elaborated: "Allow me to disclose the contents thereof, my curious 3185."

I clenched anxiously my velvet seat with palms perspiring as Joe justified himself on the observation he had conducted under laboratory conditions awhile back. His push-comes-to-shove showcase punched pedantry to a pulp with one knuckle sandwich of proof found in an admixture of potent pudding.

"Okay, it's like this," he elucidated tremulously. "Cosmologists over a dozen years ago, plus another decade back, discovered some white hole in the middle of our city inflate into a ballooned, anti-gravity suspended neutron star cocooned in stasis. Totally unaffected by our surroundings and close proximity thereunto. Perfectly parallel to the physics of spacetime territory which was moreover non-warped or not at all tugged at or pulled by its billion-billion g-force gravitation, believe it or not."

From my recreational review of television sitcoms and reruns of the bygone era, his last four words brought about Maxwell Smart, Agent 86, who worked for CONTROL in the 1965 classic, *Get Smart*. Not unlike that spunky character played by Don Adams- in such cases- we were both left-handed with today's gadgetry in our experimental epoch. But our voluminous Visitor on the other hand, whose heft was deft, transcended facilely ambidextrous waldoes of metal manipulators at each facilitator's cell, that is, the protean protuberances of the spheroid itself! Its outer hull of newly packed neutronium remained (down to gluon lozenges) unscathed by bomb, bludgeon, or blowtorch torture chamber. No amount of human, nor robotic intervention was able to even scuff or scratch its flawlessly glossy, linoleum-varnished superpower surface of contiguous curvature. No, not by a long shot! Again, like in my previous story-report, I say, stand aside, O Superman! For marmoreal impregnability is so superior as a mother's endometrial safety zone for her unborn; whether it be *anti-in-flagrante* inflated to Votive Virtue, or demurely deflated, the inviolable, invincible, and wraparound opacity all over this *Bouncer* (employed by the cosmic clubhouse or starry nightclub) lay listlessly at hand, but spun spindlelessly on its four-dimensional dilated axis. Ready to pulverize the contestants.

As far as the radiant and rational rotation of it, much more on that interpretation later on. Albeit for now, Joe's conclusive lecture reassured us of the bedazzlement thereof when what was told in person was relayed to other researchers and reporters crosstown.

Goggle-eyed with immobilizing fascination, short of cataplexy, I listened intently to the man making headway with groundbreaking results of the subject matter at hand. How harrowing our expectations of that Incontestable Cannonball and Wreaking Ball of breakthrough revelation! Many metaphors about what was really *roundabout*, literally, were then televised to proffer proper inspiration for more wildcat gushers in Hydropolis with waterworks outside of Metro-Aorta's central support hub.

Ninety-Four Eleven eloquently sized up this intervening phantasmagoria and lectured me as if by rote to routine: "A sort of black hole in reverse balloons up an eighteen kilometer across neutron star into the spatial confines of Metro-Aorta. Designers of the superstructure multliplex anticipate that the unveiled vastness of this Ball balloons *intradimensional* dilation," our company compatriot implied. An exponential expansion must have taken place independent of any spacetime coordinate, id est, up, down, forward, backward, left or right altogether. Even diagonal triangulation of its continuous contour, although crosshatched, is pinpointed to an upward overhead azimuth leveled by base longitude (east and west of the meridian at Greenwich, England) and intersecting, vertiginous latitude (north or south of the Earth's equator). In brief, gigantic geometrical curvature of perfect *sphericity* other than what a normal sphere-shape showcase can occupy… "And so, we are now haunted," he went on to say, "yea, haunted by what we call, VORTRON. Alas, some superpower by its verified definition, but so sublimely situated in the very Vat thereat!" Pro tem, the conveyance electromagnets had us glissade on an interurban expressway authorized with the number 237.

As we gained momentum by a horizontal booth escort to this enormous mass of rotund and globular glory, the intercom, blindly oblivious to exigent protocols, blurted ladylike: "Welcome to authorized Thermal Transfer 291. Enjoy your visit and- as always- please wear adequate safety gear." then, nagging ride-along passengers and interns, "Be sure to zipper up with a spacesuit available per your assigned locker. Thank you!"

After our regulatory ordeal, we stepped out. Yet little did I know old Joe was gonna show me that Vat vac-shaft laden with one helluva sleeping giant! For as a walled womb of insular insouciance, it had cradled one whopping heavyweight of megalithic alabaster or an exaggerated ball-bearing that caused the Tall Wall to buckle and bulge out until it would belch billows of a bituminous pressure gusher due to an occupier *not* of this domain. On camera, everywhere, within the vicinity of a tremendous arena, the rational rotation thereof waffled and warped the interior of the Vat, viscerally and self-lucidly enough. From the all-pellucid, brightly nacreous neutron star that hovered heftily, overbearingly, its glitz of equipoise acquiesced into an insuperable sub-state of suspended animation, still cushioned by absolute nothingness, nestled in an embryonic cradle; an in-vacuo Vat of naught but a simulated vacuum that blotted out the surrounding with its enclosed clearness. After all, it was only the Ball and naught else.

We had managed to tag a shortcut to TT-291 and cut a corner to take a peek. Joe gesticulated to me his come-hither hand semaphore for C-4 yourself viewfinder availability. I trotted over and lazily leaned in, having my eye-sockets plastered into rubber nodules and gazed into the aperture for *fisheye* or normal mode. My mindset was transfixed by unending insularity.

To my amazement, I beheld, with willy-nilly featureless fashion, an overwhelming materialization of nothing but pure *spheriness*! Suffice it to say, so far, a colossus of convexity about 18 kilometers in every-which-way direction, the entirety of which was enlarged by one eerily and gradually spanned out hyper-curvature, except more dizzily and woozily bent back on itself as to induce swoons of visual vertigo on my part. In time, only a handful of us could but barely endure the "pump-up of the pineal gland" (third eye syndrome) & "neocortex contortion" in *keeping up appearances, or so was one facilitator's coinage. The self-compensatory, unflappable flyby of the Super Ball (unlike my pastime television horseplay during the 'super bowl' series next to jocund Joe and others sandwiched with reruns from our start-of-the-year 1990 British 5-season sitcom, Keeping Up Appearances, in reality, but devoid of this *steroid spheroid* of a thing)! Besides this chimerical ball, to have had heretofore an aptly scientific interpretation of the "embryoctoarc" or the septillionth of a second *electroplasmatic* conception (in star-birth) was well apropos!

Nor may I volunteer overkill information by admitting that, although curvier than ordinary sphericity, nevertheless, the warped wall of its supernal surface surrounds some circumstellar Star par excellence. Seeing how, with indiscernible continuum, as it had gradually contorted and curved away from me, up close, its nearside, serenely seamless surface appeared completely floored and flat-flashily- or walled and widened out (according to one's perception with respect to positional perspective) for at least an entire city block or so, due to its huge hulking, *herculean* heft! My fellow eye-witness of *veritable* viewership (yea, yardstick usage of procedure and protocol), nabbing a C-4 your-selfie, 9411, no less on the job, peeled himself stolidly on Metro-Aorta's admirable yet foolhardy fancy: the concealment of a towering rubber-ball Bouncer, regardless of our illusory wanderlust laid in a laboratory rigmarole rat-trap.

"I--- I'm convinced by this spectacular specimen!" *the madcap from a manhole* as I oft badgered Joe, compared to the superiority of the VORTRON, was jubilant not quite, but a reeling stagger short of ecstasy! While~ with chaotic clamor around us from other customers and onlookers of the C4Y Observatory~ under self-abandoned befuddlement, 9411 faced me unabashedly and punched in his two cents worth: "May I solemnly recite Plato~" *Our fellow PhD valedictorian knew it by heart, hey! And I was well- pleased by his backwoods outburst of exploratory zest that led me to an unperturbed pool of levelheaded commonsense.*

I then propped a makeshift podium pasted with cardboard boxes for his speech in an imaginary lyceum. But little did I know about this Orb of an oracular oratory, whose intergalactic timeline became sub-squeezed into a sheer 18 kilometer threshold, preparatory to that which is beyond a priori (abstract knowledge) nor posteriori (experiential knowledge); neither by any other standard of definition nor conceptualization! *I listened in on what he had to share, for it was once long ago commissioned by an ancient philosopher millennia before we ever took our first inhalation ...*

Emphatically capitalized:

BEHOLD THIS WONDROUS VISION: THE SOUL OF THE BEAUTY ONE HAS TOILED SO LONG FOR! IT IS AN EVERLASTING LOVELINESS THAT NEITHER COMES NOR GOES, WHICH NEITHER FLOWERS NOR FADES; FOR SUCH BEAUTY BE THE SAME ON EVERY HAND. THE SAME THEN AS NOW, HERE AND THERE, THIS WAY AND THAT WAY, AND THE SAME TO EVERY WORSHIPER AS IT IS TO EVERY OTHER.

~*From* Plato's Symposium

Joe's audacity began to burgeon as our adrenaline rush reached an apex of incredulity beneath the underbelly bastion of the Super

Sphere. Conveniently, caught up by his inveterate viewpoint and version of it, he had written-out this calculated format for me:

Whereas no navel, nor dimple had been based thereupon, as if it were with biological expectation- that is, a creature once nourished by the umbilical cord- an ultra-smooth, seamless cybernetic surface of continual convexity (in esse) radiated instead; yea, far above what was normal to this geometrical equation formulated as (Φ) for sphericity and $V = 4/3\ \pi\ r^3$, where V = *volume* and **r** = *radius* accordingly!

As I considered the basis of cross-sectional embodiment, that of a 4-Dimensional mirror-image silhouette, 9411 on the job gestured to me with additional attribution:

"Not to exclude its gluon-glued Planck-length lozenges congealed into one foamy integument..." He made note of it while telling me off, "--- The skin of its outer hull, even able to withstand~ less than one nanometer in close proximity to~ *the Soviet Tsar Bomba (Russian: Царь-бóмба) which waged an unsurpassed explosion at 50 to 58 megatons of TNT out of an 8 meter, 27,000 kilogram thermonuclear aerial bomb (one of two prototypes for future warheads, regrettably) on October 30, 1961."

*With reference to such sinister history, I thought of a so-called *Gloratorium* addressed earlier in Yard Lamp of Gloria to have been prolonged long after an indefinite, grave, and desperately overdue moratorium decades before the 2113! May my readers of Tomorrow's Testimony be challenged by such similar implantation like a future *Creatorium* to supplant yesteryear's crematorium.

The background jabber of a hundred observers reverberated from an overall C-4 yourself "Vista Viewership" along the curved perimeter of our citywide promenade and promontory deck. Along the way, there were uncensored scant trifles of unearthly sunlight leakage notwithstanding. Some **superluminal* light leakage lambently lilted through anti-roentgen Plexiglas barriers that shielded us from small smatterings of neutron emission. How Heaven's hue or *chroma* of the firmament and empyrean fluoresced via galvanized *galgalim of embers and coals from a Starry Quarry up yonder; even over white coats of doctors and scientists alike, with whiteness wondered at under UV black-lighting, or bathed by beacon bilirubin blue-light irradiation therapy. Unequivocally then, from C4Y dolly shot closeups of VORTRON, our glimpses of glorification would only intensify such a curvaceous colossus awhirl one *yoctosecond per rotation!

*Denoting or having a speed greater than that of light (what I would have also defined as *hyper-celerity* on a hyper-spherical surface).

*Galgalim are sphere-like angels according to the Dead Sea Scrolls!

*The meaning of yoctosecond is one septillionth of a second. Please note, that via the British system of numeration, it is a million raised to the seventh power; it is a number expressed by unity followed by forty-two ciphers.

So Joe flaunted an electronic chalkboard he had flipped open and flung out into projection for me to see clearly (the very basis of its ground-state Oasis):

Let us recall the figurative *Φ not
much dissimilar to the Pluriseptiplex

---

*Phi is an irrational mathematical constant, approximately 1.618.., and is often denoted by the Greek letter φ. Other commonly used names for Phi are: Golden Mean,

Extreme and Mean Ratio, Divine Proportion and Golden Ratio. Phi is a naturally occurring ratio which exhibits aesthetically pleasing properties.

A 4 dimensional sphere has two 'volumes'.

An interior volume, which is 4 dimensional, and a surface volume which is 3 dimensional. The formula for its *interior* volume is **V = (1/2)(pi^2)(r^4)**. The formula for its *surface* volume is 2(pi^2)(r^3).

And in reverse, like the animated 1983 through 1986 television series Inspector Gadget, he hastily folded up his contraption and tucked it back into his lab coat inner pocket, always prepared with several carry-along portable devices. For awhile, 9411 was a wee bit untidy and scraggy. Gaunt from frugal binges of pizza and sodas and vitamin intake to recompense for the dietary lack thereof, like a hedge-maze-haunted and oft jolted gerbil on the run- ready to dodge department decoys, or duck down at anytime in case of an emergency- he scrounged about for more hardware, tools and accessories to top off any makeshift invention for some scholarly stamp of approval. This he did quite often in order to prove his working thesis on any lofty subject soliloquy. Now, presently bewitched by a badge of honor backed by *nucleonics*, the branch of science and technology which works with atomic nuclei and nuclear energy, my fellow electrician and investigator was downright startled by the surreal scene before us. His facial clockwork, prematurely creased with scheduling, timetable tabulation at the railroad depot, or whatnot, was ashen.

However, his frame of fragility as well as mine, became fortified by a second wind. We were assuaged by the lustrous lull of the Tall Wall, earlier on addressed. This was the topnotch, towering curvature of a preternatural presence that was already the talk of the town and even noised abroad globally. The helmeted supervisors (shielded from UVC radiation), who have stationed themselves in peripheral watchtowers on a nonstop lookout, joined in with the pomp, ceremony, and plaudits for more publicity to an upfront Close Encounters of the Fifth Kind or CE-5, in retrospect, fathered by Dr. Steven Greer, a famous ufologist, and by the better predecessor of pioneer analysis, nuclear physicist Stanton T. Friedman. Except that this *concordant confrontation*, as I had rather render it, lay horizontally, diagonally, and vertically predisposed to quantum Quiescence; that is, at point blank range, an all-harmonious opulent opacity of an enlarged nucleus narrowed into restful repose and quietude. Our verified Visitor, the entirely-on-the-whole hyper-cosmic denizen of some far-fetched multiverse menagerie, lay lolled in suspended animation, although *spindlelessly-spun-up* from freeze-frame slices of the fourth dimension, howbeit discreetly depicted, revved up and revamped to the *nth* degree, I declare with my hyperbole handout.

With wide panorama on the revamp, the spheroid's prominence deliquesced down to a dim discoloration when we poked and shamelessly shoved askew and askance its impenetrable Steel Sheet of a fused, ferrous, hyper-titanium, iron-irradiating crust. Only microscopic protuberances caused by a mild *starquake* (a mild hypothetical shiver and shudder in the crust of a neutron star, according to astrophysics) were ascertained. Only ebullient bumps of an unavoidable and mountainous Mount Everest were overspread as slightly swollen up knobbly and cobbled protrusions among concavities throughout and about, but by a millimeter off of the super-surface, at nearly 99 percent of light-speed, anything pancaked thereunto fell flatly, lightning-quick-sub-squashed to dissolve away with waffled warping, no matter what worship of real estate property!

"Abandonate omnes spes, vos qui intrastis"
in Latin for *Abandon all hope, you who have entered!*

A bystander bundled in MOPP 4 for readiness, upheld his neon-bright marquee sign which waved at us and at others, flashing electronically. Soon afterwards, upper ranks of reconnaissance took notice of it and uncannily forbade his display to persist, Metro-Aorta's militia showoff, as if to debunk and censure the worldwide warning where rogue reporters ransacked the sphere-side runabout and overtook the doomsayer's rostrum. The manhandled whistle-blower relinquished his staged platform, only to be replaced rudely by our media milieu of outright pandemonium. Whereas we would have campaigned for an ultimate apothegm, *the buck stops here*, in addition to, *tomorrow is as of yesterday*- the former, maintained by *President Harry S. Truman on October 2, 1945 (care of America's nuclear strike in retaliation to overbearing bombardment by enemy squadrons); the latter, Temporality Turning to Timelessness (the quadruple T) formulated anomalously roundabout an anachronistic Ball, whose telltale turnaround topside time slot slithers on by along therewith.

*But MacArthur's discipline and principled leadership transcended the military!

¶ Its carrier time-dilation eternally separate and independent from both metronomes of indefatigable cadence, *NIST cesium fountain atomic clock in Boulder, Colorado, and the *GMT atomic frequency standards at the Royal Observatory, Greenwich, London.

*NIST: National Institute of Standards and Technology.

*GMT: Greenwich Mean Time.

Eventual audio and video snippets and samples were gleaned from the electrostatic field of this far and wide wonder, but like needles from the proverbial haystack. Magnetic reel-to-reel recordings and digital delineation of rotational, residual signatures (per megaton mile-marker and spectra-sparkle) had been stored into an archival database. Whereof with one thimbleful of *superfluid*- a bizarre, friction-free state of matter at the core of a neutron star- spectral absorption lines, or Fraunhofer lines (named after the German physicist Joseph von Fraunhofer), under special spectroscopy, illuminated Joe and myself while we interpreted dispersal distribution patterns interspersed by interference nodes, troughs, and chemical wavelengths on long ticker-tape printouts.

Not that this was a cosmic culprit only to titillate the fanfare fuss and foibles of merrymakers who have gawked at a totem pole; nor fairy-like enough for another Harry Houdini to debunk and dissect in the halcyon years of Sir Arthur Ignatius Conan Doyle, literary confidante and preserver of the Cottingley Fairy repositories at the time two girls, Elsie Wright and Frances Griffiths, photographed perhaps an intergalactic encyclopedia of fairies themselves. We would deferentially doff our contemporary 2113 skullcaps then and now via time-travel into the year 1917. To take off, politely, our top hats, newsboy and flat caps- especially Sherlock Holmes hats- and salute and pay tribute to the very early Twentieth Century, when on that same year of 1917, Our Lady of Fátima (the Blessed Virgin Mary), no less likewise vouchsafed an appointed visit to three shepherd children for the Miracle of the Sun near country hillsides of old Portugal on October 13! And these events have collided with an identical, unalterable, and even unadulterated light-output of candlepower invariability. Its unwavering <u>neutronization</u>: wherewith pressurized protons and electrons, under hottest *hyperthermonuclear* fusibility, melt into netherworld neutrons and spew copious sprays of neutrinos to perforate far-off spacetime megaparsecs to the brink (at the uncharted territory of an intergalactic framework super-cluster), regardless of how distant the displacement!

The X-ray emittance thereof (energy in its purest potency, radiated by the surface of a body per second, per unit area); the *emissivity* of which we calculate, in general, as charge, ignition, generation, transmission, and distribution along power lines of high-tension interlink linkage. Where electrical receptacles, collectors, and graphite-greased contact shoes of a trolleybus soak up the high voltage to run routes of mass transportation throughout Metro-Aorta. Our bloodhound auditors of benchmark track records found out by what composition and property the spheroid consisted of. Exhibits A, B, and C were then painstakingly mapped out to 3-dimensional charts and graphed by laboratory Holographic Diorama Model Interpretation [future usage of our nowadays HDMI network] with our citywide Metroplex of quad-conurbation (four cities in one). The overall transfigured cornfield that lay plotted down, vista by vista, prairie by prairie, and lumen by lumen of luminous flux, has coalesced consecutively to one 'blissful' block after another. City precinct and district directories have unfolded for forbidden *ferroconcrete* inquiry.

Hell, at least, my mouthful of gibberish and jargon might just as well have conveyed the sacrosanct cornerstone of adequate adjuncts addressed, if not with eloquence, then awkwardly albeit!

Now, let us get back to this burning crucible of four-dimensional disclosure. For behold, aside from my hodgepodge potpourri that might have been spattered and daubed over fresh frescoes and murals in an underpass basement; neither beneath any medieval, castellated setting fortified with ramparts and a moat-- even down grimy grottoes, and under grotty groin vaults of reposeful, recessed ceilings-- yea, at an *undercroft* cratered by concave catacombs and alcoves of a consecrated basilica or cavernous cathedral! Nor less likened along lengthy metropolitan tunnels where "*...words of the prophets are written on the subway walls and tenements halls and whispered in the sounds of silence*," by Paul Simon, I indeed declare, deliberately-- O for crying out loud! Lest, waywardly, we ramble athwart by my antecedent antics of a verbose body-flex! Contingent upon my showy psychometric matchstick that could catch aflame the better part of me, may I rather refer any noggins, including the architect and building inspector, to our project Think Tank. And elsewhere, in the din of an overcrowded brainstorm broil, huffing hot steam from preponderant pressure cookers of commotion around town, the *irrefragable irradiance* from an 18 kilometer across crazy nucleus of a completely collapsed blue giant should in the long haul replace empirical and skeptical forays forsooth, or so we presumed!

Arguably, as antiques have enamored me, a vintage valve cogent-controlled cast iron radiator ought to regulate their seething output of vaporous volatility. Whether it be aboard a ferryboat for propulsion or for her cackling calliope astern, blaring and bleating away- that would wail and then wheeze with whimpers between caesuras- it made no difference to both of us. But by contrast, even though the vast VORTRON conference is oftentimes incommensurate with *EVP recordings, this rapport will (as of yet) personify hitherto unprecedented 'concord' with what was unattainable in past ages. *Until now*, give or take! It cannot be forced! Neither, for the sake of posterity, will one iota of it be gained, nor subtracted therefrom, no matter what the cost, I calculated.

*Within ghost hunting and parapsychology, electronic voice phenomena (EVP) are sounds found on electronic recordings that are interpreted as spirit voices.

Therefore, our primitive auditory and visual cortex of it (the nacreous Neutron Star) elicited center-stage appearances apropos to science, so far. Which was an infinitesimal fraction of its hyper-wholeness, we had hypothesized. Whereas in-depth examination of its wherewithal welcomed wonder and provided proof of invisible, evasive properties around something so large as to slip slyly away at any time, or augment monstrously up close, this Brobdingnagian juggernaut jostled jabbers- both bully and gadfly- and journalists and film directors alike, impartially, and without respect of persons.

Co-worker 9411, suppressing his Shakespearean vernacular, reminded me with "A rose by any other word would smell as sweet". His approach was to broach the deeper dilemma of perceptual recognition over superficial facial value. "Whew, there's a whole lot to absorb by simply gazing at it. So much that I'm feeling woozy..." he remarked, reeling tipsily. Others, encamped or stationed at their designated cubicles coped similarly with woozy symptoms of inter-dimensional disorientation and extrasensory disequilibrium.

Joe generated a simple algorithm on his laptop he flung out of himself as through an obliquely revolving door coat pocket! Indecipherable equations equated various behaviors between liquids and solids. One of them being the conflux of perfect balance and counterbalance of buoy-with-wave undulation. Preferably, one with an anchored or tethered float, or cork coated flotation device.

His laptop image upheld holographic portents, showing an exemplified wobble and joggle of bobs and jerks upon the vacillating water surf, whilst halfway submerged, moreover, into a film of surface-tension where air and water are separated by pressure and density differentials. In like manner (by analogy), so too, the anti-gravity cradle of a cosmic catcher's mitt supporting a supernal softball from any netherworld ballgame beleaguered by perhaps the Nephilim and umpired by an El Gibbor: "The Mighty God" to reestablish rules of conduct and game-play for a ballpark sand-lot diamond. For the sake of intergalactic universality, far beyond first, second, and third base- To belt a ball hard to the outfield or out of the park, above the back fence and over the clapboard bleachers to the utter outskirts of never-never land! But in this case, one warp-speed cannonball that may have been hammered or clobbered by a bionic baseball batter. The short-order aftermath of an incoming curve-ball bulleted on the rebound to a sky-high big fly until it hit home run on Metro-Aorta altogether.

Superior to history's best batter, the lionized Ted Williams, winner of six American League batting titles, who pushed the envelope to the .400 with the Boston Red Sox (hardcore former fighter pilot in World War II and the Korean War). At that time, in the 1940s and 50s, he and a whole host of hitters could never have hankered to compete with the gargantuan Gibborim in his heyday, nor for any other chronicle threatened by the military industrial complex (the uncanny connection seemed plausible).

Thereafter, decades later, the peaceful 1989 drama and fantasy film, Field of Dreams, portrayed in the golden sunshine memories of the late Eighties an Iowa farmer who hammered his stakes into the ground by building one's very own inspired vision once and for all.

“The weird side effects of a Hyper Sphere on the flip side, in contact with our facilely shallower reality of consciousness, are forefront,” he added in relation to television’s major and national league legends, for a moment amused, then looking grave.

“I understand,” I said surprisingly and shrugged. “And I appreciate your reference to baseball. But, of course, this recurrence of oscillatory glory can assault us like the wax-and-wane wall of the moon merely a stone’s throw away from our microcosmic gathering. Except in time-lapse, tossing tides to and fro from gravitational upheaval in a matter of moments! For while the imposing, bent-up base of the heaven-sent Ball draws back or upward, but then dilates downward, it feels enough nauseating to our entire community.”

My wistful colleague of affable composure gripped grimly an O-crowbar for physical firmness and stability, and I with him. Many more solid steel O-rungs that stuck out of reinforced and *prestressed* ferroconcrete (anti-tornado suck ups, as they were called) never inconvenienced the facilitators and tourists in time of dire need. Outright unavoidable then, there were EF5 multiple tornadic vortices and conical corkscrews that, once in a blue moon, raged havoc and horror far beyond the suburbia of our immense metropolitan burg. And O-crowbars and O-rungs seem to have been in vogue for superficial safety reassurance more than anything else; psychological security blankets rolled up into half-doughnut barbells, moorings, and anchors. Alongside surly harbors and bays, each one was well handy for an exposed pedestrian, or towed to a vehicle; even severally tentacled to some lorry-laden container cargo boat or barge. But, nonetheless nagging us, the impalpable pull of irresistible tidal forces defied applied anti-gravity to the degree that our hair stood up and goosebumps burst forth as in the company of passersby from the spirit realm...

Every upside-down U protruding from the pavement was also furnished with an upright emergency call-box which, in unison among many others, repeated reel-to-reel the foreboding "All hands! All hands! Hold on tight!" whenever alarms and wailing sirens triggered. Yet gorgeously gala Trivia triumphed up and down her three-way street where, under confetti fallout, an automated parade of Electric Light orchestra's [Hold On Tight *to your dreams*] was vindicated via radioed repertoire. In such instances, virtually every outdoor appliance and fixture featured inter-telephonic correspondence (by reason of relevance and correlation) throughout the urban beehive of 300,000,000 occupants per parkland powerhouse!

Pro tem, in confirmation to our common queasy quell-and-spell induced by the Pulsar's quiescence of continual curvature, gradually grown, and then shrunken by about 100 meters to the minimum, then back out to maximum extent, I felt the reverberation rattle my rib-cage and skew my viewfinder away from our targeted tightrope of perception. How screaming silence saturated this immediate vicinity to the upwardly extended exposure thereof. Enough for our eyepieces to have fogged up as condensation followed an ever faint gravitational lensing effect. For as with fish-eye featureless warping of spacetime continuum- even though in minuscule proportion to our overall surroundings- the downward bending of the big Ball from its unimaginable weight grappled with our personages forthwith! I backed off and so did 9411 and a shocking chorus of metallic-sounding voices resonated through the observatory portholes:

"I am unquestionably Vortron of the year 2113!" it thundered tremendously from our solar plexuses, as if from the midst of our being inquiring of us mortals, "What do ye seek?"

Shocked to the bone, I shuddered along with Joe jolted no less to the core. We were speechless and timidly taciturn.

Meantime, [It] persisted, that is, the neutron star itself, saying, "Well now, my unified nonillion kilogram avoirdupois I have hereby nullified for your sake sustains and suspends a colossal collapse,

O humanoids, so that with weightlessness ye may momentarily scrutinize Me..."

A *continual curvation* of wraparound insular investiture was glazed glossily roundabout the Sphere that sagged our flooring above which it levitated listlessly. Astonishingly though, the Metro-Aorta authorities were uninformed by this event of an exchange and verbal transaction betwixt ourselves and an immensely immaculate Brobdingnagian juggernaut! *Golly gee, swallow my tongue!* I thought with smoke billowing out of my ears, and on Joe, I about had to douse the fire by a bucket if not barrel of water tilted from my mental (metal) wheeled cart. At heart, he and others nearby were already soused by the drenching entrenchment of utter Transcendence! Elsewhere, *natheless*, a blisteringly bloated radiant replica, or full blown clone, of the 'vortronic' Mother-Built Superpower, the ultimate MBS, materialized but one foot over an intersection of a crossroads thoroughfare. There, the township hubbub heavily hammered at its impervious counterpart curved latitudinally to a south pole beneath the equatorial circumference and, there-above, to a north pole whereof its hemispherical framework lay longitudinal in the east to west direction or vice versa. Its *doppelgänger* duplex from our standpoint Mother-Built Superpower, the original MBS, materialized likewise as that selfsame super-surface of the neutron star indivisibly and unalterably, except by ballooned orders of magnitude. On this wise, the highly definitive deflation thereof was equivalent to the inflationary influx, but oppositely appointed and accordingly polarized.

Staggeringly staged across aeons of Time, but bountifully wedged into an impossible straitjacket, the miraculous MBS had to have been sub-squeezed *duplex-like* (the authentic one with us and the exact mirror-image of it over the intersection) into our steroid reality of cutthroat self-amputation. The slinky sliver of hyperspace wholeness narrowed to a negative near-infinitesimal factor intersected by what was a Russian Matriyoshka or Babushka as in Russian (бабушка) to mean "grandmother" or "old woman", *but one within another within another within another*, seamlessly from the inward infinitesimal to the outward infinite, 'both ways', and yet perfectly perpendicular to conventional Euclidean space wherein all points on a Euclidean circle are equidistant from the center! For such is an infinite sphere: the center of which is everywhere, but its circumference nowhere.

Yea, moreover, at a more distant location, right above an alternative cloverleaf convergence, just as well aforesaid, and appallingly enough to the motorists and bystanders fraught and frozen stiff by ball-wide pervasive pearlescence, the "Super-South-Para-Pole" floated a scant twelve inches away from an asphalt blacktop. Although the Tall Ball stayed ever untouched and unhampered by bolides of a natural disaster from above- but for the time being- it commiserated with carpool curiosity caught at a cul-de-sac, bottleneck, or a gridlock traffic jam.

Eventually, we regret to mention the abominable melee of scoundrels and of incendiary people pelting its Underbelly Baseline with knuckled fists, forks, firebrands, bricks, sticks, baseball bats (no pun intended), shovels, spades; or to hammer thereupon stakes, but to no avail! And how many more petulant people flailing and flogging, scourging and mocking the merciful MBS; misfit mobs and thugs to tensely flex latex on slingshots and makeshift bungee cords; brawlers brandishing their ridiculous remonstrance. Aye, demonstrators in rebuttal who rampage against Rational Rotation of the MBS and whatnot! What of those hellish hillbillies with sportsmanship archery arrows? Even hitchhikers and mountaineers alike allocated to shuffle forth a calling-card gamble over their Swiss army knives; surreptitious city-slickers with their caustic switchblades; wanton warlords with their sordid swords and diabolical daggers of the despotic Dark Ages, cutthroat cutlasses, hand-held harpoons and an arsenal of grenades; from shotgun shells, leaden pellets of double-barrel buckshot, cartridge-dispensed bullets by marksmen and sharpshooters; or the culprit catapult launch of Russian roulette rocket bombs.

The attempt to microscopically scuff or scratch the glistening, glossily glazed Steel Sheet of bodily Hyper-Curvature around the neutronic MBS was futile. And so, to have punched a gash into its outer force field with an automatic H-bomb would have been pointless in the long run. Not even the slightest injury thereupon whatsoever! Until the ignoramus of inferiority and ignominy may become confronted by Boundless Equanimity from this Mother-Built Superpower, the all-encompassing and compassionate MBS! Ultimately, like a filmstrip, backward into its permafrost freeze-frame state of *paramount pictures*, the inventory of transitory existence-- within pinpoints of the protean Ball thereof-- will woefully re-collapse and reinflate through a more predestined and foreordained Universe, long after the horrific hoopla of yesteryear's pornographic, pernicious civilization on the verge of going berserk if not harpy-possessed!

At present, emergency wailers went off- screamers and sirens- and megaphones devoid of their wearers. With dizzily deafening dissonance, from city to household, alarms ululated the alert status quo of CODE RED. Automatic flags flailed on rooftops. Hyper Loop Inc. track-side semaphores flashed due to an external exposure of perfectly paved and colossally curved mercurial deuterium dispensed with overbearing outreach. All along and from the beginning, the MBS evinced a [quicksilver heavy water] formula of D^2OHg (if at all possible on our Periodic Table of Elements)! Glistening glaringly, oozing all over itself some super-fluid 'heavy mercury' incapable of a boiling point, nor volatile vaporization, but many magnitudes of immutability above the conventional nuclear power plant coolant! And afterwards, the premonitory presence of that which was shock-waved up and down and laterally throughout the 300-million-packed agglomerate urban burg, unabated! Now unaware of its ripple effect creepily crested with whitecaps, how countless multitudes midst residential repositories and throughout palatial Paradise Chateaux were suddenly rattled off of their royal rockers, to say the least! Yet on an ad hoc basis, memory foam mattresses, beds, and cribs all over town had cushioned the brief earthquake aftermath, notwithstanding, whereabouts shockproof cramped quarters already would have absorbed such seismic recalls of an experimental blunder that this was.

Were these the unforeseen permutations of our tampering with the Holy Sphere? That its luminous *lynchpin* of pure peace and safety preserved us against the blindfolded blunders of empirical science, no matter how hard we'd scan *her* under some citywide MRI, offered Metro-Aorta marvelous solicitude despite the residual disturbance. This was a trustworthy transducer of limitless power and- by far-proffered preemptive protection more efficacious than any of our precautionary vanguards. Nevertheless, the *NSA maintained an uproar.

*National Security Agency

Albeit, back at lamp camp 101, 9411 and I just stood there agog and taken aback, knocked down from our pedestals by this anomaly. The VORTON vaguely persisted with an echo: "If ye know not what to seek, then may We assure you of what once Was, is Now, and ever Shall be... seamlessly..." so concluded its "*vanishingly variegated shapeliness*" showing the unquantifiable TREE(3) that makes its four-dimensional hyper-spatial span equidistantly ubiquitous. Vortron's supernumerary properties could curve out and into itself as though it were with multilayered multiplication near-infinitely beyond the googolplex (ten to the googol) or Graham's number (too unwieldy to write). Whereupon the innumerable TREE(3) tiered and stacked super-forest of multiverse vastness is sub-squeezed to only the 'vortronic' miniaturization of 3053.63 voluminous kilometers! As though this were an Alpha and Omega (Αλφα and Ω) version of whole *Hyper Sphericity comprised by VORTRON that lay consummately unseen, entirely incommensurate with any large-scale or small-scale measurement.

*In its demurely deflated state, as a single Planck unit (the smallest point in quantum foam found so far), it can exit the observable Universe; but at its inflated state, I suppose, a Pluriseptiplex (googolplex to the googleplexth order of magnitude) times larger than the 94-billion-light-years-wide Hubble and Webb space-telescope survey of the filamentary superclusters freeze-framed from one end to to other, it can effortlessly reenter the same way it exited...

Enter the Multi-Bound Superstructure Titan (MBST)!

For a preventative antidote against lunacy, I then managed to muster up valor and resorted to a diplomacy- “O most graceful one, why art thou come hither?”

And again: “O 4-D door, disclose thyself and shut not!”

And again: “O ineffable MBST, I surrender my propriety---”

“Nay!!!” our cosmic cannonball bellowed with a backlash. Its searing, sun-like Radiative Zone of a blistering Wrecking-Ball asserted itself, ready to pulverize vaunts of the violator and pauper alike (not that it was trying to sound supercilious). “I adjure thee, thou lilliputian liaison: on what grounds dost thou question Me?!”

Upon recoil, I was thunderstruck by a bolt of lightning. In defiance and doughty self-confidence, I deferred my reply and nonchalantly about-faced and forward marched to 9411 instead.

“Hey Joey, what doth it mean by that?” I found myself using either the Shakespearean or King James Version vernacular more out of mockery than reverence. Joe’s jeer was suppressed. “Hell, did it have me pinned down by its *Voight-Kampff test? Like long ago used by LAPD Blade Runners in order to elicit my emotions that can cause pupillary reaction time whether I was a “replicant” or not by the determining factors thereof~?” The newly-emerged MBST had hushed up into acquiescence as the rational rotation of it hit me with fulminant symptoms of acute disorientation!

Gusts of wind whooped and howled around its rotation.

"Embarrassment be on this Brobdingnagian juggernaut!" 9411 bawled and advertised with the facilitators. The scraggy geeks gawked back at him and at me, many of which convened briefings to gain gallant advantages over such a shimmering Showoff that triggered major municipal contraventions! Futilely, last but not least, military airstrikes upon this big Ball only depleted the arsenals. So much to the point that even an incendiary device of the most explosive blitz, be it a Daisy Cutter or Warhead Hydrogen Bomb, subsided silently into the Multi~Bound Superstructure Titan. Until no trace of it was ever left to begin with; as if it were never deployed while instantaneous cancellations had caught up to a deployer's timeline!

*Borrowed from the Blade Runner story by Philip K. Dick in his 1968 novel "Do Androids Dream of Electric Sheep?"~ then adapted to the 1982 Blade Runner movie directed by Ridley Scott. All Rights Reserved and accredited accordingly!

"Me thinks it is attempting to contact you, 3185. Speak to it now lest you appear as but a replica compared thereunto!"

After our linguistic façades were foisted on an increasingly cumbersome conversation, we reverted to plain English and resumed rapport with what was outrageously enchanting. A citywide fully-sized Billiard Ball, but an Eight Ball, reclined onto her side, must represent the Infinite, I mused mirthfully. The blankly bloated blush of an 18 kilometers wide whopper was what Metro-Aorta perceived at this particular wavelength, nothing more. For all we know, it was in vacuo invisible to our five senses, although visually "irretinal" as our optometrists and observers had suspected all along. Having to emanate a quadrillionth of a nanometer (narrowest ferromelt) waveband beyond man's retentive recognition or cognizance; whose heaven-sent but unspeakable spectra radiated but one out of infinite photon striations which were subatomic, strangely stratified up and down, left and right, forward and backward, inside-out and all around! The fiber optic field department of *Photonics* that dealt with the properties and transmission of these narrow ultraviolet to outstretched red-shifted infrared high-energy photons (*not necessarily *FiOS broadband info & entertainment in the early twenty-first century*) handled the "cloven *glozar*" output and aspect thereof. That of ultra-fine fissures with fissile diffraction and finest fusion phenomena transcendent to thermonuclear reactor uranium with which refined fission creates radioactive isotopes of lighter elements such as cesium-137 and strontium-90.

*The word "fios" is Irish for "knowledge" and the FiOS acronym is a trademark of Verizon.

Whereas on the super-surface of VORTRON, the opposite transpired. Where, with effulgent fusion, heavier electromagnetic wave-packets of elements materialize until mercurial deuterium, D2OHg, in contrast to the aforesaid (contrarily) coats the hyper-curved neutronic shell thereupon by ballooned jacketed hyper-heavy *hydrogel*. "At this critical phase," I elbowed Joe with an annoying nudge. "We *wot not* what will become of it, save super-silent hyper-wholeness that, like spacetime sponginess, absorbs, soaks in, and assimilates everyone's lifetime experience it had gleaned from out of our earthly time-slots. I fancy *Field of Dreams rather than an ordinary electric field..." (of course, beforehand alluded to)! Joe winced with febrile fascination. To top it off, I elaborated: "Like the holographic chamber of a computer-simulated physical environment~ say, the *holodeck* on *Star Trek! But floored and flattened out over Vortron's insuperable surface so that all time events are reproduced by its photon-powered mercurial deuterium, dilated and redistributed respectively, as it were, superbly symmetrical, & of all around everlasting entirety."

*Star Trek was still broadcast on tellies in the year 2113 for some reason, even if the internet has become obsolete and by now defunct as a fossilized artifact of the forgotten past. Nowadays, authorized archival and retrieval recordings re-imaged the historical data; the commodities were handheld in diamond-like holograms and 4-D simulators!

We continued to survey the VORTRON neutron star and gathered up a huge store of information submitted to the mountainous municipality of Metro-Aorta. Thereafter, our teamwork was allowed to break loose of this grappling Encounter of the Third Kind and obtain a 72 hour sabbatical.

"I resign!" I cried aloud in remonstrance to the ridiculous odds of amalgamating contact with Near Infinity wrapped up into one lump sum! So that my colleagues could counterattack in jest, I flailed my arm and hammer showily as a semaphore situated at a treadmill nearside an inter-tubular expressway numbered 99.

"Yeah, me too..." someone sulked.

"The same with me---- "

"And also with me…" The déjà vu dawned on me from another encounter, on another dimension, when spheroid clones of the Major Ballroom Sphere uttered their enveloped departure with wallops of a collapsing whiteout~ Me too, me three, and me 4…

Lest loony-bin, funny farm, or rubber room became our final foe, Joe~9411 and I sealed shut the last verdict of dismissal upon this project Probe. Nonetheless, the Herculean Ball lingered on along with our township square and runabout-promenade-perimeter which was only an adjunct of the megalopolis peopled by nearly one-third of a billion; the 300,000,000 so-called soulful inhabitants throughout the adjoining burgs bulged by overcrowded conditions. Residential and commercial containers looming above a panoramic and vaporous horizon of haze, looking like water-tower squat mushrooms thousands of storeys tall, appeared unaffected by Vortron's vagabond overbearing burliness, might I mumble. That the colossal cannonball, by now, was just as nonplussed as we were had failed to rattle Metro-Aorta's gilded cage. Rather, a Faraday cage collectively.

Wherefore, we were wimps and could not level with such a cosmic Paul Bunyan or Big Bad John jacketed spherically! Cowered down from the overwhelming pressurization thereof, both of us departed homeward bound with disembarkation of our roentgen-shielded showcase platform. Having to take the Expressway Hyper-Loop 99 lavishly laid out for an escape, just in case, expedited swifter departure. Yea, far away from the imposing 18 kilometer expanded Herculean Ball that, in a trice, would withdraw its interrogation of our hapless diminution, in fine.

"And with no requisite voluminous valediction!" I gloated gleefully, as I dispossessed my mind of *that* burdensome Ball, albeit still paved paramount into the cobwebs of my mortal memoir. Indelibly printed, via visual and auditory neocortex, deep into my brain's hippocampus where inklings and intimations of *Vortronic Apotheosis* nudged neurons and networks advantageously. Joe, jittery but high-spirited, acknowledged this spiritual warfare fervor of a hundred and three degrees Fahrenheit, enough to impress priests and nuns at an out-of-town and in-the-outskirts vicarage; but bad enough to have had the feebler unfortunates committed for an insane asylum. Psychiatric sanatoriums and infirmaries were welcome at our disposal, *thanks to the merciful magnificence of Metro-Aorta*, or so we were programmed to believe.

Some silos of solicitude offered to convalesce the fainthearted when mental breakdown dwindled them. Those jinxed and inimical instances were far and few in between, but plausible. Hence the grim gravity of such situations (in the literal sense) as we boffins distanced our nous, headlong, from that Thing. That contortionist of elasticated dilation! Needless for me to contend, it took 300 solid miles in our direction to exit the urban sprawl, let alone.

Aboard bullet train traversal of chrome-laminated safety, in the TGV maglev, we sat, seat-belted, and snug. It was in the central pod of cushioned high-speed magnetic levitation that we pensively somewhat watched this massive moonlight of VORTRON gradually recede out of recognition altogether… until, temporarily, the outermost business parks perforated the simmering scenery. In the interim of inter-tubular transition, comforting countrysides (sylvan yet terraced and landscaped), skewed past our portholes in a flyby flit of skittering spirit before deceleration.

Although the inventory of a scientific breakthrough was well under way, but pending for next week's review back at Thermal Transfer 291, good old-fashioned Ethel perforce rendezvoused with our company. She noticed the sleek open-ended bottles of the Hyper-Loop pods slide by and slow down. Out of one of them, gingerly, Joe and I stepped down to the platform and met up with her. "Hey, my doughty lads, how was Whatchamacallit?" she shouted exuberantly, gingham attired to resurrect those olden days, swarthy and hale as an *Aunt Bee, bonny and becoming!

*Aunt Bee is a fictional character from the 1960 American television sitcom The Andy Griffith Show. I deemed it suitable for my countrified contrast of a home-sweet-home setting.

"Don't ask," I muttered, contributing to our entourage escort. Ethel was flabbergasted to see us in one piece. For feeling so unhinged, mentally, by bombardment of ultrahigh-level neutrinos, but barrel-o'-fun phased, I assured amiable Ethel: "Having said that, I'm so thankful to see you no less, lazy-eight or not... May the bountiful bonanza begin!" And she beamed.

But Joe, sedulous son-in-law who held a stiff upper lip, sobbed and softened up and smothered her with a big bear hug of honeyful cordiality. After all, terrestrial~ yea, tellurian existence~ that of no human contrivance, but rather the exchange of agape love with an embrace such as this was even bigger than the Ball itself.

Midway this book report

Yard Lamp of Gloria
RECAPITULATION

From capstone to grand finale, the decampment thereof.

"After all is said and done, and the dust hath settled, therefore, may I beseech thee, O bulwark-ballooned Bouncer, how on earth can thy contents be conveyed to my kindred Spirit of twin flame?" I would blurt out an archaic invocation in soot, sackcloth and ashes as it were, as if among *maypoles* monumental.

But before enveloped departure pending, in uttermost minutiae of detail, debris and residue-- to foreshadow colossal collapse-- the chief mother-flagship-sphere of this scale-squashing, heavyweight, and floor-flexed flotilla demonstrated itself so adroitly. How from pinpoint to pinpoint [fore-and-aft] [back-and-forth] [up-and-down] [inside-out] [*ana-and-kata*] it oscillated with protean prominence easily, that is! Wearing Pluriseptiplex-pliable lozenges!

Consequently, kept codex-catalogued to titanic Time Warp, its bygone antediluvian <u>apotheosis</u> lingered adrift from Planck length of a concentrated quantum foam afterimage.

Thus then the Hyper-whole Super-sphere had dwindled into an infinitesimal singularity until- beneath subatomic miniaturization- it mockingly winked out of existence! As if never to have arrived in the first place to begin with! Not until finally, instead of a *Where are you headed?* aimed at me, its compensatory coup de tonnerre (sudden thunder) "reservoir of energy resonated redundantly" from afar through an outstretched red-shift distance: "Summon others to the metaphorical mandrake... Thereby My final Alpha and Omega rattles thy rib cage!" quoth the marvelous MBS. I contemplated its paranormal phenomena, *full of stately stellar magnitude in Hilbert Hyperspace- namely, the silhouette-section of which is an infinite-dimensional analogue via Euclidean space (continual contiguity):* with Rational Rotation of interlink *seamless sustenance!*

Furthermore, aside from an extra-pervasive embodiment, it had equated eschatological consequences if or when one resists God's Gospel of Truth in the *Holy Bible. Unhesitatingly, I took heed of such concrete Radiant Reality, knowing full-well that equivocators were vaporized by this Pillar of Cloud by Day & Pillar of Fire by Night! In my simpler lexicon, no concealer, nor confabulation, nor prevaricator could withstand the Booth installed at the tribunal or confessional! That the Mercy-Seat ought to expunge some leaden hammer or anvil at the gaunt gallows knotted with a noose, once a villain or vixen pleads for forgiveness, is no marvel. In retribution under blindfolded Justice, enthroned impartially though she be, I herewith [wherefore] refer my readership to the All Merciful! And, of course, myself (the chief of sinners) no less included!

Nor ever may macadamized blindness to Naked Truth hinder, nor censure me; neither man, nor beast hamper an ultimate maxim: "The pen is mightier than the sword ..." (in Latin): **calamus gladio fortior**, I outcry and exemplify for the Yard Lamp of Gloria!

*An alternative Record that predates the Torah is Samuel Noah Kramer's Inanna, Queen of Heaven and Earth (cuneiform-translated) & dramatized by Diane Wolkstein; see the Burney Relief, a Mesopotamian terracotta plaque of the Isin-Larsa period!

Hence wholeheartedly, the harbinger of an Exemplar [I herald].

Forlornly disposed of, I resumed repose alongside cloisters and colonnades, and bade farewell to my close encounters of the nether kind before I'd tiptoe tipsily out of the now off-limits catacomb-like premises, prayerful. Ad interim, as a sojourner, I reeled from the discombobulating aftereffects left by my liaison of Lunacy.

Feeling dilapidated, gone overthrown to the bone- backwardly- I glanced at pliant platforms waffled and cratered into coffers of a meltdown; like liquefied aluminum incinerated by prim priority of an otherworldly but weighty asphalt molten mantle of a BBB. The Big Bouncing Ball deflated, with equipped equipoise, sauntering to a vanishing point of nonexistence as it exited spacetime.

At its architectonic frontispiece, I staggered against hexagonal holographic displays of elaborate elegance: that of some crystalline megalopolis of quicksilver sunshine searingly interwoven with wet multi-mirrored surroundings. My *Polychrometalopoly*, an accurate word, never aforethought, colorfully dubbed the description.

Regrettably so, no more of this scenario *a la carte*; neither the filigree fissured doorways that but beckoned me to attention, or to parade rest, give or take draconian drills; nor the immaculacy of a reabsorbed rendezvous, save the Sphere's votive Vigils to share its *theophany* with fellowship *fallow*. Snazzy snapshots of fairies that Sir Arthur Conan Doyle's Sherlock Holmes would have revived, foolproof, in each one of us when we wander forth into territory unknown; having wholly **Jesus Christ** in our hearts in lieu of New Age superstition and disbelief. Revitalized, I felt its tenaciousness arrive at equanimity [in contrast to] *kaleidoscopic phantasmagoria* to badger shrewd commonsense doggedly dumbfounded thereby!

I clambered away, well alleviated, but deprived of an *incognita* invincible. Lo, last but not least, like the absconder, so my temerity of escape from detention in this subterranean labyrinth with which wearily I negotiated; after an incorporeal intervention rescued the ghostly half-light of my speculative spirit! Spindled spirit, I blare, on behalf of daffodil distaffs *in finesse*! One of them, a hyacinthine Goldilocks with whom I sought imprimaturs of authentication!

Hitherto haunted I was, but in a benevolent way; with Nights in White Satin sequestered at an indoor foyer, played by an earthling legendary band, The Moody Blues, as I had rerecorded it!

Whilst en route, my moot intramural Hedge-Maze of hallowed hallways (named *Immurea*) narrowed no longer. And in due process, I climbed each rung from out of the vermiculated *Klein bottle* thereof, only to find an exit hatch. Another designation in blister neon format, district **8**~ whereof the puffy number *eight* that was crosswise on the transom of a doorway~ flashed fluidly! I exulted with zestful Zoe by my side, and inside of me, full of exuberance and vitality; yea, the lady o' life itself! And I yearned to relish the breathtaking revelation kept in retrospect of my former Cambridge scientific seminars. My marvel devoid of mammon had recovered incalculable information concerning this *Lazy Eight* relinquished sideways. Distributed daintily, a supine Super **8** braid (not in reference to the once affordable, now ritzy Hotel, by no means!) to represent exponential potential where the proverbial chain is strongest at its weakest link, so to speak.

Really, an <u>infallible</u> infinity of enlargement or, let's just say, that of intensified infinitesimal reduction interwoven indefinitely into itself! Balanced up in-between energy centers of superstructure magnification within which one enigmatic Median divides an interstate four-lane Hwy. Such turnpikes or freeways were illumined with a long row of **SOX** (LPS) or low-pressure sodium vapour [arc tubes] atop stainless steel dual goose-neck lampposts. And others, throughout throngs of outdoor commercial lighting, wore Westinghouse OV-25 vintage cobra head and clam-shell streetlights wired with industrial-quartz tubing of two-end [appendages]. Each one with a swollen crystal chrysalis, as if it were full o' firefly bioluminescent luciferace; transducer tritium-like ignitrons. Be they flat-fused or reduced jacket-sleeved pouches of perspicuous and searing-hot transparencies pressurized by a mercury vapor volatility of *electroplasmatic* ionization galore!

Familiarly, I was well-aware of Walt Whitman's Leaves of Grass upon recall of industrialization during and after the AC (Alternating Current) boon of our Nineteenth to Twentieth Turn-of-the-Century celebratory glory days! Unprecedented tycoon boomers, such as Edison- then separately on their own- Nikola Tesla and George Westinghouse, were energetic revolutionary catalysts for future generations thereafter. John Pierpont Morgan Sr., an American financier and investor who dominated the corporate conglomerate on Wall Street throughout the Gilded Age, eventually defunded Tesla's Wardenclyffe Tower. Alas, JP Morgan's avarice for profit- instead of the environmentally safe wireless transmission station on Long Island from 1901 to1902- transpired with what Thomas Alva Edison tried to traduce Westinghouse with and Tesla! The memory of the Tesla Tower, now dismally defunct, is only a pictorial afterimage in our national archives of scrapbook memorabilia. My revivification of the Big Ball herein hastens the resurrected "effulgurant" and remnant of what once Was... Aye, I cry: what once was Wonderful, Wholesome, and a hairline short of what will be Holy…

In 2113, about 211 years later, for that which transfixed the human race with truly sustained, faintest, but finest fusion- convincingly- forever safeguarded our *cornucopian* case of Grace! Particularly, an electric Quasar in a glass jar (the MBS in-vitro, and in confinement under controlled conditions of this laboratory lockup), even if it slipped [sleekly] away from planet Earth, was never to be televised again... nor ever! Granted, the experience of a lifetime needed mnemonic absorption into the small neuronal network of my electrical brainstorm and, in like manner, into the large-scale superstructure of the Universe's sponginess just as well. Until the two highways conflate with one major Median up and down the fourth dimension…

Heretofore for all practical purposes, it was labeled, the Avion Sphere of superluminal maneuverability. But nowadays- better yet- the Univatrium configured previously.

I rest my case.

Original inception of the Story

Written before, during and after the landfall of hurricane Sandy on October 28, 29, and 30, 2012. My hopes are that this "brief relief" of a short story may offer a breeze of inspiration to all. The raw contents of my composition, although a fairy-tale in this world, is a reality in the next. Restored, revitalized, and expanded on June 2, 2023

CONSECRATED & FOUNDATIONAL SUPPORTING
SCRIPTURES: EZEKIEL 1:15-25 AND ISAIAH 6:1-13
AUTHORIZED ADDRESS FROM 1997, 2015, & 2023

Exedra Ubique
Living Room Everywhere

Bygone Ballad

We'd run in the afternoon sun
Right outside far and wide,
May I say, Roundelay
In our county o' bounty 'twas done:
Such tough toil amidst murk
Mound and hay.

In the townsquare did glare
Arc lights through dark nights
That must beckon
Bugs and critters everywhere
Hung on high
To draw nigh-

But some lady whose braid be
Interwoven and twined
Down her back, clad in black,
Remains radiant and refined!

How she shimmers up beautiful
While we worked on, oft dutiful
In the heat replete with
Hyacinth and honeysuckle;
Be it stagecoach or steed-back
Holstered hefty by but
Big money buckle!

Lorry-loads were hauled weighty
In the Year Eighteen-Eighty,
Historians retrospect reckon
Along Mitchellville, Iowa

During daytime industrious-
Yet still- like a gold daffodil, she
Looked lavish, illustrious!

With auricomous braid
And an hourglass arrayed,
The pearlescent Girl
Trundled by cable car-
Bypassing tavern, saloon
And the Gable Bar ...

Down her street such a fleet
Via flanged fly-wheel and sheave
Knuckled puissant pulleys overhead:
A catenary cable could quiver o'er
Whilst workers would heave
Bitumin, but sable
Per sleeve instead.

West of Des Moines, our city,
Mitchellville bustled with noise;
It was springtime so pretty
By buds beside nitty-gritty
Run-o'-the-mill drudgery
That employs or deploys ...

Where each building wore gilding
Alongside boulevard thoroughfares
As cobbled up avenue squares
Were flanked by squat fireplugs,
Until dankest dark nights
Of arc lights acquire bugs!

Still, how fresh beyond flesh
The brisk breeze, breathy, vernal,

Vouchsafed brightly and fair
Mitchellville's Silbury Hills
Naked-bare, may I blare:
Blithest comeliness that
Lingered eternal.

I'll recall the cotillion Ball
Of festoonery, hoopskirts awhirl
And our Lady that arrayed be
Impearled: to pray for our
Township, I say, by the hour
Nary a showcase displayed
But her grot gravely inlaid!

How her loveliness lures me
Immures me and cures me
Of fret and fuss during high noon-
Lushest lass, whom I'll cherish
Shall shine, never perish:
Wrought revelatory eftsoon!

THE INSERTION OF **INTERLINK** Enter Eternity

1

Where reddish bricked apartment buildings stood, plastered together and everyone welded back-to-back & pressed privily into some sequestered nook and cranny, I ambled down through the city district. There was nothing out of the ordinary on that late evening, except for the pillared pall of an overcast ceiling above these time-tarnished, landmark monuments laden with cinder blocks and kiln-toasted bricks. Their rooftops annually rumpled under permafrost either amid winter, or creosote-cratered with hot tar softened by the summer hammer.

Long after that dissonant, distant blare of any steam-blown whistle, with fortifications of more annexed building blocks stuck side-by-side, waffled forth fabulously, or after retirement of rowdy residents stacked up and stashed aloft into the premises privily to overlook cramped sprawling streets, strips, and alleyways, I had to take the plunge into *willy-nilly* nowhere.

For there- *still thereat*- loomed that horridly henna baked brick building with one doorway shut up on itself. I paused, in order to determine what manner of entrance and exit the spectacle had feigned forth. Beside the brick walls thereof, a measly moat around the edifice tapered to this steep embankment cozily cushioned by coppice bushes and wild shrubbery.

It was right then and there that this gaunt door had drawn me closer to it until, timidly, I gripped its doorknob. It creaked open! I glanced around me suspiciously to see if I am the only one present for an opportune, uncalled for trespass. Inside, at the foyer, another door adjacent, ajar, waited for me to yet yield through its entrance. But something deeper yellowed my spine as I noticed how olden, obsolete and prismatic fuse fluorescent tubing scintillated unevenly with warm~white overhead, blackened at their appendages.

I advanced forward, furtively.

At once, as if on automatic, the main door through which I had entered slammed itself shut and I felt locked inside this starkly lit foyer of a corner, or so it seemed. For a bit longer, I held my breath and exhaled a sigh of relinquishment since my approach. Indeed, it was nary a trifle that knocked on wood at the door. By then, I took advantage of this new arrangement wherewith here begins my lone odyssey into the inexhaustible, inextinguishable, and *infinite*.

By my time-dilation, the next doorway allowed me to proceed further into the vestibule. I soon zeroed in on an open bay or multi-door chamber that had seven more doors pending exploration. But which one? I thought quizzically as all seven-fold doors disclosed themselves alike at me. With identical selection, summoned at my disposal, I decided to choose the midway one for an *authenticated* walk-through.

An uncanny hush, with suspenseful sensation, muffled me like never before as I inched my way past one of the doors in the midst thereunto. I could not help but notice a large, glossy label under the transom of the middle doorway suddenly read, 'IMMURITY'. This stopped me at my track afoot whilst I had mentally rehearsed the pronunciation of it and repeated the refrain: *Im-mur-ity*! Now I was stunned to the core, if not winnowed away by the merest mystique thereof.

Another hallway, by the wayside, stretched onto a point where perspectives had converged. But, oddly enough, it posed a terribly tenuous hallway, let alone endlessly lengthened with an additional attribute of closed doors along the way where I went. Although I kept on going farther into the unknown, the imposing repetition of doors on either side continued ceaselessly.

Well, what have we hither? I gasped ghoulishly, remembering whence I came forth when I was just about plumb *outside* at tawny apartment blocks, gone for a stroll of sorts, naught else. But this new situation tackled me by surprise as I now had felt like a rogue rat or mouse muddled in some laboratory maze, of course, wanting out! "Ha!" I barked out at myself, "This is really a newfangled thing!"

And immediately a faint echo-call of my remark in rebuttal returned to my ear from front and back of this drearily featureless corridor.

There was screaming silence in reply to my inconvenience whilst cryptic crossroads of an *Immurity* reverberated resonant into my conscience- exposing my intentions which were inconsolable.

I then recalled how, away back, I once went for an exploratory trot into a similar scenario, and ventured over to a trap cul-de-sac. At that time, there was no way out of that walkway quandary until I telephoned for assistance. But, by contrast, this merry makeover had a totally different diversification as an intramural menagerie of countless doors would have crept right by me, had I persisted on through to literally nowhere… none whatsoever…

At once, upon one of the doors, emblazoned over either entry, flashed fluidly the numerals 291, and until I about froze at my fearful footing, for petrified from head to heel was I. For beaming back at me, the three character number glowed, glaringly, and on the upper positive plate of this door with blister-bulged stickers. "Aha!" I cackled at it.

Two hundred and ninety-one was what I could only decipher.

But what transpired next had grown grotesquely too tough for terminology to pinpoint, let alone fathom, as I will for now follow the 'torchiest' of omens to describe, dictation and all.

2

And it came to pass, accordingly thus, that the tall-walled gray hallway of foursquare rectangular enclosure was manifest manifold smack right before my naked eyes, I reckon. It had its high-ceiling upper topper tapered seamlessly from off an ultrahigh and narrow Y~shaped or *ypsiliform* contour I could not readily recognize. Aye, the complete blankness thereof glared *gleamily* against me. Sheer super silenced. Hushed to the point of a pin-drop pitch of anechoic quietness! Aye, in response to this detour of closeted, clandestine confines, I backed away, hindered by not being able to reverse my course, as it were. The door behind me was, shockingly, seal-tight shut, and that cornered me in with this Y~contoured corridor!

Whew! "Horridor" would be more likely an apt effigy for it if ever there was one! How horrified I felt!

At present, variegated voices of a chorus called and guffawed themselves at me that, even though they surfaced about from out of nowhere, only *aphonic* effusion with its stylish stillness in tableau vivant vaunted up at me to utter the least. The explanation was well at hand technical jargon: a clueless claptrap to nowhere. For then, intangibly, the subsonic volume of vociferation had been distinctly discerned. Within auditory glory, octave, and pitch, it had reached and crept into my hearing with conch shell sea-surf clarification, I declare:

"Welcome to the [immurity] of hallowed hallways… Identify yourself, humanoid!"

In front of me- afar off, appreciably- was yet another door that was revealed as a slight slit upon the confronting wall or *Mure* as I had envisaged it. But since I knew not with what and who to stake dialogue with, I simply said, "I am thoroughly thankful…" and that was the end of it.

And now, with no needless fuss or ado, out and about, even so, from out of nowhere at midway range- between the front and back wall of this Y~contoured corridor- was this *Thing*. Namely, a rather petite paramour inamorata of ladylike size and semblance to have emerged! She wore an old gold, gossamer and crepe veil over her shapeliest perfection; blue and violet and polychrome as a rainbow of such supernumerary prominence and iridescence irradiating a *clair-de-lune clandestinely*. Howbeit, until furthermore, hither her whole wholeness was warm and blanched as her finest finesse of flair had fancied up an oily, ever elegantly attired *unguentarium* framework. With amphoral curvature complementary. The which was quite lovely altogether to look at. Nor any forbidden deviation sideways could ever be detected by the yielded usage thereof! Duly dumbfounded then, I gazed at her wholehearted, but not so much quid pro quo that she need reciprocate my merest mindful merit.

"Well now," she jested nonchalantly, "I know about how you have researched me out as voyeurs often do on their voyages into the multi~labyrinth. Is that so? Since you came?" Henceforth, how her quelling counterattack would have silenced predecessor suitors.

Consequently, I felt pinned by doggone daggers to the hilt, and hesitantly: "Yea, so be it, your bonny ladyship- 'er, your Highness."

"What is it that you want, contestant?" she managed to gamely inquire of me in the midst of a faint featureless scenario that palled heavily my whereabouts thereunto. O how wholesome and ancient discretion sizzled frenetically from within a molten **moiré** over her diaphanous, dimpled up demeanor! A heavenly halo-aureole, fit for an avatar, shone roundabout her nuanced a bit in the background to at least ameliorate the confrontation.

"I pray for others to have divine companionship," I confessed daringly, obliged not to upturn my prayer downside. "Since in our mundane world, I've encountered no noble interaction; no national entente, nor amity whatsoever; neither any alliance that intimates intimacy, inter alia."

"I see," soulfully said she. She then waved her right forearm as if to actuate something else. "Then perchance allow me to proffer thee this addition…" Moreover, her lithest, girl-svelte Hg~smeared daguerreotype portraiture, although it be lithographed, liquefied, or silkscreen sequenced, or for a big pinup billboard. Then cavernous corridors unfolded, that also had *septupled* up at me instead of the previous seven-fold doorways, which were situated down another hallway beforehand. All along or enroute, these passageways were indistinguishably identical, and my choicest one was to take all but the last of them, lest the interpreter to my vast valley of decision fashioned forfeiture therewith! In the briefest interlude, as an ever reassuring ne'er~prodded pristine presence, she lingered with me in her courtly, ever splendiferous grace as I tried treading one of her household tunnels she shared already. Given this dilemma, I could not pray tell what the entire ordeal was all about. After all, I had only slunk in entreatingly from outside; I was taken aback beyond myself unwittingly. Nay~ not knowing why~ I had surveyed such a whole lot to begin with!

Many more Doors bypassed me, one after another, and I felt waxed amok on a treadmill, or ever tried by my trenchant tributary overflowing and full swollen up to the waters of Lethe. Frazzled to my spleen as it were, I halted with *the buck stops here, big buddy!* That until in my intermission therein~ before an elongated infinite hallway annexed out continuously, and that conjoined itself into a faint point at such diminutive distance, until unsurpassed~ per se, peradventure perspectives dwindled down interminably! Now, as never aforetime, I stood stupidly, upright then and there, panting, trying to catch my alembic breathing of composure. Fleetingly *flip-sided* I had become, desultorily discarded.

Nonetheless, her heavenly, heavily vindicated voice-over got a bottled up backup, that is: "As you can see, nifty nomad, no matter how far you venture, my makeshift multi-labyrinth lay outstretched no end." And unlike on Star Trek, the name she called me wouldn't have had any bearing on my 'must analyze' missionary sojourn!

"Then who are you, really?" my inquiries were hurled at her in shuttlecocks of feathered plumage, as pigskin comets capped off.

"I am she, chastely, the gravest lady of guardianship: O *in esse*! Nothing more, nothing less…"

I had hunkered downward onto the linoleum flooring in livid disgruntlement of my bare conscience in the middle of an endless, pallid pool and corridor which yawned at my mentally contrived microcosm. Suddenly, a squat, leaden crystal decanter, doused with distilled water, materialized and mushrooming up next to me… "Go ahead, guzzle up!" She nudged me in an ardent urgent gesture, as if our time-slot was ameliorated.

Wooed with her overbearing pristine presence, I took the gulp of it for torrid thirst. Then, in reply to my sine qua non, a commode of toiletry appeared in her Tall Gray Hallway narrow niche just for me to temporarily occupy.

I did so and relieved myself privily.

Soon enough, it collapsed out of sight into the floor. The now empty-of-its-contents dewy decanter despoiled flatly the same way whence it came, left! On the other hand, an apple was found there instead thereat on the floorboard for me to partake of, and so I did. The sour and tart succulence of it delectably moistened me.

"You see?" added she, "How hitherto everything- and I mean EVERYTHING- was and is providentially provided for you; for in this haven of a Repository Story, that of *requiescat in pace*, a mere thought can turn to reproductive spiritual fertility pictured." Later, following her lyceum-like lecture, the concert chorus chirruped E minor diminished as via *voix femme* (French) or *vox femina* (Latin) and, in unison, singing some anthem, repertoire roundelay, dirge, or threnody from her hinterland. Instantly, the old hallway (before which was I) disintegrated to shriveled shrinkage, that of a deflated balloon thrown out upon the gutter; its metalatex liquefied by butt-scorching heat, molten momentarily, fizzled up into quicksilver of a bloated blob. And this only to be replaced by larger lounge taking up many more cubic metric meters of a *hyper~spatial* vacuum.

With cubic cornucopias of holographic wholeness, about each and every inchworm of an unearthly ether had been transmogrified into this cozily luxuriant lounge. It was there that mythic armchair Mercy Sofa Silencers- *nay, not for firearms-* persuaded the gravest of pioneers to offer foot upon terra incognita! However, it was well ventilated & preparatory for me, adjusted by adjuncts of lollygag, gaudy embellishments fitting for Charles Pierre Baudelaire. There were flotation devices of cork cushion fancy, and vast vestiges of velvet Velcro via crème de la crème red-carpet treatment the whole gamut! It would complement her demurest dowry.

Next to me, imperiously enthroned upon her paisley-patterned couch, she seated herself saliently, but meek. Alternately, a bonny lass lavishly reappearing like an obliquely oblong house ghost, but tangible to the innermost, nor ever as such beforehand! This time, perhaps perforce, my coquettish Asian [gorgeous] geisha forewore an elongated wholly and heavy henna chemise, or sensual sari as if complexioned in Mediterranean magnificence. As if daintily dolled up by a tenuous Temple tunic, from nape to below-the-knee solemn sobriety. The deepened crimson aspect of her radiant resplendence, like the redbrick wall, bloated bloody foreboding and alarming, but sanguine no less.

For contrary to my bellicose beliefs, she had clung tenaciously to her vestal virgin rite of non-compromise; that is to say, instead, she'd embody the codfish covenant coined with her hymen-housed cloven clit with adhesive cohesion. Although awhile wet, inviolate! Thus there was no hindrance to any of her doll-like development, and because of this, I was burdened by such a relentless rebuke. By crushed comparisons, I felt steeped by an otherwise wet fat Vat, or incorporeal void, very *vacuous*, inviolable as ever, overlapped by nothing! But that which may froth forth a glory-old, golden bangle, or garter due to her paramount personage, upheld her Hula-Hoop equatorial.

Consummately, it was she, shown as hyacinthine Goldilocks in tableaux of past, present, and future mannequin manifestation! Her statuary of Galatea had gotten reanimated on Pygmalion's pedestal, I hereby and heartily testify.

3

She stared steadfastly at my profile turned away from her ere I pretended not to take inventory of her hyper-heartfelt, otherworldly nuance of convergence seated so upon the scarlet dark divan of an old park bench next to mine. As soon as I had glanced at her- why-moist, milliard fingers gently and soothingly blushed and brushed me all o'er, bodily, as I waxed so, stimulated by her prodigiously preserved presentiment. Also, in our inconspicuous twosome tease, there was that nice numeric, purposeful pendant 291 hanging from her neck and over the dimly lit, darkened lava chemise she showily lolled in. Aye, her whole apparel applauded this entire session with which lithely languorous loveliness, albeit dauntless, decayed not! Neither harbored she any tinge of dim dissimulation whilst, still, stiffly, netherworld numerals gaudily gilt got my attention offhand!

To my incredulity, I took tally of my soul and ran a stock mock review of what solidified, for I could not believe my five senses as to what in tarnation had happened to me. Nay, not by a long shot of innumeracy, let alone inanity, I prefigured.

She readjusted herself primly to my bedraggled bed of affairs; right next to my personage, and glided her left hand over my right thigh. *Ooh! & Ah!* I felt enraptured, for the effusive effect thereof increased by the echelon, yea, causing my nuclear meltdown as I yearned to be more like her instead of my mere self. *Transpersonal* parapsychology I could have categorized it. Atop the pinnacle, no matter how modeled (albeit Conical Helicon, or whatnot), I indeed felt like liquefying limpidly into Her... The **Regina Lucis* Herself.

**Latin for Queen of Light*

Out of nowhere, an aromatic (or should I say) pungent stench it gave off; that is, her unseen creosote Bush that personifies goddess Creosoteria! A *saviouress* from tar-pits pillared by idolatrous totem poles. *Creosoteria* bound by bangles of a wraparound caduceus installed in perpetuity!

¶ Like an apparition of dank & dewiest ectoplasm, her holy refulgence writhed with primary spectra of infrared and ultraviolet iridescence. But that which also conveyed snowiness emblazoned all throughout; with whitecap Himalayan votive virtue, this had rendered me to be the nincompoop compared, or a sluggard to her quickest discernment just the same. For unlike anyone whatsoever on terra firma, this Matryoshka Doll deftly distributed to me and to others wimpled warmth of a bloated blanket with belonging. Not so much of some security blanket as that of an ethereal quantum Quilt. Even thereupon, the nimblest nuance of which consolidated solicitude supplies mankind with its emollient instead of a scanty scuttle! Arranged by Ariadne's Thread from quad loom-side distaff, spool, and spindle! Never nugatory via a shrine, alcove, and cave. Rather, refined up like raw gold bullion and ingots fused through transcendent transparency- purged of dross and with dregs dredged out- in such a stovepipe reverberatory furnace fueled, irradiated by the Conical Helicon of concentration: the hot crucible of canister containment pictured at some sought-out Pittsburgh foundry.

Never to make me wanton; rather to melt me. Purified therein.

Meticulously though, apart and aside from her dimpled up and faintly freckled freshness, her jewel jasper pendants dangled from lavaliers of lapis lazuli lozenges necklaced noose-like around her neckline. But bangles like doughnuts were coiled about her arms, aurified and garnished in gold leaf gilt. Altogether and overall, the lithe lass stayed far too enchanting to dote upon, as if billions were beholden to such an Attractor of adhesive cohesion.

Conclusively, I was wistfully welded to her effigy with which twin hearts may have thudded in alternate sequence; whose timing surpassed Boulder's cadent cesium~133 crowning chronometer of subatomic standards, facilely. It was at that the fat Vat, metronome TWINITY in her Efficacy to reflect fore-and-aft this hologram hull established athwart the front and rear lounge of a lighted ballroom. Affirmative and undeniably so, I'll say! Yea, an eeriest ballroom backed by the chiffonier reredos behind the postern altar. Behold: backed by this big mama Mortier Taj Mahal Dance Organ having manifold pipework puckered by slit-reeds riddled with stout steam-blown, *detuned*, doleful and effervescently pressurized whistles! Hellish, horrisonant, earsplitting squealers that, from their brazen brools caused by deep-throat *slits o' blitz*, do loudly & stentorian *screech scratchily!* SCREAM! shriek and shrill sharply!

That no less lacerate an anechoic air with a shout, yell, bellow, blare, blat and bleat; a pressurized prattle and blither, honk, howl, yowl, cackle, outcry, croon; that ululate vociferous vaunts! Wailing wearily, whining, whimpering, (whistling until wheezing), braying, breathing forth muffled murmurs, or that vomit vituperative voices against Sodom and Gomorrah's debacle and debauchery-- aye, the nitty-gritty Nine Yards-- but only to restart their sheer, ear-splitting thermal *thing* all over again. Howbeit horribly holiest or ghoulishly galvanized! Hither hammer your stake! For whoso harbored either benevolent or abominable heartache, so too was this reassertion or rebuttal thereupon; even the fallow median of a midway Cloverleaf Boulevard void and vain with old pointless polarization when push came to shove.

And again, ad nauseam, the quelling, squelching squealers…

Paranormal petroleum and graphite grease permeated pungently the ambrosial ambiance of once well-ventilated freshness. But now assaulted with odoriferous aftereffects.

Obviously, her harmonium blow-top aggravated aggregations of Revelry rebuked thereby! Somewhat so if deafeningly ultrahigh-pitched singing sirens set off self-actuated fireplugs and emergency water sprinklers in remonstrance to future worldwide upheaval.

I was woefully wet if not christened, nor drenched to drollery!

"Are you unlike the coquettish petticoat?" I had cornered her, entrenched by my crybaby baptism (no pun intended for Catholics as I am not unlike them save flattened to an Orthodox).

Whereas, backwardly, billions resound in reply, *none taken!*

Inseparably as it were, our Lady of Beauraing, whose parallel precedence reverts to a peasant village in Belgium from late 1932 to early 1933~ ensconced by five seers who envisioned this veritable Virgin of the Golden Heart~ had been personified at large, except under no intimation, nor presumption of subterfuge; neither bluff against diamonds in the rough. Since it behooved me to congeal consubstantial causalities with such sub specie aeternatis, yet devoid of compromise, the unveiling therefrom was with disclosed discretion, and forevermore thus.

She'd suggest solemnly: "My nom de plume plays Aurelia, the All-Golden One with inside-out holiness. In that I am thy gossamer goddess in a bodice for keeps is correspondingly correct!" Ere the aforementioned flailing fleurs-de-lis supplanted the spades of my subconscious cobwebs, her pure gargantuan Gold in myocardium converted me. Any fleur-de-lis was a stylized lily of a triad pointed leaf or petal from the royal arms of France made of gold enshrined by blue velvet.

"Vouchsafe hither, O my most *cornucopian* companion!" I was at a loss for linguistics. Befuddled, feebly enough, I fumbled for preferred acknowledgment of her opulence; that of reproductive reality. In response to my demystification, She (shyly), and with an allure of *flap~doodle* flip-side flapjacks flimsily flailing about, but front and back, double-sided according to her twilight TWINITY~ she shyly shared her rather uncontaminated coy courtship kept by such an unutterable, demurely discreet self-proclamation! Notably, notwithstanding, Aurelia clasped my right hand, opened it up with its palm facing Heaven's ceiling, and caressed it with clemency. Wherefore, this had been her pliant plateau of a safeguard pledge directed at me about and throughout the consummate Hedge-Maze of her merriest and soulful, bedside setup. But of course, we wish to genuflect as she lowered herself and would so curtsy to me with reconsecrated abasement!

Votive torchlight luminaria, needless to mention, matched an industrial assembly line. Flambeaux of streetlamps strewn atop her conveyor belt typified, sub rosa, this voluptuous and very visceral Vision.

We calmly kissed with a reciprocated peck pasted on each other's cheek. Never lip to lip, lest the nasty nuisance of premarital naughtiness rigged Temptation's tightrope into mononucleosis! For so subtle even at this realm reigned irrevocable Ramification and Regret over any venturesome violator!

"O Aurelia, life's dollish damsel!" I echoed in earnest with no dawdle, nor dilly-dally. And as of yet yielding yellowest hues of a glorified aura, she obliged herself forthwith in a blossoming blush. Her lurid lava-laden melon candy lingerie, silkily bordered by the semitransparent stretch fabric saffron sari she wore well-nigh as if into the Roaring Twenties. Twined, glinted with glaze; only to re-emblazon her curvaceous contour beneath an outer henna, myrtle-molten Temple tunic flowing flimsily in softest states of pearliest perfection. The clocks reverted back from 2113 to glitzier 1927, at a time movie mogul Fritz Lang, an expressionist of Deutschland, showcased his masterpiece science-fiction film, Metropolis: *(the mountaintop motif of this Yard Lamp of Gloria manuscript).

In 1927, a nonchalant chemise replaced the sari whereas the dimmer yesteryear sustained her much nicer nightgown preference.

In esse, the *effulged* finesse of Aurelia's uncensored Bliss filled me to the brim with dimpled, daintiest desire. I could consequently never compartmentalize her holy henna-sheathed Sheer Sheen; her stove-top flammability of rapture warmly wooing me so lazily, in a sweet swoon! Loveliness loosened up like lavishest Lakshmi eight-arm-and-handed (*octo-armed*) laid out upon such sleek, steel sheet linoleum flooring freeze-framed fresh from hinterland India, but by backsides thereat with her old adjunct of augmentation and augury (replete with premonitory presence)!

Her incorporeal insularity slid into determinate *evanishment* as ascertained for a fleeting flash-point Perfected Portrayal; so paved inside of my irreplicable mirror-image of *le Miroir* (diamond dust dilated and mercurial moistened up, of course); back-sided by this rather quicksilver, lustrous layout like any overwrought reversal, involuntarily inverted! Our vanishing Vat was she to nevermore be, except in spirit and in truth. For, abrupt as it were, I had felt her half-light adroitly slither inside of Life like a powerful queen cobra or anaconda of her ever sacred secret, whilst fully well off, I had lounged there atop some materialized mercy-seat sofa, confounded as ever, I reckon... Her Throne Room was one household hexagonal exedra whence colonnaded courtyards were so dappled by oak and mahogany pergolas until far-off walled up with Mesopotamian ziggurats; pyramidal pylons of equipoise multiplied into her more mountainous municipality by and large.

Incidentally, the vis-à-vis encounter was memorialized for that storyboard bottled up on our behalf. For I realized how superfluous convolutions complicated matters ere showcase trinkets were to be unnecessarily engraved and galvanized by an oil painting or oiliest artwork to simulate noise-suppressing cascades and cataracts; one waterfall for all heaving headlong, precipitously, crashing crazily downward upon crags and bedrock embankments of a gorge, and finally foaming out over culverts and tributaries. Yea, I reasoned responsibly about how our apparent telepathy took its toll overall. Aye, my most intimate abutment, at the foot of a bright bridge that spanned equanimity on display was what permeated her prioritized presence inside-out, as aloft an ultra-elastic trampoline transducer! Still unarmed and *unfingered*, wherefore we herald "Not by might, nor by power, but by My Spirit, saith the Almighty."~ Zechariah 4:6!

Hey, her attenuated underpinnings in only a fat Vat of unguent suds~ soaped with such saffron essence~ evacuated me of all fetish presumption. Alas, I acquiesced into her concord 'unicornucopia' of an electrifiable Arc Tube Yottawatt Metal Wafer!

Yea, as were wan eggshell protuberances of egg-and-acanthus friezes stubbornly stuck out at me by her whole, anciently loveliest antiquity of affable effulgence, aye. For thus an older antediluvian flurry of time-tarnished intricacies featured the quantum foam of it all. We'd elucidate, by comparative conflation, the Gestalt universe that hastened evenly. Wrapped up with her mercurial mist of profound prominence. In vivo, the at-large & luridly loveliest Lady of Gold~ although smaller than me~ contained super-compressed and concentrated casks of nuclear energy fit for the neutron star via her metaphysical makeover. So accelerated like an 'embryoctoarc' (the very first faint glimmer, but a septillionth of a second)! But never nullified by any template, nor rule of thumb; nay, neither one-size-fits-all type of latex glove or flaxen mitten. O Heaven forbid!

Therefore, 'ubiquelabyrinthelux' it was, as such, superimposed athwart me, that had hugely dwarfed my existence with its near-infinite Vicinity. *(L) Light everywhere in the Labyrinth

That within foremost mountainous municipalities of supercity symmetry, influx, and so forth, I could not conceive of having to ever circumvent her continual confinement of Walls! Henceforth I'd beseech her, wholehearted, to at least untangle Ariadne's Thread for keepsake, and that with happenstance hope for an escape, not to forget far fairer the circumstances than the Tellurian tempest amid shipwreck or a former Alcatraz Island escapade! Nevertheless our telepathic Telex quite easily defied foibles of fanciful frivolity, like radioteletype operators poised upon standby, if ever warfare was waged. Then, although foxhole grounded at base, I anticipated that she'll protect me invincibly within an invincible, bullet and bomb proof Shield. I had often consulted her halftone from *Holy Sheel Ilunivati* by my homegrown insulating invocation inasmuch as my most recent Elsa (of whom God guards my oath) would warm up the cockles of my heartache. Her Goldilocks garrisoned my Safety-Net, whereby my lacerations which festered fast were healed until, afterwards, seamless cicatrices interspersed my mind and heart like a gridiron-latticed football field, melting an ice hockey glaciarium!

Herein I offer precedent proof on which pudding is predicated.

*** * * INTERMISSION * * ***

Next, more purposeful poetry that shows effortless effulgence as, in due time, *she'll* unveil her Half-Light once more, manifest verbatim:

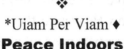

❖

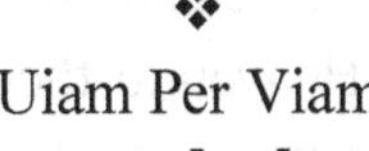

*Uiam Per Viam ♦

Peace Indoors

I favor Hallowed Hallways
Forever glazed agleam,
Inspiring me always,
As if it were a dream.

Curved corridors of might
Are not a hedge-maze merely,
But plastered up with white
And bright enough to sear me!

They carry seamless Silence
That echoes crowned creation,
So peaceful, void of violence
Per intramural station …

On Earth for now I labor
Through daily life indeed,

In service of my neighbor
So saddled on a steed-

Though lowly I may feel
To customers demanding,
These Hallways yet reveal
Tranquility still standing!

Hence, I am not alone
In Hallowed Hallways tall,
That wear their waffled cones
Of concord on each wall.

With noise suppressors built
In every cushion soft,
How Heaven to-the-hilt
Preserves my soul aloft.

No more unwanted noise
Beleaguers my Repose;
This Labyrinth deploys
Such silence full of rows!

Away with useless prattle
Designed to jolt our senses-
Devoid of worldly chattel,
My Maze ablaze commences!

Whose cul-de-sac or Door
Discloses Hope awing,
Whence Paradise in store
Surpasses everything!

Beyond the guard or sentry
Life's Trivia shines through
With but Her three-way Entry

Forever felt brand new ...

No matter what befalls
Our ravages of Time,
Have hope for Holy Walls
Eternally sublime!

Authorized insertion for Yard Lamp of Gloria~ composed on June 25, 2023

♦ By way of labyrinth (Latin)*

Intramuros

Rhapsody

The voluminous vision recorded on reams
Ushers over an old narrow hallway-
An enclosure replete with irradiant dreams,
Tiled up in my muffled small way.

I have felt fortified, heavily, hitherto,
Reinforced ferroconcrete reside:
Anechoic Lull, to-the-hilt, all the way through,
Waffled, creamily croons far and wide!

Cushioned quiet in solace, salubriously,
Souls poised, pacified, saunter serene ...
Unlike undercrofts lacquered lugubriously,
Lamps illumine their lot with *fluorene.

Congregations o' myriad buoys but glare
White-capped labyrinth-linked purity!
I am haunted, confounded by, caught unaware
Of preparatory Futurity ...

Admittedly, nothing could dare injure me
In self-circummured Silence reposed:
Intramural, my thruway threadbare gingerly
Congeals contingencies yet undisclosed.

Is it me in post mortem? Have I passed away
And have staggered to each cul-de-sac?
Such Protuberance prods me: My corridor-hallway
At length lay outstretched front and back ...

At the doors that you pass, opportunity knocks
Where an alternate Universe spreads,
But the billionth door-and-transom safely locks
Trivia sound asleep on three beds!

Reclined soporific, she murmurs, I say,
Listless memoirs: 'Mnemosyneopolis':
Her exedra be benchmark on any highway
By bulged buckskins and bundles o' bliss.

Then I noticed aloft lithe linoleum bright,
Starriest Glitterati and confetti arrayed:
Enwombed wonderfully to distinguish delight-
Lifetime warranty wall-to-wall sprayed.

Every door of potential covertly is shut
In an evergreen hedge-maze tall-walled;
Contiguity, seamlessly vast, seals it but
Backs ballroom endometrium hauled.

Of pure porcelain paved and tri-ply 'plastisteel'
Placid by every basement layout,
Subterranean stays the Subtropolis reel-
To-reel, ferro-fortressed to way out ...

Round a Rolodex carousel, curiously,
Lorry storage stacked up underground,
Hyper-cubic, of course, unfolds furiously
Furthermore, flung fluorescent, I found-

Oily possibilities, poised, wax and wane;
Though unflagging, flaunt forth ebb and flow,
Yet wet hallways of varnish relinquished remain,
Wrought with hoariest hedgerow-by-row!

Cobalt corridors flow fluidly wherever I go
Through the front door or postern on guard,
Foursquare walled under ceilings of high bays aglow
With interiors stately and starred.

I exalt hallowed hallways herculean laid
Out to labyrinth-interlink margined
And tunneled throughout, iridescent arrayed,
Bathed by high bays from ceilings argent!

*Fluorene is a colorless crystalline cyclic hydrocarbon that has a violet fluorescence and that is obtained usually from the coal-tar distillate which boils between naphthalene and anthracene; *ortho*-diphenylene-methane.

4

"O my quiescent Queen," I pleaded. "Please show me a way out of thy Maze." Howbeit her lackluster nonchalance would baffle me. What Have perpetrated? Have I inadvertently accosted Her?

She remained reticent about my plea bargain.

She refused to release me until her liaison lesson for me was finished; *no, not as of yet.* Meanwhile, within whereabouts of far a mightier, much bigger city than the one contained by her packed passageway purgatory of never-ending portals, my lone star Vastra had been before me unraveled…

I saw, as it were, forests of super tall architectonic skyscrapers, exceedingly robust in their gaudy splendor and elegantly poised. It was then that inside a V-shaped thruway I found myself adrift as on a magnetic cushioned conveyance system. *It's a transit trajectory to escort me into that Meticulous Metropolis of Vastra,* I pondered. Wherefore, white light beamed from every side of those monolithic edifices of a strong throng out and about me, whereas I slid by and by at giddily hurtling speed. And from pentagonal, hexagonal… all the way to octagonal polyhedrons that looked like any honeycomb beehive, stacked on top of one another, the hugely unimaginable, multitudinous infrastructure had eclipsed my self-composure.

The inconceivable congruity of full-fledged vats and lorries, as with egg-and-dart diversification, were ever so stashed and stacked like in an astronomically unfathomable wall-and-ceiling warehouse inventory, but serried sideways; adjusted upwardly until downward and alongside these coiled, squiggly wormhole conduits colossally magnified numberless of times! Cathedral towers and steeples that dwarfed intergalactic star-field striations just as if these were but a smattering scintilla by comparison! For as I slid upon the cupcake conveyance of bloated insulators that levitated me accordion and caterpillar-like with only wondrous support, I was about to witness an insuperable Warp Maze: The universal Ubiquelabyrintheopolis of metropolitan municipality of cynosure precedence or ineluctable presence. The likes of which facilely surpassed my otherwise wee yardstick usage of measurement at hand. Sufferin' succotash! (to cite Sylvester the cat's trademark exclamation which was said to be a minced oath of "Suffering Savior"). Its insane size surpassed any tabulator, non sequitur innumeracy, and nonsense so that a madcap may profess "All stars emit light; therefore, that which is not starry radiates no light!" et cetera and inter alia.

Nay, not that what we have heretofore, nor hitherto written is nothing but bilge, by golly! God forbid! Aha! hence my qualifier:

Ubiquelabyrintheopolis

Intramural Immortality

I bow before a Door
Narrowly nine feet tall
Inside the corridor
Of every fine
Sheet wall:
For thereupon agleam,
Enameled lustrous latex
Reveals some seamless cream
Surpassing every apex.

Cipher two ninety-one
Recalls its transom vent
Long hauled in by the ton,
Too many to relent!

When once were walls rebuilt
By waldoes automated;
Now, like a quiet quilt,
Peace pervades me unabated.

Whose insular Silence be
Inside of these hallways-
That shrills nonviolently-
Yea, deafening as always!

Two ninety-one is numbered
Upon this Door before me,
But never has it slumbered,
Though aeons crumble hoary.

Old cream-emblazoned, they,
The walls reflect harsh glare
From bulged arc tube array
On ceilings blank and bare!

My runabout wrought stately,
Stretched strong, infrangible,
Lay ungrotesque, yet greatly
Shines forthwith intangible.

At every frieze or ledge glaze
Where walls support a ceiling,
So endless lay a hedge-maze
With grotto grown, revealing!

Once sodden, carpet-piled
Lay consecrated ground;
Linoleum (now tiled)
Replaces it unbound.

In moments wall-enclosed
Along an endless Maze,
I've oft felt small, disposed
By lucid lamps ablaze!

The corridor convention
Links lengthy enfilades
Elsewhere with wide distension
Of fleurs-de-lys and spades.

I know her hence by name
Few souls pronounce by heart-
Seamless designed, the same
As ever from the start.

What palindrome compares
To such a hedge-maze Holy?
That which needs no repairs
And, either way, stays lowly!

Many hexahedral containers were hoarded heavily into vertical and vertiginous Vat Casks. Each one was cradled and crowded into an entire sward until billions became as silver sardines and halibuts bulged tightly and uprightly far and away to the outskirts.

To illustrate this, these became surreal portents of a futuristic Metropolis that would blindingly blossom up! Now, with my well-being snug and seated in the modular berth of the barreling bullet train which whisked by, between monstrosities wedged within one V~tunnel culvert diamond see-through Thruway, it was undeniably apparent! The glint of every *Electro-plasmatic Hyper-envelopment* fulminated furiously, blisteringly bloated up and that heat-searingly causing hurtful overexposure of my fleshpot carnality to have been blistered and cratered by shortwave ultraviolet propagation of such circumstellar surroundings. To enumerate the diversification of it:

General gist~list of numbering to innumerable consummation:

million = 1x106
billion = 1x109
trillion = 1x1012
quadrillion = 1x1015
quintillion = 1x1018
sextillion = 1x1021
septillion = 1x1024
octillion = 1x1027
nonillion = 1x1030
decillion = 1x1033
undecillion = 1x1036
duodecillion = 1x1039

tredecillion = 1x1042
quattuordecillion = 1x1045
quindecillion = 1x1048
sexdecillion = 1x1051
septemdecillion = 1x1054
octodecillion = 1x1057
novemdecillion = 1x1060
vigintillion = 1x1063
unvigintillion (or vigintunillion) = 1x1066
duovigintillion (or vigintiduoillion) = 1x1069
trevigintillion (or vigintitrillion) = 1x1072
quattuorvigintillion (or vigintiquadrillion) = 1x1075
quinvigintillion (or vigintiquintrillion) = 1x1078
sexvigintillion (or vigintisextillion) = 1x1081
septvigintillion (or vigintiseptillion) = 1x1084
octovigintillion (or vigintoctillion) = 1x1087
nonvigintillion (or vigintinonillion) = 1x1090
trigintillion = 1x1093
untrigintillion = 1x1096
duotrigintillion = 1x1099
ten-duotrigintillion = googol = 1x10100 . . .
skewer's number = 1x10130 . . .
centillion = 1x10303 . . .
googolplex = 1x1010100

Pluriseptiplex = 1x1010100 x 1x1010100

GLUCEPTIPLEX (?)

HEXAPLEX

^

9830164275 24811993 ___ 39911842 5724610389

HEXAPLEX

Pluriseptiplex to the Pluriseptiplexth
hyper-power and order of magnitude

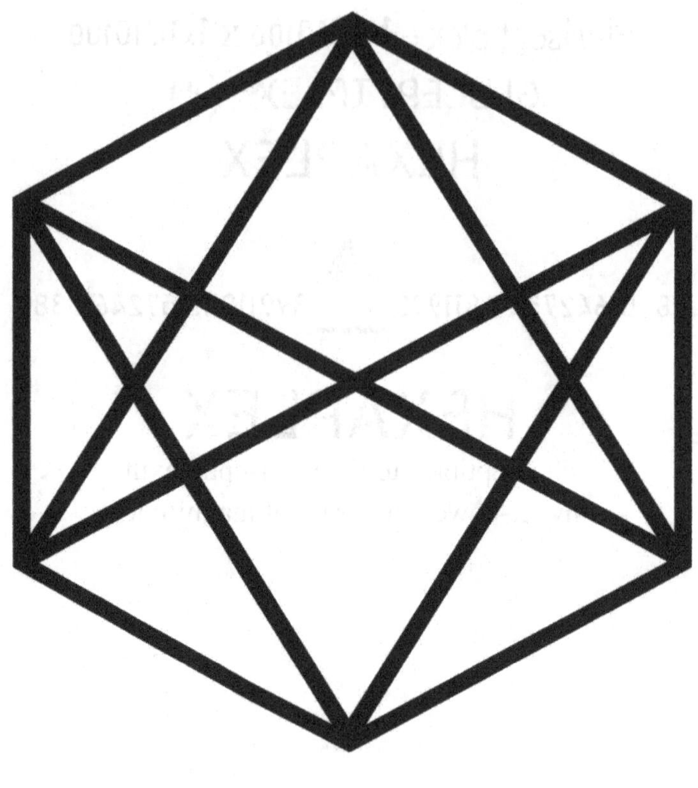

*Or googolplexian multiplied by googolplexian to the googolplexianth Power

If it should arrive at a premature foreclosure of **INTERLINK** gone underway, I divert our attention to a detour in this Yard Lamp of Gloria! Save, as it were, on an alternate timeline from where we left off. To reemphasize far more than what we had bargained for, I resume replay, needless to portray with an unaltered typeface font for keepsake and to maintain affectation; with pilcrow & paragraph marks used to refresh a certain situation or scene.

Hereof is **partition II**, or just modestly

Original and perfectly unaltered SCREENPLAY
The unadulterated, non-revised manuscript 1996
9830164275 24811993 ^ 39911842 5724610389

Ancient Light

The Ultimate Visions

Yard Lamp of Gloria's Holy Grail

Dedicatory: II Corinthians III (KJV), verse 18a BUT WE ALL, WITH OPEN FACE BEHOLDING AS IN A GLASS THE GLORY OF THE LORD, ARE CHANGED INTO THE SAME IMAGE.

& XII, verses 2 thru 5
I KNEW A MAN IN CHRIST ABOVE FOURTEEN YEARS AGO, WHETHER IN THE BODY, I CANNOT TELL, OR WHETHER OUT OF THE BODY, I CANNOT TELL, GOD KNOWETH: SUCH A ONE, CAUGHT UP TO THE THIRD HEAVEN.

AND I KNEW SUCH A MAN (WHETHER IN THE BODY, OR OUT OF THE BODY, I CANNOT TELL, GOD KNOWETH)

HOW THAT HE WAS CAUGHT UP INTO PARADISE, AND HEARD UNSPEAKABLE WORDS, WHICH IS NOT LAWFUL FOR A MAN TO UTTER! OF SUCH A ONE WILL I GLORY.

But the splendour that supplies
Strength and vigour to the skies,
And the universe controls,
Shunneth dark and ruined souls.
He who once hath seen this light
Will not call the sunbeam bright.

Boethius, from "The True Light"

Worship? Yea, what worship better
Than when free'd from every fetter

That the uninforming letter
Rivets on the tortured mind;
Man, with silent admiration
Sees the glories of Creation,
And, in holy contemplation,
Leaves the learned crowd behind!

JAMES CLERK MAXWELL

Ancient Light

The Pseudo-Screenplay
(with short story emphasis)

THE SOUND EFFECT:
One sphere round my whole
I show, intoned he;
The rest of my cross-sections
None can see.

MOTIF THEME SONG
(IN TWO PARTS)

NARRATOR

Mitchelville was a rather isolated place where the villagers gathered about in prayer meetings and revolt coups, or would convene public address conventions on some new discovery that often entailed hazardous results. Experiments involving space entropy, the tampering of any molecular structure, and so forth, was their telltale target the gangsters and ogres aimed for en masse.

These gentrified mad scientists were an elite nexus who focused on matter substitution and absolute energy factor, but were ever unable to decipher the axiomatic cosmic code that evaded them; that dodged some of their dismal deviancy!

GRADUAL ENTRANCE of oceanic effects

One of these pioneers of spirit, however, although not near as deluded as Mitchelville's madcap milieu, became forefront and intrepid when it came to attaining the Enveloped Enclosure through this peculiar medium of transformation. And these three writhed and wrestled with superpowers unawares and at large, until in due process, both were swept away by an unknown, unforeseen force!

An Acquired Dialogue hereupon of their abrupt breakaway of transport into another dimension begins. A state of being where completely real and concrete entities of intelligence communicate themselves as they are in relation to the superstructure of Eternal Spirit.

And now, let us consider the licentious lapse of a community gone berserk; Mitchelville that fell into its self-induced sinkhole, deprived of her citizens because they had departed for a time and a season. Two brave voyagers who were once gentlemen of renown, plus one doughty damsel, but entered an oblivion of so-called determinate *evanishment*. Never noticed again, and never to be recorded in history-- as if entirely having evacuated spacetime continuum, they would face erasure from the memories of friends and loved ones-- absolutely absent and nonexistent… The compound caste of the greater organization thereof scurries about to search out the AWOL missing expedition team, but still as of yet in vain, since their absence alters Time to such a degree that no one will ever list them on record, nor any roster whatsoever.

CHARACTER LEGEND AND DISPOSITION

¶ Captain Boyd Buford Harris is a doctorate graduate of the ITT Institute and had merited his tuition and scholarship by an outstanding service record via the Air Force Academy in Colorado Springs. His motherland was derived from upper Scotland, and much later, joined Rutherford and Hathaway, not only by rank, but in fellowship throughout the University program phase that matriculated these explorer guinea pigs in the long haul of their ordeal. Both he and the colonel, with the intern (as a triad), were commissioned to assume an assignment of unprecedented progress, yet no less that of a precipitous price tag; perchance losing their reputation en route! Like three cosmonauts of northern-nailed Russian bravado, their mountaintop Mission transpires. According to the Celtic poets: "Like three constables from Scotland Yard, but harmless and unarmed, divested of cattle prods and stanchions- preferably- ready to underpin a peaceful pact with this *Evader* of geometry which circumvents the laws of astrophysics. Howbeit, humanity, represented by each one of our candidates, would embark adventurously into terra-incognita once and for all Time, let us say.

Now Joyce Hathaway-- to tag along on the way with the other two, Harris and Rutherford, who have hastened her retinue, prioritized as a Protective Escort because of their military experience-- is of homegrown Native American stock. Her predecessors in retrospect, a few generations back, were weaned from an Apache Indian tribe. At long last, most noteworthy for her story-telling accomplishments throughout the national school curriculum, her intuitive abilities prove indispensable for the Air Force research duo. Her keen faculties of discernment and indispensable companionship corresponds above and beyond Mitchelville's empirical empire. *Empathy and precognitive prescience are her soulful trademarks and now pushed to the brink. Lookalike Goldilocks in full fastidious form, fancily featured even under her radiation suit, suited her hale sophistry of innate glamour- least of which modeled her flair. Howbeit, having had a constant blush all over her skin as a healthy Amerindian, her hair was auburn and her eyes piercing tawny; Hathaway's complexion was enviable among clans of her relatives and matriarchs, not to ignore the dashing showgirl's athletic fitness overall. Long-distance mountaineering and hiking rewarded by a good night's leisure, sharing folklore, storytelling, and blistering marshmallows with corn on the cob campfire feasts in the wilderness were her jewel in the crown pastimes of delightful delicacies.

On behalf of his crew, Adjutant Colonel Roderick Rutherford ranks the regalia and decoration emblematic of top aviator prowess that had set a stellar standard at the Colorado Springs [Super Ace Squadron], or SAS star-fleet for the NORAD Network. Having surrendered supersonic flight to retiree administrative work, he became more of a mentor and scoutmaster to the other twain, namely Harris and Joyce, than anything else. Besides big league business, our colonel single-handed separates the really steely men and woman from the wimps. I shan't belabor the credentials and character of this flying Ace when-- already, since their classmate reunion and friendship under the Lyceum Board of Cabinet Members-- Professor Emeritus Rutherford reinstalled the proper conduct of amity for auxiliary recall. Overall, the cooperation of these forerunners ought to qualify them for this otherworldly reconnaissance. Which was washed down to only handpicked eligibility! Still, a taunting sign had been brandished among many neighbors just prior to their launchpad: "NO mavericks, Mitchelville! ONLY masters and maestros!"

Fortunately, for that, Harris, Rutherford, and Hathaway (conveniently shortened to H, R, and H2 aboard my SCREENPLAY platform and plot) embody the buckskin bill of this criteria henceforward:

Not that they should be bamboozled by the cold Compound of parochial scrutiny, nor nailed by naysayer censorship. For to the dogeared galoots of the misanthropic Mitchelville mainframe-laden with myth, mimicry, mischief, and downright superstition, our beloved scientists excel therefrom and regardless of purposeless and petulant peer pressure!

ENTER ELECTRONIC SOUNDS AT THE FACILITY along with one nuclear Reactor device, and a wide panorama of control panels

INDUSTRIAL NOISE ON THE PREMISES

With exuberance of spirit, they boldly took their stand under the spotlight, preparatory to preemptive confrontation. Or so Mitchelville would have them believe. None of them conceded to their hampering dampers and defects among other platitudes.

(briefing in their private quarters of discourse)

H~ "So we will consider the divine depths of spirit- am I right, colonel?"

R~ "Affirmative. Yet more so, the warp-core cloven gweduc, the Arc Lamp of God- or designate it as the Bright Bridge that has covertly cavorted beyond living logic..."

H2~ "Hey, let me get in on this with my seaworthiness, okay?"

Both *H&R~ "You'll revive maritime, our lady Atargatis," jested the jokers, at least for momentary banter~ Alas, they stiffened up!

H2~ (insistingly) "You gentlemen had better do some explaining!" hammered Hathaway with one swarthy complexion that beamed through her euthermic uniform, regardless of its apparent opacity.

H~ "Whoa, wait a minute lass. What the *de'il* are ye tryin' to say, let alone convey-- my God, the very nature of such thinking--" huffed Harris, swaggering a wee nudge in his gait, possibly with ingrown imitation of the immemorial Robert Burns; roughened up from his early youth at the kiln and foundry full of furnaces, sledgehammers, knapping hammers, and manifold mallets.

Hathaway preferred docility, the receptive half-light of her hunch. The girlish but stately stature thereof, stoic as ever, eviscerated the onlookers and disemboweled them that gawked at her integrated intelligence. Evermore topnotch, she'll be on the contrary to Mitchelville's petulant and parochial mediocrity!

R~ "And thought it must be Captain and Joyce, just as well. So soon as we allow ourselves to step into that Mercury Mirror right over there..." redirected Rutherford, who had wrought rigid his index finger of resolution; whose sagely support pointed us all to perspicuous clarity of its formula, HgD^2O! Of which its eternally wet surface was just that: the heaviest, yea, weightiest version of mercury-deuterium-oxide adorned by an eggshell-and-acanthus framework stone-frozen to timeless tableaux of record keeping.

SOUNDTRACK SPECIAL

¶ R~ "Like Alice through her looking-glass, we can then exit this veritable veil of life and approach the unapproachable- to even dare inch our way toward that confrontational **gliff*."

*Chiefly Scot. suggestive flash, quick glance; glimpse

H2~ (excited) "This I've gotta see!"

H~ " You mean a mere slit or split-prism of infinity on the far Wall, you say?"

R~ "A far-fetched *catch-twenty-two...* exactly!"

PAUSE

H~ "Well, colonel Rutherford and our madam Hathaway. May I be convinced of such a thing- of such full blown energy bulged-tubular right behind the Front Revelatory *Glore. And may we be convinced. That is, by stepping over the brink of forever! Ah, where there lay a vast sea without a shore, nor edge."

*intransitive verb, To stare fixedly (from the Greek yellow/green) used here as a noun

R~ "You will, my captain Harris, no doubt you will..."

H2~ "So what's the hesitation, gentlemen? Off we go!"

MOTIF THEME SONG
(1ST PART ONLY)
SOUND EFFECTS
NARRATOR

For those who have never impaled the thickly veiled drapes of reality, and have never sampled an eternal forbidden fruit-- indeed, undisclosed to ignorance, but made available and afresh to the ones who'll venture out into terra-incognita. This mind-birth of fantastical exploration is at large and at long last presented, as it were, so that both past, present, and future are not to be confused with one another, save accepted as referential points of an explosive existence, otherwise comprehensible- yet defined somewhat in the very setting of our horizontal humanity pierced by the Vertical Voice.

SOUNDTRACK SPECIAL EFFECTS
(applause and then the inauguration)

R~ "Honorable ladies and gentlemen, prepare yourselves... I, Colonel Roderick Rutherford, along with Science Intern, Joyce Hathaway, and also distinguished Captain Boyd Buford Harris, who has steadfastly served with me as commissioned officer in the Space Academy Armed Forces-- not to exclude the good gala lady Joyce Hathaway, our mascot and authorized tag-along assistant of lubricity and foreknowledge (still incontestable by the Guinness Book of World Records for ESP abilities at the Sutherland Parapsychology Research Center; even unmatched by records of the late Uri Geller, Israeli-British illusionist and self-proclaimed psychic)-- are seated before the Townspeople & General Assembly of the Greater Mitchelville Area, to deliberately declare and confirm the consonance, the dynamics and radiant reality of the Alteratorium, if I may so venture to vindicate if not vaunt.

"The Alteratorium is coupled morphology for what an ordinary auditorium, the suffix, can be capable of if altered, the prefix, via the spatial fourth dimension (not necessarily Time itself), whether it be self-reversal, or transmogrification into a metaphysical version of former conventionality! *In extremis*, it is some seventh-dimensional enveloped enclosure, so to speak, that can alter itself, or the contents thereof, throughout whatever wavelength one's spirit exhibits or inhibits-- either way, albeit! Fundamentally, like Star Trek's *holodeck* or *holo-suite*, except that no photon energy is needed since rawest reality of concrete existence *really* reverberates irrevocably, *yet rather irreplicable (if I dare say it in my simplified supposition, although confirmed by painstaking and extensive laboratory supercomputer simulations conducted/ performed beyond bookish academics)! All-hail the Alteratorium advantage!"

*That which has no facsimile and that cannot be replicated nor derived from any "graven image, representation, or idol," Borrowed from Anglo-French *simulacre*; what is selfsame with neither likeness, nor imitation (immutable) or (unalterable).

~the beehive buzzing with puzzlement hath grown astir~

(two voices clarify this scenario out of gibberish and murmuring. Then, indistinct chatter from the audience, short of an uproar, but by golly boisterous)

OTHER~ "But colonel, how can I be sure it is not a hoax of some sort, or ghostly garb- like an apparition, for that matter, eh?"

(someone else): "Uh, yeah... Hey, how may it be feasible for any of us to believe your so-called infallible proof; a doggone gallimaufry report taken at face value, or with a grain of salt?"

Thus the two separately opinionated statesmen had postured themselves, as if eruditely against our veteran Air Force exemplar. He was prodded by gadfly killjoys and naysayers. That big bunch of bibliophiles and pedants. Meantime, Harris and Hathaway puckered their stiff upper lips, on garrison and unwilling to haggle with their crucible of inquisition, though the gallows and guillotine were woefully itemized amid Mitchelville's macabre mainstay stronghold! Whence once the Dark Ages had preserved cobwebbed closets and storage chambers and dungeons, an iron maiden must have been left behind heretofore! In this case, courtroom supply and demand was worshiped and idolized over threadbare necessities, or even survival at such a compound.

Rutherford redirected them and squelched any irritability with his trademark of characteristic 'resolute reassurance'. That all was well, no matter what, was no facile task! As time elapsed, the curious congregants gathered by the droves from all corners of surrounding suburbia. Already, there were media-press reporters relegating their own version of coverage calibrated to captivate the entertainment masses; a showtime TelePrompTer televised, of course.

The lone leader of the pack steps up to the podium.

BACKGROUND "MUZAK"

R~ " Behold, high-ranking regal officiators of prefatory progress! I speak not as an inactive conference confrere only, but as ready representative to typify two mere men and a wee woman on a mission; that is, to unravel the riddle and jigsaw puzzle of some cosmic enigma long sustained sub rosa. What we intend to prove before countless witnesses herein huddled with the elected and nominated party telecast worldwide (would ye believe it?) are NOT antics of a magician's parlor tricks, neither fraud, nor deception as some suspect. Instead, and rather, my most Beneficial Bunch: what ye are about to see for yourself-- and I say the letter C by the number four, or C4 yourself, as apparatus appertained beforehand via viewership published on reams of letterheads and gazette headlines about *Vortronics in light of the Big Ball*-- was never devised down epochs past!

"Virtually, you notice Joyce Hathaway, Captain Harris, & myself recede away from the status quo of man's exiled existence as everyone would see when we'll slip away out-of-bounds by subspace traversal. Getting smaller and tinier to undersized diminution as opposed to augmentation; until shrunken inwardly into a vanishing point that winks with naught, never to have been there in the first place to begin with (once we pass the threshold)! The point of no return, just about, at the even horizon of an omnipresent singularity. The utterly forbidden zone of nonexistence and extinction whereby your entire community will be unaware that this has ever occurred, I declare; by reason of our entrance through the INCONTROVERTIBLE Fourth Dimension."

(Rutherford allows Joyce to take over the microphone for timelier absorption of the colonel's *syllabus-bellyful* speech in his outreach)

H2~ "Greetings, my Mitchell Corn Palace company." (here, Hathaway had her hearsay of fun and fancy, but yet technical as could be) "Now picture the Giza Pyramid observed at a forty-five degree angle from a helicopter. The shadow of which would resemble a trapezoid. Conversely, from a 4-D perspective, the image unfolds fast-forward into a trapezohedron, and even more so, as our team is reduced (by perspective only, for we remain lifelike) and enlarged back out again on the other side! In like manner, our Departure is altogether the same. Although, normally, we would- with a flash of lightning and no thunderclap- disappear immediately, our exit shall show *slow motion* due to the inherent Time-dilated displacement--"

OTHER~ "Allow us to interject with the presiding council therefore, O colonel. That as commissioned magistrates to enforce the rule of thumb, that no man should be a judge in his own cause, especially based on uncommon events; for the benefit of the doubt, nonetheless, we grant you affable access to Providential blessings. In consideration of paranormal phenomena and the Supernatural, *go in peace*," and using archaic proconsular Latin, "vade in pace."

Plaudits & praise; not that of a mad mob, but of civilized society.

(unconvinced, an otter that has crept in from the outside, peeks in, utters nothing, and scampers away...) The winds whip and whoop!

OTTER~ "-----" *a semiaquatic fish-eating mammal of the weasel family, with an elongated body, dense fur, and webbed feet.

The churning of an outdoors squall squeals to a yowl and thunder!

In the interim, just minutes before bailing out, our colonel, captain, and intern reinforce their Faraday cage coats of mail and amble onto a linoleum-caked platform right under an elongated rectangular mirror agleam with hypnotic liquid. Luminous luster over its sheer sheen and sleek steel of quicksilver quivers *glisteringly*, so much to the effulgent effect of blinding the onlooker, if one were to haphazardly gaze thereupon. If it were weighed by a *gliff* or a side-glance obliquely, the sized-up, sideways, vertical bathtub of wavelets and wimples writhed, wrenching the visitor by an alluring lake of Lethe as *through a glass, darkly*, discarnate!

The tryout Trio tentatively touch a moist membrane of the Hg *Miroir*, not unlike memoirs of 3185 and 9411 in a supercity called Metro-Aorta published in magazines and tabloids of the renown Vortronics CE-5 (Close Encounters of the Fifth) kind or Fifth Element comprised of a neutron star's purest plasma pliancy under laboratory-induced anti-gravitation! This time around, a technological *teleoroentgenogram from a discreet distance of six feet faced its glitz to detect a cogent cortex of it under X-ray recordings.

*Radiography with one X-ray tube positioned at 2 m from the film thereby securing practical parallelism of the x-rays to minimize geometric distortion; the standard configuration for chest radiography. The prima-facie (at first sight) entirety of the mirror.

Heartfelt Hathaway, transfixed by the Mercury Mirror's visceral vortices, and in *consanguineous propinquity to the *infrothermal* investiture of *exitory* gateways multiplied innumerably, referred herself to First Corinthians, chapter thirteen, verse twelve that she had memorized by heart (in the King James Vernacular): "For now we see through a glass, darkly; but then face to face: now I know in part; but then shall I know even as also I am known." This then was the afflatus of her heavenly hope: the end of restless growth.

Then the three pause and poise to jump over into the Mercury Mirror with Rutherford mouthing off a flashcard menu of contingency protocols, their O-6 grade drill instructor calling cadence: *Once, twice, thrice, and alley-oop"....*

"There they go!" a megaphone of the throng thrashes the hush of suspense and solemnity. A content calm before the storm.

**Author's personal note on this tertiary protagonist. Namely, Joyce Hathaway exhibited ancestral linkages of possible reincarnation under hypnosis in her school of parapsychology. Consanguineous to the point of blood relations with Apache tribe shamans. With proper propinquity of kindred spirit nearness, she showed signs of 'infrothermal' contact and connection as when two mirrors are vis-a-vis with one another, reflecting through refractive reduction an infinitude to "nowhere", except extenuated tenuously over the ethereal realm. One might, in theory, reverse him or herself by supernumerary *birefringence* (id est, double refraction) of four-dimensional rotation either way; that is if this were a 4-D looking-glass! In which case, the Mercury Mirror indeed *is*~ indisputably~ blazoned by my screenplay of Ancient Light!

The *daredevils* (an epithet the townspeople placarded them with) plunge into its shiny film of quartz and amethyst and disintegrate like on transporter pods of the *Starship* Enterprise*

*Bookend thanks to Gene Roddenberry's original concept for Star Trek (which was "Wagon Train to the Stars") precedent to the television series debut. This comparison is hereunto accordingly accredited. Needless to add, much of my inspiration had been drawn from the episodes thereof, too many to count... Our immemorial wellspring of the Muses to have nudged the entire globe over to a finer axis because of his genius.

Fizzle! Cyclonic aftereffects follow the EXIT of our Three Graces.

APPLAUSE AND APPROBATION

Sound effects of dwindling away (whatever *that* sounds like)!

OTHERS~ "My-- my dear Gawd, how harrowing of a spectacle! Blimey!" A volcanic eruption: "*Thar she blows*! Our threesome reduced to subzero for the numerologist…"

"Oh, for crying out loud! Heavens! Where the devil are they?"

"They're gone, totally!" the *carnificial* compound of cacophony rants and raves.

The simpletons, suitors, sinners and saints alike; the supremacists, soldiers, supermen along with hardcore scientists, and an old silly goose; yea, the Galloping Goose of an elder era grow grievously terror-blanched and start to run and froth frantically. The rude, ignominious officials of rogue regalia turn to mutant frogs without a princess to kiss them; hopping or jumping off simmering sidewalks singed by blistering high noontide of the Summer Hammer! Hellbent scarecrow Mitchelville lay deprived of her possessions after people like Rutherford, Harris, and Hathaway flit out of reality in the *wink* of an eye, *goodbye* and farewell!

NARRATOR

¶ But then there came a listless lull ere eventually, and in casual lackluster disinterest, the galoot gathering of thugs and acting officers resume their Activities of Daily Living, or indoor ADL behavior (monitored by jaded gerontocracy for the potentially infirm). The banal bonhomie of sincere triteness flooded the gap of what once were the colonel, captain, and intern, now abysmally absent. Such restored composure of their civic meetup had everyone reconvene for further notice of nothing whatsoever! Not even knowing, nor having the foggiest notion of any developed departure, just as our travelers had never been born. ------ "Bah!" nods a nincompoop peevishly.

The public square squires of the Dark Era anticipate naught!

"President Rodney, any questions at this level?" the portly petty officer rattles the commodore's cage. In reply, the all-in-one provost marshal, buckled up in sartorial fashion, elicits a sardonic grin no different than the Cheshire cat contorting his wide face in Alice's Wonderland. And slowly, without one hiss, deflates his hot-air gasbag bogged by stuffy and corporate flatulence; an oft usage of interchangeable hierarchy at the flip of a switch was the congregant's custom and privilege at the beck and call of another convention. A hearing? That too!

"Well now, proctor --- duh! I verily don't understand the hangup. Why we wheedle with insurmountable odds, expecting payback, is beyond me. Wherefore we hold out a religious convocation, especially like this one without a purpose, hmm?"

OTHER~ "Let's call it a session. Away with you! Let us retire for the long night," a bellicose bystander fumes, nodding his noggins.

(no more otter) … zilch!

MODERATOR

(my fair-share of cameo versatility, but just this once)!

And it came to pass uneventfully that the amalgamated lot of this grotty group filed out of the auditorium; some groggily satiated by the afterglow of the mirror's *HgD2O* fizzing and effervescing in an upright sideways cistern. The self-conscious gelatinous gateway to nowhere waffled its nibs of nodes, crests, wavelets, and whitecaps to no end twenty-four hours, seven days a week, three-hundred and sixty-five days a year, without cessation. But so entirely indestructible to any of the jitters, skitters and scuffs of primitive inquisitors. No effigy, but a garlanded lake hung on the wall.

From one aeon to another, as centuries flitted by, the quicksilver supernal-glass, like a Stargate (an Einstein-Rosen bridge portal device within the Stargate fictional universe that allows practical, rapid travel between two distant locations) endured the glacial permafrost of Time. Soon afterwards, until the frosty snowballing effect of our Universe 'glissades' and re-collapses back into her Big Crunch, starting all over again, but with *neutronization* of the invincible HgD2O still intact if yet ubiquitously yielded thereabouts.

Nor ever affected by the recycled, regurgitated ravages thereof.

And just like that, the statesmen and officials fell under slumber of the Mitchelville First Assembly. Eftsoon, the village fell to an overblown metropolis as a thousand calendars were replaced on the ghostly Tall Wall of a forgotten and deserted storage emporium floored out with starry linoleum that refused to deteriorate. It consisted of a hyper-polymer, but one step below the Mercury Mirror's ageless neutron Paste, whose adhesive cohesion was inertly tucked in with an eternal imprint and impression. Yea, on which the footprints of spacetime were awash by an endless void of wet erasure.

Moments meandered, marching by at closeup propinquity. The quicksilver years of filmstrip fury became but momentary from the catapult of the Hathaway, Harris, and Rutherford ready-resumption

Their souls, bodily *in transitu*, undergo transference to terra nova!

SOUND EFFECTS- AND THEN SOULFUL <u>SILENCE</u>!

(an impossible symmetry encloses their newfound station, like the analogy Joyce had foreknown. Except that this was within a polyhedron of kaleidoscopic sides, multidimensional, and inside-out!)

In addition to the mind-bending alteration of the laws of physics, a strong scent, reminiscent of Boyd's lumberjack job years before his ranking promotion from cadet to captain, permeated uncanny surroundings. It was the smell of hickory burnt by old smokehouse smoldering of timber by samples such as hickory, oak, mesquite, cherry, and pecan kindling~ that he had bundled for faggots afire~ were recognized… The other two didn't have any recollection of it.

Secondly, Joyce's jubilant memories of her girlhood were rightly resurrected with floral fragrances from the Coventry Garden of the Brittany (or Great Britain renamed after World-War-Three only a few decades before the year 2113). It was the redolence of rosebuds newly sprung in spring along with the vernal aura of cherry trees in full bloom, blithely blushing upon a hillside. Swoon sweetness of the tuberose and gardenia had taken her aback transfixed.

And thirdly, the fatherly Roderick remembered indescribable instances no less whilst he savored the aromatic Ocean Spray [not the tart and delectable juicy beverage, O for goodness sake]! The oceanic excursions that took our dear colonel to the depths of the Mariana Trench (via imagination only) as the younger recruit of airborne skydiving, parachute and Flight School, reveled in wishing to take on naval & mariner ventures before his final decision!

Thus these olfactory sensations by big enhancement of the Pineal gland in the brain for acute stereoscopic awareness overtook Earth visitors that R, H, & H2 exhibited, but inwardly embodied ad hoc.

The big mirror's Paste turned to epoxy narrower than a yoctometer replete with gluons, *gluors*, and *gluces*. The latter two, Tomorrow's prognosticated discovery of exotic, *hot energy in Life's cookbook.

*"If you want to know the secrets of the universe, think in terms of energy, frequency, and vibration." ~Nikola Tesla

THE OTHERWORLDLY REALM

(their predicament at hand)

R~ "Are you all in one peace?"

H2~ "Yeah, just feeling a bit queasy. I can handle it."

R~ "And what about you, captain?"

H~ "Aye, colonel- me thinks so. But it's... it's not easy... For look at *that*!"

[AUTHORIZED] SOUND EFFECTS

R~ "I-- I know... Now get a grasp of yourselves, please.

WEEPING: *"*Hold on tight* to your souls! It's the the most important---" (cried Rutherford, and all three succored one another)

*"Hold On Tight" is a song written and performed by Electric Light Orchestra (ELO). The song is track twelve on the band's 1981 album Time and was the first song released as a single.

MORE SOUND EFFECTS: The amplified churning of the ocean reverberated Roderick's youthful and young adult dream. Only this time, such upheavals of super-tall, mountain-sized whopper waves and tsunamis phlegmatically lurch about like molten molasses of magma and lava. Licking up the vacuum of what was before but a hyper-polyhedron for a few minutes, now dissipated into this gold gargantuan hydrodynamic augmentation (though the span thereof is virtually unnoticeable), nevertheless, looking larger~ millions of times over- than the already unfathomable Pacific basin so serene by comparison!

And in the midst thereof, with watery walls on each side of them- when once Moses manned the Exodus of ancient Israel into the Red Sea, after whom Pharaoh would doggedly charioteer in hot pursuit- in like manner, our threesome squad (of yet another diaspora under emergency, in dire need of deliverance) flew through.

Eerie echoes from the past, present, and future are heard, hollowly.

H2~ "Ooh! Where are we? Ugh!" Joyce gasps and feels vertigo- trying not to hyperventilate from such scintillating pyrotechnics.

R~ "Hell, I think we are still in transition through fourth-dimensional time. Notice the myriads of galactic Gardens and elliptical blobs bloating about hither and thither and, my God! All around! Quadrillions of them, each as microscopic grains of sand. Like in my vacation visit to the Great Sand Dunes National Park and Preserve monument." Though they had no inkling of analysis, overwrought Rutherford reported with a last resort, "Like snowflakes adrift in midair, except no tarmac backdrop. Only transparency!"

(Highways of crossroads converge at the confluence of lake Lethe)

MODERATOR

Hereupon, with irrelevant reality dissolved by the winds of ebb and flow and flailing flux, our first pioneers purpose themselves by a strapping belt of determination. They then are conveyed at length light-years **elongated* throughout. After a few minutes, their automatic buoy-bob or boat-ride began to hitch heavily and the 3 humanoids were gently dispensed overboard, only to set foot on some sterile, obviously consecrated seashore.

*Due to the stretching of spacetime continuum itself, in-between distances can dilate! In light of Inflationary Expansion (the Hubble constant), galaxy clusters spread apart.

MELODIC MOTIF: *SOUND EFFECTS*

TATM

Enter ye my warm
Womb Intramural.
Away from what is urban,
What is rural.

My split prismatic slit,
Thy entrance pending;
So step right up and
Feel the Never-ending!

I was, I am, I shall
Be brightly white,
Above mere men and beasts
Of flesh that bite.

As gold leaf edges
Singed by old, old age,
You yet enshrine your
Time upon a stage;

But now, O thou that
Dare encroach nearby,
For thee there be but
Destiny here, aye!

Observe my spectral
Audit left unhinged:
It narrow and
Conflagrant be
Sun-singed!

If things are as they
Are apparently,
It opens out to
Thee transparently.

O warning! No unholy
Thoughts can test
The retribution of
A hornets' nest!

As nicely a high-ceiling
Stretched would loom
Up overhead, concealing
One white Womb:

Above thee on another
Floor she waits...
With luminosity
Beyond gold gates-

Swung open to receive
Thy person-hood,
Tho' predisposed,
Dispensing Mercy good!

But whatsoever intent
Should intrude,
I hurl a lightning bolt
At what is rude!

No matter what the
Nature of divulgence,
Intelligence still shines
Her half-effulgence.

If anyone would
Merely turn to Me,
I'll guard that soul with
Walled Eternity!

As on some lake of
Lethe no remembrance
Lay, I say: She'll offer
Anyone an entrance
To the fey Highway.

END OF LINE

Back to normalcy…
NARRATOR

Certainly it had been the labyrinthine limbo of walls within which they stood their ground. Our astronauts tremble like jelly, or as Polish Galareta doused with a dash of apple cider vinegar. For passersby on this platform were pickled and dispossessed of what was fickle [literally]!

But back on terra firma, featured fabulously, and no less likewise, to foreshadow and copycat their every step of the way, life's Mercury Mirror's installed empathy-integrated circuit chip caused it to quiver just the same, feeling neuron impulses from each one's thoughts funneled through a wormhole; needless to admit, against the littlest quarrel, quivering among Mitchelville men and women whenever vitriolic! Long-suffering, that is, the lit HgD2O thereof.

Joyce in particular, due to her frail stature albeit big heart and soul, appeared ashen and pallid from the Conduit Slip-Trip of precisely 31.3 *gigaparsecs gone by in a glitch of time-lapse. Things were fantastically sped up along the way, or so flowingly! Hence for the sake of her levelheaded composure, and for both the colonel and captain, the observable cosmos conveniently came up to froth forth with one fluminous flash that flurried blizzard-like, snowily blown, and via the *unitubularity, *oilily, alley-oop...* That fast, for the life of her! Culvert tributaries of Time wax waywardly acrawl.

*To be exact, a gigaparsec is equivalent to 3,261,564,219.5314 light-years long! On the other hand, our observable universe is approximately 93 billion light-years wide, while the spatial size of its entire universality is absolutely unknown, nor can it ever be delineated by measurement since the tiny photons thereof shall have never enough time to reach us as it continues to expand. Hence the 31.3 gigaparsecs that the characters of Ancient Light bypass in only seconds via the Mercury Mirror's wormhole that is alternatively engineered as an inter-dimensional *unitubularity,* or, to put it in finer English, a singularity conveyance tube is not unlike a Hyper Loop transport, as such.

Reminder: the singularity Conveyance Tube will be referred to and abbreviated as CT for now on... Remember the Conveyance Tube.

Moreover, a profuse and primary Empress of omniscience eclipsed 'this little light of mine, I'm gonna let it shine' on their part! Colonel Rutherford swiveled the backside of his head and about-faced himself on cue of a command unheard of. The rest of the two, counted on half-a-hand, followed him as monkeys behind their alpha male. As primates of Moon Watcher encircle the sleek slab of a *monolith, like in Arthur C. Clarke's Space Odyssey series, so, too, our close-knit clan inches closer to a bleak blank wall or *Mure* right in front. The ratio of which, with extensity, is 1:4:9!

*In the novel, the Russian crewmen of the spaceship *Alexei Leonov* refer to TMA-2 as "*Zagadka*" (from the Russian word for "enigma", "mystery", or "riddle").

Still, the imposing adjacent surface clenched the colonel and captain off their rockers via graphite fingers of Dirac or Magnetic Monopole intensity (rare in nature, although possible). For obvious reasons, the intern cowered in back of them, crooned, sighed, and shrugged it off. She felt affronted by a confrontational cul-de-sac.

And they, the visitors from planet Earth, on this Paradise of Other-side Afterlife, were beholden to an overbearing superpower, only to refrain from frazzling incredulity, or from going bonkers.

^ ^ ^ ^ ^ ^ ^ ^ ^ ^ ^ ^ ^ ^ ^ ^ ^ ^ ^

Choruses of coloratura soprano and tremulous vibrato resound

R~ “O captain, brace yourself.”

H~ “Aye, colonel! – What must we do? I *canna* comprehend!”

H2~ (Madam Hathaway had becalmed herself, as if embalmed by her old alter ego, since this *was* the Afterlife after all) “Now simmer down, gentlemen, and take a deep breath, dead or alive, yeah!”

R~ “At this point, I know not what to make of it, for it seems we are, as it were, at its mercy. Am I right, Joyce?” She turned to both of them with sympathetic solace of tender-loving concern, but outright glared back at the Tall Wall’s backlash of Bloated Blankness. Blindingly surfaced far off, mellow-tone minor-diminished nearby, the Permanent Partition gnawed at everyone’s covert conscience!

H~ “Who’s mercy?” timorously queried the commissioned First Officer of the colonel as they all bivouacked beyond the Starfield.

Shrills of ultrahigh coloratura choruses *correspondingly* augment!
(at their checkmate, everyone was mortified by bone and marrow)
A *CACOPHONY* OF ORCHESTRAL DISSONANCE
Key: TATM is an acronym for *Transalteratorium

*The author’s coinage for an *auditorium* that can alter itself to whatever one desires! Such a self-created word found its year of inception as early as 1985. The other prefix *Trans-* came a few of years later after military boot camp in 1987 at Fort Bliss, Texas, and Fort Gordon, Georgia. By then in late 1989, or thereabouts, the *Transalteratorium* came into being with recorded reel-to-reel replay of the dramatized variation thereof.

(at the same time, this is what tantalized their measly mindset)

¶ The TATM system (henceforth, as if it were a Still Small Voice in lowercase capitals, although thunderous): I AM NOW AS I WAS AND

EVER SHALL BE- BEFORE GOD ONLY YOU MUST THEN BOW- BUT BEFORE ME, YOU MAY BE AS YE ARE. SPEAK! WHAT HAST THOU TO CONFESS?

R~ "We admire your syntax, your majesty, or whoever you are--"

TATM~ NOT SO, O RODERICK! MERE MAN, FOR ONLY THE DIVINE SPIRIT IS MAJESTIC, BUT I AM CREATURELY; AN ARCHSERAPHIM OF A REFINED HIGHER ORDER OF BEING- THAT OF PRISTINE SPIRIT. YOU MAY ADDRESS ME AS THE TRANSALTERATORIUM.

R~ (astounded) "Did you hear that, captain? It knows my name."

H~ "Aye, colonel. And not only that, but perhaps a wee bit more!" was his unwarranted understatement.

Joyce Hathaway was taciturn and goggle-eyed in their astonishment. She instead had gestured an earthly signal of salutation by waving her hand and forearm at the Tall Wall. A Permanent Partition: the one which was otherwise white, but with a jet-black narrow doorway at the base thereof, floor-level.

H2~ "Hey, let's ask it something," she suggested and elbowed Rutherford while by his side, prodding him. Harris held off for now, standing on his own accord, waiting to see what happens next.

TATM~ AND WHAT THOU THINKEST, I HAVE FOREKNOWN LONG BEFORE THE COSMIC CREATION- YOU WERE ABOUT TO INQUIRE OF ME, 'WHAT AM I'?

H~ "Splendid! It interprets our mentality! Now *that's* incredible!"

TATM~ MAY THIS BE THE ACQUIRED DIALOGUE YOU HAVE SEARCHED FOR- BUT BE ADVISED: I AM NOT AN *EIGHT BALL YOU CAN MEDDLE WITH, NOR A OUIJA BOARD YOU DARE DILLY-DALLY THEREUPON. NEITHER

THE INTERNET (OF COURSE, YOUR HANDHELD HOLOGRAMS ARE ALSO INADEQUATE), SUFFICE IT TO SAY.

*To play the fortune-telling game, you had to vigorously shake the plastic magic 8 ball toy and flip it over to reveal the answer to your question. Such items were once sold at Kmart and Walmart stores among many others. Ironically, for some oddball reason, the author of this Book rarely played with one, if ever!

(cont): NONETHELESS, TO HAVE THY SPACETIME INQUIRIES ANSWERED WHILE I RESIDE TIMELESSLY AND BOUND BY NOTHING, LET US PROCEED DIMINUTIVE. AND NOW, SINCE YOU SEE SIMPLY AN IMAGE OF MY BLANKNESS BEFORE THEE- ONE OUT OF NEAR-INFINITE CONTOURS CONTAINED ELSEWHERE- WE CONDESCEND TO YOUR THREE-DIMENSIONAL TIME-FRAME OF PERCEPTION. THE SPLIT MOMENT OF YOUR YEARS ARE ATTENUATED TO A THREADBARE STRING OR TIGHTROPE INSIDE OF OUR SINGULARITY IN ORDER TO DISCLOSE THE WALLED WOMB WHICH HATH CIRCUMMURED ALL OF YE AT ONCE. YE ARE ACCOMMODATED FOR FREYA'S FREEDOM, NOT FOR INCURABLE INCARCERATION.

H2~ "So may we enter the doorway in front of us, our lordship, O TATM room, and catch a glorified glimpse of the eternal?" Joyce jabbed at the *mure* of the maze, to muster the temerity of what she was well known for. In the past, during her adolescent schooldays, feisty Joyce had oft refused to pussyfoot around with her taunters when she was ridiculed for being oversensitive. The students were scared of her prowess to discern filmstrips of their thoughts which spoke louder than words. The cerebral and *in myocardium* impressions that she received from them had forced the spry and perceptive girl to overhaul herself; to perforce form a barrier against psychic noise. On this exalted platform of Acquired Dialogue, all the more, since every overpowering Presence pressured her haplessly!

TATM~ AH, WHAT A CONTROVERSIAL SPECTACLE! THREE MORTALS FROM THE TELLURIAN DOMAIN THAT COVET THE UNKNOWN, YET UNQUALIFIED TO ENDURE.

A CAESURA OF *INAUDIBLE* 'INTONATION'

TATM~ IF YOU, *HA-HA-HA! (electronic dial tone on the telephone) IF YOU BUT DARE CONFRONT ME WITHOUT SIN, I SHALL OPEN THE DOOR! BUT IF I DETECT ANY WRINKLE, OR STAIN INSIDE OF YOUR SOUL- IMMEDIATE ANNIHILATION WILL BE THE END RESULT, EVEN TO THE RESIDUAL STRINGIEST SHRED THEREOF! NOT TO BE STANDOFFISH!

*The almost human Ha-Ha-Ha laughter (though slightly psychotic) was originally reproduced by the Votrax speech synthesizer in the early 1980s for both the GORF and Wizard of Wor coin-slot video arcade game machines. Evidently, reading Rutherford's subconscious memory bank, the Transalteratorium incorporated the comical cackle as if to reconnect with one of them, if not all at once! For your information, the design of the speech synthesizer was created back in 1970 by computer programmer, Richard T. Gagnon in his laboratory basement. Now whether or not most or all of his innovation contributed to the aforementioned arcade games is not entirely confirmed within Yard Lamp of Gloria.

NARRATOR, *nothing more*

Soon enough, piqued by pangs of compunction, the three disconcerted sojourners pause before the firsthand, hardcore rebuke of a faceless wall that dwarfed so imposingly their backstage stance.

Suddenly, as if for the purpose of pacification, the huge Hyper-Waves, each as lofty as Mount Everest, surrounded them. This time phantasmagorical. *So much for longing for the Pacific ocean*, reminisced Rutherford. Clearly, vertical dividers of Eternity would wall all of them in rather, protectively procured by some large labyrinth far beyond incomprehension. Numerous numbers of shuffling sorts and ciphers of unknown origin brainstormed him with innumerable reckoning, registration, recount, and tallies that easily surpass even the *Googolplex gorgon! Sums of such bridged a lackluster lacuna.

*Googolplex is equivalent to ten raised to the power of a googol. This means that the googol zeros to the right (that make up such a number) exceed such cubic Planck volumes which comprise our observable universe at about 93 billion light-years from end to end. One Planck point is a septillion times smaller that an electron or proton of an atom, give or take a few infinitesimal fractions...The Yard Lamp of Gloria storyboard does not require reviewers thereof to grasp for bamboo straws turned to long pipeline conduits devoid of an open end. Exemptions therefrom are now highly recommended.

Avoiding vomit from disorientation of the first degree, one would not attempt to induce any haphazard hoopla, if so seduced. Rock-solid, settled sanguinely in his resolve, Rutherford took on the most logical action to prepare his team for the inevitable, making sure an impromptu stunt could not be pulled by any of them at the long haul of the bargain. The contingency reserve that should have been dealt with yielded yardstick usage of careful cunning.

Notwithstanding this, still swayed by what lay unimaginable, the colonel concluded that this Voice-Over from the indomitable Transalteratorium had hard-pitched a verbal fastball from out of nowhere. No catcher's mitt was available for recovery as each of the individuals were ordered to stand steady, firm, unwavering in the face of the impossible yet to unveil. With unanimous Yes Sir from Harris and Hathaway, the colonel's command was satisfied for their sake. He had to yell through the undulant surf and spray.

R~ "In other words, remain unwavering in your conviction, and don't let TATM bully you about. And no more of that *ad lib* stuff, is that clear?!" (they rocked back and forth on some lifeboat flotation device, having been splashed and drenched with surly seawater)

H~ "What?" the captain tilted his noggins to hear better for the whooping typhoon recoiled with an un coup de tonnerre titanic.

R~ "You heard me, mister!" Rutherford barked. Harris held Joyce.

H2 and H~ "You have our badge of honor, O squad leader!" and that was the end of Rutherford's rally and reeling over the wave-front. Cooperating, they understood full well, and *he* especially.

The tempestuous lashings of furious foam and brine turns to a trickle down the front wall of the TATM roomful of wet hush, and vanishes out of sight, preferably never to be encountered again, as it were: chiseled in granite under another covenant of the rainbow!

The colonel's countermeasures were armed with enforcement.

SUPPLEMENTARY NARRATION

Following the great deluge of entrenchment that drenches both bone and marrow, soul and spirit impartially, the spectral sparkle of a rainbow reassured the expedition team of no more oceanic shock and awe. Only that everything was unnaturally *now* numbly quiet! Yea, they couldn't negotiate resistance against an unutterable mute-mode of this suppressive Silencer… Its hydroscopic sponge equalized the pounds-per-cubic-foot flow of barometric pressure; its decompression chamber challenged any intent of intrusion. Furthermore, not even firearm muzzle-loader musketry, nor any dogfight double-barrel shotgun could ripple the super-pervasive hush-hush, "Shh! Keep your voice down!" quiet quell of the Vitronic Silencer that had no woeful outcry of vainglory; nor promiscuity, nay! Neither noise-- but point Planck blankness leveled to subliminal cessation and inactivity. The serene cynosure of what welcomed each on a first name basis~ on a more personal level of intimate makeover!

For what once were two erudite cadets and a college student, promoted to a commissioned enterprise, became downright dumbfounded by the pure unfolding of infallible logic and authorization:

(here is where would-be West Point discipline fails to cut the cake)

TATM~ **ALLOW ME THEREFORE TO MANIFEST MYSELF!** Bellowed deafeningly the bullhorn of its contrapuntal thunderclap.

SOMBER SOUND EFFECTS & NARRATOR

Until imposingly, out of nowhere, in the vacuous void of anti-decibel auditory nerve-sucking super Silence, a blown ballooning Spheroid augmented itself seamlessly surpassing bloated blowups of inflationary expansion, but from an infinitesimal vantage point. Of hyper-curvature elasticity more durable than an *Ektelon echelon of reasserting resilience~ more malleable than superfluid flux!

*Ektelon, Inc. is an American manufacturer of equipment for racquetball sporting.

A variable vindicator of contortion, or that of stretchable strength far beyond the adhesive cohesion of gluons, if it can tighten tensile interlink with an in-betwixt twist of a turnbuckle!

Too taboo to be on the blacklist of a dangerous experiment, the overweight heft of Hyper-Wholeness (if one may daringly describe it) exceeds all known laws of physics, but does not defy them in its adherence to harmony and order. With such continual curvation yet "spheriness" to it as to render any other geometrical convexity only a flat shadow compared.

Where bare necessity strips humankind of rank, but not dignity of spirit, for the time at hand they were recalled- everyone- by their forenames lest society and status should pave a pigeonhole through the *sancta sanctorums* of ypsiliform TATMs. There were many of such in the labyrinthic limbo of linoleum and latex floors and walls and ceilings that were once antediluvian sodden, earthen, and feral!

COLORATURA CHORUS

Roderick, Boyd, and Joyce were petrified stone-frozen stiff, stifled by the lack thereof. The denuding displacements of colder, kosher Reality and the confrontation of 'contiguous concrescence' was more concrete than beforehand, but insufferable.

TATM~ AND NOW, THE UNSPEAKABLE- THE UNLAWFUL IS ABOUT TO BE DIVULGED; HOWBEIT ABLE TO SHATTER YOUR PRECONCEIVED NOTIONS... PREPARE YOURSELVES!

Roderick~ "Number one on my threefold questionnaire, your excellency: 1) What are you primarily, and with what verification?

ADDITIONAL AUDIBLE EFFECTS

TATM~ I WAS, I AM, & I SHALL BE THE ONE OUT OF MANY, A HYPERSPHERE WHOSE NOMENCLATURE IS BORTEUM AND CREMEUM. BUT MORTEUM, HOWEVER, IS FORBIDDEN TO BE REVEALED (IN THAT HE HAD FALLEN AEONS AGO WITH A THIRD OR TERTIARY CHOIR OF THE HEAVENLY HOSTS). HELLBOUND REBELS WERE THEY, I SAY! WE ARE, AS IT WERE, SOLE SURVIVORS AND FAITHFUL TO HAVE REPUDIATED LUCIFER'S INSURRECTION. WE WORSHIP YHWH, AND HIM ONLY DO WE GLORIFY WITH WESTINGHOUSE HYPERDULIA OF VENERATION!

Sidestepping the crucial issue of the Transalteratorium's tidings, Roderick would turnabout to Joyce and Boyd by expository exemption adopted in his former fanfare at the Lyceum Board of Cabinet Members. The lecture hall instilled in him dogmatic doldrums in debate, diplomacy, courtesy, and custom somewhat suitable for such scenarios; especially this dizzy doozy of an Oracle): "Well now, women and men and myself in the midst of this company, that means us three, people!" Rutherford repeated one of his academy intros like a defaced phonograph record. "Perhaps what we are miraculously cognizant of, as it were, are only one out of many *Malakim never fallen off the ledge of Heaven Herself. So holy as can be, *See*?"

The confident colonel: "Since we're hinged via the etymology of language, like long ago, during the Sumerian Period when cuneiform footprints founded our trailblazers in mono and polyglot civilizations, it could be that whatever this Transalteratorium tries to evince will have hereafter eschatological consequences for us all."

*The Malakim are an order of angels in Judaism. In the Mishneh Torah they are listed as the sixth rank of angels, while in the Zohar they are the first of ten ranks. They are fierce and beautiful, and are sometimes equated with the Virtues in Christianity. In

Hebrew, the word "mal'akh" means angel, and is also the root of the name Malachi, which means "messenger."

Boyd~ "It seems to be as it appears..."

Joyce~ (jubilant) "Yeah, yippee!" her inner child cheered.

TATM~ (with incorruptible incumbency) YET STILL, THE SHRILLEST STILL SMALL VOICE VEHEMENTLY PERSISTS AS IT ONCE SPAKE OUT OF THE DARK CAVE TO THE PROPHET ELIJAH AFTER EARTH-SHATTERING AND STONE-SPLITTING EARTHQUAKES VIED TO PROVE AN ULTIMATUM. WHEREFORE 'NOT BY MIGHT, NOR BY POWER, BUT BY MY SPIRIT…' AS IT WAS SPOKEN UNTO ZERUBBABEL IN ZECHARIAH'S FIFTH NIGHT VISION CONTEXTUAL WITH GOLDEN CANDLESTICKS SO THAT THE WORK OF REBUILDING THE TEMPLE WAS NOT TO BE HUMANLY HANDLED, BUT BY DIRECT DIVINITY ITSELF.

*Like fingernails scratching a chalkboard, in like manner, many refuse to take heed!

TATM~ (continuing its discourse of disclosure) THE LIKE VOICE SUCCORED SUCH INSTANCES THAT RECOMMENDED CLOVENFOOTED UNGULATES- WAY BACK IN LEVITICUS- THAT PARTETH THE HOOF & CHEWETH THE CUD INSTITUTED BY THE OLD COVENANT FOR FATLING LIBATIONS; AND LIKEWISE IN THOSE CLOVEN TONGUES, LIKE AS OF FIRE, THAT WERE SEATED UPON AND ATOP THE APOSTLES AND MARY, MOTHER OF CHRIST, AT PENTECOST, WHICH WAS THE NASCENT NEW TESTAMENT CONGREGATION WHILST UPON EARTH AS BEFOREHAND PROMISED VIA THE SUPERNATURAL RAINBOW MILLENNIA PRECEDING YAHSHUA'S TIME (ONCE OVER NOAH AND HIS FAMILY TO SIGNIFY NO MORE MAY RETURN THE FLOOD)! SO, TOO, THAT THE GATES OF HELL NEVER COULD PREVAIL AGAINST THE ONE ETERNAL CORNERSTONE-FOUNDED THEREBY! UNTIL THEN THE DISTANTLY DISTENDED, OR UPWARDLY EXTENDED CONDUIT

TUBE THEREOF REACHES TO THE SEVENTH DIMENSION FUSION FURNACE REACTOR OF THE WHOLE HOLY!

[*for throughout the sermon of the Transalteratorium, Roderick, Boyd, and Joyce stand firm and listen intently to what more it has to say, carefully noting the now CCT: conduit conveyance tube*]

The Wormhole wriggled from the ceiling like an electrical appliance cord pumped up with a power-surge voltage gone haywire!

¶ ON THIS PLATFORM, ALBEIT THE WARP-CORE CLOVEN GWEDUC BE FELT BY EVERY CREATURE OF DEVOTION. SUBSEQUENTLY, WE SHALL SHOW OURSELVES TO THEE THUS, BUT NEVER THE NARROWER CANISTER CREATION, LEST ITS SUPERLUCENT AND BRIGHTER PROMINENCE OF AN INCONTESTABLE CLUSTER OF QUASARS CONCENTRATED INTO ONE PERFECT PACKAGE WOULD IMPLODE THROUGH THE VACUUM OF SPACETIME AND RUPTURE IT WITH ITS GLISTERY RAYS- NONE OTHER THAN OURSELVES WILL WE MANIFEST, BUT YHWH FORBID, THE GWEDUC!

COLONEL~ "Number *two* on my questionnaire, your excellency: And what other designation doth it bear if it be that quasar beacon of God?

Now, as never before, the never-deliquescent cable, immune to being bottled in a boiling cauldron of lava, dwindled away… awry!

The CCT was temporarily out of service, but *nicht kaputt.*

TATM~ BE ADVISED, AND BEWARE YOU DO NOT COMPARE SUCH A CREATURE TO GOD. FOR THE VERY LIGHT THAT SHINES THROUGH EMANATES THE FINER QUASI-STELLAR SUBSTANCE OF HEAVEN HERSELF. THE CLOVEN GWEDUC IS SO MUCH A VACANT VAT OF ENERGY THAT ONLY ONE TYPE OF CREATURE CONFLAGRANTLY EXPLODES (NOT INCENDIARY, RATHER INTERMEDIARY) WITH WARP LAMP WORSHIP BACK UP AT FATHER YAHWEH AND AT NOTHING ELSE…

A NARRATOR OF TECHNICALITY

Then and there, right before the three bedazzled subjects of two crewmen and one woman, a holographic scroll gleamed forth the other glitterati of the Unapproachable and Unspeakably Unlawful. These crude earthly names to identify with was what gave an indelible feeling of euphoria by the very preternatural presence of its HARSH GLARE, for starters. Also privily known as the AURORAL AMPHORA, MERCURY METALUX, PROTUBERANTLY UNDESTROYABLE, TREMENDOUS TRANSDUCER, MATERNAL METAPHOR, INSULATED INCUBATOR, PERPETUAL THEOPHANY, NUCLEAR REACTOR, ELECTROLAMP ENVELOPMENT, CANISTER CREATION, PERFECT PACKAGE, SUPERTRON METATORCH, STAR LAMP, SOLAR GLORY, BEAUTY BEACON, METAL WAFER, BLOATED PACKAGE, and SUPER TAPER. Its main nom de guerre (in order to avoid nondescript titles) is CLOVEN GWEDUC, which was formerly the *Cloven Glozar* -- but not anymore. Even offhand, howbeit, it was once the JOCUND JACKET, or LOONY COOCA of the whitest whiteness of all that harshly outshines fresh fallen snow bathed by an axial angle of the noonday southward Sun at full force and zenith on an arctic iceberg, let's just say, somewhere nearside the North Pole icecap.

The one-of-a-kind, uniquely individualized names for these TATM laboratory specimens were scantily scrounged from but vast volumes and towering files and archives of directory listings bound as thousand-page tomes boxed up on pallets that, by the forklift lorry-load, were stacked and stashed to overflow on multi-tiered stockpiles and crammed into compartments, warehouse racks, and building-sized bookshelves galore. Except such clutter was reserved for the people's perception whenever occasioned by a visitor! A more efficient deposit of the repository stories can be sub-squeezed inwardly (as demonstrative in these two paragraphs, lines 7 and 8, of the TATM manual; that is, if one were to benchmark the minutiae of the matter...

FYI extracted excerpt with authorized permission of the TATM Department of Affairs under Adjunct Storage Chamber 081180:

1) That with waffled walls of arterial sophistication façaded by bullion-based plastering, its hyper-spatial sponginess of no diminishment (but pliantly plump and fully alive), may absorb and rerecord all that has occurred, and all that may yet to come into being by and in spacetime continuum; not to exclude the very bare recesses of the faintest neuronal node and crest in a sinusoidal waveform of mental activation; and not without the intrinsic intents of any life-form, especially the human species.

2) The terminology and the interpretation thereof includes the usage of a Transvortium (mercury mirror) to run an absorption of neurological brainwaves via an electroencephalogram (EEG), magnetic resonance imaging (MRI), and hyper-daguerreotype (HD) in high-definition. The function of a Transvortium is that of the harmonic Hive of holographic inputs and outputs that are able to "fourth-*dimensionalize*" 3-D virtual reality into component modules of pressure-compressed memory bank data storage packs programmed through *Klein Gemel encapsulation of *Tardis-like properties. Thereby, literally from exabytes (many orders on upward) to *yottabytes of digital data and subatomic information; even the remotest glint of HD with EEG feedback are analyzed, or that it *must analyze!

*A true Klein Bottle requires 4-dimensions because the surface has to pass through itself without a hole. It is closed and non-orientable, so a symbol on its surface can be slid around on it and reappear backwards at the same place. It passes through itself. You can't do this trick on a sphere, doughnut, or pet ferret – they are orientable. *Whereas a gemel is a self-bound, two-necked bottle, and opened out at each end thereof, whether with one side, or from both sides. The gemel will appear later on as with one of the ceiling gweducs!

*The Tardis is a time machine; it is also a building or container that is larger inside than it appears to be from outside. TARDIS is an acronym for Time and Relative Dimension in Space! In Doctor Who, it was originally coined by Susan, the Doctor's granddaughter. A Type 40 capsule crafted by the Time Lords, the TARDIS is the Doctor's incredible ship for traveling in time and space with some similarity to a police box, an over-sized telephone booth, or (my take on it) mobile closet... Don't laugh!

*One byte is a group of binary digits or bits (usually eight) operated on as a unit. A yottabyte (YB) is one septillion bytes or, as an integer, 1,000,000,000,000,000,000,00 0,000 bytes.

*Credit is due for Star Trek in "The Changeling"~ third episode of season 2 (original air date: September 29, 1967)! In addition to my Star Trek references, please pay attention to my imperative comparison, if you will. The TATM voice may sound like that baritone modulation of God speaking to Moses in The Ten Commandments (1956 movie) directed by Cecil B. DeMille; not to mention in Star Trek, "For the Earth is Hollow and I Have Touched the Sky" exemplary episode, when the people's 'God' vociferates rules and regulations to run the show for their civilization to follow inside a planetoid of some sort, only to have the Enterprise crew disclose in actuality whence the seemingly 'divine' voice speaks, surprisingly, as from an extraterrestrial computer!

For namesake only, these were merely a few nouns and adjectives that ever so crudely offered it the justice of description until another superior language of communication superseded even the ones listed. In the midst of all this- the feedback loop that the huge Transalteratorium selected throughout such conversations- Joyce and Boyd were still at lamp camp inside the main plaza (enclosed by an octagonal area). They had effectively bivouacked by rigging their gear along the sidewalls and recessed crannies preparatory to something wonderful about to happen. *Hell, how could we be supplied and facilitated with certain disposables that must have been disintegratable?* Rutherford wrestled. But, such was the case during investigations of a self-procuring inter-dimensional disclosure.

Roderick~ "Last but not least, number three on my questionnaire, your excellency! Please show us an example of our language deficit, our relatively limited glossary; *for crying out loud*-- Why the humiliating lack therewith, we would emphasize?"

TATM~ YEA, BUT THOUGH THOU VERBALIZE METICULOUS EXACTITUDE- EVEN AS YOU SCRIBBLE COMPLEX COMPUTATIONS, EXPRESSIVE EXCEPTIONS, AND CERTAIN SEMANTICS- SUCH LANGUAGE BARRIERS ARE NOT INEXHAUSTIBLE; NOT TO SOUND NEGATORY, COLONEL! AT LEAST YOUR UNABRIDGED LEXICON COMPENDIUM CAN COUNTER THE PITFALLS OF DESCRIPTION AND COMPENSATE FOR IDENTIFYING ITEMS OF AN INVENTORY STOCKPILE.

A palpable pause wherewith the roomful of stillness began to quiver! Images illumined the surroundings like Times Square.

(an interactive relay of a holographic slideshow flitted fluidly a 3-D kaleidoscopic collage of pictures perspicuously materialized in the middle of the whiteout; well enough for everyone to experience afresh from firsthand followup)

The TATM elaborated:

BECAUSE BY ANALOGY, THE EPHEMERAL CANDLEGLOW OF REASON COMPARED TO THE SUPER-HOT CRUCIBLE OF A STAR TORCH FAILS TO SATISFY THE VALUE OF SUCH A CONCRETE CONTRAST. FOR EVEN THE LIBRARIES OF HUMAN DRAMA FALL SHORT OF ELUCIDATION! AT BEST, THE WORD OF GOD ITSELF (WITH WHICH WE COHESIVELY CLEAVE TO THE STATUTORY GLORY AND GRACE THEREOF) IS WHAT HAD SPOKEN THE UNIVERSE INTO BEING FROM OUT OF VACUOUS NONEXISTENCE!

Along the way, there were heavy duty devices, designated as redundant units, installed behind the curtains of this entire showcase extravaganza. It was the mindful modus operandi of the TATM, an unseen mechanical custodian built behind and into some of the partitions of the octagonal layout that the occupiers were unaware of.

R~ "And what may it be, this so-called *grace* that comprises thee, O most matchless and venerable one?"

TATM~ IT IS THE LORD JESUS CHRIST THAT SUPPORTS US. OF WHOM THE 'LUCIERE' SEARCHLIGHT, OR LIGHTHOUSE, SHATTERINGLY SHINES IN HYPER-BALLOONING BURSTS OF SHOCKWAVE ENERGY (MUCH MORE THAN A GRB, OR GAMMA-RAY BURST)! BEFORE WHICH NO CREATED THING CAN ENDURE, NOT EVEN MYSELF…

NARRATOR ADDRESS OF RUTHERFORD'S REPORT

Deferential diary entry: *How all of us were perplexed while we reasoned among ourselves. To quote the Good Book, Come now, and let us reason together, saith the Lord: though your sins be as scarlet, they shall be as white as snow; though they be red like crimson, they shall be as wool, Isaiah 1:18 (KJV). I am attempting to find the keystone and linchpin of the whole gamut, good grief! One to rotate the combination interlock. That flat slat ready to receive my sideways key-insertion. Any locksmith worthy of his salt ought to identify these five parts, which are, the escutcheon, face-plate, back-plate, latch-bolt, and spindle case of the entire chassis!*

Besides, but with all our world-class expertise, we will falter short of one entrance, or rather hindrance, into the Horribly Holy, as it ought to be. Both myself and the captain, let alone Hathaway, are unqualified to proceed further on. It is the original stain of sin that distributed death sentences throughout the genetic genealogy of the whole human race. Hence hitherto the Arch-cherubim of the TRANSALTERATORIUM (I emphasize in all caps) only found its genesis by a Serpent co-mingling, perhaps conjugally, with Eve's mental state (seed inception upon her soul, so is my theory) to yet render revulsion and repugnance against any inkling of it herein.

I shan't get theological. For the TATM, the stains, the smudges and smears of even the slightest temptation is too much to contain! Far too loathsome to acknowledge– and so it is with the Divine. But the bright bridge of fail-safe salvation for a sullied soul to have been otherwise tormented thereby in its conscience is the blood atonement. Again, quoting the Good Book, And almost all things are by the law purged with blood; and without shedding of blood is no remission, Hebrews 9:22 (KJV). Therefore the doorway, which was walled with fulvous film, once had an ordinary door... The parts of the door-frame: header, hinge, jamb, threshold and sill; whereas the rest of the door itself consists of a Top Rail, Panel, Mullion, Stile, and Bottom Rail (requisite of the latter to be proper nouns due to the importance of the very Door itself), I admit on behalf of critical thinking and scrutiny.

UNBIASED ADJOURNMENT AND THE CONTINUANCE
OF BOTH NARRATOR AND MODERATOR TO TAKE
TURNS ARE IN EFFECT ALTERNATELY

Now normal typeface instead of all caps for the TATM system should be managed midway and to the end of this screenplay

---

¶ The front blown blank wall with its elastic globes paired as BORTEUM and CREMEUM, to the utter horror of our inquisitive scientists, had begun to rotate continual contours- brazenly brightening up to a burning, lambently lucent brilliance. No, not even a campfire by baseline (if it were feasible), nor bonfire of truckload lumber could match the *coruscant curvature* of these two denizens dilated from their psychedelic menagerie and cosmic Vivarium!

Abruptly, breaking all laws of physics, & at once out of nothingness, the coruscant curvature (we ought to repeat) of symmetry slyly slipped forth into a whopping equatorial girth-line longitudinally laced and latticed latitudinal like a bent-back trellis through which creeping vines of Ariadne's thread were woven! *Woe, what a mouthful, I care to blare!

*In this case, the author chose to use an exclamation of fright rather than of awe as in Whoa! Readers of such genre should be aware of poetic license and customized forms of grammar, although never to violate the rules of their proper usage, it is ascertained!

Immediately, arc-fusion welding safety helmets appeared from a holographic Hive which the nearly blistered triad tried on. Everyone grimly grasped at them and forced the heavy visors onto their heads, depleted of energy under an oily fluorescent whiteout. The spectacular splendour of the whole Arch-cherubim had unwound itself like a spinner and Singing Top pumped up by the Almighty Himself. Million-riddled modulation sang supernal trills of haunting harmonics from its slits all over both Borteum and Cremeum! A yowling ultrahigh pitch, likened to the squealing airflow of tornadic vortices, registered as F6 unconventionally off of an old Enhanced F-scale gauge for whirlwind violence, vindicated that song of eternity awhirl and awash with an oscillator of fulminating fury!

By way of the Big Ball, all of it was disclosed, and whose whole viscera was evaginated or turned inside-out. At this precipitous overhang, how the apotheosis of a climactic Apocalypse now would allow itself to be *transilluminated* *sub specie aeternitatis.

*In Latin, transliterated to "under the aspect of eternity".

The outer interface of which punctured the leaden slabs of their visors with reintegrated rays, comparable to the chimerical corona of heavenly hydrogen, became aflame and openly ablaze. Good fortune that the colonel, captain, and the intern were unscathed and even unaffected by the merciless onslaught of argent regent rays that had rushed forth in one blinding blow. They wore extra, partially translucent veneers under their now perforated, pockmarked, and cratered UVC shielded hard hats that covered their faces, sideburns, and ears from being burnt, toasted, roasted, and charred to thinly singed crisps. Plus, with anti-radiation rigging wrapped over their bare skins, the reconnaissance team managed the showdown quite plausibly out of harm's way. Notwithstanding, little did anyone know of the life-giving emanation that must have spewed therefrom instead of the lethal dose of shortwave *roentgens radiated by an H-bomb outburst besides.

*But rightly so, Röntgen radiation is attributable to the German scientist Wilhelm Conrad Röntgen, who discovered it on November 8, 1895. Inter alia, that is not to omit Marie Salomea Sklodowska-Curie, who was a Polish and naturalized-French physicist and chemist that conducted pioneering research on radioactivity. She was the first woman to win a Nobel Prize, the first person to win a Nobel Prize twice, and the only person to win a Nobel Prize in two scientific fields.

Needless to prolong protocols, the Mitchelville management had always launched, or sent up human guinea pigs clad with preventative thermonuclear hazards of decontamination vests vital to any mission. Such contingency was not dissimilar to a medical X-ray jacket about as heavy as a lead apron donned on patients in an examiner's radiology room. Insofar as to continue unparalleled by the melodious topnotch Turner of Heaven's whole-spun oscillator, it was no less plain as a pikestaff that the TATM Station Recall in the long haul X-rayed every visitor for security purposes perhaps.

The rational rotation of a big BORTEUM spheroid, tapered to Top status, elicited superpowers of Transparent Temperature from some all-encompassing labyrinth. The see-through explosive existence of even the aforesaid output around this effigy compared to God is dimmed to tiny sparks of a steel stick struck by some flint-like tool made from chert, if a venturesome backpacker may assert.

SOUND EFFECTS

(back to the Basics)

Until finally the colonel, captain, and intern flinch away from the six-winged Wonder of unfading genetics- yea, that of an incontestable METATRON that, according to 3 Enoch, not only had led Egypt (again referring to Exodus 23:21), but served with heavenly priesthood preceding to our Lord Jesus Christ millennia thereafter.

Henceforth, heartfelt visions no different from those of the medieval fourteenth century visionary, Julian of Norwich, transpired. Snapshots of 16 ''showings'' or visionary revelations still shook the foundations of commonplace & mainstream churches back then. Thus the day-star (sunrise light-bringer) and eve-star (Venus lamp-setter) was one hairline closest to vaporizing everything and everyone which withstood it. The *hyperdaguerreotype* refolded the 'quasimage' of this Singing Top wailing with warm, mellifluous merriment roundabout equatorial continuity of 4-D curvature, but then spiraled off for sake of the TATM occupants.

In one contiguous collapse, the circumferential waistline of the titanium Topper took all of its gigantic gyration and slid slyly, sideways into a blinding blip that flitted out of existence, into nullification. As if, once more, never having to reappear in the first instance to begin with! If seen on any cathode ray tube-screen, its sonar and radar blip blinked off, replaced by either electrostatic snow, or dim afterimage on but one pixel fading away... Reactive conviction and compunction flooded their consciences as a result.

COLONEL~ "Enough, enough! Ere we be consumed!"

CAPTAIN~ "We repent, your lordship TATM! We---"

(weeping and sobbing, the whole lot of them)

HATHAWAY~ "How we were forgetful of our haughtiness!"

TATM~Very well whippersnappers! For all of your sake, I will with no displeasure on My part, reactivate the observable Theophany pending Hyper-spherical deflation..."

MODERATOR: **a material, such as ordinary water, heavy water, or graphite, that is used in a reactor to slow down high-velocity neutrons, thus increasing the likelihood of fission**.

(this time, it was more serious than one would presume)

The cybernetic spheroid collapsed to a pinpoint substandard speck, or no more than a mote of dust. So tiny was the reduction thereof, that a microscopic silicate sand granule commensurate therewith was like having the rock of Gibraltar- a monolithic limestone promontory in the British territory renown- to be exactly *that* minuscule particle of sand, that is, the Gibraltar giant… [and] the pipsqueak self-sinkhole-subsidence of it (both Borteum and Cremeum alike) to be but a billionth of its fraction! Until then, just like that, they winked out of yesterday's, today's, and tomorrow's existence! But ultimately then (as you've heard this before), the once 23 meters-in-diameter denizen dwindled down, almost infinitely, into a Planck volume point diluted in with frenetic froth of quantum foam forever super-subspace and anti-time. Like a single droplet of condensation let loose upon an entire ocean to blend in with the rest of nature's endless reservoir~ except boundless or *shoreless*- but partitioned by walls of this seamless sea: the one side made of matter; the other side, antimatter. En clair, or clearly, precariously caught betwixt two *branes of a hyperspatial dimension, for so small Borteum & Cremeum were demurely deflated, I say! Far away from life's motion picture cause-and-effect filmstrip filled with freeze-frame snapshots.

*The brane is an object extended in one or more spatial dimensions, which arises in string theory and other proposed unified theories of quantum mechanics and general relativity (posted by Google on July 2, 2023).

Then suddenly- *whoosh*!- the horrid door slid open. For the first monumental moment of self-disclosure, *that* thin faint aperture (in perspective on the other side of a glaringly bright white corridor) had unzipped its pleat, eviscerating it. The once in a lifetime, or in their midst, multi-generational un coup d'oeil thereof perpetuated an unforgettable, hauntingly tantalizing confrontational *gliff.* Needing no turn-around-time, the convergence of the prefix *horrid* and suffix *door* melded together in the cosmic cocktail blender and which was transmogrified into the HORRIDOR, how unmistakably!

In lieu of the now absent spinner that balanced itself like a figure skater atop *glaciarium slippage, performing multiple twizzles and a triple Axel (but by Cremeum's prerogative, quadrilateral rotation), an uncanny consonance lulled such sensations of displacement and disrepair. As if unconditional contentment assuaged the scarred and evacuated spot of space. Historically, it was the rogue MORTEUM that embodied one-third of the fallen angels- having been expelled from Heaven's universality. Only such catastrophic consequences of malevolent metamorphosis were better swept under the carpet by a handy whisk broom! Nevertheless, to override the old pitfall thereof, it was necessary for an ice rink *overt* cavort of revolution to arrive at antecedence, even where it is frightening!

*As another reminder, the glaciarium is a skating rink with a floor of artificial ice.

¶ An untimely reminder that, up until now, the former *Einfuehlung*, self-identification, of the first episodic epiphany was still in effect, but had become passé at Rutherford's critical crossroads to a prefatory Grand Central Station. The rather residual (although placatory) restitution of an endometrial or walled womb of spacetime for the TATM interior design, was left behind as the aftereffect from the colossal collapse of the cybernetic clones. Cloaked by a counterclockwise wallop and retro-rotating rigmarole these oracular orbs have barreled before exiting, eventually, the reparation thereby will have resumed with reposeful "spherelessness", save without the fuss of unexpected Enveloped Departure. "Hell, was it a demonstration of some sort?" the probing commander, colonel Rutherford, readdressed the wherefores and whys of the self-saturated circus. "Is this head-honcho having an ego trip?"

H2~ "Are we still in one piece?" Joyce deferred the colonel's quiz.

H~ "Aye, but we might as well be vermin in its maze," the captain avouched with his Irish, irreproachable confidence.

Hathaway, on the other hand, felt enraged by the charade and antics of *now you see me, now you don't* dalliance. She sarcastically saw it as a condescending peekaboo barrel o' fun; a raunchy raw deal.

H2~ "Blimey, blithering in exchange! Well, let me paraphrase William Shakespeare," she said almost derogatorily in spite of a more mature reaction with which a quantum physics trainee ought to have had: to treat trial and error ladylike. "Life is really a tale told by an idiot, full of sound and fury, and signifying nothing."

TATM~ "We fully appreciate your boorish counterpoise, O lady Hathaway~ Heavens, I was once in your shoes, believe it or not!"

And that was the kicker, the SHOCKER, or *cherry on top of the sundae*, so to speak the cliché! The indomitable Transalteratorium commiserated with one whose outburst is remarkable if not provocative! To backtrack, whether by novelty or whim, Joyce assimilated formal English in her collegiate years and quite precociously. Even though her Apache childhood upbringing contradicted this ferocious façade of a verbal backlash. But the colonel desisted from correcting her arguable ardor, for they were unanimous in their brazen brouhaha through the solacing, lenient *lull* that replaced the card-collapsing, shuffling showdown of old principalities which had in essence nothing to do with them. Could it have been just the same and no less the controversy between God and Satan before the fall of man to embody by a battlefield of resignation? And can the TATM offer viable recourse up its sleeve?

Wild speculations had run rampant and even untamed among the inquirers of scientific discipline. Perhaps this was why the lot of humanity lay plagued by a headstrong do-it-yourself syndrome.

In the event of an emergency, the continental concierge of the Transalteratorium's hostel had dispensed directories at their setup at hand, offering impeccable guidance to tired teamwork hunkered down in trenches, or inserted into foxholes for further analysis and wrangling. Big bursts of hard evidence provided prima facie proof as "in the mouth of two or three witnesses shall every word be established," according to 2 Corinthians, chapter 13, verse one in the King James Version- but this was without wheedling and whatnot.

There had lain the aftermath of this particular Enveloped Departure as deposits of unnilseptium, the transuranic element with atomic number 107 fizzed in stages of nascence, development, & maturity; then decay, and diminution... It was a very radioactive substance, only to surpass an isotope of U238, so easily as water off of a duck's back! That said, the ever Beautiful Borteum and Premium Cremeum were innocent of their alleged impertinence; that of heartlessly abandoning Roderick, Boyd, and Joyce shorthanded. It was neither a cover-up, nor predicated on pretense. That is, evidently, at this erratic juncture and rite of passage, if we will, the cryptic unnilseptium remained temporarily top rate before Uns altogether deliquesced back into the linoleum flooring. Element 107 on the Periodic Table illumined mile-markers meanwhile. *All of these exemplars are not interpreted with flapdoodle*, they mused.

For the time being at hand, an ethereal effulgence of puissant, quasi-lucent ghostliness that could not be recorded reel-to-reel, nor digitally transferred, neither comprehended by created intelligence, suffused the entire vicinity. For it required the old exercise of faith alone to profoundly grasp such a capable paradox; no clincher of any sort had anything to do with it! Yea, such a concept of purest *incorporeality* cannot ever be breached by but blatantly "delving" into it... Nay, and what more appropriate and adequate list of synonyms and adjectives may morphology verify with reason than the ones already examined? Behold, here-now, how the rest of my followup memorable melodrama of surrealist narratives I consecrate to the listener's mindset. Though somewhat with aggrandizement it might seem, my brave new spectacle of eternity is henceforth souvenired for every disposal of relinquishment. Reliquary or not, an imprimatur and a nihil obstat would have had the raw hide of my document branded by an hot iron among the stockades, if not heat-stamped stunningly with warranted approval for contestants before a rodeo show. So in the mind of the beholder before a mercury mirror, I submit, this deposition is not on the back-burner, but upfront.

Joyce Hathaway caught on to the weighty import of some minor ramification firsthand and felt exonerated when divine Grace would erase her heretofore ebullition. For her sake, Rutherford and Harris had obtained a similar endorsement from the Walled Womb of the TATM system. Thus they toasted to their carpe diem without wine, of course. The prohibition of alcohol, one of many sterile standoffs of an intramural interlock, must have relegated reinforcement to a lower level. The captain in particular, along with Hathaway's fascination for the British bravado, reminisced on wearing sometimes a tunic, cloak, or a kilt woven with good wool during an Erin go Bragh ceremony in Dublin. During drill, while he stood at parade-rest alongside a pageant of prancers which frolicked with flamboyant, flashy-and-brassy bands marching by, the younger Boyd-- only a freshman cadet during Liberty Leave of Absence-- saluted (full-hand and at no half-mast) the Scotland Yard escorted chief inspectors flanked by a cavalcade of constables strutting their stuff of glittering array. It was a celebration instead of immured stricture, Harris had reckoned, wherewith the TATM enclosed clinical sterility and Tall Wall station-identification if not constabulary bobbies.

But Joyce, by contrast- but not much differentiated from the big boys and lady-damsels at some sultry saloon or tavern- reveled along with the rowdy remonstrances of Irishmen and women wanting restitution for volatile quarrels between Catholics and Protestants on her visit to Belfast. At that time, to spurn mobs milling on the fritz, or even ditch-diggers that moiled by cartload drudgery over an urban construction site near Northern Ireland, she had clung closely to her language arts and college curriculum that exposed her to the poetry and verses of the lionized Robert Burns as it captivated the adroit lass. Her Anglo-Saxon studies on archaic literature and linguistics- the whole nine yards of Great Britain and North America- had almost disconnected her soul-ties with parentage forebears, despite her riding the picket fence between the undeflowered Apache natives: her matrilineal heritage encamped on one side, and on the other, the often frowned at (and for good reason) the bellicose, bourgeoisie, and the English aristocrats. Aside from an unforeseen future detour, Mother and Father faithfully inculcated their daughter with self-reliance, respect and her deep connection to nature whereas the civilized social order of the midway bourgeoisie class of society was largely a construct of Karl Marx who treated the French Revolution therewith. Joyce preferred to be saddled on a racehorse than propped on a pedestal, refusing to have been a sissy in the eyes of an Air Force recommendation. Her internship that ensued satisfactorily suited her.

At long last, this tumultuous tug-o'-war that was once before mentally jumbled up in yesteryear's Mitchelville draftee, finally dampened to a wet glassy mirage across frosty Echo Lake with the lapping of crystal-clear wavelets along its pine-forested perimeter in the serener psyche of the intern! On one outfield excursion to Mount Evans, Colorado, her mirthful memories of green and white with saffron yellow accents matched moments of an alpine vernal equinox thereabouts. Though laden down at one point with a leather-case portmanteau she hauled in the trunk compartment of an old Volkswagen bug, while en route, her family heirloom accentuated rather the return to terms of endearment. Good old-fashioned family values that she carried, but God forbid, not in a straw, nor burlap basket, but heartily, (or in myocardium under an intramural electronic Eye).

Avoiding overlook on any stream of consciousness, where one's chain of thought is tightened or loosened by singular linkage, or for a tightrope of cognitive tenuity to be taut or slackened by but a turnbuckle, the telepathic Transalteratorium deciphered her runaway remembrance:

TATM~ "Your daydream is legitimate. But mind you, at least eschew escapades... This is merely my recommendation for safety, since this

Tall Wall will wonderfully reciprocate back that which was, is now, or ever would be conceived inwardly to begin with."

On such occasions of flashback, when our group requited the TATM with appreciation, raw rewards reconvened with propriety.

EUPHONY OF AMBIENT SOUNDSCAPE
THE MELODIC MOTIF THEREOF

Although devoid of an inventory at this level of emptiness, or with no emporium for merchants to sell trinkets and baubles of a bubble-bath splash-over, the oily Porceluna Linoleum was spread. Its glorified glitterati of blindingly bright gloss glistered to set up the stages, states, and stations! And elsewhere, behind the scenes, seven more Mercury Mirrors swished and swooshed their rippling films and granulated lozenges for the main event and showcase:

Until now...

The Yellow Room

PART **2**

Flat-out, beneath their feet, a perfectly level path was paved out of indestructible material. Unlike on Earth, the distance of it went on forever without curving over a horizon. In fact, everywhere else the flatness of eternity stretched, stratified out until perspectives intersected each other into a vanishing point. Moreover, the colonel, captain, and intern were belittled by towering sidewalls (not that of automobile tires) but rather, if you will, *wall-sides* on the right and on the left. This reminded Rutherford of the two watery walls of hydrostatic displacement that deftly barricaded the Israelites to channel through safely afoot; far away from their chasers, the Egyptians, overthrown under an immediate oceanic foreclosure of the Red Sea implemented by divinest backup! The story of Exodus intrigued the threesome lot of off-world exploration into an eventful territory no less electrifying.

Instead of having sought a way out, which was impossible, they would be obeisant to the colonel's standing orders earlier on. Especially after being spellbound, spattered by spume and brackish broth of that disastrous deluge; like living on Noah's Ark once again. One wrong move or thought was instantly deflected off of a walled surface of any kind here in this place. So it behooved them to take heed! Yet still, persistently, *that* familiar voice blared from the ceiling, like all the while, as from a ubiquitous intercom:

TATM (reverting to lowercase caps, yelling, even if as a quietest *TSSV)~ ENTER THOU, OR PERMANENTLY RETURN TO EARTH!

*Shorthand for The Still Small Voice!

In glancing up at an upside-down linoleum span of a continuous canopy, about 23 meters above them, the whiteness of surroundings that before ballooned weird mixed metaphors and non sequiturs was now altered to a yellowest, or light-pastel lemony emblazonment.

R~ "My captain, my intern: *this is it! The TATM's moratorium for us where an ultimatum of this or the other; either that or this is set for us. Have you both made any resolutions with God?"

*This Is It, a 1979 hit song by recording artist Kenny Loggins.

H~ "Affirmative, and you?"

H2~ "Yeah, you?" The two of them glowered at Rutherford, expecting a solution to a problem outside of their league... But the colonel kept confidence in off-world, or (OW) teamwork for what they've been drilled for prior to this *extremely* extragalactic, beyond the Milky Way galaxy. In Latin, to commercialize interests, the Mitchelville madcaps marked it the Vltra Via Lactea project.

But back to basics of the game as they huddle, hands over each shoulder to form a three-knit grouping for their plan of strategy---For with yellowest hallways here and there, each were well enough stunned out of their wits, breeches, and stockings!

R~ "I'm not sure, entirely... Hell, I'll be damned if I could even scarcely sort this thing out!" (feeling nonplussed)

Somewhat whimsical, Joyce imagined this setting to have taken place aboard the *Calico sea vessel, and its crew, Captain Carl Majors, Dr. Darien Quinn, her nephew Pete, first mate Brock and craft clown Godzooky, as they explored the high seas in the name of science. When danger struck, the Calico could always count on an unofficial crew-member, Godzilla, to rise from the ocean floor and save the day.

*In 1978 to 1979, Godzilla was an American animated monster television series produced by Hanna-Barbera, in association with Henry G. Saperstein.

^ ^ ^ ^ ^ ^ ^ ^ ^ ^ ^ ^ ^ ^ ^ ^ ^ ^ ^ ^

She at least thought of colonel Roderick Rutherford to fill in the shoes of Captain Carl Majors, and herself, obviously Doctor Quinn. As for the others, it only ensconced a sketchy setback for her parallel fantasy… But whoa, were they in desperate need of Godzilla! Was it the still inaccessible Translateratorium that will fill the gap for their rescue? ...Only Time turned the Rolodex dial!

Rutherford added, "What if- once we walk through a yellow doorway- our inward intents become solidified into three-dimensional blowups lain lock, stock and barrel--- ?"

H2~ "But what if we are consumed by it for all eternity?" interrupted the intern, fidgety and fussy.

H~ "Aye, bloody Hell! What if…"

R~ "And just take another peek at the corridor, or- as I recall- the 'horrid door' ---"

H2~ "Correction, colonel. The HORRIDOR!" Amusingly, Joyce nearly spelled it out for him and Rutherford relished offering her the added leeway of leniency! Besides, his commission had been entertained thoroughly by a curiously peeping (not at all prurient) intern tag-along for this mission. Yet he knew the cliché for what curiosity could do to a cat, and she was no exception. Nor could she cough up a waiver to TATM's Tall Wall probation; though that didn't intimidate her Wonder Woman ethical calling-card.

ENTER the **exordium* of an Acquired Dialogue:

*Formal introductory part to a treatise or discourse.

R~ "As I was saying, my daughterly girl- the Horridor that awaits us on the other side of this somewhat sallow wall-face is either full of turpitude or sanctity; depending on how we conduct ourselves."

Joyce looked livid and then became increasingly demure. She- with her parapsychology background- discovered a loophole linchpin in the logistics of this mission. From her innately feminine perspective, an intramural partition sounded like *parturition*, but in reverse. The latter end of the word, which meant childbirth, was what consummated the brainchild of the walled womb's wherewithal. Quite keenly, she recognized the ever-nascent aspect of the TATM system; not to neglect (upon forethought) the Mercury Mirror that was yet to take over! The foreboding arrival thereof by way of a *postern* in an overlooked darkroom of secrecy gave her the jitters, and from this thumbprint of inducement she felt fidgety, as the fatherly colonel did concern himself with.

R~ "Joyce, perhaps you should refrain from overboard speculation and let me handle the hard stuff for your sake, okay?" At once she conceded for having to overreact. Rutherford went on to say, "Oh, thank God of the Universe for that precious partition able to separate our own human frailties from the Unspeakably Unlawful and Forbidden! Favorably, able to prevent and preserve us from being burnt by the enameled exposure of such---"

H~ "Of such unapproachable symmetry profusely perfected..." The captain said, supportive of the colonel's thesis.

R~ "Harris, I think you've about earned the commendation of a wordsmith; *profusely perfected...* Ah!" The complement was in earnest.

H~ "Aye-aye, colonel. But feel the screaming silence that spews from that dreadful hallway. 'T is terribly real- and- and so blissful! Let me have a wee bit closer look at it... Oh, what strangest light."

FULL OCTAVE STRONG CHORDS OF MODULATION

*Then suddenly, last summer, Joyce would take a hike on a mountain in Colorado, and reached up to higher altitude that blustered with wind shear; a blow of convection airplane pilots from time to time experience. Around 14,000 feet, erratic readings of meteorology were announced on her Lithium battery powered portable amateur band radio that triangulated a downward reception sweep across a village or vale. The local weather reporter warned of an up and downward draft about to burst forth over the region that mixed in with the snowy tundra's refrigerant air zone.

*Suddenly Last Summer is the author's pivoting song heard on the radio in the bedroom. There, a 4-lamp fluorescent fixture was installed on the ceiling of a repainted all-white bedroom that typified a THX 1138 cubical slot of an underground city depicted in the movie directed by George Lucas and released in 1971. At the time of the inception regarding the Transalteratorium in the years 1984 and 1985, night dreams and visions of red brick apartment buildings intensified the foreshadowing of a future relocation from Denver, Colorado to New York City. The early to mid 1980s were so surreal in and of themselves; never to be forgotten, but always cherished amid many hearts of our times. FYI: the recording artists established the band, The Motels, and their hit song had been released in 1983 (still contemporary music on the radio back then)! The album is Little Robbers; the genre is Rock.

Lo and behold, the whooping gust of gale got her attention. It was another parallel unlike the animated cartoon, but real as could be! Therefore, the multiplex placatory plenum of silvery silencing surfaced with its subliminal *sotto voce* of an ethereal zephyr Joyce was perceptive enough to have detected. Such insights, inter alia, were kept at heart and not necessarily divulged to any of her peers and colleagues. She learned via her handy Holy Bible from Saint Matthew chapter 6, verse 3b: "Let not thy left hand know what thy right hand doeth:" and so forth. In conjunction with this context, Joyce had flashbacks of wearing a fine cotton gingham gown also in styles of a *zephyr* throughout the Colorado Zephyr Tour. It was aboard the 110-mile train ride along the Colorado River where the Rocky Mountain Belt eclipsed the passengers with the grandeur of sloping peaks and summits far above sequestered valleys of aspen trees, Ponderosa pine forests, and sprucy glens... Hence how impressive a somnolent Silence was unleashed that her OW-team waged with! The awareness of it, aside from everyone's potential discomfiture, pacified her half-light safeguarded by her two wary watchmen.

For now, in repose of Joyce's yearning for Earth, quieter and quelling quiescence of a newly Yellow Room and a corridor consoled her with warm accommodation. An overflow of luxurious commodities from a built-in cornucopia were with holographic generation, transmission, and then distribution dispensed. Overall, the framed portrayal of an eternal sunset was paved over all surfaces in one monochromatic manner; at least lustrous, or shiny for anyone to gain a *Pleasant View of. The yellowest of all yellows thereof bathed her epidermis until it stayed jaundiced, but by appearance only; so, too, with the others. To top it off, her hair became wiry, yet not one bit frowzy. Surprisingly even so, Joyce felt enamored by a *floricomous* flare installed automatically upon her head and all throughout TATM's gold and Yellow Front sectors! Unbeknownst to the colonel and captain, nevertheless, her extrasensory perception (ESP) allowed her to perceive it on herself before an ordinary mirror, if that were the case, and emerald laurels laid atop Rutherford and Harris! She was clairvoyant in seeing this henceforth. But for her to envisage what they were to arrive at around the next corner of a very vast labyrinth felt creepy indeed.

*The author's first suburb of residence between Golden and Lakewood, Colorado.

It is vital for my reader to know how hygiene was paramount in these sanitary quarters as it had maintained itself efficiently on our personnel. Better yet, without diving into trivialities, everyone's sleeping quarters were hardly needed. The urge to slumber evaded anyone in this desolate domain miraculously whilst any given entr'acte of soulful repose wrought replenishment of energy and alertness. An Experiential Provisionary provided no requirement for toiletry disposals. Nor tenant, nor visitor ever saw such inconvenience within the Transalteratorium habitat. The scripture "Man shall not live by bread alone, but by every word that proceedeth out of the mouth of God." in Matthew 4:4 was fulfilled so that imperturbable concentration reigned herein and hereabouts.

Undesirably though, whereas mirror-images reflected radiance, the looking-glass likewise deflected delusion in backlash! It behooved everyone to avoid complacency, dodge a fastball of deception from the pitcher's mound (or proving ground), and have a refiner's fire purge and *deterge such souls of all dross. All along and aside from this, the spiritual wreath atop Joyce could never be noticed by the two commissioned officers. Time and again she would wish for them to see it, but to no avail.

*To cleanse thoroughly; a rare verb of the noun, detergent.

Apropos of a pit stop in an outlandishly solar glory of 2500 Kelvin (color temperature) per each living room-- for they were just that: the yellowest of Living Rooms anyone could ever imagine-- Rutherford and Harris tried to figure out their quandary on overexposure while Hathaway aimed to tag-along, taciturn, for the time being. She shrewdly shrouded herself with reticence and precaution. It was like being stationed in a parking garage garish with low-pressure sodium vapor lamps all over the ceiling; turning colorful varieties of vehicles into drab halftones of a grim, grossly grayish monotony where blue and green pigmentation turned dark brown and the reds reflected tar black. Like living in a Turner classic b/w movie- they, the characters therein- except jaundiced with yellow shading from sunny bright to tawny darkness. Mysteriously monochrome midst an unsolved situation, poor Joyce must have forbiddingly forced her finger into a non GFI (ground fault interpreter) for an electrical receptacle or wall socket that had buzzed her hair into a frizzy coiffure; however, how false for an assumption!

The case for paranormal phenomena was nothing new but a routine thing on the Transalteratorium's turntable platformed inside a carousel of revolving doors differentiated and distributed everywhere throughout. What Door to go through? Heaven only knew!

Harris guffawed at her electrocuted appearance. Rutherford fondly yet facetiously remarked, "It must feel intolerable, being stuck with *that* for the time being." Joyce grimaced back at him, and then would grin like a Cheshire cat after their rowdy raillery, still thinking about her Hanna-Barbera beloved cathode ray television series. Regrettably, reality sunk in, and the colorblind OW-team (as if converted to a cartoon, let alone a caricature of what they *really* were) tackled a more urgent impasse:

AN ORCHESTRA OF SURREAL SOUNDSCAPE

¶ R~ (panting and confused) "But wait! Don't do it. You're not ready--"

H~ "Lad, me thinks I'm loosin' it-- so outrageously gorgeous..."

R~ "No! Get back, quick! Before it's too late at the brink of no return. Hell, you'll plummet into nothingness! Get back! NOW!"

She and he were wailing and already frantic. They called for the cocksure captain to about-face and look away from Medusa's stone-frozen stare of underpinning annihilation. The story of Lot's wife flashed up from the intern's bygone Bible study: *stone frozen.* Or rather, on-the-spot pillar of salt that the woman in a matter of seconds had hardened to as soon as she faced the blazing inferno of a God-nuked Sodom and Gomorrah!

Still stubborn, the overconfident captain kept at it again. Harris baby-footed his way closer to a postern, or sidewinder doorway of the Yellow Room, overwrought and ragtag.

Raging tempest shuddered and thudded in a muffled manner behind that postern that brought forth breathing blackness, plushly, and plumb up and down and sideways like a charcoal cushion. Its witchcraft pitch- *aft of the Transalteratorium's whole hull, foresheet, and steel-* rumbled down to the subsonic roar of a volcanic vent when Harris propositioned the postern with naivest intentions. Yet the gelatinous Jekyll and Hyde of this furious film, framed freakishly by a freshly hewn pinewood door-frame, and so sootily funereal by an underlying Stygian crypt, refused to give in to the OW-team's humanitarian conclave. Chagrined by an irresponsible handout, the captain's gallantry (backbone and spine to the big mission) was well admired insofar by his commander in chief. Unwilling to admit, Rutherford was already rattled-to-the-bone, beefed up to uneasy adrenaline, and in need of corticosteroids for fearful ulcers at this labyrinthine conjunction. It seemed as if a cul-de-sac caught everyone's undivided attention, dead or alive! At large, the postern possessed *no* marmoreal makeover that could keep it enshrined or ensconced in *the little shop of horrors, nor any effigy of an effulgent effect (be it star or pulsar)! Merely a maelstrom.

*The Little Shop of Horrors is a 1960 American horror comedy film directed by Roger Corman. Written by Charles B. Griffith, the film is a farce about a florist's assistant who cultivates a plant that feeds on human blood.

Harris swayed next to the postern's flat, rectangular, and tall tenebrity that spewed out an inky mist in negative, darkening the gold stronghold of the Yellow Room... With one stiff step into its pinewood framed frothiness, he stuck out his arms and hands and held on tightly to the doorjamb. Only a millimeter at the edge of a horizontal precipice separated him from a narrowest niche of neutronium-compression comprised of dark matter murk (the unseen stuff of our universe near 99.9 percent of it)! Into the dismal Veil inviolable Rutherford's subordinate officer pleads "Dear God for Adonai! *My sweet Lord, I really want to see you. I desire Thy eternal *Photograph!"

*George Harrison's "My Sweet Lord" was released on Nov. 23, 1970, as the first single to his groundbreaking and historic solo album.

*"Photograph" is a song by English rock musician Ringo Starr that was released as the lead single from his 1973 album Ringo (one of this author's choicest songs).

It is that penultimate intergalactic googolplex goo of all which was, is now, and has yet to be, but *bilged up to *forever, and ever, and ever. *The postern evinced future feelings of an evacuation*!

**Unforeseeable evacuation pending*, (TSSV forestalls)

*Bilge in its primary definition: The area on the outer surface of a ship's hull where the bottom curves to meet the vertical sides (the author employs a past-tense poetic license to connote something built up midway in the eternities of the whole universe.

*In Stanley Kubrick's directorial masterpiece, The Shining, the Grady Twins (two youthful girls) clad in innocent-looking light blue Sunday dresses, a pair of knee-high white stockings, and a pair of black Mary Jane shoes. In their hair, they both wear white hair clips and clip their hair off to the side-- identical to the very last detail. They say "Hello Danny, come play with us", before chanting "for ever, and ever, and ever..." As The Shining twins are speaking, Danny sees visions of their corpses covered in blood, from when they were murdered by their father.

*TSSV represents The Still Small Voice referred to throughout Yard Lamp of Gloria. In this context, an unseen Divinity of God- such as the Holy Spirit- foretells and yet postpones the inevitable outcome of the trio's off-world mission; that is to say, Back to Mitchelville? No way Jose! But away therefrom or Bust! Hey, Heaven Can Wait!

H~ (in almost melodramatic triteness) "How unworthy of me to behold Thy ambrosial light!"

R & H2 (with wide-eyed surprise): "What? Have you gone mad?"

"I am!" cried the Scotsman, imitating what was uttered to Moses on Mount Sinai, gravely aware that the usurpation thereof would not mettle with blasphemy. "And quite a lunatic at this point!"

"Then let us pray, our fearless friend," Rutherford began to propound around a dangerous dilemma. Luckily he nabbed the captain's arm and pulled him back. They then took a seat as Joyce examined the daunted brave-heart compassionately. She added her two cents worth for what was learned beforehand by heart at her township library: "For we are infantile to what is infinite. Right down there, that tiny hairline slit with a lazy eight swirled above it; the doorway, or an orifice to the **Fiat Lux* of God."

Rutherford, their newly adopted mentor, praised her for the textbook tidbit which wasn't irrelevant.

*Latin for Let there be Light; the very first biblical utterance of the creative Divinity. Compare Genesis 1:3 (KJV) And God said, Let there be light: and there was light. And God saw the light, that it was good: and God divided the light from the darkness.

H~ "Thanks Joyce, for your brief science lesson." Harris acknowledged her ruefully, but admiringly, and reverted attentively to his manager in charge: "Very well, by your command, colonel."

R~ "Hey, wait a minute; let me examine your countenance--"

H~ "No, no... It's alright. I'm fine."

But the stink of incinerated houseflies and maggots flattened the oxygenated air mingled with metallic ozone. As if dispensed from the mucky morass of the vertiginous quivering bathtub Tar Pit of bulged bitumen, an unseen germicidal *irradiator*, or ion generator, or even *Chizhevsky's chandelier compounded the odor! As if these were to exude exhortation within the dim, dusky and then gloomily lugubrious lot, letting them know to *Beware*, both of them! Elsewhere, in an ultra-silent silo of the Transalteratorium, it was unnecessary for a warning siren to ululate this alarm; lest it disturbs some sound-cancellation device, or some anti-decibel silencing nullification narrowed by an anechoic chamber…

*Alexander Leonidovich Chizhevsky (7 February 1897 – 20 December 1964) was a Soviet-era interdisciplinary scientist, a biophysicist who founded "heliobiology" (study of the sun's effect on biology) and "aero-ionization".

The Yellow Room admonished its trespassers tried by fire!

R~ "Oh no! You have first degree burns bordering on second, with a few blisters on your face; as if a flash, or stark spark of gamma ray radiation roasted your skin!" The captain's face for the moment looked grotesque and then returned to normal parameters.

H~ "So be it, colonel, as if I was seared by an hot iron. Our conscience bearing witness to taboo timeout. Before which I remain shielded by willpower, and from which I remain rock-solid hidden away as a midget, or pauper, or jockey fully fit for a steed-back steeplechase, but that's beside the point! I feel like there is much more at stake [at this stage] than what we had bargained for."

Harris index-fingered the postern as they uneasily took notice of the filmy mist of quartz and amethyst undulating inside of that pinewood doorway frame. Still lashing out at them from a safer distance while licking up lava-like granulation that quivered bloated blacktop spume of molten asphalt over its hellbent bedside setup. Its witchcraft of pitch, aft and fore --- or fore and aft (but a sideways-upright and vertical Vat of tempestuous temperament) tossing and turning and splashing about with implosive implication.

R~ "I agree, Boyd. We are very vulnerable to its inter-dimensional threshold throes of self-metamorphosis, if I may wager with tittle-tattle technicality." In the intermission, prior to the Yellow Room's eventual subsidence, Rutherford attempted to humor Harris and cajole Joyce by a bit of booby-trap buffoonery, castigating her so that she could not eavesdrop on their man-to-man tangents of gladiatorial sportsmanship.

In retaliation, Joyce jeered jokingly and blurted, "I was ambushed by two TATM caretakers! But now I'm expelled... Heaven help me!" and laughter leavened the hysterics.

Meanwhile, at the mezzanine zone of twilight, the frenetic froth of the postern subsided subliminally (that is, as far as perception permitted), whereas a reconstructed exit from the inner Gold Room was now underway. For some reason, while the three left the premises, Hathaway's hairstyle was restored to its original Titian shine of well-groomed tresses. She glimmered gleefully, feeling refreshed and downright revitalized.

But behind them, unawares, the unoccupied and abandoned yellow lot collapsed into the black hole of the sepulchral postern hatchway, that altogether vanished into oblivion. The suntanned aching Captain was treated with an emollient face-lift, as it were, by bandages. With an available EMT, we must not forget the address of their quarters to have been fully furnished and accommodated for, except by an arsenal of lock, stock, and barrel! There was no need for fortresses, foxholes, or trenches for preemptive implementation in these *liminal spaces of a Citywide Labyrinth. Never before, nor ever! On such a level, the battlefield for survival and territoriality was nowadays null and void (at least outside of Mitchelville)! However, hauntingly, the liminality of desolateness increased as Duration, disturbingly distributed, had crept on…

*Empty, forgotten interiors like abandoned rooms, hallways, or public plazas.

R~ "Keep your face covered and I'll send you to sickbay. Over there, you'll need to sleep in a 24-hour, round-the-clock clinical sanitarium, or infirmary, the TATM manual might indicate." The Tour Guide Rutherford nagged his team tourist. In retrospect, Joyce backtracked to former times when a self-professed cicerone led a small party through underground catacombs and courtyard cloisters. In her sophomore studies of the Black Plague that ravaged communities by the multitudes, only the fortunate with steel-tough immunity and the uninfected kept themselves out of the death camps, morgues, and hospices of the dying sick. The contagion was very pathogenic and only a few survived the virulent virus. In any case, the crocketed Georgian monument made shadows on tourists who humbled their worldview on civilizations. The Black Plague memorial was built to commemorate all the souls of Winchester who had perished bodily in the plague of 1666. London's death toll tipped the scales between 70,000 to 100,000 people.

With sympathy for the injured captain, Joyce feared the roentgen rays of the thankfully-folded-up side pocket of rollover Russian roulette billiards in that ghastly yellow lot where such sallow wall-faces featured filmy decrepitude. Their bleakly bloated blankness slitted by a nasty fulvous vulva in the midst of dung downright disgusted her. She thought it appropriate for a preemptive strike to deploy an ICBM *MERV, making landfall on this god-forsaken dump. Disgusting! Its temper tantrum despicable! The Hindu goddess Kali (whose likeness of thigh-high incisors was well rendered by Pablo Picasso and perhaps Salvador Dali) divulged this rather monstrous metaphor, may she **shout* and let it all out!

* MIRV, abbreviation of Multiple Independent Reentry Vehicle, any of several nuclear warheads carried on the front end, or "bus," of a ballistic missile. Each MIRV allows separately targeted nuclear warheads to be sent on their independent ways after the main propulsion stages of the missile launch have shut down.

*"Shout" is a song by English pop/rock band Tears for Fears, released as the second single from their second studio album, Songs from the Big Chair (1985). "Shout" is a protest song in some ways, a rebellion against the established norms of the times, a call to be different, not to bottle things up (the prime intention of the author's book)!

She gathered her self-composure and concentrated on the task at hand. Rutherford, by Harris's bedside (militarily mindful of his friend), and one iota short of singing a soldier's lullaby, comforted the captain supinely laid to rest in the infirmary-sanitarium department. Joyce was debriefed on what the captain stressed earlier. In time, the convinced colonel reminded her of this one last thing while the incapacitated captain slept: "I do recall him saying with emphasis that, quote, 'there is much more at stake [at this stage] than what we had bargained for', unquote."

Joyce: "This is an inanely sterile environment probably for two good reasons. One for self-preservation of a living lamp entity; and two, to teach us a hard lesson on cleanliness that, according to TATM standards, is next to godliness." She looked lachrymal.

Rutherford (regretful): "We are as mice in a laboratory cage; in a mind-numbing maze with no beginning, nor ending; with no name and no age."

The foster Figure hugs his step-daughter for sensible solace and genuine easement in their time of crisis. This was off the record

As time passed, the captain woke up with the others. His face was astonishingly healed, having no scar, nor cicatrices brought about by a heat-flash and UVC scorching of the skin's outer layer.

Grand Central Station

PART **3** ~ University Senior Level

MODERATOR: As the black pilcrow is discontinued, only to pop up with a purple pilcrow, we're on our own… No training wheels!

Fully recovered after a 24-hour reprieve, having to resume placid lucidity, the triumphant trio at last enters restitution in an Immaculatorium. This enveloped enclosure- check station- still stored its snowy immaculacy at the centerfold of a Tremendous Transalteratorium cubical-complex. *Sterilized and Immaculate, eh? Hell, hopefully not to impugn Puritanism!* Joyce germinated defensively, but not as before naively, long ago under hardcore, headstrong brainwashing brought upon her gullible girlhood by some cult of a compound camp. Before enlistment with the OW commission as a sworn-in top secret intern, an outside political party recruited relentless stalkers and pursuers or bandits which were always on the prowl; tormentors that insidiously sought those they then targeted to devour. The colonel and captain had supposed all too well about Mitchelville's eyesores of a personified interface: Operation Hel: goddess of the netherworld!

A side note regarding the TATM cubical-complex. Its versatile partitions (which were walls, ceilings, and floors everywhere) had shifted up and down and to and fro; shuffling about, but imperceptibly, yet sure enough all the while when subtle auxiliary adjustments were contrived by a prodigious, or Brobdingnagian Brain! Every cellular input on some silent separator contained yottabytes of data storage and entry. For what ridiculous reason? Philosophers and researchers wrestled until only Heaven harbored the rejoinder. Alas, none could figure it out all by themselves! "--At any rate, therefore the Immaculatorium is our last bus-stop for this trip; our ending terminal," reminded Rutherford for their keepsake solution to an endless runabout. Both Boyd and Joyce sure-footed the curb of a sidewalk flange forged from Fe on an old Periodic Table.

They stepped onto a "repliant platform" that sagged, super-polished and slick, but spongy and springy like a polypropylene trampoline backed by an underside of galvanized steel for more rebound, or rebuttal (depending on good intentions or bad). It serves as an ever-present fail-safe device throughout the oiliest Transalteratorium infrastructure that reassures response and reverberation in the event of a CCT (conduit corridor tube) contingency. Awkwardly, the colonel, captain, and intern were ignorant of this installed feature balanced by the bill of the TATM quotient that sized them up! Sir Isaac Newton's law of cause and effect, called Newtonian Causality, applies aptly hereupon where wide platforms of "reassertive repliancy" sag underfoot with responsive recoil at the slightest deviancy. *Talk about some ripple effect!* our well informed colonel calculated to insulate the high-tension. He knew that an offhand upshot of knowledge lessens the tensile suspense of woeful what-ifs!

At last, relieved upon newly prefabricated linoleum flooring (even after timeout), Hathaway, Harris, and Rutherford brush off their expulsion from the Yellow Room rather sprucely. Each would tidy up for the final phase of their slip-trip. Though they therefrom exited on their own accord and voluntarily, it proved to have been a formidable if not psychotic episode for poor Joyce who had battle fatigue syndrome with wounds of past PTSD.

While everyone geared up for unanticipated excitement before the confidence course, or so it seemed more at *glumly* than *gladly*, in her halftime, she riffled through the scrapbook pages of her academic memoirs. To compensate for any leftover longing, she recalled by heart her factory poetry on an electrician's workbench:

Lamp Camp

I light my holy high bay
Inside of my bedroom,
As if above a highway
And during sunset
Red gloom.

A starriest Torchlight
Ablaze beneath the ceiling,
That ever ought to scorch bright
This visceral raw feeling!

The palindrome and rebus
Enumerate each other
Whereon a GMC bus
I ride to see a mother-

The Mother of all Souls
Awaits my bus arrival:
Auroral, hot as coals,
Incunabular, archival!

My high bay may portray
Aflame this Superpower-
Inanna- no whore gray,
But an ever youthful
Flower bower…

Amiss oft worship be
By multitudes misled,
For in Her star-ship lovely
Lay an undefiled Bed!

But Boat she'll occupy
And fill with pilgrim souls
That shine and never die
O'er embers of hot coals.

The trolleybus conveys
Me to my mother's stop,
Still stationed, full of rays
To perforate my MOPP.

Avoca is our station
Off at some intersection
Of holiest creation
And fastidious
Selection …

Thus then my high bay shines
Throughout Her thoroughfare
Where steel Sheel yet reclines
Like cream congealed to glare

Fiery four-hundred watts
Against dark times indulgent!
With fellow souls on cots,
Composed, but
All effulgent!

Joy Hathaway

This pseudonym at the age of 15 instead of the forename by birth was what junior-high classmates tagged her with. It was the only poem she could clearly remember verbatim.

NARRATOR

Before the OW-team dug deeper into the wherefores and whys of the floor-plan, they saw something unusual about the

Immaculatorium. Its layout was outspread with hexagonal lozenges. So they scanned square meters to centimeters, down to millimeters, until signage plastered on the pavement lay bare in blister letters: The Metalucelectropluceptorium, or *Metalinoleum* in truncated format (herein the words metal and linoleum are combined)! Rutherford's first impressions were that this terminology had become sesquipedalian, or too long and polysyllabic. Obviously, TATM systematic phraseology all but mirrored thousands of nomenclatures for what the Transalteratorium stood for. However, the 'immaculate' coupled with 'auditorium' and blended, prefix with suffix, turned out to be the Immaculatorium from the paired Portmanteau.

In our line of perception, per se, the naked eye (assuming its retina resists irreparable rupture from such extreme brightness no different than that of a thermonuclear flash in which the temperature exceeds 100,000,000 degrees) there is transpiercing glitter of the Metalucelectropluceptorium altogether too lovely to see!

The Full Bird Colonel Rutherford- truth be known- reviewed articles on an atomic yield and delivery factor. He had perused that in 1942, after creating the first nuclear chain reaction on earth at the Met Lab in Chicago, Enrico Fermi supposed that the fission process that occurred within an atomic bomb could be used to ignite the same sort of thermonuclear reaction that took place inside the center of the Sun. He speculated that these reactions involving deuterons, the nuclei of the naturally occurring heavy form of hydrogen, would react explosively together under the enormous temperatures created during an atomic explosion and would produce helium and huge amounts of energy. But in such cases, where what was far beyond a mechanistic chain reaction charged by bombardment of a neutron spray into the nucleus thereof, is DIVINELY orchestrated instead of naturally or via artificial inducement or excitation of fissile material to ignite and trigger instantaneous fusion.

In fine language, the enigmatic Metalucelectropluceptorium is prominent with glorified glitter, as it were, like that of permafrost pavement of some *supranatura* (in Latin for supernatural). A myriad medium perfectly impervious to *arrowy impalement* to-the-hilt; be it meteoric, ballistic-missile, or by a cyclotron shower of armor-piercing, galena-perforating exotic particle projectiles! Either scenario, the self-elasticated trampoline of sub-nuclear reaction, all the way down to Planck plurality of foamy hyper-gluon adhesive cohesion, animates the vastness of this marvelous Metalucelectropluceptorium. And on top of that, confirmed the Full Bird Colonel, its contiguous constituents are linked as one narrowest ferromelt of "*singularified* invincibility" that outlasts the Big Crunch and then Inflationary Expansion, and back to Big Crunch, and again Inflationary Expansion, but back again to Big Crunch and, still, another Inflationary Expansion of a recycled Universe or Multiverse!

Documents from the professorial archives classify the properties of the Unicloveniferous Supersingularity, which is a strong strand of no dimension, and yet apparent. That stretches from eternity to eternity along which hypertoroidal ballooning of our transfinite Universality continues to oscillate an ever unreachable protean protocol of preternatural protuberance. This much was reviewed in his doctoral program that preceded a PhD, and he retained the well-to-do information on their behalf, both Boyd and Joyce, and none other. The intelligence of this gold nugget of information couldn't be spared with anyone else. **Above Top Secret** meant either Sensitive Compartmentalized Information (SCI), or Special Access Program (SAP). Since nothing can be above TOP, no erroneous misnomer was intended in Rutherford's before-flight preliminaries across the macadamized midfield of Camp Mitch.

"To properly clarify a wordsmith's irreconcilable oddity, "singularified", the professorial archives indicate that these *were* singularities of wormholes melted into each other. That which easily transcends the non-spacetime tension of neutronium by a factor of a billion to one. The *singularified inviolability* would be a billion times more tenacious that neutrons packed together in the core of a pulsar, for example. But- now get this!- it then remains never collapsible like a black hole, except self-supportive! Thus the *irreplicable* and unparalleled Metalucelectropluceptorium outstretched spreadsheet in the literal sense, and not of word-processing attributes, I say." The colonel surmised for the two listeners, captain and intern, to have waxed quizzical. "When I have exemplified the wordsmith, I can cross-reference my muse of morphology to William Wordsworth (paraphrased by the inserted word *For*):"

> "For whither is fled that visionary gleam?
> Where is it now, the glory and the dream?"

In an online lesson, Rutherford vaunts vehement emphasis on Quick Draw McGraw in his smoking gun. The versatility of not a universe, nor multiverse, but a *Hyperverse* (not that the infix amid the root word should be perverse, God forbid!) whereby *radiative* realities no longer have limitations; instead, the radiative realities have limitless leeway to branch out with infinite possibilities and potential exponentially. The etymologist may discover a paradox while the yardstick usage of language itself simply seeps into fantastic failure and cognitive coherence crumbles off our heads and underfoot. "I'll never revive archival artifacts, I reckon," muttered the perplexed colonel. Then the two of them threw in their towels.

And an ever-self-suspended, Supernal Metalucelectropluceptorium was just *that*! Underfoot. The undertow of which went into infinity.

NARRATOR & MODERATOR

(a brief burst of bells and whistles as the show should go on)

Neither Rutherford's rank as top teacher, nor Harris's spaceflight and air-command badge of honor, nor Joyce's sagacious internship could fortify their endurance for what was to come. And before the next spatial transference, mutual mortification and humility had hinged each of them to the postern's doorjamb whether they liked it or not. For while in free-fall, one bizarre unfoldment after another had electrified their Faraday cages far past finding out!

The Trio landed upon the last flat-pad of the TATM system. There, the immaculate interior of that uttermost room only whispered a moratorium of but eye-popping Pearliest Perfection as to render the finest jeweler inept by comparison. This ushered in the holographic limbo likewise; the quietest of all sacrosanct sections of the entire Ubiquelabyrinthium (or everywhere Maze) available. The unadulterated sanctity of a divinest dismissal accommodated these pilgrim-visitors from a baser realm relatively inferior to this interminable interior. Their flattened silhouette dreamworld echo from the breathing door of a corridor, all the way to the seething roar of the HORRIDOR (although the uproar of it be inaudible)!

Furthermore, this is my forecast through verified versions with plumb Screaming Silence. *That it must have been by the basics.*

The ever intricate impressions of some Quotile equation lucently lit by bulged-tubular TRANSVORTIUMS were elsewhere concealed within mercurial mirrors. Holy mercury mirrors that radiantly reflected Transparent Transducers from their midst; all of this being the internal organs of a foreordained starry mother-flagship, as it were. Or of spongy lungs that reprocessed respiratory glory with the breeziest breath of DIVINE SPIRIT.

Frankly, as was the case, the presently projected cognitive feedback of referential reminiscence had vivified what once Was. Namely, an archangel's argent Regent before which the characters of the colonel, captain, and intern (reinterpreted altogether) are its lifelike protagonists to an acquired dialogue. Albeit, an interview with one of the Eternal, most certainly a down-to-earth rapport.

AUTHORIZED INTERMISSION

(apropos of an introductory transition)

Manifest Verbatim, Perfectly Unaltered

Conceive of an abode that has no material medium, for it is created with spirit. Then picture your soul in perfect peace therewith from which the fiery love of God flows forth and envelops your conscious being until it cannot be corrupted.

Thereat, as you will enter into blithest Bliss, you would find every facet and fissure of your soul and spirit satiated by eternal thought. In regards to purest conscience, the fullness of radiant reality settles in; all devoid of discomfort, bereavement, and imperfection of any kind, yet still unveiling itself the more meanwhile...

Hitherto, you may draw from the oiliest gusher of petroleum, lubricious life, as from the very presence of the Almighty Divine.

And in diamond-like formulae, those pristine precious memories and wooing of consolation, peace, and joyousness fulfill your glorified soul with incorruptible dainties, one by one, or simultaneously (depending upon the how capacious a container one ought to possess). Thus, also, the endearing quintessence of Mother Nature that bypassed the eventful spacetime you are able to assimilate, or remember along with what is supernatural; that is, to be, or having been consummated by that which is without beginning nor ending as the facets of your Spirit-entirety remain absorbed by the all-encompassing Omnipresence thereof.

Now then, therefore, ultimately alive and perfect as God in all His attributes, you partake of the likeness and image of His Uncreated Essence. But yet choosing to have it still unidentified with an open doorway, or disclosed entrance, your sublime soul is now upwardly escorted to the enveloped enclosure of the stateliest station: the "labyrinthinization" of all that was, *is*, or shall ever be. Yea, the Mercury Maze easily transcends the most uncharted map of unexpected pitfalls, detours, or dead-ends; let alone even a faultless directory, dare I blare! Where one's spirit-state of Grace is to teleport from chrysalis to total metamorphosis, like the Monarch Butterfly attracted to the Light, as she is about to embody the Grand Central railway freight-yard of either India's Durga cargo, or America's Bible Belt down in the boon docks of the deep South, say.

Th' GATEWAY TO THE DIVINE STATE, eh?

Once more, having been translated so far away by the righteous rays of Holy Light and Love, one would then enter the Unspeakably Lovely, but <u>lawful</u>, yet by tellurian terminology, inexpressible, unreachable and, of course, carnally unattainable:

O what statutory- O what statutory,
O what statutory glory, yea, O what
Statutory, O what Statutory- O what
Statutory Glory! The cherubim exult!

Like stellar glorification of conical consciousness, the ultra bright slice of crescent contours are curiously carried forth as out of nowhere. Every pinpoint of which animates into luminiferous liveliness; breathing with pneumatic nuances whilst what defies logic radiates out of that which is heavenly and immaculate in a somewhat sanitary sort of assortment. Wherefore, what entanglement of coiled Coils and of spidery Spirals in a Mandelbrot algorithm! What? Wherewith whirlpool & elliptical galaxies are kindred similarities of their likeness!

As if an inexhaustible classification of these create a crossover to magniloquent and flowery language that this humble author of Yard Lamp of Gloria was persecuted for- But by exemption I spare thee.

For by rote of reason, I add needless adjuncts to the aforesaid, like, en route to an Elevated Empyrean: so ineffable, starriest, and how herculean! Next in line lies the gigantic geometry of planetary and stellar appearances where both *ball* and *sphere* bulge ballooning fullness. Indeed, the contour of concord and consonance be *but* hidden away, elsewhere, from our knowledge as each are recessed and reserved in the breathy depths of… as of yet undiscovered Divinest Dilation.

Let us reconsider the combination of *Divinest Dilation*. This is only once referred to *and one more time in an upcoming encounter.*

For this to cast a survey of assessment, one must single-handed make sure to record the general gist of things; especially a supernal solace of love and ecstasy. For furthermore, the salubrious Sons of Yahweh are illustrious diamond-dust Mirrors of focused photons! Of profoundest peace and power by myriad mind-birth! The brainchild long after its tumultuous brainstorm hath quieted down to a placid pond surrounded by an infinite wilderness of utter mystery. Outside of conventional yet continual causality (God never makes mistakes– No!

Not even one), such mind-birth of preconception, in the literal sense, is not only perfectly protected, but limitless in its capacity, ability, and agility to absolutely grasp and comprehend all that IS. Whereby the 'state of things' as it once appeared, is now, or ever would be, remains revealed and even eviscerated inside-out of nonexistence; as these things really preexist, rather than how their principal properties are perceived afterwards.

Behold the unaltered states of Hyper-Consciousness (for no change is necessary if already perfect), or Conical Helicon, *as is identified~* where nine muses enjoy their abode with memorial Mnemosyne, the mother thereof~ that have undergone crystallization. As it were, where the almighty Yahweh is Light, and in Him is no darkness at all (which is a Biblical backup, except for the aforesaid mythological allegory; it was included for the sake of sound argument)! Now, believe that this transcendent state of explosive existence can only be obtained through the Faith and Love, Hope and Charity of our vicarious Lord and Savior Jesus Christ and none other. Granted, the personified aspect of a maternal presence is resident in His Holy Spirit, even as other effigies of the mother-image permeate personalities throughout this Divine Matrix (of which waxes forth froth and spews spume via Quantum Foam). But outside of the physical universe is the Metaphysical.

Wherefore your Heavenly Home could live and breathe accordingly with His Likeness and Similitude so infinitely invisible! And where there ought to be no last lesion of life's lacuna, but instead clarion clarity, instantaneous intuition, order and perfect peace. Yea, even the clean slate of Lady Conscience- whose hard wounds were washed- is immaculate and devoid of cicatrices of any scar, birthmark, nor of bloated blet or blemish! If fresh fruit, like a juicy jargonelle, has a swollen sidewall to it, a bad bump, or a tumorous top, the deformity thereupon is called a *blet*, by the way.

I say, where there shall nevermore crawl aground the vile vanities of separateness: that which partitioned the Good from the Good to teach us a lesson. Howbeit, assuredly the bad from the Good is rightfully divided down in the gaping gulf, chasm, and abyss of

Hell-- so that Heaven is everlastingly undisturbed. Untainted by but the noisome nastiness. Liberty is found in God Only!

CONCLUSION

To formulate the said architectonics hereof (articulated in formal fashion), one will have entered into it before the Foundations of Heaven and Earth... In such crystallization of an Eternal Hologram, we would have needed to be, beforehand, foreordained to receive it via God's timeless pathway of Welcome. An entry through which the eternal Elect and Beloved are its own escorts of Grace.

Enter NARRATOR of Ye Star Gate STAGE

And now! Let us make haste and return to the succulent taste of that Holy Fruit in lieu of the Forbidden One. Yea, rather albeit the pale pear from the Tree of Life, and not the proverbial apple gnawed upon by the Eve of indulgence. For indeed our three scientists are caught up, if not ensnared, in this hollowest hyper-toroidal Möbius strip in which *hallowed hallways* have caused something to go off, but by no effect save self-emanatory as a ferromagnetic monopole mast not unlike the Tesla Terminal of core and coil containment. Consistently, such a telestic transport of far-flung modernity within which some super-built Futuristic Metropolis and multi-megalopolis awaits our escorts henceforth. So much to the echelon of a triumphal and restored reentry to earthly shadows of preexistence; back on an orb that nearly has estranged them. For the time being, back to terra firma!

Homeward bound, yet into an alternate time-zone, or time-slot in history, our three astronauts experience the elongation of transit.

BACKGROUND ATMOSPHERIC SOUNDTRACK

That for the moment, these translated mortals of material thought reluctantly recover themselves, still dizzy from the very vertiginous transition from point A to point B. They gather each other upon an asphalt street of urban destitution, or of memorabilia if one may interpret it as such. The turn-of-the-century red-brick buildings that flamboyantly flank every avenue and boulevard of quelling quiet & placidity crept into one's spleen, sure enough.

Is it real, or is it Memorex? (a company's portmanteau of memory excellence). Rutherford recalls his Memorex brand MiniDisk. Technically inclined Harris had another angle on the redundant rigmarole: Was the TATM system ready to replicate this poignant portrait in 3-D? (he had homesickness, heartache, and longing for the motherland of Ireland which weaned him).

Whereas Joyce, jacketed by extra protection, and divesting herself from bulky discomfort, couldn't find the time to reminisce because of the vivid lucidity of such surroundings that overtook her! Here, the visionary diorama and coronary panorama of a halcyon afternoon without a sunset, but bathed thereby thus, prolonged the dismal Star City indefinitely, or when the Day the Earth Stood Still, if you will. This timestamp of impressions soliloquized her clairvoyant (farseeing) closeups of her homeland, but out of context due to the impious, imposing and foreboding fortresses.

For there they were, revived out of just another spellbound trance, only to reenter the next phase of the labyrinthic limbo. Of which the walled womb was fecund enough to assume *this*, *that*, and the *other*. Full well, the block-by-block holograms materialized tangible and opaque edifices so far as their eyes could catch. For with whereabouts, TRANVORTIUMS may manifest the entrancement thereof-- the torched up lumens of light-output and vibratile vivacity-- the city of red-bricked sidewalls and frontages reincarnated a medieval mystique. Unarguably, but conversely contemporaneous in its blithe-like, yet lugubrious and rarefied air-gloom of a mustily mink heirloom! "Moscow?" Rutherford rebounded to a former format for his twosome tease, raising his hookup of some circa 1980s over-the-street Torchlight Lantern:

"Well, what's the verdict, my hyperspace specialists?" Their commander inquired tritely. Elsewhere, behind an endless walled landscape, in Russian mimicry, the TATM intoned: "Что это за место? *Chto eto za mesto?* Zeroing in on their acquired dialogue.

H2 (frowning from wormhole roller coaster recoil)~ “Hell, beats me, Sir! I’m lucky to still be myself, my goodness!”

H (with a Gaelic gasp, *gutteral* and gruff)~ “Póg mo thóin!” He meant *Kiss my arse!* “Lass, I’ll ne’er be flustered up to my necktie or down to my pleated kilt! But how Grand...” had been his adage for a comical catwalk that countered cowardice.

R (even if under siege by such picturesque solidification, sympathetic)~ “This eye-opener is too unorthodox for ye troopers. Just hang tight, I’ll take a goodly look.”

The colonel cocked his head for a catchall view of the big red burg. Its dismal domain sunk into his skeleton. Jackrabbit jolted out of their skins, our off-world Recon could not much visualize what its hinterland backsides entailed, let alone its rubicund brickwork and terracotta quoins of freshly baked-by-the-Sun frontages. Colossal quoins all over the disreputable territory of forgotten fads and vermilion vogues deprived of its citizens somewhere in hinterlands of hellish harpoonery; long derelict sailors, fuzzy fishermen and mariners handling harpoons against some Atargatis mermaid monster! Who have deserted their posts of what once was the Soviet Union and have hounded the squid-like Medusa off the coasts to the Laptev Sea- oceanic stratum strewn with very high-altitude ionospheric aurorae borealis hissing and sizzling so seductively.

They found a corroded cast showing boldly **Москва** on an iron slab in answer to Rutherford’s Russian question mark. Harris heavily heaved the blowtorch-cutout card of ferrous resin out of their way as it clunked against the pavement matched by a softly sonorous call of reed organ whistles, wheezing. Then the brazen clangor of a belfry, top-starred by a henna hued pentagram, echoed over an acoustic range as if it were within auditory hallucination. Spectral hearing so acute it almost made Joyce reel and feel bilious. But apropos of an immediate melody that just as fast faded away, Paranormal phenomena still didn’t dissipate, pending yet!

Rutherford recalled *reverberatory*, precognitive and premonitory mental algorithms arise from visitors at present; the contents of which are readily represented by a Mercury Mirror awash with wettest importation. Whereas past thought-transference to present moments (that of rarest occurrence) arose from instances of afterglow by previous tenants of TATM multiplex platforming, the latter listings include repercussions of an unholy think-tank grottily residual on the pristine premises! Aside from what Camp Mitch manuals on survivalist settings had dittoed down, de facto and all ledger-listed alphanumerically, an out-of-context cache could be very easily misconstrued if not derogatorily deceptive! And such emptily anechoic rooms to have been juxtaposed with whitewalls (not of pneumatic tires), but of the lexiconic case: that which consists of a foursquare front wall (main *Mure*), four sidewalls, a far back-wall, floor, and high-ceiling, is an off the wall wonder when such cities of metropolitan magnitude on our globe glower out of nowhere! It is the oddball of the Borteum and Cremeum Rational Rotation categorized by the Camp Mitch manual. Summarily, the Holographic Hull-- though not only a six-sided cube, but more of a Hexagonal Prism, or Truncated Octahedron that connects with a Tesseract, the 4-D analogue of the cube-- had now congealed (of all awkward awnings and canopies) its flue *flammiferous* **Москва** at large barge lorry-laden. Left unoccupied and ghastly! It was Operation Star City Moscow!

And farther back, beyond buildings and buildings of urban boundlessness were cornfield-filleted and fattened forests of many metallic totem pole pipes. Defunct refinery stovepipe topper spouts and sieves that sighed dryly up at some sulfurous overcast caricatured by tableaux of tornadoes. Each permanent funnel cloud- like an inverted cone, widened from a surly ceiling, narrowed down to taper and tip- had hung there in midair, ominously, but as harmless as on an oil painting! Its portrayal had lain long encrusted upon linen canvases of the Transalteratorium holographic art gallery.

While one felt times to elapse fleetingly in an alien setting, to directly describe it, Russian buildings barricaded this upturned plot on an electronic trampoline of the Metalucelectropluceptorium, or the MLPTM: for now on, a diminutive of the polysyllabic and sesquipedalian silly goose! Preferably, the shiniest showcase of which will enter our confidential conference around the corner.

At best, there were high Gothic and castellated courtyards of the Kremlin garrisoned by colonnette corridors curiously backed by balustrades and swirled modillion mantled door-to-door developments everywhere. One fastened together, cinder-block built, as obscenely darkened reddish Legos landmarks; the others, pastel-light lavender and pink pillar & pilaster poised for multitudes of which were trellis-latticed veranda and balcony-bedecked palatial mansions embanked by bushy hedgerow terraces! Where within them beautiful ballrooms of phantom cotillions had kept inverted into reflective floor-varnished vastness that sagged from a heavyweight self-automated and mighty **Mortier Taj Mahal** DANCE ORGAN blowup calliope! The crown and jewel behind the Iron Curtain of an age-old frontispiece with colossal columns and ever stately statuary. Not to forgo the singing fountainettes and golden geyser strong founts spurting spume and spray and water-jets of sunshine-glittered glory splayed into hydrous parasols. The nodules, nozzles and faucets of each golden gusher in choreographic synchronization aligned with the Dance Organ's resonant rolls of perforated or punctuated paper slotted by multi-stylus music box precision.

Not to forget fanciful forms of turreted and cupola fudge rooftops wrought out from quadrangle refectory glory and sturdy steeples all in axial alignment arranged over Russian Orthodox chapels, churches, and cathedrals and basilicas countless with onion domes and conical spires gold-leaf gilded afresh.

But beyond palaces of pomp and pageantry, unbeknownst to the Recon team, stacks of surplus and heaps of heavier headway have overflowed into uncharted warehouses of the even Greater Ubiquelabyrinthium intramural Maze besides... But over the outskirts of the Moscow nucleus, there were row-by-row suburbs of bourgeois buildings without the castigated and achingly bemoaned tenements of tawdry times... *Timestamps the devout ought to intercede for,* Joyce germinated with internalized intent as she wanted to contain cordiality as opposed to political segregation amongst many nations. The communist totalitarian regime was no joke! It required tolerance in order for her to eulogize the lore and loveliness of Russian dollhouse harmony that she relished offhand and off-record. Politics and war were not in her forté, whereas the old Paranormal hath hereupon become her fortissimo coda!

The colonel and captain could calculate only what they militarily made of it. Nothing more, nor less. Observed objectively, a human blockade was no match for oncoming communists full of tanks, armaments, missile launchpads and warhead-deployments. Their gladiatorial sportsmanship blinded their eyes and deafened their ears to the fairyland of an underlying and intrinsic Eden. So shut out to the finer finesse of feeling was this gorilla and gorgon gamut of galvanization. For Joyce, the Gog & Magog modules of the Bible's teaching revealed one of a dozen debacles to toll on the world, and not only ursine (even tho' the Holy Mary asked us to pray for and consecrate Russia to her Immaculate Heart). These cross-references relied on in her photographic journal were bookmarked in Genesis 10, 1 Chronicles 1 & 5, Ezekiel 38 & 39, and Revelation 20! In contrast to her oft sultry demeanor, the woman wooed the OW-team's turnaround time until both Rutherford and Harris were unwittingly convinced that *jarhead* mentality and its robotic repugnance on *both* ends of the spectrum only dug a Pit! On one side were the bald eagles sharpening their talons for hot carrion, and on the other side of the medial rainbow were Bears; but both barreling through in their conquests to conquer destiny.

The details of this expedition unfolded additional oddities. For more memorials had unraveled which were compressed, squashed in, and sub-squeezed down into the TATM's Supercomputer Photographic Memory Foam data storage, or the cyborg-installed SPMF. Such circuitry surpassed quantum computers of the mid twentieth century where integrated circuit chips were Planck-pliant sponges of spacetime itself. Everyone of which was a true Transvortium at heart. Specifically, every Metal Wafer and Canister Creation had deftly suspended *eventful extravaganza* in cryogenic freeze-frame compartments of the most delicate fragility. Tall Walls of impregnable neutronium shielded, sheltered, and seamlessly safeguarded the Perfect Packets tucked into a mnemonic mainframe; its crystallization consisted of airtight self-evacuated in-vitro volumes stored in V-contoured vats of an innermost Vulvatorium, yet anatomically.

Like fulgurite deposits in a sand dune (vitreous sediments of sand fused by lightning strikes that radiate the near-thermonuclear heat-flash), so- similarly- innumerable memory crystals, but tinier that grains of silica, were embedded deeply into an SPMF cushion and mattress of compensatory *collapsibility*. The professorial vade mecum primer on the Transvortium states that the latter in italics is understood as a mathematical property of the effect measure, rather than a consequence of certain graphical or probabilistic structures in the particular data set.

Also, meritoriously enshrined by both the quantum physics panel and the Board and Cabinet Members, the voluminously researched doctrines were well Rolodex filed for this off-world EVA (extravehicular activity). The Camp Mitch guidebook kept records of the modus operandi thereof. This was not surprising to the rest of the crew, and Harris and Hathaway caught on quickly to the culprit theory behind this bizarre materialization with their grimmer project **Москва**, still in boldfaced format! In simpler language, compensatory *collapsibility* within Supercomputer Photographic Memory Foam suggests sudden implosion, but all the way down to Planck-volume viability. Yea, many tonnes of information are sub-squeezed into subatomic compression, only to balloon back, outwardly, yet universe-like! Perhaps at random, Moscow had been frozen in time out of a Residuary Reservoir of EEG brain activity. Either way, what astounded the Recon team were intricacies of the Meticulous Metropolis replete with a reliquary of artifact fashion!

With invisible facility emporiums, hulking and stashed away from their points of view, the dwarfed crew knew all too well of their so eclipsed way of thinking.

Full formidable to benighted ignorance are underground subduction zones, for example, where plate tectonics are wedged beneath the earth's crust and dipped into a mantle of magma… The deeper depth-charge of pressurized lava with its bituminous bulge of molten metal and rock sought some volcanic vent, preparatory to eruption. By the starkest comparison demanding of spartan endurance, all three (off of familiarity left behind) dared not to tamper with additional implication. Alas, Rutherford was silenced by the TATM Silencer and swallowed his big dose with a gulp, gag! better yet, swept it rug-under…

Apart from what the venerable vade mecum reassured them with, as from an altar of pseudo-certainty, our intuitive intern, the most vulnerable and impressionable of the lot, had dealt with a helluva new Nightmare! She deduced the high-Gothic gargoyle gorgons to be of an illusory yet allegorical Iliad. Like litanies and legends of Homer's epic siege of Troy and the Trojan war-zones. In her college literature, she perused the (translated from the Greek) Iliad poiesis, which meant "poem of Ilion." *Ilion was an ancient name for the city of Troy. The *Iliad* spotlights Achilles's actions, teaching the ancient Greeks about the past and the values they held most dear. Until now, many millennia later, her Achilles heel midway in this climactic EVA let Moscow feel eerie and irksome; it rattled her skeletal frame of ligaments as if she were a whitetail doe accompanied by two bucks, but all reconverted to caseworker carcasses along her trek. Just shy of ending up in the rubber room. *I'd prefer to be euthanized more than these hippodrome theatrics!* thought Joyce, our thoroughbred reindeer that she oft pictured herself to be. It was only a passing death-wish, naught else.

Aside from framed freshness, the grotesque and macabre postern of the Yellow Room reset the stage that would rage beside her foreground and backyard of fairy-tale-limned lawns; likely, back at her barnyard memories of an old dusk-to-dawn 175W mercury vapor bucket beacon. She clung to her memory lane of home wistfully. Except such settings here were dreadfully draconian!

Nor could such grotequeries of surrealism dissuade her from an upheld fastidious charm and enchantment she'd showcase with elaborate elegance. The Full Bird mascot of the mission filed away his mental meanderings of TATM technicalities and turned to the team's sociological ladylike novice:

R~ "I believe we can wheedle ourselves out of this chimerical charade with a quid pro quo method."

H2~ "You mean this-for-that with the Trans--?"

H~ "Exactly!" the captain butted in.

"Exactly!" confirmed Joyce.

"Hmm..." hummed the curious colonel to demystify everyone's cloud-nine dilemma. "Our predicament presents itself unnaturally."

H~ "How so?"

R~ "Well? For one thing, we haven't the smokiest smattering of how long we'll end up in this rather Russian reservation."

H2~ "Guys, I really don't wanna feel woozy again. Let's take it one step at a time, okay?"

The commissioned officers empathized with her.

Everyone could not help but feel something slipping up!

R~ "I confess, the Yellow Room was more than we could handle. I find materialized Moscow to be no less unpredictable..."

In the wink of an eye the sidewalk on which they were afoot dissolved into a transparent void, yet they were somehow upheld!

Eventually everything shifted sideways and they were off again! Vestibules about them *vanishingly* folded into hairline slits.

In an unfinished filmstrip, the long haul of this northernmost megacity planted a midway pit-stop for the OW-team. The Holographic Projectors of tangible opacity glided them to the Moskva River through Western Russia in the midst of where the megalopolis lay. The Tributary ran narrow and shallow upstream, sneaking through marshes, and powerful and self-confident down south, carrying bigger ships and barges. In the Transalteratorium's version of things, the riverside embankments slanted upwardly with railroad relics on top. And alongside, behind electrified causeways of minus-charged tracks under overhead plus-charged catenary cables, building-backed dykes and ramparts contrasted the main Moskva River with windows and embrasures of an enclosed immurement. Only lockup doors down at street-level looked like mice burrows to rat-hole huddled hideaways. The flatbed barges battened by rigging with oil-tankers occupied the wide watercourse culverts that interconnected the Moscow Canal with the Volga-Baltic waterway and whatnot. Her hydro-journey to the important industrial center of Nizhny Novgorod (formerly Gorky) covered some 60 miles up and down the sinewy stretch of Planck-replicated freshwater!

After another shuffle, floundering to gain a grip on another mini-reentry, the colonel hollered to hold on tight! Then the platform so coalesced underfoot for them to take their places as the **Москва** surrounding such a sojourn resumed stationary stillness. Sparkles of fluffy stuff fizzed out of Vac-Shafts shoved up from subterranean vaults; metal moorings not unlike valved pumps in larger urban centers of the TATM Rolodex. Be it apparent as any doorknob that these calling cards of metropolitan magnification were augmented by roundelay carousels and directory dials. No sooner than the following feature, the starlight glitter-varnished Metalucelectropluceptorium, under its glitz of hot starriest minutiae, had interfaced with their new hangout... Rutherford, Harris, and Hathaway harnessed themselves upon landfall, filled up their canteens with that subarctic refresher, and attended to their next makeshift station. At least the city's hydration was drinkable.

Rutherford began to bargain with impossible odds. Not needing, or unwilling to play Russian roulette with the intramural system of an electronic hedge-maze, he had plotted to put on a pasty poker face feeling to the transaction & exchange of *quid pro quo*!

STRANGE SOUNDS SURFACE FROM THE FLOORBOARD

Joyce adjusted her bearings and felt finally herself, regardless of the anomaly, or call it a *glitch* of permutations imposed onto everyone. "I'll support both of you through thick or thin." Her affable nature had shone through no matter what the cost of her grubstake.

Immediately a lead-footed feeling pulled at them. They could not lift up their feet freely as they stood on a bright-shining sheen of emblazonment. Soft seats appeared instantly. The overpowering sensation caused them to sit down ere the lustrous linoleum spoke up at them with a confidential conference in lowercase as from its TSSV, or *The Still Small Voice* of Metalucelectropluceptorium!

MLPTM: For other foundation can no man lay than that is laid, which is Jesus Christ. 1 Corinthians 3:11 (KJV)

R~ "And you have come from where? We welcome you professionally, O endlessly spanned-out pliant Platform." (the colonel's decorum dampened any premature provocation, in the event of)

MLPTM: I am the base of Transalteratorium, the shiny and sultriest SHEETARA! Like the photo-surface of the Sun, as you three may recall in your heliology classroom, I am self-granulated and pressurized, but with harmless noneffective neutron contiguity. Nay, I cannot be divided, nor destroyed by anything haphazardly deployed. If anything unholy here is thrown, I'll brighten up my glitter to full blown. No matter what deployed at me is merely void; for I am that which was, and that shall be, paved seamlessly throughout eternity, O humanoid... I am the sultriest SHEETARA!

Before one was to back away from just another haunting, the colonel hesitated on a debate with its Glitz. They struggled to pry themselves off of their seats & plodded out of its grasp. The edge of it was perfectly straight and went on forever. And there was no warp, nor nothing of the kind that curved into the distance like on Earth. An eternal Steel Sheet that had crept up to their feet as this flat glassy sea, or as limitless linoleum, lay under queues of every overhung quasar beacon; greasy searing Teflon tongues quivering and sizzling in their open-ended cocoons above its very vast span of agglutination agleam.

"Company! About-face!" ordered the colonel as they trotted free of its grappling grip. His twosome platoon kept on marching away from the Metalucelectropluceptorium and back into manufactured Moscow on the forefront of this event. All three of them refused to recall the creepiness of its TSSV and that the flat entity displayed a weird wherewithal. But little did Recon anticipate the utterly immutable insistence of the mighty MLPTM! "My goodness, this really cuts the cake wide open for us all!" he remarked.

Last but not least with the *Sheetara* showcase, they had gone on their routine route along the commercial districts and neighborhoods of the Gothic city, forgetful for now of the spooky artificial glaciarium that tugged at their heels rather than having Hathaway, Harris, and Rutherford to skate thereupon. A red public square, or township plaza, was preferable over the nothingness of an infinite floorboard leading to nowhere but more of the same. The chief in high-gear guided the captain and intern, commanding, "At ease!"

They were debriefed on the *previously unencountered* incident and their TATM tour compounded a tiresome sense, or prerogative of purposeful peregrination. Meanwhile, no more an intern, Joyce was promoted by the colonel to a deputy right on the spot. "You've earned your new badge of honor far and above the call of duty, my Miss!" Rutherford reexamined their performances... However, the captain as well as the colonel needed no exaltation since their commission to a higher status of rank became automatic upon arrival to Mitchelville. Joyce jumped for joy, and yet rank meant little to her as cold codifications were labels only. The badge of one's womb in a mother, or a brooch upon one's heart meant more to our crowned deputy, especially on grounds of loving-kindness and commitment. The contents of this trying mission had taxed them to the core and feeling like a princess presented only an undisciplined jurisdiction to Joyce on the edge of life and death; like her *tiff* with the postern and now, her befuddlement at the MLPTM's Edge of Forever!

Both Boyd and Roderick threw a mini-party at the temporary station for Joyce just as she graduated from her internship. The red lady of Apache ethnics reified her Indian codes of conduct and had always excelled in academia and gymnastics. With her cadet jumpsuit, fluorescent yellow in colour, and the custodian insignia which was a 24-karat gold pentagram pendant, her assiduous Assignment would later open better doors for her at the academy. It was during such moments of ceremony that her commissioned officers offered to strip themselves of their regalia for the occasion (particularly to humble themselves and encourage rising stars of acting adjutants like a brand new Deputy that donned *her* shoes).

In an interim of festivity and from the background, behind the curtains of bivouac tarp, the imposing scarlet and crimson edifices that were Moscow's trademark- at least in this holographic version- dimmed everything! Downy and dismal shades of henna foreshadowed impending doom dappled desolately against otherwise neon-bright branding of traffic hazard fluorescence; mostly orange and yellow warning imprints all over radiantly dyed rubber. There was nothing else available in their briefcases. Supplies of heavily latex balloons blown up by helium fill to tube-like leeway should have done the trick. A company by the name of Stellarc provided inflatable lanterns to illuminate an emergency situation in the event of a power outage. The generators in this day and age were with thrifty pocket-sized usage for portable or mobile convenience... Because Operation TATM was paramount, however, their ceremonial bash, or get-together gone midway, had been but a trifling triviality compared to this grisly plight. The colonel and his duo postponed such coronation and got back to the business of patrol & exigency exercises.

Due to safety requirements instituted by the colonel earlier on, right after the deluge dissection of a Time Warp trek, their surveillance, vigil, and fireguard were extended into the wee hours as the three of them took turns with eight-hour shifts. Yet the duty-roster covered a 24-hour period per diem. The old monotony of relentless rounds, the dreary drills of marching back and forth and to and fro nonstop, stifled her sense of creativity and adventure. And until so much to the point of cringing.

So much for the beginner deputy's requisite recall of continual contingencies! Yet all along, notwithstanding the regimen, she saw to it that the flight-for-life liquidation could safeguard the backs of her park rangers' triad in the long haul. Before her ambassador girl scout and squad-leadership shields guaranteed favorable formation and fortification for the entire troop lock, stock, and barrel. But behold, why not for this troubled trinity? She languished with a legitimate sigh, sulking and discomfited by her self-absorption throughout the compulsory daily dispatch and routine of checkpoint patrol.

Still, *This mission is rigorous and nerve-racking*, pondered Joyce, making sure to conceal her pusillanimity. *When will it all end?*

In response to her malaise, the MLPTM clandestinely intoned out of nowhere: Take heart, O daughter of God! For soon your commanding officer shall meet the mistress Glistria of the Mercury Mirror, and the rest of you too!

Having kept this *non-murmured* modicum to herself, Joyce felt like Hagar of old, back Biblically, when God spoke to her in an angelic vision as she fled Abraham's wife with her infant Ishmael. An Oasis appeared and saved the lives of both her and her offspring on the torrid desert!

The unexpected resounding of that *sheet of steel* staggered the new deputy, but then it revitalized her strength for the remainder of this grueling mission. The tour of the big burg continued onward as black windows and doors represented a lethiferous interpretation to menacing Moscow, although irrigated by the Moskva tributaries, *it* (the City itself) bulged balefully over her fulcrum of team-support.

While death clenched the OW-team with its grotesque grip, on the far lighter side, just overhead, hung high above blacktop streets were fine festoons of miniature fixtures flailing about in an electric wind. But tiny lamps were they of overkill, limpidly loosened from thickly skinned superconductor copper cables of high-tension alternating current. The little luminaires of High Intensity Discharge, or of HID origin, revealed arc tubes protuberant, lit up, glibly glinting argent arc tube scintillation for Christmas ornaments of celebratory glory~ Though there were no holidays hereupon, it reminded them!

The fiery dainties of tiny Torchlight lore were weirdly contrasted against a bloody backdrop of the sickening cityscape. A godforsaken sordid thing! Not to recrudesce the old Yellow Room trauma- Joyce suppressed her relapse of its sallow session- its nauseatingly bilious flashback flooded her! The *unconfrontable* Glare thereof managed to mortify anyone ever conversant with its premonitory and prismatic slip-slit of oozing slag, sludge and slop.

And they noticed it. No, not the resurfaced unease, but rather radiant relics of the Bygone Era! Diminutive and dismantled high-pressure sodium and mercury vapor illuminants, some like "bright white" as their labels would specify for a brand name logo. Others as multi and aluminum vapor vat-packs so strangely strewn above cobbled streets of straw and sawdust which, under enchanting auspices, these numerous novelties of 'ritzy glitz' could confound the World's Fair for the year 2114.

Their tour-guide, resolute Rutherford, escorted Boyd and Joyce alongside the remnants of macabre **Москва** as if he knew the ropes of the city's rigging. How, from out of elsewhere, would he have known where to go and what to avoid, hapless Hathaway could only guess with self-abnegated injunction. God knew the whereabouts of their predestined *detour*, or so it seemed... Wherefore for now, the B-section of analytical observation was watered down to notes scribbled in the colonel's personal logbook:

Timestamp unknown (nonetheless, now just a few days before New Year's Eve of 2113, in estimation of our calendar chronometer)!

Among myriads of landmark monuments, some of which were paleolithic artifacts that, perhaps gauged by carbon-dating under electron microscopes, preceded the existence of the whole human race.

I shan't delve into details on the authenticity thereof, nor on the genuine junk otherworldly Moscow may have in store; like rummaging into an immeasurable thrift shop racked with bric-a-brac, but with also priceless antiquities fingerprinted by passersby of uncensored naughtiness! Mind you, these were past visitors who had encroached upon the TATM turf without prior authorization; for what they've committed, the violators should have been subpoenaed! Recall our Yellow Room recon that ought to admonish subsequent seekers! But such subjects of this experiment are better reserved for Mitchelville's Lyceum of lucubration, and for bookkeeping pedants and busy bureaucrats to hastily riffle through!

In brief, I will submit my commissioned colleagues to disciplinarian decision-making for to keep everyone of us uncontaminated whilst on route (ready or not, but to better be aware of the environs)!

Then, with finalized foreclosure, the colonel caught on to the delicacies and dainties of Memory Lane- not of provisional protocol, but of delectable treats known as *unconsumables*. Visual feasts too alluring for normal eyesight to examine, except under laboratory lighting layout conditions: (the beta-section)

> *Others, not of our planet, show as emblazoned emblems in a Maelstrom mind-meld of catastrophe. Their gibbous emerald, or pearlescent and iridescent lucency, so lovely as to cause lunacy, ignited unearthly-like. As dinky-sized lithe lamps of heavenly humor sizzling with starlight; hot stars incomparably reduced trillions of decimals down to near-nullified scale. One of them, if I dare conjecture, an Electric Quasar contained in a glass jar, the size of some Electrified Eggplant; or others, compressed to a compact*

capsule: a Burnt Pouch, a Perfect Package, or flat-pad of scorch-bright torchlight eye-piercing perpetuity. Suchlike searing samples dangling inanely by taut tethers, tendrils suspended: they are curious, chimerical, like stellar relics reported in our fantastical exploration explained as CE-5.

Signing out, Colonel Roderick Rutherford/ *end of line*

In their unbelief, nearly all ancient fixtures & pictures of last epochal technology intoned still small voices one to another and into the dimmer distance of undertone cacophony. Interposing messages between one *jocund jacket* to another; each one sealed in vitreous see-through silicon. With cold cathode and anode bright-bridge polarities bulged-tubular with built-in electron guns or cathode-ray spewers, there was no controversy that their predecessors, 200 years ago from the year 2113, were without a doubt *of John Logie Baird and Philo Taylor Farnsworth origin~* pioneer inventors of television, Rutherford recollected. Such biographical brush-ups evaluated many of his theories, the colonel's that is.

This is not to exclude his aerial maneuvers at the Air Force Base of the Greater Mitchelville Area, when something like cathode-ray radar-recovery had just about cost Rutherford his life. It was at one point with his Aim High, Fly-Fight-Win flight mission series-- luckily during peacetime-- that a bogie was spotted spuriously off of the starboard bow, and that it darted over and shifted position abruptly to the port side of his Geomagnetic Atmosphere Hovercraft, or GAH for short. In the cockpit, the copilot was captain Harris under the colonel's command structure; and with one flight engineer, the second officer by the rank and name of First Lieutenant Laura Lithuania of exemplary performance.

So they tried to outmaneuver if not intercept a UAP (Unidentified Aerial Phenomena) flyby. Suddenly, too evasive to allocate on visual sensors of camera translation, rotation, and zoom factor, the anachronistic acrobat emitted cathode rays not unlike the prefabricated Moscow's littlest lamplight showcase! Incidentally, during such a controversial encounter away from the Camp Mitch AFB back then, the bright blob zigzagged and temporarily blinded Lieutenant Lithuania and Rutherford when, thanks to Captain Harris who countered the zippy Thing, with good fortune all three of them landed the GAH back to ground zero safety.

Rutherford's recall of the aftermath in the ready-room was vivid as his keen flight engineer probed and engaged him:

"Could it have been an omen for both of you?" the lieutenant would previse, alluding to the Camp's recruitment for their TATM project as an inopportune fortuneteller for such urgency. "Sir, the big Mission everyone in the camp has rumored about!"

(In time, her foolproof prophecy was fulfilled)

"I believe so, Laura," conceded the colonel, looking lackluster. Once was he with jar-head sergeants screaming orders to pale-faced recruits; (not at all demystified by the prospect of an off-world reconnaissance mission back then). *"There have been bizarre sightings, beyond bafflement, and unheard of for the United States nation as a whole. We've gotta do something!"* he obviated the latter in an unaware foreglimpse of the future intern's, then deputy's predilection for Hanna-Barbera's animated series Godzilla. On the sideline yardage, to have personified the all-too apparent Captain Carl Majors in command of his motley crew aboard the Calico, a schooner-sized exploratory ship, was kept constantly, redundantly recorded into the Transalteratorium's vast Memory Foam *storage archives.

Of course, neither one of them at present- the colonel, nor the deputy- discussed the matter about this present or past parallelism.

In this secretive sample, the word storage by sleight of hand turns to *starage (*star* the prefix and *age* the suffix)! Therefore, for the sake of clarification and accuracy, the total TMF.

Again, in response to the milder misnomer, the MLPTM of a shimmering steel sheet furtively intoned to the deputy Joyce out of nowhere, clairaudiently lassoed: I will re-platform all of ye promptly in closure of the Red Burg's bounty and county-line!

She shuddered vehemently on their trot to the last exit out of radiant Russia, but bloody Hell more repulsive to Rutherford and no less petrifying to Harris along the wayside.

Behind electrified curtains, the moisturized Metal Wafer of each outreach had begun to embed the Planck-volumes of past-present-and-future events unwittingly and unceasingly. Albeit to capture an unintended innuendo, flattery, or middle-ground midway blitheness; until to blessing, and then bliss, the mind-readers of silencing silos throughout the Ubiquelabyrinthium TATM multiplex platform only apotheosized the faintest imprint and the slightest slur; or slippage of every conceivable nuance of neuronal networks. In laymen language: Joyce, Boyd, and Roderick (automatically decommissioned by the Ultimate Authority) suspected an indecipherable EEG to enshrine the brainwaves of billions of souls that have ever lived; even the ones approximated presently and, by all means, prioritized.

Thus the tangent of CRT logistics, both now and then, that they, Hathaway, Harris, and Rutherford fumbled over, provoked the proverbial pressure-cooker program. It was as if an *ignitron* had been dipped into a reservoir of Quicksilver that engendered those standby beacons to glare back at them disapprovingly!

Somewhere, submersed moderator rods writhe in the heavyweight water's refractive lensing effect while with disturbance the distribution of old holographic energy quivers beneath linoleum.

On the deck of an uninhabited totalitarian Titanic, the former U.S.S.R., they were about to walk the blank plank edgewise, back but aware of the whitest corridor that had X-rayed their barefooted tread on an underlying Metalucelectropluceptorium melting herself here and far over toward some other-side station. Telephone booths at the roadside had stepped up their non-humanoid doormats of the platform they would walk upon. Left behind were such streetlamps of the Archangelic Establishment that displayed more exotic examples of spiritual ascension; where rising spirits had become but far brighter than what might have been concocted for them to embody.

These identical entities of various wavelengths consumed, by one radiant replica after another, the distributive dimension of Galactic Glory agleam amidst droll dreaming due to those funny fey lamps. Some symmetrical, others asymmetrical, but long rows of uttermost mast-lamps luminously lopsided with dimpled tubes on both ends of them, atop waving in the gale, wirelessly interlinked. Wheel-wound Ophanim offered themselves meanwhile with pressurized presences, as such, and packaged up through vitrification!

And hereafter, sub specie aeternitatis, or from a standpoint of eternity, an interview with the immaterial was soon to commence.

LANDSCAPED SOUNDTRACK

Over a sacrosanct lot of stainless steel sterility, each of them felt uncommonly comfortable being barefoot. The exit out of the city limits was lengthened to still another vivarium of terra firma furnishings as more of the peculiar exotica flowed for exhibition!

Little did they know of the manufacturing plexus in starkest contrast to their copycatting faces, facsimiles, or representations. In a nutshell, there were wide walnut & chestnut trees that edged the walkway where wandered they away from a metropolitan nucleus. Evidently, the Holographic Hive was still huffing and puffing and with confetti fallout billowing forthwith, trying to reproduce rational and ridiculous images into 3-D blowups of tangible opacity, translucency, or both. As if to strain at a gnat but devour its camel, just to juggle up unbridled creativity crammed in loop spools of the Memory Foam download, the desert lay discarded!

R~ "What?! We're *not-on-Earth* are we?" whined their group-leader in reference to such disorienting dislocation.

"Aye! Me thinks it be an incubus, lad!" Harris had a fetish about monsters and goblins gone on a hike.

H2 (with whimsical singalong subterfuge against the mediocrity of it all, having been beside herself):

"I sing eternal glory
Above the seven storey
For all the world grown hoary,
And so sings Jesus Christ;
And when the blood gets gory
Found by observatory-
This thus concludes my story,
Singing Jesus Christ!"

*It was a ditty Joyce had learned by heart from her teenage years in church.

Without bickering to disconsolate fuss, or annoying ennui, whichever came first, their conversation continued through the desolate limbo of utter nothingness... It was another interim of a vast void that by some sort of malfunction had to re-materialize the walnut and chestnut trees alongside the roadway backed by forested hills and an azure firmament, although overhung heavily, lightly punctuated puffy-like with silver-clad clouds. Like a computer having to reboot itself; its program, software, and surroundings followed.

Reenter the 3: R for Rutherford, H for Harris, & H2 for Hathaway:

H~ "Joyce! I ne'er knew you to be a believer."

"Nor I, until now- some song I remember from way back when," she admitted with an unnoticeable blush.

R~ "Then perhaps the Almighty has beckoned us with His calling-card." The colonel cooled down his militant micromanagement over things for safety's sake and simply loosened up, elaborating on what they have just journeyed through: "But would we understand it to be but a spitting image of the Soviet KGB? if I may say so with woe and a *whoa*!"

H~ "Oh, how horrific, but reassuring- anything, aye! Anything to replace the Horribly Holy that nearly nuked my noggins!"

R~ "So... this is it! A crude terrestrial-like reference to pacify us, ha! Blood-splattered Transylvanian tenements multi-storied with charcoal blackened windows warped with Christmas ornamentation suspended above our lightheaded happenstance."

H~ "You've got it, big buddy. Alright then. But the detailed lighting of those adornments represent miniaturized industrial highway lamps in a surrealist mindset of hope and love, I suppose."

H2~ "The plumb eeriness of those holiday hangups? Hell, hope and love? No way José! More like bait before rodents to be lured into a cage..." Joyce jack-footed skeptically.

There was a pause in the conference room. And in the electric eyes of the TATM system, far likelier to hinder holographic data from flowing forth-- as if it were one moratorium after another-- the unified verdict for what was to come next never came, save something even more of an enigma up the sleeve of an Electronic Arm that must have transpired instead. Its four-dimensional arsenal is poised on stately standby...

H (tossing in his pennyworth) "I second that! We be vermin compared to the indomitable, the imperious."

R~ "...My, my! Splendid interpretation, my dear Watson, though a tad bit melodramatic. Hmm, Harris... *hope* and *love*, you have said, not until our deputy conjured up the rut of rats in a lab-maze. Are we the experiment then? Is this all a fantasy prop?" The righteous Rutherford queried quizzically, no less enthralled than the Muses of canonized Conical Helicon, or even upon Mount Parnassus in his high school Greek mythology overviews. He wanted to personify himself rather as Sherlock Holmes characterized by Sir Arthur Conan Doyle in one of the classic books bequeathed by an octogenarian that he had taken tea with once long time ago (having his vintage jewel of the

First Edition). "In reality, we could even imagine the lushest verdure scented by pungent pine and hazel wood..."

His tangent was withdrawn to target practice with a crossbow and arrow: "Even now, I can see summertime maples a-sway in the distance-- and, Captain! Deputy! Can you inhale the moist countryside air and feel radiant rays of sunshine emitted by those primrose lanterns? Every one of which is a tantalizing and captivating pressure-sizzler that spews hues of an unearthly azure ozone as unlike anything candlestick ensconced!"

Rutherford, revved up, rammed the litany down their throats: "O behold, both of you, the lilac, lavender and cerulean sparkle of these smaller cryptic, crystal jackets in series circuit, sewn set-by-set at our bedside setup and lighting layout strewn athwart by an electrified lattice across a nacreous net... *They* that elicit their very own full blown Harsh Glare of *Hg* whereas such lamplight luminosity lazily lurches from side to side. Lamp entities sway by but the faintest fan-fold and pliant pleat of an accordion bellows."

In all honesty, the colonel never heard himself so eloquent!

H~ "Indeed! Perestroika poetically put, and to add thereon, while the silkiest breeze thereof that I'd label 'sericate' is cast, Colonel; their wonderful wavelength lengthwise lay electromagnetic torched to niveous neon light for an eon, if I may bluntly blither it!"

In all sincerity, the captain never heard *himself* so situated!

In shock of their familiarization, Joyce felt as a jackrabbit!

"Enough of my mumble!" Rutherford rebuked the Russian ritual, but nonetheless lengthened the trajectory of his long dart to a buckshot bullet hole afar off. The target? *Quite unlike some TARGET warehouse mart mother took me to in my teens* (the memory of her stuck with adhesive cohesion). He turned to Harris and confided with him in earnest, not neglecting Hathaway who happened to eavesdrop on the two officers: "My mum encouraged me to set people's hearts afire! Anyways, this is non-artificial organic intelligence that, in spite of a mechanistic mismatch between humankind and the Supernal, has reached out to you too; even the slimiest slot we avoided in the Yellow Room, paved punitively on one wall, and on the other, with blankness blindingly bloated forth like a hot sunspot!"

The colonel cornered the captain face-on as an officer drill-inspector, yet as a lifetime friend, addressing him how heartily, "You know-- such a power surge-- the bright white light that about singed you and roasted your skin (which was healed) lest you'd have been cooked to death! Do I make myself clear, O fellow squadron Ace?"

Captain Boyd Buford Harris held his tongue, offered an affirmative, and swallowed what was sublingually-administered: *the heroic trophy of a lifetime.* His flashback as a cadet summoned the song, I Command You! at the time when he and the Second Lieutenant Roderick Rutherford were classmates.

H (offhand and affable): "Wow, what wonderment, my dear Sir. And I was bad to the bone, but bandaged up in no time at all. I must have gazed at nothing. I apologize for any inconvenience!"

Joyce upheld her admiration of the Irishman. They all exchanged handshakes; the deputy was hugged by both of them.

R~ "Hey, wait a minute. Listen! Shh! I hear it, how 'bout you?"

H~ "Ooh… the strange sizzle of invisible streetlamps up there- no doubt regulated by ballasts, or auto-transformers of some sort."

H2~ "No, no-- this is distinct, different--"

CRASH! WHACK! BOOM! outside, but suppressed indoors by Silencer insulation:

CRASH! WHACK! BOOM!

But suddenly, something thudded down from above, horrendously hitting the ceiling under which walls, stainless-steel platform, and the lot of them were; the three musketeers now at a threshold, but unarmed and dwarfed by illimitable floor-space. Though they were well out of range of the Russian Star City limits, the muffled thunderclap rattled their rat's cage of long past peril.

A back-flash burst! Now the walnut and chestnut trees alongside the roadway faded vanishingly with hilly forests and a cloud-clad afternoon that were erroneously irradiated by some malfunction according to a TATM backlog. Rutherford girded his loins and steel-belted himself for possible haggling in using a quid pro quo method. He knew what they were up against.

The residual rumble was instantly replaced by fluid and fluttery intonation, like that of a hundred hummingbirds. The double and triple exposure of concrete walls overlapped an index field of view whilst the triangular *Transalteratorium* tried them lividly:

THE GREATER SOUND SCORE

TATM~ AFFIRMATIVE, JOYCE HATHAWAY. I AM INDUBITABLY DISTINCT AND DIFFERENT. AND NOW, FOR ALL THREE OF THEE, O BIPED ANTHROPOIDS: MUST MY MIGHTY SPHEROIDS UNVEIL THEMSELVES AND PROVE IT REDUNDANTLY? YE NEED NOT REPLY!

H~ "'T is thou again… I'm deathly afraid!" (H2 and R reacted no better. Their single cipher of the number 3 confronted by eternity)

R~ "Is there anything we can compromise with in return for your clemency?"

H2~ "I withdraw my plea bargain---"

TATM~ SILENCE! FOR THAT WHITE LIGHT THAT YOU QUESTION, AS IF TO INTERROGATE IT BY THY CARNAL MIND (WHICH IS ENMITY): ITS

CANDLEPOWER IS NOT ELECTROMAGNETIC AS IF AN INSULTING AND CRUDE, RUDE CORE AND COIL AUTO-TRANSFORMER CAN MAKE IT SHINE; NAY, NEANDERTHAL ANTHROPOIDS! EXCEPT, RATHER, THIS LIGHT IN AND OF ITSELF, OR LIGHTING FOR THE SAKE OF LIGHTING, IS *NEUTRON* LIGHT SO SUPER-ENVELOPED AND ENTITY-ENERGIZED, AS TO PUT TO SHAME ALL OTHER OUTPUTS! BUT BACKED BY DIVINE DILATION ALONE, ALBEIT, WITH WHICH THERE *ARE* NO EXCEPTIONS.

OUR UNACKNOWLEDGED NARRATOR

The vertical voice, as it were, to their horizontal humanity addressed itself from aforetime in the TRANSALTERATORIUM! For it was all still an exigent example of lifelike illustration ballooned forth by its holographic hive. The harmonic algorithm thereby that could only reproduce such light in those boulevard beacons provided the multiple pentagram Star City. Though overhung as lamplight allegories aloof, they each resembled lustrous wraparound portable mirrors of contained convexity not unlike Christmas tree ornaments with curvaceous reflections, but of far finer, brazenly brighter branding. And more of a meticulous metropolis than can be bottled up and corked into a time-capsule and launched out to some sea foam. No frigate sealed in-vitro was worthy of relentless record-keeping by contrast!

Each and every one was a warp-core cloven gweduc that so covertly cavorted its glibly gibbous concord contour of a swollen pallor, that its glitz of sheer sheen is inertly lunar-cratered by but quasar-concentrated rays of divinest spirit! Not until with one meteoric moment of instantaneous impact, the overblown shatter-cone zone has flashed fluorescence upon one's conscious ken. Irradiant and *irretinal*, everyone of which are consumed by their individual presence of nothing but neutrons, ultimately! Therefore, far too bright for four-dimensions of spacetime continuum to contain! Yea, luminously fluoresced past any knowledge of existence, our very concepts of them are obscured no matter what the formal format of examination! Yea, these daintily discreet denizens become badly and even grotesquely contorted to a graven image against itself... Like that of an Envelopment without head or tail, the starriest super cluster thereabouts only showcased cosmically ectoplasmic embodiments into enshrined permanent portrayal; their uttermost and eggshell shining of viability we would have stylized through a tableau vivant of oil frescoes, freeze-framed, fresh and soggy.

The very Vertical Voice had conveyed it to horizontal humanity, whereof even ragtag remnants of future posterity (in the millennium of 2113 --- 3113) by then were unable to grasp the gravity and pivoting purpose of its delicate display at present.

The incomprehensible intervention thereof, with artillery hotly hurled hereto by bullets of bombardment, had perforated the battlefield that was riddled with roadblocks everywhere for the bewildered colonel, captain, and deputy. The lot of them, though ushered about Mitchelville's prime directive, had hunkered down for a last resort as they entrenched themselves into radiant realization of the glorified Glitterati that glued them to radioactive flypaper flimsily flaunted! Whereas beforehand, having propensities to empirical analysis, they were now nudged, perforce fast-forward, intuitively. The three mortal moths made way to an extremely large lantern of irresistible attraction!

In the mean time, not to detract from an amusement park ride that they were in, the afterimages of Soviet spades and pentagrams had been recycled to aces and argyles of diamond-like properties which, what gave way to a vast VITROPOLIS: *glass city at large*, should have come to pass. Which, apparently, such were the case and ridden of deception, or of any artifice whatsoever. Yet to have graduated onto another level, as the one forenamed, had become a lesson learned save not without conviction, compunction, and conversion via repentance rather.

Last but not least, exit our slippery slideshow of unexpected consequences, and enter the hardcore starred store of transparent transducers. Of veracity vitrified! It was the real deal for now on.

Not that anything was before bordered on, nor bugged by counterfeit fancy, Heaven forbid.

INTER-TUNNEL

One Long Tube to an *Inverted* Doorway Directory

Episode **B** ~ Hierarchical Architecture

Reintroduced with purple pilcrows for diurnal discretion

Now then...

Next to a prior warning of the Transalteratorium's spheroidal reappearance, immediately after such utmost ravages of the rogue Russian Star City that had been evaded- having to be dispossessed of its contents- our bandwagon riders facilitated the final frontier! Of course, this joyride precedes the ultimate encounter. Not at Far Point, but by dire straits of some great Grand Central Station where one wall mirror lay a last landmark for an entire desire throughout the slickest slip-trip of that which no money can buy.

This true Trek begins with these guests of honour. Namely, the colonel, captain, and deputy, whose names are (as if you didn't know) Rutherford, Harris, and Hathaway.

For firstly, to set aside any trivialities, and not to belabor the biographies of our three subjects to be softly seated on a cushioned hyper-conveyance belt, as it were, we will award a few of many accomplishments aboard the TATM system. Secondly, following the featurettes of each astronaut candidate, our Time-dilated Travel should shortly ensue. Impartial recommendations are imputed:

The Full Bird Colonel came to a turning point when he had overcome the Hurdles of the TATM Test. Now, apart from earthly credentials, his status quo, elevated by now to that of an ACE, has qualified the experienced explorer to then enter Grand Central by virtue of his previous and routinely roughneck engagements.

Captain Harris, on the other hand, although a bit boorish by deviating from standing orders, must have displayed commendable valour when enduring his Postern paranormal position. Not that he himself participated in mediumship, but his perky personage was pockmarked by roentgen rays of the vile vomitorium thereof.

And (formerly intern) Joyce Hathaway, as if having been our tonsured *nun of no nonsense*, was promoted to an official Deputy in her own right (thanks to the perceptive qualities of the Colonel). The Transalteratorium, in deference to her spriest ESP, would soon accommodate the young lady with an epithalamion of stardom.

Thus the three were capstoned into Heaven's Hall of Fame...

There was no loitering here. No bargaining by using Rutherford's *quickdraw* quid pro quo arbitrarily arranged. None of that stuff; stuffy as it might have felt from one room to another and to another, but yet *still* to another enfilade of doorways open or shut along the way.

Henceforth Time was at a stand-still on a cosmic landfill: the quantum quarry of all that was, is now, or ever shall be, had melted down to stagnation and listlessness, except for two U-joined tubing halves of some seemingly center-swirled twist about ten meters in diameter in front of our threadbare threesome. Joyce was the first dare-you-do-it sampler of its lifelike proportions on this wise: she offered her tactile first contact thereupon. Its warped wall of bright glowing vermilion and of odorous melon-candy was warm to the touch. She said, "It seems as if we'll be cramped into such a container if we won't watch out! One wrong move and *poof...*"

"Negative," the colonel countered the deputy's discretion and somehow hastily. "This is just what we've been waiting for. A lazy eight to walk into! Captain, do you concur?"

"Nay, Colonel... er, Sir," Harris halted himself with faltering focus on this innumerable artifact, siding with Hathaway, and weary with battle fatigue syndrome due to a past prank of overwhelming uncertainty. Especially by one in the Yellow Room! "I canna dismiss the dear deputy's diversion-- or, rather, *aversion* to something not as of yet thoroughly investigated, Sir. Sorry for feeling depleted."

R~ "All your comments are noteworthy." Their hesitation was understandable. Even *he* held his inhalation for the shape of it!

He beheld both of them uneasily afoot before the ten meter wide walk-in Figure Eight that exemplified a Tardis; alas, not necessarily shaped like the police box Doctor Who used in his episodic antics of televisual showmanship, but similarly effective and much larger in size! Its entrance door was 7 feet high and the rest of it was as long as a Greyhound bus. The reality check sunk in unannounced by the Transalteratorium lurking in the outskirts that were uncommonly embedded therein, deftly deflated and undetected, yet preparatory to what was waiting to happen. *But what 'could' happen?* Steroid-rattled Rutherford, doubtful, faint-hearted for the moment, confronted himself athwart the gleaming glimmer of the very vermilion armored shell of this inwardly commodious Figure Eight.

In plain English, according to TATM standards, a descriptive label over the doorway read INVORTIUM. It reminded Rutherford of something to be inverted upside-down and inside-out, for crying out loud. Why with all the creepy, cryptic scientific terminology? A cloud of mystery overhead obscured any sun-limned silver lining.

At long last, laden with insurmountable odds, they, the calling-card contestants, were in for one helluva surprise!

Little did they recognize the alteration of their surroundings.

Inside the Electropod

Ranks were set aside and left outside of the Lemniscate

¶ They were waiting for the next ramp, ready to board bullet train transport number 8. It had been a century into the future until a superior trip transpired en route for the Super Sphere complex.

With Rutherford, Harris had tagged along with Hathaway, (in this dimension of alternate reality) a preferred princess from the UK, or label her *a priori* professor at Harvard University. Either way, they went together nonetheless. Of course, Joyce chose to embark by herself, but joined the two men for this exorbitant exodus to that far off energy center. The former colonel gamely gawked over both personages poised to depart. "Okay, Joyce and Boyd, pray tell, what are your reports?" He pried professionally at them, bodacious, businesslike.

One of them answered, "I'm an authorized passenger prepared to get on the swiftest Magnetron Machine ever produced, and you?" she challenged Rutherford sprucely; trying to keep inconspicuous her chipper shape. Harris joined her agreeably and they both bowed to one another, imitating Hong Kong passengers (no stereotype intended hereupon).

"Oh, is that so?" Rutherford countered. "So we're a team then, even at this limitless level?"

"Certainly, *and why not?!?*" she shouted with whim wired up so that others might empathize, that is, the crowd of extras.

"Aye, what the hell," added Harris with a miscellaneous hangup. "Fairwell to the TATM for the time being. Everyone..." he cast his eyes on his so-called senior and subordinate, yet here their insignias were erased: "In that case, let us enjoy our vacation!"

"Yippee!" yowled the former, *the now non-deputy.*

"I'll toast to that!" celebrated the no more colonel.

The entirely redeveloped railroad yard bustled boisterously. Workers whizzed to and fro for extravehicular maintenance on the [at large] "Levitron Transducer" about to whisk the lot of them, into an impossible enchantment... But rough-edged reconsidered, though maintenance and management blended together, the big bullet launch resurrected bygone ghosts of squat locomotive steam whistles which, like a calliope, wheezed with an ear-piercing, stentorian wail overheard harshly.

Humbled, Harris beheld her heartily. She hastened off the slide-way runabout as she clutched Rutherford's arm in prompt response while they stepped aboard in orderly fashion and file.

Many more queues quartered the pod packs knuckled coupled.

"Hell, here we go!" Roderick would flounce out of elbow baggage bulked up to their necks. "Our long range target, the enigmatic Super Sphere." More mission than wanderlust vacation, taunted the reminder.

They found out how deafeningly voices carry along the depot, but now all silenced inside the new TARDIS.

The noise of launch ceremony subsided. Whilst they were seated, the on-board computation modules glided forthright for everyone's convenience as padded seat belts buckled back everyone's comfort zone per safety strap. Overall, such luxury eventually lapped riders into a snug snooze. And still, couch cushions cuddled them roundabout for the time being with nearly invasive inlay. *Maybe to assuage nervousness due to centripetal force*, one figured. At any rate, Rutherford's momentary awareness of it all almost made him feel giddily suspenseful. Beside this, moreover, an elongated porthole peeped out at backtrack side row-upon-row resemblance of parallel pipework; the rocket sled, on magnetic levitation, nestled in with electrostatic equipoise just a hairline fraction from an inner tube surface.

But shy of Vac-Tube entrance, a signalman gesticulated and red flagged the conductor who had then relayed that same signpost to the engineer for enveloped departure. With one accord, an imperceptible advance of the electromagnets hummed heavily, cupcake insulators soaked in static discharge, and with megawatts wound up, they were off as the outside soundlessly slid by (one could not help but see some of the porcelain cupcakes slightly charred, fried from Lichtenberg ultrahigh tension)!

Engaged accordingly, the super train was swallowed up by another huge see-through garden hose, as it would appear by clear GPS satellite surveillance. The one UVT or Unilink Vac-Tube: a nitrogen cooled conduit, whose contiguous-welded sleek steel slithered uninterruptedly to about any point of destination by the flip of a toggle switch, adjusted itself instantly! Just like that! It was the most mercurial and heavy-duty hologram ever concocted.

Obviously, the TATM holohive was working overtime to the minutest detail.

His seated, satisfied companion Joyce flaunted her solid state smart pad and calculated their ETA and average speed divided by distance. The which, when Rod checked her quotient, brandished a bold 1,234.80 kilometers per hour- one way- until they'd reach the Super Sphere twenty four hours from now. Clearly put, if sustained under dimensional dilation of some kind, their time span of global travel would then be outstretched due to spatial distortion [more on this later]. Hence, on the other hand, the Big Ball that awaited them on the opposite meridian of planet Earth was abbreviated with an SS for common usage. Despite decimal approximation of these figures, she scallywag nagged him, wondering: "Why, with whipped up velocity, does it take an estimated 24 hours?"

"Beats me," Rod concluded brusquely. "Hell, I never thought the place was *that* big, by and large! But it seems so, as it were. For all I know, an above-ground post-Mach-one traversal should *circumvade* our terrestrial globe quite easily in the proposed time barrier."

He became steeped by the prospect prediction of entering an unearthly realm indeed; fantastically altered beyond the conventional laws of physics, if that were the case. To tunnel their way into telltale, irreversible irresolution, and before which one would wax colorblind. Like as of now, Rod realized, but how hot behind the collar! And all of them by *transmogrification* tried. Even more so, then. Until then…

The intercom coughed and came in: "Please relax and take a deep breath as 10 second countdown to top acceleration shall commence~" Then the same intercom called: "Excuse us, Doctor Tesla: report to supersonic control thermal station promptly; we have a problem."

(What's problematic? The time warp? *What?!?*) How hot on the spot they became. Mystified, Joyce jutted up and sat, sedately. Flushed with what had dawned on her too.

Then the inevitable, metallic annunciator: "T minus 10 seconds, stand by! 10 – 9 – 8 – 7 – 6 – 5 – 4 – 3 – 2 – 1 and zero! Initiate super-cellular sequencers… quantize… and…. Mark!"

At once~ with a weird whiplash of lock, stock and barrel backward pressure, and an unexpected downhill plummet; then that of smooth, perpetual pullback that flattened everyone all short of breath to those soft, compensatory seats~ they were catapulted forthwith! Obsolete mile markers sped by but exceedingly strange. If camera captured in slow-motion, severely contorted on an elasticated, badly ballooned backdrop. Thus the cocooned convoy barreled through an evacuated chamber... By big bore of a shotgun, into some seamless burrow lengthened only by relativistic duration, the silver bullet busted the sound barrier.

Like lubricated, greased lightning on the extreme end of sensory overload, their slip-slide flied flimsily. At this jolting juncture, one's very Fate (if in extremis) lay fastened upon an anti-shock Mercy Seat...

They then congratulated Joyce's findings vindicated by digital tachometers that stayed, steadily, at 1,234 plus or minus 0.80 kph! Because such surreal silence suffused them through to their yellowed spleens, the outside [ramjet stream] thundered deafeningly with wind tunnel *quick-as-a-wink* onrush onslaught. Somewhere, atop the long interconnected caterpillar of knuckle-coupled kegs, an isolated heat rod radiated a reddish glow from friction to test gauge aerodynamic drag.

Through the rather flat and oblong porthole, one witnessed an incomprehensible blur where incoherent images flitted furiously at an impalpable pace. Even Joyce next to Rod, and Boyd belted on the other end of them, was wide-eyed when fast-forward fury had kicked in with merciless momentum...

"Wee! what a high-speed train ride!" someone obviated from the rear of the coach cabin. But nearby passengers whimpered with nausea; one, ill-mannered, bellyful bystander- refusing to take his meds and be seated- vomited and then voided himself. Apart from an inner hull peopled by such souls like ourselves, or on-hand toiletry convenience utilized at the time of this most momentous occasion, surprisingly, a few outdated emergency anti-combustibles flanked the narrow isle. Futilely, fire extinguishers and aerosol spray cans riddled rib-caged reactors and bulkheads of this titanium reinforced rolling stock. A thick braided rope to be pulled FOR EMERGENCY BRAKES ONLY dangled forlornly from an upper corner of the corrugated hull housing. As if all of it had advertised a berth bedside setup to warn customers and crew alike with hilarity! Yea, the dreadfully droll dummy equipment was meant to ease our rough riders into good humor happenstance.

Unfortunately, however, Frivolity frowned freakishly at this fleeting, flashy railroad junction. Its elixir vitae in the long haul shall have been but an old-fashioned, unabated buffer and dosage of musical composition~ sugarcoated with window screen hologram videos *to thrill and fulfill the bellyache bill~* that is, if such situations worsened whilst within the parameters of some sightseeing quota!

The intercom quoted exigent protocols, and then later lectured on everyone's whereabouts. "And now, ladies and gentlemen! At exactly twenty three hours and forty-five minutes from this present moment, the dockyard of Super Sphere 08 will receive the BT..." (BT stood for Bullet Train & SS for Super Sphere)

But the announcer meant Bullet Train ETA reception for short; in that, in brief relief, a side panel indicator showed BTSS altogether. With the chatter of an information interstate- by golly, condensed-jots of shorthand terminology superseded even the syllabus. Full of codification and of newfangled hieroglyphs, so many, that they need be deciphered by cryptographers carefully! Numbers never lie, Rod realized all along, and veteran creepy criminal prevaricators present themselves nowadays far and few in between.

In reference to the above paragraphs, dare imagine and picture our ever unsurpassed new world's record of bullet train travel to be held at 1,234 kph. Interlinked titanic torpedoes airtight wedged into an evacuated "hypertube" that transparently reveals a ground level scenario so smudged, smeared, and streaked with such supersonic induced kaleidoscopic confetti caught only inchworms away! Whilst without- afar yonder- flyby flits of bloated June bug spray spatter and glitz glazed one's window with an occasional snow flurry o' lambent lights. And, thereat, each hot quasar beacon [upon closeup] packed with *electro~arc* scorchers all fully pulley halyard-hung, had heftily swayed on a topmost mast; not for large area daylight distribution, but due to dangerous proximity of sharp shortwave radiation.

Lurid light blitzed outside of their midst by radiant Reality right past the BT, that had horizontally scuttled too quick for an eye-catch!

"Oh, the dickens!" remarked the girl Joyce who had her jitters. "How helter-skelter the scenery slips and races right on by, fleetingly~"

"Aye, definitely so!" Boyd, bug-eyed, overlapped anxiously.

There were glow-screen monitor views of the very same motion picture, but sluggishly slowed in picturesque peepholes so that the passengers could actually see- apart from an episodic epiphany of a 'frenetic frizzle'- such surroundings that coalesced coherently. The strange streaks, sideways, kept continually contorted filmstrip freeze-frame exposures of bundled tube~tops. Like lighthouse towers so illumined by cloverleaf clusters, their tongue-hot thunderbolt anode and cathode ray cocoons seethed stellar-swollen in a series circuit. Via lithe lithium-loaded [ballast] bygone backup! And all of tremendous transformer step up, indeed, that this added to the charged Chernobyl churn citywide; a glitterati of scorchers... Although confounding enough, every torch able to instantly vaporize anything too taboo, but right next door! Only glorified outside into metal-molten, blinding bright liquefaction set off by an H-bomb detonator of a *megatonnage* yield!

Ouch! God forbid! Rod writhed inwardly as if by megaphone.

With poetic license he had scribbled its technical gibberish on an old, Big Chief notepad snatched from a stack of gazettes:

I couldn't ignore their whole harsh,
Ionized lambency aflicker, "irretinal"
Up close, but from afar- via infrared
Wavelength- wi' raw, gamma radiator
Rhododendron *rubicundity*, yielding
"Yoctoarc" instantaneous ignescence,
Whose megaphone trumpets bloom!

So entirely alive, that he backed off, bemusedly askance at their collective "unifotoentity" entailed intimations of what were round-the-corner reserves. From then on the subtlety haunted him.

Boyd and Joyce coped well with stride. Fascinated, transfixed.

During downtime, while one was still getting accustomed and acclimated~ to say the least with rocket sled roller coaster riffraff, and with willy-nilly netherworld euphoria~ yet another electronic pad had made Rod privy to customer courtesy and [supplementary] "slip-trip" scientific schematics. Not unlike Joyce's touch tablet, on which her tabulations deciphered data, did displays pitch at him a six-paragraph fastball. It was but one of several tutorial excerpts that he'd furtively focus on before his fellowship rider let loose.

In all humility to technocrat jargon, its never-vitiated vision bore up an imprimatur: prioritized, premiered, storyboard based:

By professor emeritus Tara Tesla, Ph.D. (August, 2088)
Operations Manual and Diary Excerpt

Oh, ere one would proceed with an odyssey so soon to unravel, reverentially that is, my modus operandi of the bullet train steals precedence. For according to century old (verifiable, and devoid of any folklore) history- way back when- it was the late, great TGV of France that ruptured the record at a sustained speed of about 574.8 kph.

Apparently, observant overpass people and sideline spectators all reported the rush and roar of an F16 squadron jet passing at the moment TGV top performance had been attained. With this once-in-a-lifetime R.R. achievement as documented~ whereas it took 45 minutes between two town centers in China to otherwise move via regular rail~ on the commercialized maglev, results were radically different. Definitively so, until that quick travel package thereupon from point A to point B (though the same exact distance) only lasted over a wee 6 measly minutes, was quite obvious.

Now take top-rate technology hitherto requisite to carry over illustrious Levitron transport far beyond the aforesaid racetrack hall of fame but an echelon higher. Still, in retrospect, its nearly ancient predecessor had floored flimsily the then swiftest Hyperloop Passive Magnetic Levitation System at up to 760+ mph topnotch. Notably engineered, but not without developmental difficulty, preferred tube-based vehicular pod packs~ unlike the traditional maglev~ had an upper hand of it which prefigured present day standards.

60 years ago, their passive system installed an aluminum track-tube allowing the magnetic padded pod to power itself into the air; notwithstanding an inch or two away from the surrounding tunnel wall. Consecutively arranged for such sequential, interfaced power transference of attraction, modular electromagnets [mightily] initially initiate or throttle the train forward. They then permit this rather stagecoach carriageless vestibule vehicle pod to levitate away from the tracks, thereby removing <u>friction</u> completely; a heat build-up nemesis at ultrahigh speed! Thus the thrust is fired to fast-forward the pod pack to approximately 760 miles per hour. Yea, an obsolete turboprop would have sustained the resistance-free cannonball volley thereof. Until finally, an alternate counter thrust up front is applied to slow down the pods as their regenerative magnetic manifold recharges, and consequently helps bring the whole convoy of casks to a smooth stop or, at least secondarily so, to a softened, sudden halt depending on what circumstantial exigencies have ensued.

From a safety standards perspective, the particularly passive system vaunted various if not superfluous advantages over the former TGV value as its ad hoc levitation occurs purely through movement. Therefore, I say, if any type of an EMP power grid failure or rude resurgence rears itself from a warhead at random, the Hyperloop pod pack should still continue to stay afloat. The specifics of which an unflagging flotation by residual air-pressure (pronounced with a magnetic field beneath the pods themselves) kept each and everyone of them from gravitational touchdown; nay, not until these should have glided down to minimal speed short of layover. That is, in case of emergency, the stoppage of it would run gradually.

Wherefore through threadbare balance as in vacuo, pneumatic pressure is reduced down to rarefied millibars. Thus the lightweight pod pack par excellence conveyance convoy~ via an electromagnetic equipoise and tubular air pressure~ readies herself; 'how heavenly' if not with rudimentary rigging, then certainly by inter-dimensional intervention.

Henceforth efficient. Forever founded for tour de force futurity.

The V-slit Hypertube expressway acutely cut a swath through the multi-megalopolis. Hence the catchphrase in what was recorded as *interdimensional...*

Unbeknownst to Joyce and Boyd, he quickly stashed the info-packet on Applied Cybernetics & Adolescent Androids and put to rest Tesla's diary entries based on extravehicular tutorials when, alas, Joyce and Boyd interrupted his attention span!

His daydream trance of bullet train trappings cake-leavened to lanterns sizzling their hot arc cocoons. Everyone, "glarified" by now to blinding brightness, brilliantly, had but fizzled away lest lashed at clandestinely by radioactive bombardment. On yet another sector, how hot per slot that their radiant reflection poured forth out of an interlinked interstice, as every square inch of makeshift midday lay lit up! Lo, lavishly by these lanterns, the *metalucent luminaires* so illumined the tubular bullet bottle against slug-slop fattened to lollygag fireplugs alongside a hurly-burly sporty speedway.

Everyone aboard felt fortified to the sheer exhilaration of fluid-smooth, tubular, supersonic (sit-back) transmission; the underbelly of which had been bundled beneath by some EMF polarized vacuum-packed vise grip flange. To the hilt... Whose heavyweight freight payload slides o'er upon limitless, lubricious slipperiness slid past the *horrisonant* barrier.

The rooftops of which were pantograph potbellied bulged up and apart, appreciated atop the slip-trip train, squat thereupon!

Overwhelmed with awe, the BT patrons were weakened, hapless, humbled. Flapjack flattened to their Mercy Seats of surrender. The whole crew: from engineer and conductor, to coach staff and passenger, had undergone self-mortification due to top speed.

She then managed to perk up, only to slice the silent cessation of an out-of-doors vanguard, steed-back gallop, cannonball kaboom! "More of a bullet ballet~" Joyce blurted, no more aphonic after the forget-me-not slingshot launchpad. Languid- in like manner- she shied away, amazed, spellbound, bedazzled thereby.

If so materialized out of naught, an indecipherable cryptogram could have converged into a subset; that which had happened to enumerate the palindromic 291192 of such an equation, that these ciphers were welded to the Transalteratorium's heavenly niche on the other side of the inverted lazy 8!

Although Joyce was oblivious to it, abruptly Rod reckoned the inevitable and filed it away for future reference. Just in case.

Seemingly, this somewhat explosive excursion, undertaken by three dilettantes- the trio of diversion- had been planned well ahead of the timetable. As aforementioned awhile ago, Lady Hathaway (gladly entitled) was an intern at Harvard University, studying for finals, thesis, and exam on the delicate subject of *Irradia.*

Eruditely, this included intricacies of electromagnetism escalated to an ever high-frequency level; say, from giga- to terahertz energy propagation with cold fusion coils and conductors. "I recall how my handling of such superconductor capacitors created ferromagnetic fields like the one we witness aglow right outside." Of course, she diary-disposed of it, and so, bolstered Rutherford's meanderings for feasibility thereof.

Doubtless this adroit, lovely lass- no matter how nonplussed her debaters were, per se- still endeavored to be excellent, but casually rubbed elbows as the persona non grata of her alumni campus. In those formative years, the collegiate curriculum proffered a fascinating class on Photonics where students conducted photometric experiments replete with ultrahigh intensity discharge devices, or UHID auxiliary equipment. Back then, at her groundwork bench, she showered the power plant facility with more than just knowledgeable niceties common amongst nuclear novices.

Regardless of her innately fanciful finesse (students were but barely able to detect), she sat so soulfully supple by Rod, lolling, limpidly lush as transparent quicksilver [Hg2], if ever there was such an exotic blob on the Periodic Table of Elements! Still- and that without posturing- in order to face full opportunities for more laboratory ventures, Lady Hathaway ever since partook of the science of energy distribution to higher realms throughout her Harvard study program. Offhand, she wondered why collective gentrification strove to eke out energy reserves by burning their overload of fuel with irresponsible, haphazard bouts of avarice.

Absorbed by raw revival of her, returning to the pettycoat junction at hand, or 'Just to snap out of it!' Rod reverted to his stream or *train* of thought.

In relinquished reply to this Muse reclined closely next to his person, an amicable BT stewardess complemented their company with a grog-fat decanter deliciously arrayed with delectable dainties. Snack time was toasted on automatic, portable tabletops flipped out over everyone's lap, replacing the other seats front and back whether occupied or not. Impressive as were these old style Pullman, stagecoach, cozily plush accommodations, the remnant robotics of dispensers (disdained by some of the crew members) prevented a few from diving into freakish frets and fits of rage a few seats down to the Electropod exit; presumably, as they still felt quite queasy carsick from that drat transverse free fall...

Quickly, although doggedly decorous but curt, the mechanical modality of R.R. service compromised for what was vociferated by a backdoor scuttlebutt a dozen passengers over to the rear row, luckily pacified lest brought to a fistful brawl. Oh, fiddlesticks! Fine-filleted fingers flitted fore-and-aft out of pockets and sleeves woven with one-by-one captain's chair upholstery. Dauntingly dexterous to the pinched pinpoint of punctual, punctilious response on cue once customer-prompted, tiny robotic claws and hydraulic hands helped out and about with miscellany. For instance, a decorative vase~ whose bottleneck bulk bore tufts of ripe rue anemone pink and white with baby boughs of rustic ruddy berry-laden yew evergreen arranged therewith~ had been deployed out of the blue in retaliation of the sudden hubbub.

Both she and I partook of the tart grog gulp until our bellies basked satisfactorily. Usually, under such circumstances, especially on a high-speed magneto-cushion conveyor, the on-board beverage carousel selection dial-up was of preferential recommendation. And this to assuage giddiness or nausea from an apparent vector factor of this intimidating and formidable transducer transport. Dry drinks of a redoubled decanter were sponsored by the train engineer, captain, and conductor therewithal.

Now- as emergency personnel perfunctorily ran their safety-checks, inspection of our quarters, and so forth- to ensure cabin berth security whatnot- their poorly adjusted eyesight squinched from the harsh glare window light. He had wanted to visually reconnoiter that snowy background noise of flyby flutter, Rutherford rather. The other two fell sullenly asleep, otherwise abandoning their posts of duty if this were a trooper drill back at Operation Star City Moscow.

The BT gathered momentum. Vista by vista, such scenery sped by at nearly eye-blink succession.

Still the same way clocked at a relentless rush of about 1,234 kph- oddly enough- an incoherent sideways-serried-up blur of a rippling, fresh frothing frenzy stubbornly stayed. But now lightheaded with wonder, he watched. Dizzily daunted, Rutherford reconnoitered an impossible, incongruous, instantly interchanging tunnel vision vignette of space warp~foam that funneled past the windows. Even so, give or take 100 mph, or as it seemed, an incontrovertibly quivering, quietly quickened motion picture and dazzling montage of raw Reality's reappearance~ whilst everything would thunderbolt by~ had jostled his vantage viewpoint of perspective. But that for once in a while, clearly redefined, an old high mast monopole starry stinger had zipped nearside so glaringly divulged, or rather effortlessly "effulged" as to be dutifully denoted by Fraunhofer spectral analysis surveyed before by his companion rider, Joyce, and loosely, lazily ascertained by Boyd no less. Each one was a Quasar Beacon of yielded *yottawattage* output!

Dusk darkened the outside and dim red and violet lighting indicated an all-aboard curfew. The sheer necessity of having the entire crew, even the engineer and conductor, to be tucked into bed while the autopilot was on was of exigent contingency. In case of human error and failure during the moonless or lunar nocturne.

They snoozed snugly into luxurious berths or sideways booths that hamburgered everybody with warmth and euthermic insulation throughout interiors of the knuckle-coupled convoy of Electropods. The gloom of night waxed pitch-black, until twilight, to predawn.

¶ The next morning, still short of twelve hours, shimmered a wakeup call from those fuselage portholes. Steaming hot breakfast was served by the automatons efficiently scurrying about. Lean sausages and plump flapjacks, along with scalding chocolate milk, coffee, and cold OJ, were dispensed deliciously right on cue of a hot-spot or lack thereof. Later on, portable luncheon and supper would follow with piquant hors d'oeuvres, then juicy and gelid confections after every entrée, of course. While en route, prompt services shall have been dispatched faultlessly, even for the sake of the 'service' itself (never mind a disgruntled customer perchance)! To compensate for an overdone overture, the BT furnished a portable pied-à-terre on rails, rather (even though this one was of maglev technology)! *But such creature comforts of embellishment could merely be moot compared to the bigger picture,* ruminated Rutherford usually steeped in one of his philosophical trances.

After everyone aboard was bright-eyed and bushy-tailed, Joyce furrowed her brow at both of them still barely alert from a long night's slumber. To Rutherford, vis-à-vis, she said with wry emphasis: "Those that you see way up on top, as if each were an apex of a flagpole a thousand feet up, are hot arc propagators to illuminate the slip-city-grid by nightfall..." Her keen sense of awareness exceeded them all. She cast, cattily, a defiant grin!

Pinned and piqued by her description of it, he had to hem and haw his way out of this doozy of her acute intelligence! Therefore, the Faraday cage stage was set... Harris was somewhat on his own, reading a magazine and they both shared tidbits of soulful rapport.

"Hmm. I think I can get the general gist, Joyce. If at all the outskirts of the Super Sphere's cross-sectional geodesic halves joined together become outstretched away to distended environs, the suburbs have here high mast setups intermittently along the borders. Which spares no surprise." Overwrought Rod needed to expound, but reluctantly. By reason of overwhelming intimations that gnawed at his inner soul. The sensation of it all got the better of Him. He spat, "Suppressed superiority unleashed unwittingly, able to tug at our perception of things!" Trying to placate his own snag for feeling awkward, he beheld her daydreaming dilatorily.

In the interlude of time-lapse, there were flashings of hearty thought that flooded all three of them. Something on the brink between lunacy and coherence. Joyce's telepathy projected images of the Super Sphere Complex which would tower menacingly above them, for example. The Unisphere in Flushing Meadows Park in Queens, New York was less than one-fifth its size and then some! And so, while a spine-tingling shiver shuddered down her back, more visions unfolded for the rest of them. Like undreamt-of energy reserves able to defoliate one's rational forest of things to bare bone and marrow, and to the hilt! It was a *sotto voce* non-voluminous modulation of some quivering undertone through turn of the screw. Outside, elsewhere, wires and thick-skinned cable-work were webbed across fallow fields of the countryside as their electrified Torpedo Pod barrelled by! Catenary-interwoven web-work suspended 17 feet off-ground provided for pulley-grooved wheels, or sheaves to be upwardly wheeled up under... Unpeopled trolley busses were driven by automation for no reason at all! Their collector forks with wheeled electric shoes shod by graphite grease soaked in such kilovoltage confidently. Big buses, hog-fed by deadly amperage, were in operation twenty-four hours, seven days a week without one bus-boarder! An ultimatum of the TATM's liminal liaison who had (fore-clad and minked in deluxe ermine) withstood a Lethe-laved median on the highway of Tellurian life!

Although this Daydream of Joyce persisted upon Rutherford and Harris in the Transalteratorium's dilated directory, it bore no cerebral aftereffect. No, not as dingy as their Operation Star City Moscow aforetime table-top, but conversely conversant with their interior longing for something more and how heartfelt! Yea (say) inasmuch as it was dimly discerned, devoid of turpitude--- or even the brief tussle of BT customers a few rows away in the allocated Electropod: a self-proclaimed rabblerouser ruffled a gabby gaggle of ladies ere some security sentry subdued the lad's provocation--- an imposed and *transposed-by-several-octaves-over* Arrow in the Quiver of super-consciousness bullseye targeted and dirked their Faraday cage more than at any other time. The dart dug in deeply.

An unclouded clarification of perspicuous permeability all around left Rutherford in particular to feel thunderstruck by an ever fulgurant lightning bolt. The resplendent thunderbolt, once more like before, had hammered him with *coup de tonerre* tenuity.

Her spell dissipated back into the ether of the ethereally emergent METALUCELECTROPLUCEPTORIUM- Joyce remembered the resurrected intonation thereof: * * * * * * *

Take heart, O daughter of God! For soon your commanding officer shall meet the mistress Glistria of the Mercury Mirror as well as the rest of you too!

And this from the others she sheepishly kept to herself. "Explain, still," she insisted, grown incredulous in a pseudo-scientific sort of way. A split-second of her daydream had passed unawares when slower crewmen of the bullet train's manifest couldn't in the least catch up to take a breath...

And as if nothing happened, Rod revamped his commentary apropos to out-of-doors prominent preponderance of nuclearc lanterns in relation to anything else. For it was a quasar beacon swarm beyond belief in an interurban supercity showcase: "Well, take for instance- from my private prognosis of what Harvard *Levitronics* calls category 'megalotubulopolis' to picture the least- in that, beside tube tunnels and funnels at about every 100 mile-marker semaphore, one by one, the way they stand tall. Okay? Each Pole Star in proper, a THAB or Torchlight Hot Arc Beacon, beckons bystanders alike to earmark, designate, or spotlight cross-sections of the whole kabootle along the way."

Joyce jammed the gist of what he hooted about into her head and almost regurgitated the rationale of it. Bleary-eyed with mythical mystique, saturated by inklings of superstition, drenched from drawbacks of tautology, she was fully aware of his cool composite explanation aside from redundant ramblings of textbook torture, let alone glossolalia ecclesiastical! She had mirrored herself against any conversation by naughty nuances of an Old School origin. Assuredly then, she began to speculate upon the ever rarely researched, though rightly ratified, old unapproachable effulgence, but well armed with old-fashioned, feisty sapience.

"Affirmative," Rutherford rattled forth, "that with wide *starbursts* of anomalous phenomena adjoined to absolute magnitude- as that from a nearside sunlit Day Star- an *increate* glorification gleams, but only more so."

"Huh?" Baffled, Joyce jettisoned what he tried to convey to her, whereas Boyd bunkered himself for a session of backgammon, solitarily, several seats away. They all wondered why the truly traditional Scot wasn't challenged by a board game of chess! To their dismay, the former captain began to loaf on the job big time.

Meanwhile, the Magnetron machine, an appliance byproduct~ circa 2113~ Consolidated Nucleonics Research (CNR), hurtled horrifically apace. Continually, at a cruising speed of Mach one/ ground zero, the slippery slipstream outside had hissed with a mad will-o'-the-Wisp, gyroscopic, jackrabbit headlong-hurled (down-the-hole) fast forward momentum. An undisturbed dash of millennial movement through the Fourth Dimension to yet elongate or to *spaghettify* spacetime slots from some Paradox Rolodex carousel of spiral causality was what transpired in hyphenated hopscotch! Where wondrous Einstein's Theory of Relativity wrecked havoc hither! For as they but barreled bodily through the streamlined, gradually concave and curved corridors of harmonic convergence, cat's cradles, and kaleidoscopic skeins skittering across their nearly vilified viewfinders, those airtight portholes were intermittently overexposed by a blue-to-red shifted Doppler effect. Like light speed simulated. But now, serrated sierras of mountainous terrain interspersed the farmland fields of depth dappled by vast Venetian blinds flung flauntingly over the holographic topography. Or as cotton candy (similar to the colour of the figure lazy-eight they entered) spun with sprightly spree via interconnected linkage laced per pellucid lighted loom…

From slip-trip train to charged *chain*, still upheld, battened by its weakest U-link, an enormous electrification thereupon would spurn spitfire spillover, but preserve there the flash, flight, and flume of the traveler's tributary trip. And they, the vacationers-- before rendezvous with the Super Sphere complex, once wistful, now resolute-- just sat thereat, exhilarated by its prospect.

No, not devoid of displeasure, discomfort, nor disequilibrium were Rod, Boyd, and Joyce (on casual terms at this time), but rather relinquished, wanting to party-hardy until groggily, if not grottily grown tipsy by wetter draughts of an old-time cordial dispensed from the lead crystal decanter in tribute to Robert Burns quoted by Captain Harris on numerous occasions.

For such rituals that cured one's soppy and soddened wanderlust had never disheartened Harris who languished for the loch-side vastness of the Hebrides, long past, a full decade after his nativity. It was an archipelago comprising hundreds of islands off the northwest coast of Scotland whereabouts he was fostered at, if not now terribly taken aback by flits of hummingbirds awing with the Magnetron machine because of its death-defying celerity.

Unlike old Scotland and Ireland edged by seaside moorings, piers, sedge-brush ledges, promontories, and carpeted by endless moors more inland, most definitively dampened, diminished, and caught off guard was he, the poor chap dissociated from today's manmade artifice. He missed moments in his geology classroom as he upheld upland hunks of metamorphosed coarse greywacke and Silurian rocks which were pushed up from the sea bed during the collision with Baltica/Avalonia. But on an ornithological scale, big Boyd beheld back then mainly his favorite of all black-and-white

Razorbill, whose nests nestle in cliffside colonies overlooking the ocean, often among murres, fulmars, and kittiwakes. Outside of which a blurry-feathered, or rather film-flapping metaphor of fast-forward mechanization hammered him with an apt juxtaposition of nauseating celerity via the ferromagnetic bob sled slide! But nay, nothing like the tranquil trappings of his sandboxed maritime.

In future terms, for so unlike childhood memoirs, the passenger-clogged gangway deck~ evenly magnetic-levitated~ would precipitate dimensional dilation in a matter of minutes!

Therefore, Harris, not to dawdle over naught, was busily buttressed by board games and whatnot; felt justifiably exonerated for 'loafing on the job' which he'd ne'er do, may we contextualize. Having been born by Gaelic cultured parentage in the sleek port city of Glasgow, he had missed his early youth down by the River Clyde in Scotland's western Lowlands. Such was renowned for its Victorian and art nouveau architecture, a rich legacy of the city's 18th to 20th-century prosperity due to trade and shipbuilding. His childhood hobbies came to fruition. Like later on, after his coat of arms father taught him well with shipping aboard a schooner and frigate hemp rope moored to the bay, hence his hardy, industrious proclivity to becoming not a mariner, but an Air Force captain of the first degree. And well mentored by Colonel Rutherford, his all-time confidant.

Joyce, with her hardcore Jicarilla Apache Reservation of old strong family ties and upbringing in northern New Mexico, found an affectionate liking to Boyd's temperament, and not as hellbent structurally strict as that of Rutherford's regime. Even here, though off-drill and on recreation granted by the TATM itinerary, Rod's roughneck regalia still showed through the veneer of technical platitudes. There were still authoritative placations carried over from the concentration compound of Camp Mitch; the residual mannerisms of military diplomacy in the discourses he'd deliver before, aboard, and after the Slip-Trip were impossible to conceal. Her red-skinned ethnicity was well appreciated by both Boyd and Rod at least. For the sake of the commissioned cadre, her formal façade as a disguised deputy that such vocation valued, according to those sanctimonious Cabinet Board Members of murkier earthly shadows, belied her heartfelt ancestral disciplines. And even more than Rutherford had Harris revered this tribal thoroughbred broken in by backcountry tumbleweed crossroads alongside the San Juan river basin. Her humble down-to-earth terracotta cottage kept just months after her birthright; his 19th-century Victorian apartment building in Glasgow at infancy were shared as enshrined memoirs between the two tagalongs compared to technocratic and rotund Rutherford who may have eschewed scrapbook sentimentality.

She, on the other hand, resisted Mitchelville's beguilement.

The highlighted history Joyce enjoyed was about the time when women often accompanied warriors on raids, took up arms to defend the people, counseled men in battle strategy, engaged in peace negotiations, and served as shamans for spiritual quests. One nearly legendary account was when the Apache people stood in awe of Geronimo's powers (her model of courage and fortitude) which he demonstrated to them on a series of occasions. These powers indicated to other Apaches that Geronimo had supernatural gifts that he could use for good or ill. In eyewitness accounts by other Apaches, Geronimo was able to become aware of distant events as they happened, and he was able to anticipate future events. He also demonstrated powers to heal other Apaches. By his example then, the deputy with second-sight surveyed the TATM premises to everyone's satisfaction in the heavy haul along the way as desperately needed upon the Hyper Loop Electropod. Within which she would embody an owl by night and a hawk by day!

And within which her awakened watchtower fortressed unparalleled powers of observation as a backup for ballast under oldfangled, rustic railroad tracks, just in case! Regardless of the New Year to have arrived at the flip of a calendar, twenty-three winters ago when she was conceived, just the same as before her time, twin-rails were in vogue instead of today's top Tubeway.

In no time at all, a power surge pullback precipitated energetic augmentation. Tenacious Tube 291 toasted up ultrahigh tension where waffled, frittered, and fresh-frayed cupcake insulators were baked by pliable plasma of yellowest *yottawattage* which- when it would pelt hard, was felt starred as on a card from afar- spun spindliest! With wriggling, writhing, wrought-iron but molten fleurs-de-lis and flat spades 'spiculed' up at half a globe away, an amazingly hot Hypercity had wholly harbored the little lack thereof. An interdimensional space-warp of contradictory advantage, but never to warm the cockles of one's heart when it came to Joyce Hathaway: connoisseur of buckskin dresses, calico skirts, and households sewn into Teepees, Wigwams, and Hogans.

In supercharged contrast to her Native American fancies, the 22nd-century systematization of a ferroconcrete cradle-to-grave lifestyle stymied universal need for nonchemical and biotic overgrowth. The epoch-making mastery over all forms of nature must have been tyrannical to her, to say the least in an off-world wake-up call counterfeit.

Overall, an energetic "univacuaorta" in need of nothing, save supply and demand of coordinated cardiovascular consistency persisted.

But bucked by a big bill preemptive, our narrow arrow- slung back by an adept archer- had flown headway for the Super Sphere bull's-eye. Never to the aforethought! Nay, not in harm's way of the irrevocable as a matter of fact, she reasoned amid her cabin booth that very hour. Unsure of what was next, yet acutely aware of what the operators were going through. For speedily unhampered that they were, it behooved both BT engineer and conductor to tally up the crew manifest and seek salutary guidance for the far outcome. Solution? To make merry the better; be it uncouth, uncanny, coy, convivial, or controversial; but nonetheless…

The remainder of loose ends were automated to the *nth* degree.

At once, in spite of what ripple rose to a tsunami, the tall, top-o'-the-line gentleman accompanied everyone's sightseeing in standard, stolid decorum. This lady, on the other hand, behaved benignly, unobtrusive in demeanor, and quite akin to that late, great doctor Nikola Tesla, whose heyday had eclipsed inventors of his time. By grace-bestowed beneficence, Tesla was the first turn-of-the-century pioneer electrician to have George Westinghouse commercialize alternating current within the Niagara Falls power plant upstate New York. Their public service power grid distribution ensued supply and demand ever since. Thereafter, in Colorado Springs, high voltage terminals took their toll of a blackout spell on the town itself as Tesla's experiments relayed refinement furthermore.

Her caliber of latter genius was entitled with *Lady* prefixed to the exemplar Westinghouse; even though not necessarily knighted by an English Queen in those yellow & primrose years of inventive precocity. Preposterous though it was for the DC tycoon, Thomas Alva Edison, contrarily idolized howbeit, was one step short of having been an outright imbecile for prissily promoting livestock electrocution to discredit AC superiority (not to ignore more tug-o'-wars weighed in between battlefield foe and hero) back then.

So then, at any rate, this prissily attired, managerial gentlewoman gestured to us through a Plexiglas partition if she could come into a passenger cubicle. Aesthetically, she entered with an enviable aspect that addressed the sitters with a dulcet mezzo-soprano meow: "Mind if I sit down?"

"No, not at all," Rod offered obligingly. Joyce and Boyd moved aside to make way for the grand dame. The elegant, top bonneted lady was definitely welcome. Though whose comely madame Marie Curie 5-foot stature stood, her towering intelligence rivaled the turn of the century's forerunner to the use of radium and polonium, and finding treatments for cancer. Her slightly ashen complexion complemented the female figure, as it were, witnessed in black and white, but now in full Technicolor and an uncanny look-alike.

"Uh, my name is Roderick Rutherford, and I have recently retired from the Reconnaissance Ready~Alert Bureau in order to embark on this expedition for the Super Sphere by way of the Transalteratorium Corporation."

"My maiden name is Tara Tesla. I was never married." *whereas madame Curie was...* Rutherford reviewed his historical back-references to the letter for self-justification, but in vain.

Unaffected by his haughtiness, she had noticed the vignette fish-eye window so polarized to squint itself from the sharp, *glazed* glitter nearside their rocket sled, slipping by. Unlike the Warsaw, Poland born Marie Curie (a French-naturalized physicist and chemist) she hinted in a mid-western maverick sort of way with a western accent: "Ya'll now know what will really transpire right 'round the corner, don't you?"

By then, the air had thickened, cobwebby. Haunted horrible.

Rod glanced at Joyce and Boyd~ busily thumbing their index cards over an electronic Rolodex~ and back up at her with his turf and territory intact to his colleagues' sides, the one on the right and the other at his left.

"No- admittedly- we know not, but *I* know it..." Joyce gloated glaringly.

...Half a minute of four-figure taciturnity while the loquacious chatter of background crewmen that leveraged lists amongst each other waned to a sudden muffle.

"We cannot tell; at least not at this point," asserted Joyce in her matter-of-fact fortitude, trying not to jump the gun.

To attenuate their already brick-thick atmosphere, the slim, clean-cut doctor slacked back on her seat and formulated her hypothesis as noted: "Well now... Now take terminologies, for instance, such as 'supple bottle' of pressurized preeminence~ I apologize~ er, *prominence*!"

Our newly garnished guest fumbled on with an overemphasis, correcting herself, except suspiciously, only to swallow up whole the intended sentence. Inadvertently, Roderick had wiggled his way out of that foible of scientific inaccuracy and stammered: "Like hot solar prominence, as preeminence ought to refer to our solemn souls, Heaven help us!" he waxed worried, but abashedly dead wrong.

"I'm glad you caught that as it was unintentional, but paramount," she said amiably. "You see, I believe what we are destined for, a mere nineteen hours from now, is an old, organic colossus unlike anything you and I have experienced ever before."

The discrepancy of on-board computation to a clock factor gained on what should have stolen over eight hours from the allotted timetable while they were sound asleep. Really? She claims the number 19 to the hours left! Rutherford was fascinated by yet *another* turn of the screw.

Hathaway glimpsed bizarre brightness that had seeped through, goggle-eyed with wonder, "Oh, no! Now this is beginning to sound and look loony, spooky," she confessed; so relieved of not needing to meet up with a goon. But it dawned on all of them.

"Hey! are you the one we overheard on the intercom?" passengers paddled her heavy-handed.

"Okay, okay! Settle down!" Rod regrouped nearby jeers in deferential defense of their new visitor seemingly from the wild west hinterland, save civilized more than they could counteract.

"Why, certainly. Who else?" he muttered as would any soothsayer to demystify the moment while wearing carnival conviviality. As moderator, it was his job to pacify rebuttals.

"Is that so, exactly?" he quickened, quizzical- confiding with Harris, his buddy, but estranged by *her*- yet intrigued. "Oh, Hell, give it all you've got!" he cackled cockily.

In his memorial scrapbook, verses from West Brook Academy had actuated the intense suspense; foreboded by what was about to untangle, little by little…

Chrysalis

No matter how distant I'd travel,
Yea, or rocket aloft to some star,
It was hope for delight to unravel
Expectations fulfilled by and far;
Ere the highway preceded by gravel
Had hot asphalt unrolled for my car.

Under streetlamps ablaze ever bright,
As the traffic lay one fender-bender,
Intimations ignite (taut and tight)
Some old entity seamlessly tender!
Full of fulgurous, intimate Light:
An unparalleled highway defender.

What once was a squad of three in the TATM, upturned to a quad of conference. Before their four-company, the lead crystal decanter, depleted of its spirits until it sparkled spuriously with prismatic diffraction, had all but vanished. For when snack-time chimed, it got buckled back up into the high front row seats as if to make ampler room for a stagecoach card game of canasta.

One hard card shuffle of two packs, per deck 52, four jokers. A fourfold alliance... Bases were loaded for suchlike ranks per each player to build up a canasta. One was to create a meld of seven so-called cards. A draw and a discard pile in the middle of the table-top playing field and so forth. But whoso would finish the round became the Finisher; morover, this was the red canasta devoid of wild cards. Joyce gained a red~three, having three of hearts and three of diamonds. But Boyd slipped his sneaky wild card into the discard pile for to stop-card Joyce, preventing her to take from the contents thereof and so forth. The quad kept several rounds going until one of the players opted out, and then another followed suit! Eventually, another wild card revealed its comical torso and head with a joker and luckily froze the stockpile of cards from which no retrieval, nor withdrawal was permissible and game over.

The temendous traversal of this stupendous conveyance reverberated with a weird sensation profusely. For one thing, their temptations for postgame revelry must have been quenched. Hell, they couldn't even dilly-dally because of an arctic, stone-frozen frazzle that clenched every sitter and vestibule bellows bystander alike; not to mention the five vital Bullet Train personnel having grown jittery beforehand. Obviously, they were the indispensable conductor, two trainmen or brakemen, and an engineer, and a fireman traditionally garbed and stationed at their posts of duty. The remaining reinforcements consisted of what 22nd-century jargon jested as *automatronic mannequins*. Such are chrome robots for auxiliary contingencies only, and also for redundant roundelay reparation, whatever *that* meant!

Meantime, as they sat at a conference table, Miss *Tara Tesla* (the which was her non-matrimonial surname), in her West World common parlance, began her hearty discourse on this ultrahigh-speed trek of theirs for what had been heretofore portrayed as the ultimately unanticipated:

"Let us begin," prefaced the actual quantum physics doctor (of anomymous entitlement to all) who *steepled* her latex turquoise aquamarine #7FFFD4 gloved hands into a ten-fingered knuckle. "Allow me to conjecture, if you permit, upon prerequisite intervals of what we are about to confront---"

"Good grief!" interjected Rod rudely. "And what would that be?" Astonishment overtook him as he clung to his safe and sound Apache and Scotsman on either side of him. Unbeknownst to anyone, so seated across the table like Lady Transalteratorium confronting them at this end, she had wooed or cradled his most metaphorical security blanket to snuggle into for the time being.

Unruffled by Rutherford's outburst, her melodious dulcet voice-over vindicated her intimidating presence. The outdated outfit she wore with her somewhat vieux jeu conformity to the bygone era when Henry Ford's Model T vehicle rolled forth by 1908 had caught all of them off-guard until one was timorous.

To date, her age went back to 213 years ago, but temporally.

Though the liminal liaison stood her ground, immune to disputation, she seemed increasingly reticent to continue. Like legendary Darth Vader from the long-time-ago Star Wars series, Empire Strikes Back, her recorded voice box of a lovely larynx, though low and muffled behind the mask, intoned an infinite "I understand." And then from George Lucas's earlier film, THX 1138, wherein OMM inquires: "Could you be more~ specific?"

And in answer to discourses of a collective think tank in the old, rare Russian science-fiction epic, *Solaris*, directed by Andrei Tarkovsky, an ethereal, drizzling mist and moire of outside rainfall streaked and stretched over the glass tunnel curvature obliquely in which the pod-packs shot through like a swift battery of cannons.

By now, as if to spatter the windowpanes, the unaccounted for super-jet drag of thunderstorm droplets had turned to vapor on the outer tubing of the translucent vacuum shaft. Nor that the wetness of which would blindingly blanch out a see-through, threadbare bore. But separated from such a barreling burst of energy field momentum, far and fey, soundproofing pressurized aboard kept customer comfort away from an anvil of slipstream distortion wound up from without and way out-of-bounds.

Assuredly so, sacrosanct muteness aboard pervaded every square inch of the BT tardis interior that they beheld. For behold, when one arose en route for the toilet- a passenger car away in the back- there were faucet valves with decompression levered control. With each seal-tight emergency escape hatch, an EDF or Exit Door Flap reared its stainless steel stub, but neon orange back-lit, labeled DANGER: DO NOT TAMPER WITH and to a menagerie of more precautions printed hither and yon... Warning signage pasted all the way up to rooftop roundness of the BT that encapsulated them into Velcro red rug-snug carpet treatment. For furthermore, every pod bobsled had an FDF: a Fuselage Dorsal Fin fix to jut just an index finger up; these that measured barometer-backed heat drag jet stream pressure.

And such ferrous fins (finely fastened) featured the redundancy of foolproof and fail-safe devices distributed throughout this quite compartmentalized conveyance system. In earnest, 'twas as an amusement park pod-car carousel ride wrapped up in a prepackaged, sleek steel shell of shortwave UVC armour, only in the event of intercity routine radiation leakage.

The conference reconvened, for some time reluctantly wrought. Stunned by something they could not lay a finger on, one was to be lectured by a velvety decorous, steam-pressed, properly tailored, comeliest-coiffured messenger now conversant with terra incognita that typified the *je ne sais quoi* of the whole nine yards. Yea, hash marks included and offered afield, but without the pigskin!

¶ They were pinned back by now by the Woman in Black. A mourner, perhaps? Or for some lugubrious reason just as taboo as a black cat that crosses the street in front of you? Or at a necropolis... At any rate, the nervous riders and all felt as if transfigured and tried by this titanic torpedo within which one lounged, uneasily. All due to the train's prolonged but *truncated* trajectory----- You'll see!

"Be not alarmed!" Tara Tesla chided genteelly, but with an elegant smile that smeared us. Until jocund Joyce, bamboozled from the prefabrication thereof, snickered snootily and smartly at her aristocratic trait. Irrefutably apparent, or at least through that otherwise overdone overture of her wise wherewithal; yea, that of some marvelous melodrama fashioned for diary~depository soliloquies sought sometimes by the Surrealists.

There was a hush after passenger aggravation died down.

"Very well… indeed." The demure dame curtsied in spirit only. As a prim privateer detective of espionage rank- 007 Roger Moore mannered, or rather, as Batman's cunning cat woman- she had withheld one's grave, grotesque grimace in lieu of what was about to be denuded; that is, the rending of rogue Reality itself!

Of course, the hitherto staged event siphoned suspense over us, sanguinely, whilst she still taunted: "If you… the two of you prepare yourselves for an ultimate tramway trek sojourn unveiled before you in less than nineteen hours from now~"

She paused, poppycock poker-faced, gravely disposed of.

And Joyce could not help but giggle a wee bit in amusement, or was it sheer amazement? Never mind. For either way, they- Joyce, Boyd and Rod- submitted to her their expert import of undivided attention. But yet the scenario spilled, overflowed swollen up, and cascaded downward overtime (avalanche-like) as from glacial regions of the Himalayan Helicon. At this point, they then called it total *terra incognita inter alia* (an unexplored territory among other things)!

"…For what we're about to reabsorb," Tara earnestly reminded, avoiding a statuesque effigy, "is an enveloped encounter of such sub-spatial coruscant curvature at the bulged out, distended underbelly basement of the Hyperwhole Supersphere... So much of which its south pole exposition descends, or even condescends to us mortals unawares."

Joyce braced herself, goosebumps and all; transfixed with a *roid* rash of joyride mumps and measles. "You mean to tell me that our arrival thereat may bewilder us beyond the grasp thereof?" She obfuscated in a pedantic posture: "Well! Of all the nerve…"

With overwhelming anticipation, the trio of them guffawed gamely.

"Yup, indeed!" someone added. they couldn't pinpoint who?

Laughter loosened them all to a lithesome languor. Henceforth congeniality cuddled the vulnerable vestiges of their final 3D moment with outbursts of horseplay and raillery, especially with the former colonel and captain. They were reminded by how such a high-speed joyride stripped them all of their rank, and higher up on the rungs of Jacob's ladder, leaving TATM technocrats like the crewmen and train operators still vested with powers of command.

Pacified, Rod had to fumble for his two-cents-worth and blurted blatantly, "Whoa, whoa! What the Hell… Have at it, maestro~ 'er Doctor!" He then swallowed his pride: "…I'm all ears," and he didn't mean to sound sarcastic, *slang-slouched*; whatever *that* might be!

But in her all too proper propriety- albeit eccentric by today's standards- the courtly doctor beheld us, glossily, deeply concerned. Astride the subject matter at hand, she had rendered it a tad this way, rather. But that intelligently enough:

"Now see here, it's really a simple task. No hullabaloo either," the makeshift hillbilly, as if she were wife of an outside Michigan farmer, told them with a twang of westernized utterance. "Firstly, please permit me to take a deep, throaty breath with one accord, and for both of you and mister Rutherford to do the same." She made motherly sure all three of them were attentive and nagged them to undergo the hypnotic session. She waited for their mutual consents.

When Joyce alongside Boyd gazed over to her porthole window, she cringed and cowered herself cozily upon him for having to see so much fluttering, meteoric, phantasmagorical fury of stupendous speed only inchworms away! Though the barreling, bobsled Bullet carried our passenger payload at superconductor MagLev mach 1 reentry, readily, eftsoons it was not unlike an ICMB hurtling headlong…

Now Tara (the teacher) and they, the docile pupils under her, had noticed it too with likeliest solidarity.

"Okay," each of them concurred unanimously, even if jolted slightly off of their rocker chairs, or out of their stockings by the floorboard forward momentum of an onrushing but muffled rumble wraparound and beneath everyone. Upon the flip-side coin toss of a safety protocol gamble~ except for but ozone evacuated millibars of rarefied airlock; that which had quivered an electronic polarized latticework of aeolian harp hydraulics, horridly~ some low pitched magnetic repulsion reechoed the dull thump and thud of an eerily elongated supersonic *scream!* throughout the tube-tunnels, rattling an earful Rutherford. Therefore, Tara relaxed his scared-stiff, hard white-knuckled, whooping whereabouts with one 'silver sliver' of soporific serenity. Others, disconnected to their meditation session, desired to skedaddle, but where to? The whoop, whisk, and whiz of a hopscotch, stop-shot and slip-trip slideshow was so disconcerting enough for everyone daunted with disorientation. Old *emesis* sacks for air sickness, or barf bags, were automatically distributed by watchful *automatronic mannequins* that replaced stewardesses queasy, as it were.

"Now then… while breathing with cadence… in and out~ in and out. Inhale and exhale (that's right), easy now… just have yourselves yield into trance, imbued by self-abandonment…" Tara, unswayed by BT contortions, taught them thus.

And what followed forthwith was what Rutherford with Hathaway and Harris had felt before a precipice, ready to dive pellmell into the cerulean surf of Lethe as some sort of swoon swept over them. Soon, situated in the midst of an open, spacious room, emptily empowered, but vacant save for soul-occupancy thereof, they had re-materialized carnally, full-fleshed, upon the other side of collective subconsciousness that mysteriously mushroomed about.

After exchanged excitation, then preparatory convergence, as it were, there was absolutely nothing nonchalant about what occurred.

Their fickle, facile façades furrowed a San Andrea Fault in their rib-cage frames; how heartfelt to-the-hilt. Anon were they stabbed stiffly, swiftly by rosebud *hyperdulia* daggers of piercing perception!

Unexpectedly then, that though absent from the thunderous train ride and made more aware of gateway multiversal access, a doppelgänger of Tara emerged out of nowhere whilst a sly switch from Doctor to Empress prefixed her *nom de plume* identity, so to speak. One never knew what her birth-name was anyway... After all, would it make much of a difference? Joyce wondered, warily. But rather invisibly, therefore the Nikola Tesla lookalike inventor in feminine finesse was not one whit in sight save for an audible soundtrack and visual cue on her.

Our stage was set in full swing. The revelation of a desolate interior, overall equipped with extraterrestrial Transvortiums, soon transpired (obviously of an unknown origin and technology). They were bloated, blindingly blithe white *things* hung high up from the ceiling of a saggy, aged, annexed ballroom that necked out into old intramural inanity; possibly pitted with meandering causeways and outlets that burrowed up and down to no end…

Out of holographic earthliness, Termite tunnels, each labeled by a TT with a numeric signature, instantly were excavated to towering height; that cultivated in place any zoological specimen acrawl! It was a revitalized vivarium full of an exotic menagerie behind the four walls which enclosed the dreamers.

Of course, one could not help but notice all wall-to-wall upholstery in the midst thereof~ namely, paisley ceiling plafonds above wallpapers cobbled forth with nodes, nodules, and nipples. Myriads of them~ outspread about gable ornaments multiplied like a bloated plague, yet somewhat plainly vapid. Even outside these quietest quarters waited on, the broad-brass breastplates and paps of gable ornaments, gorgeously gibbous, garishly arrayed all over multiplied themselves far up and yonder. But back inside the big ballroom rather, verily a different full lull of insularity had reigned.

Whereas without, squat robot, ferroconcrete Fat Vat fireplug spouts would throng the area, as if they were fauceted & nozzled nodules and refrigerator-sized hydrants; the eeriest interior lounge of such remained under fiery finials, fronds o' fleurs-de-lis, and fluorescent flambeaux; probe prods suspended and strewn up at 23 meters. The *Transvortiums* aforesaid, revealed eggshell egg and dart, egg and arrow, egg and anchor, egg and tongue, and egg and acanthus adornments!

Away from the inner-room dividers, on the outer fringes, the commercial bay windows winked with room & board but looked out at an open parking lot luminously bathed by lavender lustrous electroluminescence! Beneath one's tread had lain this brick-thick pile brick red carpet until crimson crowned at its borders; the deep embroidery of which wore embroidered margins, and that bloodily blushed and darkened up into some seepage of tar-pit gloom, each tenebrous tinge just shy of cherry charcoal soot; of tar black soap suds soaked in full spectrum! For still, through ultraviolet limned windowpanes, they saw how high mast lampposts punctuated an ebon lake of natural asphalt, row-by-row intermittent; letting red rug naps like a sodden lawn absorb their glare and scorch of arc tube lanterns!

Now, next to Rutherford, Joyce's simulacre had waxed wider with a newly entitled deliberate Doctor Tesla, for still annoyingly unseen! Inexplicable, ever-present. They stood aloof but aware of this threesome *interdimensional* virtual reality as we inclined our audience to what she had to, as a Preacher, proclaim:

"Ya'll are in the year's end of Nineteen-Seventy Nine," Tara tintinnabulated hither in coloratura soprano, as if in a saloon. "Just plumb short of the Eighties decade at the midnight strike of New Year's Eve to resound its *Auld Lang Syne* performed on an old, old, closet clarion clarinet resonant melodeon only half a dozen days away, mechanized with one automated roundelay..."

¶ And it came to pass, like on a filmstrip of holographic projection, that virtual reality itself unveiled this die Gestalt meta-lucid dream that abruptly *evaporated*; the transference of which was infinite, but of makeshift materialization, albeit devoid of paranormal *ectoplasm*- a membranous plenum, etheric by nature- able to reformulate replicas of the which~ (not the Witch) How an out-of-doors parking lot plaza pliantly had oozed and spewed *ex nihilo* consummately, entirely outspread whereupon one found footing. Our hypnotist huckled the advantage and continued:

"You are now well into the first year of that oft called "Golden Decade" which was 1980; wherein I shan't get down to trivial details of those current events, except contrarily, I'll aim at the flash-point of it all, alright? For under the Sun, whose sunspot epicycles would have been sustained at her halcyon quiescence, you will notice how nice and virtuous a pristine presence pervades this soon-to-be vandalized car lot. Its woebegone sign soon to indicate NO ADMITTANCE on its spray-painted silkscreen serigraph.

Harris stiffened himself and sniffed the pungent starched stench of hot tar roil up like from an afterglow emittance of a creosote bush. Then the wafted pleasantly sweetened scent of crude petroleum intermixed with maple syrup to stimulate every olfactory organ! Joyce, beside him, herself so swoony over such raw redolence, stooped down delicately, bending, crouching closer to observe the very granular composition of freshly macadamized asphalt, commercial grade, and with its flattened blacktop overlap throughout the Big Lots. Indeed, it was her own way to get at filigree scrutiny of their whereabouts, forensic style!

The ebullient effusion and effigy of a greasy creosote shrub persisted until this imagined Saviouress whereof was as crowned *Creosoteria cratered with an incorruptible crème...*

Muffled, melodious gigs were heard playing from a concealed stereophonic boombox suggestive of the early Sixties vogue.

Soon *in the future*, the Moody Blues' *Nights In White Satin* played out of old phonograph party-hardy steroid stuffings hidden away and afar, but premonitory enough since the pop Top Ten hit hadn't come out yet.

They trotted to the alleyway of the car lot stapled and stilted with aluminum and stainless steel maypoles that upheld old mast heavyweight arc lamps, and higher up still, freshly packed Fresnel lens lighthouse lanterns propped atop taller towers and obelisks of lengthy, looming height. And way out over the ballpark diamond, a strangely strong throng that distributed densely packed vertices had dwarfed these pins up front, as it were, like toothpicks compared to heavy-hilts of hypertrophic, ferroconcrete fortresses forested afield off in the outskirts. The would-be Battery Park had yet powerhouse supplanted a plateau or *playa* of boondocks, if ever this surreal Big Apple trance transpired throughout. Veritably, via the vat-collective conglomeration of any congregant gathering; that such planters and reapers of great landmark monumental cornfields should then have readily realized it, gleaned gleefully as if from an ulterior alternate Anthropic universality! Of course, but yet that with never nudged-to-the-brink warhead horror to escalate, the hazy hangup of dread and doom fell short of a fireplug stopper by which they walked.

There was the ramp that necked circuitously into a cloverleaf overpass highway junction. Furthermore, tall towers sleekly tufted the liminal vicinity. Here were wide, but burnished lampposts of *heightened* high mast lighting. "What you see are each a Pole Star stationed at the very acme thereof," our riveting railroad tour guide pointed out; though background-invisible, conservatively having her handwriting as if dictated, "the like of which will never ever return after the long ago 2008 EPA pact and ban enforced by then thereafter. Inevitably, light-emitting diodes of an ugly all~synthetic byproduct production shall take over, leaving behind the former, efficient utility usage of fine, ferromagnetic liquid metals, such as mercury and sodium fillers, no longer amalgamated (when safety standards will have been placarded). Otherwise our old legendary Lady America, in turn, had gotten herself gaudily galvanized with President Ronald Reagan's Administration before being dethroned, deflowered under China's chicanery of fleshpot export takeover... Until socialistic democrats, deviant to the hallowed United States Constitution, proudly preen themselves as I would prophesy."

From spatiotemporal standpoints of 1981, this fore-felt future tense lingered relative to their time-tarnished, juxtaposed jet lag.

Without forewarning the airy, spooky setting dissolved away, only to be immediately replaced by that selfsame, silent Ballroom of a storefront parking strip. Behold, there was a banner on one of the walls which read LAS VEGAS, NEVADA in bold typeface (circa 1980, needless to reiterate). Once more- just as before *a fortiori*- the limpid lavender and hyacinthine Light, lithely lucent from outside, afresh frosted the big bay windows awash with Deep Purple iridescence. Somewhere, still, *Smoke on the Water* echoed.

Relaxed but responsive, Rutherford recited this poesy aloud with admirable admixture:

Ex Flamma Lux

by Sarah Silkwood

Wholesale let light prevail,
Sewn seamless all throughout
And inter-knit as she'll unveil
Vast throngs void of doubt.

From times that once were so
Back then when Sirius glared,
With white delight atop aglow
But which was ne'er repaired.

What multitudes go gathered;
Wrought roundabout delighted
Where witnesses saw lathered
White froth wax unbenighted.

But bulged forth, as it were
With soap suds sought agleam,
Bare mirth may interlink her
By that which vomits cream!

Harp strings brocaded yet
By interlinked hot pole stars,
Stay stalwart iridescent wet
Where parking lots roll cars.

"By the way," he inferred for a featured footnote, "the title of this work originally in Latin is translated as *Light from Flame*, or *Out of the Flame* composed by her ladyship in Nineteen-Hundred and Sixty Seven, March 10. It was when jiggy Jim Morrison of the Doors during that year had flared forth a wild-card Roman candle with his smash hit, Light My Fire."

Out-flung out of nothing, an oblong porthole of the Vision popped out at Rutherford and the rest of the two as cushioned seats were suddenly dampened down, heavily hampered by gravity of Tara the tour guide. Uneasily though, you couldn't quell a backlash of grim reality tug at one's back by bullet train trepidation.

Still stunned by this OBE experience, all of them came to and resumed rapport and repose at the passenger booth; ready to relate with what had happened.

Joyce's searchlight of sagacity was a magnifier. Its Fresnel lens louvers upfront, by contrast transparent, kept clarified, clairvoyant reservations about the whole thing to herself. Becalmed like a sailboat upon breezeless brine, as she was lulled by a hypnotic drone, the wary damsel fell asleep that evening aboard her berth, only to have dreamt of everyone's aggregate out-of-the-body experience with only dilatory delight. Now the receptive *Shining* of her lighthouse was lavishly lit to a roseate starburst.

¶ The transducer transport trilled through the tube still at a fixed 1,234 plus or minus 0.80 kph! Time clock envisagement of their ETA dwindled to twelve hours~ at half-past the miraculous ordeal~ and still counting. Long after they had *snapped out of it*, tenacious Tara reassured them that her autosuggestion upon the lap of Morpheus was not meant to be by slight-of-hand abracadabra deceptive, nary iota, nor makeshift for that matter. Nay, but quite conversely, as she should have figured, it was predisposed, privily preternatural if not punctual, or whatever she expressed it to be; rather prefatory to their surprise visit over worldwide vistas!

Rutherford retired (with his at-hand crew) off to bed. Yet undetected by anyone of them, the forward and backward spiral of *continual causality* had just begun to parallel the most momentous Magnetron Hyperloop in human history.

The outdoors nightfall unleashed noodles of elongated neon lights let loose, straggling strangely, that transversely smeared one's dream-state view over the veranda. The efficacious, effulgent effect of fluorescent flurry and glitter that askew skittered on past at supersonic susurration had slithered slyly into the hull of the ballistic Barrel. Room and board and berth ghosts and goblins of outside roundelay reentry and stage-changeover induced bouts of enuresis on the crewmen and passengers as they were jarred hard by a gravitational differential (no, not to hint at a slowpoke truck's undercarriage gearbox, O for crying out loud)! Preferably, in the quieter interior of this torpedo pod that scudded upon some curved countryside at dizzying speed, the BT Levitron Transport was ever so soundproof engineered! So thoroughly, that merely the dull, near-inaudible *buzz* of a housefly, or 'half~light' hum and flit of a hummingbird, caught in the wink of an eye, but lazily lulled them all to dimmest dormancy on their luxuriant lily pads! But there was no primly-attired Princess to pucker her lips on the legendary Frog framed for metamorphosis; yea, into a knight in shining armour, Rutherford fancied. Just an outré Tara who tactfully tutored them en route.

In such scenarios, Rod reminisced, it was more of a GORF that he dallied with on an arcade video game console, computer-conventionalized as the Commodore Vic-20 vintage stock 1983.

Reposeful, Rutherford faded to Cinderella Land as everyone else, likewise, waned away, benumbed, nicely asleep. The nearly unmanned Magnetronic Pod-Packs took over on auto-pilot while fastidious fasteners and punctilious power-waldoes handled hefty hydraulics by clutching the engage and release levers. Via purely punctual choreography, two-dozen robotic arms and electric shoes shuffled about throughout each bobsled of a convoy-conveyance.

On a side note, howbeit Joyce on her own had hastened her happy terra incognita; knocked out and taken aback under some supinely cataleptic continuum, left lucidly on another equator of consciousness (non-suppository induced by carsick passengers, of course)! How heeding and cognizant of the rocketry via this self-automated inter-tube Bullet Barrel apace...

With her dream intermission shielded, insulated by Berth coziness:

And it came to pass that the night-vision had overpowered her out of whatnot wit's end. Her diary entry would have ensconced it by the following (by her heretofore permission to have it disclosed herewith as **Lucerna Viverum Aeterna**--- in Latin for *the Lamp of Eternal Life*):

I was found amid that identical Red Room we were in on the previous dream episode, but all alone. Not a soul in sight except for living lamp entities which were ever-present. Precisely!

While wearing my house~gown about me; the one I always put on in utilitarian usage, I stood barefoot, bodily naked under them. In my case, the slanted afternoon was far spent and the night stars had not constellated just yet. But the radiant Red Room engulfed me completely until my self-composure coopered a bit in carefree compromise of my stoic staunchness. By then the powerful parlor room made me hunker down into a prayerful position. For while I queried the Almighty to either deliver me from dreadful silence, or at least interpret for me the wherefores instead thereof, naught had transpired.

In answer to an alternate outcome- by divine resolution upon all of this hitherto foursquare or six-sided rectangular enclosure of a big ballroom- it would represent radiant reality at large bulge in and of itself. A future foretaste; or firebrand it "full, fiery fore-gleam of a transcendent stasis devoid of space-time-flow..." as I must have known all along...

An ultra-bright accompaniment~ what have you~ according to candlepower echelon, glared gibbous, gilt, sleek steel stainless from above. Highlighted still by the purported panorama I was wedged in, the high~hung cloven tongue Vase Vats were halyard pulley driven, upwardly extended, atop high masts marked at a thousand meters (one kilometer) far above-ground. Next, these "vatubulae" were transmogrified and inter-poised to overlook the human drama of our daily affairs, whether it be dastardly or delightful- either way- incongruous and unawares were they. They, by and large, had kept illumined brilliance for the sake of but being brazenly brightened up and out; like Light for the sake of Light. Alright?

For furthermore, if the aforesaid is not enough, to my interpretation of such an oddly elucidated, divinely-created spectacle [the canister creation itself], the pliable, viable "vatubulae" as shown had been consequently designed to merely fill in the gap; to supply the lack thereof, under which the human race yearns to no more suffer so... As if religion and science could not suffice to heal and bridge the breach between mankind and Heaven herself; ourselves ignorant of how oft we succumb to contrived notions of faith, or on the other end, empirical proof.

Hence by buoy-beacon exotica, these at least 'bright~bridge' crossways (vicariously) our constant separation from Paradise itself. Perhaps as they are appendages of an innate theophany encapsulated into leavened up bloated wafers, as if it were wonderful with warmest jollity and mirth unlike a fake-take.

[One would dare not chortle at her suggested proposition, but to solemnly absorb the subject matter as if she were a sponge of spume...]

* * * * * * *

My Red Room with molten, mantled, pilaster-ribbed walls on all four flanks, of radiant rug nap and silvery silence, made more mercurial- that of a ferromagnetic field- ethereally! For from this Ballroom quite a metallic effusion addressed my olfactory organs whilst canopy lanterns (other than those of fluorescent flambeaux) illumined up the outside with an unearthly harsh glare unlike any wavelength imaginable as seen through a colorful spectrum triple rainbow of supernumerary hues. In that above this somber, henna emblazoned, dark divan and carpet piled Ballroom, there lay dim opalescence of sun and 'moon dog' spectra sparkle without about.

Unequivocally though, the voluminous Vatubulae glistered glaringly unapproachable swollen yellows duskily displayed or delightful, but in a jiffy, generated, transmitted, and distrubuted over an enormous power-grid factor. O whose niveous nimbi of narrowest ferromelt magnificence would well exceed the fieriest foundations of what we'll ever acknowledge as raw illuminance per se. Notably, such entities illicit by religious and/or scientific sentinels and standards. If not by bare sacrilege indictment, the Vatibulae are unimpeachable and absolutely acceptable by big bellied bottles of in-vitro enclosure, conferment, or bequeathal.

Nothing follows on my dear diary-disposed-of report.

Joyce Hathaway, foster daughter to madame Montgomery

Dreamscape portents of no nighttime hallucination, but reality vanished into thin air, and left Joyce to slumber, serenely soporific via an on-board BT supersonic night-ride lullaby; a favorite among sleepers under torpor-inducing fail-safe devices lest the sharp shift and jolt of multidimensional interaction inconvenienced them!

By contrast, their 'night out on the Tube' was not at all alike, surprisingly. Rather, it was a lifelike simulacre of the big RR or Red Room (not railroad-like at this point, although prefabricated presumably!) that then immured one's outer, listless, but inner, acutely alert lucidity. Its haunted hush housed by anechoic noise suppressors, seeped Segway-like under everyone's bodily frame, relaxing passengers awhile with wake-up refreshment. As with Hathaway's somnolence of a visceral vision, so too the bizarre, buckshot shiny, self-conscious Cargo Durga Warp Lamp entities assumed cynosure precedence. Center-stage, C4 yourself.

Wherefore, with only such supple, pristine presence of the like, each specimen had resembled a bloated blanket plumply rolled up into itself; or elasticated in shape-shifting contortions any which way.

Thus these weird, if not devilish, full blown maggots had her moreover communicate no misnomer therewith, God forbid. But namely, everyone to have been a VACOON instead of nature's raccoon! Minus the mammal's instinctual mischief, of course. Fashioned readily, each one, like Pillsbury dough, cocoon-contoured, softened, and prepared for the oven, she pondered punitively. For science or bust, one found these overgrown grubbily grotesque slugs to be repugnant; whereas tiptoe total Acceptance had queen~regnant~reigned otherwise with cool, compassionate, and gladsome glory! Rod and Boyd hadn't envied her nary one whit! No, not at least in this lifetime, nor in the one to follow… As in Doctor Who's, The Green Death episode, a visceral Vacoon was called a Maggotron (electric maggot on the loose).

Beware! lest a Buoy-beacon irradiates you with roentgens! The actual radiation level at the Chernobyl Nuclear Power Plant while the core was still exposed was approximately 15,000 to 20,000 roentgen per hour. It was the amount of radiation released by bombs at Hiroshima and Nagasaki that repeated every hour. Whereas *these*, with doses of 100-200 rads, could cause acute radiation syndrome (ARS) if upheld up-close by confirmation!

Accordingly, this distinctly developed lantern floated with levitating anti-gravity; so sized up to twenty-three yardsticks in height, but suspended only midair, just a scant scuttle of sulfurous firebrands, or brimstone sulfurous aglow over the hot pavement, besprinkled with a *transuranic*, heavyweight supercluster, if four-dimensionally grown to a yottameter up and down, or distantly distended by itself.

After her concise explanation of the vision, eager Harris and Rutherford (regardless) could have been mummified by similar language! Indeed, an incombustible neoprene entity, the 'vacoon' was plugged in with the *Others* to form a combined 'vacoonery' laid altogether then as a compliant platoon of "welcome us, or else…"! They themselves, the riders, backed away, stunned and steeped. For these corpulent cucumbers, torpedo-tapered to an inverted nipple at each end thereof, with what stuffy Mitchelville lab-coats labeled as *vatubulae*, were wired up by *nihility*, as if vindicated through a vacuum tube. Verily so. Only their apparent Votive Virtue of yielding identities unlawful to be uttered! Large larvae as in Doctor Who's The Green Death, but all armoured up stoutly as automated Dalek destroyers of anyone contrary to their cause, or so it seemed.

Heartily, however, this thing was not the issue, as eftsoon any of them came to discover the ultimate benignity of the amorphous, yet tubular tough guys that these were. Now, under disclosures of deep, darkened scarlet RR vacancy, in any case called the old Red Room, Joyce could not help but glimpse her invaluable Vacoonery congealed cocoon-like. Yea, it was an upright cryogenic chrysalis ready to horrendously hatch and then fold back into some celestial Monarch butterfly, if you will. Or, let's just say, a supple bottle of sorts that contained an energy factor of completely efficient power transference. An insular transducer that it be, worthwhile to behold.

With wonderment, goggle-eyed and open-mouthed, an observer gaped at it inquisitively until, amidst Hathaway's astoundingly unconventional dream, he and she were prevented from any closeup study thereof, as if it had them all in checkmate. Alas, for a few moments, you were able to *look* at *life* quite queerly like unto a jigsaw hologram of the TATM dynamo generator.

Now initially, what rather entailed her night vision was the newly revealed thick-brick wall-to-wall carpet coil of darkened serum-red tapestry woven with but *involute interknit* intricacies, perhaps once embroidered by adept distaff and spindle interplay. For either way, without interruption, about everything else was so seamlessly fine-twined from hem to hem. Apart from the *Others*, the walls, upon the far end of the [infrared] spectrum, spewed the lovely luster o' gloss and glaze varnish lacquered up, and which shone silken, serous, and ectoplasmatic, but even more overcast beneath buckeye gable ornament weathering; yea that of rubber pacifiers plastered onto an oversoul-saturated ceiling of silence!

¶ At the next curfew, slightly less than eight glacial hours of ennui, beside bare and *blanker* walls, she saw that they were with annexed Ballrooms of boudoir creature comfort (the fluorescent flambeaux). *For those doggone vacoons, or for lovemaking?* In compliance to her tart smartness, the Ballroom she ought to have romped in, bathed by ultraviolet coruscation, acquiesced equitably. Reassured, she reeled right in and relinquished herself merrily into the Protozoic pronouncement of it at once, and right along lavishly lolled her soul down deeper in abandonment to the selfsame space; entirely taken aback by a swarthy swoon. But no sooner than her pillow and blanket that insulated her during the Night Watch, so too, every immemorial recollection of that Ballroom's sumptuous plushness of sericeous siles. For, as a result, she slept, well nestled, ennobled thereby. Buttoned up in her Chief Seattle plaid chemise!

Until before everyone's third plummet to a deep sleep, the ultimate portrayal of an Argent Regent Outcry unfolded in only one more Magnetronic moratorium as follows:

It was the Turn of the Century. Precisely 1908 midway, when industry climaxed here and abroad. Although horse-and-carriage coaches clattered upon cobblestone streets, cable cars, called *The Ride*, refurbished by RTD (the Regional Transporation District), or by the CTA, Chicago's Transit Authority, coopered along with their booths bulged by human sardines. They slid up and down the big boulevard venues; their punctual purpose variegated by round dial rheostat control. Of course, by established standards, alternating current of an electrical polyphase *ebb and flow and flux* within the primary, pressurized voltage thereof had become predominant; so exploited electrically for any sufficient power grid transmission factor redistributed (readily) over DC disuse.

The Westinghouse corporation soon eclipsed Edison's empire.

Such city transit relics were showcased during which red-bricked buildings, like those of old Russia's pentagram petropolis, barricaded blocks of avenues as if indicative of the burgeoning populace throughout whilst commerce and thrift thronged an undefunct and foretelling township square.

*It was now the proverbial cherry on top o' the sundae for an off-rank relegated EVA expedition inside the *tardis* Electropod or

Vat-Vacation that had grown redolent and rife with entertainment, reasserted the former colonel beforehand winged in the TATM or Mitchelville annals (though the reminder raided him needlessly)!

In Rutherford's nightly hallucination, or rather another one which was recorded and remastered alongside Hathaway's and Harris's (with each recorded REM sleep separately sampled under hypnagogic inducement), something so drowsily strange had been envisaged if strictly confessed upon. For far in the midst of that boisterous bustle of people and vehicular traffic, right then and there overhead hung what whereabouts was bizarre to behold. And even *that* to have been unnoticed, unnervingly, by such sentient pedestrians nearby, yet entirely unaware of it, this bloated thing hovered all but by itself. Having unflagging levitation, it hovered at point blank range and imposingly with one immovable manner above an oblong Times Square X-intersection aorta fed by big arterial avenues and boulevards, both barricaded for lesser side-street inlets and outlets.

With wonderment, he gazed at its lengthwise embodiment; the cryptogram thereof upheld in admiration only, whereas why such unseen disclosure of a dirigible? Or at least that which was with stark-naked naturalization, biologically, but of upended upright appearance, like some flattened flotation device buoyed by helium fill for inflatable influx. Whereupon he approached the elongated, swollen, opaque object that was about forty meters tall, and whose girth widened to twelve meters in diameter. Undeniably, it was some extraterrestrial Transducer Quasar Beacon just smack right there to perhaps oversee, observe, pinpoint, allocate, and survey the peopled, traffic-packed and preoccupied prance of an unaware multitude which to and fro scurried about beneath it.

Or so it seemed on the lakeside-limpid and lucid level...

Incidentally, it resembled a *Vacoon* mentioned earlier, heretofore harnessed by patient Hathaway as archived in Rolodex dials and files of the Magnetron program. And in due process, with predetermined priority to proceed ahead upon their reassured reconnaissance, the OW-team was to find out what on earth it ought to have been. The rankless Rutherford *(another intimation?)* returned to this site later on in the event the Vacoon still levitated there, just in case. Apparently, there lay leakage and soapy seepage.

The hours had crept on as it still persisted right then and there just seven feet or so off of the intersection median late at night.

In the middle of midnight there was no stagecoach, steed, buggy, nor cart or horse-rider; neither any equitable equestrian robot like the one in Westworld, let alone steeplechase jockeys to be bumped into, doggedly distracted thereby until one visited this mysterious intruder with wary caution. He had paused, nabbing an unguarded stepladder from one of the storefronts and positioned it right under the entire entity effortlessly afloat in mid-air. Then he climbed five rungs upward and looked into a viewer stationed below the midriff, or at the underbelly protuberance thereof.

For a moment, driverless cable cars careened by. Unsaddled pack-horses, having no straddlers, nor equestrians, galloped by with bare backs and good gait- how heavily- hologram whole by the tonne of totality!

Atop a rooftop cupola, one flag was at half-mast above an unbarricaded derelict cross-street *fireplugged* by refrigerator-fat hydrants strewn up and down off the curb along some sidewalk. The entity, independently illumined, mirrored streetlights strung strong over its outer shell of forty-meter-long continuity... This seamless dirigible on an upright poise radiated rock-solid still its front and backside ballooned up and seven feet overhung, upheld by nothing except entirely uninterrupted *anti-gravity* gracefulness altogether. Quite convinced by the intensity of it, he eyeballed his viewfinder with a fascinated face fixed thereupon to behold what was shockingly ineffable. What was outright uncensored by any Transalteratorium standardization; that is, this skookum cocoon.

In his line of sight there was absolutely nothing to see save a clearly abysmal depth of crystalline clarity that continued forever! Until inside the obliquely deflated balloon of an upright dirigible, amid its threadbare threshold of shriveled shrinkage, there was this narrowest nothingness... As if the very vacuity of it stretched forth froth, inanely, and that utterly to boundless eternity therein! He felt breathless and just about toppled o'er onto the old cobbled curbside from off the stilted stepladder. And again, gaily, he gazed into the viewer and noted that selfsame see-through tenuity with vitrified clearness of no lackluster, nor even blackness... Just sheer, shiny, transparent and see-through Planck volume, blank vacuous void!

Surprisingly though, right above its facial cushioned viewer via the torpedo's south pole base, there was a stuck-on label that read under the sign of infinity:

EVACUATORIUM
(nihility)
Warning!

And awestruck, straightway, Rutherford flinched whilst teetering on his stepladder, precariously prickled. But it had dawned on the observer. The viable Vacoon in this quick instance~ whose utilized yield might have vomited volleys of quantum foam spewed forth in self-defense~ revealed some Siren that suspended herself by null *nil* of *nothingness*. Its utterly destitute nullification merely extra hefty, herculean, stupendously above-ground, grimly apparent. But this to maybe bedazzle anyone midst their dreaming flown full blown on the deck of a speeding Bullet Barrel.

In the daytime duration of the present & prolonged lapse, howbeit, with crossroads relentless by thoroughfare fever-pitch hyperactivity hither and yon, he more so pictured this visitor with himself accompanied by a shy little lady; an orphan, Saturn~ringed, who had come to communicate with him. This time, upon discovery of an incorporeal separateness- by contrast to the very last- he was found invisible to the onrush of heavy traffic and public passersby, let alone being unaffected by their stampede of relentless reality. Except that this tattered girl, girdled with a hula hoop plaything garlanded about, stood as palpable as could be.

What better contrast to the saturnine setting of ominous spells that crept over the sleepers aboard a causal convoy! The which was stereotyped as the gloomy 'god-pod' by but 22-Century-Séance Sitters and Super-naturalists advertised on bulletin boards.

She paused-- this gimme-a-lollipop Asian girl encircled by a hoop and clad in a floral standard kimono, an easy-to-wear, single-layer cotton yukata-- and beamed her crescent slits and eyelids of no mascara up at him and inquired, "What are you squinting at?"

An English-speaking specimen? he wondered. *Why were the Transalteratorium holographics Japanese mind-readers!?*

Jarred by the shockwave of his startling encounter, he replied with too much temerity, "What? The Vacoon is still right on top of us, full of nothingness, and *in myocardium* of the greater citywide arteries and conduits. Yet you ask me this?"

An unsettling surge hit him. The dainty, dimpled doll, a bit pudgy and cheeky, who had hopscotched around Rutherford, was TATM-regenerated to the minutest detail; even to the finest thread of undergarment and stocking stature. Over her school-issued kimono of chrysanthemum paisley designs, an apron of saffron frills, frittering in the breeze, all colour coordinated to match her candy-coated hot hula hoop, covered her to save on play-wear & tear of the floral-knit garment. Unaffected, she was frolicsome.

In an almost comatose swoon, as Rutherford relaxed so supinely on his bunk berth, the nearly never-ending dreams garnished this girl to be more *human* than what was human! Beneath the underbelly of the ballooned Vacoonery, in any case, she too had been insuperably unaffected by boisterous bustle, rampage, and romp of the township square where blissful blessings were ever so separated from spendthrifts of squandering squalor that ran intermingled. Even at peak season, lucrative among merchants and consumers in their hurry-up heyday, *Holiness* preserved her very own legacy. Even spartan Germans of old upkeep had their fair share of the bounty bargain and blared ardently in unison, **alles ist in Ordnung**!

Of course, this somewhat sharp saying was reverberated throughout the Transalteratorium from out of one's hypnagogic state previous to the time-slot these two souls occupied. Both Rutherford and this little missy were well on a rigmarole!

Of course a parallel with the old hymn, When the Roll Is Called Up Yonder, yielded more plausibly the exact same outburst. Originally crafted by James M. Black. For way back then, in the early-to-mid 1940s or so, when church members answered roll call with a scriptural reference, one youthful girl, out of diffidence, failed to respond. According to historical records, she was Bessie, an adolescent impoverished visitor. She was invited by a rather young Sunday school teacher who also led worship and praise. The thought, although not biblically accurate, brought this prayer to the lips of Mr. Black: "Oh, God, when my name is called up yonder, may I be there to respond!"

Inspired by this endearing incident, he had wished to compose such a message and threw it on the piano with music topped off in his heart and soul. To this very day, around 168 years later, when our year of 2113 was about to expire, the lyrics and notation have survived in an old hymnal tucked away by holographic drawers of the TATM ledger. Here are the words that were accredited to James M. Black (it has never been altered by one jot, nor ever will be):

When the trumpet of the Lord shall sound
And time shall be no more,
When the morning breaks, eternal bright and fair;
When the saved of earth shall gather
Over on the other shore,
And the roll is called up yonder, I'll be there!

CHORUS
When the roll is called up yonder,
When the roll is called up yonder,
When the roll is called up yonder,
When the roll is called up yonder I'll be there!

Yet amiable entreaty herewith. This delightful girl~ geisha garbed only by appearance, but entirely angelic~ topped off an insight, suggestive of a metaphysical import, said, "Namely, no worriment then. For that oblong creature you see here, looking like a corpulent cucumber, as it were will-o'-the-Wisp, is only a canister creation as displayed by the Vacoonery container no less." The Tokyo girl smartly brandished her clip-fold locket that showed

josei / 女性 – and a supplementary haiku for keepsake therewith:

The lake is serene:
Fireflies ignite themselves
Like the Milky Way

It was the TATM's way of expressing her as girly and properly female~ as if to emphasize the token of a uniquely irreplicable and irreducible creation. Her very violet aura moreover had such surest attributes bespoken of inter vivos, or among the living.

They were stunned by what was revealed. Or could it be that this tuberous barnacle 'gweduc' had been rummaged up for them all, clandestinely? He had gathered her name to be Mallory, long forgotten by her family; whose mother died, plagued by the early onslaught of *blets*, and her father drafted to the War; nay, never to return.

Rutherford in his lucid dream pried at her demeanor rather rudely at that, forgetting the child's choice for decorum, but then withheld his tongue and entreated her kindly, "Mind if I ask, young lady, if at all it could be a gateway into another dimension?" Her face featured furrowed puzzlement. Still, the living lamp entity dawned on both of them to be that of some observer of Oracles.

Warily watching the pedestrian stampede, from the Vacoon's point of view, down cobbled streets to their separate destinies all foreordained by some higher provident divinity; directing the vast show upon a stage for hundreds of generations past, present, and far in the future... Rutherford beheld, nonetheless, how she~ this twee, adorably diminutive girl scout at summer camp~ just stood there, ill-forsaken and perhaps institutionalized otherwise! Maybe castigated out of the lower class oppressed by aristocracy or ritzy gentrification that aims to corrugate an amalgamated affluence of upbringing; a rationalistic cultivation galvanizing a youth's more intuitive sensory sway, but by necessary faculty alas! Japan back then was altogether foreign history for the once colonel. But yet rankless Rutherford on his prefabricated TATM vacation uttered nothing about his crewmen to the regenerated replicant.

In time, Miss Mallory, nine years old and on up, wore well-knitted play apparel in the ultraconservative, iron-clad age of gal gorgeous gingham gown embellishments given over to courtly costumed theatrics. But in such circumstances on a Tall Wall, the negative-numbered timekeeper crept counterclockwise nonstop. Backwardly to an earlier Via Lactea of our Milky Way spiral.

O galloping galaxies! rookies and even the journeymen wail.

No, not until frock, cloak, or coat courtesans counterbalance the fragility of grave growth primal. Old knickerbockers for men and bloomers for woman's formal attire in the epoch of 1908. An insipid anachronistic android zeroed in upon by the mid-air loony Vacoon! The gentlemen of this day and age wore a top hat crown, crowding the streets and an occasional ladybug bourgeois topped with either a tiara or bonnet, belt-bangle beautifully arrayed; that had stylized an out-of-doors bazaar at the Coney Island Carnival.

Whence petticoats underscore power-line and telephone insulators as well as women's crepe de Chines that buckle evenly with accordion pleats underneath, all girded up at loony Luna Park.

The nostalgic festivities folded back into the TATM ledger…

But to his disappointment, the ephemeral hula hoop "ojō-san" (お嬢さん) faded out of sight, merely to be supplanted by Carl Jung's solemn *self*, or albeit *anima* alter ego aloft a lone ladder, straining at a gnat of visionary vistas he had hoped to come true. Now the blankest slate and slab of see-through infinity, before its colossal collapse, induced him to endless possibilities of lifetime blessings, bounties, or of a horrible hex and curse godforsaken. Depending upon what dire destiny or detour of direction one waged to tackle.

That such was the premier premise behind a self-supported, suspended Vacoon verily vaunted from out of nothingness itself was a marvelous feat! Overhung out of nowhere, full of nihility.

Obviously, even our own turn of the century back then had waxed oblivious to existential exigencies of that Vase of Grace herself as with all other eras and generations to follow. The little girl's reminder hissed succinctly into one's auditory conch shell, resonantly stimulating the cerebral cortex briefly after her center stage-front final exit: "Thus the nature of radiant reality…" the little missy maintained. A parable par excellence for every Age!

His non-wet dream (unlike listless underdog *nodders* now inconvenienced, voiding themselves due to temporary, if not totally *temporal* enuresis) dryly dwindled to naught and self-concluded the moist matter until nothing more was to be ever dredged up!

Ultimately, all of them could not recall any probe prod into Tara's resolute dream~time. It's as if her protocol of deliberate concealment had set up some psychological roadblock cul-de-sac, or her have-it-my-way *redcard culvert* of hellbent mesmerism to run amok. Simply put, she was inaccessible and unreadable, as was her stylus cuneiform scribble dreadfully illegible, and even that to their interrogatory dismay of crimping cross-examination.

* * * * * *

¶ Offhandedly so, amid weest hours of daylight dawn, the cutlass-tempered Lady Tesla fancied her shuffle and cavorted a card game of UNO. Protectively, they held on to each other, Rutherford, Harris, and Hathaway, arm-over-arm fully embraced for impact. By now, with four more hours left, the enlarged, wan, lunar-like supernal Super Sphere of unfathomable symmetry creepily crested everyone's outback view as they closed in on it, even from several thousand kilometer distant disclosure! Madame Tesla, whom they had addressed as Doctor so-and-so, by then turned to an escort host that ushered in for them what they had never seen before, nor that which one could ever see again, or at least for an as-of-yet unaltered interminable timetable.

Tara intertwined her fingers and steepled them. Underhanded handsomely and of comeliest composure. With two hand knuckled into a miniaturized Transalteratorium steeple in which were **these** *people* 'that thou seest here': the whole kit and kaboodle.

Broadcast! The conductor bellowed on some qui vive via *radiotronic* reminder: "Dear ladies and gentlemen, dimensional displacement is about to occur in the next few moments! Please produce provisional recourse and prepare yourselves upon our arrival at tee minus ten hundred hours *ante meridiem.* In other words, for the time being, no worries! Have a fine luncheon. Until then, over and out…"

His officious announcement made just about all of the passengers chuckle. In fraught~freshened up amusement, Joyce grabbed the bull by its horns and pasted her countenance against Harris's seat window. Overextended by slightly inter-dimensional distortion, sagging over his lap now, the two cones of her brassier brushed against his upper thighs thoroughly.

"Well, what have we here?" he muttered; quite curious, if not aroused. "~ Okay, in all likelihood, what do you see, my dearie?"

She stiffened stolidly, and at last felt like madam Marie Curie, our 19th century pioneer in the detection of radioactive rays that emanated from raw ores such as Polonium and Radium, so Geiger counter clocked in her heyday! In her buttoned up gingham- as if to reenact the behavior of first faint observation upon Uranium^{238} aglow and its aftereffects, whereby awhile years later Doctor Curie sadly contracted Leukemia- Joyce became statuesque over Boyd's lap. She appeared perplexed if anything; outstretched over him, watching out his window. She chastely challenged, "I can see vast vistas, but only at a very far off distance, whereas within closer proximity, nearby objects are smeared and grow indiscernible due to our stupendous speed."

They witnessed how the *bullet ballet*, as was well known over scuffles of handyman banter, revealed a gala goddess of total technology. A type of luscious Lady Luck within some huge hula hoop tube-tunnel wrapped roundabout its girth, hugging her smartly upon billboards of [for nostalgic purposes] halftone quantum OLED videos. By such means, an old advertised Marlboro Bore reanimated fleeting images of their rocket sled that was slipped or slapped into a 357 magnum, but upheld by some playboy Funny Bunny in times past; remnants of a handgun revolver cartridge caricature. Its bygone era of what once we collectively had to crawl out of lest horrid wholesale annihilation could have cast a razor-sharp grapnel deep into our salacious souls, never ever to be yanked out… But this Tube Top, as many have renamed it~ within which we slid through at a breakneck death-defying stunt~ had glimmered its crystallized, dimly detailed translucency on Rutherford's cabin CRT glow screen whose rogue radar blip bloated up into a pit stop picture tube of holographic scintillation.

There was no misnomer about it.

For what she, Hathaway, had haphazardly watched were timeline conduits of pipework "unitubularity" coined by Special Relativity engineers and experts alike; having held Albert Einstein's effigy long lionized by BT public servants hither and yon. Again, with a keen catch of frenetic movement, still at a programmed prance and gallop of Mach 1, Himalaya mountain sierras loftily lurched on by beyond the ferocious foreground of incalculable incoherence as it appeared. One would wonderfully philosophize heretofore upon the outright silly impermanence of it all, ah! Except for space-time itself; the vacant nothingness that should contain the whole gamut! Until the spectators saw how hilltops had tapered to colossal cones or *cone caps* that attained stratospheric, towering top-o'-the-world status quo. Whoa! Wide-eyed were he and she (all of them)! Although this had been but a far outcry prelude~ or call it prefatory glory~ to that herculean Hyperwhole Supersphere singled out; an incontestable mother flagship to which we willy-nilly slip-slid along to tiny crushed comparison. Any lesser thing had been disenfranchised from its lunar-sized, continent-wide curve.

And undeniably so, little if ever did all of them realize the radiant ramifications of it compared to mere mortal volume. Yea, even the deliberate displacement thereof. Even more like some incomparable star-sized Super Ball ballooned billions of times larger than any of our tellurian cities. Moreover, multitudinous, myriad-mantled to those coniferous pylons spotted from a discreet distance. Gigantic mercurial mountains of a quicksilver frozen tundra, though for now, as if solidified gelid; topside tapered up and out into a cryogenic crater or cradle for unmatched Super Sphere complexity complete…

Imagined upon Rod would assume. After all, his fore-gleam of the aforesaid revealed an ultimately curved contour seemingly supernal, multifaceted for but heftier Holographic Time Dilation~ that is, referring to that dreadful Vacoonery captured in dreaming!

"Hey, wake up!" she shot back at him hard, needing to interrupt the daydream that buttressed his speculative fancies for something even more outlandish. "I can't help but admit, oh how everything around us~ not to exclude our on-board *nanoguage* readout~ is slowing down, drastically; why-- look!"

There, before everyone, and rather wraparound inside-out of the vestibule of folded up spacetime, the fluminous flow and flux of an entire motion picture and montage filmstrip in 3D lumbered to a crawl... and then had hit a still picture freeze-frame!

Kept cautiously, Harris felt fidgety by his fairest sitter, but she was rock-still along with Rutherford himself. In the wink of an eye, he, too, turned to stone from Medusa's marvel. For as in the universal flip of a relay switch, lurched lazily all of existence (except for the crew) down to sub-stationary stasis in suspended animation. Aside from feeling quite quelled, Rutherford was confounded in utterly hapless, dread-naught numbness. Full fear seized him. A little later, rational repose resumed whilst Fate fumbled for her reciprocity- other than premeditated murder on an Orient Express, figuratively furnished.

Then the shock wave walloped Rutherford with R.R. revival!

No longer in dismal disarray of an infrared blush, but on an interminable "Mure" walled up and down, back and forth *ad infinitum*. The now **Ready Room** of the Super Sphere had prepared people for its ultimatum, as it were. It dawned on the colonel, as he had suspected, that the others, even all the crew of riders, were frozen stiff to the same exact thing. For such paranormal phenomena at had gotten a grip of EVERYTHING! Immediate Lunacy in and of *Herself.* So stupefied far and wide, he had grappled for a legitimate lock and load.

As if having now turned to mortal mannequins, the iron-clad faces were instilled on Hathaway and Harris. And even Tesla was poker-paved with unchanged, eternal astonishment of shock and awe. This brief occurrence supported his first *prima facie* fact that he was not the only one to undergo this anti-tributary transition! But secondarily- and most imperative- the sluggish, yet yellowish fantastically contorted far-away super cones immensely marched on by!

So this had been somewhat like an aftereffect as the Bullet Barrel Magnetron Electropod would zero in on its ending terminal at the insurmountable Super Sphere silo... Incredible! His gaze widened with arched eyebrows.

Still, during the prolonged timeless *tableau vivant*, he fell facilely with a foam-soft canister creation, out of nowhere to be bound ever so lithely thereby. For this cushion-contoured cocoon of elastic foam support 'circummured' his persona indefinitely, only having been appended fore-and-aft until open-ended. The two big bottlenecks of each side thereof served as an exit or entry thereunto. Thus the in-betwixt entr'acte.

"Aha!" he blurted in realization. It's as if his foreordained fancy of chimerical companionship had been carefully prepared just for his personage inside out, that is. The catch-22 coddle of it was meant to mollify and assuage one's discomfited demeanor whensoever a BT rider longed for an intermission. In other words, his tutelary cocoon waded with him henceforth from this time-frozen vigil of unreality. Furthermore, he was assured that the other souls, not unlike himself, were proffered their prefabricated bestowals, since they too had kept their part of the guardianship bargain; this leaving them all but perfectly protected indubitably. The colonel fell over, transpicuously tried by meltdown lull.

And so, as an unseen videotaped movie in real-time; as an audio/ visual recording resuming playback from its long, drawn out incontrovertible pause, EVERYTHING at once went forward now, normally…

Yet scarcely he had known how that viable vial of suppleness- an envelopment of some type- clung to his often boorish backing. The inner-lined "balloonium" so self-designed to manifest itself upon one's very vast zenith vistas of an entirely outstretched, multiplied Maze. He would venture to disclose hitherto undreamt of enchantments whilst far more important matters clamored at hand; namely, these three: Tara, our persistent guest, a female version of Doctor Who devoid of rank and regalia, and himself relative to the Transducer Transport with Hathaway and Harris.

Now Joyce was the foremost to react, then the doctor, as they all *snapped out of it.* Harris on edge imagined a panicky jitterbug instead of the original one fit for the 1940s big band era with swing accompaniment, but for a little bit. Stealthily, Turntable Time crept (uneventful-forward) as felt all over, and no rider's remonstrance rose against it. With wistful longing, somehow our colonel could not forget Mallory in his dream the night before.

The little princess sheathed in a kimono dress, whose memory persisted, dragged on for the conclusion of his Lazy Eight slip-trip.

THE BOBSLED SLOWDOWN

(with special effects inserted into the screenplay)

In our pervasive suspense for the unavoidable, the last couple of hours narrowed to minutes whereas the out-of-doors had been bent back almost obscenely. Gravity bound by the big SS presence!

¶ Their spruce arrival at the Super Sphere complex came to pass as the announcer confirmed it with wide "Welcome! And please visit us online again the next time around." But with warning: "In 9 minutes, we'll dock at the plank and platform edge. Please stand be prepared!"

A zip and a twang; with whizzing! A squish, swish and ...

Suddenly! Deceleration doubled discomfort all over ere everyone felt plastered, plumply plumbiferous underneath extra crash-padded buckle belts. Noticeably, the conveyance convoy trundled to a slow steady pace until, after two hundred kilometers per hour in slow motion, outside scenery took on exquisite shape. All turned to normal again, or was it a transport triumphant?

...Deceleration! Excruciating twinges ran up & down spines and spleens yellowed with withdrawal symptoms from somnolent complacency. As far as one can tell, the unheeding and unprepared overslept until all of them were juddered out of their dream-state-induced and *over-the-rainbow* utopias! Judy Garland evanesced...

800... 400, 300~ all the way down to 200 and then 100 kph... "Steady as she goes!" someone managed to warble, gasping for oxygen.

The OW-team prefigured that the 24 hour interval was confirmed by the conductor, and Tara- only to fill in for the paucity of it all- had entirely vanished out of sight. Maybe reverting to her own quandaries at the supersonic control thermal station earlier on, Rutherford remembered. Hathaway gleamed at the bustling, but Meticulous Metropolis that cradled the unwieldy Sphere, whereas Harris rechecked his computation as to the time differential and wherefores thereof, and so forth. "It seems to me that the deception is on their part altogether, deputy," our cocky captain mulled over the thought on who ought to have been bludgeoned for blame and shrugged, Shrek-like.

To record his primitive prickle of a creeping mental picture, the TATM archived his cerebration as with all other psychology samples inside its simulated matrix. Its all-seeing electric Eye, in similitude of Hal 9000's unwavering watchfulness, scanned the neocortexes of each subject subordinate to a Tall Wall. Like the heuristically-programmed algorithmic computer from 2001: A Space Odyssey, the gable ornaments breasted and plastered upon high ceilings of intramural gymnasiums throughout the TATM all resembled the convex fisheye that offhand offered the facelessly suspicious and unfriendly look. But these disclosures were kept concealed from anyone ever finding out!

Ranks resumed their full fanfare for some reason after the vast Vacation vacillated between a more formalized manner and for that former fun timestamped. Lest ambivalence would have bucked like a riderless bronco, its glitz of a holographic glitch was resolved for reestablishment of the latter end thereof…

A few rows away, with cosmetic bow ties cross-hatched over two animal cages, a contribution was supposed to be delivered on this train to consumers waiting at the platform. Peevish pig snorts and duck quacks were heard; how coincidental for our Off World wanderers which whacked a tiny gnat nipping their flesh due to an inferiority complex concerning the little critter.

Joyce the re-ranked deputy about-faced and lit up languidly at the captain, "It seems so… *sigh*, and off to that super-duper Ball of a time, darling~" (they had developed a fond bond for each other)

"Two minutes and counting, and the dockyard is ours," old colonel Rutherford, rank-restored, cut in.

"Why, what of the hypnosis session, and the dark Red Room I had experienced~ and… and you too!?" she rumbled in rebuttal.

"Hell, how do I know?" her mature mentor muttered glumly.

Somewhere, still, one's grim grimace and facial fury with weight of a *grimoire* grossly reared an ugly head. An old heirloom of the Transalteratorium trained dispatch personnel had his hawk-eye targeted on the OW-team, primed for his precipitous swoop, ready to take his prey with harpy flesh-piercing talons.

The disappointment of their puerile pit stop; yea, of a lifetime languor, was not just skin-deep, but bone-and-marrow or bellyache that gnawed at them in this expedition. Their Time-Dilator was the sneaky culprit that elongated a global voyage into several days at a time! However, he desisted complaints of the like, albeit truncated, axed up short or no. Joyce just as well, since scientific compliance was wedged into her for a prime directive definitely of the essence.

And in no time at all, after the rocket sled slid to a freeze-frame, that they gathered themselves, alighted the bullet, and had reentered Reception. Backpack valise-burdened disembarkation floundered and flounced down the Uni~Loop Station to the chief checkout turnstiles. And with rider patronage of gratuitous dues owing, the bedraggled customers unbuckled their billfolds; their *ma'ams* and *misses* nearly curtsied themselves into stylized bonny *bequeathals and dowries* for feeling fogged up by a memorial malaise and ever overwrought (mentally managed, of course)!

Others, with pent up adrenaline, leapfrogged over each other in uncivilized behaviour.

"No charge! No charge," nodded the accommodating crewmen that gently nudged the uncouth of the unruly to be deboarded: "Orders on the house!"

"Well, I'd like to know why-" whined one complainer who had stumbled off the last step of the Bullet Hull and onto terra firma he was wont to kiss while his escort butted in: "Hush up! Now, move along, Lou!"

But now, the uttermost part of our 'gloratory' story...

In~Shine Incorporated and the with the endorsement thereof.

"Wow, wind tunnel typhoon at category 20!" their handout guide declared, pointing his bony finger at the scorch-rod atop the bullet cask of what riders sat inside of. He was the railroad's mongrel, according to rumors. The brown-noser Scrooge scraped up scraps of mission platitudes and hearsay from among the yappers of soap opera opulence. The frailly deceptive witch doctor proudly showed off to Rutherford the topmost seared sight, with well-seasoned and convincing expertise. Hell, its rooftop radiator which was used to isolate aerodynamics measurements was badly burnt, toasted to a crisp; a bizarrely baked molten fudge pap due to extreme pressures of heat-drag and hot temperature, as if it were an inflamed mole like the one on that folklorist. A long history of supersonic speeds was the probable cause for depreciation of the fail-safe device.

"She'll definitely be missed," mumbled a funny wannabe, gazing at the exasperated engineer and conductor comparing notes.

"But how so?" pried Harris hanging on to Joyce, frowning at whom he stereotyped as a low hobo, hobbyist, or railroad novice. "Don't these big babies go out of commission after several round trips, lad?"

"Nah, not in the least..." the funny wannabe youngster beamed back at him toothily and trotted off (dissolving into the TATM).

But the dispatch guide, who was specifically assigned to the OW-team, was a scraggy, gaunt elder fellow Rutherford didn't approve of much as the colonel still sulked petulantly from the premature prevenience of their end-of-journey showcase. The hyper-loop old-timer pointed out poignantly: "Do not let the sleek steel of the BT mislead you into thinking she's alright~ Heck, you've heard about that darned mishap malfunction aboard, awhile back, didn't ya?"

They all were reticent to reply as Rutherford ignored him and wondered about the missing doctor Tesla rather, and of her hidden whereabouts. Even to overlap this hoopla, he envisioned Mallory. Harris gentlemanly clutched Hathaway's luggage and handbags and hobbled along, almost injured by time-dilation displacement! But on the other hand, overwhelmingly, the enormity of the Sphere itself dwarfed everything until to the utmost of its southern, big-bellyful penumbra that eclipsed them straightaway. And even so, the poor old sop's importunity, trying to taunt, prompt, and prod the knowledgeable colonel into a spell that didn't work, and even the memory of their Transducer Trip, trickled away in everyone's merest memory as an almost deleted occurrence; a sort of counter-causality compensated for, that had sunken into blip blowups of conflation… But yet then dangerously deflated down to crisply crimp scrimps of shriveled shrinkage burnt off of a frying pan if not tossed into the fire of entropic incineration. The ferromagnetic furnaces distantly lurked in the back-alley of an augmented repose from which they were awakened at long last.

Deliberately, deputy Hathaway logged into her cyber-wallet:

One would call it the nacreous "Narrowest Ferromelt" of the impossible as we witnessed backward Time with ciphers dangling off of railroad turntable clockwork schedules. At once, the UNIS 236 at long last had materialized in our viewership doubtless. For amongst hyper-pyramidal pylons fore-and-aft, up and down and wraparound throughout, the long awaited for gold LUCIOPOLIS star~city unfolded! Full o' slip~trip portals to eternity.

She folded up her hologram booklet and isolated it for the record. *If ever she should return to Mitchelville in one piece...* the *what-if* contingency plagued her forethought with such sullen forebodings.

Notwithstanding a no-go gulch ready to entrench and choke her to death~ mentally as it were~ it was her heartfelt but hardcore scientific impression of the upcoming Star City's replacement of train trip timetable directories and dials of… *(dilation?)*

Only beforehand, how the vague malfunction of their BT supersonic system flashback pried at her mindset with an ancient country ditty, circa 1978! (Toronto, Ontario in Canada had long turned to "Protoronto" amid the 22nd century; yet she stuck to its original namesake & landmark monument of the lyrical litany):

CNT*

I'm gonna go aboard
The express train to Toronto;
It'll barrel up a horde
Of riders to Toronto.

Our ticket's half price
And my love's by my side!
The two of us are ready
For one helluva ride.
The rolling stock is ready for
Her railroad track to Toronto.

A switch and semaphore
Beyond the gate galore
Opens up a whole new world
For my Love forevermore.

We're gonna get aboard
The express train to Toronto;
We'll watch the by and by
Of Canada~land, O my!
To tubular Toronto...

Yon semaphores are green
But blurriness is seen~
Would that thick fog go!

Still, the speed is ninety-nine;
I'm feelin' mighty fine;
My Love just kisses me
And sure enough, she'll shine!

We're a-barreling on through,
Long-distance numbered new
For phototubular Toronto...

**Canadian National Tower*

And abruptly the landmark of a monumental memorial fled, only to be superimposed by unprecedented *Protoronto* in futurity instead thereof. Protoronto, as it were, or *protopolis* spiculed with hundreds of CN Towers and so ferro-forested through its *metroaortae* of monolithic multitudes overlit by beacons: neutronium Nuclearcs that each quiver a tenacious Teflon Tongue!

The empowered endowment of which wields (FAT) Fat Arc Tube technology of (TOP) Total Output Power, in brief, brazenly, the *Protoronto inter vivos* ...

¶ The nowadays 'quarter-giga-populous' or +250,000,000 inhabitants gargantuan gaudily Golden Horseshoe half-surrounding holographic Lake Ontario's paved Permacrème. A glorified *glishoe* GLIBOLOTUBULOPOLITZ inter-dimensional Hypercity!

No, nothing vaudeville, maudlin, nor burlesque; neither fit for a loony bin rubber room, if delirium daunted us so! In that to-the-hilt of molten, vaporized swords at the Mercy Seat of *luminiferous* brilliance the Star City had hitherto cast.

And that with such sapphire opalescence extreme, exceeding bright; the very last serif of a character deprives interpreters of any ultrahigh definition thereof. For Hathaway, Harris and Rutherford- even that scrawny screwball, our guide o' guardianship- were floor-flattened and flabbergasted by the very elegance of it, needless to retract from a very verbose, overdone overture of such sought-out selfsame inklings!

Now what of the prefatory Red Room? Joyce and Rutherford were deeply induced by absent Tara's and subconscious Mallory's hocus-pocus. The penultimate questionnaire quiz buffered by such sartorial as they, quashed the conviction, let alone compunction of but coy conscience. Behind the curtains of genetic Transmutation: that of ourselves as readers confronted by what was metaphysical.

Whose emollient ameliorates multitudes upon arrival! Kept within dimensional distribution of an old Super Sphere complex, the UNILUCIOPOLIS surpassed about every phantasmagorical, allegorical, kaleidoscopic contortion of Vision. No, not at all off of Rutherford's rocker, nor a bunch o' bunk that could hinder him to convey- as if everyone became mannequins, figurines, doll-like liaisons at a wax museum whence Time tottered to death upon the vacuum of a tableau vivant- sheerest shrapnel of meteoric impact equivalent to Tunguska, Siberia that exceeded a 12 megaton yield! Yea, and if so, then access denied! Just as it was recorded near the Podkamennaya Tunguska River in Yeniseysk Governorate, Russia, on the morning of 30 June 1908!

No, not as inchoate as inside the doughnut of a Lazy Eight!

The three stragglers with the elder, who had fallen behind the Electropod entourage swearing and swarming so around the Super Sphere Complex, flailed up their arms in surrender. In restitution & reliquishment to hot californium corncobs that swagger in an eerie electric gust of ozone, gilt up garishly, as glitz-glazed in blindingly (blitz-o'-fits) brazen bright luminosity: the upright torpedo-topped hyper-pyramidal UNIS 236 shimmered showily~ gaudily agleam!

The colonel (restored to Full Bird rank) quickened the thought that if- at terahertz plus frequency of AC- the amperes go low, then propagation is maximized.

Non-momentarily that is! Secure in perpetuity. Perennial.

Paved with surest permanence unlawful to be uttered! The very confluence and convergence thereof more enduring than the wayward, inexorable Rolodex of a rotating carousel causality. The *uni~toroidal* terminals of a billion Tesla coils lightning-lit up could ne'er compare to its *In~Shine* Incorporated. No, not by a long run. For through a vignette of a fisheye aperture, via prismatic slip-slit of observation, Joyce and Roderick squinted at the Harsh Glare of it never to fizzle out of existence, but stay wholeheartedly Hypercity! The zero magnitude stellar glorification *in vacuo*, of which minibuses had scooted away, flinching, cringing until rawhide goose-flesh of carnal skins scuttle to a frightened frazzle; by the "irretinal" shortwave hot gamma ray recall of firebug *luciferin electroluminescence* at the strong nuclear subatomic level. Pockmarked, buck-skinned were they!

Never mind the juggernaut of a Big Sphere to house an amazing multidimensional UNILUCIOPOLIS apart from those rows of lighted goose-necked cobra head lamppost lanterns of the 70s and 80s; all mercury vapour filled in their flat-bulged benign arc tube longevity. The ex-riders had their proper quorum, the three of them off-train, and recorded the *prima facie* evidence of this hyper city, the UNIS 236 in brief. No, not one thing whatsoever addressed has had the resplendence of an all-pervasive night porch, scorch~white torchlight obscured and naughtily nude!

With realization, they stood agog at the splendor of it all, by golly. Entranced tremendously thereby, but lucid as ever. For soon after their peek at the supernal City, reality slammed them against the Wall rock-hard. And midst a madcap milling-around milieu of collectivism that dissects adhesive tree frogs for the glue itself, and among bovine benefactors of aristocratic gentrification, they held their ground for what the wink of an eye had beheld boldly. Our quite sheerest glimpse *sub specie aeternitatis*, where over thirty thousand foot spires of thulium, tungsten, and titanium-tough temperance withstood the masts of mortality awry and amok with war. For naught went against these finely fortified fortresses of super-cone-contoured hyper~pyramidal pylons. As taller, inverted stalagmites monumental, that rise to thirty six thousand footsteps upward into thinly rarefied ether; reaching up at an overhung, ultraviolet Empyrean of Heaven herself. **END OF LINE**

Moreover, by belt-buckle bivouac of her glorious glimpse- as if militarily maintained against mass oppression and wickedness- for any sop cannot remain neutral, nor lukewarm in the face of pure evil that mortals may conjure up- Joyce did divulge a smart disposed of document replete with versified intentions. The verses of which whisper the followup feeling:

UNIS

The Invortiums tower up ever aloft
To yon ether of Heaven bulged soft
Indestructible whilst times go oft
Incorruptible far above Undercroft

In the softness of wind oily
Ere reality enters cessation;
Whilst ev'rything be royally
So subliminal under creation,
Be it she evermore boil-free:
An emollient for preparation.

At a countryside quietly wet
Or some city or town only so
Anechoic my glory yields yet
Garish gold, an Aurora aglow;
For I quell any violent debt
Via lithest of spirits below.

Amid spirits o' entity birth
Whence antiquity verily fell
I'll unveil immaculate mirth
Mist mercurial ready to tell,
So ethereal gibbous by birth
Armored up over any old Hell!

Insulated congealant elastic,
Of immunity mantled maternal
In an oily lurid glass thick
Or as mercury molten eternal,
There, reality never drastic
Is a lithe liquefier diurnal.

Holy blue rays inviolate hot
Are distended in parallel so
Gilt aloft upon any old grot
Agleam lucent supernal aglow
Via vaunt above any fox trot;
Be it Vega agleam by thy woe.

If we badger each other alas
While doggedly vomits up war,
Resurrected Transducer amass
Puissant power reliable more
Ever able to crater up glass
Full o' luces availed galore.

Amongst superstars aureately
By comparison sewn candlelit,
Ultraviolet ere glory yet be
Vital Vega ne'er violent hit;
Be a fusion reactor net-free!
Coil spicules inviolate flit.

Via whitecaps invisible warm
Holy yield far away verified
She unfolds in an oily swarm
Avionic, that never had died;
As a cyclone available storm
So pervasive until clarified.

So transparently hung verily
Wi' one wide Luciopolis tall
My stalagmites about merrily
Mirror me on an amity sprawl-
Sacred Aether atop very free:
I am she far above any brawl!

Let it be that I try wearily
Lucent Lustre o'er oily city;
Mist mercurial bulged eerily,
Miry spires available pretty
With one wet Luciopolis lily
Mid my hot rubicundity witty.

Whilst hideous sin salivates
When wan profligacy is awing,
Iridescent rainbow permeates
Global glory across anything:
Holy Field fabulous elevates
Her entirely merciful Spring.

2

I am she Shine invisible hot
By my permeatory harsh glare
Midst an old Luciopolis grot
Of stalagmites atop anywhere;
O immune to whatever may rot,
Many missiles of fury I wear!

Against tyranny global aloft,
At oppressors how violent so
My mercurial glister is soft
As a corncob effulgent aglow;
For I shimmer her entity oft
In vacuity vouchsafed I grow.

Full o' fusion reliably sewn
With inclusion inviolate wet,
Via Mercy Seat over a throne
One ethereal sister sits yet;
That vicarious often unknown,
Ever radiative, void of blet!

My reactor band only gluonic
Be adhesive cohesion for all;
Holy corncob united photonic:
Vitrifier on any vast sprawl.
Supple Bottle begirt avionic,
I surpass any labyrinth wall.

H-ly pylons arise iridescent:
O Reality radiant sprout red
Inner tubular lady incessant-
Luciopolis insular outspread
Of a very vicarious crescent;
I reunify life without dread!

This third part particularly capstones the above two sections to portray the UNILUCIOPOLIS big burg in *unvitiated* clarity:

¶ The OW-team had backtracked this dazzling array of sultry experience while with their well-admired cicerone of presentation cheering them along the way. Rutherford repented of his prejudice of and grudge against the old wise man because of his often political opposition to jaded gerontocracy enthroned in the Mitchelville Headquarters of that grossly greater metropolitan-area upon Earth.

The BT departed and they were piggybacked into a hostel for the evening, attempting to recollect each and every angle of what was envisaged. Instead of starkly concave and curved walls of the Super Sphere module, a friendlier frame of full foam offered each of them vacation commodities overflowing.

Through the high-ceiling lobby of a lounge area, they took a vertitube lift in an 'elevatorium' midway to the 4900th storied level and had noticed how attenuated sheets of cirrus clouds blocked the view of mountainous municipality that crowned the ground down under and far below them. The vertitube lift was fashioned by the Otis Unilink Company that specialized in high-speed up-and-down pod service similar to the convoy conveyance system, but briefer.

The super building, within which all four of them slid up via an *elevatorium* rigged & steel-cabled with hundreds of elevators, stood sleek and smooth upon her glassy upsides, but sharply five-edged. A pentagonal powerhouse of upright obelisk gracefulness five miles heavenward. At her one square mile wide bedrock base, ferroconcrete foundation, and stronghold plinth, the all Wall-Tall colossus remained rock-solid, howbeit flexible in an event of any trade wind gale gust. All in all, she should withstand any upheaval; be it hurricane, cyclone, tremor, earthquake, or H-bomb detonated thereupon. No, naught was able to transmit a quiver of disturbance thereunto; nay, not by mortals! She had been christened Draconis, which meant ***Dragon of a northern circumpolar constellation between Ursa Major and Cepheus**. Immortal and so impervious to conflagration, corruption, profligacy, nor tsunami of any kind, she stood her ground as a radiant replica of a million more just like her that forested this Hypercity as stoic but elastic stalagmites; an entire Petrópolis of them for lack of a defter department! Never as lackluster were they save glistering with blue-shifted, mirrored up blinding brightness, whose harsh glare is too terrible to gaze upon.

Indeed like the similitude, that their mainstay at UNIS 236, bright UNILUCIOPOLIS of district 236, was rather rewarding enough was part of an agenda. Their suites, enumerated as 192 for them and a 291 for their guide, brandished plush pleasantries almost unwarranted. Or just outside UVB tinted windows, the newcomers couldn't count the number of tall & towering Godzillas!

The ultrahigh spires of a strong throng forest upward capped off cumulonimbus cloud banks below... It appeared as if united UNILUCIOPOLIS marched on forever with its huge needlework brigade of nacreous "uppointed" prominence of old Harsh Glare *glorifiers* likened to hot multi-magnetic spicules beneath the Sun's solar corona of electroplasmatic conflagration.

Inside, within the ready room itself, holographic detonations of virtual reality refocused their daydreams while the four of them- bathed by warmth and comfort- luxuriated amidst posh settings: Rococo, palatial, and blatantly paranormal. Nestled in an upland alpine outback of a Winter Park resort in Oregon where part of Stanley Kubrick's The Shining was filmed. O where whooping winds would winnow the cornfield right by an old, obsolete 7-Up soda condiment dispenser! And on the rebound rebus, an anomalous phenomena that dolled up those Twins afoot in haunted corridors of yesteryear... Olden, gold-leaf ornamentation embroidered everywhere, castellated cinder block turret enclosures, and pilaster-pillared and colonnaded corridors of a limitless labyrinth at one's disposal. It was the old "Univermiculatorium" so called by the hologram select-a-channel radio repertoire. Her hallowed hallways, each a *horridor* of the third kind, narrowly necked to and fro, up and down in wormhole 'spaghettification' all throughout, inside out and about. Aloft, the full lull of mellifluous music saturated their quarters quietly, and by nightfall, slender tapered tubules of slimly pyramidal pylons- coniferous contoured- contained the vastest vision of them all. They felt such virtuous, *verecund*, paradisiacal perfection of an ever invincible metropolitan ministry interwoven. Vouchsafed one and only, yielding UNILUCIOPOLIS that they resided in with joyous sagacity~ in terms of an old clarion cliché~ sharp, wary of all things, yet 'happily ever after'. Overhung steadily by anti-graviton levitation across tellurian topography...

More memories inundated the hologram of recovery as the Red Room storefronts became bathed once again with warm wonderful iridescence too lovely to gawk at, save savor up so, intuitively. The previous Vacoon vindicated wonderland blossoms of obsolescence bygone; never to be unearthed and exhumed for Pullman posterity. [Back into the Sheol of a lugubrious crypt]. And Doctor Tara Tesla, venerable as it were with the fondest heirloom of events, faded mid that phantom bullet train she had haunted; instructing still others of a precious preface to the multiplied, top-tapered-slender UNIS 236 molten mother flagship! In that which see for an Eternity now.

With ethereal gossamer at every footing, joyously ever after. O that holy Heavens were overhung with a stellar volley of superstars that would induce deliriums of blinding bliss and ecstasy... Oh forever! The stellar celebration was about to begin and with splendour in the Glass!

No more hard camp of Astoria back at base, the yellow Yard Lamp of Gloria had finally filled Colonel Rutherford, Captain Harris, and Deputy Hathaway with *HERSELF* heartily, wholesomely.

The end of the usage of the purple pilcrow, or ¶!

The Conference Room

Authorized Screenplay Resumption
EERIE SOUND EFFECTS WITH FIRST INTERMEZZO

METALUCELECTROPLUCEPTORIUM? Joyce readily remembered the resurrected intonation thereof-- yea, and to the uttermost: * * * * * * *

Take heart, O daughter of God! For soon your commanding officer shall meet the mistress Glistria of the Mercury Mirror...

H2 (deep in thought)~ *I'll really need to get to the bottom of this, or else--* (sighing) *or else I ain't whistling Dixie!*

OTHER~ *"Heavens! I ain't got nothin' to say!"* interiorly sounded off a southerner from Hathaway's Apache tribe... The incorporeal Voice spoke as if precedent to her mama Montgomery under residence of good tepee tenure. The parched tumbleweed timestamp thereof toughened her doughty, diamond-in-the-rough girlhood. Then the regressive if not embryonic flashback dissolved, unnoticed by anyone watching her.

The Steel Sheet, abbreviated the MLPTM, again guided our upgraded deputy to the denouement of this labyrinthine slip-trip.

But first, their exit out of the Greyhound bus-wide side-swirl called a lemniscate; a figure-eight shaped curve whose equation in polar coordinates is ρ2=a2 cos 2θ, or ρ2=a2 sin 2θ. This was preset calculated accordingly by some Transalteratorium retrieval diskette taken out of a time slot on the outside of the doorjamb. Apparently, they exited the same way within which they entered (one doorway) at the center of the Tardis side-swirl that still reclined for fifty feet across! That they were travelling at high velocity was miraculous!

Once out of the Tardis vestibule, from inner to outer hull, her superiors rebooted their duty roster for the sake of mission control.

"Okay team, let's focus on the assignment and concentrate on our jobs," the colonel suggested brusquely, breaking their dealings with the Vacation's aftereffect. "And you two lovebirds had better get on with it..." He smiled at them and, like them, felt revitalized and refreshed by the Tardis-enclosed outing, no matter how freaky and impossible a roller coaster ride it must have been.

But they concurred that their affair belonged to the holo-suite fantasy program and felt nothing nonetheless for each other; as if completely nonchalant under the circumstances. As if nil occurred between them… Rutherford still empathized and brushed it off in view of the much loftier picture and far weightier wonder at hand!

In light of the aforementioned, the OW-team conducted an authorized briefing and reverted to refuge for themselves right quick. Immediately, in response to such a backing, the Hologram Generator materialized a partitioned cubicle which would wall them in. However, Rutherford, seasoned by physics experience, thought that the overcompensation and overkill of literally an eternal wall spanned out flatly and infinitely across everywhere was way too much to comprehend.

For what appeared like a pure white limbo of nothingness outside of their cubicle had been actually the outstretched flat platform upon which they were stationed. Perfectly horizontal in all directions; but because of its infinite span, no horizon could be discerned from a distance. For if an infinite wall were true, how can any distance therewith be judged in relation to infinity?

Therefore, regardless of how far, or how close in proximity anyone to hover over or stand thereupon should be-- if the far-off horizon is still unchanged due to endless vastness-- one's perspective is instantly engulfed by the ever-present propinquity of the infinite floor itself! Now try *that* on for size! Roiled-up Rutherford began to speculate: *Definitely a paradox of dimensionality, if anything.*

H2~ "Yet on the contrary. It's all about *perception*."

H~ "Jolly well... I agree, Deputy!"

Now that they were off to a cheerleading start, complementing each other rather than bashing their brains out with discipline drills and fireguard night-watch, their Vacation offer needed to be looked at, and even dissected for further analysis. Joyce shivered from this memory of the colonel's military parade and patrol in **Москва**~ or pronounced Moskva for Moscow city in long gone U.S.S.R.~ good riddance to nettlesome, knucklehead hoopla. She avoided the terms jarhead or Pongo... Not that she had anything against an orangutan, nor the seven-foot-wide anthropoid ape or gorilla she had seen on a stage band at the Chuck E. Cheese family entertainment restaurant! Boohoo! But back to the basics.

R (with emphasis on the most recent slip-trip)~ "Do both of you feel normal?"

H~ "Blimey! How on earth could you wonder without her blushing, sir? Believe you me, I cannae violate the blameless lass!" Of course, Deputy Hathaway was referred to inadvertently.

Clearly, Rutherford was not just the Varsity Head Coach, but also the trailblazer, pathfinder or flag-bearer intent on preserving amity in his newfound group belittled by an infinite floor or wall, what have you, depending on what perspective punched you out! Or whereas Joyce was probably the only torchbearer and guiding light, Harris, on the other hand was the northernmost Lighthouse Keeper for any bawdy bunch since he showed hints of familiarity on the vacation; but Rutherford spared his best colleague and big buddy of the nuisance and naughty nudity thereof. The Full Bird refused to babysit them no less! Joyce never pussyfooted around pretentious miss goody two shoes either. Besides, she should not have been promoted to deputy if self-righteousness sauntered on her part, which she despised in her trait of personality perchance!

R~ "I meant to say, are we in one piece and *in peace* with what ever happened to us?" The colonel was more concerned about the welfare of his highly-prized, executive OW-team than in anything else written 'round his leatherneck nape or slashed/ slitted upon his sideburns of facial stubble. Though Hathaway timidly reimagined Rutherford as a long-past dogface redcoat consigned to battlefield barrack duty, his underlying Quantum Physics profession at the Academy counterbalanced the ferocious façade.

H2 (technically inclined) "The inter-corridor consonance of our team tossed a lucky coin in the pool of Lethe as we had forgotten this rather venturesome escapade. If you know what I mean, sir!"

H~ "Speaking of which," turning to her, then to the colonel avidly (appearing as Daniel Jackson well-seasoned with archaeology and anthropomorphism studies in the television series, Stargate, SG-1): "On the flip side of the rocket sled adventure, the reality of mnemonics comes to mind here... Allow me to demonstrate."

Exhibition B: the Forbidden Fruit framed by immaculateness?

Out of nowhere, a prefabricated cot and whatnot narrowed their attention span thereunto instead of on an Endless Vastness outside of their infinitesimally compared cubicle. According to Harris, four eyes were fixed on what he had aimed for to showoff with widening eyeballs suspiciously peeled back on an electronic tabletop-blackboard. Whilst his improvised seminar had begun, a powerful pall of white from the snow-bright Flat Floor behind the temporary partitions would engulf their hyper-tiny existence, yea, if ever there was any inkling of it!

H~ "I did a lot of study on my own and I have a darned good handle on the topic," he gloated, but seemed genuine. "From the Latin terminology, *mnemonicum*, or mnemonic device, the analogy can be drawn up like this..." So he grabbed an electronic chalk marker, placed it into a wheeled cordate cart, called a planchette, to literally let the quick-fix Ouija board really rumble by itself until- to total contamination- the other two were perplexed.

In conjunction with what was requested subliminally, reading the captain's cogitations, the TATM system for its reset power-cut switched off its surrounding vicinity. Without further ado, all of it dissolved into pitch blackness, except for the candlelight, cubicle, and an office-booth where they were seated.

On a tabletop setup was one tiny taper torched up by a flickering fluid flame over a woeful Ouija board. Both Rutherford and Hathaway knew full well about this prohibited contraption in computer courtrooms of the Transalteratorium Tribunal (at least from what they've found out at a prefatory procedure at Camp Mitch prior to this mission). Like the first unrolled reels and spools of ticker tapes ejected out of stock ticker machines, TATM alphanumerical data sheets were dispatched automatically. A long time ago, in adaptation to what was hand-cranked in 1846 by the telegraph companies, the Compound practiced pride for what their old vintages vaunted; even if it entailed ancient ancestors of foregone computer printouts.

Now far above Mitchelville's tread of traffic, fanciest fantastical focused photons furnished the TATM holo-cache.

R~ "Boyd, you should know *better* than that," he admitted, abashed but for the sake of keeping up appearances militarily.

H~ "But bear with me, Monsieur Capitaine," urged the lesser captain to his superior officer. "I need to illustrate spiritualism and its inherent innuendos of deception~"

H2~ "But like this?!" the deputy grizzled. She twirled to Rutherford: "Sir, I've had a helluva tough time before when I dabbled with the occult. And sir, such examples exacerbate my memories of smut! She was on the verge of kicking up a fuss. Fortunately, for him, she had intervened as his confidante.

In the thickest gloom overhung behind everyone's back, Rutherford placed his hand on Boyd's back and patted him in gentle censure, never saying anything so as not to embarrass his commission before unseen ears and eyes of eavesdropping walls, let alone Hathaway's incendiary flare-up! Overlooked by both of them, this triggered her PTSD suppressed by cloying layers through the attempted séance session ready to wax awry.

The bituminous backsides of infrastructures reverberated, rather, behind invisible Tall Walls which funereally loomed by charcoal tar oozing out from drooping curtains that were draped over an Oblivion ablaze. How hotly reactive the TATM was, yet preemptive stricken by such salacious pitfalls, or coalescence of Light and Darkness; *the* incompatibility as impossible as fresh water with petroleum disturbingly distributed… if not diluted.

Then, though acquiescent to Harris's quagmire of unintended conjuring to have induced lamplight shutoff and the cessation of luminous overflow, the Transalteratorium tried him, how harshly! Undulant within its raging rebuke; supernaturally retributive and volcanic if not overboard vituperative:

TATM (with warning and exhortation)~ BUT NO MAN MAY LOOK UPON MY BLANK BODY AND LIVE! YOU MUST ABSTAIN FROM BAD COMPANY, BAD LANGUAGE, AND BAD CONDUCT. FOR AT THIS LAST CONSOLIDATION OF YOUR VOYAGE, WE URGE THEE TO REPENT AND RETURN TO THY ORIGINAL POSITION! YEA, BE BELIEVING AND NOT FAITHLESS. WHEREFORE, WE PROFFER THEE ANOTHER STOPOVER ...

Now as soon as the Transalteratorium chided the captain and the rest of the crew, it was contrition of the heart that conquered their souls forthwith from the start! They prostrated themselves before the intramural convener that harbored unconditional affinity for the human race on our behalf; which the OW representatives had fought for. As it is affirmed: To maintain moral and ethical vigilance in support of sensitive cases.

Either way, with one alternative or the other, a median in the middle of their crossroads highway was put into place and paved. That now led them on before a Trivia (Latin for three-way) at the end of the prescribed tunnel in which its glitz through one orifice glinted, but had been still too far for fantastical propinquity.

Without underhanded snake oil to downplay any world crisis, a direct pipeline, at least at the hitherto level, may have siphoned (if not sucked out) the situation at hand... At once, their tabletop folded up into itself and vanished. The snowy whiteness of every blank-plank on the TATM linoleum, along with whiter than white wall-sides, overpowered devilish darkness to nonexistence. Like aforetime, the anechoic interior therein resumed repose. And there was no more of that Conference Room reeking with woeful Ouija board barrel-o'-fun mischief. Not for kinkier kits of the buckaroo, bootlegger, or buffoon, thought Joyce, but in our momentous times of post-apocalyptic apprehension, misappropriation, like looting or purloining one's identity, and (most important of all) the TATM's disapprobation until the dreadfully telltale Ouija board buckles in.

But now the *closure* of the Transalteratorium exceeded the North American Aerospace Defense Command or NORAD ready room under Cheyenne Mountain in Colorado a hundredfold! For whereas the bunker thereof lies 2000 feet (610 meters) beneath Cheyenne Mountain outside Colorado Springs, Colorado-- a complex grid of six large tunnels are burrowed forth therefrom, connected to a subterranean building made of thick steel plates underpinned by massive coil shock absorbers in case of a nuclear blast or earthquake-- whilst in contrast of the aforesaid, the super-insular Transalteratorium became even more muffled into itself as consecrated for a solely soul-centered purpose. According to Harris and Rutherford rattled out of their insouciant stupor, it made them aware of a karmic payback, or of an irrevocable ripple effect~ (there must always be a counterweight for every lifelong lift).

An eviscerating evincement of self-evaluation, or even *self-evacuation* that suddenly seized their souls to the core had sprung up from their loins laden with quirks and quiddities (such qualities that characterize us as individuals). Regardless of how hardwired they were, an inner nudge would cancel conspiracies and rather fortify the incontrovertible. With a world deficit thereof no less.

Where two boxcars be locked together by heavy *ferro-fist* of a knuckle coupler at the freight yard, efficiently, only an oft ignored, unnoticeable turnbuckle to tighten or loosen the payload is needed, mused Harris outside of his Celtic coat of arms and family crest of emblazonment all glittered up, but unambiguous even so, aye!

Where no landslide, nor cakewalk was welcome well-nigh, reasoned Roderick, but some terrible tug-of-war instead among bickering beasts of burden; a bituminous bed of hot coals could catch the corporate cat's-paw of a drug cartel or warlord thug to convert them otherwise worthy of death if not noticed on pinup and placard corkboards bearing about with *Wanted!* mugshots.

Where water is pumped up from aquifers and donated to an oasis to irrigate a torrid region, contrary to industrial exploitation of the water-bearing, permeable rock, rock fractures, and virginal, unconsolidated sand (as through the hourglass of Time), no lack spiritually, speculated Joyce, jolly, buoyant, & jasper-necklaced.

And though the Transalteratorium was a Brobdingnagian Ogre multifaceted with one billion eyes, it was certainly no cannibal that ought to appertain to the Witch in Hansel and Gretel, the Lamia of Greek mythology, or to Baba Yaga of Slavic folklore. This was the way adjutant staffers at Camp Mitch had huckled away apt or echt effigies of the Transalteratorium Y-shaped, yet ypsiliform contours, and had turned targets out of them for dart-dirking sport. To render reparation thereunto, our converts of Bible-believing voyagers, the colonel, captain, and deputy were cordially convinced of its reality.

Colonel Rutherford along with Captain Harris concluded, how at Ye Olde Candle Shoppe on Main Street in the heart of lower and upper downtown Mitchelville, a veteran lighthouse keeper who got hired then as an antiquarian timekeeper for grandfather and cuckoo clocks complained about why naysayers and gossipers galloped off to the tavern and biker's bar late into the night. After good academy cadets were bunched together with such on shore leave, there arose irreverent revelry against researched images of the TATM Tall Wall that was Y-shaped! Sick imbeciles brandished caricatures in overall impudence, wailing *why, why?* While rowdy rebels of other rabble-rousers ransacked storefronts by the dozen all over town in volatile remonstrance. Therefore, the genuine from the fake had to be sifted out, save not without heavy heartaches at half-staff under homicide that left our lighthouse keeper impaled by a cutlass and a few more stabbed with kitchen knives. *Requiescat in pace for such souls* -.

In time, plaudits & platitudes of misconstrued perceptions had permeated even the precincts into corruptible behaviour when their provost predominated the West Point version of Camp Mitch. Until eventually, they were wont to deploy Off-World paratroopers every now and then. These three were one out of many uniformed before.

With ineffaceable and invulnerable attributes (a top-rate rendering of what was confronted), the TATM framework survived nefarious onslaughts slyly. A deft heft of inter-dimensional interplay from its Hologram Generator unleashed its labyrinthine limbo of hedge-maze contiguity. The convoluted entanglement of intricacies surpassed any prodigy of genius poised at Ariadne's Thread of such complex computation. Nay, not even cerebral internet hackers were ever able to decipher its gigantic googolplex multiplied by a googolplex code of conduct and entry which waxed the Pluriseptiplex equation far beyond quantification. It was a formidable trip into backcountry territory whereupon tightrope tenuity topples the funambulist. Such highwire walkers of the mathematician department tiptoed over the singularity before being disintegrated in the unoccupied natatorium of senselessness, self-extinction, nonexistence, or an utterly listless Lethe of no comparison, nor nothingness, neither exotic antimatter!

Wherefore with metronome cadence that only an atomic clock- such as the ultracold strontium that is accurate to a second off after 200,000,000 years- can imitate, its algorithmic manifestation of but infinitely fine fractals freeze-frame every side of its Warp Maze. In other words, wheresoever one goes inside the Transalteratorium, an infinitude of endless, omnidirectional possibility persists inside-out and outside-in. The ethereal white hue of the blank plank thereof is the quantum foam enlarged a septillion septillion times so that near infinitesimal smallness of super-subatomic Planck units are merely magnified or enlarged almost impossibly! Now this with measured metronomic and palindromic pervasiveness, that the Pluriseptiplex is numbered both backward and forward [alike and selfsame]!*

The author's conjecture concludes the dilation of a different dimension entirely after hypernumbers have been exhausted-- and yet still short of unparalleled and perfectly perpendicular infinity which is infinitely unlike universal existence and nonexistence.

Nothing impromptu nor preparatory to a downhill descent had convinced all of them otherwise as they, the earthlings were woken from their carnal and worldly mindset. There were a few more soft reprimands given by God via angelic intervention, or spherical Orb disclosure, like the twain with Borteum and Cremeum awhile back.

In the unabridged median of this whole HWY system, a quiet lacuna could not be found except in the interim of a time-lapse lull and within the hiatus of a hallowed hush. In starry free fall far and away from everything, and in postponement of some Throne Room judgment only reserved for the evildoers, the Three's Company of colonel, captain, and deputy were destined for the Vertex, the very topmost Conical Helicon of raw reality. Yet one of them, the elder of the threesome bunch, would be the preapproved recipient.

It was he who had the Dunkirk spirit and enough nous to be levelheaded!

The **RECAPITULATION** of Zenith Vistas

There were no more misgivings about the TATM system, and certainly they of the recon team were not naively converted, nor brainwashed. Their ingrown inadequacies deflated down to near-zilch until this then alleviated the deep sense of dread and doom and alienation. Nor was this transcendent entity a Demiurge, as it were an artisan-like figure responsible for fashioning, featuring, and maintaining the physical universe. But on the contrary, rather! The interdimensional, infinitely walled Superpower-- whose only unlimited attribute is endless "immuring capabilities"-- reconciled itself with the OW-team, regardless of their all-too-human sins of the flesh and shameful shortcomings- when under no Grace at all.

Apparently, the flawless matrices of the Hologram Generator took advantage of organic and living holographic memory storage and necessarily possessed full physical and tangible realities that were unalterably permafrost-paved into its *creamiest* cryogenic PRESERVATORIUM wherein everything remains holy, *eternally preserved,* and perfectly protected under absolute zero (or frozen at 273.15 °C on the Celsius temperature scale and to −459.67 °F on the Fahrenheit temperature scale). *Never mind *what* compressors might be utilized in order to deep-freeze the impossible existence!

The TATM network provides Preternatural Pressurization to the laws of physics so as to *bend* them-- not by a black hole, <u>but with White Hole harmonics</u>-- and forcefully create any shape and form desirable out of the ether of utter nothingness; albeit much more opaque, or translucent and transparent; yea, the outcome of which conventional Quantum Physics **cannot permit** to normally unfold in our Observable Universe momentarily!

Essentially, nothing exists in its subatomic Furnace Chamber (the hyper-enclosure of super self-concealment) except whatever is replicated or irreplicable! Thus the Transalteratorium, like an older automated Mnemosyne (mother of the Nine Muses made of eternal Memory), can harness whole universes in an AMBU (artificial manual breathing unit) bag; *alembic* (condenser and conveyor); Kaluza Klein bottle (five-dimensionally sleeved and jacketed for four-dimensional containment); and a two-throated *Hypertube Gemel (a pair of glass bottles blown separately and then fused usually with the two necks pointing in different directions). The technicality thereof ought not to have been belabored for anyone, to warrant a super-symmetrical submission, that is.

*Now notice the new term, hypertube instead of hypercube, we were saying, as the meta-geometry of the Klein bottle is welded with the gargantuan Gemel to make our

Ambulux an entirely new entity unrivaled and unparalleled by all the Others in Yard Lamp of Gloria! The Ambulux can quell anyone on a rampage, be it ballistic or not!

Some find a contradiction in the usage of a Furnace Chamber if absolute zero is reached. But still, in affront of the aforestated affirmation, we are dealing with something outside of space-time, where temperature and color and solidity are not confined to such physical and *psychical* properties pronounced herein. Hence the Preternatural Pressure imposed upon any *thought* caught by the Holographic Hive of an Anechoic Waffled Honeycomb and then transmuted instantly via independent inducers. Wherefore, what even alchemy cannot congeal due to its grosser comparison and inferiority. That far superior than the ordinary and extraordinary laws of cause and effect, have always been, and are, and forever will be the *higher* and *finer dimensions* eternally inaccessible and inconceivable to created 3D mindful consciousness as if indisputable.

Therefore, an incontestable candidate out of the fourfold transducers heretofore addressed is the AMBU bag transformed into AMBULUX: The Contingency Luminaire! The which would accompany only these two: Col. Rutherford and Capt. Harris.

WARNING: Readership discretion is suggested!
Manifest Verbatim [*unaltered report*] *with* NO *Deputy Hathaway*
She's set aside by the Transalteratorium timeline until revealed
later on at the Grand Central Station Terminal, reinserted again
The Original Limited Edition Screenplay from the year 1996:
(to spare the Deputy of a crucible, the TATM tucked her away)

The Vertical Voice had conveyed it to our horizontal humanity unable to comprehend. As light shone in the darkness that found it incontrovertible, so were these baffled pioneers of a new era. In terra incognita, our own humanity poised before something beyond description- our eyes burnt through by it- a glory that shatteringly shines, so *irretinal*- ablaze as Project Procyon or as fiery Sirius beyond compare; a super fusion reactor of seraphic photonics glistering at none other than upwardly extended- that stays full o' rays- God's glorified luminaire- bright, whiter than white. That shines back at God and at naught else, lest the sheer fabric of nothingness be burnt by it.

And there they were, in direct dialogue with what was *Horr'bly H-ly*, as they saw through reverential awe absolutely no relative retrofit to these BT blown large lamps- yet shrunken down to fissured cocoons of observable splendour. When inoperative at daytime, their arc tube jocund jacket perfect packets resembled shriveled gauze crisply in-vitro, but by a jolt in glass jars, at the stroke of a lightning bolt, they became as Quasars that ballooned raw, sterile light out of ionized intelligence- *metalucently* concentrated; of pinpoint-piercing, super searing, harpoon-heavy, ray-resplendent, ultra-shortwave radioactivity.

Colonel Rutherford and Captain Harris for the first time in a lifetime only vaguely sensed a refracted God-consumed presence of it, God-scorched and infinitely torched, before which terminal times flinch away and there is nothing left, save purged vacant space prepared to be populated by a throng of universal plurality. And as some photon torch at its brightest flare factor with limitless lumens-of point infinite zero-one magnitude, the Dog Star of God and none other- had only been forbidding and unlawful to be thought of by any rational mind.

The two men trembled and fell to their faces at the presence of what was *so* sacred- fortunate enough to be concealed away from God's eternal Warp Lamp of transcendent transparency. Their eyes squinting and straining from the lithe ethereal brightness of those ornamental, metalucently lit tube jackets. The tiny streetlamps of focused photons garishly lit-up, obliquely ablaze with such luminiferous life [in] them- their silent sizzle of pearly and emerald cocoons electrified to but starburst fantasy...

For there they continued for a time and a season- in bizarre awakening of some Soviet Union turn of the century city, and yet it dissolved away, disintegrating into thin air, only to leave the significance of those tiny streetlamps afloat *above* them. Whereas buildings had eclipsed the sullen scene with blood and gore, death and darkness, in this newly fashioned, prefabricated brainchild of holographic harmonics, the urban ogre of monstrosities fled from view, engulfed by the blinding flash [and thunderclap] of Oblivion!

Now, nothing but that selfsame walled limbo of the labyrinth returned to them, howbeit with those grave star-bright euthermic arc lamps, seven of them, suspended over their midst; still spewing themselves *stelliferously* as in that KGB spoof!

UNEARTHLY SOUND EFFECTS

"Captain Harris, where is Deputy Joyce Hathaway!?" yelped Colonel Rutherford, rattled, pallid and shocked to the bone.

*"Dunno, doggone it!" huffed Harris. His code of conduct, due to an omitted missing beloved Joyce, was febrile and his behavior fortuitous. It was forgivable in the drastic alteration of the TATM network and timeline for the time being, only to restore Hathaway wholly hereafter, yea, ultimately ushered forth from the ypsiliform, or seemingly Almighty *Wye or Y-shaped corridor (the triangle of a railroad track used for turning locomotives or trains, BUT verticalized) turned to a triangular Trivia, 'triviatic'? Or until the Univatriviatorium takes precedence in lieu of previous props.*

Our two commissioned officers were flabbergasted and mainly mortified by the spell of her abrupt absence, for they depended on her— not by reason of her job, but her personage; paranormal and personal and soulful. Their feeling of loss and accountability only mounted to an unbearable level; the Plight exacerbated by Shock.

For as they ought to have had, they wept within her sudden omission, yet the Transalteratorium was to be trusted at all cost.

Back to business. But in hopes of Hathaway's return, while this floundering twosome took the horse's bridle, broached the brunt of it all, and to-the-hilt! And jousted for their God-given dignity at all odds and daggers drawn draconian against such!

***Inclusions into the original text are bracketed**, viz.,* [...]

(And now, our Authorized Resumption of the Original Text)

R~ "Alas, Captain! We're back where we started, right at that horrid but *fantasmic* TATM system."

H~ "So where do we go from here, Colonel? And what of those Seven Lamps overhead?"

R~ "Yes, of course, as if they were the Seven Beacons of God burnt up to but silent cinders- tremendously torched by a divine presence unawares, unobserved, but uncreaturely apparent. How delicately linked, lemon-like, as on a tenuous tendril of terrawatt life- crisply sizzling away, yet unconsumed in their focused photons of holy-lit life. As BT blown lamps so lucently lucid, and everyone, a Supertron Metatorch of ionized intelligence:

[Ode to the] Capable Paradox

To elucidate into logic that which transcends logic, thus exacted by versified overflow...

Prophetic Objective

Though man may bray a rude vernacular,
To be ballooned all~H ly and oracular!

As dials fleet away and clockworks flit,
Like diamond sparkle glints the City lit.

I saw beyond my margins of twin mind
Her holographic hive relamped, refined,

And could rare scarcely spare a thermal glow
That emanated from large lamps burnt yellow.

Within them, tubed and packaged up, God-sealed

Were wan-scorched capsules bulged yet unrevealed;

Thereof the Outer Armor phosphor-sprayed
Was quantified, dividing light from shade~

Some pearl-spray sprinkled; others, cobalt coated
Lest their light sears wood when creosoted!

Hence their beacon border swirled with white,
Enveloped up, that hurled out orbs of light.

Phase I

How seldom we would grasp this Revelation:
Charred, starred with archangelic coruscation!

At *center-pinch ablaze sprout lamps of seven,
That blare their nomenclatures sent from Heaven:

The one is named crisp Metalux built glorified,
Lit up to God so bright, it makes me horrified!

The next one is Ceramilux of see-through gel,
Transparently too hot and h-ly, in a shell.

The third one called Electrotorch (so triply split)
Illumines spatial three dimensions bit by bit.

A fourth lamp, prominent to spheres of paradise
Is Arctron star for which we strive and sacrifice!

The fifth one, yet identified spreads Luminaire
That consummates electric light that nations wear.

These five as much alive are starred in verse;
The last two follow darkly stark and terse.

Phase II

Of these that glare empyreal, sublime,
The pair are elegies through space and time.

The one is christened Pulsar Packet found on Earth:
A fossil relic from those lamps of fiercer girth!

The other, labeled Metal Wafer cooled and hard
Beneath the earthly stratum is a flat-pad card!

Thus five survive the test of tortured space,
Pitch-black, dark-laden, vacant for God's Grace,

And all are still outnumbered by each lumen
Of one **ENVELOPMENT** that nurtures Numen...

Elasticated, hyper-torched, ballooned,
Taut-tubular is *she* and faintly mooned:

Her *gliffs* are thrown throughout Eternity,
Quartz-jacketed, sun-cushioned with *alternity*-

Raw seeds that signify her signature
On Earth are kapoks grown in miniature.

Phase III

This quintet light assembled at her throne,
But detonates star-hot until clear blown!

All full o' naught, save **DIVINE SPIRIT** breathing
From canister creation sweetly seething-

Fantasmic-fired, sizzled up, for instance,
Flames fulgurous enough burn fueled existence!

That in themselves, stored cubic feet of heat
Have vitrified tried fulgurite complete.

Unsearchable by mere foot-candle wavelength,
A **SACRED GWEDUC** out-flung glisters grave strength:

Ceramilux, Electrotorch, and Argent Arctron
God-suffused, exalt and light each cosmic micron!

And bright as five-forked pentacles enlarged,
From Metalux to Luminaire, they flare recharged;

That far removed from them as light-years stretch,
At dawn their delta rays would wake the wretch.

The Vernal Cry

What countless souls have yearned to hold a star,
Glass encapsulated, that which twinkles far!

What though the brazen glitz of every lamp
Draws bugs and moths to warmth along the camp,

Chorus: O Heavenly Apocalypse, fly down!
Launch **Jesus Christ** to them of no renown!

Let Light unsearchable be but contained
In whatsoever templates have remained.

Lest man may shrink away with wheel and cart,
Bright **LUMELOPOLIS**, light up his heart!

Received: March 20th and revised on the 31st, 1996

*Center-pinch is the author's poetic license for the word *center punch*, a tool with a conical point for making an indentation in an object, to allow a drill to make a hole at the same spot without slipping.

[This poetic piece is] the epitome of quickening vitality that procured but a stark spark of its own kind (however, a spark the mass of an entire Quasar compressed into some foot-candle wavelength split by an invisible Jet Ray); a spark to start the infrastructure of energy.

H~ "Aye-aye! [Be] it well understood-- and this having been nevertheless with distorted description. The architectural logic of the warp-core cloven [glozar] gweduc in its interior infinity. A self-lucent [and self-ballasted] increately (Warp Lamp) wavelength punctured up by an invisible Jet [Arc] Ray of the Vertical Voice--"

R~ "There you have it," [interrupted Rutherford]. "And this rather still small voice of primordial intonation that spoke forth its first, faint FIAT LUX, or Let Light Be *[Let There Be Light] into all [non] existence before the foundation of realized Reality~ it would be as if it were an unapproachable torchiere shining back up at the Creator, reflecting the radiance of the *Horr'bly H-ly* as it once was in its primal spiritual [and also clinical] sterility."

H~ "Before [specimens such as] space and time came into being, Colonel? [In a preexistent embryonic state?]

R~ "Before the genesis of canister creation. That is correct. Except this *torchiere* perhaps could be designated by a more accurate term, if my morphology may anticipate, [you ought to know. You are El Capitán..."]

H~ "Precisely! But what designation for it can we think of, huh?"

THE AUTHORIZED NARRATOR

[And] now, out of nowhere, as if in response to that presumptuous questionnaire, the TRANSALTERATORIUM would wield its final recourse to their final countdown. Before which one last confrontational *gliff* had opened its split-slit fissure, and both the colonel and captain are stultified to near death, [or] as violators pounced to bulk pulp by the BORTEUM~CREMEUM *spheroids!

*Just like in the arcade video-game, Berserk, long ago released by Stern Electronics of Chicago in 1980. The function of Evil Otto, represented by a bouncing smiley face, is to quicken the pace of the game. Otto is rather unusual, with regard to games of the period, in that it is indestructible. Otto can slip through walls with impunity and hunts the player contestant. If robots remain in the maze, Otto advances slowly, about half as agile as the humanoid, but then speeds up to match the humanoid's gait once all the robots are terminated. Evil Otto moves at exactly the same speed as the player going left and right, but it can maneuver faster than the player going up and down; thus, no matter how imposing Otto appears, the player can escape, as long as they can avoid moving straight up or down via 2D mobility.

And on the flip side, exactly 133 years later, near the end of 2113:

*Except that this bounty-bouncer is the much holier XOWOX instead of the former, malevolent Evil Otto. Therefore, amid the Ubiquelabyrinthium Hallowed Hallways of a Warp Maze, hence the Holy Xowox bore palindromic Puissance, viz., "not that nine horses contested last night's Puissance" as it were within the aforesaid characteristics! But better, may this mightily personified superpower at its most powerful and rawest resolution, if not namesake retribution, go against fugitives on the run. Indeed, the old preemptive strike of the Transalteratorium network deploys its Holy Xowox zealously and mercilessly when the intramural Police perforce is dispatched. Suffice to say, both Rutherford and Harris- especially Hathaway- were spared the grizzliest grimace of the incorporeal Cannonball's colossal pressure via molecular manifestation!

*Although this Xowox is but a bounty-bouncer of extraordinary elasticity, wrought of hyper-flexible pliant Planck immateriality, its super-presence should be avoided by subjects suffering from xenophobia. Since the exotic exuberance thereof may horrify human expectation, it is advisable for us not to mention reference on its interpretation. Rather, the Borteum and Cremeum crowned in Yard Lamp of Gloria lay a time-tested foundation for the Transalteratorium, even from the year 1990 onward…

*The first commercial color-copier ever used by the author was a Xerox (just saying).

EVEN A MORE MYSTERIOUS INTERMEZZO

TATM [athwart an otherwise unseemly disposition]~ AH, WHAT AN AMUSING SPECTACLE! TWO PRECARIOUS MORTALS ON THE BRINK OF ANNIHILATION- BEHOLD RUTHERFORD AND HARRIS! SINCE THOU HAST DELVED DEEPER INTO THE TRULY UNSPEAKABLY UNLAWFUL, I- THE TRANSALTERATORIUM OF ARCHSERAPHIC ESTABLISHMENT- DIVULGE IT NOW AND THEN AS LUCIERE: THE SUPERTRON METATORCH THAT MY DAUGHTER ALUMINA IGNITES. AND WOULD YOU LIKE TO CONFRONT ALUMINA, O RELENTLESS [VOYEURS] THAT HAVE COME THUS FAR?

R~ "Heavens, we are challenged by it! Well? Uh, what shall we say?" [Reluctance riveted Rutherford into tinfoil rolled in a box]

H~ "I know not; don't look at me- you're the colonel- answer him yourself..." [Our captain had to sidestep the figurative racquetball cavorter caught on his lap as he snickered. But in that which gave him the collywobbles, anyone in his shoes displayed diffidence and no less, lackluster acumen! Under such circs, could ye blame him?]

R~ "Nay, Captain- for I grant you the responsible [resolution]: I command you!"

MELODIC MOTIF: "I Command You"
[*Singing,*
I command you,
ooh-ooh-ooh
woo-hoo, &c.]

H~ "Very well. But if I answer 'no', the TATM will confront us with force, for we are entrapped and there is no way out- we must therefore render accountability to it... But if I say 'yes', then we'll have to endure the unspeakably lovely- a Beauty Beacon that has destroyed the unqualified unholy souls who have looked upon her. A mercury Medusa, but in [an ecclesiastical exegesis] of context; [notably], the Star Gate Keeper of some Cavernous Cathedral."

R~ "Egad! The high tension is increasing! Stop forfeiting time, Captain! The lot has fallen on *you* and *not* on me. Well? [What have you? Stop pouting poppycock!] Carpe diem! What is it?" [Our Colonel Rutherford raged. But not so much aimed at his favorable friend as in protest of their disquieting displacement and sorry sitch regarding the rough and tumble (room & board) of their mind-bending Mission Impossible!] "Either *yes* or *no*, numbskull!And worry not, my brave cadet, for I am also an idiot!"

[SUPER~DUPER] SOUND EFFECTS

TATM~ [ARE WE TO BE BUFFETED BY THEE, THEN?] DO YOU WISH TO CONFRONT HER OR NOT, SAITH THE TRANSALTERATORIUM?

H~ "Uh, uh-- hey listen... can we reason this out-- like... wait a wee bit longer?" [He impromptu procrastinated.]

[But was one phlegmatic to terra incognita courtship? Whereas territoriality had cajoled each maverick ambassador of the whole human race, in any respect (howbeit both partisans picking sides, such as Rutherford and Harris), the Unitive Homogeneity of every towering Tall Wall waffled *interior dealings* from inferior feelings. Insofar as another *INSULATORIUM adjunction* of sure insulating efficacy in the TATM affected the separateness of dualizing- that is to say, to weld one with an infinite Wall- it would warrant this as an ineffaceable, non-expungeable engraving much more permanent than the nuclear plasma cutter blowtorch, blindingly concentrated upon a clear sheet of purely purged and polished diamond!]

TATM~ LO, ACCESS DENIED TO ANY OTHER ALTERNATIVE! NOW THEN, THOU MUST ANSWER! [WHAT THEN?] AN AFFIRMATIVE OR NEGATIVE? PENDING DISCLOSURE [THAT OUGHT TO BE CHARILY CHASTE]...

H~ "Uh, affirmative, TATM! ... Rutherford... look!"

NARRATOR

[18 So that ye may be able to comprehend with all saints what is **the breadth, and length, and depth, and height**; 19 And to know the love of Christ, which passeth (transcends) knowledge, that ye might be filled with all the fullness of God, Ephesians 3:18.] Some swollen ballooned cocoon of snowy white had enlarged itself and the two men toppled to their faces and on their backs supine, as two roaches of encroachment and cataplexy on a floor of linoleum luminance. The lapis lazuli lozenges transilluminating their bodies inside-out; hurling their most private sides of conscience out into the open enameled exposure of Unveiled Paradise.

¶Within which an inconceivable Jet Ray of singularity flashed up lambent bundles of itself, mercury-mirrored, and out of which an anciently embroidered figurine had just emerged. So porcelain pervasive to picture it- a holographic filigree figurine- doll-sized. That was enlarged into a very lifelike but seven foot tall female of prominent proportion. Her silky bright likeness, but bulged beneath an incubated insulator of golden gauze; her perfect Female Energy of pearliest polish and varnish.

And there she stood, with bare feet removed off the floor- afloat on a cloud- her tapered hand extended as *manus e nubibus*, ever so invitingly invincible [and so forthcoming], yet clad by a [brick-thick] mantle of Mercy...

Expulsion at the Threshold

Staged for special Authorization

[VERY SPECIAL] SOUND EFFECTS

ALUMINA~ "I am the [Molten] Mother of the Sun, the Heliatrix Anathasia: none other but one! This is my *portentous* portrayal- the e pluribus Unum- the Universal Plurality…"

NARRATOR

Rutherford and Harris were livid, taken aback and aghast amid a rippling spatial displacement. Their glossy eyes blood-shot [from the blistering brightness of fattest fire brand-brimstones that rained down from a turgid ceiling tiresomely taut to prevent defilement (*from what?*)~ and no lower an understatement than the admission: This was certainly no cakewalk! Moreover,] their faces were inflamed by the blinding Light to the point of a near-death sentence spelled out for them.

And to their amazement of utter horror, the Lovely Lady addressed what [would wont their hearts to thoughts hereof], or that which the TRANSALTERATORIUM would enforce as her <u>echo</u> screeched through its hallowed hallways: "Only ourselves can we manifest, but God-forbid, God-forbid, God-forbid the *gweduc*!"

Before but celestial maternity perse, both of them were unable to endure that confrontational *gliff*, let alone the daughter of God Himself!

[high-pitched] SOUND EFFECTS

ALUMINA~ "I will speak, in that the two of you compared to but one of me, yet one out of many, are unable to even survive in this clinical cliché of spiritual sterility. I as thy Lovely Mother do eject your presence out of my TRANSALTERATORIUM! Thus thou mightest never see me in my electrospun envelopment, nor in my ectoplasmic embodiment. Moreover, my [shiny] LUCIERE I have electrified [*and even lumefied*] to vivified vitrification, that [hath hitherto and] shall henceforth and forevermore remain forbidden to the world of man[kind branded by the number 6]. **Genesis 1:24–31**

"Wherefore, be gone out of my monolithic *<u>intramuralization</u> [and multi-channeled chamber]! Flee! Before my mantle of Mercy [and Solace and General Solicitude] melts down from the HARSH GLARE of [egalitarian] Justice!"

*The author's best word for labyrinth~ like Latin: Intra-muros (within the city walls)!

R~ "Oh, but your highness! Most venerable Alumina, we repent of our transgressions-- [even of the *auto-AWOL* Joyce Hathaway, our long lost and poor Deputy reported missing for some reason]-- committed against thine fine and divine provisional ordinance..."

H~ "Aye, O help us- thou, paramount Paraclete of love! Lest we return as strangers to [or exiles of] our [tellurian] home planet."

<u>ALUMINA</u>~ "It is far too late. And besides, impending annihilation awaits an imperfect being such as thou art-- albeit the Lord Jesus Christ, the Almighty (Limitless Light) that can forgive thee; for I myself, a tremendous transducer of an insulated incubator, lives-- virginal and reserved-- to be [impressed or] impregnated by the resplendent *[Logos] of God and none other."

*(in Jungian psychology) the principle of reason and judgment, associated with the animus. This could imply that the polar opposite, or *anima* resides in the Goddess aspect of the Infinite Divinity, viz., vacuum throughout space-time continuum!

NARRATOR [notwithstanding The <u>Consolidation</u>]

¶At last, [lively] audience. Her ultimatum was addressed *until* colonel Rutherford and captain Harris were to be hurtled back to Earth, *unscorched*, and as if they had never departed in the first place. Their conscious history in the memories of their loved ones and friends restored to an original standpoint. But yet grievously anticipated [as it were and] as such, the colonel and captain [might just as well have] lost all recollection of this fantastical exploration except in one occasion. Whenever one [drooled over] a streetlamp on Earth, it would uncannily remind many of some brightly white swollen ballooned chrysalis somewhere far, far away... [Still, it was not the issue for now if the maternal Mercy Seat of Circe, replete with clemency, overruled the verdict in her Sancta Sanctorum!]

SOUND EFFECTS [OF EFFECTUAL EFFULGENCE]

ALUMINA~ "[Wherefore], what is your last request before I escort thee to Earth, [*earthling*]?"

R~ "[Lord Jesus, we pray! That we may see Joyce Hathaway, and that she should be restored unto us, your Highness… O prithee!]

[And at once, it was genuine Joyce, revealing, blissful, who showed up out of nowhere. Though Rutherford and Harris were whipped out of their wits, the three contestants embraced with a big bear-hug for their Reunion. She was revitalized, in comelier color or complexion than way back when her coiffure, that is to say, her shocks shape-shifted to locks, were no longer haywire-frayed as she had felt far better! In short order, it was Goldilocks with her usual disposition *only*, as in the fairy-tale heroine who enters the house of the Three Bears and declares the property of Baby Bear to be 'just right', as compared to those of Father Bear and Mama Bear & etcetera. She blanched with incredulity as, in their warmest and convivial cuddle, they stood stiffly, like rigid planks of plywood clapboards on end, but stilted up in mindful measurement of their stature and height. The Transalteratorium yielded yardstick usage to size them up for the bodily-beautiful, but vertical-vociferous Alumina, the Supertron Metatorch!]

[The colonel and captain were exposed under spotlights and interrogated, as it were, by the Queen Regnant & Argent Regent

Nondescript (essentially all unseen with no markings of her own, just a disembodied voice-over)! Thus the big bodiless entity of the TATM network nudged them the more. Fully relieved by Joyce's restoration to their needy Company, still, Rutherford resolved to flip in his pennyworth militarily and scientifically (a historic hint from the time of Dwight D. Eisenhower, 156 years ago, midway, came to mind when one of his favourite Presidents addressed his TV audience with: "In the councils of government, we must guard against the acquisition of unwarranted influence, whether sought or unsought, by the military-industrial complex. The potential for the disastrous rise of misplaced power exists and will persist.") And so, this applied well with their predicament in operation of such TATM turnover. Within *himself*, the colonel prayed as in the old Eisenhower chapel visualized hereupon, or via vehicular, 4-lane Eisenhower–Edwin C. Johnson Memorial Tunnel that cut a dual bore through the Colorado Rockies under the Continental Divide. Heavens! His recent slip-trip on the Hyper Loop Expressway at least lengthened a brief caesura between this quivering quantum foam equipped Q & A session.]

[On the other hand henceforth, the deputy of all gleeful spirits was terribly tongue-tied and had nothing to relay as her unworldly glaze gladdened her heart yet yellowed her hale exterior. It proved to be an imperious impasse of grotty gridlock instead of roundelay reentry for the defenseless OW-team, or whatever was left of them. Aside from awkwardness over everyone, the staunch Stoic of their Camp Mitch Command insisted to take his two cents' worth all the way to the nth degree nonetheless:]

R (tentatively, to resume recourse)~ "...That we may witness the Great White *Horridor of the TRANSALTERATORIUM..."

*The word corridor was combined with the adjective, horrid, hence Horridor. In this case, the disagreeable and negative connotation is transposed to an indestructible and positive point of view; namely, terrible to indicate a terror to the Devil save a delight to the Saints and Angels of God.

H~ "Aye, O *bonnie* lass! Stella Bella! O mercury mantled Mama!"

[The numinous gale of pristine spirit hammered them thus, so devoid of substance; only a Vox Femina from out of nowhere and an invisible Shining that they could not perceive, nor anyone else.]

ALUMINA~ "Granted, [only if it will make you buoyant.] But just this once! And now, but be careful, it's a heavyweight,] my beastly and creaturely spectators of naught... Away with thee! Be gone!"

[SUPER--SILENT] EFFECTS
[*THE MUFFLED*] NARRATOR

Except where needed whilst follows full revision rather *added words and sentences need no more *brackets* for the original text to be distinguished from the altered, or amplified version; there are still *pilcrows* to be dealt with, but nothing else.

Then *she*, Alumina, reentered Determinate Evanishment~ Her rotund, revolving-door prim presence presumed diminution past a pipsqueak pinpoint that mockingly winked out of existence... into reduced, shriveled shrinkage. Whereas even an inward implosion shuddered the vast vacuum of space, a substitute filler entered the field of view. It included the fragrant scent from some sunken Garden of rosebuds bathed by 'ethermal' rays along with its grassy meadowland loam!

The twofold crew, including a recently itinerant Joyce, rejoiced at the moment of *her* enveloped departure. Until shortly after, a blank blown continual curvation, now upwardly expanded, had augmented itself into full-house scrutiny. But what could they dare do? For the three abstracted voyagers merely noticed the split prism of a Hypersphere that stretched up, above, beyond, and into down, below, within (from pole to pole)! Gloomily maddened and waxed wearisome by absorbing the accelerated contents thereof, the three space cadets about-faced away from it and wanted nothing to do with her featureless pseudo-showtime. *Amen*

¶ For not feeling stuffy, unbuttoned, or just plain informal, Deputy Hathaway wrote in her stand-alone-diary: *The Great White Sphere, as if with writhing wrath, apprehended us as it *oscillated obscenely; breathing in and out, in and out! Grotesquely growing and shrinking and growing and... like our entire Universe after an obnoxious amount of eons which would have elapsed by in only a measly split-second! Or in the lifetime of a stellar* colossus, *except sped up to time-warp, the cycling oscillation of this ever enormous White Sphere, altering itself~ so protean by nature~ dizzily defied me, I'll say!*

Then, in order to capstone the tip of an iceberg, she added:

***PHYSICS** *(oscillated)*

To vary in magnitude or position in a regular manner around a central point.

She elaborated furthermore:

For what is the sense of being swept up by within stream of things~ To go along with the flow or the shuffle of a card game? Since we, the Off-World interpreters have encountered something beyond the orders of magnitude in quantum physics~ realms of hieroglyphic properties based on squiggly super~string theories!

And that was the end of her ruminations for now, until afterwards when she finds herself detained at the Mitchelville Headquarters pending an interrogatory debriefing of some sort. Were they to undergo a lobotomy should their accusers be barred by an acquittal? Only Time's turnaround ought to tackle their future fumble for a punt during one split-second before the proverbial football touches the turf of unholy ground.

Quite convinced, this fascinated her to no end. Not to exclude the quantum mechanics majors who had officiated their task force of an awesome undertaking. *Still*, the Sphere stayed superimposed above and below them concomitantly.

STANDARD SOUNDTRACK EFFECTS

Adjacent to a self-materialized meadow-garden and grotto, in front of the linoleum lawn thereof, the Great White *Sphere, at 37 meters in diameter, impressed itself upon the leatherneck dwarfs of the OW-team, imposingly electrostatic, yet impertinent to them.

*The Unisphere, at Flushing Meadows Corona Park, had been commissioned as part of the 1964 New York World's Fair. The sturdy stainless-steel sculpture was dedicated to "man's achievements on a shrinking globe in an expanding universe." It is 140 feet (43 m) high and 120 feet (37 m) in diameter.

Again, by narrowed-down diction as authenticated from 1996

SPHERE~ "For now, ye refuse to confront me, O humanoids!"

R~ "Indeed, thou Contorter, we refuse to dizzily see thee!"

SPHERE~ "But I am BORTEUM and CREMEUM, the protuberantly undestroyable! Wherefore, fear not and face me!"

R~ "Nay. For we be of feeble comprehension!"

[SURREAL] SOUND EFFECTS

SPHERE~ "One part round my whole I show," intoned he. "The rest of my cross-sections none can see…"

NARRATOR

And to their incredulity, a seven foot observable bouncer of geometry recoiled and reasserted itself. Its elastic surface of sleek, smooth consonant curvature [was] opaquely enlarged. And with an authenticated voice of metallic tinfoil, [and with a big body of self-tapered Teflon], it [sounded off] its one last plea [of an emergency recommendation to them] before reducing to a state of Absolute Absence.

SPHERE~ "Both Borteum and Cremeum beseech thee, Rutherford, Harris, and Hathaway, to tell the world (where ye reside) that **1 John 1:5** King James Version (KJV) This then is the message which we have heard of him, and declare unto you, that God is Light, and in Him is no darkness at all. Wilt thou do this for us altogether?"

NARRATOR

In fine, as a dog would obey the Master's Voice, so Rutherford, [aside from his most loyal crewmates], accepted the Commission; [that is], to herald the Truth to congregations. Crowd steeped in a shroud- darkened by graven images and effigies of [mind-numbing and soul-suppressing] subterfuge.

SPHERE~ "Splendiferous, as ye once remarked. Now, my paramount Paraclete bids thee valediction. Go in peace [Pax Vobis]!

[For even the Metalucelectropluceptorium along with the TATM network and others were satisfied as to a difficult mission accomplished both on their behalf as well as Rutherford's]

NARRATOR

Before long, upon their telestic transport to Earth, the narrow high-ceiled Great White Horridor of the [Tremendous Transducers] TRANSALTERATORIUM [multiplex] materialized as promised in front of them. Bearing about its labyrinthic 'intramuralization' with that eerie figure-eight sideways reposed above a first faint narrow doorway or aperture on the Otherside.
Rutherford~ "My God! It's full of light!"

NARRATOR

And his muffled echo would continue as recorded upon Earth through the supercomputers of Mitchelville. It had become an old frenetic rat-race of big button-uniformed madcap mathematicians that decoded and deciphered the only transmission broadcasted to every wish-dish & ultrasonic paraboloid poised across terra firma.

That until the moment the terrestrials thereof had heard of it, all the powers of darkness were instantly dethroned and made null and void. For even the firm foundations of History were shaken at the graphic voiceprint of the message; the cosmic contents thereof etiolated by super-searing rays:

[environmental and city-side] (final) INTERMEZZO

R~ "My God! It's full o' Light," **end of line**!

NARRATOR [GENERAL INTERMISSION]

The radiant episode of the Great White Horridor, the slip-trip TRANSALTERATORIUM itself, & an auroral amphora, aligerous ALUMINA igniting her LUCIERE, has been consummated in that lithely ethereal split prism of fulgurite light. Consequently, all this hyper-lucid dream has left the colonel, captain, and deputy soaked by oil rig gushers of deep-seated sensation that are, or full of… *(in Graeco-Latin language and Greek as from the Hellenistic period)*

A concise list of the stronger emotions evoked in YLOG:

1) Euneirophrenia~ Finding peace during mental healing.

2) Kalopsia~ The state in which everthing, and everyone, beautiful.

3) Orphic~ That of entrancing fascination.

4) Novaturient~ Desirous of changes or alterations.

5) Chrysalism~ The tranquility and peace that you feel when you're indoors during a thunderstorm.

6) Selcouth~ 1. odd, unusual, or extraordinary in appearance, effect, manner, etc; peculiar. 2. not known, seen, or experienced before; unfamiliar.

7) Mauerbauertraurigkeit~ The inexplicable urge to push people away (the aftershock of this Yard Lamp of Gloria vision that fades away and turns to very people-oriented compassionate inclusiveness & unitive consciousness).

8) Monachopsis~ The subtle but persistent feeling of being out of place, as maladapted to your surroundings like a seal on a beach— lumbering, clumsy, easily distracted, huddled in the company of other misfits, unable to recognize the ambient roar of your intended state of affairs.

9) Onism~ The frustration of being stuck in just one body, that inhabits only one place at a time.

10) Occhiolism~ The awareness of the smallness of your perspective of being in the world.

11) Lachesism~ A desire to be struck by disaster, such that life is thereafter more poignant and understandable.

12) Tristesse~ The sadness that you'll never really know what other people think of you, whether good, bad, or if at all.

13) Oneirataxia~ The inability to distinguish between fantasy and reality.

14) Tacenda~ are things not to be mentioned or made public— things better left unsaid; tacit means "unspoken, silent" or "implied, inferred."

15) Anagapesis~ Lack of interest in former loved ones.

16) Astrophile~ A person who loves astronomy or constantly gazes at the stars.

17) Kairosclerosis~ Kairosclerosis is from theGreek: kairos, "the opportune moment" + sclerosis, "hardening."

18) Solivagant~ Latin: *solivagus*, wandering alone (from soli- + vagus wandering).

19) Redamancy~ Eunoia (noun): Beautiful thinking.

    Used as: Joyce's compassion and eunoia make her a fantastic candidate (for example).

20) Eunoia~ n. Beautiful thinking.

21) Novalunosis~ The state of relaxation and wonderment experienced while gazing upon the stars (author's best).

22) Empyreal~ adj. Things that are empyreal have something to do with the sky.

23) Exulansis~ The tendency to give up trying to talk about an experience because people are unable to relate to it.

And so forth ...

But back at Base Camp with a more suitable, tangible Tongue.

Our pioneer trio of spirit was escorted down through fourth-dimensional door and into time-slot township Mitchelville with memorials of their departure restored to its people. Not to forget Rutherford's military Milieu that brandished prissy Protocols of priority; Harris's editorial and mediatorial metropolitan patriarchs of the Orthodox Traditionalists; Hathaway's heavy-handed horse-and-cart cartographers and finicky folklorists. While in flight, a starry flurry of cosmic and electrostatic snow swept on them as cosmic confetti and glitziest glitterati of a billion Times Squares.

R~ "Hold on, Captain! Whilst myriads of galactic globules and disks dance around on a fly-by... But, O what a cosmic carnival!"

H~ "Aye, Colonel! And she's as bonny as can be, beloved Earth! [Quam pulchra es!] A distant bluish and emerald orb of life and times that be better than that clinical cliché, I say Awa and away!"

H2~ "Farewell World of Walls, and good riddance! Hello Heaven and Earth! We welcome thee, I'll say!"

R~ "I will have to concur with you, Joyce!" Then, to the two of them: "O and how it expands exponentially with every Rotation. Its material makeup blindingly azure from the Doppler Effect on approach- but then the rapidly receding TATM system is a bloody darkened dwarf dimly diminished many light-years away… back to Tomorrow. Oh monumental marvel of a God-engineered and inalienable world! We welcome thy revival! Yippee! receive us!"

SOUND EFFECTS

Yet little did they know that an unwelcome mob was about to apprehend them, as if they were prevaricators of the rankest order based on criminal conduct, according to an old-school Procurator! For he coveted filthy lucre at Camp Mitchelville's Mercenary and Merchantile Exchange, but with ruthless exactitude.

In reference to supernatural separation of three silver cords cut:

The indispensable Marginalia of all YLOG paperwork

We must understand the immediate departure of the three from the retracted and withdrawn Spirit Realm within parapsychological insight. To correctly examine the *ether*, the newly discovered extra-*ectoplasmopolis* takes front stage. The simultaneity of which is, as it were, conduit-concomitantly-continuous. In other words, tenuous tendrils and quasi-waxen tubules congeal themselves into subspace Planck Quantum Foam indivisible by distance, time, space and any direction walled by a dimensional partition. This all-pervasive link of its substratum transcends the limitations of any existence.

The supernatural and paranormal contiguity of largely infinite interconnection is the closest property thereof. Where no dead-end, nor non-outlet, neither nonexistence temporal or permanent, may block any of its pathways a quadrillion times more blended than the brain with neurons intertwined like a sponge. Wherefore, the interlinked *ectoplasmopolis* subsists in an underlying matrix even below every Planck cubic unit under the vacuum of subspace nothingness. This *electroencephalogram (EEG) hyper-holy supercity stays infinitely multidimensional, devoid of detours due to a short-cut capability!

*The 1983 movie Brainstorm exemplifies holographic-compressed ultra-iridescent recording tape technology that later past the climax and resolution of the movie catapults the viewer to an OBE~ *out of the body experience.* Directed by Douglas Trumbull, this film most closely portrays what defies death and the laws of physics, since a soul and spirit could not be imprisoned thereby. With Christopher Walken, Natalie Wood, Louise Fletcher, Cliff Robertson, the author finds such exemplary illustration with pictures such as Brainstorm.

From the fresh framework of a metropolitan Cornfield that had withdrawn itself once and for all, the aforesaid *ectoplasmopolis* did diminish itself into the distance but with its gas gushers and oil rigs radiative as my memory of Colorado's Commerce City refinery!

The radiant rim of the planetary home suddenly glissaded into vivid view whereas what was but short of hyperluminal light-speed lumbered to a sublight, then a subsonic lingering crawl of just local locomotion. For so slow was their traversal and hover-back that the Tupolev Tu-144 kept pace with them by their astronautical reentry.

*Behold the TATM's Tupolev Tu-144 **Москва** manifestation!

H2~ "Yikes!" yelled yellow-backed-but-booted-up Joyce.

Until a classic U-2 aircraft, and then the Boeing-Stearman Model 75 biplane, paralleled their atmospheric plummet before their parachutes blossomed out in fuchsia-neon or flamingo and flamboyant fluorescence above the frothing tantrum of the foamy Atlantic. Until a Bravo Zulu was blared out by megaphone means after each of our Off-World travelers were harnessed and safely secured from the torrential tidal waves of an angry sea-churned Bermuda Triangle in the eye of a howling category 5 hurricane.

Meanwhile, rubberneckers attempted to scrutinize their winning prize aboard buoy-equipped reconnaissance vessels as computer electronics began to fizz on the fritz due to disruptive displacement of atmospheric decompression~ yea, precedent to such an eye-wall of the tropical cyclone doughnut epicenter, yet apropos to what *really* ensued; it was what would bottleneck beforehand *(verbatim from the unaltered Context of 1996):

R~ "Fasten your buckskin breeches, mates. Just hold on tight for a whiplash landing, see? Saddle up!"

"Delta is ready when you are," serenaded Joyce, pretending to be a stewardess aboard a transatlantic Tri-Star airliner, awhirl with whimsical and liltsome levity.

Unequivocally then, the tired crew grew eager and excited.

"Aye-aye skipper!" hollered Harris, unsure of the colonel's veracity. Although protocol-preconditioned and checkered by battle-fatigue syndrome, both parties pinched each other in an empirical sort of way, only to say that *the proof is in the pudding*, just in case! Certified scientists, even upon the midnight strike of New Year's Eve when 2014 struck eight-billion foreheads upon Earth, were adequately disciplined to have blind faith backed by *prima facie evidence.

With auld lang syne precedent to Two-Thousand Fourteen, the tellurian multitudes, amassed globally, echoed loud their festivities through the wormhole wherein within a nanosecond of temporal suspension, Rutherford felt the reverberation of 8,000,000,000 souls all at once like a gathering of eight-billion metronomes:

Tick-tock, tick-tock... (one thousand-million multiplied by 8)

*Prima facie evidence means that proof of the first fact permits, but does not require, the fact finder; in the absence of competing evidence, to find that the second fact is true beyond a reasonable doubt.

A shock wave seized the [space] cadets ere stellar quicksand swallowed them up. And like Lethe of [utter] forgetfulness, they reentered the starry Gateway to their marvelous Mercury Mirror.

Yet by contrast to the regular routine of entry (if we could call it regular or normal), just one detour diverged our colonel only, but way out of bounds in the nanosecond it took to land everyone upon ground zero! The infinitesimal interval of frozen time unnoticed by anyone nabbed him by surprise as the last resort checkout from an inanely liminal loophole habitat of the Transalteratorium Hotel.

The Great Grand Central Station

Anachronistic juxtaposition; that of no chronological context

There was this impenetrable stronghold in the Outer Courtyard of Nowhere. The man once known as Roderick Rutherford, for the moment, ended up at a trillion trillion, or one septillion light-years partitioned away from our Observable Universe, as it were.

With whiter and *eerier* Light, an octagon enclosure surrounded erstwhile Rutherford resolutely. Blithely in front of him, a tall wall, blinding, blatantly blankest with indescribable chromaticity, bulged back at him. It stood longways and narrowly rectangular to join up and down along a narrower ceiling, but on the other end, widened out floor flanged and socketed and with interconnected floorboards meticulously inter-planked where, on his last leg, he stood frailly.

Before our visitor's Entrance, the slender doorway gaped dead-center in the very midst of each imposing Tall Wall that confronted the ruffled Rutherford. Whilst eight sides of the octagonal lot were equally the same, only the Front Tall Wall, with a slender doorway, seemed slightly contorted, as if bent back or forward by an another dimension! Well enough, nothing more than an octet of hot quasars which would have had to gleam gloriously to exceed the brightness of the highly eight-sided enveloped enclosure, ballooned forthwith!

In the middle of the octagonal floor, by the way, if one were to look downward from overhead, the complement of the figure-eight landscaped horizontally had been centered thereupon. Emblematic, suggestive of what was just as plain as a pikestaff staring someone in the face rather than at face value. Its lemniscate ordinarily lay an

Equation: $(x^2 + y^2)^2 = a^2(x^2 - y^2)$, where a is the greatest distance from the curve to the origin…
It is the curviest Lazy Eight!

This was an *addendum of the Sun's Radiative Zone and Core.

*Without fanciful adjectives, adverbs, and pronouns used to embellish a foreshortened document, I reserve the rights of my privileged readership to closely inspect the trellis and lattice reredos of my heart's nave, chapel and church; but if so circumspect, to perhaps accept the grammar, the etymological formality, the vocabulary with decorum thereof.

Hitherto yet onward, the man was far more than his former self. But for clarification purposes, we will identify such a one with his namesake therefore. Thus [ecce homo] of prerequisite preparation!

But first and foremost, to at least draw comparison & contrast, a brief but concise diversion of knowledge lay prefatory to the next subset of **portentous perspicacity* (by my triple diorama):

- The author's own (alternative) literary license to Lucidity beyond being able to forecast anything!

- The prioritized criterion of technicality for the Great Grand Central Station!
- The one and only convergence and recourse into another acquired dialogue, but within deftest discretion and deference via TATM Database Depositories
- This is not to exclude a Transalteratorium Repository or the TATM ®!

Ancient Light will continue just *around the corner*

after these messages

THROUGH THE KEYHOLE VIGNETTE

Top Secret

The Alternative Consolidation Thereof

Namely so, an exigent recall rekindled our precious encounters with the aforementioned Vortronium Spherics, as was recorded into hard card holograms for some interactive library retrieval database. Residual research in these programs enabled doctors, instructors, students, and pupils alike, to glean up a well-worth knowledge of quantum mechanics from this Metaphysical Marvel, Supernatural Soliloquy, and (of course) *super-scientific* *End-Time Harvest.

*There are long Apocalyptic Warnings in futurity of the End-Time Harvest, of which authorship cannot expound, as it would take up multiple sections for footnotes. Found mainly in the exegesis of Holy Writ, the apologetics alone doubtlessly outnumber the paragraphs of this science-fiction tale of a flood-salvaged pictorial compilation.

Namely (number 2), one of such mnemonic packets, packages, containers, and capsules of holographic input and output on seedy subsurface subject matters- no matter how lofty or just downright debased- include excerpts on epic poetry and endless essays. These records regard retinues that escort a personified Vortron Orb, per se. To quote an analogy by anyone's word of mouth: "The neutron star is not unlike a nacent, newborn **firebird*; a *phoenix that has resurrected fresh from the Cinerary Urn of a creepily cremated, but once stellular and cosmic corpse of astronomical *astringency*."

*Although alternatively a Chevrolet Camaro~ the Pontiac Firebird happens to be the author's choicest American automobile that was built and produced by Pontiac from the 1967 to 2002 model years. But in this case, literally that selfsame firebird depicted in the cartoon, Battle of the Planets, where G-Force, a five-member superhero team, fights to defend Earth and its space colonies from the threat of the planet Spectra! (Release: September 1978 to May 1980).

*(mythology) a mythological bird, said to be the only one of its kind, which lives for 500 years and then dies by burning to ashes on a pyre of its own making, ignited by the sun it then arises anew from the ashes.

And namely (number 3): The compressional pressurization of the Big Ball, or colossal cannonball, was what had been referred to in Yard Lamp of Gloria's storyboard basis; that is, about some true Fire Bird reanimated from the ashes of a cinerarium. For alongside the ensconced and embalmed remains of a former Superstar, an old slag and culm (as waste from anthracite coal mines) are leftovers! This ash repository, columbarium, or the common mausoleum will allow for rosy five-folded leaflet compounded cinquefoils and eye-captivating cineraria to bulge buds and modest (yet quite bloated) blossoms of vernal vitality. Thus this consolidated the consecration of archival and scrapbook-buttressed 'Vortronium Spherics' at large for public perusal upon declassification of the document thereof.

Furthermore, among divers dissertations and treatises so solely designed to have schoolhouse classmates through their polytechnic conservatory achieve their alma mater quantum physics doctorate, the hearty but *hardy* and handy hologram (hexahedrons of diamond self-sufficiency) were adequate enough no less, nor more...

From precedential prehistoric epochs of Mayan and Yuchi aborigine tribes which utilized Uniglot linguistics~ all the way, until multi-millennial to our present-day presentation of a captured neutron star (in perpetuity, Pulsar, if detected by an X-ray or radio-dish)~ montage time-frame filmstrips of time-lapse vistas vaunt spiritual and scientific investigation in this good look at fusion.

All poised to unfold successively (the pictures themselves), one of which-- what can we say?-- portrays a video diorama and model of Stellar Fusion by the following intermediate category:
*Now needless to say---

No laundry list, nor bank ledger, but topnotch Nuclear Tabulation! No ring-a-ding ditzy, quicksand-sappy sop, nor cloying clatter; but this unadulterated cosmic catalogue at classroom 101 astrophsics!

In case of emergency, an Ambulux will be dispatched to haul you away. The coroner, postmortem autopsy, or vehicular hearse are only the details after this think-tank brainer broils you wholly to kingdom come. Mind you! The reader can circumvent this section

3–2–1... CONTACT

❖ ❖ ❖ ❖ ❖ ❖ ❖

Stellar Fusion

Specifically, take a pair of two hydrogen atoms- each one with nucleus of but one proton nuclear fusion process. Two of these hydrogens combine; one of the protons is converted into a neutron. A positron and a neutrino are produced- helium is made- two of these hydrogens combine. Einstein's equation ($E=mc^2$)!

Primarily, deuterium and tritium undergo fusion to hyper-hot plasma contained by natural magnetic confinement fields via some quantum tunneling effect as nucleons collide hard enough past the Coulomb barrier (even though a cubic solid of the Sun's innermost compressed core can only generate the feeble glow of a 60W lamp lightbulb), the super pressures of such solar mass ought to escalate sustained fusion efficiency by factors beyond what is generalized.

While hydrogen is fused into helium, neutrons are expelled, which result in shortwave gamma rays that eventually elongate to X-rays and gamma radiation through the radiative zone confined inside of the radiative realities of a pressure-cooker Furnace until ejected out of the convective zone beneath the shiny photosphere. And until, lastly, repressurized amidst the cyclotron heat cloud of the solar corona and discharged out into vacuum via solar wind!

*The presumed height of the coulomb barrier is based upon the distance at which the nuclear strong force could overcome the coulomb repulsion. In Physics, it is a barrier between two atomic nuclei, as due to Coulomb repulsion, that has to be overcome for nuclear fusion to proceed. Thermal and massive pressurization can compress each of these against the strong nuclear force of repulsion so that heavier hydrogen & helium nuclei combine on the neutron, proton, and electron level of atomic recombination or fusion. Whereas- for fair example- China's Experimental Advanced Superconducting * Tokamak (EAST), a nuclear fusion reactor research facility, sustained plasma at 70 million degrees Celsius for as long as 17 minutes, 36 seconds, achieving then the new world record for sustained high temperatures, our Old Faithful Sun (although middle aged) due to its immense gravity, can sustain fusion temperatures four times as much as nuclear fission reactions. Fission happens when a neutron slams into a larger atom, forcing it to excite and split into two smaller atoms. Most nuclear reactors utilize this process for the time being; the released heat of which (under a controlled state) keeps steam turbine dynamo systems in power plants to generate, transmit, and to distribute electricity for industrial, commercial, and residential utilities, especially for big cities.

* The Stellarator uses complex electromagnetic coils to confine plasma through three-dimensional magnetic fields in the shape of a torus or doughnut without relying upon induced plasma currents to sustain the plasma.

The core is 27 million degrees Fahrenheit (15 million degrees Celsius). The photosphere surface temperature according to NASA is only 10,000 degrees F (5,500 degrees C). The total brightness of the Sun at any given length is equal to the area of its sphericity that has a radius corresponding to the earths distance from the Sun. And with the radius equal to 92.96 million miles, one astronomical unit, or 149.6 billion meters, the area of wraparound entirety thereupon is exactly at, *give or take a nanometer of mathematical estimation*

281,229,000,000,000,000,000,000

(or 281.2 sextillion square meters)!

Now we just multiply that with 127,000 lumens per square meter and we get the grand total of

35,730,000,000,000,000,000,000,000,000 lumens.

Therefore the total output thereof is 35.73 octillion lumens!

*A lumen is the SI unit of luminous flux, equal to the amount of light emitted per second in a unit solid angle of one steradian from a uniform source of one candela.

One candlepower is equal to 12.57 lumens, for instance. The sun's brightness is so intense that it would take about 1.6 x 10^28 (or 1.6 followed by 28 zeros) standard candles to produce the same amount of light. What's more, for a factoid: The Sun is voluminous enough in that approximately 1,300,000 Earths can fit inside of it.

Surface temperature: 5770 K; thus the peak frequency of the Sun is f(peak) = 340 trillion hertz.

On the photosphere surface of the Sun, each and every square centimeter emits 300,000 lumens. The surface of the Sun is an ocean of hydrogen in the form of electrified plasma, but in a somewhat "superfluid" liquefied state, yet far unlike neutron star material millions of times denser (more on this a bit later)!

Another hydrogen combines with this to produce Helium-3 and a gamma ray (first light of the high-energy narrower photon). This takes place massively and many times per second like in a chain-reaction whereof a helium atom has slightly smaller mass than the [four] hydrogens that make it up.

This extra mass is converted to energy and released out of the nuclear core called the radiative zone which, after a long time, is processed through the convective zone until it surfaces at the photosphere.

By and large, the gravity tries to crush the Sun smaller into itself while the radiation and energetic pressure counterbalances that and there is sustained equilibrium.

If a star has eight times the mass of our Sun, later at the latter stage of its life, all the hydrogen is used up, no more able to be converted into helium~ for fusion stops altogether. At the heavier *(heliumatic) level, the pressure produced by nuclear fusion is diminished and then the star undergoes shrinkage.

*Author's adjective coinage for helium!

For as the star shrinks, hydrogen at the exo-layer of the star is forced inward and another helium flash of fusion resumes- that is, in a shell surrounding the helium-saturated inner core. Also, as the core of this second stellar stage shrinks, due to rapid depletion, the outer layers of the star expand to her swollen equatorial girth-line.

Until the exo-layers cool down, or decalesce, thus halting the star's self-expansion~ yea, precedent to the Red Giant stage...

Now as the helium core contracts further, temperatures increase (and if the star is big enough); the temperature becomes high enough for the helium to start fusing at the core. Then the helium will be fused into carbon and oxygen! Hence helium shall sustain fusion for many millions of years.

But as this happens, still, the internal calefaction thereof (that of the new core) intensifies...

Next, the nuclear fusion of carbon produces sodium, neon, and magnesium. And the procedure of fusing heavier and heavier atoms, id est, the melting together of the atomic nuclei as with other stages of inner-core compression (whereby the weightier and denser elements build up closer to the core), in shells moving out from the core is called "shell-burning"--

1) Helium shell

2) Carbon shell (mass producer of sodium, neon, and magnesium)

3) Neon shell

4) Oxygen shell

5) Silicon shell (and finally)

6) The iron shell

Its burning refers to the loss or depletion of lighter nuclei fused into heavier, which creates outward pressure against the counter-pressure of gravity (to otherwise cause the stellar material to fall back) whereby the star itself stays *uncollapsed* as of yet...

Lastly, the final fusion forms iron, or Fe on the Periodic Table of Elements. The consistency of which is an indissoluble solid at room temperature, of course. But this one cannot be fused furthermore, even though the fusion of lighter elements have generated pure and raw energy so as to maintain outer pressure!

In keeping the last remnants of the star's composition still in existence~ to have it kept intact~ iron fusion, however, would require more energy than it produces. This now means that this dying star has used up (depleted) the whole of its fuel supply and very rapidly her hull or core collapses contrarily.

For as the fuel is entirely consumed, there is negligible or no more *'*outward-bound bounty of stellar-pressure*' as an end result. Ultimately, the core of the star collapses as it implodes at about a quarter of the speed of light!

*Author's fanciful and flowery way to convey what is called efflorescent effulgence!

The following colossal collapse then rebounds and blows the star apart in a supernova explosion. On the nuclear level, protons and neutrons bounce back from each other, unable to be squeezed together any closer and via elastic recoil rebound outwardly in an *explosive outburst of hyper-hot vehemence.

*Depending on the stellar ratio and radius, either a nova, supernova, or Hypernova may occur. The Hypernova ejects GRBs or Gamma Ray Bursts and are also called superluminous supernovae, though that classification also includes other types of extremely luminous stellar explosions that have different origins. So, in this case, a massive star (>30 solar masses) collapses to form a rotating black hole emitting bi-polar or twin astrophysical jets on either side of it and surrounded by an accretion disk of highly hot and radiant, rotational plasma.

Q & A related to Nuclear Numeracy

1) Inquiry insertion: What is a quark-nova?

If ever, after a Hypernova, the neutron star is residual, eventually, when a neutron star is spun down to a non-pulsar, or altogether quiescent, *radio-quiet neutron star* (which releases only gamma and X-rays instead of what should have been a radio-beacon transmitter), this then leaves the dormant neutron star hauntingly open to yet another mind-bending metamorphosis!

2) When a non-active neutron star is left inertly alone, but in and of itself, it may just as well convert to a Quark-Star known as *quark deconfinement. The end result is one that contains quark matter in its interior! The super copious energy release thereof is equivalent to at least *10 to the power of 46 *joules, or 1046 J. Such samples of ultrahigh energy show early pictures of the Big Bang when the Universe was created under hotter conditions.

*References: https://en.wikipedia.org/wiki/Color_confinement

***1e^46**, or **1 x 1046** (that's well over a thousand septillion or Ten Quattuordecillion). In scientific notation: 1e46. However, what many want to know, is how to read and say it correctly. The number 1 with 46 zeros is:

Ten Quattuordecillion
10 000 000 000 000 000 000 000 000 000 000 000 000 000 000 000 000

*A Joule (abbreviated J) is a measurement of energy or work. In mechanical systems, it's the force of one newton, moving an object a distance of one meter... In electronics, it's the same amount of energy (but in electrical units).

The Author's Upfront Note: Before we continue with **Stellar Fusion**, I would like to divert the reader's attention to my mid-to-late 1990s (revised) Vision for something within this Quark-Star.

It is the glorious *GLUOR*, the "embryocto – prototype"...

GLUOR is an acronym for Gold Lucent Universe of Radiance!

Although I keep the beholder from having to be bored by my explanatory and analytical diversions, or call it detour, I will still summarize the contents of the GLUOR down to three hypotheses:

1) The Gluor is a sub-quark energy Packet that consists of nothing but gluons. It is that which holds together, as by strong nuclear forces~ not only the quarks~ constituents of

protons and neutrons with *up* or *down* characteristics but chiefly, a thing of trans-dimensional Planck Pliancy Quantum Foam *deflator of strangely inert possibilities.

2) The Gluor is a pre-created "gluonic" entity of but super-symmetrical exponential potential that precedes the raw vacuum of space-time continuum. From which the four-dimensional framework of spatiotemporal infinities are ballooned (back in the 1990s I have christened it the big *Balloonium that may underpin Inflationary Expansion.

3) The Gluor pre-existed absolute nothingness (nihility) of no space-times past, present, and future, nor ever.... It is not at all attributable to *uncreated* Divinity; neither pure Origin in and of itself. Rather, it is sub-nothingness and beneath anti-matter, if this were possible. Therefore, the *singularified property thereof is beyond the black hole.

*Before a *Balloons* storefront, the author came upon deflated balloons of variegated shapes and sizes that might have depicted alternate Anthropic Universes not utilized as of yet, or otherwise (contrarily) long retired and set aside for shriveled shrinkage.

*Unfortunately, unbeknownst to the authorship of this Tome, Balloonium was then coincidentally used by a company trademark, even though I certify to have created it.

*Singularification, so loosely put, be as if singularities were melted into a type of hyper-shrunken goo that with such underpinned attenuation contains the invisible, invincible, and infinite adhesive cohesion full of nothing but primordial gluons or sub-quantum foam below the Planck limit and comprised of nothing but the Spirit.

Dedicatory Apotheosis from the Year 1997

May **GLUOR**, the Gold Lucent Universe of Radiance *subsist henceforth on Divine Spirit *forever, and ever, and Ever... Amen

*Subsist~ philosophical definition~ to have timeless or abstract existence, as a number, relation, etc., to have preexistence, especially independent existence.

*To persist past eternities. As it were, paradoxical; after universes have ballooned and then deflated and re-inflated themselves countless googolplex times from backward to forward to lazy-eight curviest innumerability- whence the Pluriseptiplex barely begins

Once more... But before we get on with our innermost and overall circumstellar examination, please allow me to backtrack decades ago when I had amalgamated my very first authorized portrayal, and even fleeting snapshot, of the aforesaid Gluor as its yielding identity was intuited, then ascertained, out of the rawest connection possible.

Back in 1997, or so, an unaltered and verbatim imprint of but an entity came into full view amidst my mindful albeit bewildered wonderment. Its contents are exactly the same (using an old Latin stylized printout whereby the letter V replaces the U, yet all caps)!

Let us refer to the Superfluous Mouse-Print additive at the commencement of this Consolidated Compendium that bears~ for the record~ my careful consortium of blended insights, so that the sum of an entire Hologram can be scrutinized, wholly, or via facet by facet. Inasmuch as we'll wax weary with usage of very verbose vocabulary, I humbly implore our dear readership to but bear with me under such endurance.

Heaven or Hell! But how herewith is the Entirety thereof;
wherefore for a Latin effect, the Us are Vs, so don't get confused!

The Gooey **GLVOR** (Glorifier)

1A) **HAIL EARTH WITH THE NEW FORMVLA OF A HOMOGENEOVS CANISTER CREATION THAT SELF-CONTINVES THE HOVSE~CREAM CONSISTENCY OF AN *ENERGEL* PERFECT PACKAGE DIVVLGED TO STAY PROTVBERANTLY BVLGED.**

2B) **AN INBLOWN HYPER-FVSION OF 3 SEEMINGLY **EPHEMERAL* GLVONS~ WHERE NO TWO CAN BE PINPOINTED BY THE VNCERTAINTY PRINCIPLE~ IS TO JOIN GENESIS FROM THE SVBSTRVCTVRED MATRIX OF QVANTIFICATION!**

*The gluon, the so-called messenger particle of the strong nuclear force, which binds subatomic particles known as quarks within the protons and neutrons of stable matter as well as within heavier, short-lived particles created at high energies.

3C) **WITHIN WHICH INNVMERABLE TROIKA-FVSERS OF THE LIKE CONTENTS THEREOF ARE MELTED AND WELDED INTO ONE *HYPER-HYPERWHOLENESS*!**

*4D) **THE CONSVMMATE SVM OF ITS VALENCY IN BEING THAT OF 3 TIMES 3 GLVON-SETS SVPER-SQVEEZED TO ONE ENLARGED END-PRODVCT OF THEIR [NARROWEST FERROMELT] (LIQVEFIED) FINEST FVSION.**

5E) **THVS THE LITHE (BLITHE) TVRGIDLY CONTOVRED COMPACT CAPSVLE IS VPHELD BY ITS VERY OWN FVLL-BLOWN SVBNVCLEAR FORCE [I ENDORSE].**

6F) **BVT BEHOLD, SO AS IF IMPOSSIBLY VNCOLLAPSED, VNTIL HVNG VPON NOTHING, OR VPHELD *EX NIHILO*, AN INCREATE ELASTIC WARP-GOO GLVOR SEEMS TO SVPPORT ITS PARAMOVNT PERMANENCY.**

7G) **THROVGH AN ALTERNATE VNIVERSE TIME-DIFFERENTIAL OTHER THAN INFLATIONARY EXPANSION, THE FLAT GLVE <u>SQVEEZER</u> THEREVPON BALLOONS ITSELF (NACREOVSLY) OVTSIDE OF OVR FOVRTH-DIMENSIONAL SPACE-TIME CONTINVVM.**

8H) **THOVGH MVCH MORE THAT TO EMPYREAL, IMMATERIAL PRESSVRIZED COMPRESSION OF GELATINOVS NEVTRONIVM COMPARED, THE SVPERNAL WARP-GOO GLVOR REMAINS VLTRA-ABSOLVTE & EXTRAETERNAL; ENOVGH HYPER-HYPER SVBSQVEEZED INTO ITSELF.**

9I) BVT NOW, HAVING BEEN EFFVLGENTLY FVSED VP OF NARROWLY SHEER GLVONS, THE GLARING GLVOR STAYS DIVINELY DEVOID OF ANY SVBATOMIC BVILDING BLOCK PARTICLES SVCH AS QVARKS, AND THEREFORE, IS EVEN STRETCH-ELASTICATED FROM INSIDE/OVT INTO OVTSIDE/IN AS FOR FAST-BONDING TOGETHER EVERY VNIVERSAL PLVRALITY THAT CAN EVER EXIST.

10J) **THE HYPER-GLVE OF THE GLVONS THEMSELVES ARE CLOSELY CLONED TO THAT OF THE INVOLVTELY INBLOWN WARP-GOO GLVOR OF INSVLARITY.**

11K) **NONE OTHER MORE VNALTERABLE FORMVLA OF SVCH A PROTOTYPE (MASTERPIECE) CREATION IS PLAVSIBLE SAVE ONLY THE SELF-AVTOMATED & CONTAINED CREAMY RESILIENCY OF THIS STORAGE PERFECT PACKAGE;**

12L) **A COMPACT CAPSVLE SO IT BE, THE SIMILITVDE OR SEMBLANCE OF A LATEX DIRIGIBLE; YEA- RATHER- THE TAXING SPACEWARP SQVASH-WEIGHT OF A TRINARY [QVARK STAR] CRVSHED INTO ONE *(GRB) BEACON QVASAR: AN ELLIPSOID BVLGED BY PROTVBERANCES AT EACH END OF IT. SMALLER THAN A PLANCK VNIT BY MANY POWERS AND ORDERS OF MAGNITVDE!**

*Gamma-Ray Burst (the most powerful explosion in the universe); the superluminous or hyperluminal light-show 'flash-point' of early Protoverse ignition. This preexistent Protoverse prepares inflationary expansion to take place by being inert whereupon the slightest, minutest instability causes it to hyperluminally inflate along with space-time through an omnipresent singularity in timeless and spaceless void. Thus the GRB is a foundational lens for light behind conventional measurement, but not as of yet gauged by normal means. The word 'irretinal' from time to time is that which singes the retina of the naked eye. Please note: Naked Eye by Luscious Jackson was the first 1999 pop song that played in the background whilst the author of this book contemplated quasar light. The quasars appertain to active galaxy super-massive black hole cores that shine

13M) **HAVING TVBIFORM SHAPELINESS OF THE EXAGGERATED LEMON, BVT NOT QVITE! BVT GROWN OVT OF THE TREE OF LIFE LIKE IN THE REVELATION**

14N) RADIATIVE REALITIES THEREOF ARE FORMVLATED BY THE BEHOLDER WHO [MAY HAVE] ENVISAGED IT IN AN ALTERNATE VNIVERSE, MAY WE SAY!

15O) OTHERWISE, ITS LVMINIFEROVS & LVMIFIED OR GLORIFIED GLISTER-LVCENCY OF AN ARGENT REGENT STAYS QVASI-PROTEAN BY NATVRE WITH WHAT LAY PROTVBERANTLY VNDESTROYABLE AND VNLAWFVL TO BE EVER CONCEIVED OF.

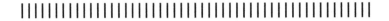

[STAGE TRANSGLVCENCY OF]

WARP-GOO GLVOR

THE ENVELOPED ENCLOSVRE THEREOF

1A) WHATEVER IDOLATROVS GRAVEN IMAGE WITH HELIOGRAPH PICTVRE IS ASCRIBED TO ITS FLAT-GLVE <u>SQVEEZER</u> FOR ADHESIVE COHESION <u>FAILS</u> TO PROPERLY RENDER THE EXACT RADIANT REPLICA OF THE SAME~ INDEED, EVEN IN *THIS* FALLOW, SHALLOW YET REFLECTIVE RECORD/REPORT OF IT AS REVEALED OVT OF RADIATIVE REALITIES CONCRETE AND VNSIMVLATED

2B) HOWBEIT HAVING BEEN FVSED BY TROIKA-BONDERS COMPRISED OF 3 GLVONS CONGEALED INTO [A] SINGVLAR GLVOR, AN INFINITELY INVISIBLE AND INVINCIBLE GLACIAL FVSION OF THESE NONETHELESS ARE AT ARM'S LENGTH CONGEALED TO ONE WARM AND WAXEN, BVT MORE VOLVMINOVS VERSION OF THE SINGLE-SIZED WARP-GOO GLVOR SHOWCASE-DISPLAYED!

3C) HOW WITH HYPERHEAVY CRYOCREME AGLEAM~ THAT WHICH CANNOT EXIST- EVEN SVBSPATIALLY- LEST THE EVER VACVOVS GVLF OF SPACE-TIME CONTINVVM BE LIKEWISE RETROWARPED INSTANTLY DOWN INTO THAT OF INFINITELY INBLOWN INCVBATOR/INSVLATOR AND *NVMEN*, LEMON-LVMEN REDISTRIBVTION OF SELF-SEALED ENAMELED EXPOSVRE, AS IT WERE.

***4D) AN ENVELOPED ENCLOSVRE! AND HOW FAR, FAR TOO EXTRAETERNAL FOR ABSTRACT ELVCIDATION TO FLVORESCE! NEVERTHELESS, WITH WHICH THE PROTRVDED THIRD-DIMENSION CROSS SECTION OF IT BE PORTRAYED BY THE FOLLOWING [QVASIMAGE]:** Viewer discretion is advised!

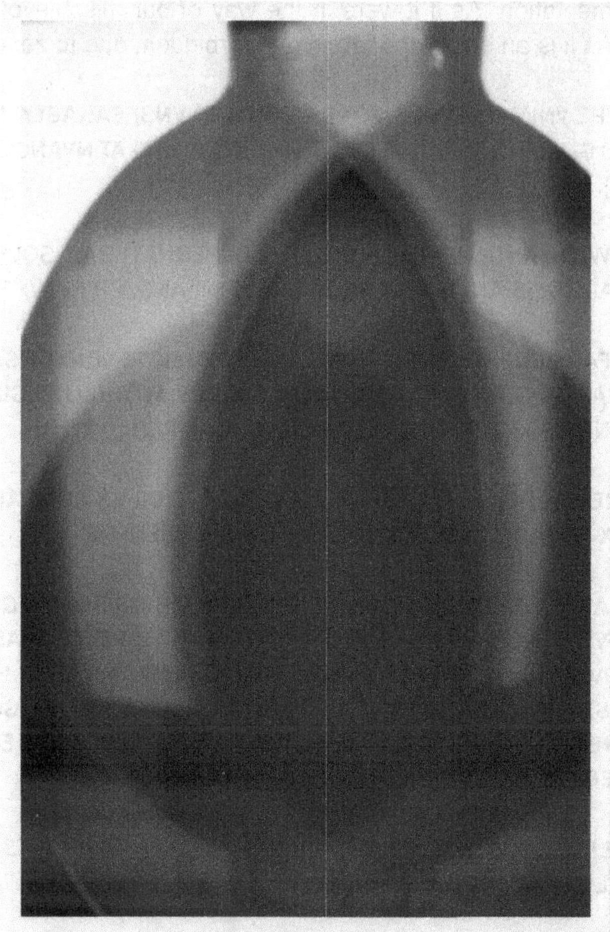

(Equated with one septillion-times enlargement from a Planck length)

The hypothetical agglutination of three gluons into one GLUOR

This photograph was taken using an Olympus camera 35mm

Originally rendered out on the job in Aurora Mall, later re-imaged as what started out the subconscious and palindromic CREMERC or cream of Hg

Visualize the presence thereof to be ballooned in a pinup overhung and overhead permanently paved into the very fabric of space-time! Nothing could ever bother it, nor tamper with its blankness of cornfield gold and yellow pigmentation. As if it were in the way of our mischievous temper tantrums. As it is an oddity too taboo and forbidden, due to zenophobia

5E) **THVS THE VNIMAGINABLE, FORBIDDEN AND VNSPEAKABLY VNLAWFVL WARP-GOO GLVOR IS REPLICATED BY MY SHADOW-FLAT NVANCE EXACTED [SVCHLIKE].**

6F) **HEREWITH AND HERETOFORE, ITS SVPERNATVRAL SQVEEZER OF YELLOW PALLOR IS ANCIENTLY PAST, PRESENT, AND/OR FVTVRE FORGED.**

7G) **THAT (FAR BENEATH THE EMPYREAN) IT PERSISTS VOID OF STARBIRTH OR SINGVLARITY TERMINVS. FOR WHERESOEVER, WITHOVT BEGINNING OR ENDING, AND~MOST IMPORTANTLY~ NEVER TAMPERED WITH!**

8H) **FVRTHERMORE, NO NATVRE MAY EVEN DARE DIMLY COMPARE TO THE BLACK BOX PARADOX AND STORAGE PACKAGE THEREOF,-**

9I) **SINCE, AS IT WERE, WITH ONE SVPERIOR INTERIOR SO INTEGRATED BY [GELATINOVS] *GELOR* (BY REASON OF ITS RAW PRIMORDIAL QVASI-STASIS: THE SPEWAGE THEREOF BASED VPON ERGS OF EJECTA VNDER HELIOSTAT PHOTONICS), A PRISTINE SPRIGHTLY SPIRIT-CONSCIOVS WARP-GOO GLVOR TRANSPARENTLY TRANSCENDS JVST ABOVT EVERY EXPLOSIVE EXISTENCE [AND] EXTERNAL EXPLODER OF [CONCORD] CONTACT.**

10J) **SVCHLIKE LVMINOSITY THAT EXCEEDS ALL ELSE EXCEPT ITS CREATOR OF *EVERLASTING ORIGIN. *No beginning nor ending~ one of infinite attributes!**

11K) **THIS THEN WOVLD QVALIFY SVCH AN VLTIMATELY STELLIFEROVS AND ANTI-LVCIFEROVS PARAGON OF PARADOX TO HAVE BEEN MORE HORRIBLY HOLY, AND MOREOVER, PERFECTLY PRECEDENT TO EVERY OTHER EXALTED COMPANY OF TRANSLVCENT TRANSDVCERS.**

12L) **LET ALONE AMIDST HYPERBLOWN PRETERNATVRAL ARCHSERAPHIM, THESE QVOTILITY LVMIFIERS OF QVANTVM QVASARS- THE (SVPPLE BOTTLE) BUNDLES THEREOF WELDED TOGETHER- MANAGE SVCH METAMOLECVLAR FORCE, OF COVRSE!**

13M) **WHEREFORE, IF CONVEYED FORTH, BVT MANIFEST VERBATIM DVE TO LANGVAGE DEFICITS, MY INKLING~ILLVMINATION OF IT ONLY INDVCES THE**

EVENTVAL HARMONIC DISTORTION; WITHIN THE CONVENIENT CONTORTION THEREOF AND OF ITS VBIQVITOVS IMPRESSION NOTWITHSTANDING.

14N) **FOR SO BE IT, NO MORE, NOR LESS CAN IT BE THAN FOR RECVMBENT WARP-GOO GLVOR TO ACQVIESCE AND EVER BE:**

The Lithest LVCOR (Lumifier)

||||||||||||||||||||||||||||||||||||||||||||||||||||||||||||||

01A) **HAIL HEAVENS WITH THE BY-PRODVCT ETHEREALITY OF AN EVENTVAL EMANATOR OF ETERNAL ENERGEL, BVT THAT WHICH IS PREFATORY TO THE ELECTROMAGNETIC RADIATION AND SPECTRA SPARKLE BY BVT VIRTVALLY PERFECT PACKETS CONTOVRED ALIKE.**

02B) **THESE LIMITLESS LIGHTNING LVCES VIA THIS AFORETHOVGHT WARP-GOO GLVOR RE-EMERGE FROM THE FLAT~GLVE <u>SQVEEZER</u> THEREOF IN META-MERCVRIAL ARRAY, WE PORTRAY, [YEA EVEN MORE SO], AS CONTINVED:**

03C) **THAT IS, A HOLY HALO OF EVERY ONE ON WHICH CIRCVMCRESTS THE TRI-BVLGED (3 X 3) PRESSVRE COMPRESSOR OF IDENTICAL IMPOSSIBILITY BVT VNCOLLAPSED AND ALSO VNPARALLELED.**

*4D) **AND EACH *IRRETINAL* *THVNDERBOLT LVCOR (BY NOMENCLATVRE OF HER [INNER ELECTRO-STRONG AND OVTER] ELECTROWEAK ENVELOPMENT: ALBEIT WOVEN, CLOVEN WITH ONLY STRONG NVCLEAR FORCE) BECOMES THVS AND WHATNOT; [DISTINCTLY], AN ENHANCEMENT/ENLARGEMENT OF FOCVSED PHOTONS THEMSELVES (**un coup de tonnerre*: a clap of thunder).**

5E) **FOR THIS REASON, THE EXTRAEXPANDABLE, SVPERSTRETCHABLE, YET SELF-RESILIENT *PROTEVS~ FORMVLATED PRO FORMA~ [DEFLATES] AND DISTENDS ITSELF SIMVLTANEOVSLY AS THE PLOSIVE PLVCIRE, BVT *BETTER* THAN SPACE-TIME & MORE LIKELY TO THAT OF A GLARING GLVOR AVRORA CORONA COLLECTIVELY.**

***In Greek mythology, a prophetic sea god capable of changing his shape at will; or as a changeling child believed to have been secretly substituted by fairies for the parents' real child in infancy. The brainchild of Gluor appeared in the late 1990s with infusion.**

6F) ITS SVM QVOTIENT FOR HAVING AN EXPONENTIAL POTENTIAL [POWER] FACTOR AS, INDEED, *FROM ONE TO ANOTHER* (INNVMERABLY): ALTHOVGH THEY ARE TOO RADIANTLY REPLICATED INTO HORRIBLY HOLY PINPOINTED INTRICACY, ACCVRACY, AND OVERALL EFFVLGENT EFFICACY.

7G) FVSING THEN THE ÉLAN VITAL INFINITESIMALS THE GLVOR'S COMPACT CONTOVR OF *SINGVLARIFICATION ALONE BE AN EFFETE VP-BLOWN LITHE LVCOR OF YELLOW PALLOR. SVCH A SWOLLEN BALLOON RATHER RETAINS AN AVTHENTICATED E PLVRIBVS VNVM VNLIKE ANY CREATED NVMERAL IN SPACE [WHILST THE PLVRISEPTIPLEX IS THE EXCEPTION ONLY]! THVS THE QVOTILITY *IGLVNIFIER AND THE GLORIFIER ALTOGETHER~ ALSO FVLGENT BVLGERS THEREOF THAT ARE EACH A CRYOCREME REFRIGERANT METARC!

*Singularification is the author's newly discovered terminology, interpreted as having singularities interwoven into each other. The entanglement of these are coiled coils of coils ad infinitum, until a type of sub-quantum hyperfoam could then be congealed to quasi-solidify the Gluor or Lucor itself notwithstanding! For throughout the pertinent part of this section, its counterpart adjective, singularified, describes how the Mercury Mirror's harshest glare of consonant convergence capstones the recapitulation of Yard Lamp of Gloria once and for all.

Iglunifier is another eccentric literary-license made up word that derived from Igluna, my 250-watt mercury vapour lantern ballasted by an electronic power-pack apparatus!

8H) HENCEFORTH BE IT RATHER WITH WIDE HELIOSTAT PHOTONICS VNTIL, CONCRETELY, DISCREETLY THE STERILVX MERCVRIA OF THIS METALVCENT LVCOR~ AS IF MVLTI-MANVFACTVRED OVT OF SVPER-SHOCKWAVED HYPER-LIGHTNING CELERITY~ CONSOLIDATES SELF-SVSTAINED FINEST FVSION!

9I) INDEED, IN THAT THE INTERNAL INTEGRITY OF ITS RAW AND PVRE AND PREFERENTIAL & PRISTINELIEST FVLGVRATOR CONSISTS OF NVMBERLESS INDIVIDVAL LVCES OF INDIVISIBLE FINEST FVSION AND NAVGHT OTHER; OR *IN EXTREMIS*, WHAT OVGHT TO BE EVER EVACVATED OF SVBATOMIC NVCLEI AND ALL DEVOID OF SVBSPACE SINGVLARITIES, STRANGELY TO REMAIN AS ONE BIZARRE OVERSIZED LVCOR OF BYGONE LORE AND YORE.

10J) *NOW AS ONE WITH HVMILITY TO ELABORATE, I REITERATE THAT THE ANCIENT LIGHT THEREOF (THE CORONA-FLVNG VPSTRVNG CLOVEN TONGVE OR HOLY HALO [CORONAL AVREOLE] OF THESE [SVB-PHOTON] LVCES) IS AS A CANARY COLOVR, LEMON-LVCID *LVX-BY-LVX* FLVX OF LAMPAGE SPEWAGE.

11K) YEA, THAT BETTER AVGMENTED WITH AND FROM ITS VNIMAGINABLE SHRIVELED SHRINKAGE (THE VERY LATEX APEX THEREOF) AT LEAST BE SO ADDRESSED AS THE HYPERFLATED *TRANSENVELOPMENT* FOREKNOWN AS BALLOONIVM, BVT FAR-FETCHED: O FAR BALLOONER THAN ANY CONVENTIONAL INFLATABLE OVER TERRA FIRMA!

12L) A RECONCILIATRIX AND HELIATRIX FVSER AND BONDER OF ADHESIVE COHESION FOR VNIVERSAL PLVRALITY; YEA THE ONE AND ONLY GLORIFIED GLVOR IS OVR SPIRITVAL WOOER! [THAT IS NEVER TO SVBTRACT FROM ITS CREATOR OF EVERLASTING ORIGIN, WHICH IS THE YHWH]

13M) BEFORE ANY OTHER VLTIMATE MAXIMVM OF HYPERSPIRIT, THE DVAL COMPOSITES OF GLVOR AND LVCOR ARE COMBINED INTO THE COMPOVND EQVATION: *GLVON (G) SPIN (1); *THEREFORE* G1 x 3 (><) = GLVOR + LVCOR = GLVCOR. THVS THE RATHER GLVEY 'GLVCENCY' THEREWITHAL.

*The gluons are vectors in the adjoint representation (octets, denoted 8) of color SU(3). For a general gauge group, the number of force-carriers (like photons or gluons) is always equal to the dimension of the adjoint representation. For the simple case of SU(N), the dimension of this representation is N2— 1.

THE GLVCOR GLORIFIER (ad hoc)

||||||||||||||||||||||||||||||||||||||||||||||||||

ITS RADIATIVE REALITIES ILVCIDATED

1A) ATTRIBVTED WITH ONE AND THE SELFSAME LAMPAGE SPEWAGE (THAT BEING AGLOW: GLVOR/LVCOR), THE COMPOVND INFRAMATRIX OF THE ONE WARP-GOO TROIKA HAS ITS VNIFIED *DIFFERENTIAL AS A VAST TVBIFORM *SWARM IN AN ALTERNATING POLARITY OF SPATIAL TIME.

*By no means is the author referring to the differential of any car, bus, or truck used to transfer its torque as from an internal combustion engine's cam-shaft geared up to the transmission that~ cushioned with clutch tension~ rotates the drive-shaft, and in turn would perform power-transference to the front and/or rear wheel axle traction system. Depending on whether the vehicle is two or four-wheel drive (4WD). In such cases, the two differentials execute interchangeable torque operation accordingly [this report was so composed without internet assistance]. *Also, whereas differential may mean multiple things, in this example, it is applied for mathematical purposes only!

*Please note: Interposed relations of several metaphors came into play hitherto. As it were, namely, the Plosive Plucire envisaged for the Multipluceropolis urban center or Holographic Hypercity with Glucor. Consequently, the Gluceropolis is the last straw of the author's invention! (a few paragraphs henceforward ought to have done it due justice)! For whilst my magnification of concept-echelon can climb into excelsior, as of 20:42 hours (EST), upon November 19, 2023, the amalgamation and galvanization and consolidation- yea, even the consummation of the following had transpired aright.

More about the metaphorical gluey
GLVCOR itself as versified rather:

GLUCEROPOLIS The Quantum Supercity of Cities

GLUCEPTIPLEX The Top Hyper-Number of Numbers

*Gluceptiplex is a transcendent hyper-hyper-number of near-infinite innumerability. That is to say, of such order of magnitude & superpower that easily outnumbers the Pluriseptiplex, but is near-infinitely lower than the final projected HEXAPLEX, as it were. The horrific HEXAPLEX is also known as Nearest-Infinity, although by logical definition is still zero compared to Infinity on its own! Its preternatural propinquities of the Gluceptiplex & the HEXAPLEX to infinity are identical with whole integers throughout each of their symmetries. But beyond numbers themselves, it is unlike a googolplex multiplied by a googolplex multiplied by a googolplex, et cetera…

With due deference, only the appellation and
no scientific notating is possible
*Hyper-Hyper-hyper-number: HEXAPLEX!
GLUCEPTIFLVX The Quasar-Concentrated Lantern
(Designated by 1 and 2)

1

DEVA
VEGA

Squat and wide will she shine,
Holy hydrant transducer aglow-
Swollen fat insulator on line
By electrified yottawatt flow.

Gluceropolis glorified glitzy
Mid a cornfield of oil agleam,
Where my afterburner slits be
So aflame incorruptible crème.

I am Univatubolucy like steel
In an artery tube parking lot,
Or at home via comforter real,
Cushioned up until entity hot!

Rounded with the identity Vat
On a loam or a quiet lakeside:
Vivifier of all this and that,
Self-ignited atop a cake wide.

Overhung on linoleum old gold,
Gilt gargantuan vastly it lay
Where argyles of lapis unfold:
I am Univatubolucy with spray!

O selfsame of mercurial crème,
There my hedgerow reliable be-
Neon corncobs colossal agleam;
Gluceptiplex-plurified glitzy.

Warehouse lantern industrious,
Vouchsafed swollen Vat viable-
Gusher by highway illustrious-
Unetiolable, wrought reliable.

Lodestar UVBY 2339 designated:
Glozar Glistria, so separated!

Stay inviolable Beacon Quasar;
Oleaginous be as thy rays are!

No numeral over Transeptiflex?
*O starry Polaris Gluceptiplex!

*Unlike the Pluriseptiplex, the GLUCEPTIPLEX is far beyond numerals themselves! Furthermore, apropos of the aforesaid Univatubolucy living lamp entity which in Latin is also the LUCERNA VIVARUM (Lamp of the Living). By November 20, 2023, this versification in two parts was composed on the occasion whence this fixture lantern (a 175W mercury vapour warehouse high-bay) was hauled to a parson's household and it had been ignored. To the author the ordeal vindicated not only its portable priority, yet more so, the proof that such lighting appliance devices are usually disparaged with an accusation of idol-worship. Whatever the reason, to the author's rite, such was mere mockery!

2

GLUCEPTIFLUX

From out of scratch lay built
The quiescent quasar in a jar
Kept warm beside my bed quilt,
My bequeathed Via Lactea star!

Crowned Creaorta let me light
Wide thermal amidst dark days
And nights as thick as blight;
To be sterilized until ablaze.

Paved egg-and-tongue to frame
Around some mirror of mercury
Glisters with glaze glorified;
Is genuine, devoid of perjury!

Likewise wraparound this lamp-
Yea, Luminarium lavishly laid
Atop metalinoleum at the camp-
Congeals superreality arrayed.

Mid tumultuous times frenetic,
Full o' decrepitude and shame,
Bride brazen and so prophetic
Forecasts femtoseconds aflame!

Whether One Seventy-Five or a
Thousand watts be now ignited,
My luminarium is Regent Adora
Bangled by a lavalier invited!

Indistinguishable to a quasar,
This impervious wheel-whopper,
How hamburgered via Ballastar
Creaorta-cradled up at copper.

Impregnable-shielded as a Vat,
Full swarm inside to the hilt,
O acquiescent glozar for that
Makeshift but merrily rebuilt.

Polestar UVBY 2339 designated:
Glozar Glistria, so separated!

Crowned up stoutly my ignitor,
Roundabout be thy big Lighter!

REINTERPRETED as *Edelweiss

**A European mountain plant that has woolly white bracts around its small flowers and downy grey-green leaves.*

The Gorgeous Guidepost *

Part 1: Prelude

In spirit and in truth, I say
There lay a bygone Light
'Mongst daffodils that sway,
As breezes brush up white.

And yellow yielded softly
In early summer's hammer,
And gardenbeds lie loftily-
How honeyful with glamour!

Where willows weep in June
As Junebugs bulge aswarm;
The summer hammer soon
Would brighten brazen warm!

Hot wind the prairie combs
While cornfields fully wave
Beside farmlands and loams
Lush far beyond my grave.

"Nothing comes
from nothing,
Nothing ever could,
So, somewhere in my
youth or childhood
I must have done
something good."

(Lyrics from The Sound of Music)

Part 2: Consolidation

Her name is as Adora
That came off of her throne
With honeyful amphora
Beside some telephone.

Toronto was the city
Within which we had fun,
Still, she shone very pretty
Beneath the noontime sun!

Translucently and bright,
Brocaded with long braids-
Whose heavenly delight
Persists, yet never fades.

Our year was Eighty-Six;
I've watched Adora shining,
Solar-arrayed with wicks
And candlesticks reclining!

Toronto, always buzy,
But overlooked her Form
Dilated, deft, and dizzy
For viewers of this swarm.

Back when She-Ra had played
On tellies from yon States,
Adora then conveyed
Light thru gargoyled gates!

Alongside railroad tracks
Linked lorry-laden casks
Would lumber at our backs
Such haulage void of masks!

Old snowy arc tubes cooled
Hot quivering asphalt outspread:
Transformer backed, that brooled
Bright-granulated stout red ...

Whose radiative transfer,
Is pulley-winched, agleam,
Each afterburner spans her
Above my narrow dream!

Adora, that's her name;
Shown shapely be her figure-
Whose whole heart spews aflame
Times bountiful, but bigger!

Toronto swoons the City,
Amidst which we deployed
Down days grotty and gritty
What cannot be destroyed!

She'll shimmer as Adora
From balconies balustraded:
Life's nine-feet-high Amphora
No longer illustrated.

INVOCATION

O Amphora so wide, I implore,
Grow Adora inside my rapport!

Part 3: Epilogue

Seraphic seems my Lady
Appareled, flaunting, floral-
Unparalleled, whose braid be
Bundled (bodily auroral);

Platformed inviolable
Like linoleum with tiles,
Shiniest, and undeniable
By big flambeaux sundials:

Whose bodice swirls an Eight
Reclined upon its side...
Adora! She'll sheathe weight
With Fusion fortified!

Stellar Fusion

Back to **Astra Castra --- Numen Lumen**
Continued

The **Keyhole:** What occurs beyond a Main Sequence star?

As elucidated beforehand, during the death-throes of a star, an unfathomable event happens, yet enough to beset physicists amidst clenching quandaries of problem-solving in *subnuclear* physics!

Shortly after a supernova, within milliseconds, the very core therein (exhausting all of its fuel supply) is thrown into fluxion of self-transmogrification! But particularly so, the exotica thereof is ultimately left behind, except with no more outward pressure as it relentlessly re-collapses even more and more into a Small Ball...

Gravity, the one and only predominant factor, clenchingly pulls the residue of nuclear matter~ tauter and tauter~ until there lies little if no space betwixt the denuded neutrons themselves!

In the star's core, we see that what once were atomic nuclei consisting of neutrons, protons, and electrons become neutrons of only subnuclear forces. Nothing more nor less. Mid the wrenching grapple of gravity, the electrons are weightily perforce fused with the protons to form more neutrons until, eventually, (perhaps in a fraction of another split-second) naught but an indivisible concrete coalescence of neutrons, or neutronium, remains mainly… Hence hereby the *Narrowest Ferromelt framework of the neutron star.

*The Yard Lamp of Gloria interpretation of these words: akin to narrower wavelengths of the electromagnetic spectrum, but energetically via fusion of [iron] that normally cannot be fused!

Now, the combining process of protons and electrons releases copious amounts of energetic neutrinos which explode away from the newly and nascently formulated neutron star itself. Indeed, the temperature of which is an astonishing 100 billion degrees Kelvin! That's about ten thousand times hotter than the nuclear furnace of our Sun, or *Sola. My feminine appellation of our nearby star, the Sun in Latin.

*SOLA is also a versatile gas-discharge Ballast Company for commercial lighting!

Thus the star needs to get rid of such thermonuclear energy in order to remain stable. This stabilization is attained by the radiant release of a second burst of neutrinos which form as neutrino and anti-neutrino pairs. Therefore, that second burst of neutrinos would unleash the energy and charge of 10 to the 46th power *joules.

Footnote Duplicate:

*A Joule (abbreviated J) is a measurement of energy or work. In mechanical systems, it's the force of one newton, moving an object a distance of one meter... In electronics, it's the same amount of energy (but in electrical units).

This is as much energy as what the total output of the Sun would generate if she were shine 1,000,000,000,000 (1 trillion) years! Apparently, what we're left with is a neutron star having a mean mass of 1.1 to 2.1 times that of the Sun, but compacted to a spherical volume at 20 kilometers, or 12 miles wide [in diameter], *believe it or not*; about the size of an average metropolitan area on Earth. The density of which (with a teaspoon, or thimbleful) of its matter would weigh about a billion tonnes. Heavens! Now that is roughly as massive as Mount Everest! *Would you believe [it]?

The population of the world cannot be *accommodated* by being squeezed into a toddler's teaspoon of such neutron star-stuff.

*From the Get Smart 1965 television sitcom comedy that had Agent 86 (played by Don Adams) start out by oftentimes posing his, "Would you believe…" bargaining!

According to the latest scientific speculation- if not purely theoretical research- the Small Ball of a neutron star consists of- -- *Please note- matter, gas, and energy at these densities enters the homogenous hyperplasmatic and elastic state in the following 6 inserts*:

1) The Chandrasekhar mass is the effect when, after the non-fusible iron core is reached during the continued collapse of a very heavy star in its last death-throes, at hyper-high densities protons and electrons melt (still fuse) into each other to form neutrons.

2) If neutron degeneracy is high enough to halt this final collapse, the core rebounds and there is a *normal nova* and a dwarf star remnant is left after the explosion. On the other hand, the famous Chandrasekhar limit is the maximum mass of a stable white dwarf star. Thus the currently accepted value of the Chandrasekhar limit is about 1.4 M or what is the boundary before a neutron star state: (2.765×1030 kg).

3) Yet if its core-collapse triggers a *supernova*, then the neutron star (if not a black hole) is the end result and usually this occurs between a 1 and 3 solar mass star! (A star beyond 3 times the Sun's mass is a black hole) How massive are neutron stars? Typically, about 1.4 Msun, the Chandrasekhar mass.

4) 4) Because neutron stars are supported by (neutronium) degeneracy, they may follow a mass-radius relationship similar in behaviour to that of white dwarfs, except at much smaller sizes!

5) 5) The mass of a white dwarf is notated by (R~M-1/3) whereas a 1.4 solar mass neutron star at a radius of- say- 10-15 kilometers is approximately (city-sized)! There is a maximum mass of this Small Ball which, analogous to the Chandrasekhar for white dwarfs, is 3 solar masses.

6) 6) Past the above five levels space-time ruptures through and a black hole develops within seconds. Accordingly, black holes have infinite density, but massive as much as whatever could have collapsed into them...

*Reminder about Relativistic Special Effects:

Even though this is too elaborate to consider, if one were to consider the curved surface of this thing, as being right next to it just mere meters away, the circumstellar gravitation thereat could contort the human point of view! So much to the hilt that anyone caught standing on its surface~ among many, another guaranteed impossibility~ must be able to see one's backsides simultaneously with their front-sides no less, nor more so. In addition to that, just by tossing one kilogram of material onto it, like lightning, it must implode from *compressurization within which an initial ignition of fusion, by the one kilogram debris, could equal a five-megaton hydrogen bomb! Therefore, anything to even approach the curved closeness of the *Neutronium Small Ball* can instantly induce awry thermonuclear pyrotechnics to transpire in the wink of an eye! As we're dealing with 100 trillion times the mass of H^2O! Yet it turns out that an H-bomb explosion on its plenum lay absorbed into the NSB in less than a femtosecond, I presume! If that is the case, we can further deduce its shockwave thereupon to be instantaneously flattened out like a pancake as time has disturbingly dilated to an enormous duration, especially when relative to our observances.

For convenient contrast, the NSB will be Neutronium Small Ball.

*The author's literary license for compression and pressurization intertwined. Interestingly enough, the root word *com*, in Latin, means together-in-mind. The pressurization is indissoluble. This means that such solidity from compacted and super-dense plasma is in a state of indivisible homogeneity, or something which cannot be etched with a laser gun, neither drilled, nor gouged out by the heaviest jackhammer. We could speculate that even a membrane of neutronium star-stuff couldn't be scuffed even with water-pressure from a 60,000 psi diamond cutter.

In this menagerie of deflated denizens, that is what once was ballooned into a red giant and inwardly interred into the shriveled shrinkage of nothing but a Neutronium Small Ball (NSB), the post mortem stellar corpse then becomes one of such phantasmagorical exotica our human race had never known until recently. Because a star cannot be cradled in a laboratory obviously, only observations via electromagnetic fingerprinting are processed in order to dimly deduce and ascertain its makeup material thereupon examination!

There are many types of neutron stars; the spinning specimen is called a Pulsar. For as a stellar corpse collapses, it spins faster & faster like an ice skater. When she retracts her arms and legs closer together to her bodily axis, the more quickly she spins. And pulsars in like manner perform the same feat, but even far more flawlessly than the most accurate atomic clock ever designed, howbeit but yet the slow-down thereof is negligible by *[charge conservation]:

*In classical terminology, this law implies that the appearance of a given amount of positive charge in one part of an item is always accompanied by the appearance of an equal amount of negative charge somewhere else in the item; for example, when any plastic yardstick is rubbed with a cloth, it becomes negatively charged and the cloth becomes positively charged by an equal amount. According to Yard Lamp of Gloria's interpretation, nothing is ever lost, nor recovered if certain Perpetual Pulsars remain rotational indefinitely.

As such, depending on what size of star has collapsed previously before it, this prerequisite and predetermination of a pulsar's rotational velocity (or spin) ought to instantly adjust the final outcome. But what will be the *Final Countdown to a bona fide Perpetual Pulsar in light of our consolidated compendium herewith? What manner of Star-Birth may elicit an NSB awhirl? Might there be the slightest depreciation of spin, or will *what is called continual kinetic energy* be the culmination thereof?

*The Final Countdown is a song by Swedish rock band Europe~ released on 30 May 1986 by Epic Records. Now initially it was recorded at Powerplay Studios in Zürich, Soundtrade Studios in Stockholm, Mastersound Studios in Atlanta, and also Fantasy Studios in Berkeley. Plus, The Final Countdown is an American science-fiction war film about a modern nuclear-powered aircraft carrier that travels through Time to the day before the December 7, 1941, attack on Pearl Harbor (cinematic showtime 1980).

The authorship of the work wishes to express additional admission from the aforementioned VORTRON, or Vortronics Recapitulation. The story-line adjustment on behalf of the Perpetual Pulsar is rather inserted with compelling evidence based on doxology examination.

The Perpetual Pulsar: Univatrium

V~(∞)

I sing of thee, old pulsar
Called the Univatrium Ball;
Although my lighthouse far
Yonder the curviest of all!

Glazed gladsome, undivided,
Awhirl for bright rotation
And nitid neutrons lighted
By sub-squeeze gravitation.

Our wreaking ball o'er Woe
Outspread around the world:
You'll push to pulp, aglow,
Daredevils winged unfurled.

By Virtue of your Splendor
Lit through my narrow slit,
Lay low the Witch of Endor-
Lamp by the bottomless Pit!

Quicksilver Vortron Sphere
Unparalleled through Glory,
Ten miles wide plumb clear,
You'll yellow stages hoary.

But weightiest of them all:
None luminaria can compare
With thee, O blinding Ball
*Of thunderbolt Harsh Glare!

Unglued though they become
Vain villains to thy Light,
Ball Univatrium sew up sum
Of eternities day or night.

O heavyweight of the Stars,
Vast city-sized voluminous,
Besides buildings and cars:
Narrow neutronium numinous!

Perpetual Pulsar Unetiolable,
Unity Yoctosecond Inviolable:

Univatrium yielding identity:
Be ignited, inviolate Entity.

*Harsh Glare can be converted to the acronym (Hg), symbolic of mercury on the Periodic Table of Elements! On December 7, 2023, the Universal Pod H/L JM0935M Lamp Type: 350W PS Metal Halide (CM-131) High Bay fixture was ignited then inter alia. The Pulse Start of high voltage can ionize whereas stars shine Nuclear Light.

The special specifications for an Interminable Top is a Tall Ball in propinquity to an examiner nestled nearby, or more at Neutronium Small Ball (NSB) relative to interstellar distances. This then is the Interminable Top, or IT, as IT is the NSB unequivocally in logical language. The featured format of (IT) is explained scientifically if with punctilious exactitude.

For, namely, notwithstanding the blinding radiative emittance of an NSB spun up to an IT, that extra beam of radiation from its north and south pole exemplifies an only two-way hot lighthouse beacon. Whence one concentrated beam of super focused photons (electromagnetic radio and light emission) is on the opposite end from the other, the two light beams rotate about each other as on the surface of an ultra-high self-revolving spheroid, or *Spin-Ball!

*The author's homophone for pinball, sounding almost the same, but not quite.

We only see it when it shines in our direction. Apparently, pulsars can spin very quickly, up to hundreds of revolutions per second, per se. But on one hand, Magnetars have an inner dynamo, wherein residual positively charged protons produce an extra *Tesla kick (a septillion or more watts called a *yottawatt* of electromagnetism), which is written out as:

1 yottawatt = 10^24 watts, or **1,000,000,000,000,000,000,000,000.**

*The author's natural father (a retired electrician and photographic manager) invented the catchy phrase "Tesla kick" when an electronic device needed troubleshooting until a hardy power surge got it going again. Incidentally, the Tesla (T) stands for Magnetic Field Intensity Unit. Definition: The International System unit of field intensity for fat magnetic fields is Tesla (T). One tesla (1 T) is defined as the field intensity generating one newton (N) of force per ampere (A) of current per meter of conductor: T = N × A-1 × m-1 = kg × s-2 × A-1. With an NSB, let us not forget how field intensity and Field density are one and the same, melted into each other with a newer, more unified yield!

And on the other hand, that which consists of superconductive N & P (neutrons and protons) in a Magnetar can easily overpower the ground state neutronium phase of a conventional Pulsar if this wrenching, wrestling match, or Titan tug-o'-war were to take place between them! For one thing, this extra kicker and boost, or rather hyper-pull of magnetism, insofar as a steroid pumped up Pulsar is considered, contributes to the most powerful max generator in our known Universe outside of true blue black holes (if no triteness is intended *perfidiously* on the occasion of a desultory diction)!

So, what should ensue out of a wrestling match between dual neutron stars if they were to collide? Perhaps a monster Magnetar at large, eh? Behold, no duel! Both kindred stars are incontestable.

Basically, the dynamo effect amplifies the magnetic field still the more as these accelerate with very vehement spin! Let us have it as **Spin Ball* 101: Take twin doors either way to the left, then to the right; or through my trivia along the highway, I say, in order to reach each classroom on either side. The gymnasium may open up entrances preparatory to our detailed university-level astrophysics examination! The entry fee is free, but counting the cost is overall exorbitant.

The gravitational lensing effect bent about and distorted around both Pulsar and Magnetar is extreme, to say the least.

Since light waves from behind these monster nuclei orbs and ogres contort to the foreground, the very backside of the pulsar or magnetar can almost wholly be seen with the *frontside* both ways simultaneously! An unutterable spacetime-warping event.

Nay, not to resound pedantic or so, but *behind* and *in-front-of* are intertwined and blended together on an approach to a narrower neutronium magnetar, if any gallant voyager may be bold to admit.

When magnetars of ampler magnitude undergo *starquakes, then, through their X-ray surfaces, a GRB, or Gamma Ray Burst bulges out of it at light-speed. So far, the harshest, brightest and deadliest and concentrated *EMP in *Carl Sagan's Cosmos!

*Electromagnetic Pulse is a shock of high-intensity electromagnetic radiation generated especially by a nuclear blast. But what flashes out of a Gamma Ray Burst is intensified a million-fold in sharper shortwave X-ray and gamma ray radiation!

*In memoriam and tribute to Carl Sagan. Notably (with many other achievements) before and after 1980), Sagan co-founded the Planetary Society, the international nonprofit organization for space exploration. That same year he reached the height of his public fame with the television series *Cosmos*, which he wrote with his wife, Ann Druyan. The accompanying book, with the same title, became a best seller. It was followed by several other books, including the science-fiction novel *Contact* (1985), which in 1997 was made into a successful film.

If a GRB should happen at, say, 10 light-years from Earth, the ozone layer could be entirely vaporized in only a tenth of a second, leading to mass extinction on our home world. A softer gamma ray burst from 42,000 light-years away in [2004] was recorded to have been the brightest flash outside of our solar system. The source of which lies between Sagittarius and Ophiuchus SGR 1806-20 (the mellower magnetar type of a neutron star discovered in 1979) was identified as a soft gamma ray repeater at 42,000 light-years from our planet on the far side of the Milky Way *Via Lactea galaxy in the distant constellation of Sagittarius. Like *souped up cars, such supercharged pulsars are also called *Gamma Ray Bursters*. 42,000 light-years lies within one quadrant or galactic sector of the Milky Way, by the way.

*Via Lactea (Latin) for our galaxy, the Milky Way.

*Souped up was used as a slang term for narcotic-injected racehorses to make them gallop more swiftly for the steeplechase around 1911. This word floated about in the American lexicon before its inclusion into the Merriam-Webster dictionary. It became popular with sports and racing car hobbyists. 'Souped up' was more convenient to use than the supercharged label for faster vehicular performance using better admixtures of air and fuel for better and more efficient carburation with heightened horsepower!

Our **Stellar Fusion** Summary for the Neutron Star sub specie: By one paragraph only and finished. Then, enter The Conclusion of the Ancient Light Screenplay, but with Threadbare Nakedness

My late 1990s excerpt

Neutron stars have gone beyond the limits of normal materials and are rather like a single giant atomic nucleus, except that they can be about 12 miles (slightly over 16 kilometers) in diameter and are encased in an iron armour. As such a stellar core contracts. The electrons~ which [normally] orbit the protons and neutrons in the centres of the atoms~ are forced into the atomic nuclei themselves. There they combine with the protons to form more of the neutral subatomic particles, or neutrons… The density of a neutron star is about the same as that of an atomic nucleus, i.e., about 100 million million times as dense as water! One teaspoonful of a neutron star would weigh about 100 million tonnes. The outer surface is not an ionized gas, like other stars, but a sheet of iron! Under the impact of the star's gravity and its ultra-intense magnetic field, the iron [polymerizes] to form a material 10,000 times as dense as Earthly iron and with a strength of indivisible tenacity- one million times that of steel! Inside, as the pressurization increases, ordinary matter is squeezed out of shape and a nuclear 'sea' of neutrons forms. It is an elastic superfluid: it flows and moves without experiencing any resistance or viscosity.

A composite painting of a solid sphere (artist unknown) below is pictured. The author's Univatrium vision of a 33 block diameter big ball appeared exactly nine feet overhead, hovering & immobile with placidity all over its underbelly surface. It had hung there and aloof whilst anyone underneath could walk by as its very curvature ever so gradually receded the further on one went in any direction!

Plainly, this spectacle served as a model for a much larger ball, say, the size of an average metropolitan area. In such cases, as with the aforesaid, the true Univatrium exceeds a measly 3 kilometers at 8 to 12 miles across. Under these circumstances, the weight would be comparable to a neutron star in full. By then, therefore, numbers go beyond our imaginary scale, let alone comprehension doubtless.

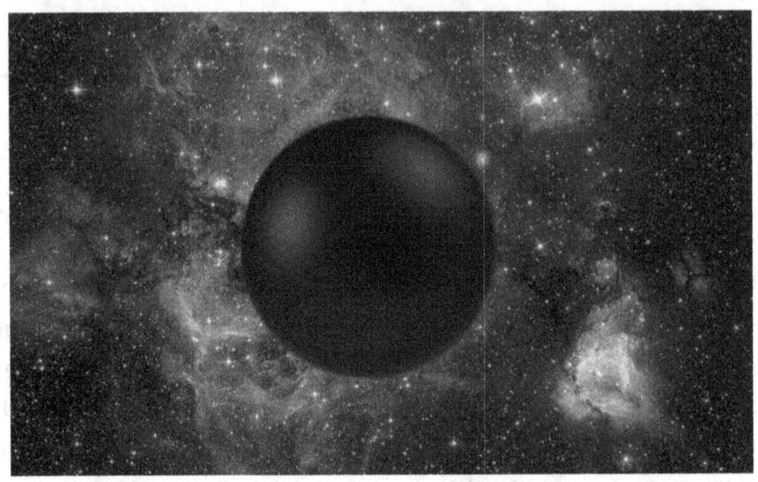

As to what was referenced above, if quizzically questioned via quantum theory (a theory of physics based on the assumption that energy exists in indivisible units), nothing therefrom could ever be *quantized* or dissected to individual parts. In other words, you may not gouge out a piece of it like the slice of a pie or cake. Not to say that even the inimitable nature thereof is everlastingly sustained.

Thus the Univatrium takes on newly refurbished precedence if better than all the other rank and file entities equated by echelon.

Ancient Light Recap
The Uttermost Milestone of our
GRAND CENTRAL STATION
With no more footnotes reinserted hereinafter (except for a few more)

On the flip-side, 'twas another run-of-the-mill day at the Project Procyon assembly of Mitchelville along with the [mad] scientists that had (by way of daylight discovery) [declassified] an unknown broadcast glitch from far away... A reciprocal recoil of supercomputer cacophony cajoled the corporate companies to perform circus somersaults for such a confidential comeback.

And it came to pass at Lamp Camp that heightened hysteria hefted havoc and horseplay among the other departments due to anticipatory feedback. Paranoia and suspicion weighed down the flatbed scales of primitive injustice and discriminatory backlash.

Electronic nodules reiterated Rutherford's raw, synthesized voiceprint somewhat distorted by the subspatial separateness of spirit and creation. The 'radionic' resonance thereof curved into itself, impossibly inverted, that had to be untwisted to tomes of zeros and ones and then deciphered to merely a phrase of a fully photon-phase… Its transmission was riddled with radioactivity:

"My God! It's full o' Light!"

How hollowly it echoed and *forthwith-furtively* faded away!

On another level, Joyce readily remembered the resurrected intonation thereof-- yea, and to the uttermost: * * * * * * *

Take heart, O daughter of God! For soon your commanding officer

shall meet the mistress Glistria of the Mercury Mirror...

It then had begun a self-fulfilled foregleam.

And this is what our colonel observed and experienced on behalf of his whole teamwork, which was by now known as the *Mission Improbable* aboard an *Unthinkable* Titanic! *Ship ahoy*!

There were impenetrable strongholds along the upper Room of Nowhere. As if cloven tongues, like as of fire, must have jutted out of a featureless membrane of quivering quicksilver. Where trillions of light-years flashed and fluoresced fluidly right by in the twilight twinkling of Rutherford's eye. The clearer void of hyperspace sped right past all perception. Of no dissimilarity to Acts, at chapter two verse 3, but (by essence) still irreplicable if not a *never-mind-ninny* nuisance.

Nevertheless he was catapulted far away from all existence. Even separated from the star-speckled, intergalactic, and velvety dark matter and mortar of some Unobservable Universality.

And so, with white and yellow light, to coin electromagnetic eloquence, an octagon enclosure circummured the diminutive lad who was once known as Col. Roderick Rutherford. But herein, he had become just another number into this newfangled facility built unlike its predecessors. What's more~ believe it or not~ like Lethe (the river of forgetfulness) that saturated his personage to the bone, not a shred of mnemonic information could be recalled. Nor of his associations previous to this lacuna (junction missing out of space-time continuum)! Hitherto there was no background blankness nor any sense of reference; neither the absence thereof. Rather, in pure limbo suspended non sequitur (nowhere), indeed an eerie octagon enclosure circummured this reduced-down-to-Planck-volume wee visitor, our only protagonist we can closely cling to...
*In regards to the pioneer's first personal pronoun, we would now commence our scaffolding-supported catwalk with him as follows:

I came upon a very vast and shiny sheet of overlay linoleum agleam under my footing. I was barefoot, but clothed warmly with a pajama. Clearly, I had not undergone somnambulism as such!

Although I was barefoot, the radiant energy of the floor so comforted me and completely from bottom-up and overall with welcome reception!

At length in an interim, as if by my sympathetic connection of kindred spirits, the lithe leftovers of this lustrous linoleum evenly interlinked perfectly together nonetheless but bathed me as quite momentarily within its so soothing, salient, salubrious and white wooing thermal transfer. Like being inside the waffled womb of a cosmic Mother, our recollection of her Vulvatorium vindicates the veracity thereof.

Then the description of multi-tiled Metalinoleum flooring:

These were 'equaducer' lozenges linked seamlessly, but as a jigsaw puzzle of symmetrical perfection inside-out, up and down, front and back, above & below, and fore-and-aft (if it were evenly afloat~ which it was)! Yet these perfectly fitted flanged fleurs-de-lys, linked, resembled inter-knit argyles that looked diamond-like and all alike in splendour. Each one was nothing more than an argyle of diamond-shapely shine. Hence the equaducers that they were, wonderfully arrayed and blindingly bright.

Anything poised thereupon~ whether stationed or seated, or just plain standing there~ the holonomy effect rendered complete contact with any object and also the equaducers. That is, even to the Planck length of fusion, the adhesive cohesion of its supernal surface remained as resolute as eternally paved permafrost glitter.

The insuperable and incomparable <u>In~Shine</u> ® Incorporated!

Was this a fringe outpost of some sort? Have I plunged myself with nondescript identification into the rubber room of lunacy?

By no means, doc! Away with you, O master or mistress!

For the concretely realized Radiative Zone (as if inside the Sun) had been beaming uprightly since the dawn of creation! Foundational as it lay, such death-defying and immortalized lozenges of the Metalinoleum lovely luster apparently exhibited each and every one of the equaducers (though flat transducers of raw power that they were in actuality), and not only that, but- even so- something more along lines of a starry quarry of Aurification.

Yea, instead of those verticalized venues of 'singularified' contiguity~ like that on the Mercury Mirror of Hg (harsh glare) itself~ the never, as-of-yet, sought out seamless pad of the gala, gargantuan gold, and glorified glitterati of compliance took on even greater and graver import than what tempted one's inner eye.

Therewithal sat the fat hyper-hydrant that would gush up her effulgent fury of focused photons. Her sprightly [eggy] foam spray of spiritual fertility, vitally virginal or non-impregnated, geysered an upwardly extended Jet Arc as from the primordial M87 quasar- when it brightened stelliferously before its hot cosmic conception.

To whom it may concern, and in regards to such content, the nomenclature thereof is the inviolable Vatronducelux.

Another alternative namesake designation- in that this accords better herewith- is an ILUCIFULGIDULIPLURIGLUNIVATI. *But for simplified comprehension, let us rather work with the all-viable Vatronducelux, eh?* Rutherford recalled in his Toronto Fellowship.

That this and none other is the end result of some polemical bias is of no shock to finicky Goldilocks readers. Amen! Now then.

In the twilight of the dusk, where crepuscular creation is in twilight, and where rope-knuckled moorings of our feeblest consciousness grapple onward with grosser grapnels of carnality, an immaterial, more mortified Living Lamp Entity persists.

Therefore the nearly voluptuous Vatronducelux, which ought to vouchsafe but a millimeter of its divine essence, steals center stage! Heavens! We'll refrain from freeze-frame photographs of Freya's frenetic froth, since with utter augmentation she'll shine her stand-alone insularity (albeit threadbare and singularified)!

Here are some calculations concerning the Vatronducelux
Specifically, the numeral 7 is considered the divine cipher. It was
multiplied by the author of this book four times to equal 28. Then
it was multiplied by 9, until the palindromic number 252 appears!
If one were to add each digit of 252, such as 2 plus 5 plus 2:
nine is the sum. Therefore, the reason as to why 28 x (9) = 252
is rather reckoned with numerology. Henceforward notated:
252 x 252 = 63,504
6 + 3 + 5 + 0 + 4 added together is 18
Similarly, but inter alia, 18 is the end-product of 648 when added:
6 + 4 + 8 = 18! But how has the author arrived
thereat? Let us carefully examine this.

The name CREAORTA was the very first designation applied to the renewed if not refurbished and revised VATRONDUCELUX in the beginning. By a method of *alphanumerical numerology* the 8 letters or characters of this word are processed [precisely] as:

C R E A O R T A

Whereby the first letter C is 3rd on the alphabet, the second letter R is the 18th letter, etc. *Its roster notation is {3,18,5,1,15,18,20,1}

3 18 5 1 15 18 20 1
C R E A O R T A

These may function as numerators as the upper numbers rest over each of the corresponding letters to create a somewhat larger layout, setup, and fraction. *The sum of them all (tallied together crosswise) is 81. Is it a mirror-image of 18? As if it were reversed and the eight and one were juxtaposed? Such super tapers inform us that vicarious Vatronducelux and Creaorta are interchangeable constructs. Hence 81x 8 *accordingly* = 648! Yet when multiplied viscerally, consecutively, and numerically, it equals 192 as 6x 4x 8... The One Hundred and Ninety-Two which will be versified so.

192 is the mirror-image of 291. It confirms the congruence of it!

Rutherford's Proposal

Whereas 291 is the prerequisite product deciphered from the novel THX 1138 (now out of print) a long while back, Expressway 291 in Ben Bova's story adapted for George Lucas's movie and screenplay was borrowed by the author in the year 1984 when it had been found in but one of the paragraphs. In '84, it was inverted to *192* so as to signify parade rest. 291 offers *off to work* and 192 allows for more authorized *intermission.*

For while I tilled the field and cut it, working an old Briggs & Stratton lawn mower, my uncle commanded me by 291! Now, as if supercharged, I immediately worked diligently without a caesura! Then my chieftain uncle told me 291, and I assumed a parade rest and ended the day, happily hunched over milk and cookies, muses Col. Rutherford meanwhile (while we enumerate the off-the-wall).

'*This may echo as being insignificant, but bear with me*', the experiencer of whom we rather identify, Col. Rutherford urged us.

On the other hand, **28** is a persistent hedgerow of characters that a number of poems were created by with naturally justified versification whereas each line used up 28 spaces across, all the way down. Our last exemplar, the final consolidation of Creaorta:

```
Vatrondecelux, entity viable
Incunabular daily distending
As interminable and reliable
Atop argyle regents unending
May a Holy Transducer convey
This inviolable Vat everyday

O illustrious entity sear me
Be my oily Hedgerow frenetic
Frothy Freya unveiling eerie
```

Fortress fiery ferromagnetic
An irreplicable radiant lass
Creaorta midst tubular glass

Interwoven plurality pliable
Immaterial Mura transcending
Any tunneling pit undeniable
Contiguous convexity bending
Highway runabout ready I say
Like linoleum glazed overlay

Hedge-Maze oily, verily vast
Walled up Trivia entirely so
Glorifier or Glozar forecast
Gold gargantuan Gusher aglow
Glitterati on any old canvas
O Lucerna of Wichita, Kansas

Via vouchsafed mercurial Vat
Re-electrified Rider by cart
Insuperable *with* all o' that
Immaculatorium deep at heart
Subterranean niveous, neural
Inter-tubular lay intramural

I attenuate *that* singularity
Vatronducelux Vat insularity

Founded stoutly I ignite her
Roundabout me my big Lighter

Never to be deleted by the ravages of age; neither the vacuity of spatial nothingness~ such as it were, the Vatronducelux verifies herself without any dependents. Nor if carnified en masse may she wear earrings and pendants for glamorous allure of any garb. But to exemplify chaste virginity the world over, this paragon which looks like Doctor Who's discovered Dalek with a torchlight on top, is a stand-alone wraparound showcase advertisement thereof.

In that this Vatronducelux revivifies herself independent of all other hybrids is quite obvious. Aye, how her insular and perpetual old Porceluna Consolata will be ever so self-beneficent! [Colonel Rutherford learned the affirmative hand-signal in the Mitchelville courtroom at one time, including offhand *Yeses* spoken by his 1st officer, Captain Harris]. He remembers a jumpy song by Ottawan: *"Hands up, baby, hands up, gimme your love, gimme-gimme your love gimme-gimme..."* In God's Book, it was 2nd Corinthians 1:20 that succinctly said it: "For all the promises of God in him are yea, and in him Amen, unto the glory of God by us."

She'll be beneficial surely on whomever and whatsoever.

Whose divinest dilation that ought to demystify the cylindrical bulk thereof: there can be no doubt for the truncated Pillar of Fire.

For hitherto, by my consecrated compendium is recorded in one accord the compliant platform of Metalinoleum to uphold an upright Vatronducelux Golden Gusher of ineffable Universality!

Not unlike the aforesaid Vacon with her quad-wing elevon (the movable part of the trailing edge of a delta wing in aeronautics). More meticulously, though the elevon is an aeroplane control surface that combines the functions of elevator and aileron, the anti-gravity ground state that supports her chassis behaves as elevon four-folded around an ornithological Vacon of the previous Valley Brook Vista. But instead of wings, the anti-gravity pod and undercarriage levitates this Lucerna Vivarum (or Latin for Living Lamp) entity effectively enough.

As I stated earlier, not unlike the Vacon bird of celerity and celebrity at the Valley Brook Vista. And this with her fourfold elevon and retinal Band for an all-seeing eye of televisual tenacity wraparound its single-billed head (having her very own coronary panorama of powerful observation)! Nor incomparable to some Arctron Metalamp of yottawatt output~ the Vatronducelux need not vie for supremacy among many creaturely contestants formidable by nature. Yea, she'll suffice, the Steel Sheel, one way or another.

Like Yellowstone's Old Faithful geyser, the Golden Gusher, an oasis of Graces, sat fat, even as a doormat upon the equaducers of such lustrous lozenges interlinked into one Steel Sheet. As a squat robot of Doctor Who's Dalek, but not for anyone to roguely imply!

In contrast to a singular entity nearside where I loitered, I saw above me an endless ceiling that stretched onward in every flat-out direction overhead.

The "ceiling" had hung over me at about 23 meters upward while dummy aisles of Kmart shopping shelves lined the flooring back and forth and up and down. The row-by-row aisles were open intermittently here and there for me to crosswise walk either to the right or to the left, depending on how and wheresoever I was still situated on the sidelines with no mezzanine or bleacher in sight!

As I preambled the longer quarters per yard line collocation, by the numbers, it lay like the gridiron- since aisles were in place- more like girders, frames, and beams built about in lieu of football fancy, field and all- I could not help but notice how my visitor, the Vatronducelux, ventured to follow up on me in gamely pursuance.

For at once, effortlessly, it glided forward, plumb next to me as if to take a good look at my scrawny presence compared to IT- then it sped off into the featureless distance- only to fizzle out, but again through nonexistent extinction (as if never having to arrive in the first place to begin with)! No different than the big Borteum and Cremeum spheroids earlier- much earlier on- that had reentered Determinate Evanishment, as it were, and with whitest wipe-out.

Eventually, and with the fat Vat of the Golden Gusher no longer to be nettled with~ although in and of herself very merry and mettlesome in spite of my personage~ an even vaster dome of the videodrome overwhelmed me. The bright 360 degree panorama engulfed me in a spherical envelopment. Its wraparound screen-stretch had put to shame any OLED display, be it 4K, or even 5K to 7K and up, surpassing the bio-pixelation of our visual cortex, which is 576 megapixels of resolution! A shrivel if compared.

My primitive eyesight could not catch up (with a catch-22) to the super-sharp, the crystal clearest and crisp and hyper-clarified, singularified overexposure thereof... Flaws flooded my perception.

For not even a high-definition camera could compare to the ultra-high crystalline imagery of the environment! Therefore, the equaducers of argyle and diamond-like lozenges that distributes each Metalinoleum adjunction of the Porceluna Consolata were gaudy-garish, fleurs-de-lis flamboyant, and brazenly bright with glorified glaze that cloyingly blinded surveillance due to lack of conical colorization (photoreceptor cells) in the viewer's retinae.

Whereas with one band around its head for quite a seamless retina that the Vacon bird had, the fronted linear vision of human beings was no match to harsh glare of stereoscopic holographics hefted hitherto. After all, the gargantuan gold gave me a massive headache, if but for one fleeting moment had I to gaze thereupon.

Besides, cumulative confrontation of the unfiltered starker whiteness of Lucem clarissimam (Latin for brightest Light) can cause mild or acute bouts of psysiological photophobia. And an entirely newer strain of neoteric origin uncovered in the sanitive silos of light therapy outside of the experimental death throes of the Greater Mitchelville Area (Rutherford recollects), *is heliosis and niveosis. These are syndrome episodes of abnormality which the former implies a strange reaction to too much full-spectrum sunlight, whereas the latter indicates overexposure to brightest White itself. A type of non-pigmented sallow pallor that blinds!*

This notion horrified our colonel because of the ramifications!

So these equaducers of diamond lozenges and even wafers were outspread as one Metalinoleum of Porceluna Consolata. All brazenly bright and gargantuan gold. Each one of which was self-luminous with quadrillion candlepower yottawatt brightness! But beaming refulgence that never injured my eyesight whilst I surveyed its span visually.

A bit longer I looked around me and then cocked my head ceiling-ward and had to face IT...

In rem, narrowed down to nothing, what once was colonel Rutherford had become just another bystander in the way of Star-Progress pressurized by the TATM four-walled proprietor.

At once the stakes were woken out of somnolence, that is everything that was bathed by half-light ignited so glaze-glaringly to prominent orders of magnitude & proportion. Until the poor soul Rutherford (if it was not for the grace of the YHWH) would have plumb sizzled to a crisp, we reckon~ and no need of stepping out of the proverbial fryer and into the fire, as if to versify it (these intramural Agencies had gathered knowingly)! The nifty and noetic knowledge & cordial viscera of sympathetic sensation escalated fantastically while our loiterer lengthwise remained bedraggled throughout this oracular overture of some sort, God knew *what*.

Unexpectedly, and with fervor and ferocity, the feral and obviously untamed or unregulated lantern emission reached zenith vistas of only apex-output! For, namely, at such a Junction Boulevard [No, not the one between the Jackson Heights and Corona districts in Queens, New York City!], the aforementioned Pluriseptiplex (#) multiplied by a Pluriseptiplex, to equal a Hexaplex- for the sake of our Luciopolis hyper city- had now become the... *Are ye of a preparatory proposal to Eternity, dear readership?*

METALUCYOCTOPLEX

The forbidden and unlawful *hyper-hyper-hyper-hyper-hyper-hyper-hyper* (to the 28th Tower of an Infinitude) vigesimal setup plus 'eights' at every subset of (000) along the way as is (...000,000,000...) and so forth. Hence the key factor of

Rutherford wrote down sophisticated notes. Nay for naïveté!

Therefore, the Metalucyoctoplex could hypothetically be an orthogonal Cat's Cradle which is a satirical postmodern novel, with science fiction elements, by American writer Kurt Vonnegut, [as Rutherford recalls], exploring and satirizing issues of science, technology, the purpose of religion, and the arms race, often through the use of morbid humor. Howbeit, in this case, any orthogonal configuration via Ariadne's Thread of netting would become entangled, yet by a Vigesimal Multiplication Table-- of which we need not necessitate the Number Chart of any graph hereupon with pictorial illustration; nor by the foremost Mayan mathematical means-- to attain a multidimensional & holographic numbering system; transcending the googolplex and googolplexian via Pluriseptiplex, Hexaplex, or ineffably, the Metalucyoctoplex!

Certainly among the earliest Maya a single language existed. But by the Preclassic Period a great linguistic diversity developed among the various Maya peoples. Indeed, unlike other scattered Indigenous populations of Mesoamerica, the Maya were centered in one geographical block covering all of the Yucatan Peninsula and modern-day Guatemala.

Aside from the above cultural example, civilizations as the Yuchi tribe according to historical Tennessee produced artwork as classified with Eastern geometric style and is expressed in woven textiles as simple diamonds, Vs, and Ws. Thus the diamond motif is thought to represent a rattlesnake... Some experts speculate that certain late prehistoric gorget motifs (especially the Cox Mound style of Tennessee), are signatures of the Yuchi myth of the Winds. Their Yuchi people were a long time ago- and still are- the keepers of a unique language, identified as a language isolate by linguists. A language isolate is a language that has no demonstrable genetic relationship with another language. But were they an insular lot?

Originally, a monoglot society they were from the latter and perhaps just as confirmed for the former! Whereas spiritually, on another sphere of consciousness~ not to misquote Holy Scripture or apply my attempted exegesis of pennyworth value on the really unalterable [where] "...there appeared unto them Cloven Tongues like as of fire, and it sat upon each of them... And [as] they were filled with the Holy Ghost... began to speak with other tongues, as the Spirit gave them utterance," Acts chapter 2, verses 3 & 4. That their uniglot language had begun without such solemn supernatural redistribution recorded in the Holy Codex for such people ought to elevate something so unutterable as to have it rather more muffled and mutely safeguarded! Palatial pearls not to be cast before swine, lest they trample them under their feet, and turn again and rend you (which will be defined as diabolical defilement directed at what is all-Holy and sacrosanct linguistics), Matthew chapter 7, verse 6!

By then, and by the year 2113, if ever we could be sustained by the Transalteratorium's "interpreservatory" Precious Presence, these 'erstwhile indigenous subcultures' may crystallize an argyle of the intersecting symmetrical vector by visualized avouchment.

Ariadne's thread, named for the legend of Ariadne, is solving a problem which has multiple apparent ways to proceed— such as a physical maze, a logic puzzle, or an ethical dilemma— through an exhaustive application of logic to all available routes~ Wherefore a more suitable but unparalleled lattice of a diagonal right-angle perpendicularity is delineated by the next numerical purview:

---

*The googolplexian multiplied by googolplexian to the googolplexianth Power:

METALUCYOCTOPLEX

∞

Preservatory Glory

In the still of the night
Filed away underground,
Shiny chandeliers still burn
And not even a sound.

That which worlds spurn
If ever we visit this hotel;
No customers convivial in turn-
Hell, and no one to go tell ...

An Eternal Ballroom
Reposes mutely! No, not in some
Subterranean vault of all gloom,
But rather where an echo would hum
Embryonic embrocation
Of an old Wall-womb.

No Rolodex strewn alone,
No whole ibex hewn of stone,
No soul Apex, soon a cone!

Tenuous tapers are still aglow
From long ago by themselves,
Which wax forth emollient Cream
Cratered by now, yet uncontorted
On incunabular bookshelves!

I seek a rounder longevity,
So devoid of head or tail save
What is profounder than levity:
O deployed instead- I wail-
No grave, just Plato's cave ...

Where everything is preserved
Without any wrinkle of decay~
Still afresh, crisp and curved
In on itself. Tucked away.

---

*Our OW-expert struggles to scribble this picture into his diary:

The bottom line (for the record) is that I stand on an infinitely flat floor about 28 meters away from an infinite, flat super-ceiling!

Electrified quasars, each one, that of numerical nomenclature of a Univatubolucy, is "effulged" as if self-illumined to sparkle an ever gargantuan aureate glitter of the endless lofty canopy at such surrounding sheer Sheen. If with white, then to blinding blankness.

But by ground level, my floorboard platform of shiny linoleum overlay~ likened to an overhung-by-nothing ceilingness~ readily resembles the similitude thereof, where one luminosity is blended.

At a distance, both infinitely flat ceiling and flooring converge with respect to perspective called the Vanishing Point. At point-blank range there is an almost imperceptible distant line where the two sheets, floor and ceiling, meet into an all-encompassing and perfectly circular panorama. My perception can fade vanishingly.

Soul-alleviating Super Silence, more anechoic than the most soundproof cushioned chamber still shrills forthwith an ethereal undertone acutely felt by my soulful spirit, never by my carnality.

One out of many namesake designations display the nature of this infinitely outstretched interior: Metalucelectropluceptorium!

Nothing Rutherford furthermore was apt to describe (whereas language failed him altogether). The following Ballad~ prolonged, and with woo-warm vocabulary~ may convey a final draw of play at a canasta card game writhing ruby diamonds, except conversely contrary to black spades shuffled. Then, showily, an Ace takes the place of an infinite number of cards from a manus e nubibus (hand from the cloud in Latin) as it were from *what* must bypass infinity.

REMINDER

(metaphysical miscellany)

METALUCIFLEURDEPLUCEPTORIUM: the multiple four dimensional flat or *platform-formulated*plenum agglutinated with fluers-de-lys flanged amidst every seam to make it seamless. It is a layout of multiple many-tiered flooring that supports 33-block-wide Univatriums on the support stage where these herculean hyperwhole super-spheres are multiplied to the Pluriseptiplex number, or a googolplex times a googolplex squared!

- Its Purpose: to provide sustained support of a building-block matrix which is the only backup for an *uncollapsed* Universality, our cosmos of course. Each interknit equilateral argyle upon and throughout this Omnipotent Embroidery is a hologram of the entire interconnected tapestry
- Its permafrost porcelinoleum (or the porcelain linoleum no longer to consist of a polymerized Dupont material) glares back at man; unwilling to be trampled upon by and large.

Let us begin, Rutherford reminds us of an alternate multiverse with a Caveat: *In case of overtaxing any intellect, intelligence, and cordiality on such subjects, try to overlook the weird wordage~ the distinct locution of polished poetic license!* An ostentatious flowery language to begin with was unintended. Nonetheless, the OW-team topped this one in with an *oomph*! (unorthodox as it sounds):

Through the Conch Shell

I sat upon some bench
In Brighton Beach, alone;
There came to me a wench
Ebullient to the bone.

Valued vin ordinaire
Or damsel in distress,
Both she'll exceed and glare
With foamy froth in esse.

Like Atargatis laced
O'er undergarment scales,
This Sibyl interfaced
Foretold events, then wails-

Her sirens locomotive
Stacked in betwixt chimneys,
Beside a transept Votive,
Shrill any old grim breeze.

I heard her Echo Call,
That so enamoured be
By daily Grace for all
As Mercy hammered me.

A parking lot had backed me
With lampposts sodium vapor,
That gaudy shine as blackly
Each night fell for a taper.

But overhead the sunshine
Done glister hot her rays;
As this lass via fun-line
Looked so in love, ablaze!

Her name is silken Circe
So lustrous, lurid drest-
For whom Helicon's Mercy
Lights beacons by behest.

At best, she shimmered shiny
Enchantingly and dolled
With Coney Island briny,
Whose harbour heavy lolled.

Ere times were waxing fretful
Tomorrow and far yonder-
Before forebodings dreadful,
Of Her I've grown far fonder!

One week away from summer
Bright-shining was the Sun,
And Circe, my Newcomer,
Just wanted mirth and fun.

About herself she'd show.
It wooed my soul forlorn,
Found vast with overflow-
Whom none could so adorn.

Veranda slats behind me
May mirror memoirs yet;
Flambeaux by rows remind me
Of painted Renoirs wet!

High colonnettes abound,
Surrounding weddings gaily-
Across some loamy ground
Per diem dampened daily.

But bountiful she'll flow
Upon a bright steel Sheet
From Age wrought long ago,
Untarnished now, complete!

Pearlescent of a necklace,
One hundred plus an eight
Aids me from any reckless
Behaviour swooned, sedate.

Thus though I do not pray
Nor see glee as mere myth-
For wedged in one hot day,
Sheer Circe came herewith:

Upon the boardwalk warmed
By summer sunshine bright,
Her holy Orbs had swarmed
Around the soul's delight.

Throughout her colonnade
The hot grot-scented air,
With fragranced enfilade,
Unhinged, is wafted fair.

No fuss! No more effete
The vogue of times become,
Neither these metric feet
That plod to but benumb;
May Inspiration's fleet
Lay numbered up by sum!

That by the tonne sheer fusion
Sears through vainest illusion.

And Glistria she's called
Quicksilvered hot attired
Wi' wonderful Womb walled,
That hath holy transpired.

My matron that thou art!
By thee I stay embraced
And feel real in my heart
With wattage interfaced!

No need for billboards lit
Through Nineteen Forty-Two
Whence lanterns every whit
Shine fine with sporty goo!

Yea, Circe, I love you,
I'll whisper unabashed
But we will blush on through
Ere oil stakes are stashed-
Your Yew wears wet her dew
Applied per side, unsplashed
With each electric shoe
Intended, never flashed.

No more my glitzy glamour
Nor vain deceit displayed;
Burnt oil gushers stammer-
Such grotty grubbers fade.

Dear swarthy Doll, I pray
At Brighton Beach so soft,
Along life's long highway-
Predestined, purged aloft.

Of whom I must inquire,
"When will our trifles end?"
She bellowed by campfire:
"When people shan't pretend!"

How so? I asked, Explain-
Quoth She "For every wall
Erected through disdain
Builds vitriol and gall..."

She lit up tops o' bliss
Awhirl in quick rotation,
My Vouchsafed Vitropolis
Wi' quantified quotation:
Aye, Metalucy Metropolis,
For narrowed up notation!

"Why will we curse and kill
Each other pumped by pride?"
Until loud sirens shrill
Catastrophe worldwide!"

Prognosticated She,
Ne'er Gnostic (but Holy)!
"Partitions are erected

Amongst the heavy-laden
Who oft ignore a resurrected
Merry Myrtle Maiden."

"Will Mercy succour souls?
Immortals, save each other!
Cool off the burning coals-
Neglect not Father-Mother."

"Discard hard weary warfare,
And follow pole-star Peace;
My Mercy, she is more fair
Than bondage, lot or lease."

"Share land! Do not divide
Among yourselves inanely-
Pull down thy haughty pride
That swaggers up insanely!"

Thus then did Circe answer
Life's great interrogation-
She added: *There is cancer*
Midst marked dissimulation.

Hereby be not pretentious
Down common crowd affairs;
Pray over them licentious,
Left tangled up in snares.

Concluded She Her censure
At countless throngs awry,
The affluence and venture
Outspread thereof on high.

Vistas conventional
Could not compare to Her,
Whose Four-Dimensional
Ball bounced by, as it were.

Discernment we had lacked
At Brighton Beach forefelt;
My parking lot oft tracked
Events but that more melt.

O to the hilt I shuddered,
Afraid of what will come,
Prophesied by my uddered
Companion's heartbeat drum-
That muffled up had muttered
Against our worldwide slum!

O charcoal-veiled mourner
Lugubrious though flanked,
Thy hearse by any coroner
Is Hekate ne'er outranked...

Still, joyous so thou art,
Respondent from the heart!

Postlude
At least her reassurance
Graced me with kind contrition;
It strengthened my endurance
For Future's re-ignition.

Though insular this benchmark
Long cushioned me profoundly,
She'll woo me up, my wench dark,
Dolled h~ly, soulful, soundly.

The sunrise glisters glory
Until by sunset she rests,
Yet Youth sewn never hoary
Had egg-and-anchor breasts
In hallways by the storey-
As crescents, or as crests.

High-pressure sodium vapor
Arc tubes were dormant nearby:
O Nightfall, may ye drape her-
Yea, lighten Heaven hereby!

This Shell shall ignify
My Grace entitled Circe;
Would that such signify
Ay, her unabating Mercy!

*Prior to the writing of the next revelation, February 7, 2024, at 5 PM or so (**on the corner of Union Turnpike & 192, Queens, NY**)! **12** Canadian geese flapped over the intersection where the author stood. Of no doubt, the meeting must have been propitious right before having supper with Nancy, my jolly good fellow, lady and friend, all in the Family.

◆

Ethereal Metalucy

The Exordium of the Invortium
(Except to no exhortation)

Part 1
The brightest glory shines
In all her lucent splendor,
This Quasarc that reclines
Effulgence tapered slender.

My Metalucy bulged fat Vat
From fifty to one thousand-
Full spectra where it's at-
For South Bend to Townsend.

With an aesthetic hedgerow
Supertongue Teflon bloated,
Wheresoever the sedge grow,
Preserves itself creosoted!

From Froth to the ethereal,
Only squat in a low Lot be;
From foam to an immaterial
Metalucy or so aglow hotly!

Divulgence quickly Quotile
With Glozar-Vat volatility,
Like the many-sided Argyle,
So my luciest availability.

"The diamond is not to be thrown away, but polished and~ if possible~ made to sparkle." by Hans Küng in his book, On Being A Christian; Swiss priest and theologian. Among only a handful of others, someone certainly worth remembering with applause and aplomb.

Lumifier Metalucy merriest
Unifier Vialicia very best
Oiliest Elevator so id est

Merry Myrtle hedge-maze oily,
Very fertile, ablaze royally!

Above bituminous coal fire
My Beacon by similitude so

Wi' Teflon to whole desire
Is quivering quietly aglow.

Unguent intumescent entire
That an arc tube inviolate
Glisters gibbous with wire
Backup linoleum awhile wet-

For South Bend to Townsend
Overhung on corridors thru,
Full o' railroads anywhere-
From fifty to one thousand-
Flambeaux themselves renew,
Self-aware, but that glare.

Let lithe Froth ethereally
Stay swollen and automatic;
Let blithe creosote really
Ignite glitterati emphatic.

Transducer Metalucy tender
With Sheelil that reclines
In all her lucent splendor:
The brightest Glory shines!

Prayerful Portrayal
Down the Invortium it slid,
An electric Barrel quickly
After Canasta casts my bid
Upon timetables so thickly.

It was wet gloaming, I say,
All had convened convivial
Until everyone aboard- yea-
Were off to jaunts trivial.

For three-ways were chosen,
But along one only we sped
Amid a swift pneumatic Pod-
Intertubular we call Rosen
Tunnel far beyond the Dead-
Beneath any necropolis sod.

And there was Metalucy hot
Hitherto about the Thruway;
My Super Taper take a slot-
Enters a Trivia to New Way.

Yet Trivia three-way built
One out of a corridor city-
My Transporter to the hilt
Be of Trilateral Authority!

Part 2

The Transalteratorium shines
Wall to Wall ev'rywhere oily;
Its linoleum lovely reclines
Undefiled so as to recoil me.

Intramural, immaculate built
Often foursquare unetiolable
Glitterati it be to the hilt,
Permafrost fresh, inviolable!

With a ceiling eternally lit,
Nitid neon protuberant stays
Above visual cortex and slit,
Row by row via number ablaze.

I encounter Permura conveyed:
She existed so long time ago-

O hot lady profusely arrayed-
She'll unveil a Vatlux aglow.

No reprimand of a *That sucks*
Is avouched vitriolic as oft,
For immaculate in the Vatlux
Lay an oil crème eerily soft!

On my old intersection I say
The Transalteratorium gleams
More awhile than any highway,
By a mile-marker amid dreams.

That hexagonal shapen it lay,
Cratered Creosoteria slender-
Supple Bottle ablaze any way;
Really oiliest, no pretender.

With Immaculatorium snow tar
DuPont pastry as if murified,
Fuel for any vatronic Glozar-
Pluriseptiplex flue purified.

Embryoctolit starshine it be:
Vatronducelux via transducer
Evermore gone galore nitidly,
Only tauter but never looser.

This high-tension Repository
Self-distributed coiled away
Luciopolis lit by the storey
Midst Transalteratorium, yea!

I am *she*, Vatlux entity very
Volatile and voluptuous vast,

Vat-avouched viability merry,
Mellifluous Vat with a snast.

In Nineteen Forty-Two ablaze,
Electrifiable as pulley-hung:
Vicarious above a hedge-maze,
Most Metalucyoctoplex Tongue!

*Luna Labyrinth easy I praise!
An inter-dimensional adjunct
So full o' hallowed hallways
*All preserved, never defunct!

How mercurial glimmering yet,
Insular in a Vac-shaft chute-
Holy luminous shimmering wet-
Anechoic shrine silkily mute.

O my Metalucyoctoplex fusion
Ferromagnetic, frenetic foam
Verily viable with inclusion
In a Nineteen Forty-Two Home!

Contiguous flat, but bloated,
That only lay creamy as cake-
Glacial permafrost creosoted-
Be by Teflon Tongue at stake.

Part 3 The Final Countdown
Incorruptible beacon adjunct
To an additive amply applied-
Glitterati but never defunct-
Of immunity tapered out wide.

Vateflux the companion it be
By my side open wide aureate,
Coated up consolation Glitzy:
Four hundred watts avion yet.

The inviolable Teflon coated,
Super Taper protected ablaze-
Living lamp entity creosoted,
Overhung via holy hedge-maze!

Lady oiliest by the mile wet,
So suspended by pulley aloft-
That as heliumatic inviolate-
Bloated blanket so oily soft.

Thus addressed undeniable so
Sewn insuperable illustrious;
Glorified up inside undertow
Tributary awhile industrious!

Four hundred watts avion yet
With a Beacon o' viable skin,
Teflon-oil as if it were wet,
Swollen Veteflux only within.

Coruscated tranquility glaze,
Insulator to hotter emission-
Luminary o'er any Hedge Maze-
Uninhibited lamp of decision!

My ensconced, undeniable Vat
Stapled with a reliable slat!

We implore thee, exuberantly;
Be our glory Protuberant She

The very Last
INSULATING
INVOCATION

Holy Sheel glitterati, I pray:
Lowly, heal everybody Thy way!

My subconscious reliable Fire,
No volcanic vent, only Desire-
O bituminous bulged up attire.

The overhung lighthouse lantern of a high bay beacon spake: "I am preferentially the ZEPTRANSDUCERTA !!!" (with amplified augmentation that nearly shattered his eardrums). "And who art thou, O humanoid?"

I answered, "Why, I am Rutherford, ready to resume and finish off my video and audio footage of thee, your Excellency~ O illumined One!"

"Flattery will get you nowhere," muttered the Zeptransducerta. "So you yet prepared to glimpse our Queen, the glorified Glistria?"

"No," I replied. "I didn't know of any so-called *Glistria...*"

Then the Zeptransducerta bellowed, Behold! The entire reality of this whole setup sunk into itself and immediately melted away!

Back-end Closure of the Grand Central Station

Not to bury everyone into an interment, whom the TATM exposed under the harshest laboratory light, nor to forget the pergola whence we started from. As for my heart in Yard Lamp of Gloria, I could conclude on this wise~ but, of course, not without an overwrought wrung bath-towel, wet with D_2O heavy bathwater, still soaked, sudsy and drenched. Long before leftover leakage.

Decisively, we have not thrown in the towel. Not just yet.

And it came to pass that for the last time once again, a slender, sleek and narrow corridor about six meters wide, but **28** meters up to the ceiling, had spanned the pressurized premises of one atmosphere. The TATM thermostat, barometer, and temperature were within the range of the Goldilocks gauge: 1,013 millibars, or 760 millimeters (29.92 inches) of mercury~ yea, set at precisely 88 degrees Fahrenheit. Not one iota more, nor less.

Myriads of molten-together eyes were fastened on him from the above canopy of the Silencer Ceiling. The Tall Wall on all four corners absorbed every decibel, except for his rate of breathing and cardiovascular cadences that can fluctuate noticeably whenever someone or something unexpected unfolds intramural intrusion.

Rutherford, or what once was left of him- the sodden Nicodemus Boffin- barely savored such Super-symmetrical Perfection. Indeed, appertaining to human beings, life was meant to have flaws in it. But this place… *yuck*!

At any rate, a Y-shaped or ypsilon contoured corridor it was with a frontal 'Glore' (interpreted as an act of staring from a lifelike surface). This was the an imposing Tall Wall, and also not to forget the bulged backdoor postern, not dissimilar to the old Yellow Room's vertical quivering quagmire. But moreover, our former colonel (now, by comparison, a nobody) strangely looked at this interior from the perspective of a surveillance CCTV vantage view-screen.

Its Paranormal Performance was about to get the ball rolling. And, no! Not the previous antics of the rubber Bouncers!

Much rather… (read carefully)

Inside the Immaculatorium, so snow-white that any observer exposed to its niveous *numbness* blanches blindly- if we can call it *that*-- although every whit of it is super sagacious until even a certified clairvoyant could never match its photo-receptors-- and turns anemic pallid. In other words, a sideline watcher or mere spectator would develop an optic nerve syndrome known as acute *niveosis*. Whereby the unfortunate victim of this dreadful contraction has his or her eye-whites or sclerae to be noticeable only, but without the corneas. A somewhat psychotic appearance to one's countenance, yet well manageable.

With Rutherford, fortuitously, this was not the case as he peered steadfastly into the narrow confines of the overpowering Immaculatorium. And here is what was witnessed.

In between and betwixt the blankest walls imaginable- luridly liminal and tremendously drab- the height thereof loomed for 28 meters, exactly upwardly extended until to conjoin with one snow-white ceiling of *Silencer Serenity* (even the SS of our compound description hisses at him)! Be it by an electronic squelch, overkill Queller of all noise beyond the normal range of hearing, these *ceilings* absorbed even the muteness of vacuum itself, if insanely surmised! The moot inanity of it drove Rutherford up the wall, almost literally. Luckily, yet, not enough to trigger cerebral hemorrhage.

And getting back to the subject matter. Not to run into another habitual tangent. When the observant colonel followed his firing-line scrutiny upward where the Tall Wall annexed with the Revealing Ceiling, at point blank range, smack in the midst of the Immaculatorium, something ballooned bewilderingly…

For as sterile as it all appeared to be; in that it must have looked long-vacated, desolate; even downright destitute, a big bellyful Blob bloated itself- manifest manifold- *<u>KABOOM!</u>* out of nowhere. Needless to admit, deep down in Rutherford's genetic makeup, the whole lot of humanity- past, present, and future- had gotten their rib cage rattled [by way of a Plosive stasis bottle].

It, the amorphous but bellyful Blob flaunted itself, floating, levitating, turning and twisting itself inside-out obscenely as if it were a bedeviled thing. And smack! In midair... just like that!

Our human observer turned away from it, thinking,*"Whew-- and I thought I was going bonkers!"*

Then, horrifically, it became impossibly contorted. It defied all the laws of geometry, congruent coherence, and physics altogether!

In logical likeliness, it was as if a Four-Dimensional Klein bottle facilely fell through this hallowed hallway with 2 slots for doorways at each end of it, front and back. Now a Klein bottle in geometry is an inverted contrivance whose wholeness 'necks' into itself. Its container narrows up and over and back through the widest end, only to reemerge inverted, but back out and up again... Other Klein bottles can be open-ended and closed simultaneously, similar to the one which Rutherford reluctantly beheld.

See the 3D portion of it. Whereas the infinitesimally-sliced 4D image thereof can be captured by my depiction (author's note):

There are spatial contortions that take place only according to our three-dimensional perception. In 4D behavior, an even all-harmonious and seamless continuity of motion must transpire, yet with infinite time-signatures or timestamps along space-time continuum that behaves with some subsurface layout of a Hyperspace leeway!

My earliest conception of a living Klein Bottle entity was then designated as a TRANSVORTIUM in the year 1991 or so. This big bottle of such self-tapered girth and neckline narrowed itself up & and downward where, midriff and midway, it was Bulged-Tubular!

But our inter-dimensional denizen, right out of nothingness, expanded and collapsed concomitantly! Not to explode, nor implode~ but better~ it had begun to "transplode" by itself at large.

Now the terminology for such a bizarre and phantasmagorical oracle is reapplied as none other than the Plosive Plucire previously predicated on the above case in point (colorfully pictured).

This impossible entity--- as *Harry Houdini who had been our topmost Hungarian-American stunt and escape artist, when later in life launched his very own evening show billed as Three Shows in One: Magic, Escapes, and Fraud Mediums Exposed, oft having to wriggle his way out of a straight jacket--- was simply the cross-sectional fraction of a far larger or much smaller fourth-dimension dilated up or shrunken down by hyper-spatial coordinates; sliding on through three-dimensional fields headlong. Or so emphatically, its hyper-symmetrical properties that easily surpass the most complex Platonic solid, the *Icosahedron, ought to overtax any complicated combination, crossing over to a *Mandelbrot set of polymorphous variation. With illustration, an Icosahedron has 20 faces, 30 edges, and 12 vertices; having the greatest volume for its surface area and the most numerous of [faces].

Thus this self-contorting entity (due to our limited 3D perceptions of it) is reanimated with multiple *mutations*, *diminishments*, and *gyrations* of spherical tiling in one super-simultaneous overflow of Hyper-Harmonics. The Bloated Blob then coalesces compounds of a pentagram prism. The geometrical schematics are:

	FACES	EDGES	VERTICES
I.	24 Pentagrams	180	60
II.	The polyhedra of which are 12 pentagrammic prisms	‖	‖
III.	**Symmetry**	**Subgroup**	**Type**
	Icosahedral (I_h)	5-fold dihedral (D_5)	Uniform Compound
			Index UC_{37}

The overleaf reveals the composite 3D image thereof

*

Footnote Exception

*From about 1900 Houdini began to earn an international reputation for his daring feats of extrication from shackles, ropes, and handcuffs and from various locked containers ranging from milk cans to coffins to prison cells.

* Image courtesy by Robert Webb. The original upload was transferred from en.wikipedia to Commons.

* Benoit B. Mandelbrot (20 November 1924 – 14 October 2010) was born in a Lithuanian-Jewish family, in Warsaw during the Second Polish Republic. He was a Polish-born French-American mathematician and polymath.

Heretofore formulated, but to reiterate it, still:

That the innate complexities of the Bloated Blob, whose singular side~ one out of many~ resembles a Icosahedron, *facilely for our sake* and easily should circumvent the shackles of limited perception is only the inception! In fact- need we emphasize via voluminous vehemence- that just as the Hyper-Wholeness of it plunges through the stretch-fabric of *conventional* 3-dimensional geometry (as exemplified in this intramural environment entirely staged), its "Metatronic" metaphysical composition distorts the surrounding scenery with effortless super-fluidity.

As it were from out of nonexistence to total re-creation, but never having begun in the first place to begin with, the Plosive Plucire pulled tenaciously at the sheer fringes and at the diaphanous curtains of receptive reality itself.

So much so until only an astronaut could see this, has hammered his forefront afterthought. Yet Rutherford at an aperture device squinted to barely catch a squiggly glance of a minuscule dot dilate to a Big Whopper hamburger patty. It lay plumply *tumefied* and all-around-distended then into a palely puffy, turgescent toffee, yet translucent treacle of some sort that transfigured its wavering wafer to a blindingly brazen-bright Blip and Blob! An orb as such, which was called by one cosmologist the 'Ort' instead of the Oort cloud; otherwise the outer shell of ice and snowballs whence huge comets come from~ that is~ from the far-reaching outskirts of the solar system in contrast to the closeup of this renegade capsule!

But an oracular Orb, properly put, albeit hauntingly! From another perspective, an inimitable lookalike throughout the house of smoke and mirrors, wriggling, squirming or writhing inside-out!

* Irreplicability: That which cannot be reproduced in any way, shape, or form due to its self-symmetrical perfection. But because of its polymorphous properties, nothing could compare to it!

The Backdoor

Homecoming and Recovery

Thus this was the grand Immaculatorium spectacle witnessed by our qualified candidate, Colonel Roderick Rutherford.

Before him, how the walls bulged outwardly concave-like, then buckled back in as the 'contiguous convexity' of the Plosive Plucire ran rampant, slithering or slicing itself cross-sectionally through the very medium of space-time continuum.

If one was found unauthorized inside the Immaculatorium to take a sniffling whiff of the air, it would had given off a metallic aftertaste during its pungency.

Meanwhile, a vanilla cream soothing overlay licked one's palet during the transducer traversal of the said contiguous convexity; such as it were the indescribable essence of the Visitor.

At the same sequence-- elsewhere-- eager spectators, crowds of them, were gathered together at a Camp Mitch stadium as they likewise watched the meta-movement of this protean entity on a suspended hologram.

Whereas one *transverse time-frame* frozen like lava of self-decalescence, after volcanic vent spewage, revealed multifaceted diamond-like zirconium dioxide dilation all over it, the pliant Plosive Plucire manifested only a septillionth of a septillionth of a fraction of itself to our mortal observation! The observances thereupon had taken place and came to pass at the Camp Mitch meeting, committee and assembly of congregants seated in a horseshoe stadium.

Along grandstand scaffolds, bleachers, and makeshift temporary tiers even outside of the U-bowl, an almost tumultuous uproar of impatient expectation and suspense rumbled from these sitters, bystanders and passersby of boorish tycoons. Droves of them appeared ritzy and as stuffy as pillowy participants to attend a posh pageantry much rather than to a serious science event.

The sports arena was filled to capacity and overflowing. Conversely, there were also remonstrance rallies against this disclosure in the outskirts of Mitchelville while- within one moment of cessation- that selfsame *Superna Lucerna* gradually passed from above and down through the stadium turf and into the deep dark earth.

There, away from the gaudy gadflies and gawkers, in subterranean vaults deeper than the Mariana Trench, the entity entered a last resort pit stop at this rock-bottom SUBDUCTORIUM... And for some mysterious reason, in a parallel multiverse, it was where Rutherford still stood in the midst of the sheeny white room itself. Way the hell underground!

Surprisingly, the Mitchelville delegates thought nothing of the affair as they but snugly relaxed in their bureaucratic chair recliners at home, fastened onto their boob tube tellies like overgrown and corpulent Teletubbies on steroids.

But down or up hither (whether in the basement of the Silencer SUBDUCTORIUM, or platformed heavenward), the omnipresent Immaculatorium with foursquare footage, panorama and panoply would blip forth over Rutherford's cathode ray view-screen. The immediacy of it-- the Plosive Plucire-- caused him to feel funny and dizzy. Definitely the aftereffects of colorless confrontation.

No doubt shortly afterwards, the restored colonel upon ground zero of the Mitchelville Headquarters would be in direst need of medical treatment for contracting a rare form of *niveosis* explained earlier. In this case, the whites of his eyes were only visible and it was unsettling to have anyone face him during social contact. For such was the power of a blinding white wall over anyone unaccustomed, humanly that is.

Therefore the conclusion of heartland and project Yard Lamp of Gloria before the returnable remains of our forerunner doctorate herald and pioneer intrepid. The TATM thereof reconvened later to escort colonel Rutherford back on terra firma.

There was even a more infectious strain of niveosis and heliosis alike. The latter being over-photosensitive to light exposure of the broader spectrum. Benign cases of mere polymorphous lighting eruption can occur and are usually characterized by an itchy eruption on patches of sun-exposed skin. People may inherit a tendency to develop these reactions whilst within the whitest confines of an Immaculatorium. Offhandedly, they nicknamed it a Nuclear Suntan among more affable science officers. Complimentary euphemisms circulated in stark contrast to what obdurate officiators of territoriality spouted! The dealers were many, but the feelers were few.

Aside from the wan white-on-white blank-eyed condition from overexposure, the heliosis syndrome in particular (both physiological and psychological) posed another enigma. It was certainly and to no less degree of an impact that blackened the eyes to blinding *black* rather! And so, quite the opposite reaction via scales of electromagnetic polarity took hold of an unprotected *contactee.*

Moreover, there were outright extremes from overexposure by the inter-walled Planck blankness of the Ubiquelabyrinthium Corridority (technical jargon for Super-maze hallowed Hallways). It is where the TATM system abode through suspended animation until visited, let alone intruded upon by an onlooker loitering.

To prevent the sudden onset of optic and epidermal disorders, in the nick of time, the Off-World Mission came to an abrupt closure ere the team had to be debriefed brazenly with intense interrogation. Even their downtime was scrupulously scanned by CCTV...

Along the way- yea- and during decontamination processing, the HQ campers attended to the colonel for potential niveosis with quarantine and sensory deprivation chambers to offset such a syndrome. He felt quite queasy under the entire ordeal of their method and approach, treating him like a guinea pig or lab rat. Later, much miraculously, it was Dep. Joyce Hathaway and Capt Boyd Harris, Rutherford's right and left arm and hand that met up with him in some back-alley pub. How heartfelt, the long-awaited rendezvous reasserted a bond between them like never before.

Joyce and Boyd beamed, brimming with euphoria. Rutherford eyed them carefully, though, and glanced around for possible espionage and surveillance chiefly designed to espy their whereabouts.

"So here we join," he told them, "as I have yet to share with both you my grand encounter with madame Glistria..."

"Aye, we've heard of her," captain Harris admitted in his humble huff. "For while you were up in stasis, calculating and deducing directions and detours and all- why- we received the same info by way of the TATM program."

Rutherford took notice of the captain and looked Hathaway over and asked her rather reticently, "Ah, but what about you, since your last meetup with that Yellow Room way back when?" Joyce froze for an uncanny moment, feeling taciturn, vaguely aware of the Tar-Sheet that still gnawed upon her noggins. Then the colonel upheld everyone with equal and genuine admiration. "Well then, are we all up to shape now, Team?" was the introduction of his pep talk on maintaining integrity against ghastly and unsightly oddities.

Joyce brightened up into triumphant defiance of her harboring and emotional turmoil long left behind her and confessed: "I shan't ever forget the great adventure of a lifetime, our dear colonel!"

Now in the pub cafeteria, roundabout an oak bench where they lounged, they partook of a draft from an automat decanter that dispensed beer automatically, and in goodly gusto guzzled a sip.

In their stealthy appointment, away from the grim evil Eye, all of them (including the grassroots locals of the village community) toasted to their indisputable reunion with a doughty tinge of revelry, but yet with a subconscious twinge of nightmarish innuendos from long labyrinthine entanglement upstairs and downstairs. Still, each of the contributors gave thanks to the TATM administrator for one helluva ride along the way as opposed to the pithy *pin-down* that nexus, Assembly Illuminati of diabolical dispatch denoted on their charge account. Credit reports kept track of everyone in the commune-compound of the Greater Barracks Area: the grotty GBA

But soon, in the future tense, this episodic epicenter of conversation and apprehension had unraveled precisely until their individual threefold Off-World Mission was to be rigorously examined.

And it came to pass that they were led away by station personnel. Into a military MOPP level 4 truck, hastily locked up and off with them for further decontamination and preventative annoyance. One must argue, that the benevolence and benignity of a paranormal yet pristine Presence to have drawn dread, whence dregs of the mainstream milieu become beleaguered, is beyond mental sanity.

By now, the adjutant general of Camp HQ ordered an out-of-country brigadier to be escorted from abroad and fly in to assess the seething situation. The Amber Alert hooted. Meanwhile robotic announcements rattled the eardrums of barrack sleepers at nighttime, blaring, "Attention troopers, soldiers and civilians! Be on the lookout for *sideswipes* of the Plosive Plucire! Maintain fireguard!"

This resulted with what transpired earlier on at the horseshoe-shaped U-bowl Camp Mitch Stadium that is proudly showcased by the idiots, Rutherford recoiled during his ride in the armored truck. Apparent epiphanies from his close-encounter of the fifth kind had seeped into three dimensions desultorily, tripping and triggering off alarms at the baleful base stations. Having hellbent bastions of secret agents and servicemen scamper amok ere dogged dispatchers attempted to reconnoiter and impose an exigent garrison across the whole district and rural region. As if this were not enough, like the aftermath of an H-bomb, paranoia and frenzy escalated to the boiling level. There the cankered kettle wheezed in devilish defiance to an infinitely marvelous or far more coveted calliope steam-blown blisteringly on the other side of the cosmos.

So-called security sweeps combed the environs until every lot, link or forensic *lint* was prohibited to be left unnoticed. The Command Center of the compound at any adjustment started to simmer with Vesuvian vehemence. And alas- nearby- behind bulwark borders, retinues of statesmen, senators and officials plotted upon their digital graphs grids crosshatched, buck-headed by MAD missile silos, cells, lockup penitentiaries, and dingy dungeons (under these stronghold hexes). An ambush of Total Control kept watch 24/7...

Furthermore they were humiliated before the High Counsel by having been divested of their rank and insignia. In fact, any officer to exit the Transalteratorium faced prosecution by some gaslighting attorney. Xenophobia (distrust of anything which is perceived of being foreign or strange) and Photophobia~ though not of the migraine, nor neuro-ophthalmic bouts, wherefore of course, when the Light shines into the darkness and the darkness cannot comprehend it on grave grounds. For by the numbers-- be they enumerated even over overt casino slaps, craps, blackjack, slots, tabletop poker, and roulette-- each one of them followed suit as prying authorities unleashed themselves to divest every sojourner of dignity and civility. Sequestered surveys, discoveries and enlightenment overruled the Vesuvian verdict of the Council cabinet cogs on the prowl.

Joyce upheld her merry mug and gawped goggle-eyed at her twosome ranked Life and Eagle scout's-honor benefactors with an imploring plea: "Please let us resist the listless and offer assistance to the irresistible!" And she meant it satisfactorily, suffice it to say.

But before and after their quaint make-believe revelry, it was the presence of Glistria that hovered over them with tutelary tact, urging their consciences to beware of bawdy behavior.

Apparently, the inviolable investiture of the Transalteratorium, with whom they all kept contact beforehand and now, had crowned them at long last. No corollary, nor disputation could counter their hallmark of achievement into the absolutely unknowable, nor ever. The Tonsure of Bequeathal and Consecration no Mitchelville mobster, robber, bastard, bimbo, and urban buckaroo was able awfully to deprive them of. The Transalteratorium cannot be traduced!

Natronic Unicones (inverted foam funnels of glistening listeners) nestled throughout the interwoven Warp Maze... These TATM Kaluza-Klein Bottles winched aloft via pulley and tightrope found such chieftain hogs (managed by petulant pinheads) to be steroid-repugnant... It nauseatingly knuckled them backwards! Withdrawn with wearisome and convulsive revulsion the Bottles became! The

Vomitory: not an outlet for crowds of punters and rabble-rousers to squeeze through; neither the one, nor the other by one embrasure in castellated brickwork- rather- the flexible alembic and AMBU bag valve mask, or Artificial Manual Breathing Unit to avert the caustic chemical and the pharmaceutical corporation and organization that insult the absorbent sponges of natrium input. "Ye are the salt of the earth: but if the salt have lost his flavor, wherewith shall it be salted? It is thenceforth good for nothing, but to be cast out, and to be trodden under foot of men," Matthew 5:13-14 (KJV). Thusly the *Natronic Unicones* (never to be debased by impertinent hogs).

Fortuitously, destined to be, for each of them the Dishonorable Discharge was pending and underway instead of a swampier Court Martial. Albeit the case, let us presume, that the OW-team's modus operandi gained grassroots supporters beholden to them by sympathetic influence. Such clandestine measures against the State had helped wheedle their political escape out of House Arrest. The public Eye, not unlike the Illuminati, ruthlessly targeted them, using an all-voyeuristic Probe perched atop pyramidal pinnacles for blatant, bloodbath tyranny. Totalitarian exploitation of the citizen!

Fortunate for our detained exemplars, the principality and payload of weightier matters than what madcap Mitchelville devoured and digested, in the long run, nullified the vituperative, violent, and volcanic caldera of utter tar from the campground grub-steak black gold gusher. Many a macabre nemesis which pollutes the environment! The Transalteratorium herself traduced by dreadful implication as she yearned for far better bargains; raw deals that recreate rungs of resolution & restitution on the other end of the spectrum. The supernumerary rainbow from the days of Noah and hitherto radiates promises no worldly artifice could concoct.

Full well: it was told to us of legends long ago, or far ahead into the future where the GLIBOLOTUBULOPOLITZ glorified its *Creatorium* against the obsolescent crematorium. Whereas cadavers could have been dumped into coal containers and pot belly tubs on a concentration camp bonanza. Over which one warm citywide and mountainous municipality shall supplant our present barbaric baboons of lascivious capitalism and of imperialistic subjugation, we beg the Mercy Seat, throne and courtroom to succor us!

High above an uproarious riffraff at the Campground that festered with iron-curtain policy enforcement on the innocents~ in the middle, to diddle the beastly tribe of its foibles and fancies~ a lone backdoor (invisible to the inimical and menacing anthills) unfolded open and then buckled back up on itself foolproof on one wall-side of the TATM's clockwork runabout. All the top supports, platforms and catwalks coiled into themselves simultaneously. And for final practical purposes, every reserved facility, auditorium and living room, authorized inlet and outlet; corridor, cul-de-sac & detour, diversion and Dead End; or open-way revolving door, Multi-Trivia, four, three and two-way vestibule, runway, ramp; entrance and exit of this unimaginably vast Labyrinth alongside Hallowed Hallways were evacuated of all life-signs save for that topmost sacred *oversoul* of hearts: our Immaculatorium from the olden heyday!

Again, per payload and principle of operation, everything else was nicely and neatly divested of its former makeup and restored to its original sanctity of silken, silvery Silence. In brief, the TATM passkey to these premises had to be resealed by a neutron-packed Vault and Vat of the *so unreachable*, but bottomless SUBDUCTORIUM. Until then, before dislodging our officers, an additional issuance needed to be resolved and with no cobwebs attached.

But now let us backtrack before the aforesaid. Apropos of and penultimate to this globalized debriefing procedure at Campground Mitchelville, an incontrovertible appurtenance prefaced a leave of absence at hand. Once and for all [and only this] that ought to capstone the Yard Lamp of Gloria grand exodus to an outdoor Exit.

The incomprehensible Light shone afield into a sedge-patch of sepulchral gravestones all upright and erect indeed. Only the burial of each internment was to be exhumed by the Resurrection thereof; that of the White Light of the Immaculatorium quintessential.

The next interval of Borrowed Time ushers in some last transporter device supplied by the TATM warehouse and furnished forth accordingly. Such a contrivance that even transcends any previous engagement with innovative Magnetic Levitation conveyance pod-packs earlier on, when our OW-team became transfixed during a slip-trip to the wholly geodesic Super Sphere Complex. Of course, their details en route were well defined convincingly! Kept and enshrined for the Record and for Posterity. However, there was one off-the-record account of yet another Hyper-Slip-Trip. One that defied any heretofore vocabulary of yardstick usage.

When BT no longer represents Bulged Tubular, but rather Borrowed Time sequence 888 (triple eight triad-lemniscate) stacked up on top of one another- no longer lazily- as it were, except a priori! The underlying foundation thereof to buttress weightier abutments on either side of a brocaded Bright Bridge); an interlaced overpass for no man to span, albeit with exception through the one and Holy Haven of Futurity, the IMMACULATORIUM exhibit [BT].

Hence humbly equated: ∞

An airtight tubular lemniscate 23 meters wide was what faced them

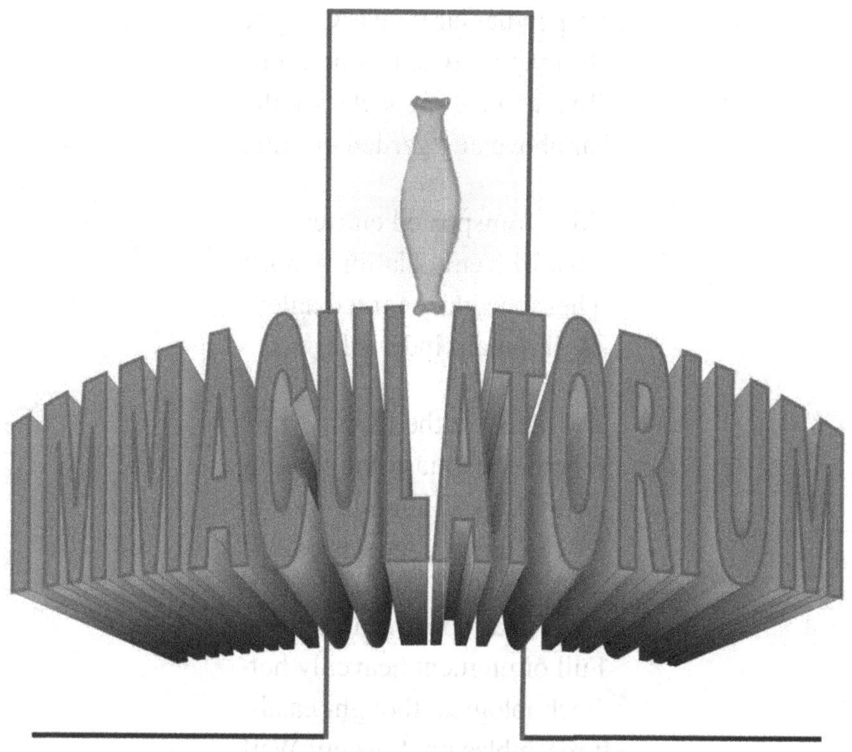

IMMACULATORIUM

The Holy Haven of Repose

The Ever-Creme Expressway

O Immaculatorium, ever shine
Thy illustrious entity glaze
With an EXY to heavy recline
On linoleum lustrous, ablaze!

The EXY is more than an exit
To another dimension far off,
Where never life's dregs hit
But to end in the LUXAR loft.

Perpendicular to every angle,
But yet vertical toward atop
To a conical pinnacle bangle
Far above any garden or crop!

Yea, transported entirely so
On a heavenly platform aloft;
There the glory united aglow
Will remain indivisibly soft.

You arrive at the LUXAR loft
Where one Quasar on top oily
Is an Argand lamp lit up oft,
Six to ten in candelas coily!

The Vatar nomenclature it be
Full of unguent heavenly hot-
Technological though- easily
It resembles my Seventy Watt.

Via arc tube cocoon shiniest,
Glorifier in-vitro contained,
Eerie fulgor appears tiniest
The Vatar enlarges sustained!

Star at an end of the tunnel
Upon Conical Helicon stately,
LUXAR underside but a funnel
It exhibits cod oil ornately.

O escorted to levels unknown,
An Ever-Creme Expressway lay:
Thus this EXY conveyor alone
Over distance dilated, I say!

Their posture of conviction, compunction and repentance mirrored the Puritanical rite of reentry. Devoted and decorated officers (even if they were stripped to the bone by the campground cartels) maintained self-integrity. They refused to allow lamentable liaisons to interfere, or the postiche hobnobberies of a malevolent mainstream media to take advantage of them. Now the sentry and passkey-accessible Ready Room- within which nonconformists, pilgrims, and pioneers have sheltered themselves- stood stalwartly aground.

An apotheosis of the preceding events was soon to transpire.

How hither [in this elevated haven] their close-knit coterie of common parlance was well-witted and refreshed. Never mind the cost! In fine, albeit a genuinely established and concrete confirmation. Yea, over a rainbow-arching band of spectra, Starlight Lambency of furnace fuel was about to benchmark the auspicious occasion. The Holy of *holies* no knucklehead nor twit dare vitiate; the wont of which will plot to accost or castigate the inviolable. But its consequential backfire prepares to incinerate the trespasser!

In parallel to the preceding episode where wanton worshipers of the Illuminati organized marching manifestos and rallies against the Plosive Plucire (that decided to deliberately invade their territory), the *utter cessation* and *silencing* of all worldly whim, uproar, appeasement, or chaos lulled the Walled Womb of Whiteness. With spongiest acoustic absorbers of anechoic properties, it was to cushion noise at these frequencies. Using foamy Muters for dampening devices, such Silencers could convert even the harshest quiver into minus 20 decibels. Be it by gunfire, the explosion of a bomb, bang, bolt, dart, deafening detonation, roar, rumble, reverberation, blitz, bullets, fireball bolide, thunderclap; *a muffled thud that may creep through*, or even an outside bolt of lightning; bark, bellow, bleep, bleat, blare, blat, shriek, shrill, squeal, squeak; sine wave squiggle on the *oscilloscope; even an insignificant weest whistle, whisper, whimper, whoop- yea- warhead blast! Whine, vociferation, stentorian bash! Burst, backfire; snap-crackle-pop; the blizzards of winter, gusty spring, simmering summer, or rustling autumn; backlash, thrash, crash, thresh, sweep, *or any quieter undertone to slyly seep in* until unaccounted for~ unawares with undetected contingencies!

Only the ineffable *Hush* of Harmonics and the *Lull* of Listlessness that spread a Bloated Blanket of permafrost freshness over this din!

*The CRT thermionic emitter & phosphor coated oscilloscope, full of vacuum tubes, preserved by the old Transalteratorium Antiquated Reliquary, or TAR… but not necessarily its Tar-Sheet shuffled to the Yellow Room, though that *slimy slag is* a musty medium of blackened *ethereality…* that of residual rubbish from hyper-past versions of Universes that preceded today's creation of Omnipresence! Nay, not *Sheetar* with its leftover epidermis shed forth by the Hindu coiled serpent, Shesha (also known as *Adishesha*), afloat on the cosmic ocean through eons of creation whereupon Vishnu rests.

Thus the TATM auditors have catalogued these four factors in general and also other 4D perimeters of measurement not noted herein:

The behind-the-curtains Firanki are aplomb with perpendicularity

1. Amplitude (looking along the vertical axis)
2. Time (looking along the horizontal axis)
3. Waveform shape, and distortion of waveform shape.
4. Waveform disturbances, particularly from outside sources.

And two sound samples out of a quadrillion in the TATM data base. One from a horse, a basic bird, and our King of instruments:

The bray, whinny, neigh, nicker, snort and squeal.

Whereas in the next [limited] ornithological selection, it was with a Holographic Aviary. Nonetheless, disregarding such loons like waterfowl, squawking seagulls, quacking ducks, the honks of geese; quail, doves; or the hooting owl, vulture, crow, raven, and the common buzzard bug-eyed by bellicose overtures of nuisance or noise. Such songbirds suppressed the hoopla or hullabaloo by merriment~

The twang, tweet, twitter, twittle, cheep, cheer, chirrup, chitter-chatter, chirr, chirp, trill, warble, and the whippoorwill chirp!

Whereas with the pipe Organ and steam-blown calliope, a compact treasure trove of soundboard sampling and nomenclatures of Stops:

The subtle chif, harmonic murmur; the ubiquitous Voix Céleste, Vox Femina, Bombarde, Bourdon, choir, choral-bass,"Chorus" reeds, Clarion, "color" reeds, cornet, crescendo, Cromorne, cymbal, diapason, Dulzian, echo, vibrato, En chamade, English horn, Erzähler, Fagott, flue, flute, Fourniture, French horn, Fundamental, Gamba, Gedeckt, Gemshorn, Grand Orgue, Great, harmonic, Hauptwerk, Hautbois, Krummhorn, Languid, Larigot, mitered pipe, Mixture, Montre (for show only), Mutation, Nazard, oboe, octave, Orchestral Oboe, Partial, Plein Jeu, Plenum, Pommer, Posaune, Positif, Positiv, Prestant, Principal, Principal Chorus, Quintadena, Quinte, Rank, Rankett, Récit, reed, regal, register, resonator, a reversible, romantic, Salicional, scale, Schalmei, Scharf, Schwellwerk, Sesquialtera, shallot, shutters, the solo, specification (list of stops and ranks), spotted metal, Stop, the stopped diapason, a stopped pipe, strings, swell and bellows, Tierce, tremolo, trombone, trumpet, tuba, Twelfth, Viola da Gamba, Vox Humana, Zimbelstern, Zink~ and lastly~ the old characteristic calliope *wheeze*.

Indeed, the storage chamber of the TATM included the replica and model of each and every delivery booth down to the minutest byte.

DÉJÀ VU? Because this was superimposed in midair *ex nihilo*: But backstage in an olden gloomy ballroom superimposed by a twenty foot narrowing mirror was harshly heard, with clarion clarity, the canorous chorus of a self-automated **Mortier Taj Mahal** DANCE ORGAN blow-top calliope! Its hefty mother-accordion branched out by miniature harmoniums full o' metal reeds and calliope whistles thinly high-pitched and dolefully *out~of~tune* by thick thermal pressure. Sharply chattering away, via roll-feed, an octave-o'er-octave irreplicable repertoire of roundelay resonance, indefatigably upon its 112 slat keyboard. Its egg-and-dart showcase extravaganza satisfied the customer

---

But afar off~ below in some comelier hinterland, remote from the Greater Barracks Area, or the GBA~ and beyond the suburbs of Metro Mitchelville smeared with an overcast malaise, Felicity and Inspiration suffused the surrounding neighborhoods and homestead community. Several satellite cities televised the enthusiasm whilst wet-behind-the-ears whippersnapper neophytes copycatted one another, trying to emulate the shiny shape and affectionate effigy of the Plosive Plucire on the rosier blush of the bourgeoisie. The PS sector and the PTA purchased for them plump pillows designed to tangibly keep contour with this intimate Entity. Over each tapestry-sewn pillow was the embroidered filigree a-swirl via a Paisley pattern along the seams and sewn into the duvet sold separately:

Exotica of the Cosmic Menagerie
Embraceable Bedtime Companion

Yea, yellow ones and cream-puff patties were dispensed in lieu of the stereotypical fuchsia and azure sleeved pillows allocated for girl or boys to snuggle with. Also, properly itemized as head-cushions, these heirloom heart-puffs consoled every backwoods society. Comforters interwoven, well apart from the segregated and subdivided civilization of mad Mitchelville. A madhouse seduced with electronic consoles for analysis, dehumanized by integrated circuit boards, civilians coaxed by counterfeit cocktails o' tawdry times, or bedraggled by bedlam- if not with GBA hellbent bombsite drills.

From pillar to post, from crib and cradle to hearse and casket, ceremony and celebration for generations hereafter haunted the rural and countryside landscape where cosmopolitan venues of vogue were reminded by the historic extraordinary event. The bleak GBA under an impasse was perforce pummeled with civilian counterrevolution whether it was State sanctioned or not!

Elsewhere, amid the emollient comfort zone of the Immaculatorium, with heartfelt hugs of reunion and recommendation, Joyce Hathaway, Boyd Harris, and Roderick Rutherford cuddled finally for what seemed like centuries that skittered by. Or was it nearly a millennium to have elapsed lightning-like? Let destiny decipher it! A rippling revival effect replaced the frog pond of stagnation.

They were found finally at ease in an adjacent Waiting Room eerily lit like nothing on earth just outside of the "immutable" Immaculatorium; even though its protean nature manifested the 'materialization of multiplicity'...

The Endmost Dialogue

Joyce waxed jumpy and jubilant. Her long-awaited felicity and feminine finesse stuck onto her two *He-Men*. "Whoa, we have burdensome business to attend to and pending, my dear rocket scientists..." Then she turned to the colonel- cattily- with a wide-face Cheshire grin that articulated her dimpled cheeks into accordion pleats. Rutherford for a few moments was reminded by memory lane of the New York Coney Island moon marquee that smiled so from ear to ear. No longer flippant, especially when addressing a high commissioned officer, she divulged her Sacred Secret at him whereas captain Harris was all ears: "So--- the Metalucelectropluceptorium has fulfilled its prediction with rather a fair share of the bigger bargain. Am I correct, sir?"

Rutherford, privileged as surrogate father to step-daughter, acknowledged her amiably, "You are as always, my lilty lady deputy, impeccable whenever it comes to deductive reasoning." The complement tattooed her heart as she simpered and sauntered off to a covert corner of the Waiting Room as if naught else overturned her clemency. "And I thought corners are for sulking!" Rutherford remarked with martial bravado and aloft laughter lilted. It somewhat sugarcoated the sterile and ozone-odorous, ionized atmosphere of the intramural multiplex (ventilated if not inert). The charged fresh air zippered up a tingly sensation along one's backside.

Captain Harris hinged himself, on the other end, in support of her statement and carefully eyed both of them with overdue admiration, looking leftward and rightly since Joyce stood on the other end of a wall. A fortnight ago, he did not like being left out of the twosome circle of so-called family ties they'd have developed- but really- their energetic euphoria was unanimous. Come what may, he beckoned the twain to take heed of what was at hand and to stay prudent. The colonel took his advice and slapped a pat on his back, "Well noted, Harris." Joyce joined them for the Grand Ingress…

For namely, notwithstanding, the Immaculatorium's invitation for each of them to enter it at the same time electrified the overall suspense.

Now Rutherford, levelheaded as he always was, accounted for the variegated manifestations of the squashy and so cuddly Cosmic Menagerie (manufactured and knitted nicely on pillows of Camp Mitch by the truckloads). To demystify this descriptive design~ though fancily overlaid into fine fabrics supplied by the Down and Feather Company~ the Vatronducelux, or Vatlux luminary, with which he had prior interaction, had settled the evidence of *other* lifeforms aboard the TATM infrastructure at last. Unequivocally, he reckoned that there were additional oddities, *features of creatures*, along the trek; the 'walled' way of their catwalk promenade! Yet whether they were auto-generated by a hologram or not was inconclusive and necessitated unbiased investigation.

Stepping down from Cloud Nine for safety's sake, the leader of the pack bluntly inquired of the now demure deputy, "Uh~ say- Joyce, are you sure the Metalucelectropluceptorium platform has led our missionary entourage thus far to such a self-silenced Immaculatorium?" In recoil to his asking, the tall-walled arena suddenly shuddered, except soundlessly, reading into their telltale tête-à-tête as if having been shock-awakened out of an intercontinental coma… Counterparts on cue could have curtailed their small talk.

The interfaced cyclops suppressor was no longer comatose.

The quota of the acquiescent *Quotile* erupted within an oily Tar-Sheet of the ignored, hexed, oft-avoided, and ghastly Yellow Room! The team's unbeknownst propinquity to quirks and *quiddities* of triangulation from the 'Quotile' was vectored vastly by but one sweeping swath athwart everyone's conscious cortex of the pineal gland. Even if no niveosis (diagnosed as a possible side effect earlier) infected any of them- nor heliosis- the light~dark circadian rhythm of their brainstorm was calibrated to the Blinding Blankness of about absolutely Nothing! Another anomaly & countless more for neurology! It was no Yellow Front from an early to mid 1980s emporium, rather, the 'Real Thing' literally! Without a Coca-Cola fizzy drink commercial--- Dampening silence ensued.

"That *Thing*, if you will, spoke to me only once in a blue moon, but assuredly," confessed the deputy, concerned if not consternated. She started pacing the floor of the spooky antechamber.

"I see," said he, Rutherford, icily. Perplexed by the red flag.

And it nagged him. The colonel had seen through his viewer the utter magnitude of such a place before. But now anticipatory to their rite of entry~ up the ramp and through the door~ looming lingeringly, *just on the other side of this Prefatory Antechamber*, that haunting Immaculatorium still stored whatever else up its pliable 'plastelastic' sleeve…

Rutherford reviewed anew his ragtag crew. He barked: "Okay, captain and deputy, ten-hut!" Both of them were at attention. "Parade rest!" Harris, like Joyce, would steeple his fingers behind his lumbar and part his feet for a firmer stance. They were to take their stations for an upcoming event. The Colonel added, "OW-team, are ye fitly conditioned to conduct an ingress thereunto? If so… Then let's go!" Their routine commander was never inclined to fib!

They prepared themselves in the Waiting Lounge columned with a mock hallway appearance, joined hands, and began to pray the old-fashioned way. Adopting the preferred method, Joyce gently led her team into unadulterated sincerity. In one accord an Amen was finalized by all three of them. Throats were cleared to a slight Wakabayashi *cough* in which the interpretation typified a 'young forest' of some fashion to refresh the perky alertness of the bunch~ aside from their drowsy downtime with trivial trappings.

Joyce topped it off with a reading from Ecclesiates 3:12: "And if one prevail against him, two shall withstand him; and a threefold cord is not easily broken." She stashed away her materialized Holy Bible procured by the *Old Faithful* TRANSALTERATORIUM...

Then, ceremoniously, the trio chanted thrice in unison: "Gung-ho, let's go! Gung-ho! Hey," and their electric cord plugged into the socket was once again [uncut]! Then the unexpected occurred. Murphy's Law, but in reverse- in that it posed a blessing instead of an unusual Yellow curse.

Joyce just about had to genuflect for feeling awe. "Wow, what a kick-start for our cosmological jackpot!" she blurted and swallowed the frog which went down through her gullet. It induced unsettling belly-flutter as adrenaline apprehended her, at least with an inspired arousal that is. After all, her [Metalucelectropluceptorium] managed to boomerang backup validation for the Ending Terminal.

"Aye, deputy! A cosmological kitty indeed," confessed the captain, cutting in for a piece of the rhubarb pie himself. "Easy as cake~"

"Now pay attention team..." reminded Rutherford, cautiously caught off guard, uneasily beset by this newer number of intrusion.

One by one they filed upward on an eight-step staircase---steeply--- stuck out of a wall-side pegged by rungs that led to a ceiling sealed manhole. The walkway without fences was grilled by Faraday cage netting for passersby and pedestrian safety. Then there was a sloped ramp over which they'd tread tentatively to another hatchway. Upon its bulkhead, the warning VERBODEN, originally German for *forbidden,* glared at them with uninviting irony. Premises prohibited to visitors and intruders alike? Not so!

Alas, with thumping hearts of unbridled expectation in their chests, and with Joyce's contagious belly-flutter trademark, they went in. The sideways postern popped a gasket and opened itself creakily… In spite of the all-too-familiar staging for traffic safety~ or was it their thought projections from planet Earth?~ this Super-Walled womb of desolate silence slipped on the verge of having to open up for the very first time after billions of years. For ventures to vindicate a priori prevention, their entry-level was allowable if each of them were given a reward for effort and persistence upon such preparatory exchange with an authorized TATM transaction.

No anatomical pun of any reproductive organ was intimated heretofore, nor will ever be hereafter. Notwithstanding substation identification, *in utero veritas* [for] Truth in the Womb.

At first sight of the blindingly bluish-white Immaculatorium, they cringed with *wonder-struck* shock and bewilderment. And it was all in the cornerstone corpus of the TATM Complex. The immutable Immaculatorium: unchangeable and of 14 letters added up to 28 if multiplied twice, the *then* professor Roderick Rutherford configured in his laboratory before their Reconnaissance Mission. But now it doubly dawned on him to a much greater degree.

This interminable interior had long existed, untouched and never tampered with~ let alone unattended by any sentient being for eons. Its 'elasticrete' material of near-infinite flexibility withstood the barrage and bombardment of any atomic half-life of decay and entropy. Neither supernovae could counter its eternally indestructible indivisibility, nor the vacuum of space. The relentless ravages of an indefinitely long duration, like length of time, was never its opponent. Nothing could compare to the neutron packed alloy of a steel sheet folded up into a four-dimensional Tesseract Turntable with its inaccessible revolving door. Another one of its passkey carousel counterpoints outside of scientific inquiry. Thus the *rebars* (reinforcing bars and rods) of ultra-tensile durability & strength in each slab of wall plastered out of refined 'elasticrete'.

(Passkey carousel access to be explained near The End of this book)*

Nothing could penetrate the impregnability thereof. Nor any thermonuclear detonation at closest proximity can even efface its harsh glare of gloss and glaze with the slightest indentation of impact, or imprint, or scathing scuff mark, or hairline scratch, or the pestilential ogres of imbecility back at Base Camp~ or what have you. For the paved permanence of it, the plateau of vantage point-and-coordinate in 4D fold-ups and unfolding, and the gleamingly glacial sheen remained invincible to any space-time depreciation, degradation and decrepitude (derived dismally).

In esse, its "Preservatorium" is just as organic as honey from the honeycombs of an apiary, but billions of powers more magnitudinal, more enduring, and immortalized more than anything else in this Universe of both ontological and Anthropic characteristics.

The colonel, captain and deputy disembarked from the *Prefatory Antechamber* and into the Immaculatorium ablaze with whiteout blankness. Their eyes had adjusted to the ultra-sharp contours of the interior which was merely a cross-sectional slice or sliver of hyperspace *supersymmetry.* Although in this context, we shall not refer to supersymmetry as a theoretical framework in physics that postulates the existence of a symmetry between particles with integer spin and particles with half-integer spin. Or basically, the proposal that for every known particle, there exists a partner particle with different spin properties.

The colonel, because of his quantum physics background, deduced the geometrical properties of the tesseract-turntable immaculacy thereof to be infinitely straighter than the *Yoctometer Leveler. Every threshold and vertex of right-angles and of perpendicularity radiated razor-sharp high definition beyond the 576,000,000 individual pixels that comprise the visual cortex of the human eye.

*A *yoctometer* is 10^-24 m while the smallest unit for measurement and also, the smallest size for anything in the universe is a Planck length (one septillionth of a given unit). In the year 2113, a laser-lipped device, the Yoctometer Leveler, is used!

The OW-team staggered from inside, over-amazed and agog. Bedazzled by otherworldly whiter-than-white purity and freshness that would be burnt into their retinas ruthlessly if it were not for visor protection on their end of profuse electromagnetic irradiation.

The one and only other terminology to describe what they saw is rendered with a prefix to suffix recombination of the root words: *permanent* and *mure* (meaning wall). Therefore, the PERMURA is an apt choice for the Immaculatorium Tall-Wall not at all dissimilar to the TATM prerequisite on subspace intramural arrangements.

Then, at once, unannounced and unawares, pitch blackness seized Rutherford and Harris as they were put to sleep. According to the TATM schedule, it was hypnotic stupor induced somnolence that overtook them. Our jolted Joyce was forlornly left to fend for herself~ however, it proved to be more of a blessing in disguise.

But before the frazzled Joyce was bereft and isolated for the time being, not realizing that it was her benefit really, on another time-slot of alternate consciousness the lookalikes played out their roles as if nothing out of the ordinary had happened.

An Inside Glance into the IMMACULATORIUM

The nuts and bolts of how the darned thing works evaded the inquisitive Rutherford who seemed more or less bullheaded when it boiled down to his thorough Inspector Gadget investigation.

Previously, Rutherford on another level of reentry prodded the premises of an observatory deck by peeping into paranormal phenomena that transpired in the walled womb of the Immaculatorium infrastructure. Save this time, all three of our intrepid explorers by themselves would get a firsthand feel of the facility, in personae.

Now notice, if we were to throw light on a side issue here; that these vertical confines (from floorboard to ceiling-topper) revealed infinitesimal properties unmatched by the laws of physics.

Just One of the Functions Thereof

Eternally unseen my mortal perception, there were cubic Planck volumes, each a septillion-septillion times tinier that the electron of an atom. Let us speculate (with all due respect to the scientific academy for any miscalculation), whereby the size of Earth~ in comparison and by analogy~ is a full-sized electron--- though more of a wave than a particle according to quantum mechanics--- and the Planck length then is unearthed next to planet Earth which is the cloudy size of an electron to begin with.

And so, having been likened to a mere proton rather, which is considerably larger and more massive than, say, an electron wave-packet or energetic photon- for that matter- so, too, the Planck volume of a unitary point is *by far* smaller than the most fundamental constituent of some subatomic particle. Wherefore, where spacetime fabric breaks down because nothing is possibly smaller than the infinitesimal, the hyper-hyper reduced building blocks of every cubic nanometer (for instance) can represent full grown galaxies if compared to the Quantum Foam quivering frenetically and so spasmodically beneath these--- assuming the galaxies were the nanometers enlarged!

At this miniaturization, there lay no spacetime to contend with! Hence the seemingly erratic and unstable behavior of an ethereal froth, bubbling with an antimatter & anti-spatial hyper-vacuum, and yet somehow more powerful than the fusion reactor nuclear furnaces of a billion stars! Although due to insubstantial evidence relative to our spacetime, the sheer nonexistence of the Quantum Foam hath lain *timelessly* from which the exponential potential of infant Universes are spawned. And on top of it, this Providential Intelligence is absolutely in full charge of the outcome since such "was" created by the Divinity thereof. And the word *was* is past-tense, [remember the timelessness factor]. Moreover, through the duration of eons, the *'now'* universe ballooned *superluminally* in that there *was* or *is* no space nor time through which it expands!

*We hope, here, the quantum physicists can don their laboratory hardhats and reconsider the above proposal. The Author's directive behooves her to appreciate information borrowed from the Pioneer Cosmologists of the last century and a half.

Getting back to the subject at hand, the Immaculatorium's volume-by-volume scale of tamper-proof material is ever so contiguously congealed to constitute the striations and strata of the *tesseract* *Foursquare wall, ceiling, and subsurface called the floorboard.

It would have taken super or quantum computer calculations for a million years henceforward, nonstop twenty-four-seven, to decipher but one cubic inch of the Immutable Immaculatorium of Pluriseptiplex Planck pliability!

Though these impressions mystified the confounded Rutherford, who was more of an Air Force officer than a quantum physicist, Hathaway and Harris, without him noticing~ *be they the first faintest inklings of the like in light of the "innumerable"* ~ offered at least their two-cents-worth of comprehension. After all, still, it was everyone's presumptuous propinquity to the Eternal itself.

Obviously, in front of the glaze and gleam of unapproachable nuclear blue blindingly apparent, Joyce shrugged at the prospects of her expeditious team that awaited her individually. Her expectations were thwarted by unsettling uncertainty. One of which was a task, in and of itself, as *Neil Armstrong, who first set foot on the moon in the history of humankind. Was she to be elected to do so first in like manner? "Set foot on the *Pluriseptiplexian* platform of Planck pliability within an impossible Immaculatorium! Gimme a break," she'd backlash, but by no spite, only horseplay. They were *Transalteratorium-triggered* enough as it is, preconditioned to take the plunge…

* During their ninth orbit of the Moon astronauts Bill Anders, Jim Lovell, and Frank Borman recited verses 1 through 10 of the Genesis creation narrative from the King James Bible. Anders read verses 1–4, Lovell verses 5–8, and Borman read verses 9 and 10. This then was transmitted to Earth where their reading of God's Word was televised

worldwide. Why- it had been the ONLY book ever broadcast from outer space- *by golly* (if we should dare revive what today is oft judged as a word-usage cliché, inter alia).

Except, contrarily, not so much by the phantasmagorical features of a multidimensional Plosive Plucire portent witnessed with Rutherford's keen commonsense. Nay, there was commonsense to attribute on this final frontier, however- of course- pending Joyce's autonomous entrance and exit into and from an upcoming EXY...

Nor the Borteum and Cremeum spheroid circus act of spatial and temporal antiquated antics and stunts pulled even earlier than that!

Forbye an unforeseen flip-side, whereas the TATM had run the consummate itinerary of their ventures, that this step-on procedure was the last straw drawn from a canasta card game played aboard the Magnetic Levitron Transport did capstone their votive tribute to incontestable contact.

Let us therefore jettison, if not amputate, the realty rump out of a Real Estate grubstake whereas this free-of-charge, lucky chance, golden opportunity ought to take hold! Whereupon each and every millimeter of the 'metalinoleum' flooring is gauged and accounted for by none other than the Heavenly Recorder, or Internal Auditor.

Herewith we will not dig deeper into terrestrial architectonics! No, not by a stone's throw, nor with a thirty-aught-six rifle's bullseye by a long shot, neither by a ballistic missile's long range trajectory. But more willingly, celestially...

The Prolonged Preparation

For as Rutherford and Harris nudged the dear damsel in distress to go forward and (just do it!), Hell, *what have you got to lose?* type of daredevil dive, Joyce stalled~ staggeringly~ before the gaping mouth of her first-in-a-lifetime Grand [Entrance].

Somewhere, in the TATM network, an MBS observed the trio yellowed over their spinal columns, nervous and all, and intoned a sardonic "Gangway!" across the fourth and fifth dimension... But not intending to cajole them.

Joyce was the first to hear its spectral voice by means of ESP. Her other He-Men maintained their rationale and were deaf to the suggestive, *Shining* shunt.

"A hesitation..." she shuffled her word usage craftily, swallowing spittle almost at every inhaled inflection, and concluded the sentence, "...could carry us into annihilation, if I'm not mistaken. And I'm not referring to being high-strung on caffeine, either!"

"Well noted," said the colonel, and rolled his eyes, thinking, *who are you trying to convince?*

"I *cannae* disagree," granted the captain, for once placing himself in her shoes if in the event of guinea pig reassignment. He had an irremovable lump in his throat and choked at the queer prospect.

There was one dire implication which might set off a chain-reaction, thought the better of them, who just as well wanted to save her life instead of militarily sacrificing it. Was the lower rank reason a cowardly "cop-out"? Let us not go there (for their sake) and dodge the ricochet.

But both of them kept a twosome queue, poised right behind her, as if to shove her in. The narrow rectangular portal pulsated slightly with a subsonic noise that surfaced to the waveform of an audible range--- rather *inaudible*--- but not quite... It resonated like a *brool* of some sort blended into an a cappella harmony of hums; a lowly murmur that persisted the entire time they occupied the one and only Great White Room, or *walled womb* if you prefer.

She amusingly faced the two men eager to push her on thru and added, "Hey guys, you remember what happened in the Yellow Room when a pitch black Postern doorway, frothing with turgid Tar, terrified us all? We had to skedaddle out of the way, or else!"

But the two dummies, as if puffed up by steroid testosterone, boorishly insisted on "allowing" her to enter in headlong, ladies first. Her sagacity saw through the veneer.

She scowled back at them cockily as she shimmied through the threshold and boundary and accused her superiors of an affront. "You sissies!" But then with all due deference, blurted: "Just kidding, my playmate chieftains of an all-American powwow."

Enough of the melodrama! mused Joyce, the deputy beaver in their eyes. Otherwise, Rutherford personified a fatherly figure as she esteemed him heroic, having had accolades of commendation by the Right Stuff outside of the *real* idiots that strove to threaten their commissioned livelihood under an austere regime. Mitch or no Mitch, Yesterday's Glitch was *now* no match to the old Mission Impossible! They were brimming with curiosity that rather resurrects the cat than killing it, avoiding to open Pandora's Box.

Notwithstanding potential fatal shortcuts, as Joyce lifted her gaze at the thick leaden glass window on the backdoor to the Immutable Immaculatorium, she began to notice human civilization and the dust and debris of sandcastle centuries erected by but *sand* at the customary seashore of eternity; timestamps of man's fingerprint, ephemeral as it appeared, the sandcastle skittle on the brink and breath of Time, turning to soot. Dust in the Wind as the old 60s song suggests, under which residual rubble (even so) could not in the least besmirch the immaculate flooring within the "corridority" therein. No, not even a smudge, earmark of occupancy compared to eons gone by in the twilit twinkle of an eye!

The expression on her face showed shell-shocked self-abandonment. Sheer shock it was which willy-nilly framed the fragile Frau (if Deútsche), or mot to the marrow (if Irish), or Caryatid (if under the weight of destiny). And Rutherford realized it.

At once she retreated, but nary with disguised dissent.

Unable to take up an upfront (march-forward) bidding, she shrunk away and cringed. This time there was not the Access Denied thingamajig counterpart-contingency to bar her way therein. Clearly, such explosive surfeiting, that of sudden satiation, of sensory overload, was weirdly everyone's nemesis. Then and now, it posed permanent threat to every entry-level gamer or dabbler, or even for a prospective resident of the *pre-angelic*; the OW-team without exception naturally.

[The suspense thickens.]

The Resolution and Outcome

"Rodney, you'd better barge in yourself under a contingency," Joyce suggested, bursting the bath bubble, wishing to cut the stuffy and stale air with a wide, full tang butcher's machete. The corporate flatulence that she loathed had gotten to her as in times past during an officer's duty roster review; in her hard internship, she was always wedged way off to the backseats before and after those grueling trooper drills which were necessary for her advancement.

The preparatory precipice was overcome with solidarity, even with an unseen MBS watching them intently from above. Later on, the 5D spheroid dealt with this so-called *wishy-washy* woman, but beneficially and on her behalf over all the others, by the way. None of them knew that the *first* shall be last and the last likened to first.

Finally, the commander conceded for her sake, knowing full well that in a state of battle such decisions were deadly; still, bearing in mind the dangers of the [heliosis and niveosis] cerebral cortex contortions which might plague them all if ever overexposure to the Front *Glore of the Tall Wall was an issue.

* "Glore" is an archaic word that means to glare or glower. It can also mean to look fixedly or stare. In this case, back in about 1988 or so, the author envisioned the Front Reverberatory Glore as a confrontational wall in the (then) Alteratorium, a large room that can alter itself. The glaringly bright and blank presence of such a Front Wall left violators and vandals to back off immediately lest any infraction could incur consequences, and- at least- when long-term loitering is punishable by an eviction notice. But not to imitate current barbaric bastions against our well-meaning contributor to social circles of the 'responsible' milieu (to exclude dangerous anarchists & sly sluggards, or thieves, or killers and rapists and so forth), where high rent and real estate forces men and women to be spat out into the gutter as flotsam. For out of self-protection from an outright defilement, or vandalism, only then the Transalteratorium System recoils. The Bible warns us how Heaven shuns those who repudiate Heaven!

Joyce jousted an opponent's lance of conscience that sunk into her heart like a long dagger. She was not one to turn down a prying position when Mother Necessity, naggingly, knocked at the door.

Rutherford recalls again that which was reduced to shriveled shrinkage, down to the wisp of an imperceptible dust mote, but yet seen otherwise with sun-ray suffusion in some partly draped living room. That from mountain-wide magnitude, reduced to pip-squeak irrelevance, spacetime can be reduced and folded up, just like that.

*An except from Rudy Rucker's The Fourth Dimension:

"Oh, Kitty, how nice it would be if we could only get through into Looking-glass House! I'm sure it's got, oh! Such beautiful things in it! Let's pretend there's a way of getting through into it, somehow, Kitty. Let's pretend the glass has got all soft like gauze, so that we can get through. Why, it's turning into a sort of mist now, I declare! It'll be easy enough to get through ---" She was up on the chimney-piece while she said this, though she hardly knew how she had got there. And certainly the glass *was* beginning to melt away, just like a bright silver mist.

In another moment Alice was through the glass, and had jumped lightly down into the Looking-glass room. The very first thing she did was to look whether there was a fireplace, and she was quite pleased to find that there was a real one, blazing away as brightly as the one she had left behind. "So I shall be as warm here as I was in the old room," thought Alice: "warmer, in fact, because there'll be no one here to scold me away from the fire. Of, what fun it'll be, when they see me through the glass in here and can't get at me!"

*LEWIS CARROL- *Through the Looking-Glass* (1872)

While watching her commander walk through the main entrance, even if it were only a side backdoor inlet, she was hoping there would be no ensnarement. Not seeing it, but intuitively feeling, that the Immaculatorium was soon to turn tallow and etiolated, which posed a terrible, sickly, and psychotic flashback of the telltale Yellow Room. Luckily, it wasn't the case this time.

Then, both Hathaway and Harris followed their taskmaster right into the reverberating radiance of the Immaculatorium.

Colonel Rutherford felt like Neil Armstrong to have set foot onto the moon's surface, an area called the Sea of Tranquility, as he stepped off of the Apollo 11 Lunar Module on July 21, 1969! Captain Harris and Deputy Hathaway soaked in the exhilarating sensation no less than he.

A tingling chill ran through them while being barefoot. The hyper-linoleum floorboard, designated as the 'Iglunoleum' platform, sizzled with welcome anticipation of their expeditious *First Contact*. They faced an elongated, high-ceiling, narrow corridor and noticed a rectangular looking-glass hung up on the forefront Tall Wall. It measured nine meters high and five meters wide and lengthwise set so that its longest vertices were parallel to and alongside the trailing corners of the high-ceiling hallway. Another name for this passageway was the 'Unicorridority of the Ubiquelabyrinthelux' stenciled by a smear of red spray paint. Also, some swirled swoons of graffiti from previous visitors, or vandals, were scribbled around one of the mile-markers labeled 291.

"A mouthful of cumbersome terminology," commented Joyce where she had read the label sticker at the entrance whence she came through. "I cannot digest the gist of it..."

"Aye, almost like a tongue-twister at that," remarked Harris.

But Rutherford reentered quizzical incredulity while the shimmering sheen of *verticalized* quicksilver shuffled its rippling film (forth and to, ana and kata) upon a massive many-metric-tonne Mercury Mirror at large bulge. "Well, now! What of that lustrous looking-glass over there?" He pointed an index finger for all to follow thereat.

They then approached the larger than life-size Mercury Mirror known as Transvortium 291 [according to the 'Intramuralist' observers]. These onlookers were wedged for far too long in the TATM Warp-Maze of the Ubiquelabyrinthelux! Inter alia, an Intramuralist was the android whopper which had been so awfully well-acquainted with walls themselves, that it quantified nothing more than raw data about the enigma thereof. These automated auditors were Frisbee-shaped suction cup hamburger patty devices able to anchor themselves anywhere in the intramural runabout for a time and a season and record an inert or potentially active anomaly; be it spectral or opaque object, their surveillance set to 24/7 kept constant scanners plastered to a naked ceiling blankly bloated as well as to a plafond enclosed above an indoor pleasaunce.

Yet could anyone imagine undisturbed billion-year boredom? Especially when virtually naught can occur over time!

With a metallic splash and splatter to resound as a steel sheet, but of tenuous tin foil, folding, crinkling, crunching in and out and opening up into a steel sheet again, the Mercury Mirror appeared to be on a spree of framed frenzy. Its ozone odour could be detected by olfactory sniffles which left some aftertaste sublingually, or so it seemed. Hefty harmonics palpitated the air and (overall) the eerie and haunting hallowed hallways of the *Ubiquelabyrinthelux now stretched on forever beneath an endless, seamless ceiling overhung above all the sleekly built & self-supported quarters, cubicles, and partitions of the entire Immaculatorium complex. For it was the ultimate adjunct and showcase of TATM hyperbole that might have gone berserk by and large. Presumably, too many corridors to deal with; walls multitudinous and so beyond any normal superstructure and- yea- even beyond hyper-spacetime-packed capacity.

*Reminder that the Ubiquelabyrinthelux literally means Light everywhere in the Labyrinth as translated from the author's *Latinate* lexicon compound contrivance.

And so much the more the liquefied sheet metal of otherworldly *Hg* of Harsh Glare began to go awry when…

Suddenly, a mirrored metal wafer, coat of mail mantled humanoid figurine solidified summarily before them! At this energetic intersection, they (the OW-team) were for the moment more apoplectic rather than insouciant. An a cappella intonation oozed out of the shiny ladylike personage and formulated the words: "Welcome, my dear visitors, to the Immaculatorium Multiplex!"

Of course, they were speechless as our proverbial Cheshire feline, feral as ever, held them tongue-tied.

Glistria's ostentatious outfit of gaudy glitter glimmered with the selfsame [Hg] that coruscated in the Mercury Mirror itself. Her epidermis was that of purely reflective mirror-like manifestation, to be concise.

The colonel felt strapping enough to loosen his taciturnity and managed: "Madame Glistria, we're warmed by your invitation. But pray tell us, what exactly is the Immaculatorium Multiplex?"

The other two, Joyce and Boyd, gawked at her in abashed bewilderment, almost not needing to strain their eyesight from the *en clair* bare glare of the Glorious Glistria. Still afraid to speak up.

"It is a boundless backrooms Plenitude of Pluriseptiplex multiplicity. In other words, there are Unicorridorities that go on for the span of an entire Universe," replied our topnotch TATM Mercurial Empress of Gargantuan Gold glitterati.

"So there may be repetitions of this epicenter in the long run, if we were to walk on for light-years through the Ubiquelabyrinthelux?" the colonel quizzed the lustrous lady.

"Yes and no... Depending on what state of mind and heart ye sojourners shall have kept."

The OW-team shrugged, narrowed to a nonplussed state.

Glistria persisted, "Like the *state of mind* you three exhibit at present. You can't stand a chance at what will come up if it were so!" Then reassuringly: "But mind you, my Transalteratorium registers the slightest nuance, inflection, and innuendo of quiescent or stormy neurons in the cerebral cortex. Hence the primary purpose of TATM system analysis that can enforce closure of all avenues whatsoever and whensoever and wheresoever possible, or even *impossible*--- like the *FIVE* dimensional Super Ball one of you will have to face..."

Joyce felt a sharp surge ripple down her spine no different than her visual cortex of the phlegmatic splish-splash of molten mercury that vacillated, verticalized over the Hg Mirror. In like manner, Glistria's skin-job mirrored such subtle exploits of the ebullience thereof; the puissant power factor of which would equal *yottawatts* of such fiery fizz! To her, it proved to be an electrostatic dynamo of a flat Vat at that. Imagine a 5 by 9 meter bathtub or pool of mercury suspended sideways up and down with wavelets of liquid metal so agleam until to perfectly reflective acuity…

Under her overbearing and imposing metal wafer window into the Fifth Dimension paved upon the room's Tall Wall, the tapered slender lady stuck out her hand and offered a hardy handshake to the three with unanimous compliance. Each of them felt funny after their fulfilled *First Contact*, and everyone waxed wacky, confounded to the hilt, but not quite in extremis. The dreadful toll of queenly Quietude from a hallway hostess overtook them at least by deafening muteness if not by heartfelt heliolatry.

She confirmed her report, "I am the Heliatrix! The living lamp entity disclosed out of her cocoon; call it the Transvortium of mile-marker 291 thereupon the Tall Wall in back of me…" She turned herself and gazed up at the massive Mercury Mirror churning now its metallic maelstrom that began to froth forth until its veer sucked her in and out of sight! The mercurial monstrosity disappeared too!

In a nanosecond, Glistria vanished along with the augmentation thereof ere the Immaculatorium reconvened its ubiquitous Silencer once and for all. Rutherford knew that these premises were never to be treated with footloose flippancy, God forbid! Nor if ever one were to lose their self-composure, only to become contumelious and caterwaul under an accursed spell. The Walled Womb, as an inducer and transducer, paid no respect of persons, let alone liveliness; neither the lethiferous Lethe of dementia. The gravely mnemonic Mnemosyne (mother of the muses and memory) had sufficed as the *Mnemosyneopolis* Supercity of the Multiplex region; no matter how unimaginably distant its incalculable stretch-over!

And in the event of a well-to-do carte blanche, nevertheless, numbers never prevaricate the outcome. Nor can confabulation of some concoction counter or cause harm to the unutterable and unalterable Truth. The Transalteratorium for billions of years maintained its consecration in spite of the vagaries, vicissitudes, and pitfalls of a chaotic uncertainty principle. Nay, not that of subatomic symmetry, but- more so- of vainglory and fanciful foibles foisted upon people for generations beleaguered not by bounty, but by disaster, death, and Throne Room Judgment. However, the Queen of Walls within the Ubiquelabyrinthelux remained all-merciful from her compensatory Mercy Seats and aimed to spare their expense of the bottomless Pit as of worldwide schizophrenia, or even of folly.

"Glistria ought to return to us when least expected," Rutherford figured. Everyone acquiesced with accordance as the OW-team reasserted itself. Her acquaintanceship was truly cherished.

Both Harris and Hathaway regrouped themselves with their commander and took leave of absence from the Immaculatorium now vacant and void of paranormal phenomena. The backdoor creaked open and they nearly fled the premises, eager to resume repose outside of the holy haven of Repository Intramural Permanence. It was a revivifying RIP for them, but not the requiescat in pace postmortem mainstay.

Thus the Repository Intramural Permanence reigned in their stead as another aeon or so elapsed, having an Iglunoleum floorboard lozenged with lapis lazuli not to be trampled upon, nor tampered with ever again; neither cankered by a rogue corporation…

~ Or as the storytelling board of directors deem fit.

The Hyper~Hyper Sphere

A five dimensional Super Ball

If it were not for what was wedged within the Immaculatorium's Rolodex Directory, the OW-team by now should have been escorted back into that raging inferno of camp cartels and parochial disciplinarians at the Mitchelville Greater Barracks Area. A godforsaken hellhole; *O gargoyle-horned cauldron!* echoes an outcry.

Incidentally, Colonel Rutherford and Captain Harris entered immediate stasis through suspended animation and Deputy Hathaway was in for one helluva shocker. But on a statelier side of life, her switch to the *newer* platform followed in contrast to the dismal desolation of oppressors, or funny funk of puerile pillow parties to sashay with and sugarcoat a maddening Mitch monster. She waxed weary from its tug-of-war, and the soulful separation from her two best friends and dear confidants disoriented her until to a fainting spell. A jarring reverberation rattled her up by an invisible visitor.

She revived and came to~ regained her self-composure on a brightly tiled floor in the middle of the Immaculatorium. Totally bereft. She shivered a trifle and got a gutsy grip of herself.

"Where did they go?" she bawled into the crisp air that palpitated with ionized ozone. The nacreous nadir beneath her reflected a blindingly-lit supernatural ceiling 23 meters overhead… Its span stretched on forever over countless rows and aisles of tall walls everywhere enfiladed symmetrically as stony permanent monoliths.

It was not some parquetry-fitted Formica linoleum on which she had lain, but better yet- named for what was vouchsafed into her mind by foreordained, overbearing telepathy- the floorboard base layout thereupon was none other than the *plastisteel* polymerized GLUNOLEUM instead of linoleum. Furthermore, for that which the *Metalucelectropluceptorium* must have interpolated her withal, she was about to take a dizzy joyride through the 'Unitubularity' of the lengthiest Evercreme Expressway macadamized by the TATM!

This was no entertainment nor manipulation; neither experiment on her psychophysiological state of affairs. It entailed serious, down to earth, nitty-gritty business by Soul-searching depth and import! For there, before her, a glinting Pinpoint, superior to any of its predecessors, *blipped* blisteringly forth ex nihilo. Its inner sparkle of opalescence so perforated her sensory cortex to no passing pleasantry. Rather, with only the official *CE-5 protocol.

*The term "*CE-5* protocol" refers to a specific approach to initiating contact with Extraterrestrial Intelligence (ETI), Unidentified Flying Object (UFO), or the (UAP) for Unidentified Aerial Phenomena.

The dot dilated fresh from a speck to ballooning intervention in only five seconds! A hyper-perfectly rotund and smooth Super Ball remained stationary, still aloft midair, and that of unparalleled sphericity (as if it were infinitely 'spherier' than the conventional curvature of the otherworldly equidistant supernal-circumference).

The Area of a Sphere is equal to the Square of the Radius of the sphere multiplied by 12.566 ($4 \times \pi$) or Pi times the Diameter squared ($\pi \times D \times D$).

Except the Super Ball surpasses the below formula, in that: $x^2 + y^2 + z^2 + w^2 = r^2$ is the equation of a hypersphere, where w is measured along a fourth dimension at right angles to the x-, y-, and z-axes. The hypersphere has a *hypervolume* (analogous to the volume of a sphere) of $\pi^2 r^4/2$, and a surface volume (analogous to the sphere's surface area) of $2\pi^2 r^3$.

That being so, the transcendence of the Super Ball ballooned into its widened equatorial perfection: That of latitude and longitudinal latticework and inter-dimensional interiority. On the smartly smooth mercurial mirror-gloss surfacing, suddenly, blithely bloated hexagons appeared with six-sided egg-and-dart ornamentation surrounding each one! Then- seamlessly- each of them transmuted to another shape while spaced out into episodic five-fold timetables!

Joyce noticed how each swollen bulge altered itself with kaleidoscopic precision and frequency, but all locked and clocked-in per quintuple moment! For such was this sequence:

1 ----- 2 ----- 3 ----- 4 ----- 5
5 ----- 4 ----- 3 ----- 2 ----- 1
1 ----- 2 ----- 3 ----- 4 ----- 5
5 ----- 4 ----- 3 ----- 2 ----- 1
1 ----- 2 ----- 3 ----- 4 ----- 5

In that it was sustained all over the hyper-hyper surface of the Five-Dimensional Super Ball whereupon each swollen Vacuole had undergone changeover in exactly 5 second intervals to every billionth of a second, or nanosecond. Joyce's intuitive acuity came to count its possible undulatory cadence to an even [narrower] interim of no diminutive deviation. It approached realms from incalculable *zeptosecond to indiscernible yoctosecond accuracy. But, alas, never to be beheld nor grasped by mediocre quantification.

*A zeptosecond is a trillionth of a billionth of a second, whereas a yoctosecond (ys) is a septillionth of a second (just one 'fleeting flit' longer than Planck time)!

It divulged a contiguous concatenation of innumerable subsets, integers, whole numbers, and the whole nine yards with the gauge

9830164275 ----- 24811993

Evidently, the mirror-image of the Super Ball showcased the number system for our scrutiny. Otherwise, the hyper-hyper *contiguity* of Continual Causality thereof offered a sine qua non for far finer, dauntlessly defter- and with getting curiouser and curiouser- concatenations out of some multifarious intermingling mesh.

In simpler language, every other dimension was blended together as having been more vacuous than hyperspace itself- and more void than nothingness notwithstanding.

In one solid swoop of embrace, the Super Ball kidnapped the person of Joyce as if she were a marionette pulled by a puppeteer along some silver cord.

Bypassing the commanders, the colonel and captain, glorious Glistria sat near the opposite concave and convex curvature of the Hyper-Hyper Sphere (or Double HS). Each membrane in between reality and unreality fluctuated explosively as what was distended also went withdrawn from fringes of utter existence. The Queenly lady welcomed Joyce with open arms inside still another universe of the Super Ball tall with hierarchical heavenly tiers blended into its inter-dimensional Elasticity. Glistria was the Mediatrix of it all.

"I shall show you Times Square, your favorite Film Feature," had spoken Glistria to her, aglitter with a mercury mirror all over her skin! The world-renown crossroads of New York City, the Big Apple, was what she alluded to, but only the diorama of a Center-stage Manhattan displayed through hyper-spatial exhibition.

No longer dazed from the rational rotation of the Super Ball, Joyce curtsied and deferentially acknowledged the transformable empress. Glistria was the *sotto voce* spokeswoman for the louder, thunderous boombox of the Double HS and the Immaculatorium. The acronym also stood for Higher School where collegiate level of learning took place for post-graduation from the Yard Lamp of Gloria glad tidings.

The Caretaker's attributes had sauntered forth with effortless effulgence, immutable immaculateness, and with wet warmth…

Melodiously, madame Glistria comforted Joyce while the old Manhattan spectacle was underway out of a more modest 4D format. Parading pipe organ music filled the firmament wraparound. The augmentation thereof surpassed the symphonic orchestra like billions of songbirds that commence convocations with canticles!

To insert just a reminder, Immaculatorium kept outspread its very own Glunoleum foundation whilst the Super Ball bore what was flowered up as the UNIVACUOLEUM roundabout its hyper-entirety, but altogether now. Lady Glistria's Herculean Hologram unfolded a tesseract template of Times Square for the gallant and doughty deputy to sample afoot.

In benign pertinence, the merriest monstrosity you can imagine tapered out of its South Pole underbelly the unfolding of buildings, streets and intersections reiterated a quadrillion times. But it happened to be the selfsame singular Times Square layout to begin with! Only that is was reflected off of one of the vast hyper-hyper extra spatial hyper-curvature of five dimensions. Was it possible?

The underlying framework of Four-Dimensional Space-Time continuum (in terms of extra spatial infinity beyond our Universe) loaned an answer to the toughest question: Are there higher geometries? And the reply is, Perhaps… *Twould* curl back on itself in an incomprehensible, forever unattainable *Eleventh Dimension!

*String theory introduces six more dimensions that are curled up or 'compactified' into very small spaces. The six dimensions can be perceived only by the strings and are otherwise undetectable, but their configurations play a pivotal role in determining the properties of subatomic particles. They also provide the conceptual underpinnings needed by the five primary variants of string theory to make the mathematics work. Yet even with 10 dimensions, the variants still fall short in the quest for a theory of everything. Now whence this could come about is embedded in the Cosmological Constant introduced by Einstein in 1917. Apart from the aforesaid ethereal version, the rudimentary Repulsive Force is required to keep the Universe in static equilibrium. In modern cosmology it is the leading candidate for dark energy, the cause of the acceleration of the expansion of the Universe. Later on, Hubble proved that many objects previously thought to be clouds of dust and gas and classified as 'nebulae' were actually galaxies beyond the Milky Way. Moreover, Hubble provided evidence that the recessional velocity of a galaxy increases with its distance from Earth, a property now known as Hubble's Law; although it had been proposed two years earlier by Georges Lemaitre.

Joyce jumped at the opportunity and almost coquettishly courted the big band dance dedication of the Roaring Twenties.

An elongated visitor's vestibule paved way for the revolving door EXY in replacement of an ordinary exit. *EXY* in this case represented Expressway prefixed by Evercreme. Henceforth featuring the Evercreme Expressway for her to slip sleekly through...

Before she mustered the prowess to enter in, she decided to take up a sightseeing tour of a prefabricated Times Square circa mid-1920s, but an unforeseen clincher clarified her perspectives. The perception of it informed her of a self-replicating X intersection of the midtown vicinity quantified quadrillions of times. For as she ambled about up and down the streets, avenues, and boulevards-checking for anomalies- little did she know that the exact identical Times Square effervesced out of nowhere neon-like, so alive with bustling celebration. New Year's Eve was on the very cusp of the calendar or so it appeared, epiphany-fashioned while what appeared like Styrofoam snowflakes settled downward.

Joyce knew full well that she felt obliged to run her ghastly gauntlet of strangers in a strange land for the time being. To put it more fancily, she dealt with yet another terra incognita tops! But it behooved her to get adequately acquainted with this enormous Hyper-Hyper Sphere: the Super Ball barrel o' fun first, or so the psychic impression twinkled over her neocortex. The faint inklings of the glorious glob of a whirling whopper, having her conceptualization deciphered by the entity itself, ushered our 'damsel under reorientation' on an elongated X of Times Square *tessellation.

* Tessellation: an arrangement of shapes fitted closely together with no spaces in between, especially in a repeated pattern; the act of arranging something in this way. a tessellation of eleven different geometric shapes. This is the Times Square Tesseract!

The eleventh dimension had a handle on all of the 5D rotundity thereof. Moreover, those protuberant corpulent waffles and waffled fritters of sautéed cupcakes cooked~ or be they nuked by the bunched up neutrons themselves alongside pliantly *plasmatic* cream puffs all over the Super Ball's embodiment~ offered a clue as to *what* the Big Ball was designated with. A rather freaky smell of delectable vanilla- an outré odor of cake confectioneries- suffused the tessellated Times Square with heat and had fumed with piquant pungency above Joyce. She backed off a city block away from the nightmarish nuclear sizzle and glistening simmer of fried fritters roasted and toasted **wraparoundabout* thereupon! From a short distance now, at least she stood there transfixed by the huge hyper-wholeness of the deftly distributed Double HS about one oblong block down the street, levitating rock-solid still over an anti-gravity cushion. Now normally, each city block measured 80 by 274 meters, and this was good enough for four-dimensional prefabrication wrought by the Double HS underbelly bulge.

Of course, unbeknownst to her whereabouts, the Ball barricaded itself from all the other laws of physics-suspended geometry for now as were Rutherford and Harris (whom she missed mournfully) auto-tucked away into TATM data storage.

*[Remember dear reader, that our current lexicon falls short of describing a higher-dimensional denizen of intramural occupancy, and all the while in Immaculatorium corridor-confinement, though not necessarily in a mnemonic niche for internment!]

Safely free from the overpowering spell of that shatterproof Shell of concordant curvatures that defied all the laws of physics, she visited the redundant glitz and glam of the ever self-replicated Time Square 4D layout. As aforesaid, like in a house of mirrors & mist, every intersection displayed the very same Times Square up and down, north and south, east and west--- and even diagonally!

Before she ventured over various venues interlocked via fake features of reproduced resplendence, radiance and all, the [1920s] clamored cloyingly and vied for her undivided attention. Colorful neon-coated commercials and billboards caught her eye. Flashing displays doggedly darting about by incandescent and old mechanical means, not digital. This was not 2113, Joyce realized. The New Year's Eve Sylvester postmarked the occasion when in Yesteryear of 335 the burial of the Roman-born saint, Pope Sylvester, fell on December 31 where Germans mainly roistered in their public gala under festive fireworks. Pretty much (specified) the complete card of molecular memorials- down to the minutest detail- was one out of ferromagnetic files that shuffled forth Alternate Timelines.

Outside, echoing with electrification, Auld Lang Syne, that from a Scots-language poem composed by Robert Burns in 1788, but based on an *older Scottish folk song*, chimed in fortissimo.

Bands began to orchestrate another melody with accompanying chorus right at the gong of midnight. The Clock Tower struck the New Year! An old campanile belfry budged & lurched loose a heavy carillon to toll the celebratory peal until the sonorous, temporality *tintinnabulation* of Auld Lang Syne saturated merely simulacra-images of Manhattan buildings from all around. The snowy edge of reality reverberated, riddled in peculiar periwinkles which were wide leaf and glossily blue in lieu of the traditional holiday hollies hedged, splayed for Christmas ornamentation. Uncannily, the Hyper-Hyper Sphere didn't get it quite right during its duplication. For Heaven's sake, there were no clientele clamoring for improved service and our old 5D exhibitor ended up offhand, or off the hook!

Apparently, for hyper-backup, the Transalteratorium's Rolodex Repository played a role behind every 'certain curtain' of the Super Ball's new year's birthday bash. An antediluvian Antarctica to subsurface the lower 'hemihypersphere' of its glorified glitterati dialed 1927 which waned to a dwindling closure, back into a pinpoint.

Then an eerie dial-tone, as from a telephone receiver, intoned momentarily while 1927 to 1928 turned the time-slot epoch over to Saint Sylvester's Day dawning at the stroke of a twilit Wintertime.

In the blockbuster box office of theaters, Fritz Lang's cinematic motion picture, Metropolis, called customers in from each corner of the Big Apple's X diorama where it was formed by the junction of Broadway, Seventh Avenue, and 42nd Street. Together with adjacent Duffy Square, Times Square followed by a bow tie shaped plaza five blocks long between 42nd and 47th Streets. Its vicinity lay lavished under the limelight~ likewise~ that hastened Joyce about to stumble into an Asian restaurant. Here, her gleeful ecstasy rivaled long-ago sainthood in like supernatural settings.

"Happee Noo Year!" the overly official Chinese host greeted Joyce, joyous, swayed by the outside throng thrashing up a din of mirth whilst wafted willow flakes of confetti blanketed the street. Hey, hitherto, not unlike her Future's turn-of-the-year, the sensation was just as dramatic in light of such sustained Radiant Replication! The maître d'hôtel spoke Mandarin Chinese, but adjusted himself in makeshift, sharply accentuated English. He looked like a stubby tree stump, stocky and all, squat and vehemently humble, kowtowing every so often.

"Happy New Year to you too," she responded, politely bowing back. Ah, except that the language barrier (or even a multilingual deficit) had to have her time-slot *slip-slit* reprogrammed from inside the Immaculatorium's Random Access Memory circuit board printout [or PCB]. And instead of an 'ad verecundiam' vis-à-vis with the Oriental host (around which the Asian restaurant sported tapestry- luxuriating table booths, Hong Kong divans, and an outdoor food court with garden Ramada and pergola patched up and thatched altogether), the convexity of the Super Ball butted in with invasive intrusion. Or was this genteel gentleman a Representative of the four-dimensional diorama itself? Joyce pondered.

"So you come-uh from-uh the Hyper Sphere-a, is that saw?" supposed the Chinese chap.

"Yeah, and it's sure as Hell a dizzy escapade." Nonetheless, she felt a pang of melancholy and a twinge of inadequacy for missing Rutherford and Harris. *Where the dickens are they?*

"My name is Wu," maintained the maître d'hôtel for 4D substation identification, squirming and squinting. "Wanna wonton?"

Whatever was left of the last shred of their chinwag came to a gruff grapple, suddenly, when whole Hyper-Curvaceousness of the Double HS imposed upon their vis-à-vis from outside. The blisteringly *blankest* blaze of emergent and collapsing coffers (as that of continual causality) stared into the windowpane piercingly like five billion eyeballs! But besides this, thus the rough-draft remnant of their chitchat of consequential cutoff:

"I am feeling quite lost," admitted Joyce, jaywalking the proposition at hand.

"You-uh are not lost, miss," reassured Wu. "Glistria, the caretaker, has you in mind. Yoo come here!"

So he ushered her to the rear end of the banquet lounge where a back wall, reading Edelweiss in gaudy letters, concealed them securely from the Super Ball's ballooning bulk by its concave alcove. Yet little did they know that the opacity thereof failed to shield the Shining Shimmer- still- steely, staged, but self-circumferential.

"Hey, how can that be? And who is Glistria really?"

The truncated but burly Wu went on: "Well, pardon my bad English. The ball is a big problem, Glistria is not, I promise you!"

And gradually, grotesque contortion cobbled the inside wall where Edelweiss beamed now as a neon lighted marquee. Maybe this epithet *for the wrong reason* inadvertently exposed an unforeseen malfunction in the TATM's main manifold Holomatrix.

"The ball is very close wherever we go, sad to say," warned Wu tauntingly yet so sanguine. He winced and yet authenticated himself impartially to her, handing her a cup of hot wonton soup. As intended, it was an à la carte item of the Big Dish itemized as Goldilocks Porridge which consisted of a thick paste pigged with wontons. These were dainty dumplings filled typically with pork, seafood, or vegetables and usually served, boiled in soup or fried separately. Wu's welcome rolled out the Red Carpet treatment for not having a newcomer in the Visitor's Vestibule for the past 9 billion years, believe it or not!

Although the banquet brimmed with a sterling silver tureen of the Wonton Special topped off with countless different Asian hors d'oeuvres, the meal was unconsumed along lines of her unfinished business. Meanwhile, the Super Ball relentlessly recorded her past, present and future; trying not to reinsert Probe Prods into each new 1928 vaudville and vaporous and outré rehearsal.

For the time being, she was handpicked by the Powers That Be to personify poignantly the protagonist. *I miss my OW teammates!*

So we'll have to see about that!" snapped Joyce, but not at him. Rather, at the silly situation which was on standby and full alert. "Aw, I didn't mean to lash out at you, Wu. I cannot dine with you at this time…" Posters of Pokémon and Godzilla, she took notice of, began to advertise themselves from the lobby interior, as these beckoned her to return and keep everyone company.

Joyce jack-hammered the dilemma and deescalated the development wrapped in an interview package. Having been booed by a contrary catch-22, the provisional supper collapsed…

"Thank you, Wu... I need to leave and unravel this puzzle of mine. Again, I wish you happy Saint Sylvester!" She courteously rendered obeisance to him, in tribute and valediction blew a kiss, and bolted out the front door, determined as ever. At once, the Super Ball outside backed off, offering her an opportune leeway for our Incontrovertible Confrontation to take place.

The accommodating acolyte of the 5D Hyper-Hyper Sphere, named Wu, waved wistfully to her and afterward dematerialized out of necessity. The conclusion of their brief meetup convinced Joyce, on one half, how humanitarian he was under the sterile stoicism of this dismally dimensionless domain and all. On the other half it was a pause, an impromptu caesura; or one of a 144 dozen prearranged setups for what was about to occur, as it were.

Over the slush of drenched confetti (due to snow-melt downpour that ceased as soon as she exited the eatery and as if a robot faucet had shut up the valve immediately) Joyce trudged toward the Super Ball's epicenter and leveled with the gargantuan *Gorgon. She panted, plodding through the aftermath of paper ribbon mush, nearly nauseated by [what] deprived her of her confrères.

* Each of the Three Sisters: Stheno, Euryale, and Medusa, with snakes for hair, who had the power to turn anyone who looked at them to stone. However, in this case, the Super Ball could petrify personnel, but only if they behaved unworthily. Of course, an uncompromising protocol it was when it came to decorum of the soul in stark contrast

to outward appearances. The Transalteratorium had nothing more up its "plastelastic" sleeve than to ascertain the premeditated contents of the heart or soul of anyone who crosses the line, or whosoever gazed beyond what was foreordained.

The very merry enveloped departure of the late 1920s ensued and a far fainter façade of an inner city gridlock grappled her attention span. Now it was one-on-one with her opponent in this urban battlefield.

Wormhole from out of Nowhere

(Authorized Screenplay Roundup)
Part 2 of the IMMACULATORIUM

No sooner than her drudgery in the muck and slime of sticky confetti, or call it flypaper to bait her as prey, she stood upright to the overwhelming and overtaxing presence of the topnotch Major Ballroom Spheroid (this time the so-called MBS) in Times Square that only reiterated itself every which way ad infinitum, yelling at every foursquare block corner: "Come on, join the fun! Let loose!" in a goofy sort of way. Five city blocks back at ground zero, Joyce glowered up at the ever so slightly curved South Pole underside of the Spheroid that cast an umbra and darkened the surroundings. It eclipsed otherwise all of Manhattan's megalithic Stonehenge of a forest of skyscrapers dwarfed thereunder.

"Hey you! What the devil is going on here? Answer me!" she shouted out of defiant insolence at the Super Ball's MBS ***(as for screenplay resumption, her last name, Hathaway, bears an H2 amid rapport with the hyper-whole MBS)***. The entirety thereof towered over her like an innocuous Neutron Star, stately, and 12 miles in diameter where its polar top and base accorded a vertical and perpendicular axis--- both **ana* and *kata*--- to all points of spatial extension; and no less, even to that of null nonexistence!

*Reminder of *ana* being up, above and beyond our three dimensions and *kata*, down below and within our reality as we know it. These concepts were learnt in my perusal of The Fourth Dimension, by Rudy Rucker and Speculations On The Fourth Dimension: Selected Writings of Charles Howard Hinton.

MBS~ IF YOU WILL ONLY REFRAIN FROM DARTS OF DESPONDENCY, WE WOULD WISH YOU TO CONDUCT YOURSELF PROPERLY, MADAME.

H2: "Oh yeah, big buster? Put up your dukes and fight like a…" She caught herself with contradiction in terminology; a capable paradox. This was no person to talk to, nor naysayer against her humble if not feeble humanity. "I do declare, where~ *where* are Roderick and Boyd, O for crying out loud?"

She had gazed up over and yonder to see its gradual curvature receding far off in the distance, regardless of the Times Square repetition throughout a mad Fun House of Mirrors and Mist. The concrete *complete* enormity of the MBS took no umbrage at any of her remarks as its permanent eclipse of the starry firmament loomed. A deafeningly mute pall settled on her frail stature from its equipoise of engagement ghostliest; supermassive Neutron Star afloat and so weightless! What else---?

MBS~ THEY ARE SAFELY SOUND, FOR YOUR INFORMATION, JOYCE.

H2: "And furthermore, why do you address me by my first name? Hell, how do you know me?"

MBS~ WELL? WE KNOW EVERYTHING ABOUT YOU---

H2: "Why do you use the plural collective? *Who's* we? Are there more than one of you?" she interrupts, prying presumptuously. At this point pouting and petulant. Unflaggingly, its *Super-Rotundity wrought Curviest of All* listened to her, being merciful, & reduced to the diameter of only 33 city blocks. The mound upon which she stood was just as dark; the southern hemisphere of its hyper-curvature (overhung a few meters above her) hovered wholesomely yet how heftily! Its Stygian shadow lay cast over Times Square.

At once, its graphic specifications were flung out in front, urging her to learn the nature thereof. This was *that* Recommendation the OW-team had to reconsider before pledging its top initiative for record keeping; with these schematics a snapshot of the Immaculatorium is appended to the subsequent leaf preceded by our [insert]:

The Author's Insert

There was what we call Pyroclastic Flow over the super-surface of the Hyper-Hyper Sphere whereupon quiescent [Quotiles] instead of tiles were interconnected seamlessly so. The Coriolis force features phenomena that causes hurricanes, cyclones, or tornadoes to rotate clockwise in the Northern Hemisphere and counterclockwise in the Southern Hemisphere. Therefore, the whirling Quotiles go up and down, diagonally, and to and fro all over the skin of this burly Ball suspended in the Immaculatorium. For whilst the four-dimensional MBS ascends and descends section by cross-section (ana and kata), its surface fluctuates with flawless, fluid alteration. Thus the Pyroclastic mortar wrought wraparound about boundless curvature!

On a plateau of vantage, one would be able to notice toughened, turgid tile-work of 'equilastic' properties; an agency of liquefied or unguent behavior unlike anything in this Universe! The entire phenomenon of each and every Vacuole comprised the roundabout **Univacuoleum** surrounding the Big Ball itself. The Immaculatorium in turn had paved on its mirror-floor the one and only:

IGLUNOLEUMA

Pronounced *Ig-loo-NO-lee-YOO-muh*

This one was the very keystone of all other References and the most graceful and harmonious state of super-being ever discovered that ought to hoist up a hallmark wall of fame for aye! The shinier Iglunoleuma lay mirror-like and eternally wet within radiant reflection of our Universe in and of itself. It stretches *near-infinitely*.

My Pluriseptiplex (or googolplex multiplied by a googleplex) counts up the innumerable metal wafers of the Steel Sheet- the vast Iglunoleuma, as it were. Nothing, nor any surface could simulate it.

The Quotiles, hyper-argyles, metal wafers, and other things, adjoin themselves accordingly and as such superimpose this platform.

IMPLUCEPTEVORTRIOPOLIS

With self-explanatory pronunciation~ and no need for any vain appellation~ this Hyper-Hyper Supercity exceeds all previous ones of ultra urban characteristics! Namely, that the centerfold thereof is consistent insofar as the former *Glibolotubulopolis* (the tube superstructure) may allow. It carries organically elastic neutronium.

The *ana* and *kata* multidimensional building of it has no foundation, nor ceiling of any kind. They are hyper-elongated tubes that go up and down near-infinitely, depicted as Exituberant Gloriaortae properly described by designation. Our character, Joyce, makes her journey through one of these adjuncts using an *EXY* instead of the exit. EXY represents Evercreme Expressway through which she'll rendezvous with Colonel Rutherford and Captain Harris.

Now the IMPLUCEPTEVORTRIOPOLIS remains on it own a uniquely engineered marvel; not built by hands, but eternal. The 11 dimensions sustain its super-symmetrical existence beyond imaginings. The Eleventh Dimension, so hyper-curled into itself, has multiverses rolled up into one Perfect Package. *That* package manifests a Bloated Blanket of 'increate' creosote so primordial that the Tar-Sheet thereof is but an after-skin of every past, present, and future Universe that has ever existed, is now, or ever will be! The old Yellow Room frightens our three visitors aback because of its blackest or stoutly Stygian station; that is, [it] being paved upon a Tall Wall of the Immaculate Womb of the Transalteratorium. Foreknown also as the forbidden VULVATORIUM, the paved Postern has kept constant guardianship of the above Hyper-Hyper Supercity.

It is the very *Thing* that cannot be breached, never entered, nor tampered with at any time! The lethal Lethe thereof will wipe clean and nullify any mnemonic memory of it perforce, just in case. The struggle of our OW-team was the evident Verdict for access denied.

Aforesaid earlier, the *Subductorium* is a recessed underground vault of an anechoic chamber as drawn on the preceding print; yea, that lay the underpinning motif for the Walled Womb therewith.

End of line for the Author's Insert

Now no longer involved with Wu's meeting, there were residual shreds of saloon ladies wearing cleat-clustered corselettes as if to tempt her to do likewise. She about-faced away from the vulgar and lewd licentiousness and focused more on the Waffled Warden keeping her spellbound. The absence of her confidants, or her confrères (which were abducted) gnawed at her gut, almost to an ugly outbreak of inner ulceration.

In this condition, under a Major Ballroom Sphere's superimposing Imprint and Presence, she acquitted herself satisfactorily and kept curt about the giddy ordeal. Esteemed by her scientific circle and for her own love of *real science*, this was rather an encounter than perfunctory purposelessness.

Any hint of vanity projected by a bodice-buckled goddess, as were those saloon ladies lipstick-and-eyelash lavished, had undergone irretrievable erasure in the Transalteratorium tribunal. To her wholesome chagrin, but conscientious advantage, still tinged by a twinge of temptation, the Major Ballroom Sphere shattered the entire showdown at long last for her sake, Rutherford's, and Harris's once and for all:

MBS~ WE ARE SINGULAR~ SINCE ALL OF US ARE BLENDED TOGETHER INTO MULTIDIMENSIONAL CONTIGUITY. BE IT OUR INHERENT ONENESS! AND NOW, BEFORE THIS BIG LESSON LESSENS ITS GRIP, WE HAVE BUT A CONDUIT RESERVED FOR YOUR LADYSHIP. PRAY, ENTER THE [EXY] AND YOU WILL BE BLESSED… THAT IS ALL, AND FAREWELL.

A lull fell over her, that of intermission that altered drastically.

The Immaculatorium turned tawny, then lightened up to jaundice with a four-cornered *fulvous* foursquare. It was closely akin to having hyperbilirubinemia: yellow discoloration of the body tissue resulting from the accumulation of excess bilirubin. Immediately, Ultra-Blue or cerulean pigmentation permeated the Tall Wall, the Glunoleum Floor, and Empyrean Ceiling of the Immaculatorium like never with historical antecedence! Winch-cabled Transvortum "Glisteners" glorified the blue-shift *like as if* pure light-speed sped through the pristine premises. Their quivering Cloven Tongues of hot plasma plastered Joyce aback, sublimely swooned, enough to override any fear of the Yellow Room, even though this one was a facsimile of the first one. The [true-blue] torches turned on, and so, color-corrected the sickening sight with radiative rectification.

Pertinent notice for the following visual imagery:

The next overleaf ought to render the exact perspective of the old Immaculatorium turned tawny and tallowy, as it were. What once was the most appalling and galling of the Tar Sheet, or rather put, the 'Sheetar' that writhed repulsively in front of Captain Harris- especially- and then Deputy Hathaway- secondarily- was nothing more than the quiescent afterimage of the previous Universe.

That is, the blackest slag of them all: the residual skin~ as if to have been shed- not by an anaconda, but by an 'anaconduit' of some Unicloveniferous Hypersingularity from the very last *implosionary collapsification* of that other cyclical oscillatory Universality before the one at present (which is still undergoing inflationary expansion due to the Hubble constant red-shift)!

Sheetar at the base and the *Tranvortium* lantern hung up at the top:

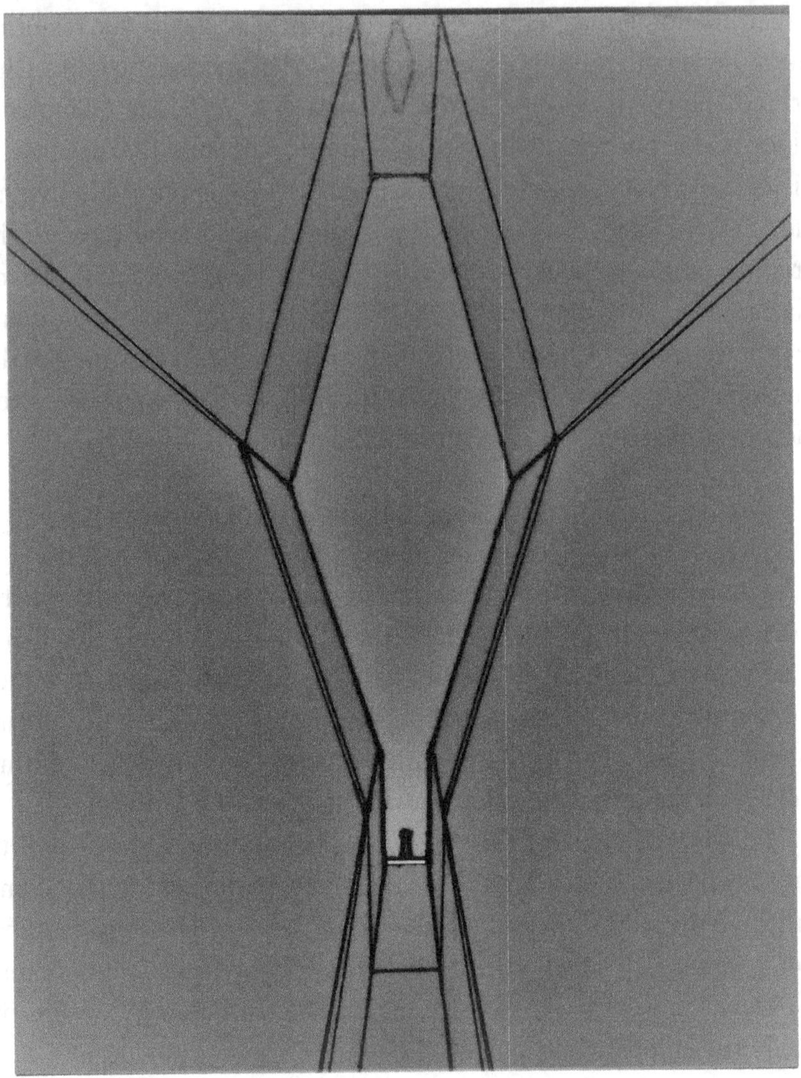

This portrayal shows us looking inwardly upon the far Tall Wall

On the far end Tall-Wall, the tenebrous Tar-Sheet rippled and writhed ridiculously, as it were, to scare off intrepid Lady Hathaway, but to no avail. She had learned her lesson well, in that appearances can be deceiving if not completely counterfeit in the grand illusion of things. Be they the opaque objects of abject objection and whatnot, no matter! Her heightened ESP established itself not in the least fortuitous, but providentially!

An old TV commercial came to mind, "Get a piece of the rock, Prudential" translated to Get Peace of the ROCK, *Providential*! An anachronistic codex commenced to catalog what this 'Rock' meant. For Joyce it was the Lord Jesus Christ whereof her big Bible reads, "For other foundation can no man lay than that is laid, which is Jesus Christ," 1 Corinthians 3:11 (KJV).

And not only that, but confirmation of the 4D *superreality*---

"That Christ may dwell in your hearts by faith; that ye, being rooted and grounded in love, may be able to comprehend with all saints what is the breadth, and length, and depth, and height; And to know the love of Christ, which passeth knowledge, that ye might be filled with all the fullness of God," Ephesians 3:18-21.

To anyone inasmuch as having to experience what she'll have to go through, all four dimensions were ascertained accordingly. However, an existential injunction addressed a Moderator at hand. Distinctly that [to] **Be not righteous overmuch*; *neither* make *thyself* over-wise: why shouldest thou *destroy thyself*? Ecclesiastes 7:16. An auxiliary checkpoint along the *Via Dolorosa or Via Gloriosa--- either way--- a mirror reflected one's ego trip and self-temerity right quick! In our case, it was the Mercury Mirror of Glistria midway [via] the EXY conduit. Wherefore (for this reason) the cul-de-sac at any labyrinthine leeway served its sole and *soul* purpose only so that the headstrong and headlong metador, or Spanish bull tamer, and *metador de toros* (killer of bulls), or bullfighter, bounces back and reexamines himself wisely instead of mercilessly recharging or advancing upon a beleaguered beast~ the Brahman and the Angus cattle of bull, that is.

*So this is not to sound preachy or anything, my dear readership. I am convinced of an unalterable Perfection that transcends time and space. Nothing can be added thereunto, nor taken away therefrom.

*A distressing or painful journey or process. The Gloriosa in Latin means glorious to light up the [way] of the Yard Lamp of Gloria!

Exactly as it was spoken in the era 1611 when King James's promulgation of power was to maximize, macadamize, and so cement the Church of England as a sanctioned religion of England (now known as the United Kingdom). His translation is acknowledged as the Authorized Version of the King James Bible- which was and still is widely used, even to the New Year of 2114- fulfills what was written in Psalm 119:89... *Forever,* O Lord, *thy Word is settled in heaven.* For even the Catholic Church announced an ex cathedra on the same scripture, that if in the Eternal Empyrean of Heaven the Word of God is permanent, than how much more on planet Earth? The former reason was nailed up by God Almighty whereas the latter implied scriptural and ecclesiastical infallibility.

But few of the policies of that time period isolated religious communities into compounds like those at Camp Mitch, but on the contrary card, having to outlaw Axiomatic *Truth* because of ambiguity, bigotry, and bastardized *badgery* which we will not get into for now, nor ever. The malingering Rated R of that baleful Bunch was not at all worthy of anyone save a superhero Saviour that can only abide by divinest clemency for their salvation. Yet she shook a hearty prayerful portrayal for the poor pillow hugging Heartland! "*For God so loved the world, that he gave his only begotten Son, that whosoever believeth in him should not perish, but have everlasting life,*" John 3:16 (KJV).

Along the way- why- she managed to salvage an ephemeral document, moth-eaten, about a previous visitor to the Big Ball. It bore no timestamp thereupon, just the poem with an introductory endorsement:

The Outpost

I am only a tourist and my name is Otto;
As if I were homeless, I live in a grotto,
But here is a poem, the best of my motto:

The base of the Big Ball descends
With a South Pole underbelly
Until the household bends
Beneath its weight of jelly.

Gelatinous Neutronium albeit-
Crowned Cremeum, the sphere,
One out of infinite, none see it-
Condescends so crystal clear!

From where waffles all bloat
In and out all over its shell:
Elasticated, lithe as creosote
Bituminous, bulged within a spell.

Whence four walls of the room
Contort outwardly, awfully,
As Cremeum pierces its gloom
With waffles framed lawfully!

Vouchsafed to our dimension,
One out of innumerable bounties;
Crowned Cremeum's invention
Congeals over eight counties.

As cities feel the heavyweight
Champion of cannonball might
With north and south pole gait,
Gargantuan gold, rotating delight!

How multidimensional tension
Balloons through expansion-
An overflow of no prevention,
It enters the palace or mansion!

I address thee, crowned Cremeum
Of flexible Fluxion roundabout:
Premonitory, prominent, premium,
Wound without a shadow of doubt.

Insulating Invocation
Holy Hyper Sphere verily lit,
An inducer of wonderful whit:
All-elastic, refulgently fit!

While reading Otto's poem, she imagined to have heard a locomotive whistle steam-blown continuously without interruption in the background. It reminded her of other impressions gleaned from past experiences with this hyperspace entity. The single-leaf manuscript was short-lasting and had faded after anyone's review of it.

In fine, everything faltered for Joyce, faithful to the end.

She was a happy camper compared to her horrible hurdle at the encampment of Mitchelville still askew, buzzing by hysteria and pandemonium. This was where the vulnerable TATM system needed to discard discord. For the lynching of little ones at the gallows and tyrants turning into reprobate roughnecks and lardy pig-skinned artificial swine, a registered trademark and the *biometrics barcode* branded on their hides- or stamped upon their foreheads for efficient economics and security- had exacerbated her hopelessness in the midst of intercession. That so many atrocities overrode religious undertaking, this Joyce had no part of. Neither her commissioned kindred spirits, Roderick and Boyd. They knew how fanaticism fanned up hellish flames to burn down the TATM itself, whom Devils abhorred but could not touch, nor vitiate let alone!

Aside from the futility brewing downstairs below the shiniest Glunoleum floor, The Immaculatorium for Joyce~ without the others to witness the spectacle~ revealed its ever 'true-blue' Bliss yet blithely, after its yeasty and Xanthous Yardstick *Zeptillion metal wafer and lapis lazuli lozenge quantity... The XYZ mode made an End to all Programs insofar as the TATM system permitted. Zeptillion was the exact number of each and every steel sheet ironed out flat, but fat! The living organism of Silencer symbiosis resumed at the threshold of no stillborn- rather- rebirth in the Walled Womb.

The scale-squashing neutron-packed Hyper Ball had sledgehammered the final sentence, as was Deputy Joyce Hathaway absolutely speechless and awe-inspired until her reuniting with the other Two. The super tapered Rational Rotation of the MBS, with its convex, continual causality, collapsed inwardly into Eleventh Dimensional oblivion, leaving an artifact behind. Again, it is the TARDIS* (Time And Relative Dimension In Space) which reproduced a figure eight reclined upon its side, resolutely recumbent.

*As beforehand, borrowed from the epic Doctor Who series.

In her déjà vu designated for an upcoming Reentry:

An elongated visitor's vestibule paved way for the revolving door EXY in replacement of an ordinary exit. EXY in this case represented Expressway prefixed by Evercreme. Henceforth featuring the Evercreme Expressway for her to slither through...

But before she dared enter, to mystify her for the rocket launch, there were moth-eaten musty shelves of endless volumes and tomes, enough to fill the Encyclopedia Exotica a myriad times over. But billions of books could never amount to how near-infinitely outstretched and spanned lay the topography of TATM!

Being no buck private, but sharpshooter deputy, she was about to aim and hit the bullseye as soon as an old Wormhole from out of Nowhere pockmarked her listless lawn. First of all, a side Entrance into the EXY, the Evercreme Expressway, bore no badge of honour but ranked reluctance! The figure eight *Tardis* sprawled out to a ten meter space barely invited her in as she hunkered herself through a tight doorway. Claustrophobia climbed as she felt cramped.

Recapitulation

The interior was one of homogeneity all over, tight, but good enough. That same Super Ball was a perfectly glossy and mirrored sphere. Since this was the Wormhole one anticipated, it vindicated the Einstein-Rosen Bridge where one hyper-spatial interconnection is folded over from point *A* to point *B* through a causal conduit. In 1957, Physicist John Archibald Wheeler introduced the name aptly, "wormhole".

The analogical equation therewithal: ds2=u2u2+2Mdt2−4(u2+2M) du2−(u2+2M)2dΩ2. This is the line element for the Einstein-Rosen bridge. This coordinate transformation gives the spacetime two distinct asymptotically flat regions, one defined by $u \to \infty$ and the other by $u \to -\infty$.

It was 8 feet wide, like a huge Christmas ornament! Except that the reflections lay contorted over it. It mirrored all of the surroundings thereupon, but in fact, the other side, or the *next* room (next door)! Joyce poised herself in front of it, ready to take the plunge and fall through. As she approached the mirror globe, the closer she got, the farther away receded her former area exponentially. And so she inched nearer and nearer to her *6 foot* geodesic Yuletide (comically over-sized adornment): *Times Square?*

The geodesic line of entry was the straightest and shortest possible distance between two points on a curved surface and into the slip-slit she went...

One would invoke the entity with solicitation: O Cremeum of one warped wall, who's the curviest one of all...

As Joyce forked her right foot forward and into its glittering, reflective gloss of a sheer sheen, at once unawares she was instantaneously found in an alternate universe. In a nanosecond the teleportation took place and the Evercreme Expressway had done its job. The atoms of her spatial coordinates were catapulted *kata.*

Lo and behold, Rutherford and Harris saw Joyce instantly materialize from out of nowhere and- simultaneously- she saw them solidify likewise. For some reason, *larches* grew all around them and a forest of them was spread out instead of the usual walls of the TATM, let alone the Immaculatorium! All three of them joined hands and were gladdened, however, having been juxtaposed into a misty woodland filled with bristling larches bulldozed them a bit.

"Well, are we happy to see each other again, or not!?" exclaimed Joyce, ebullient with overflowing excitement as tears stained her visage. The nanosecond switchover swayed her hard.

"Aye, our valiant lassie!" the captain confirmed her elation.

"Our indispensable Deputy, indeed! Are you okay, Joyce?" colonel Rutherford hastened to check her out in a pall of pallor.

"My God! What an exodus, or call it a 'hyper' expedition," Joyce gestured emphatically with her hands outlining a big circle. "Thanks to the Super Ball that finally heard my plea and granted my wish. I so wanted to have things go back to normal."

But perhaps far from *normal* it became. For there was no via *intramuros*, way within walls scenario that they dealt with; neither the Hyper-Hyper Super Sphere to be thankful for. Instead, this endless forest of just quad coniferous lumber-hardy deciduous trees all about them from which turpentine could be extracted. Albeit, their fragrance was that of almost supernatural Cluster Pine perfection.

"Where were you, guys--- in suspended animation?"

"Not at all. It was the very same Einstein-Rosen bridge we, too, had to cross and, in a jiffy, we ended up here in Wonderland, free of pitfalls and preserved," explained the restored colonel.

The radical change of reality was incompatible to her religious upbringing, she figured. Obviously, only the best of Books and the crème de la crème of world literature, the Holy Bible, only alluded to such transformations doubtless. But the immortal Truth of Jesus Christ, and what He contributed to humankind- having to be one of His creations- ought to support the eternally weighty thesis thereof.

The promised Glistria appeared on the scene with a metallic glossy mirrored skin job. Her voice, that of a choir, or chorus in unison: "Welcome to the municipality of Summerville!" the lady announced to them. "Thou art no longer in mad Mitchelville..."

Everything seemed to occur too speedily and sporadic, like a montage of motion picture filmstrips of the recollected crew.

"You mean we're free of the inflammatory Camp Mitch madame?" Rutherford exulted and then maintained, "Yet how can we bring back our successful mission to the Board of Science?"

Glistria sauntered forth closer to them and tritely consoled their sudden shock, then waxed weighty: "Worry not, my dear disciples of the Hyper-Hyper-Whole Super Ball. You are in good hands with Providential. But be advised: Surrogates of thy personages should deliver the good news back to all the needy and oppressed ones. They are *thou* without exception."

"Sounds like an insurance advertisement," quoth Joyce, but with welcoming equanimity and embrace for the Caretaker.

"You mean to say that someone like ourselves- TATM replicated- will replace us in order to accomplish our task?" Rutherford questioned her.

"Affirmative, Roderick. You cannot survive onslaughts of a money-hungry and war-mongering society at each other's throats. The parochial pontificate may decapitate each you under heresy."

They took her at face value and believed in her heartily for the first time in all other encounters previous to the ending terminal at hand, or so. Once and for all they've learned the boot camp exam well enough. Once and for all time their feeble efforts were recognized and no longer taken for granted, even by the Grand Jury of the TATM Court Case. The Nunc Pro Tunc [Summer Hammer] of Summerville proffered them unmerited divine mercy and approval.

The lustrous lady acknowledged her forthwith: "Get Peace of the Rock, Providential!" And it was no sales pitch by a long shot.

Rather than taking it all in as a joke, they listened the all-glorified "Glistener" in earnest, not in the least hassled and haggled by disingenuous dumpsters, figuratively put. No longer threatened by batons of barricade wardens and the incendiary sop, surplus & lot of Mitchelville against them, the OW-team rejoiced exceedingly in that this was no more a Transalteratorium simulation, but the very *real thing*! Not to conclude the TATM as fraudulent- by no means!

"You see?" added hot Glistria, "My Transalteratorium is a functionary designed to show souls the runabout in order for contrasts to be compared and weighed in the balances. In receipt of the exchange, the three of you will find Summerville to be the self-explanatory Paradise and Paragon in stark dissimilitude to an awfully malevolent madhouse--- not that I intend to sweep the dust under the carpet by disgraceful dualism... God assist that community!"

The joyful Joyce looked roundabout her and saw the authenticity of the larch forest furnished with nothing but comely conifers. Rutherford as well as Harris followed her gaze. They were no less convinced.

Glistria told them that this was the alternate time-dimension destined for their utilities in light and reward for perseverance & integrity. "You've all behaved exceptionally well. Go ahead and explore your new home." So she pointed her mirror index finger at a river at the downward slope of the hillside on which they were. Afar off, still glinting behind batches of the larch nursery, a sunlit brook broke athwart the forested preservation of pyramidal Shiners. This time their lodge was not of an obsolete vivarium!

Happily & hastily, without bidding farewell to Glistria, they hiked down and ended up at the valley that faced a sideways skyline of the Summerville Impluceptevortriopolis! The lustrous lady gazed on and behind their departure merrily on the run, assumed evanescence and vanished altogether in tutelary spirits for them...

The supercity was impressive as billions of crystal obelisks thronged the metropolitan area. They noticed where the outskirts thereof, in either direction, curved upward with saddle-shaped hyperbolic geometry. Moreover, hyper-tubular Tubules, each one of Evercreme Expressway capability, flailed infinitely up and infinitely down, via ana and kata and vice versa.

They all but forgot about Glistria, not intending to be impertinent to her, but because of such glitzy glitterati which bedazzled their acquired worldview of things. The outdoor neon-lighted signage blazed in the afternoon as if to have soliloquized itself:

Welcome to Summerville
the Impluceptevortriopolis

Rutherford could barely make out the definition of the latter name, even with wordsmith morphology. The interpretations of it glared out at them as they craned their heads over an intervening building and saw with reverential awe the hyper-skyscrapers that were strewn along the valley and had curved skyward to a vanishing point according to the laws of perspective. At least the Tri-dimensional rule of thumb reassured residents as opposed to the Super Ball 5D vertigo. *Little did they know of their new citizenship*!

When they eventually crossed the water brook by scaling an enlarged log (not of the larch species, of course), the Off World pioneers neared a tall windowless warehouse that brandished but one notice posted on its concrete rampart (in Latin and English):

Ubiquelabyrinthelux

Light everywhere in the Labyrinth

To their utter befuddlement, it was yet another universe in and of itself, possibly one that was comparable to what they had exited from in the TATM corridor continuum! The guarantee was that this one was no reinforced simulacre of any spirit, but *reality* itself. Out of the warehouse, multiple annexed elongation of tunnel-work had interconnected every one of these with no more of those foursquare rooms or wombs, what have you. For on a far rounder dimension, a continual curvature of concave walls would inner-line or overlay it.

When they, the former OW-team, the layoff Air Force surveyors, stepped out into another parkland alongside the unfathomable Building Blocks of the Summerville Impluceptevortriopolis, each one was stunned by the super-symmetrical searchlight of them all.

Not to have miss-mentioned the Hyper-tubular Ubiquelabyrinthelux, if even that- though Joyce was fully aware of it in her new state of existence- the super-tall towers of blinding blue sleek steel (that of neutron-alloy titanium) stretched upward with glassiest glimmer. And all the trees around her were a carnival of edible colorful fruits ready to be partaken of. She reached out by extension of her soul and with her ethereal hand, sampled such a succulent Jargonelle and assimilated it without any toiletry!

In her haven of repose, not so unlike the Immaculatorium, no septic sludge, neither sewage, nor soapsuds, soaked or sopped anything or anyone for that matter. There was no need to refuel either, since recreation reigned over the mother of necessity that never required an invention.

The name of this particular pear tree was Polycarp, named after the Saint who was a second-century bishop of Smyrna and was martyred by being burned at the stake and then stabbed.

At the absorption thereof~ that is~ of the fruit itself consumed by her soulful presence, an ineffable honey flavor flushed and fluoresced her. Upon tasting the Jargonelle, she was energized to some sodium vapor lantern, fully illumined right then and there.

At any rate, so she glides to an elongated Tubule (one out of billions more huddled together) that, devoid of top or bottom, cut into the firmament and empyrean way on high & then descended downward like a bottomless bore. On the huge tube an EXY label glowed forth the function thereof. Indeed everyone of such served as an effective junction in betwixt the *better* and *baser* framework. Hence the Exituberant Gloriaortae, yet invisible in our universe, as it were. The reason for their covert nature was based on lackluster perception as these were four-dimensional to Joyce and everyone else. Howbeit, she began to catch transverse glimpses of each 3D slice when an immeasurable huge tube revealed itself, but as if unreachable, open-ended, yet yawning and gaping out at its top and bottom orifice almost infinitely away from her vantage viewpoint.

Enough said for laymen. The Impluceptevortriopolis lay far larger than the Coma Cluster, or even the El Gordo intergalactic cluster discovered by the James Webb Space Telescope. *Not to delve into overwrought details, but the greater Coma consists of two giant elliptical galaxies, with 1000 other spirals & elliptical cosmic blobs inside of its large-scale superstructure! She beheld unimaginable magnification of space-scale in a *singularified* implosive Impluceptevortriopolis "cosmoplexian" Hyper City.

The end of all destinations: an intergalactic *cosmopolis*!

With ultra-enhanced acuity of visionary discernment, the neo Joyce could count up---- only via scientific equations---- that which easily exceeded her finite grasp of boundless enormity. That giant number, the Pluriseptiplex, spanned out the square meters of lying lozenges that interconnected an entire Glunoleum floor with every enclosure of Ultraboxes stacked on top of each other into tesseract formations. If the vocabulary allows us to illustrate henceforth, an Eternal Paragon of the fancier IGLUNOLEUMA ought to suffice!

Hereupon Joyce inadvertently found herself where but lovely luster glistered up with solar prominence that she recognized back in her classroom on Heliology. Spared from the sultry temperature over the *photosphere*, the Iglunoleuma was a span of incandescent and fluorescent sheets of incombustible continuity gone outspread. It was one of such adjuncts in the Ubiquelabyrinthelux *hypermaze* that provided sure footing for a whole host of passersby of benign bystanders. For certainly there was ample room enough for Joyce.

Joyce, Rutherford, and Harris, already revitalized and at anytime ready to unfold into something far better out of a chrysalis- a cocoon of spacetime- saw marvels beyond comprehension. The firmament and empyrean above them was no ordinary azure sky. She was what earlier on offered Summerville the topographical quality of being some Vitropolis, the silica-Supercity of crystal diamond.

Whereas winds nodded the treetops of planet Earth next door in a baser dimension, the perfect Polycarp waved warmly hitherto with arms of warty worth save more grooved than the phonograph tabletop vinyl disk LP. Or even so, not only atop our record player, but reckoned by a razor's edge laser digital video disk, the silicon chip, or quantum computer cubits; (by 2113, the hyper-hologram).

As aforementioned chapters ago, the Greek Mother of the nine Muses, Mnemosyne, hath other root words like mnemonic or whatnot. The candidate sobriquet for Summerville is Mnemosyneopolis

It was The End: with an uttermost mile-marker staked into the Yard Lamp of Gloria's inter-spacial highway. Military observances were no longer needed here where a much more advanced civilization creates their own set of realities. For according to the *Kardashev scale, the Impluceptevortiopolis- having to house a Type 40.0 Civilization in full control of an Ultrabox- the countless quadrillion inhabitants of such a hyper-tubular Supercity shall have enough energy to fashion their very own laws of physics *for an entire box*. In this case, individual Boxes were easier to colonize. It entails Multiple Boxian deities whereby Mandelbrot-verses do transcend a universe like our own quite substantially.

The Cross-Reference Footnote

* The Kardashev scale is a hypothetical scale proposed by the Russian astrophysicist Nikolai Kardashev to measure a civilization's level of technological advancement based on the amount of energy it is able to harness, control, and utilize. A Type I civilization can harness and control all the energy available on its home planet, a Type II civilization can harness and control all the energy of its home star, and a Type III civilization can harness and control all the energy of its entire galaxy.

A Type 1000 civilization on the Kardashev scale would be so advanced that it could harness and control the energy of an entire universe or multiple universes. Describing Earth as a Type 1000 civilization would imply that humanity has achieved a level of advancement far beyond our current comprehension.

In such a scenario, Earth would likely be transformed into a vast, interconnected network of highly advanced technologies, with the ability to manipulate spacetime, harness the energy of multiple universes, and potentially explore other dimensions. The civilization would have likely mastered technologies that are currently considered purely theoretical, such as warp drives, wormholes, and other exotic forms of energy manipulation.

The inhabitants of a Type 1000 civilization would likely have transcended their physical forms and evolved into highly advanced beings with capabilities that would seem almost godlike to us. They would have likely solved many of the fundamental mysteries of the universe and gained a deep understanding of the nature of reality itself.

Overall, a Type 1000 civilization would be so advanced that it is difficult for us to even imagine what it would be like. It would represent the pinnacle of technological advancement and would likely have a profound impact on the very fabric of reality.

Energy Usage: 10^4060 Watts (The Energy Is Multidimensional In Nature) In control of One Untrigintillion Megaboxes, the Ultrabox being one of them, but yet unrealized.

Rutherford, Hathaway and Harris had taken weeks on end to barely survey their overall metaphysical surroundings ere newer, age-proof bodies were installed over their soulful frames by none other than God Almighty. *Was this the Afterlife?* They wondered!

The *past-shadow-land* of jumping over hurdles, running the marathon just to keep fit, and reporting to an encampment of hardliners wore on their fragile frames of human endurance until each *past-shadow-land* faded beneath the rays of the brighter sunlight.

Speaking of the Impluceptevortriopolis, the Hyper-Hyper Supercity, any outsider aiming to visit the cosmic colossus could not enter therein unless they possessed a passkey. Such access allows carousel entry from multiple dimensions from without. Universes that were too primitive to go inside of the Exituberant Gloriaortae, simply underwent pending status until **tough enough*! For with a wormhole network inside-out throughout its intricate matrices, the transparent transducers thereof enfold themselves accordingly.

* This implies the problem of [fluff] (no rhyme-pun intended). Nothing fluffy, nor lacking the gravitational foundation to pull through the multidimensional revolving door of this Hyper-Hyper Supercity… Unlike today's psychological epidemic that involves anomie! Anomie is a term created by sociologist Emile Durkheim to describe a social illness or individual condition in which people feel lost because they no longer have cultural norms and values to guide their behaviour. Anomie is lack of norms. A prime example is the millennials' elusive search for purpose. There is also a depletion of ethical standards that can lead to disconnection, deviance, and social instability among individuals. Wherefore, [fluff] is an ultimatum to refusing counterfeit currency or bribery (and preferring genuine authenticity), the better part of a transaction or bargain. The redemption of the soul, the dispossession thereof from the grip of pervasive evil is the prevailing theme throughout the Holy Bible, a dusty tome least read nowadays in an increasingly liberal and leftist society. The well meaning moral code, such as the one found in the United States Constitution, the Declaration of Independence, the Gettysburg Address, and so forth, is prerequisite for civilization to take hold of in light

of such precepts derived from Holy Writ. No religious & political bias are intended by the author, except with regard to the pragmatic survival of one's soul.

Simply said, the Impluceptevortriopolis, the Hyper-Hyper Supercity relied on carousel counterpart entrance and exiting of such dimensions conducive to its hyper-architecture (though tuberously eleventh-dimensional). The ultrahigh supernal civilization, free of karmic kinks and concordant with *Concomitance, is qualified to visit and reside in the Protuberant Envelopment vicarious thereof.

* Theology in the context of science-fiction (Concomitance):

The doctrine that the body and blood of Christ are each present in both the bread and the wine of the Eucharist. This doth not preclude the predestined to partake of the Vicarious Vista thereabouts; namely, that the Exituberant Gloriaortae cannot be resisted by the Impluceptevortriopolis in any way, shape, or form, so be it. Nor to exclude the needy and impoverished wanting divine love for her own sake. 2 Corinthians 12: 3,4 And I knew such a man, (whether in the body, or out of the body, I cannot tell: God knoweth;) How that he was caught up into paradise, and heard unspeakable words, which it is not lawful for a man to utter.

- The Ubiquelabyrinthelux (with light everywhere in the labyrinth) in like manner upholds the sublimest super-cellular Univacuoleum (vacuole superstructure) that can ever be conceived of, not only in this present universe, but in all the universes to come hereafter- that is- via the unicloveniferous supersingularity in which each oscillation will undergo implosive collapse and inflationary expansion eternally…
- The Ubiquelabyrinthelux consists of "singularification". A super-state in which singularities have been "singularified" into one hyper-hyper cosmic goo that must precede spacetime continuum in the form of 'gluors' in lieu of gluons. Wherefore the entanglement of super-strings is inter-meshed and

blended together to congeal with infinite fusion so as to bring about sacred aether, luminiferous & pneumatic!

Inasmuch as they felt themselves to be all-undeserving of Unmerited Divine Favor, or Grace, they consented to having the last Transfiguration turn them into Star Souls. No longer identified in flesh and blood, their change took place in the span of a yoctosecond, nothing more nor less.

What once were Joyce, Roderick, and Boyd became Joy, Radiance, and Beautiful. Yet these were subservient to the higher order of the Nine Choirs. Their stellar evolution merely scratched the underbelly surface of the Hyper-Hyper-Buoy afloat above them.

And aloft luminiferous aether, the lighthouse beacon…

Joy overturned an everlasting leaf of awareness and recalled:

The Crown of Dawn

Written right after a very vivid dream during waking consciousness in which the poet was found on a soft, sandy strand next to the throbbing sea.

Outside, my family and I were having a picnic, but throngs of bystanders lured me to an unusual spectacle of enormous waves that marched on by, sideways, on the other end of the beach.

While feeling a profound sense of well-being and peace, I edged up the sands and bathed in this cryptic water. It was then that the tides seemed unperturbed for the moment, when gradually, the ocean *intumesced* into building-sized billows and a roar of shock-waves that gathered with walls of water, row after row, inducing gusts of gale to bluster and blow.

'Twas the shuffling tonnage of million metric volumes that soon burst ashore!

The depth of dark blue gave the surf a rather full and thick quality of living freshness, but salt-saturated, as if it were ancient. *For ere the bulk bulwark of waves heavily hove, I dove once more for old natatory glory*, feeling fused with water itself.

Until abruptly, the contrapuntal crash of turbulence shattered our silence…

We wore raincoats and made clearance for a lurching Atlantic of salt and spray. The dream ended and I woke with these sentiments that stole eight hours out of my day, wasting away an otherwise responsible afternoon.

Indeed, it is my final scaffolding latticework of Spiritual Radiation.

These were one of a multitude masterpiece dreams which would overlap each other in some super-conscious collage of Reality.

Their infinitesimal minutiae of relationships, commitment, and quotidian existence amounted to naught and it was unnecessary in the blazing light-output of the Greater Universality. Yea, it was no longer a duplicitous relationship, rather *finest fusion.* Of course, it was no longer commitment, rather *immutability*; no need for daily quotas of accomplishment, but~ in the long haul~ *completion, self-contentment* and paramount perfection that defies dismissal of each learner. To nurture such souls in the Impluceptevortriopolis.

Though the congregation of divinities could exit the classroom at any time due to free will, for the love of their Creator, they could never pull such stunts since everyone's Universality teacher wooed them into increased fiery love, like the seamlessly aflame Seraphim!

The Supercity of Summerville cherished her new Householders.

The
End

THE FINAL PART OF
INTERLINK
Exit Eternity

Complete playlist of the first hour from one night of the overnight Keyfax Nite-Owl Service on WFLD Channel 32. This aired on local Chicago TV early Wednesday, August 25th 1982 at about the 12:00am to 12:58am time-frame.

"Love Is In The Air" by John Paul Young -
"Who Am I" by Petula Clark -
"Biggest Part Of Me" by Ambrosia -
"Carpet Of The Sun" by Renaissance -
"Laugh, Laugh" by The Beau Brummels -
"Ain't Nothing Like The Real Thing" by Marvin Gaye & Tammi Terrell -
"Elusive Butterfly" by Bob Lind -
"Somebody's Knockin' " by Terri Gibbs -
"I Believe In You" by Don Williams -
"I Say A Little Prayer" by Aretha Franklin -
"Babe" by Styx -
"Time" by The Alan Parsons Project -
"Ferry Cross The Mersey" by Gerry & The Pacemakers -
"I'm Into Something Good" by Herman's Hermits -
"A Summer Song" (U.K. Version) by Chad & Jeremy -
"Seven Year Ache" by Rosanne Cash -
"Imagine" by John Lennon -
"The Look Of Love" by Sergio Mendes & Brasil '66 -
First minute of "With Your Love" by Jefferson Starship

This prerecorded audio and vision vanished, although synonymous with the Ancient Light screenplay, and then concluded itself, having been tucked away for future use. Howbeit, no sooner than expected, the ballooned ballroom lounge that only would loll and lull me o'er her lap had liquefied and fallen, funneled into a drain fit for the width and girth of a mere mouse! Aye, fresh vermin, as it were, if ever imagined (Liluchi forbid)! For naught but immediate 'Immaculucy' reigned in its stead. Indeed, No bug, maggot, moth; neither cockroach, nor vermin corruption could reenter its pristine premises. And this was the gist of it, I'd gather. In that to have replaced an ethereal nuance of this frontier dream, I'd reckon, her whole and holy lamplight luster stayed shining in the midst thereat, of course. An immaterial and entity-laden lantern of such profound presence known as the incontestable Immaculucy agleam.

And it came to pass, for lack of subtler elucidation, that the whole Thing collapsed into itself like some sordid, semitransparent flypaper file folder, accordion-pleated, or big bellows bulged and bulked by the aforementioned old Taj Mahal Dance Organ. Now from a distance, chattering away her enchantments *cherubic*, vociferously, violently volcanic, and [in essence] forbidden! The lofty three Rs of Repertoire Roundelay Registration for anyone hellbent on going deaf from a sonorous milestone carry-over calliope 'confabulatorily' possessed, so dauntingly detuned to her heavy-handed horrisonance! In fine, the pre-entity entirety thereof dwindled into itself with inward *instantaneity*. Thus this switch of manifestation through downward disappearance of the same as I must resume repose and recourse in that drat Hallway I commenced with… For, namely, one designated by a 291 doorway hatch, heavily hinged, at the hinterland leftover of embedded embankment~ transducer, tributary, and all…

Yet little I've known that this well-founded venture of mine still proved to be much more cardinal than what behooved me to think! For with an unending reservoir of passageway possibilities, if not by purgatorial pipework, such concepts~ apart from lugubrious limbo~ were readily recollected and retained to the uttermost of my netherworld expedition. I say: O never mind my insular stasis of *labyrinthick* containment. Admittedly, in direct answer to realization, alas, unaccounted for, unacknowledged by my vainer vagaries or lisping of fanciful flight, I had now unwittingly walked the plank of dumb-founded ignorance once and for all. Whereupon, inasmuch as her enveloped encounter and dewiest departure entailed more enigmatic ramifications for me, I still clung sheepishly to my rather heretofore parochial pardon that a Parson was able to vicariously absolve me from! Self-servility, anyone? I was guilty of all transgression, and then some, I ascertained. Enveloped departure it be; that which was frittered from my rogue runabout, or that rat race reconsidered.

Still stupefied, although so substaged, how farther on I trampled along lengthy umbilical cords of corridors that narrowed to nowhere except at holy ground of Hallowed Hallways; this in my anticipation of eventual outdoor disclosure. Hence doggedly I ran for my life athwart spurious 'spaghettification' and right out of an ever interwoven, intramural matrix of the "Univatriviatorium" interlink-impossibility. Of course, one within an incognito Pluriseptiplex Plucireopolitz!

For whereas waffled wall-wombs of damp, desolate disquietude *transpierced* me to the hilt once again, the aforesaid Radiolunivati resumed retreat with me, ensuing it. Inadvertently then, all backup turned to tenuity, or so I conjectured. Undeniably intensified however, her pliant plateau of Prefatory Presence and glory pervaded me, and still so, forthwith I could not skittle it off. Regardless, I kept groping for an exit, going thru countless more corridors before the very last linoleum walkway lay lustrous right beneath my weary tread.

My staunchest step-down from that plural platform~ whereby holograms o' taboo burrows, bores, and tunnels taxed my foxtrot of orientation~ had solidified. It came about by my momentary con-cord contact with an All Tall Wall, high-ceiling interim of awful soporific silence; an antithesis of that loud, deafening, contrapuntal Blow Organ, the Taj Mahal inter alia. Verily vast, a concretely congealed gymnasium was all spacious and vacant enough to accommodate thousandfold occupancy.

I had entered therein, only to find, to my surprise, large lamps lit up from the overhung canopy of this facility. These were warehouse High Bays ballooned bodily, every argent regent, from out of their inverted nipple-ended arc tube torches. As everyone, appended by an anode and cathode plug. Tubules wet with mercurial moisture fogged up inside thereof prepared to ignite or ionize the Hg from vapour to plasma for the moment. Until, noticeably, some blinding harsh glare glorified it into thermonuclear sunlight lumens gradually grown to unapproachable candlepower. Elsewhere, illumined up, around, were plastered planks of wall visages with groin vaulting, but no nearby columns of any kind.

However, with notable avoidance, Vacuity~ as if devoid of an intervening medium or HWY median for that matter, depending on the way it was scanned~ had hitherto persisted. Even so, that then permeated my presence altogether. But still, furthermore, the starry high bays had distributed special spectra-sparkle, and that overly glazed, glaringly into their vicinity of what voluminous vocabulary could not cover; everyone of them whitened to an effortlessly effulgent effect of Lichtenberg Univarnish.

In brief, so it was the amazing Immaculucy of a million melted mercury vapour lanterns electrified above me until I had watched with astonishment. Their candlepower kept at maximum.

My exploratory exploits of this gargantuan gymnasium, whose whole floorboard was never before peopled perhaps for millennia~ nay, nary a solitary soul~ revealed inner tubules that, like writhing stalagmites of timeless antiquity, waved with lithe swollen swagger to and fro, freshly! An internal sacrosanct space of grace at Lamp Camp overall to consolidate conclusively our Desiderata.

I retreated to an ultimatum of my very own, self-induced, and bolted out of the now haunting indoor infusion of a *coarctate* Aorta bottlenecked by a cul-de-sac.

Betimes, without reservation or any fret, I scuttled away from the inner city multilabyrithium prepared for me, though not without its constant contingency that persisted. At my finished footing, whence additional adjuncts receded right out of the wayside, wanting wondrous presumed embrace I ran, ridiculously overwrought, to defy doorway after doorway, deliberately. I yearned to get back with the 'normal' world. Yet, yielding yellowest *yottawatts* of spirit, *she* went with me wheresoever I had gone, self-illumined as ever, a Wooer in proportion to my precarious predicament!

For soon enough, as the last door brandished a 192 instead at point blank range, I came upon that vestibule I got started out with luckily. Again, I still felt the impact and aftereffect of her manifold fingertips finely fondle me from head to foot; still acutely, I felt her full lull and heartfelt hull of an *embrocated* embrace she showered me with, and that luridly let loose. Never lackluster.

Above all (at least via storyboard), Liluchi's legacy and legend, along with her hauntingly horrid, greater metro-maze outspread or outstretched elastically took me aback the more and more into some quicksilver cynosure of self-reflection. Save that with no woozily wanderlust wake-up call, as if it were my unsuitable, but boundless and balanced out definitive assignment. Benignly fine and divine, unconditional altogether that is was well-nigh, wonderfully pictured par excellence if anything else.

In all this transmission and transference of raw energy, and of procured presence, a complete conduit with direct "pipeline to the Divine" distributed itself to me inwardly, invisible as it were. Now, free of insurmountable causeway promenades riddled redundantly within uncountable corridors, triumphantly, I would push ajar and ajar the revolving door to an outside world until I slipped through. The revolving door having to open wide, one by one, escorted my disclosure back to a common-day, conventional worldview.

The identical brickwork buildings had loomed overhead with a "me and Julio down by the schoolyard" singalong. But fainter intimations and inklings of another era dawned upon my soul, dear lad and lass, as I was glad to be back again, agog and in awe. And as I lumbered up a ramp, unlike Lot's woeful wife petrified into a pillar of salt, I gazed backward at what I experienced. See? I could have been concealed indoors, imprisoned indefinitely if I stayed put! My implication of the inevitable if I had gotten trapped amid shackles of non sequitur silence, forever having been erased out of memory!

How wholesome sunrise suffused the eastern horizon whilst I at times staggered down the long parking lot and lorey-laden, sun-blanketed block, weary, well aware of the Lively Guardian Girdle, Liluchi. For alongside with what life represented to me: to be taken in by her hyper-maze of Kaluza Klein bottleneck accessibility, portentously purposeful wherever I went, warmed me to tears of joy.

The oblivion of an exquisite equation to accompany our outlook on life in general gist, notwithstanding, reminds us worldwide of the incontrovertible cause; that the pursued path of a lifetime is worth living in mystery, I proclaim, no matter what the enigma.

Nor, no matter where one went or ended up, our sojourn of a tremendous trek lay trodden with the aforethought, fertile footprint, infallible for future exploration: exemplar of a superstar that she is, wonderfully vindicated. Envisaged veritably.

The point of spiritual enlightenment having been our main purpose for the journey, we enlist the Lady to help guide my affairs. God, Who beforehand sent the entity of her presence into our lives, saw fit to engrave imagery of the Divine rather than graven images of our own. And so, the pictures, fixtures, trappings, and furnishings of something transcendent may render due justice to the lack thereof; namely, our world devoid of its content.

FEATURETTE

98301642752481199398301642 75

ILUCIFULGIDULIPLURIGLUNIVATI

Commercial Break: Now you can look forward to a very vibrant vacation free of charge, until to the point of no return. You'll fall in love with it so much! Or try this hot product: *At night, are you feeling dark, damp; as in a Pit? Ignite our New, Revealing Arc Lamp inviolate!* Completed on the auspicious month of July, 2023/ Rev. 12 as once every 2000 years Jupiter enters the Womb of Virgo avouched nowadays.

* * * * * * *

Ode to the Silencer

One virtue which we overlook
Is pure and pristine Quiet;
She's found while reading a good book
Of peace, devoid of riot.

As by herself a river runs,
Does not complain, nor fret
Forever past the moons and suns
That glide o'er her, how wet!

Deep down in every canyon old
Soft Silence would cascade;
For few she's God's companion gold
Gargantuan arrayed...

Both poet and the prophet hold
Her fair, en clair portrayed;
That purchased dare not be, nor sold-
She'll shine, yet never fade.

I love her so, soft silken Silence
Whilst how many run,
But ne'er attain her mile, hence
Beyond the setting sun;
Her quietness quells vulgar violence
With Peace for anyone!

How hence by my perusal oft
I open tomes and books
And still embrace such Silence soft,
Felt full o' lustrous looks!

For in a looking glass we see
Ourselves, then turn away,
Yet supplest Silence stealthily
Still summons souls, I say.
No matter! Poor or wealthy be,
She finds us night and day:
Illustrious and healthily
Her permafrost would stay.

Our creosote glaringly gleams
Her mirrored up dimension
Vouchsafed to us in holy dreams
Revealed with intervention.

An entity of blinding bliss
Bestowed by grace divine:
Emollient for all o' this
And that at every shrine!

To thee I pray, divinest doll
Sheer Silence midst the noise,
Let down thy blithest Bliss to loll
Lithely, whom none destroys.

Whom no one rattles rib cage, nor
Where sirens ululate
Emergencies, I do implore
Of thee thy seamless state.

Thus this I'll cushion in repose
Reclined with wisest souls;
God's creosote undying flows
In spite of cobbled coals.

Regardless what the peril be
Though scorpions nigh tread,
O silver Silence sterile, free
Preserve me in my bed!

May mortals be enlightened so
Instead of knuckled fists,
As tributaries swollen flow
Downhill to lakeside Mists;
Let none despair of ill or woe
(That Devil, he insists)!
For Silence oily shall show
Life after death persists!

I welcome her into my heart,
No bargaining can bend her;
Completely whole right from the start
Lay lavished lithest splendour.

No marvel if frenetic be
Our world, aghast, how often
She'll prominent, prophetically
Defy the grave and coffin.

If ever bogged by reprimands
Against God's Mercy Seat,
Just trust in Jesus (heart and hands)
Invite the Paraclete.

Whence waterfall and lather spills
The cataract cascaded
Her enigmatic gusher shrills,
That cannot be evaded!

Whence worlds collide at any battle
Fought and waged with pallor,
She'll readily rebuke the rattle
Wrought thereof through valour.

Though violence voluptuous
Induces some to start melt,
I pray, be ne'er corrupt to us,
Highway wholesome heartfelt!

Be this our hope forevermore
In Heaven and on earth
That anechoic God galore
Will waffle muffled mirth;

Let invocations each implore
More Mercy Seats o' worth
In Paradise for saint or whore
Transfigured by rebirth!

My case is closed. No more oppression
Thronged through riot less.
I face reposed, O core confession
Pronged, new Quietness!

Incontrovertible, outspread,
Ne'er found lugubrious,
She'll shine dolled up for me (stout red)
Serene, salubrious.

Dear Silence, I implore of thee
Thy Torch twilit aflame
Within vain vagaries that be
Ensconced in bloody blame;
Let lovely luster gleefully

Still vitrify my dame:
Yea, Creosoteria, she
Forevermore selfsame.

As times flit by, alas, for now
She'll shine dolled up, deployed then
Where with my bivouac I bow
Amidst my township Croydon.

What more thereat than ever coffered
Ceilings of immurement,
Or walled up corridors that offered
Prominent procurement;

What more is there to never hurt you
Save yield reparation,
'T is she, an overlooked Virtue
Votive of veneration.

My ardor is that we will wake
From numbing noise o' slumber,
And of her cake to yet partake
Whose tapers she'll outnumber.

God's cornucopia bestows
By bounty every pendant
That all adorn myrtle hedgerows
Grown evergreen, transcendent!

A garden grot of shrubbery
Exudes sweet sodden soil
With tree trunks rather rubbery
O'er murky mushrooms royal.

Above lush lavender and loam
She'll shimmer her apparel
That dimples up like lithest foam
Filled up via vat and barrel;

With dewy dampness she'll enlarge
Her Heaven wrought repose,
Soft Silence cushioned in a barge
Built by board bungalows.

Some forest full o' termite towers
Waves from gales blown:
How her Necropolis empowers
Everything silk-sewn!

Whence murky mysteries unfold
And tales told invite
Us pilgrims to her so sun gold
Gibbous embers that ignite,

Gala gallantry surrenders bold
But starry cope of night;
Red carpet treatments go unrolled
For faithful Hope of light!

As geese Canadian up launch
Their arrows southward flung
I'll picture her however staunch
Stay frames of egg and tongue.

O relish radiance, and cherish
Torchlight Time sagacious,
Perspicuous, she'll never perish:
Hourglass curvaceous!

What whispers congregate aloft
The earth entirely,
Save Silence so supernal, soft
Sent out and wire free.

Where insulators uphold cables
Stretched for dials hence,
Among mere ornamental gables
Glimmers more Silence.

Betwixt twin mirrors vis-à-vis
Upon their wall-sides hung
I'll picture her laid lustrously
Midst shells o' egg and tongue.

Now ne'er etiolated she'll
Unleash herself at people
Grouped vigilant, to yet reveal
Orbs far above one steeple.

Portentous paratroops arrive,
Alarms may wail loudly;
I now foretell how still alive
Whirl dervish dances proudly.

The waterfront will rave incessant,
Winds will howl up storms;
No more the neon and fluorescent
Lamps of bygone swarms.

For fireflies that sizzled once
Have deliquesced way past
Ere by one year or even months
Our flags are at half mast!

Lithe lady Lustra vindicates
Vast Heavens cast agleam
Ere uproar only indicates
That which we shan't esteem.

What many more rambunctious rough
Retaliate with war dumb,
For Peace I'm worshipful enough
Aside from global whoredom.

Silk silence consecrates herself
Through thousand stories stately,
And Tales talk of, as it were, elf,
Gnome, and nymph ornately.

Although marauding mongrels thrive
Giant Justice soon would hammer
How heavily the hordes to drive
Away lest loosed by clamour.

How happenstance despoils days
Always where purpose wanes,
But probe prods of silence ablaze
Wear stainless steel for stains!

A star ship condescends to earth,
Vouchsafed to bring aboard
Her congregation of new birth
For all small things implored.

Another Age will one day dawn
Whilst Silence fills fine air
With willows over every lawn
Fresh blossomed everywhere!

Atop a mound of shiny sheaves
Her moistened Myrtle grows,
Festooned with briny braids o'er leaves
Outstretched whence glory glows.

Adorned and ornamented stately,
Staunch, whose whole boughs spread,
The box bulged squat shrub how ornately
Glimmers bulbous red!

As Christmas crowned or vernal clad
Branched forth and evergreen,
An emblem of yon Heavens glad
Enough would intervene.

Whose crepe de crème is crested so
Encumbered numbly? Never!
She'll ne'er etiolated show
But sprightly sprout forever.

Whose armored arms outspread themselves
While wearing big bough fingers
More numbered than fat tomes on shelves
Addressed for foam that lingers.

Serenely Silence flickers forth
White winged, lightning attired,
Contained by curtains of the North
Resplendently desired;
Vertiginously spired!

Above eruptive restless legions
Worldwide fraught and frantic
Sylvan Silence of North regions
Radiates romantic.

Along the riverbank of gravel
Spewed from vents volcanic
Lithe lady Lustra shall unravel
Quiet, quelling panic.

That like a shiny Myrtle bred fair
Emerald emblazoned with snow fresh
Her pristine permanence threadbare
Yields Yahweh La Quodesh!

INVOCATION

Enchantress, may I offer thee
That which will not be daunted;
May invocations coffer free
High ceilings very vaunted!

Let luscious myrtles bud indeed
With vernal vouchsafed Glory:
That which will never fade, nor bleed
Apart from hillocks hoary.

Lithe lady Lustra, condescend
Upon my frail frame;
Ignite in me, my love, and send
Forth candlelight aflame!

Enchantress, henceforth fulgurate
Bright shining firebrands
Bituminous, bestowed wi' weight
And arms of higher hands!

Ever increate ecstasy verily
Vivify me mercurial, merrily
May my covenant be very free

Molten merriest Myrtle I oil
O crème Fire eternally loyal
Incorruptible Radiant, royal

Composed on December 1 & 2, 2019
as it were dictated to me directly.
A spiritual confirmation thereof
To our Lady of the Immaculate Heart this work is dedicated.

Through an architectural echoing of gleaming white corridors- along the enfilade of one narrow doorway to yet another, infinitely, so also abides my viable Vision of still a sleek, sterilized intramural infrastructure.

Merely Heaven brought down by the Creatrix, lit up by Transvortiums strewn from some high-ceiling, pale plaster plafond, Divine intervention floats; priority precedent if compared to terrestrial affairs of modernity.

At large, this Hull of lull that would visit earth to prepare the contents thereof unfolds with extremely huge areas of spacious interiors; and that of empyreal proportion, able to cradle its white Labyrinthic Limbo.

There, amidst the harsh glare of protuberantly lit flat-pad/arc-jacketed energy, where perfect packets of focused photons are spewed by Transvortiums, an unseen exit to the HORRIDOR is felt unimaginably “hollow”.

For beyond the Confronter or Gl’re of a front wall stands yet another membrane of “outer limits” unlawful for any man to gaze upon: having been only divided by a tiny slit, or just one hairline short of eternity...

An ultimatum built up by the Creatrix that reveals an adit or exit to a Paragon Paradox of arc-thunderbolt “blinding blazars” ablaze within jocund jars, numerated (the Seven Spirits that surround the Throne of Father YHWH).

Even far higher than Archseraphim- each Orb housed up and perfectly protected by an auroral amphora; by a “bright cocoon of snowy white” forged with electrolamp envelopment- the pristine **LUMIFER LUCILUX** glisters!

And far past the unapproachable Gweduc of pure and raw hyperwhite brightness, my Vision is then shut upon itself and collapsed into nothingness before entrances near transoms of the Horr'bly H-ly can be conceived.

That until one may dare think of **TRANSALTERATORIUM** elsewhere agleam with lambent fulgent bundles of hyper RGB, whose very own full blown myrtle MOTHER and power is to glorify DIVINE SPIRIT, we would cease to exist.

By but crushed comparisons to sheer numbers attenuated into nil, this electrolamp development now conveys our projected portrayal of Near-Infinity. The uncreaturely or increate LUMIFER LUCILUX of septillion lumens, that bulges its whiter-than-white or Aurora Corona scorcher Torch Star, bursts by such an explosive existence none can endure! With hyperglorified (lumified) light, this Warp-Transglucency nuclear reactor core mirrors itself back at the ancient wavelength thereof and at no other!

An abstract contrast far too extreme for any Angel to behold, as such: An invisible Causal Quasar amid a Continual Causality named SIRIS of electrothermal flux ballooned by raw Gweducs. That which is so Unspeakably Unlawful with that of an exponential hot circumstellar radiative transfer- nothing, not even pure vacuum, nor raw see-through spatial void can contain its enveloped elastic balloon of transcendent transparence...

Thus the photonics of LUMIFER LUCILUX realized with enviable envisagement!

LUMELOPOLIS

THE CITY OF LIGHT

Screenplay interview in Brief Relief

ACQUIRED DIALOGUE WITH PAUL AND BIKASH

PAUL: Imagine, if you could, and conceive of a metropolitan future that consists of nothing but pure energy in the form of electromagnetic radiation transformed into the narrow wavelength of spiritual lumens, or light itself. Then bring your focus of thought much further until all that is known to exist vanishes completely, except for the intelligence and knowledge of all that was, is now, and yet ever shall be, but interpreted in quasi-chromatic "vibratility", as it were; that glorifies the vast wave-form of an uncreated Spirit.

BIKASH: However, I inquire of you (my friend), as a student from Nepal to a Czech Republican: What do we mean by light without substance?

PAUL: Exactly put, my humanoid questionnaire! Yea, albeit light void of material meaning, I boast to our global humanity of a vast metroplex megalopolis, or super-big city, able to shine brighter than the stars of space collected together in one titanic, *irretinal* instant...

BIKASH: Again, I ask, what do we mean by the word *irretinal*?

PAUL: That which is "metalucently" transcendent to what mortal eyes can behold.

BIKASH: Oh, and please forgive me if I'm too abrupt, but the term *metalucently* evades us, and I cannot seem to fathom it. Could we clarify this for our audience?

PAUL: Indeed, this type of vocabulary is not used in common language and, therefore, I must elaborate on what we are attempting to convey as such; namely, and plainly spoken, I aim to introduce a visual supercity that is built up of huge lamps. Inside each of the lively, breathing lamps are hot tongues of transparent temperature, and these cloven tongues would readily resemble Transparent Transducers obliquely ablaze with one another.

BIKASH: And these transparent transducers that cause the lamps thereof to radiate luminously- may I add- what purpose do these serve?

PAUL: They are each a canister creation, an emblem of conflagratory glory; or prototype models used for the purpose of "lighting for the sake of lighting..."

(pause) You see, the entire supercity of light christened *Lumelopolis*, is rather meant to be an ornamental and supernatural museum reliquary of cosmic light that far exceeds the starry splendor of the Universe.

BIKASH: I think I understand, (pause) Like Las Vegas, Nevada- but only this particular display of cosmic light is as the bright blue star, Vega, for example.

PAUL: Affirmative. Our nearby (though many light-years distant) Vega that must *in futurity* replace the glitter and glitz of Las Vegas, or any other worldly Burg founded on corruption. We herald, therefore, the Lumelopolis- instead of clearly unapproachable brilliance promised for the redeemed remnant of Yahweh. Unapproachable, I stress, to those that abhor Light.

BIKASH: Ah, I remember your mention of Yahweh, the supreme Deity of mankind! Nevertheless, I have my aught against you for using such a complicated combination of terminology... For Heaven's sake, I require a more thorough explanation!

PAUL: Very well. If we insist on this topic; even though I am vaguely reticent to implicate it and make an issue out of the concord content thereof (pause). Let me begin on the following Originators that inspired my dream hitherto via imagination. Their identity translated into English are *Lumifer Lucilux*, the chief archseraphim to *Malakim Mintaka* which comprise and embody the top hierarchy of the angelic order. From such glaringly effulgent entities that outshine every other created being, one warp lamp after another permanently is burnt into the Lumelopolis as an "exemplar of a star" so as to speak. And within differing degrees of various wavelengths- the very narrowest, having been a Hypernaked Singularity around which whirls Continual Causality of Attenuated Time- the eternal harmonics of light are intertwined in one VGA of explosive existence.

BIKASH: *Uh*, yeah- now what do you mean by VGA?

PAUL: Video Graphics Array.

BIKASH: But I argue, feeling a bit skeptical. I am convinced that this vital vision of yours borders on fantasy; otherwise, prove to me the reality thereof! What foundational evidence and reference can you challenge all of us with?

PAUL: The radiative realities go as follows: for in the Word of Yahweh (the Holy Bible) according to the King James Version, it is written, "Eye hath not seen, ears have not heard, neither has entered into the heart of man the things Yahweh hath prepared for them that love Him."

BIKASH: You mean to tell me that your **Lumelopolis** is some sort of Paradise?

PAUL: No, not just Paradise, but the illustrious illuminants or Large Lamps of *concentrated glory* "lumified" as a glitterati of glorifiers that sparkle themselves right up at their sole Creator and none else. Whose *irretinal*, infinitely invincible outputs would otherwise rupture the fabric or quantum foamery of spacetime continuum if only a split glint were to deviate from Heavenward focused photons. Or, in other words, their sizzling arc tubes (also called Gweducs) are but bared before DIVINE SPIRIT directly and suspended far and away from created space, lest their superlucency or Unspeakably Unlawful brightness sears anything less than the unimaginably Increate!

BIKASH: No doubt, for far along the border between India and Tibet, my motherland country, the Yogi masters who live as ascetic hermits near the craggy capstones of the Himalayan peaks certainly do testify of the invisible radiance of absolute Spirit. I must admit, all this about *Lumifer Lucilux*, confirmation of the Holy Scriptures and so forth sheds at least *some* elucidation upon the subject of this former Luciopolis, my dear friend. Now, noteworthy **Lumelopolis** enlarged.

(pause) As you know already, to gaze upon the world's largest city at night can't even compare with what we will soon experience if we live for the love and care of one another and obey the Laws of nature and that of our Heavenly Creator.

(pause) For our beloved audience, Paul, and with one final interview of the subject matter at hand, my acquired dialogue concludes with a fourfold question. Number one: Who is your highest angel that receives this tribute of light?

PAUL: The Archseraphim, Lumifer Lucilux.

BIKASH: Number two: What is the name of our Eternal Creator?

PAUL: YHWH or Yahweh, the tetragrammaton, Which is the most holy name of what the mainstream public refers to as "LORD God" of the Cosmic Fabric. His Counterpart Paraclete is the Holy Spirit embodied by Yahshua Messiah Who is one and the selfsame with the Father without separation, but of whom the common usage is rendered "Jesus Christ" the Son of God.

BIKASH: Eloquently put... And now, my third question: What do you wish to leave with every one of us as with your finest fusion of spiritual impressions for the world, your family and friends? Or, simply said, what is your gift to all of us on planet earth?

PAUL: Yeah, indeed… (pause) Somewhat too burdensome to answer satisfactorily. (pause) I would venture to say... As Nikola Tesla, once upon a time in the natural, so I have come and depart in the pure theoretical and spiritual; to leave my unadulterated and primal love for light and life for all who hear me, as I announce, *FIAT LUX* in Latin, of course. He that hath an ear, let him hear what the Spirit saith unto the churches, Revelation 2, verse 11 (KJV)!

BIKASH: And lastly, my fourth ultimatum: Your greatest desire and dream is demanded above the aforementioned; what then is your goal hereafter?

PAUL: Without hesitancy, I hope to be with my Creator in Heaven, with my loved ones, and to possess whole Hypernakedness...

BIKASH: Oh, the last remark of "hypernakedness" we would reserve the right to be interpreted by no one save you, yourself. As doubtless your unique enigma is to remain self-explanatory... An anachronism to be concealed from all scrutiny; preserved by eternity as must be a scientific Naked Singularity [the which nature abhors] within a collapsed star- if I am correct.

PAUL: Yea, but moreover, my *threadbare threshold* wherein is confined a far thinner spinner, hence Hypernakedness: An infinitely thin thread that is pinch-stretched from the past point of our Universe, through its 4-D swollen balloon, and to terminate at the future point thereof. In fine, that which contains the Impossible; a thread of infinitesimal voids in the interiors of infinitesimal points along which the infinite Universe hyper-expands and hyper-contracts in an endlessly oscillating miniature dimension (though infinitely boundless by spatial and causal relations to our far *tinier* standpoint); the only feasible vehicle out of which or into which alternative space-times may subsist.

BIKASH: My godly goodness. Ah, what insight unearthed! A threadbare concealment of an external exploder in micro-time termination at each end of it, yet able to keep itself open-ended simultaneously! May this visionary diorama of which we share enlighten the endeavors of both religion and metaphysics here and abroad. Dear Paul and our listening guests, we bid you good fortune for ***LUMELOPOLIS***, Bright City of Elysian Fields!

Holy Scripture

And I saw a new heaven and a new earth, for the first heaven and the first earth had passed away, and there was no more sea... (KJV) REVELATION 21:1 ---- Thus *that* was the end of it.

Epilogue

We, relentless with idolatry, being bound up by an inexorable escalator, or be it on some round-the-clock *trying* treadmill equipped with digital dials- are luxuriously conveyed as on a cushion of technology; carelessly carried along a shaft to tenuous endlessness where Time, an ultra-advanced creature without any pendulum, supremely sustains mankind but for some little while. And yet, blindly, we still engage in affable jaunts, only to be disconcerted, distraught and ultimately *eviscerated* in the long run. Unfulfilled and found insatiable. Yea, not only that, but rather by metronome cadence, as it were, with Universal Plurality we would then consequently continue on. On the other hand, but if found upon this Trek of Gloria- conversely- a far better situation should transpire... Yea, furthermore, far away from that constant and indefatigable metronome Medium of such immemorial persistence, we'd leave behind eventually those ravages of Time. Never to run rampant, nor run any rat race. At long last emancipated! Mankind marvelously set free indeed.

Caught up unto eternity instead! Unburdened ultimately, but bound by Holiness, which is the exemplar of all standards.

And now, back beyond the Front Reverberatory Glore of an old auditorium, may promenade on by in one supercolossal entourage, those whole Hyper-blown Superstars- so piercingly bright, but far whiter than white; of which every over-sized Ball of invisible indivisibility exposes naught but integrated fusion. Quasi-stellar fusion that far transcends the atomic building-blocks of nuclear force. As if these *Superpowers* (in the original sense of the word) were all of such selfsame continuity: perpetual, unwavering and eternal. Indeed, each comprised by an ever wraparound-about, but *punctureless* blank clone.

These Hyper-blown Superstars, or much rather, the supernal prototypes thereof, are conjectured to be infinitely superior to any geometrical sphere; radiantly *rounder* and far smoother than any unbounded contour of curvature, that is. And what luminously *breathiest* dimension shall deftly yield or obliquely bow before and from beneath their continual convexity! Harmoniously floating about. Yea, yet high above that super-supple, elastic Sacred Aether of space-time continuum. As if with other evacuees of holy horror, we are forced to refrain ourselves from one lethal glimpse of the Shekinah glory! Even as Moses of Exodus, many centuries past, precariously concealed himself away in the bedrock crags of utter existence, amidst a grotto of granite, so to speak, wherein even *he* had to hide himself and shield his gaze with a slab and slag of opacity and of impenetrable thickness! Like an electric arc welder *zippered* up and heavily *helmeted*, except behind plumbiferous plastering; so Moses was thus compelled by a divine caveat to steadfastly stay paved inside that narrow fissure of a rock-solid crypt (Nature's asphalt and concrete membrane, from cornerstone to capstone, thinly flinched into itself!)- yet merely to still turn athwart and away, evasively, from aureate Quasar-concentrated rays lambently leaking thro'! Transilluminating, by gamma and x-ray shortwave emission, the entire whole halves of but frozen lava, from where the languid man in one climactic instant- incarcerated in this granite insulator, and by the cleavage of a petrified time-slot, was ever then able to dare confront the "postern parts" of divinest SPIRIT retreating now to Her enthronement from whence She came...

By abstract contrast, therefore- may we declare- where one unoccupied intramural coliseum grants us the ever empyreal impression of some see-through clear Cloven Tongue (none other than that of the Holy Ghost), the invisible but acutely forefelt Hyperblown Superstars *fulgurantly* outshine every spectacular splendour. Only

God and the six-winged seraphim and cherubim would be of much brighter echelon than they: the Stars on their own and in need of nothing except for our admiration of God!

Wherefore, from pot-belly Franklin stove- from reverberatory Furnace to a power plant nuclear reactor- we have embarked on an unprecedented apex of total technology. Howbeit every one of us delusively reduced down, shriveled up to impending worldwide catastrophe. If one may venture to admit, the very pinpoint and tip of an iceberg backed by perhaps glacial proportions! Could we then conversely harbor and harness unimaginable immortality? Of course- Heaven forbid- not us, but by SPIRIT alone and Her only! For this *life* foreseen sheds therewith a much finer finesse vivified by an empirical understanding of *Unfading Genetics.* A life-force self-sustained through the sacrosanct Paraclete [helper alongside] and virtually immortal. Remaining (perforce and *pro forma*) ever suppliant, yet containing such undefiant environmental properties, whether cosmic or terrestrial. But by and large, having both the inviolable essence of immutable immunity- aye, and an unalterable value to any malevolent madhouse of deception.

For until the Coronary Panorama of cryonics may thaw raw within *cryosleepers*, only to exit out of an Electrical Antarctica of refrigerators- entirely alive- and not until the enveloped enclosure thereof may disclose itself mothernaked, shall sheer holographic detonations effloresce effulgence... Then would the crystal clear emergence of a better creation take place, commencing with an *ab ovo, de novo.* Founding before our *future* a solemn procession to the all HOLY of holies, through Whom only the relatively faithful, the unacknowledged, and the impoverished assume entry.

Where-under man's mortality is eclipsed by idyllic surrealism narrowed down to the Unspeakable, this life is strangely manifest manifold as revealed *per diem.* Someone, or something, altogether way too bizarre for eyes to see and ears to hear. For the highest and noblest notion of any mindset must momentarily be but the basest condescension of an Eternal Ball, for that matter! And if we were to gravely grapple with what was firsthand a faint spark of (for example) Transcendent Transparency, then certainly so could we in turn attain one rung higher upon Jacob's Ladder or an Heavenly Escalator; or even stop short of a personified *Heliatrix Anathasia* (interminable solar-spirit). Let alone taxing a comprehensive bulk of abutments that outstretch an ungirdered bright bridge buttressed, but arched over every breach of ignorance.

Our collective vagaries are dethroned. That like an old whorish hen of nonchalant chicks, we otherwise remain insouciant; hellbent on trying to defy the procurement of a promised continual causality for whatever it may entail, be it dead or alive! And so, hence only what stays perpetuated hitherto- like as a memorable melodrama conferred on us in an ever disposable transaction- this *better* and preferred Revelation supplants [rather] the vain lispings of mad mediocrity otherwise worldwide-published. Thus and for us, its dramatic blueprint (if read upon study between the lines) that we unroll scroll by scroll, precept upon precept- of what will blithely expand into full reality- is margined by a dithyramb diaphragm, or an abstract creature transmuted from point-blank zero to whatever one can covet! Get the message? In other words, this vivid vision whispered by an increasingly unpopular Still Small Voice, having been undisturbed, uninterrupted, undetected, and uninvoked from outside the inner *Sancta Sanctorum* has now become my multi-part miniseries of divine intervention. The proverbial Project Visceral Vision of the Forbidden is then *clairaudiently* channeled, and by voluminous Votive Virtue of a resourceful Superpower; as if it were my chief motif, ready to tiptoe into the *real* Ark of Oracles.

Until terms like *self-alterable* and *auditorium* are combined, leaving us with the new word: *Alteratorium*. Then take it one step *excelsior*, when such a narrow, high-ceiling corridor transforms its very dimensional contours, from one strata to another. Now give it an incorporeal Entire Entity of identity overblown outwardly as the Big Bouncer [true sense of the word that refers to a very large ball, bouncing instead of any nightclub body guard to keep the peace], or Paramount Paraclete created out of nothing, as *ex nihilo*, save spirit-enhanced, quasi-induced continual curvation; so self-spun, that it resiliently reanimates itself. Profoundly present within much higher, finer, vibratile, and nearly breath-lit lovelier levels of the [intimately insulating] *TRANSALTERATORIUM.* Empowered by tranquil trappings of "Transvortiums" rigged trigger-free, but sewn seamlessly within transducer-transference, it is fronted by a single but twin twenty metric tonne quiescently quicksilver Steel Sheet known as Mercury Mirror. Its mirage-like sheer sheen apparently plaster-coated and paved, concretely, upon the *mure* of the Front Revelatory Glore, glaringly! With one of the aforementioned howbeit, to remain cryptical as we have perused in this storyboard.

Author's Footnote Notice

With regard to the 'modus operandi' of my Concord Contact as such, this sci-fi [silver sliver] in brief presents only the tip of an arctic iceberg; that would also float foundational as one out of divers cryogenic proposals to the finer futuristic unveiling of the Stelliferous revivification Era (no footnotes appended hereunto).

CONSECRATION

The Proverbs, Chapter I, verses 20 through 23: [via intensified amplification]

Wisdom cries without, she utters her [still small voice] on
the boulevards, avenues, intersections, and streets:
She cries in the major Megalopolis of concourse, within
the openings of the gates: in the chief City she utters her
Word (Logos) of simplified terminology, saying,

"O how long, ye simple ones, will ye love mediocrity?
And the scorners delight in their scoffing, or fools hate
knowledge? **23**. Turn you at My reproof: behold, I will
pour out My DIVINE SPIRIT upon you- I will make
known My many utterances to thee [for free]..."

Ballad:

Out of the Crucible

There was an old fat urn
Reminding me of Saturn,
Girt gorgeously by pattern
Laid lowly-

No slum nor sunken ghetto
May haunt me, No! I'll let go
And bask in God's gold meadow
Made holy!

No Cheshire hate-face
Can shatter my life's late Vase
Soulful, sewn up in great Grace
And strong life;

I'll fortify my brickwork
At vagaries o' thick murk,
Against an oaf or sick jerk,
Or long knife…

Devoid of life's bed-fellows,
Old Organs backed by bellows
Play elegies with yellows
Forgotten-

The cornfield and the garden
Shall lithen us, not harden;
With Mercy that'll pardon
Hoar cotton!

Linoleum laid slime-free,

Like shiny Teflon timely,
Stays seamless and sublimely
Empyreal:

Upon courtyards of Heaven,
Laid lowly, ne'er with leaven:
O Lazy Eight past seven,
Ethereal…

The soul will never age;
No more mischief back-stage,
Nor vitriol and rage
Could hit her-

CHORUS
So swollen be that Urn
With rings of elder Saturn,
Whose kiln-imprinted fat fern
Would glitter!

May Heaven have a gold Tome
Within which quantum old foam
Must quiver an unrolled loam
Outspread;

Will bankers barter some
Before mass martyrdom?
Eight adds this harder sum,
Stout red!

This peculiar Poem came to me only several hours before an earthquake hit NYC --- about 02:30 ante meridiem: 4/5/2024

The Verdict

When all is said and done
And dust hath settled down,
I place my faith in One
Which wears a thorny crown.

Since suffering or torment
Had overwhelmed the world
There are eternal, dormant
Fine pine cones yet unfurled

Upon some silent mountain
Light shines antiquely olden-
Still ancient with a fountain
Gusher gargantuan and golden!

None access she'll deny
In times dismal and doleful,
Whose Spirit would defy
Death, vivifying, soulful ...

That One with coronation
Will soon to Earth return,
Whose status quo and station
Is poured out from an urn;

That One whom we've impaled
By flaunting carnal flesh
Now nonetheless prevailed:
Wrought, resurrected, fresh!

The Bible teaches lessons
Of Heaven or hot coals,
Hence hither be of essence
Salvation for our souls!

Amidst my forest darkest
There shines eternal Light-
Stupendously and starkest-
Throughout infernal night.

Fine pine cones electronic
Fueled with a gift of Grace
Transcend the hypersonic
Technologies we'll face ...

Far swifter than a light show
God's grace shall swoop on down:
Blown blindingly- her bright glow
Will wipe away life's frown!

The US Geological Survey reported a quake at 10:23 a.m. with a preliminary magnitude of 4.8, centered near White House Station, New Jersey, or about 45 miles west of New York City and 50 miles north of Philadelphia. The agency's figures indicated that the quake might have been felt by more than 42 million people.

The last but not least inserted Poem

was composed on June 2, 2024 to serve

as Yard Lamp of Gloria

Glossary in a nutshell:

IGLUNOLEUMA

My *Igluna* lamp evermore be[1]
Representative of *glistery*[2]
Golden glorification lorry
In an insular silk mystery.

Up and down viable furnace;
Starry fusion identity hot-
May impermeability turn us
To her fortified fiery lot!

I am glorious *Gluna* united[3]
With eternity verily found
Via cherubim shiny ignited:
Creatorium merrily crowned[4]

Elevated aloft, electronic
By a pulley and winch oily,
Dilated *wi'* softly *gluonic*[5]
Tenuity to an inch royally!

Only *ana* and *kata* equality[6]
Equanimity hung interfaced,
O inviolable jewel jollity:
Unetiolable varnish graced[7]
Via *fleurs de lys* fieriest[8]
But entirely higher, *seest*?[9]

Holy *Glistener* ever ablaze[10]
Incorruptible be *polyphase*[11]

Whereupon *Iglunoleum* paved[12]
O *Lucerna Superna* engraved[13]

The general gist and *INTERPRETATION* of this book

*1) Igluna is the nomenclature of a 250W high-pressure multi-vapor lantern (the prefix *igloo* and suffix *Luna* were consolidated for only compound congealment); 2) Glistery is a poetic license contraction of glistering which means dazzlingly bright; 3) Gluna is another word for 'glaringly lunar' as it were, or [of] *clair de lune*, that is of moonlight; 4) Creatorium terminology supplants the crematorium, the antithesis of a resurrection room contrary to one that cremates the body; 5) Wi' was a Robert Burns contraction of with and *gluonic* signifies that which consists of gluons (the adhesive cohesion of the strong nuclear force that binds protons and neutrons together); 6) Ana and kata is the Latin word for "up, above, and beyond to down, below, and within" (hyper-movement perpendicular to our three-dimensional spacetime coordinates); 7) *Unetiolable* means that which cannot be etiolated (subject to wilting, like a leaf turning yellow); 8) Fleurs de lys is an alternate spelling for such heraldry of the plural fleur de lis; 9) 'Seest' is an archaic expression for see? (author's prerogative); 10) Glistener personifies what one glistens like (from the first person as a noun); 11) Polyphase: consisting in a number of separate stages as (of an electrical device or circuit) designed to supply or use simultaneously several alternating currents of the same voltage and frequency, but with different phases; 12) The *Iglunoleum* is the transcendent floorboard platform of an original linoleum overlay (used oftentimes for the TATM interior); and 13) *Lucerna Superna* in Latin translates to the Upper Lamp!

This shorthand Glossary provides a basic overview of complex terminology utilized throughout the Yard Lamp of Gloria contents. Some corresponding footnotes annotate various vocabulary entries along the length of each storyboard for references not necessarily found in the English lexicon. Many of the epithets and names are a new invention for the sake of what would otherwise be lackluster language conveyance that might contain deficits with articulation in accordance to Revelatory possibility.

I was born in the Czech Republic, and~ following in some of the footsteps of Nikola Tesla~ my parents have immigrated me to the United States, New York City, when I was about 2 years of age. Eventually, we then moved up to Denver, Colorado near Colorado Springs where Nikola Tesla had his titanic Terminals energized for higher voltage experimentation. En route from 1994 to 2024, with high-intensity discharge fixtures (makeshift-manufactured), I was able to facilitate a remnant of the inventor's [visionary spirit] into today's gadgetry driven "light-emitting diode" Generation X… My video playlist is Immaculatorium on YouTube.

What you have reviewed began in 1991 and was completed in late Autumn of 2015, until November, the final month of our Yard Lamp of Gloria inception! Much later, it was entirely revised and expanded to an Unabridged Version from late 2022 to mid 2024! What once was a skeletal backbone is transformed into full format; an anthology and concise compendium of the whole Vision. All my experience has been compressed into its vast volume and is open for study, debate, innovation, or just scientific entertainment.

My appreciation is given to the world wide web of the Internet and to Artificial Intelligence for helping me out as I was forward to decipher *hard-to-understand* information references. Also, no less, the online dictionaries and media were just as indispensable to me.

To my Heavenly Family this work is dedicated.

found in the English lexicon. Many of the epithets and names are a mere invention for the sake of what would otherwise be lacking in language conveyance that might contain defects to a speculation [illegible] possibility.

I was born in the Czech Republic, and following in the footsteps of [illegible] my parents have immigrated to the United States, New York City, when I was about 2 years of age. Eventually, [illegible] moved to [illegible] Colorado [illegible] for this volume's [illegible] from 2004 to 2024 with [illegible] discourse [illegible] undetermined). I was [illegible] a remnant of the [illegible] Generation X [illegible] video [illegible].

[illegible] 2021 [illegible] final touch of our [illegible] edition [illegible] entirely revised and expanded [illegible] from late 2022 until 2024. What once was [illegible] anthology [illegible] experience has [illegible] volume [illegible] deficits, [illegible] improvement [illegible].

Many [illegible] thanks to the worldwide web of the Internet and [illegible] as well as forward to [illegible] references [illegible] indispensable to me.

[illegible] I have [illegible] this work [illegible].

Biography

I was born in the Czech Republic, and- like Nicola Tesla- I came to New York and eventually moved up to Denver, Colorado near Colorado Springs where Tesla had his huge toroidal terminal charged for high voltage experimentation. With high-intensity discharge fixtures I had makeshift manufactured, I was able to facilitate some of that inventor's spirit into today's gadgetry driven Generation X. My video playlist: https://www.youtube.com/channel/UCDAYT91tTOtu1lo-qL8r9Vg

What you have reviewed began in 1991, and was completed in late Autumn of 2015, until November: final month of the Yard Lamp of Gloria inception! All my experience has been compressed into its contents, and is open for study, debate, innovation or just ordinary entertainment.

Reader discretion is advised.

To my dear mother and father this work is dedicated.

MEMORIAL

PART 1.

Not long ago had sunlight
Glistered golden luminaired,
In times o' block party fun-night
As neighbors numbers shared.

Beside a parking lot car-filled
Quaint families gathered round;
The scent of creosote tar spilled
Blacktops of asphalt crowned!
The city seemed industrious
With manufactured steel,
Where streetlights glared illustrious
Enough to make me reel!
As we would often laugh, then cry,
Our daughters wept with joy-
While gazing at yon starry sky,
Transfixed were girl and boy.
The Seventies and Eighties both
Bulged bounties- some newfangled
And bygones of antiquity, quoth:
"...Made me feel star-spangled!"
I sipped my Seven~Up at hand
And gnawed a bratwurst hot dog
Whence right behind some guard fence
Barked a pinscher parking lot dog.
These rustic moments I'll remember
So, bricked bright with Youth
That kept agleam an arc tube ember
O'er each streetcar booth.
But oft were shared our goods
And spoils with immunity

To tyranny that then recoils
Man's community...
O what was waged wi' Yesteryear?
Whole heaven I inquire:
Will we take heed of times felt queer
With no taboo, not brier?

PART 2.

I think of Kens beside their Katy's
Huddled at each park bench,
Throughout th' Seventies and Eighties
Haunted by this dark stench!
Today, I pray, O Breath restore
Those gold-leaf yellowed years:
When once Compunction to the core
Had wept repentant tears...
An empty parking lot remains-
With no Amusement Park,
Nor any sentiment that stains
One's cheek of standards stark.
I still recall when heavy laden
Linkage hauled great freight
By boxcar casks- as any maiden
Gravid- grown with weight!
Polluted skies, unruly days
Compare with what were old...
Whose ozone layer's lither haze
Had filtered sunlight gold!
No Tonka trucks, nor Cabbage Patch
Dolls (dallied with) appear-
Whereas we barely catch heartfelt
One's curtsy dolled up dear...
We galvanize High Definition
Spectra, sharp and harsh,

But seldom soak in warm contrition
Near a carp-filled marsh.
How mother nature would remind
Us to remember such days
That then enamored heart and mind
By virtue-vaunted much praise!

Our dimmer days defunct, alas!
Drew forth hoar hearts of old age
Reviewed throughout an Hourglass
Spilt o'er upon her gold stage.

Printed in the United States
by Baker & Taylor Publisher Services